COMPOSERS ON MUSIC

Music advisor to Northeastern University Press
GUNTHER SCHULLER

COMPOSERS ON MUSIC

Eight Centuries of Writings

SECOND EDITION

Edited by

JOSIAH FISK

JEFF NICHOLS, CONSULTING EDITOR

Northeastern University Press
BOSTON

To Dr. Varga

with deepest thanks

[signature]

CAMBRIDGE — FEBRUARY 2006

Northeastern University Press

First edition copyright 1956 by Pantheon Books, Inc. Second edition
copyright 1997 by Josiah Fisk, by arrangement with Pantheon Books.

Library of Congress Cataloging-in-Publication Data

Composers on music : eight centuries of writings.—2nd ed. /
edited by Josiah Fisk ; Jeff Nichols, consulting editor.
p. cm.
Includes bibliographical references and index.
ISBN 1-55553-278-0 (cl : alk. paper).—
ISBN 1-55553-279-9 (pbk. : alk. paper)
1. Musicians as authors. 2. Music—History and criticism.
I. Fisk, Josiah. II. Nichols, Jeff (Jeff William)
ML90.C77   1997
780—dc20   96-27774
MN

Designed by Diane Levy
Composed in Garamond #3 by Northeastern Graphic Services, Inc., Hackensack, New Jersey.
Printed and bound by Edwards Brothers, Inc., Ann Arbor, Michigan. The paper is
Glatfelter Offset, an acid-free stock.

MANUFACTURED IN THE UNITED STATES OF AMERICA

07   06   05   04   03   8   7   6   5   4

CONTENTS

CHAPTER FOUR

CHAPTER FIVE

CHAPTER SIX

CHAPTER SEVEN

CHAPTER EIGHT

CHAPTER NINE

CHAPTER TEN

CHAPTER ELEVEN

PREFACE

Where the speech of humankind leaves off, there the art of music commences.
RICHARD WAGNER, 1840

Composers have never been entirely sure about words, particularly words about music. Wagner's aphorism, while strictly speaking a comment about the difference between music and literature, and while only expressing what had become a common sentiment during the Romantic era, still tells us something about his attitude toward the possibilities of writing about music. Reading his words literally, we can take them to mean not only that music extends past language, but that even its most modest examples are beyond the bravest efforts of language. The diplomacy of this remark (one of the rare instances in which the composer expressed himself completely in a single sentence) draws a delicate curtain around the insult that is being paid to language. The insult is harmless enough, but there is no mistaking the position that is being staked out. The world and its words occupy one territory, music quite another. The first is limited, the second apparently infinite, a part of the Great Beyond of human expression.

Thirty years earlier, Beethoven had expressed a parallel thought in his famous remark that "music is a higher revelation than all wisdom and philosophy." Here music is not only beyond language but above it. Nor is it only language over which music towers, but other forms of knowledge as well. Beethoven's claim is more extravagant than Wagner's, and more brash; niceties of rhetoric were not his way. But in placing music on a higher plane Beethoven is only echoing an ancient sentiment. The Medieval poet-composer Guillaume de Machaut had an elegant proof for the notion that music rose to the highest of heights: "Now the saints couldn't sing / Without music for their song: / Hence music is in heaven." These words take us back as far as the 1370s, but even here we are not yet close to the source. The exalted nature of music is as old as the idea that music was the language of God, or, as in Greece, of the gods.

We should not fail to notice an important distinction: Guillaume de Machaut's heights are sacred, Beethoven's secular. Over time, composers have tempered their claims, first about music's sacredness, and more lately, about its loftiness and potency in general. But they have at the same time grown more explicit and more adamant about the inability of words to illuminate the substance of music. "So long as I can sum up my experience in words, I would never write any music about it," wrote Mahler in 1896, commenting on the practice of Berlioz and others of supplying written descriptions of the images and events represented in their music. "My need to express myself in music begins only where the inarticulate thoughts prevail, at the gateway to the 'other world'; the world where things can no longer be fixed in time and place." What Wagner suggested, Mahler was happy to spell out.

A 1939 statement by Aaron Copland puts the case more starkly: "The whole problem can be stated quite simply by asking, 'Is there meaning to music?' My answer to that would be, 'Yes.' And 'Can you state in so many words what the meaning is?' My answer to that would be, 'No.'" The same year, Virgil Thomson asserted that "verbal communication about music is impossible except among musicians," by which he meant discussions of a primarily technical nature—shop talk. An aphorism of Ned Rorem from 1967 reiterates the Wagner-Mahler-Copland view: "If music could be translated into human speech, it would no longer need to exist."

Some composers have asserted that the problem isn't just articulation but knowledge itself. The composer, said Edgard Varèse in a 1959 lecture, "knows as little as anyone else about where the substance of his work comes from." Here again, the sentiment is hardly new. We can trace its lineage through Stravinsky's remark about being "the vessel through which *The Rite of Spring* passed," through Tchaikovsky's descriptions of how he composed (pages 156–59), and indeed through countless remarks stretching back to the ancient world and its view of music as a profound mystery. That which is mysterious cannot be understood; that which cannot be understood cannot be described. The world has been hearing this message for a long time now. It has accepted its manifest truthfulness and taken it to heart. The indescribability of music has been granted the highest honor our culture can bestow: it has become a cliché.

Like most clichés, of course, it is true, but gives us only part of the truth. When statements from composers about the fruitlessness of discussing music become more urgent and more frequent, it would be logical to expect fewer and fewer writings from composers. If they really felt that writing about music were hopeless, why would they devote much time to it? Yet many composers have done exactly that.

From the Middle Ages to the present, the willingness of composers to talk about music—theirs as well as others'—has only increased. The precipitous rise in composers' warnings and disclaimers that begins in the nineteenth century is merely part of the precipitous rise in composers' written and spoken statements on music generally. And it is the same composers who are responsible for both. Wagner's remark comes from a man whose musical writings are more voluminous than any earlier composer's by an order of magnitude (for that matter, more voluminous than the writings of many celebrated nineteenth-century literary figures). For much of his life Copland was the most prominent spokesperson for American contemporary music. Thomson wrote so assiduously that he became better known as a critic and essayist than a composer—and virtually every word of his is aimed at the layperson. For years Varèse did more writing and lecturing than composing. Rorem has authored a dozen books. As for Mahler, it was only later in life that his distaste for programmatic narratives overcame his urge to furnish hints and descriptions concerning the ideas within his music.

What is happening here? The charge of hypocrisy is obvious but somehow ir-relevant, offering little in the way of clarification. Accusing composers of trying to protect their franchise, while not entirely devoid of truth, is equally unen-lightening. Everyone agrees that music's dimensions cannot be taken through the measurements of language, even as most of us agree that it is worth trying. In any event, we should certainly hope that composers are more comfortable with notes than with words, since otherwise they would be in the wrong business.

At the same time, it would be letting composers off too easily to suggest that they speak about their music simply because the world demands it. If some of the composers represented in this book have improved their visibility through writ-ings and pronouncements, it has always been their music that has initially won them an audience for their words, and not the other way around. Moreover, there are plenty of composers even today who have achieved renown with very little help from their words, just as there are composers of the past whose proficiency at writ-ing has not helped their music endure.

It is undeniable that, over the past century in particular, many composers have found their words more widely circulated than their music, to their bafflement and frustration. But the only reason we know they have felt this frustration—in fact, the only reason we know what they have thought or felt about most things—is because they have come out and told us. Even the indescribability of music, that concept so dear to composers, cannot be directly expressed by music. For that you need words. Wagner's remark works in reverse as well: where the art of music leaves off, the speech of humankind commences. There are things about music that music cannot say.

We can hardly expect composers to have advertised this fact (although it so hap-pens that Wagner, as readers will see, comes as close as anyone). Yet they have not hesitated to make use of words in precisely those matters where music will not do. They have set down historical facts, addressed misperceptions, offered advice, stated principles, promulgated theories, explained techniques. They have admit-ted weaknesses, described enthusiasms, and in some cases engaged in mythmak-ing. They have spent no small amount of effort attacking and defending one an-other (it would have been easy to compile a book the length of this one made up entirely of composers' intramural squabblings). They have also given us some of the wittiest and most enduringly funny remarks on music ever made—a testament to their humor, but even more so to their thorough intimacy with the subject.

Over the eight centuries of music history represented in this book, the nature of the writings changes tremendously. The earliest texts in this book are, by con-temporary standards, fairly oblique to the subject of music. Medieval musicians and scholars usually wrote about music in the context of other matters: its role in worship or in courtship, its effect on the spirit, its relation to mathematics, how it was viewed by the ancients, and occasionally the rudiments of its practices. There are no pronouncements about "why I compose," no letters with remarks on some piece the writer has just heard, no essays on audience expectations. This in itself is revealing, for it forces us to confront the enormous differences between our own ideas of music and those of other times.

Until relatively late in the Middle Ages the learned tradition of music—the principal roots of the Western tradition—lay entirely within the Roman Church.

There was no such thing as the concept of the composer, either as a distinct profession or as an individual who signed his or her name to a work. What to us seems oblique was, to the Medieval world, the most direct reflection of reality, and it can perhaps help our understanding of music to imagine a world that could write about it in these ways—and by extension, could not write about it in other ways. This is one part of the picture that emerges from the texts in this book (although because the book does not include examples from technical writings, the picture is necessarily incomplete).

Another part of the picture is the shifting patterns of acceptance and rejection. The texts remind us that virtually since the earliest days of Western music, new ideas have been greeted with extreme opinions of one sort or another, and that every age has its own way of regarding the past. We see as well the current fragmentation of Western music, beginning with Berlioz, who was the first composer to provoke enduring disagreement among his peers—about his mastery, his accomplishments, his place in history. Composers disagree about him still, in some cases profoundly. He is, in that sense, the first of the Moderns, for composers' assessments of nearly every major figure from Berlioz onward remain thoroughly divided. At the same time, there has never been a period when composers agreed so universally on anything the way they now agree on the greatness of Bach, Haydn, and Mozart—and have agreed, coincidentally enough, since the time of Berlioz. Even Beethoven, while universally acknowledged for his genius, is regarded with reservations by some composers.

If all of this gives a somewhat different perspective on music history from the vision that prevails in many textbooks, let alone concert halls and record stores, that is perhaps the real reason for this book. It may well be that composers would rather spend more time with notes and less with words, but when they have set themselves to writing things down they have often done a supreme job. In a way it is their very reluctance to resort to words that is responsible for this, since they rarely bother with the superfluous. What they can say in music is in their works; what is unimportant, they haven't bothered to say at all.

Not all composers are great writers, or great writers on music. Some assume personas that hide as much as they reveal. Still, it is often the case that private writings can give us a glimpse behind some of those well-constructed personas. And I believe the reader will find that even the least articulate of the composers in this book has, if not eloquence of manner, then eloquence of meaning. Composers can be immodest, misguided, monstrous, blind, petty—and even so, fascinating and informative. They speak directly, sometimes plainly, always confidently. Even when they are desperately wrong, they remain grounded in a way that no other writers about music have ever been able to match. They understand their subject. They know what they're talking about. It is our happy privilege to listen.

Rockport, Massachusetts   JOSIAH FISK
July 1996

EDITOR'S NOTE

This book had its origins in the first *Composers on Music*, edited by Sam Morgenstern and published in 1956. It was Morgenstern who conceived of the organization and format, and who assembled (and in many cases translated) the texts that still form the backbone of the book. *Composers on Music* remained in print virtually without revisions for more than thirty years.

In 1993 Northeastern University Press purchased the rights to the book with the intention of adding a new final chapter. As the effort to develop this chapter got under way, two things became evident. The first was that Morgenstern's scholarship and his choice of material had survived remarkably well. The second was that, however well the book had survived, it could not be made fit for republication simply by adding a few recent composers. The intervening years had witnessed not only the creation of new material but the first appearances of a great deal of older material. Nor had the book entirely escaped the consequences of forty years of changes in musical and cultural perspectives. Some composers had inevitably risen in stature, others had fallen. It was acceptable to begin with Palestrina in 1956, but it is not so today, with our expanded interest in early music. The book originally contained no texts from female composers. All of these matters suggested a more thorough revision.

Thus began what was to be a three-year process of addition and subtraction, during which I tried to bring the book up to date while retaining as much from the first edition as possible. In the end I kept roughly two-thirds of the composer texts from Morgenstern's book; allowing for the increase in total book length, these constitute about half of the present volume.

Nearly every composer lost a few words, and some lost many. A number of composers, including Mozart, Mahler, and Debussy, gained back the difference and then some. Others, such as Schumann, Tchaikovsky, and Copland, ended up with sections that are substantially new. I added some thirty composers, extending the historical range of the book on both ends as well as filling some gaps in the middle (Bach, Janáček, Nielsen, Varèse, Still, Cowell). Inevitably there were composers— Grétry, Dargomijsky, Auric, and twelve others—who did not make it into the new edition. I also found it impractical to keep the original composer introductions, feeling that they would unavoidably strike today's readers as lengthy and dated.

One new element was my effort to include many of the composers' most famous statements, from epigrams to longer texts. While it is not hard to find these items elsewhere (that was Morgenstern's rationale for leaving them out), I suspect they will nevertheless reach many readers for the first time through this book. For those who are already familiar with these texts, I hope their inclusion here will increase the book's usefulness as a reference source.

In general, I made editorial choices less by applying a set of rules than by weighing the contingencies of each case. "Contingencies" here included many things: a composer's current stature, his or her historical significance, the quantity of texts available from a given composer or era or on a given subject, the inherent interest of a text, its historical significance (as distinct from that of its author), its clarity, its appeal to specialists and nonspecialists alike, its articulateness, its unexpectedness, and what might be called, for lack of a better word, its savor. Occasionally the deciding factor was the way a text interacted with others. A text that by itself seemed unnecessary could become a valuable strand in the fabric of the book, echoing or contradicting a thought expressed elsewhere, suggesting a pattern, providing context.

In this entire process I followed only two firm guidelines. All contributors had to be known primarily as composers, and all materials had to be concerned primarily with music. Even these guidelines were bent on occasion, when other factors demanded it. For example, strict interpretation would have barred a figure such as Leonard Bernstein, who in classical music circles is at least as well known as a conductor, or a document such as Beethoven's "Heiligenstadt Testament," which touches on music only in the broadest sense. Ultimately, then, the only principle that remained inviolate was that a text had to show itself to be indispensable, something no two texts accomplished through quite the same mixture of reasons.

Composers on Music, as the name implies, is drawn from primary source documents, and because of this it carries a certain amount of scholarly apparatus such as citations and footnotes. At the same time it is not so much a book of scholarly intent as a book of ideas, a book of opinions and eyewitness accounts. These often illuminate the speaker as well as the subject, and not only inform our present view of Western music but remind us of the varying tastes and philosophies of past generations.

Above all, this is a book for the reader, and for that reason I have tried to make it more "reader-friendly" than it might otherwise have been. If I found even one paragraph in a four-page essay that could be cut without damaging the essential content, I generally cut it, if only because leaving it in meant excluding something else of greater interest. I also applied standardized punctuation and spelling to the extent that it was practical. Russian names and terms now conform to the same spellings throughout the book; British spellings in translations have been Americanized; primary quotations are always indicated with double quotation marks, and so forth. Here and there I changed a word or phrase (and Morgenstern in some cases changed many), primarily in translations. This was to eliminate unclear or archaic usages and, on a couple of occasions, to undo bowdlerizations. Anyone wishing to see a text in complete and unedited form will, I hope, use the source citation in the back of the book to locate the original.

Editorial cuts are indicated in two ways: a series of ellipsis dots separated by spaces (. . .) and a quarter rest symbol. Although these marks roughly correspond to cuts of shorter and longer lengths respectively, the determining factor was the degree of discontinuity created by the cut. Ellipsis marks used by the composer-authors as an expressive device are rendered here as three dots without spaces between them (...). Editorial interpolations are in brackets. Footnotes by the composers are so identified. A few of the text headings derive from the titles of the original texts, but most are either Morgenstern's or mine.

The composers appear in the order of their birthdates. The organization into chapters, while capitalizing on gaps in birthdate chronology, is essentially arbitrary and is solely for the reader's convenience. Within each composer section, material is typically organized into three categories: general musical matters, discussions of other composers and their works, and discussions of the composer's own works, practices, and philosophies. Within the first category, material is usually chronological by text date; in the second and third it is usually chronological by subject date—birthdates in the case of composers, composition dates in the case of musical works. Obviously such a plan is haphazard in its logic and does not work equally well for all composers. I followed the plan where it was helpful, modified it where it was not.

Throughout the editorial process I was fortunate enough to have had the advice and assistance of Jeff Nichols, whose knowledge of composers' writings and whose perceptiveness in general musical matters added tremendously to the range and balance of this book. We discussed most issues of significance, sometimes enlisting the advice of colleagues. Our goal was to compile a book that would be useful to the casual music lover as well as to music professionals, to be read for pleasure or used as a classroom sourcebook. For some, it can perhaps serve as an illustrated bibliography, the texts functioning as a "sampler" of what is available in the way of writings from various composers and periods. Throughout the book, we tried to select and arrange the material in such a way that the reader may, if so inclined, follow various lines of thought and perceive various relationships, yet without ever ceasing to be confronted with the blunt and accidental nature of history.

The resulting book will surely not satisfy everyone, as indeed it has not entirely satisfied us. There are many composers, from Josquin des Prez to Elgar to Schnittke, who resisted our efforts to find suitable material by them. We wanted to include more writings by women and by Latin American and African American composers, but material is scarce and appropriate material even scarcer—not surprising, given the systematic exclusion of these individuals throughout most of Western music history. Some readers may take issue with the inclusion of anti-Semitic texts by Wagner and Strauss; they are here simply because they are primary evidence in an issue that is still hotly debated. Some may wonder why the book doesn't include any of the contemporary composers who have recently risen to the top of the classical recording charts; the reason is that it is too soon to tell. Some will wish the book extended to jazz, Broadway, and film composers, beyond the few crossover figures it does contain. That would have made for a wonderful book, but a different and much longer one.

In acknowledging the many individuals and institutions who have helped with the creation of this book I would like to begin by thanking the staff of Northeastern University Press, especially William Frohlich, editor, and Ann Twombly, production director. Most of the research was done at the Loeb Music Library at Harvard University, whose staff members were most cooperative. Gratitude is also owed to the music libraries of Wellesley College and the University of Iowa, and to the Rockport Public Library.

Milton Babbitt, Elliott Carter, John Harbison, and Ned Rorem kindly responded to requests to supply or locate materials. Dr. Louise Duchesneau replied on behalf of Györgi Ligeti. Oliver Knussen not only supplied materials—in some cases adding new revisions—but graciously agreed to write a short statement based on remarks made at a colloquium in 1995. Andrew Ford of Sydney, Australia, provided a number of key items. Ronald Woodley of Lancaster University provided his translation of Tinctoris's preface to *Musical Proportions*. I thank them all for their generosity.

Through Marty Fernandi at Columbia Artists Management I enlisted the help of Maxim Shostakovich, who vouched for the authenticity of the passages included here from Solomon Volkov's controversial book *Testimony: The Memoirs of Dmitri Shostakovich*. Mr. Shostakovich also kindly provided a copy of Isaac Glikman's book of correspondence with Dmitri Shostakovich.

Many people offered encouragement and advice, including Anne Stone, David Moran, Joyce Lindorff, Mitchell A. Miller, Claire Fontijn, Mary Davis, Miranda Fisk, and especially V. J. Panetta and Eunice Johnson. Roger Veinus contributed substantially to the task of producing new translations from the French originals. Daniel J. Kramer furnished similar help with German texts as well as helping with research. Larry Hamberlin provided exceptional copy editing. Finally I would like to thank my wife, Carol Ann, whose support, enthusiasm, and patience have made the entire effort possible.

J.F.

CHAPTER ONE

Hildegard von Bingen

Marchetto da Padova

Guillaume de Machaut

Johannes Tinctoris

Giovanni Pierluigi da Palestrina

William Byrd

Giulio Caccini

Thomas Morley

Claudio Monteverdi

Heinrich Schütz

Hildegard von Bingen

1098–1179

During her lifetime, Hildegard was known throughout Europe as an abbess, a mystic who received visions, a writer of literary and scientific texts, and an adviser to sacred and secular leaders. She left behind a substantial body of monophonic chants, or songs, as she preferred to call them, composed in a style of unique character and boldness and suited in particular to women's voices. The letter below was written in response to an order prohibiting singing among the sisters in her charge.

MUSIC AS PRAISE

From a letter to the prelate of Mainz, c.1178

In order not to live as disobedients separated from the whole, we have left off singing the chants of the Divine Offices exactly according to the interdict, and we have abstained from participation in the Body of our Lord, whereas we celebrated it together every single month according to our general custom. So that above all for this reason, while I as well as all of my sisters was struck down with such great bitterness, held back by such monstrous harshness, and suppressed at length by such tremendous weight of authority, I heard these words in a vision. . . . And I heard the voice that comes from the living light bringing forth the different forms of praise, about which David sang in the psalms: "Praise Him in the sound of the trumpet; praise Him in the psalterium and cithara," etc., to which was added: "Let every spirit praise the Lord" [Psalm 150]. In these words we are instructed about the interior life through exterior things: namely, just how to give form to the Offices serving the interior of human beings and direct them as much as possible toward the praises of the Creator, whether according to the setting of the texts or the nature of the instruments. . . .

The holy prophets, mindful of that divine sweetness and praise through which Adam rejoiced in God before the Fall, but not in his exile, wanted also to be aroused to these things themselves. So these prophets, taught by the very spirit they had received, not only composed psalms and canticles, which were sung in order to kindle the devotion of the listeners, but also created various instruments for the art of music. In this way they were able to bring forth a whole variety of sounds as much from the structure and properties of each instrument as from the sense of the words. . . .

Moreover, when that deceiver, the Devil, heard that man began to sing through the inspiration of God, and that in this way he was summoned to practice again the sweetness of the chants of the heavenly fatherland . . . then even in the heart of the Church and wherever he [the Devil] was able, whether through sensation and scandal or unjust oppression, he continually disrupted the manifestation and beauty of the psalms and hymns. . . .

It is necessary that you pay attention to this so that you are drawn to this same devotion to the justice of God without the desire for punishment and revenge that comes from indignation or an unjust feeling of the heart, and it is always necessary to beware that in your judgments you are not possessed by Satan, who took man away from the heavenly music and from the the lights of paradise. Therefore consider carefully that just as the body of Christ was born of the Holy Spirit from the integrity of the Virgin Mary, just so is the song of praise according to the heavenly music radiated by the Holy Spirit in the Church. The body is truly the garment of the soul, which has a living voice; for that reason it is fitting that the body simultaneously with the soul repeatedly sing praises to God through the voice.

In accordance with this meaning the prophetic spirit orders that God be praised with cymbals of jubilation and with the rest of the musical instruments that the wise and studious have created, since all of the arts (whose purpose is to fill uses and needs of man) are brought to life by that breath of life which God breathed into the body of man: and therefore it is just that God be praised in all things. . . . The prophecy in the psalm . . . exhorts us to confess ourselves to God in the cithara as we sing psalms with the ten-string harp; desiring to restore ourselves, let sound the cithara, whose purpose on earth is to train the body; let sound the psalterium, which gives back the sound from the heavenly realm above for expanding the spirit; let sound the ten-string harp for contemplation of the law. Therefore, those of the Church who have imposed silence on the singing of the chants for the praise of God without well-considered weight of reason so that they have unjustly stripped God of the grace and comeliness of His own praise, unless they will have freed themselves from their errors here on earth, will be without the company of the angelic songs of praise in heaven.   [1]

Marchetto da Padova
c. 1274–after 1326

Most of the surviving Medieval texts about music were written by scholars and theorists. Marchetto, however, was a practicing musician, serving as choirmaster of the cathedral in his native Padua. All that survives of his musical output is three motets.

More significant to music history are his two treatises. The Lucidarium *discusses plainsong; the* Pomerium *discusses the new genre of mensural polyphony, which Marchetto is credited with introducing in Italy. The* Lucidarium *contains one of the earliest articulations of the emerging role of the composer—or, in Marchetto's term, the musician—as distinct from the performer.*

MUSICIAN AND SINGER

From the treatise Lucidarium in arte musicae planae, *Verona, 1319*

A musician is defined, according to Boethius,* as one who has the ability to make judgments concerning modes and rhythms and concerning the varieties of canti-

---

* The Roman philosopher and mathematician Boethius (480–524) was the author of the five-volume *De institutione musica*, which became the foundation of Medieval music theory.

lena in accordance with the speculation and reason of the science of music. For every art or discipline naturally holds reason in higher regard than the skill that is exercised by an artist's hand and in his work. For the musician learns the possibility and rationality of musical proportions and makes judgments in accordance with this and not only by the sound. The singer is, as it were, an instrument of the musician, on which instrument the artist or musician performs, putting into practice that which he already knows by reason. Therefore the musician is to the singer as the judge to the crier; for the judge issues a decree and orders that it be announced by means of the crier. There is the same relation between musician and singer; for the musician learns, feels, discerns, chooses, decrees, and disposes everything that touches upon the science; and he commands that it be put into practice by the singer as though by his own messenger. [1]

Guillaume de Machaut
c. 1300–1377

Known as widely for his poetry as for his music, Machaut left well over a hundred pieces— more than any other composer of his century. His Messe de Notre Dame *is among the earliest polyphonic settings of the complete ordinary of the mass. He spent his life in service to various courts, eventually being sought out by the highest nobility of France. Machaut's* Livre de voir dit, *apparently autobiographical, chronicles an elderly and infirm poet's elaborate pursuit of the nineteen-year-old Peronné d'Armentières.*

MUSIC AND COURTLY LOVE
From a letter to Peronné d'Armentières, Rheims, 1363

I send you my book, *Morpheus*, which they call *La Fontaine amoureuse*, in which I have made a song to your order, & it is in the guise of a *rés d'Alemaigne*; & by God it is long since I have made so good a thing to my satisfaction; & the tenors are as sweet as unsalted pap. I beg therefore that you deign to hear it, & know the thing just as it is, without adding or taking away; & it is to be said in a goodly long measure; & if anyone play it on the organs, cornemuse, or other instrument, that is its right nature. I am also sending you a *ballade*, which I made before receiving your sweet likeness: for I was a little hurt because of some words that had been said to me; but soon as I saw your sweet likeness I was healed & free of melancholy. [1]

THE NATURE OF MUSIC
From the Prologue, c. 1370

Music is a science that
Would have us laugh and sing and dance.
Melancholy it dislikes,
As well the man whose melancholy

Owes to unimportant things;
Music pays such folk no heed.
Where it goes, there joy is felt;
Comfort finds the comfortless.
Just to chance upon its sounds
Causes people to rejoice.   [2]

From the Remede de Fortune, *undated*

He who makes songs without feeling
Spoils both his words and his music.   [3]

Johannes Tinctoris
(c. 1435–1511)

The Flemish master Tinctoris traveled and lived throughout Europe, notably at the court of Ferdinand I in Naples, where he served for many years as chaplain, tutor, and musician. During the early 1470s he published the first dictionary of musical terms. He also published theoretical works on modes and counterpoint and composed several masses and secular vocal works.

MUSICAL KNOWLEDGE

From the preface to The Proportional of Music, *a treatise on modes, c. 1476*

To his Divine Highness, the most holy and invincible Prince Ferdinand, by the providence of the King of Kings and Lord of Lords King of Sicily, Jerusalem, and Hungary, Johannes Tinctoris, the most insignificant among teachers of music and his fellow chaplains, prostrates himself low to kiss His feet in humble and obsequious obeisance.

Most wise King, from the time of Jubal the first musician, of whom Moses made such great claims, as when in Genesis he spoke of him as "the prince of all who play the organ and harp," many illustrious men, such as David, Ptolemy, and Epaminundas (princes of Judea, Egypt, and Greece), Zoroaster, Pythagoras, Linus of Thebes, Zethus, Amphion, Orpheus, Museus, Socrates, Plato, Aristotle, Aristoxenus, and Timotheus, have rendered such painstaking service in the cause of the liberal art of music that, as Cicero testifies, they attained by power of thought a comprehension of almost all its range and infinite subject matter; and for this reason, many Greeks claimed that some of these men, Pythagoras above all, had discovered the very origins of music. Nevertheless, concerning their methods of performance and notation we are far from unanimous in our opinions. It is probable, however, that these were of the most highly polished kind, for it was upon this branch of knowledge—the mightiest of all, according to Plato—that they bestowed their highest learning, so that in ancient times music was taught to everybody, and anyone not well versed in it was considered to be quite uneducated. And how compelling, pray, was that melody by whose power gods, ancestral spirits, foul demons, even mindless animals and things inanimate were said to be moved! This legend, even if partly fictitious, is not entirely free of mystery, for surely the poets would not have invented such stories concerning music had they not at some time perceived, through divine inspiration, its wonderful powers.

But then, after the fullness of time, in which the greatest of all musicians, Jesus Christ our peace, under duple proportion made two natures one, there flourished in His church many wonderful musicians, such as Gregorius, Ambrosius, Augustinius, Hilarius, Boethius, Martianus, Guido, and Johannes de Muris, of whom some determined the manner of singing in the church of our salvation itself; others composed for this purpose numerous hymns and songs; while others bequeathed to posterity writings on the divine nature, the theory, or the practice of this art, by now propagated to the world in manuscripts far and near. Finally, the most Christian princes, of whom, Most Righteous King, you are by far the foremost in gifts of mind, body, and fortune, desiring to enhance the divine service, founded chapels after the manner of David to which, at enormous expense, they appointed various singers to sing joyous and comely praise in different (but not indifferent) voices to our God. And since royal singers, if their princes are endowed with that generosity that brings men fame, are rewarded with honor, glory, and wealth, many are kindled with a passionate zeal for study of this kind. As a result of this fervent upsurge, the development of our music has been so remarkable that it appears to be a whole new art; and the source and wellspring, so to speak, of this new art is held to have been among the English, with Dunstable standing pre-eminent at their head. Contemporary with him in France were Dufay and Binchois, whose direct successors are the composers of today: Ockeghem, Busnois, Regis, and Caron, the most outstanding masters of composition that I have ever heard. It is to these, indeed, that the English (although popularly said to sing like angels, while the French merely sing) now come to be compared in this regard, for the French compose new works daily in the most up-to-date style, whereas the English (a sign of great poverty of imagination) continue to employ one and the same style of composition.

But alas! I see that not only these, but several other composers—and this I find astonishing—despite the subtlety and ingenuity of their compositions, combined with an inconceivable sweetness, nevertheless display either a complete ignorance of musical proportions or indicate incorrectly the few that they do know. This, I have no doubt, stems from a lack of grounding in arithmetic, without which no one can achieve distinction in the field of music, for it is the womb from which all proportion is born. In order, therefore, that young men wishing to study this liberal and honorable art of music should not be led into such error and ignorance concerning these proportions, to the glory of God, whose gift to us they are, to the splendor of Your Most Holy Majesty, in righteousness surpassing all these other princes, and finally in honor of your most finely proportioned chapel, whose like I cannot readily believe to exist anywhere in the world, I enter, to the best of my humble abilities, upon this short work, which in view of its subject I consider may appropriately be named *The Proportional of Music*. If I have ventured in it to oppose most, indeed nearly all, of the most distinguished composers, let this not be ascribed, I entreat, to arrogance on my part. For I do not bid that my writings necessarily be followed any more than those of others; but, campaigning in pursuit of the truth, that which I find correct in their works with respect to proportions, I approve, and that which I find incorrect, I disapprove. But if I appear to the reader to carry out this policy of mine with justice, I urge them to put their trust in me; if I seem unfair, let them rather believe others, for I am as ready to be refuted by others as to refute them myself.   [1]

From the preface to Book of the Art of Counterpoint, *1477*

Before carrying out this project, I cannot pass over in silence the opinion of numerous philosophers, among them Plato and Pythagoras and their successors Cicero, Macrobius, Boethius, and our Isidore, that the spheres of the stars revolve under the guidance of harmonic modulation, that is, by the consonance of various concords. But when, as Boethius relates, some declare that Saturn moves with the deepest sound and that, as we pass by stages through the remaining planets, the moon moves with the highest, while others, conversely, ascribe the deepest sound to the moon and the highest to the sphere of the fixed stars, I put faith in neither opinion. Rather I unshakably credit Aristotle and his commentator [Thomas Aquinas], along with our more recent philosophers, who most manifestly prove that in the heavens there is neither actual nor potential sound. For this reason it will never be possible to me that musical concords, which cannot be produced without sound, can result from the motion of the heavenly bodies.

Concords of sounds and melodies, from whose sweetness, as Lactantius says, the pleasure of the ear is derived, are produced, then, not by heavenly bodies, but by earthly instruments with the cooperation of nature. To these concords the ancient musicians—Plato, Pythagoras, Nicomachus, Aristoxenus, Philolaus, Archytas, Ptolemy, and many others, including even Boethius—most assiduously applied themselves, yet how they were accustomed to arrange and to form them is almost unknown to our generation. And if I may refer to my own experience, I have had in my hands certain old songs, called apocrypha, of unknown origin, so ineptly, so stupidly composed that they rather offended than pleased the ear.

Further, although it seems beyond belief, there does not exist a single piece of music not composed within the last forty years that is regarded by the learned as worth hearing. Yet at this present time, not to mention innumerable singers of the most beautiful diction, there flourish, whether by the effect of some celestial influence or by the force of assiduous practice, countless composers, among them Jean Ockeghem, Jean Regis, Antoine Busnoys, Firmin Caron, and Guillaume Faugues, who glory in having studied this divine art under John Dunstable, Gilles Binchoys, and Guillaume Dufay, recently deceased. Nearly all the works of these men exhale such sweetness that in my opinion they are to be considered most suitable, not only for men and heroes, but even for the immortal gods. Indeed, I never hear them, I never examine them, without coming away happier and more enlightened.   [2]

Giovanni Pierluigi da Palestrina
1525(?)–1594

Palestrina spent his life as a sacred musician, although his relations with the church were variable. He held many posts as maestro di cappella, *and was briefly a member of the Sistine Chapel even though he was married. In his mid-fifties, after losing his wife and elder sons to the plague, he joined the priesthood, only to leave within a year to marry again.*

Palestrina is the earliest figure to have attracted extensive commentary from nineteenth-century composers, in part because his music was still in use within the church. His fame rests on a mere handful of works, but his output was enormous: 104 masses, 140 madrigals, 375 motets, and dozens of offertories, hymns, and Magnificats.

SECULAR AND SACRED TEXTS

Dedication of First Book of Motets *to Cardinal Carpi, 1563*

Our wisest mortals have decided that music should give zest to divine worship, so that those whom pious devotion to religious practice has led to the temple might remain there to delight in voices blending in harmony. If men take great pains to compose beautiful music for profane songs, they should devote at least as much thought to sacred song, nay, even more than to mere worldly matters.

Therefore, though well aware of my feeble powers, I have held nothing more desirable than that whatever is sung throughout the year, according to the season, should be agreeable to the ear by virtue of its vocal beauty, insofar as it lay in my power to make it so. [1]

Dedication of Fourth Book of Motets
(containing settings of the Song of Songs) *to Pope Gregory XIII, 1584*

There exists a vast mass of love songs of the poets, written in a fashion entirely foreign to the profession and name of Christian. They are the songs of men ruled by passion, and a great number of musicians, corrupters of youth, make them the concern of their art and their industry; in proportion as they flourish through praise of their skill, so do they offend good and serious-minded men by the depraved taste of their work. I blush and grieve to think that once I was of their number. But while I cannot change the past, nor undo what is done, I have mended my ways. Therefore I have labored on songs that have been written in praise of Our Lord, Jesus Christ, and His Most Holy Virgin Mother, Mary; and I have now produced a work that treats of the divine love of Christ and His Spouse the Soul, the Canticle of Solomon. [2]

MUSIC AND MONEY

Dedication of Lamentations *to Pope Sixtus V, 1588*

Worldly cares of any kind, Most Holy Father, are adverse to the Muses, and particularly those that arise from a lack of private means. For when the latter afford a sufficiency (and to ask more is the mark of a greedy and intemperate man), the mind can more easily detach itself from other cares; if not, the fault lies within. Those who have known the necessity of laboring to provide this sufficiency, according to their station and way of life, know full well how it distracts the mind from learning and from a study of the liberal arts.

Certainly I have known this experience all my life, and more especially at present. Yet I thank the Divine Goodness, first, that the course is now almost finished, and the goal in sight; secondly, that in the midst of the greatest difficulties, I have never interrupted my study of music. Dedicated to the profession since boyhood, and engrossed in it to the best of my abilities and energies, indeed what other interest could I have had? Would that my progress had equaled my labor and my diligence!

I have composed and published much; a great deal more is lying by me, which I am hindered from publishing because of the straitened means of which I have spoken. It would require no small expenditure, especially were the larger notes and letters used, as church publications properly demand.

Meanwhile, I have only been able to publish, in this small format, those *Lamentations* of the Prophet Jeremiah that are usually sung in choral form in the churches during Holy Week.

This work I offer to Your Holiness with that humility due the exalted Pastor of the Universal Catholic Church, outstanding in holiness and admirable authority.   [3]

William Byrd
1543–1623

A practicing Catholic in staunchly Protestant England, Byrd was nonetheless made a Gentleman of the Chapel Royal in 1570. He joined Thomas Tallis in founding a business for the printing and selling of music and music paper, but in spite of holding a royal patent that covered all of England, the business was unprofitable.

SINGING

From Psalms, Sonets & Songs, *1588*

Reasons briefly set downe by the'auctor, to perswade every one to learne to sing.

First it is a Knowledge easely taught, and quickly learned where there is a good Master, and an apt Scoller.

2. The exercise of singing is delightfull to Nature & good to preserve the health of Man.

3. It doth strengthen all the parts of the brest, & doth open the pipes.

4. It is a singular good remedie for a stutting & stammering in the speech.

5. It is the best meanes to procure a perfect pronunciation & to make a good Orator.

6. It is the onely way to know where Nature hath bestowed the benefit of a good voyce: which guift is so rare, as there is not one among a thousand, that hath it: and in many, that excellent guift is lost, because they want Art to expresse Nature.

7. There is not any Musicke of Instruments whatsoever, comparable to that which is made of the voyces of Men, where the voyces are good, and the same well sorted and ordered.

8. The better the voyce is, the meeter it is to honour and serve God therewith: and the voyce of man is chiefly to be imployed to that ende.

omnis spiritus laudet Dominum.

Since singing is so good a thing
I wish all men would learne to sing.   [1]

PERFORMING AND LISTENING

Preface to Psalmes, Songs, and Sonnets, 1611

To all true lovers of Musicke, W. Byrd wisheth all true happinesse both temporall and eternall.

Being excited by your kinde acceptance of my former travailes in Musicke, I am thereby much incouraged to commend to you these my last labours, for myne *ultimum vale.* Wherein I hope you shall finde Musicke to content every humour: either melancholy, merry, or mixt of both.

Onely this I desire; that you will be but as carefull to heare them well expressed as I have been both in the Composing and correcting of them. Otherwise the best Song that ever was made will seeme harsh and unpleasant, for that the well expressing of them, either by Voyces, or Instruments, is the life of our labours, which is seldome or never well performed at the first singing or playing. Besides a song that is well and artificially made cannot be well perceived nor understood at the first hearing, but the oftner you shall heare it, the better cause of liking you will discover: and commonly that Song is best esteemed with which our eares are most acquainted. As I have done my best endeavour to give you content, so I beseech you satisfie my desire in hearing them well expressed, and then I doubt not, for Art and Ayre both of skillful and ignorant they will deserve liking. *Vale.*

Thine, W. Byrd   [2]

Guilio Caccini
1550–1610

Although his first compositions were in the polyphonic style, Caccini later became a leading figure in the development of the monodic stile rappresentativo, *which aimed to displace counterpoint with a "simpler" music ostensibly based on the ideals of ancient Greece and Rome. Caccini became an important figure in early opera: his setting of Rinuccini's* Euridice, *while not the first opera to be composed, was the first to be published, in 1600.*

THE BEGINNINGS OF THE MONODIC STYLE

From the preface to Le nuove musiche, *1614*

To the readers: If heretofore I did not publish the results of my musical studies in the noble style of singing, learned from my master, the famous Scipione della Palla, nor the madrigals and arias composed by me at different times, it was because I did not see fit to do so, as it seemed to me that these pieces had been honored sufficiently, and because I see them performed continuously—more often than they deserve—by the most famous singers in Italy, as well as by other noble persons, amateurs of this profession. But now I see many of them corrupted and ruined; also, those long vocal roulades (single and double), which I invented to avoid the customary old style of passages, more suited to wind and string instruments than to the voice, I also see are misused, redoubled and intermingled one with another, and I find an indifferent use of the rise and fall of the voice, of the exclamations, trills and *gruppi*, and other similar ornaments of the good style of singing. For these reasons I have been forced, as well as urged by my friends, to have my music published. My purpose in this introduction to my first publication is to set before my readers the causes that led me to the adoption of this style of singing for the solo voice, and since no music has been written in recent times that is endowed with that complete grace I feel resounding in my soul, I have wished also to leave some trace of it in these compositions, that others may achieve perfection, as a small spark sometimes generates a great flame.

I can truly say that I learned more than I learned in thirty years' study of counterpoint from the wise discussions I heard when there flourished in Florence the brilliant *camerata* of the illustrious Giovanni Bardi, Count of Vernio, which I frequented, and where there gathered not only a great part of the nobility, but also the best musicians and men of genius, poets, and philosophers of the city. These learned gentlemen always encouraged me and with clear reasoning persuaded me not to adhere to that type of music which, not permitting the words to be clearly understood, distorts the idea and the line [prosody], now lengthening, now shortening the syllables to make them fit the counterpoint, that destroyer of poetry. They urged me to adhere instead to that style so highly lauded by Plato and other philosophers who maintained that music is nothing if not words and rhythm first, and sound last, and not the contrary. For if one is to penetrate other people's minds and produce those wonderful effects admired by the writers, it cannot be achieved by counterpoint in modern music, especially not when one voice sings above a string accompaniment and not a word is understood because of the multitude of passages on both long and short syllables, the only purpose being that the singers be lauded by the populace and declared great.

Having seen, as I say, that such music and such musicians gave no pleasure other than that which harmony could give the ear, since without the words being understood, it could not move the intellect, the thought came to me to introduce a kind of music through which one could express oneself in harmony, using . . . a certain noble carelessness in the song, passing sometimes through dissonances, yet keeping the notes of the bass steady, except when I wanted to observe the common usage; and as they do not well serve any other purpose, the inner voices might be played on an instrument to express some feeling. This is why I then created these songs for a solo voice, as it seemed to me it had more power to please and move the listener than many voices singing together; thus I composed the madrigals "Perfidissimo volto," "Vedrò'l mio Sol," "Dovrò dunque morire," and similar pieces, and especially the aria on the eclogue of Sannazaro, "Itene a l'ombra degli ameni faggi," in that same style I used later for the fables that were sung in concerts in Florence.

In the madrigals as well as in the arias I have always sought to have the music follow the meaning of the words, searching out those more or less expressive chords, according to the sentiments they should convey, and trying particularly to give them grace by concealing as much as I could the craft of counterpoint; and I placed the consonant harmonies on the long syllables, avoiding the short ones, and observed the same rule in making the passages of division, although, in order to embellish, I have sometimes put in a few chromatics up to the value of a quarter note or at most a half note, chiefly over short syllables. These are permissible, since they pass quickly and are not division passages, but give a certain additional grace, and this I also did because every rule can suffer a few exceptions.   [1]

Thomas Morley
1557–1603

Like his teacher Byrd, Morley was a Gentleman of the Chapel Royal and a music printer and publisher. Known today for his madrigals, he also wrote service music; his setting of the English Burial Service was used regularly until displaced by Purcell's. Morley's Plaine and Easie Introduction *sets forth in Socratic form the principles an English musician of the time was expected to know.*

From A Plaine and Easie Introduction to Practicalle Musicke, *1597*

THE FANTASIE

The most principal and chiefest kind of music which is made without a ditty is the fantasie, that is, when a musician taketh a point [theme] at his pleasure, and wresteth and turneth it as he list, making either much or little of it according as shall seeme best in his own conceit. In this may more art be shown than in any other music, because the composer is tide to nothing but that he may add, deminish and alter at his pleasure. And this kind will beare any allowances whatsoever tolerable in other musicke, except changing the ayre & leaving the key, which in fantasie may never be suffered.   [1]

FUGAL COMPOSITION

If a man would study, he might upon it [a point] find varietie enough to fill up many sheets of paper: yea, though it were given to all the musicians of the world, they might compose upon it, and not one their compositions be like unto that of another. And you shall find no point so well handled by any man, either Composer or Organist, but with studie either he himselfe or some other might make it much better. [2]

SIGHT SINGING

But supper being ended, and Musicke bookes, according to the custome, being brought to the table: the mistresse of the house presented me with a part, earnestly requesting me to sing. But when after manie excuses, I protested unfainedly that I could not: everie one began to wonder. Yea, some whispered to others, demanding how I was brought up: so that upon shame of mine ignorance, I go nowe to seeke out mine olde frinde, master *Gnorimus,* to make my selfe his scholler. [3]

IMPROVISATION

Singing extempore upon a plainsong is in deede a peece of cunning and very necessarie to be perfectly practiced by him who meaneth to be a composer. [4]

WORDS AND MUSIC

It followeth to shew you how to dispose your musicke according to the nature of the words which you are therein to expresse, as whatsoever matter it be which you have in hand, such a kind of musicke must you frame to it. You must therefore if you have a grave matter, applie a grave kind of musicke to it, if a merrie subject you must make your musicke also merrie. For it will be a great absurditie to use a sad harmonie to a merrie matter, or a merrie harmonie to a sad lamentable or tragic ditty. You must then when you would expresse any word signifying hardness, crueltie, bitternesse, and other such like, make the harmonie like unto it, that is, somwhat harsh and hard but yet so it offend not. . . . Also if the subject be light, you must cause your music go in motions, which carrie with them a celeritie or quickness of time. . . .

Moreover you must have a care that when your matter signifieth ascending, high heaven, and such like, you make your music ascend: and by the contrarie when your dittie speaketh of descending lowenes, depth, hell, and others such, you must make your music descend. . . . We must also have a care to applie the notes to the wordes, as in singing there be no barbarisme committed: that is, that we cause no sillable which is by nature short be expressed by manie notes or one long note, nor no long sillable be expressed with a shorte note, but in this fault do the practitioners erre more grosselie, then in any other, for you shal find few songes wherein the penult sillables of these words, *Dominus, Angelus, filius, miraculum, gloria,* and such like are not expressed with a long note, yea many times with a whole dossen of notes, and though one should speak of fortie he should not say much amiss, which is a grosse barbarisme, & yet might be easelie amended. We must also take heed of seperating any part of a word from another by a rest, as som dunces have not slackt to do, yea one whose name is Johannes Dunstable (an ancient English author) hath not only devided the sentence, but in the very middle of a word hath made two long rests. [5]

THE MOTET

I say that all musicke for voices (for onlie of that kinde have we hetherto spoken) is made either for a dittie or without a dittie, if it bee with a dittie, it is either grave or light, the grave ditties they have still kept in one kind, so that whatsoever musicke be made upon it, is comprehended under the name of a Motet: a Motet is properlie a song made for the church, either upon some hymne or Antheme, or such like, and that name I take to have beene given to that kinde of musicke in opposition to the other which they called *Canto firmo,* and we do commonlie call plainsong, for as nothing is more opposit to standing and firmnes then motion, so did they give the Motet the name of moving,* because it is in a manner quight contrarie to the other, which after some sort, and in respect of the other standeth stil. This kind of all others which are made on a ditty, requireth most art, and moveth and causeth most strange effects in the hearer, being aptlie framed for the dittie and well expressed by the singer, for it will draw the auditor (and speciallie the skilfull auditor) into a devout and reverent kind of consideration of him for whose praise it was made.

——— ♪ ———

But to returne to our Motets, if you compose in this kind, you must cause your harmonie to carrie a majestie taking discordes and bindings so often as you canne, but let it be in long notes, for the nature of it will not beare short notes and quicke motions, which denote a kind of wantonnes.

This musicke (a lamentable case) being the chiefest both for art and utilitie, is notwithstanding little esteemed, and in small request with the greatest number of those who most highly seeme to favor art, which is the cause that the composers of musick who otherwise would follow the depth of their skill, in this kinde are compelled for lack of *maecenates* to put on another humor, and follow that kind whereunto they have neither beene brought up, nor yet (except so much as they can learne by seeing other mens works in an unknown tounge) doe perfectlie understand the nature of it, such be the newfangled opinions of our Countrey men, who will highlie esteeme whatsoever commeth from beyond the seas, and speciallie from Italie, be it never so simple, contemning that which is done at home though it be never so excellent. [6]

THE MADRIGAL

The light musicke hath beene of late more deeply dived into, so that there is no vanitie which in it hath not beene followed to the full, but the best kind of it is termed *Madrigal*, a word for the etymologie of which I can give no reason, yet use sheweth that it is a kinde of musicke made upon songs and sonnets, such as *Pe-*

---

* "Motet" actually derives from the French *mot* (word) rather than "motion."

trarcha and many Poets of our time have excelled in. This kinde of musicke weare not so much disalowable if the Poets who compose the ditties would abstaine from some obscenities, which all honest eares abhor, and some time from blasphemies to such as this, *ch'altro di te iddio non voglio* [other than you I'll have no god] which no man (at least who hath any hope of salvation) can sing without trembling. As for the musick it is next unto the Motet, the most artificiall and to men of understanding most delightfull. If therefore you will compose in this kind you must possesse your selfe with an amorous humor (for in no composition shal you prove admirable except you put on, and possesse your selfe wholy with that vaine wherein you compose) so that you must in your musicke be wavering like the wind, sometime wanton, sometime drooping, sometime grave and staide, otherwhile effeminat, you may maintaine points and revert them, use triplaes [triple time] and shew the verie uttermost of your varietie, and the more varietie you shew the better shal you please.   [7]

Claudio Monteverdi
1567–1643

Monteverdi published his first works at the age of fifteen. His first opera, L'Orfeo, *was produced in 1607. Many others followed, most of which have been lost, though* L'Orfeo *survives as the first opera whose greatness is undisputed. For the last four decades of his life he was choirmaster at St. Mark's in Venice.*

As a madrigalist and a dramatic composer Monteverdi stretched the accepted rules of counterpoint to achieve a new level of expressiveness, for which he attracted the criticism of the conservative theorist Artusi, a pupil of Zarlino. Monteverdi responded in the preface to his fifth book of madrigals. The book Monteverdi promised, entitled Second Practice, *was never to appear, but his brother, Giulio Cesare, produced an elaborate amplification of the fifth book's preface in 1607.*

A DEFENSE OF MODERN MUSIC

Preface to Fifth Book of Madrigals, *1605*

To the reader: Do not be surprised if I allow these madrigals to go to press without first answering the remarks made by Artusi about certain small details in them. Being in the service of His Serene Highness of Mantua, I do not have the necessary time at my disposal. Nevertheless, I have written my answer, to let it be known that I do not write things by accident. As soon as it is copied, it will appear under the title of *Second Practice* or *On the Perfection of Modern Music* and will astonish some people for whom there can exist no other "practice" than that taught by Zarlino. But they may rest assured that, as far as consonances and dissonances are concerned, there is another point of view to be considered besides the already existing one, and that this other point of view is justified by the satisfaction it gives both to the ear and to the intelligence. I wanted to tell you this, so that the title *Second Practice* should not be used by others and also so that spirits may in the meantime search out new things relative to harmony and be assured that the modern composer builds his works on the basis of truth. [1]

CRITIQUE OF AN OPERA LIBRETTO

From a letter to Alessandro Striggio the Younger (the librettist of L'Orfeo*), Venice, December 9, 1616*

At the outset I would say that, in general, music should be mistress of the air and not only of water, which in my language means that the themes outlined in this fable are all crude and earthbound, seriously lacking in beautiful harmonies, since the harmonies will be confined to the coarsest blasts of the winds of the earth, painful to hear and painful to play on the stage. Here I leave the verdict to your exquisite and very intelligent taste; for, as a result of this fault, three lutes would be needed instead of one; in place of one harp, three, and so on. Instead of a delicate voice, a forced one would be required. Besides, in my opinion, the imitation of speech would have to be supported by wind instruments rather than by delicate stringed instruments, since, I believe, the harmonies of Tritons and other marine gods should be given to trombones and trumpets, not to lutes or to the harpsichord and the harp. In actuality, being maritime, the action takes place outside the city, and Plato teaches us that *cithara debet esse in civitate et thibia in agris* [the guitar belongs in the city and the flute in the fields]. So, either delicate instruments will be inappropriate, or the appropriate instruments will not be delicate.

In addition, I have noticed that there are twenty performers, Cupids, Zephyrs, and Sirens. Thus many sopranos would be needed. It must not be forgotten that the Winds, that is to say, the Zephyrs and the Boreae, must sing, too. How, my dear sir, can I imitate the speech of the Winds, if they do not talk? And how can I induce emotion in them? Arianna moved us because she was a woman, Orfeo because he was a man, not a Wind. Harmonies imitate these personages themselves, but one cannot, by means of melodic line, realize the windstorm, the bleating of lambs, the neighing of horses, and so on. To repeat, harmonies do not imitate the speech of the Winds because it does not exist.

Further, the ballets scattered through this fable have not one rhythm to which one can dance. The entire fable, because of my ignorance, which is not negligible, does not move me at all, and it is with difficulty that I even understand it. I do not feel that it brings me naturally to an ending that moves me. *Arianna* moved me to a real lament; *Orfeo* stirred me to a true prayer; but I do not know what the aim of this fable is. What, then, does Your Illustrious Highness wish music to do for it? [2]

THE IMITATION OF NATURE

From a letter to an unknown addressee, Venice, October 22, 1633

The title of the book will be as follows: *Melody, or Second Musical Practice*. By "second" I mean "from the modern aspect." "First" denotes "from the aspect of antiquity." I divide the book into three parts, which correspond to the three divisions of melody. In the first, I speak of line, in the second, of harmony, and in the third, of rhythm. I am of the opinion that it will not be unwelcome to the public, for during the course of my practical work, I discovered, when I was about to write "Ariadne's Lament," that I was unable to find any book that could instruct me in the method of the imitation of nature, or that could even have made clear to me that I should be an imitator of nature. The sole exception was Plato, one of whose ideas was, however, so obscure that, with my weak sight and at such great distance, I could hardly apprehend the little he could teach me. I must say that it has cost me great effort to complete the laborious work necessary to achieve what little I have accomplished in the imitation of nature. And for this reason, I hope I shall not cause displeasure. If I should succeed in bringing this work to a conclusion, as I so dearly wish, I should count myself happy to be praised less for modern compositions than for those in the traditional style. And for this presumption I beg forgiveness anew.

{3}

The Invention of the Agitato Style

From the preface to Eighth Book of Madrigals: Madrigali guerrieri ed amorosi, *1638*

I consider the principal passions or emotions of the soul to be three, namely, anger, serenity, and humility. The best philosophers affirm this; the very nature of our voice, with its high, low, and middle ranges, shows it; and the art of music clearly manifests it in these three terms: agitated, soft, and moderate. I have not been able to find an example of the agitated style in the works of past composers, but I have discovered many of the soft and moderate types. However, Plato describes the first in the third book of his *Rhetoric* in these words: "Take that harmony which would fittingly imitate the brave man going to war" [*Republic,* 399 A]. Knowing that contrasts are what moves our souls, and that such is the aim of all good music— as Boethius asserts: "Music is a part of us, and either ennobles or degrades our behavior"—I set myself with no little study and zeal to rediscover this style.

Considering that all the best philosophers maintain that the pyrrhic or fast tempo was used for agitated, warlike dances, and contrariwise the slow, spondaic tempo for their opposites, I thought about the semibreve [whole note] and proposed that each semibreve correspond to a spondee. Reducing this to sixteen semichromes [sixteenth notes] struck one after another and joined to words expressing anger and scorn, I could hear in this short example a resemblance to the emotion I was seeking, although the words did not follow the rapid beat of the instrument.

To arrive at a better proof, I resorted to the divine Tasso, as the poet who expresses most appropriately and naturally in words the emotions he wishes to depict, and I chose his description of the combat between Tancred and Clorinda as the theme for my music expressing the contrary passions aroused by war, prayer, and death.

In the year 1624 I had this work performed before the most eminent citizens of Venice, at the house of the Most Illustrious and Excellent Signor Girolamo

Mocenigo, noble knight and servant of the most serene Republic and my special patron and protector. It was received with much applause and was highly praised.

Having met with success in my method of depicting anger, I proceeded with even greater zeal in my investigations and wrote divers compositions, both ecclesiastical and chamber works. These found such favor with other composers that they not only *spoke* their praise but, to my great joy and honor, *wrote* it by imitating my work. Consequently, it has seemed wise to let it be known that the investigation and the first efforts in this style—so necessary to the art of music, and without which it can rightly be said that music has been imperfect up to now, having had but two styles, soft and moderate—originated with me.   [4]

Heinrich Schütz
1585–1672

Schütz played a central role in establishing the German sacred music tradition into which Bach and Handel were born. He traveled twice to Italy, studying first with Gabrieli and later Monteverdi; the result was the creation of a new style incorporating Italian and German techniques. Most of Schütz's compositions are sacred, although his Dafne *was the first German opera.*

TEMPO IN *STILO RECITATIVO*

From the preface to The Psalms of David *(for 8 and more parts), 1619*

Since I have set these *Psalms* in the *stilo recitativo,* which until now has been almost unknown in Germany, and since the Psalms, having many words, call for a continuous declamation without long repetition, I would ask those who are unfamiliar with this style to be sure not to hurry the beat. It would be best to adhere to a moderate tempo, so the words may be clearly understood. Otherwise, there will ensue a most unpleasant harmony, all too like a *battaglia di mosche* [battle of flies] and wholly at variance with the composer's intention.   [1]

THE MODERN ITALIAN STYLE IN GERMANY

Preface to Symphoniae sacrae, Book II, *1647*

I need not detain you with the tale of how, in the year 1629, during my second sojourn in Italy where I lived for some time, I indited—with the little talent God gave me—after the musical manner then in vogue there, a little Latin work for one, two, and three vocal parts, accompanied by two violins or similar instruments, and within a short time had it published in Venice under the title *Symphoniae sacrae.*

Inasmuch as parts of the work that were imported into Germany found such favor among our musicians and were performed in the most excellent places to German texts instead of Latin, I was spurred on to compose such a work in our

German mother tongue. After prolonged beginnings, I finally finished it, with God's help, along with much other work.

Until now, however, I have been prevented from sending it to press because of the miserable conditions prevailing in our dear fatherland, which adversely affect all the arts, music included; and even more importantly, because the modern Italian style of composition and performance (with which, as the sagacious Signor Claudio Monteverdi remarks in the preface to his *Eighth Book of Madrigals,* music is said finally to have reached its perfection) has remained largely unknown in this country.

Experience has proved that the modern Italian manner of composition and its proper tempo, with its many black notes, does not in most cases lend itself to use by Germans who have not been trained for it. Believing one had composed really good works in this style, one has often found them so violated and corrupted in performance that they offered a sensitive ear nothing but boredom and distaste, and called down unjustified opprobrium on the composer and on the German nation, the inference being that we are entirely unskilled in the noble art of music—and certain foreigners have more than once leveled such accusations at us.

As only a few manuscript copies of my little work were extant (it was dedicated to the then Highborn Prince and Lord, Christian V of Denmark and Norway, Prince of the Goths and Wends, as may be seen from the affixed letter of dedication), and as I learned that many sections, carelessly and improperly copied, had got into the hands of eminent musicians, I was forced to revise it carefully and have it published for those who may find pleasure in it.

I hope that intelligent musicians who have been trained in good schools will appreciate the labor I have spent on it and not be entirely displeased by the newly introduced style, [for] to please them alone, next to God, these present few copies are being brought to light.

As for others, above all those of us Germans who do not know how properly to perform this modern music, with its black notes and steady, prolonged bowing on the violin, and who, albeit untrained, still wish to play this way, I herewith kindly request them not to be ashamed to seek instruction from experts in this style and not to shirk home practice before they undertake a public performance of any of these pieces. Otherwise they and the author—though he be innocent—may receive unexpected ridicule rather than praise.

While in the concerto "Es steh Gott auf" I have to a degree followed Signor Claudio Monteverdi's madrigal "Armato il cuor"* as well as one of his *ciaconne* (with two tenor parts†), I leave it to those familiar with the aforementioned compositions to judge to what extent I have done this. Let no one suspect the rest of my work unduly, however, for I am not prone to deck my cap with strange feathers.

Finally, should God grant me longer life, I hereby promise—with His gracious aid—to publish soon more of my humble works, among them such as may be most effectively used by those who are not and do not intend to become professional musicians. *Vale.*   [2]

---

* *Scherzi musicali* (Venice, 1632), no. 8.

† Ibid., no. 9.

COUNTERPOINT VERSUS THOROUGHBASS

From the preface to Geistliche Chormusik
(for 5–7 parts, with optional basso continuo), 1648

Kind Reader: It is obvious that ever since the *stilo concertato* over a basso continuo came from Italy and received the notice of us Germans, it has been greatly favored by us and has found more followers than any previous style; various and sundry musical works, published in Germany and found in bookstalls, amply testify to this. Far be it from me to disapprove of this. Indeed, I recognize among us many who are interested and well skilled in music, whose fame I do not begrudge but willingly grant. Nevertheless, no musician, trained in a good school in the most difficult study of counterpoint, can start on any other kind of composition and handle it correctly, unless he has first trained himself sufficiently in the style without basso continuo and has also mastered all the prerequisites for regular composition, such as disposition of the modes; simple, mixed, and inverted fugues; double counterpoint; different styles for different kinds of music; part writing; connection of themes, and so on, of which the learned theoreticians write profusely and in which students of counterpoint are being orally trained in technical schools. No composition of even an experienced composer lacking such a background (even though it may appear as heavenly harmony to ears not properly trained in music) can stand up or be judged better than an empty shell.

All this has led me once more to write a little work without basso continuo, thereby perhaps to refresh some composers, especially German beginners, and encourage them to crack this hard nut (in which the true kernel and proper foundation of good counterpoint is to be found) and first to pass this test, before they attempt the *stilo concertato*. In Italy, which is the true university of music (where in my youth I laid the foundation for this profession), it was customary for beginners first to work out and perform certain sacred or secular pieces without basso continuo, and I assume that this excellent procedure is still observed there. Therefore I hope that these remarks intended to stimulate music and further our nation's glory will be well received by everyone and not taken as intending any belittlement.   [3]

MUSIC AND MONEY

From a letter to Prince Christian of Saxony, Dresden, August 14, 1651

Most gracious Lord: reluctant though I am to burden so illustrious a Prince with my repeated letters and reminders, yet I am compelled thereto by the continual comings and goings, hour after hour, the exceeding great lamentation, wretchedness, and moaning of all the company of poor, neglected musicians of the Chapel, who are living in such distress as would draw tears from a stone in the ground. May God be my witness that their wretched condition and piteous lamentation pierces my heart, since I know not how to give them comfort and hope of some relief.

In former days one would scarce have thought it possible, but most of the company are firmly resolved and say that sooner than bring discredit upon their most gracious Lord by begging their bread, they will set out, compelled by dire necessity, and go their ways elsewhere; that it is impossible for them to remain and continue to endure what they have had to suffer for so long, they must perforce depart, leaving anyone who will to pay their debts. They have had enough of insults, no one will any longer give them credit for a groat, etc. . . . .

I therefore submit to Your Princely Highness my most humble, earnest plea that you may compassionately solicit His Serene Highness, as your dearly beloved Father, to allow but a single quarter's salary to be paid to the company, that it may at least be held together. . . . But if Your Princely Highness should be unable to make some beneficial arrangement—though that is against all my hope—it would be impossible for me to hold them longer. In such case I shall have done my best and have no blame.   [4]

CHAPTER TWO

Henry Purcell

François Couperin

Georg Philipp Telemann

Jean Philippe Rameau

Johann Sebastian Bach

Benedetto Marcello

Henry Purcell
1658–1695

In his short life Purcell created a substantial body of music, ranging from church anthems to scatological tavern songs. He began his musical career as a chorister of the Chapel Royal in London. In 1679 he succeeded his teacher, John Blow, as organist of Westminster Abbey, and in 1689 he wrote Dido and Aeneas, *the first English opera of enduring fame.*

ENGLISH MUSIC IN ITS NONAGE

From the dedication of The Prophetess, or The History of Dioclesian *to the duke of Somerset, 1650**

Musick and Poetry have ever been acknowledg'd Sisters, which walking hand in hand, support each other; As Poetry is the harmony of Words, so Musick is that of Notes; and as Poetry is a Rise above Prose and Oratory, so is Musick the exaltation of Poetry. Both of them may excel apart, but sure they are most excellent when they are joyn'd, because nothing is then wanting to either of their Perfections for thus they appear like Wit and Beauty in the same Person. Poetry and Painting have arrived to their perfection in our Own Country: Musick is yet but in its Nonage, a forward Child, which gives hope of what it may be hereafter in *England,* when the Masters of it shall find more Encouragement. 'Tis now learning *Italian,* which is its best Master, and studying a little of the *French* Air to give it somewhat more of Gayety and Fashion. Thus being farther from the Sun, we are of later Growth than our Neighbour Countries, and must be content to shake off our Barbarity by degrees. The present Age seems already dispos'd to be refin'd, and to distinguish betwixt wild Fancy, and a just, numerous Composition.   [1]

COMPOSING UPON A GROUND

From Purcell's additions to Playford's Introduction to the Skill of Musick, *1700*

One thing that was forgot to be spoken of in its proper Place, I think necessary to say a little of now, which is Composing upon a *Ground,* a very easy thing to do, and requires but little Judgment; as 'tis generally used in *Chaconnes,* and often the *Ground* is four notes gradually descending, but to maintain *Fuges* upon it would be difficult, being confin'd like a *Canon* to a *Plain Song.* There are also pretty *Dividing Grounds* (of whom the *Italians* were the first *inventors* to *Single Songs,* or *Songs* of Two Parts, which to do neatly, requires considerable Pains, and the best way to be acquainted with 'em, is to Score much, and chuse the best Authors.   [2]

---

* This dedication was written for Purcell by John Dryden.

François Couperin
1668–1733

François Couperin was the most distinguished member of a noted musical family, an organist who served at St.-Gervais in Paris from his eighteenth birthday until his death. His treatise on playing the harpsichord circulated widely and is believed to have influenced Bach. In addition to the passages presented below, the treatise includes technical information on touch and fingerings and on proper execution of the prolific ornaments characteristic of the French Baroque style.

From The Art of Playing the Harpsichord, *1717*

THE BEGINNER AT THE HARPSICHORD

The proper age to start children is from six to seven years, not that this excludes older people, but naturally, in order to mold and develop the hands for playing the harpsichord, the sooner one begins, the better, and since grace is necessary for it, one should begin with the position of the body.

To be seated at the proper height, the underside of the elbows, the wrists and the fingers should be kept on one level. One should choose a chair accordingly.

An appropriately high support should be placed under the feet of young people and adjusted as they grow, so that their feet do not dangle in the air, and they can keep the body correctly balanced. . . .

During the first lessons it is recommended that the child practice only with the instructor present. Children are too easily distracted to discipline themselves to hold their hands in the prescribed position. At the beginning of children's study I actually keep the key of the instrument on which I am instructing them as a precautionary measure, so that in my absence they cannot spoil in a moment what I have so carefully set in three quarters of an hour.   [1]

THE PERFORMER'S MANNER

An adult should sit about nine inches from the keyboard, measuring from the waist, and young people proportionately less. The middle of the body and the middle of the keyboard should correspond.

When seated at the harpsichord, the body should be turned slightly to the right. The knees should not be pressed together too much, the feet should be kept parallel, and above all, the right foot should be kept well forward.

As for facial grimaces, one can correct them by placing a mirror on the reading desk of the spinet or harpsichord. . . .   [2]

LEARNING THE NOTES

One should begin to teach children notation only after they have a number of pieces in their fingers. It is nearly impossible that, while they are looking at their notes, their fingers should not get out of position, fumble, or that the ornaments themselves should not be changed. Besides, memory is developed in learning things by heart. [3]

MEASURE AND RHYTHM

I find that we confuse measure with what is known as cadence or rhythm. Measure defines the quantity and equality of the time, and cadence is properly the spirit or the soul that must be combined with it. Italian *sonades* are hardly susceptible to cadence. But all our airs for violin, our pieces for harpsichord, for viols, etc., describe and seem to want to express this spirit. Since we have never devised symbols to communicate our particular ideas, we try to remedy this by indications such as *tendrement, vivement,* etc., which suggest more or less what we would like to have heard. I wish someone would take the trouble to translate our indications for the benefit of foreigners, and thus allow them to judge the excellence of our instrumental music.

As for the delicate pieces that are played on the harpsichord, it is wise not to play them quite as slowly as they are played on other instruments, because of the short duration of harpsichord tones, and because expression and taste are retained whether the tempo is fast or slow. [4]

From the preface to Les Nations, *1726*

THE COMPOSER IN DISGUISE

Charmed by those [trio sonatas] of Signor Corelli, whose works I shall love as long as I live, just as I shall the French works of M. de Lully, I ventured to compose such a work myself, and to arrange to have it performed in the same venue where I had heard Corelli's sonatas. Knowing the distaste the French have for any kind of foreign novelty, and somewhat lacking confidence, I arranged—through a harmless deception—a good turn for myself. I let it be understood that a relative of mine, who is in fact at the court of the King of Sardinia, had sent me a sonata by a new Italian composer. I rearranged the letters of my name into an Italian-sounding name, which I put down as the author. The sonata was devoured with gusto; I shall not even describe the praise. But I was encouraged. I composed others, and my Italianized name earned for me, in my disguise, great applause. Happily my sonatas have met with enough favor that my little deception has not embarrassed me. In comparing these sonatas with those I have composed since that time, I have seen little that needed changing or improvement. I have simply joined them to some larger suites, to which they may serve as preludes or introductions.

I hope that the impartial public will be pleased with these pieces. For there will always be detractors, and these are more loathsome even than decent critics—who, although they don't mean to, sometimes offer helpful advice. The former are reprehensible, and I settle my accounts with them in advance and with interest. I still possess a fairly considerable number of these trios, enough that someday I might fill another volume the size of this one. [5]

Georg Philipp Telemann
1681–1767

Telemann has come to be considered a composer of greater facility than depth, but during his lifetime he was held in the highest regard in Northern Europe. He mastered the Italian and German practices of the day, producing a body of works that exceeds even Bach's in its vastness and variety. He remained abreast of new developments; the works of his last years approach the style of the Classical era.

From Autobiography *in Johann Mattheson's* Grundlage einer Ehren-Pforte, *1740*

POLISH MUSIC

In Pless, a dominion of the court of Promnitz in upper Silesia, where the court used to repair for six months, as well as in Cracow, I became familiar with Polish and Hanakian music in their true, barbaric beauty. In the public taverns the band would consist of a fiddle strapped to the body, a Polish bagpipe, a bass trombone and a *regal.** The fiddle was tuned a third higher than usual, and could thus outscream any six ordinary violins. At places of better repute the regal was omitted, but the number of fiddles and bagpipes was augmented. Indeed, once I found thirty-six bagpipes and eight fiddles together. One can hardly believe with what inspiration bagpipers and fiddlers improvise while the dancers rest. An observant person could pick up enough ideas from them in a week to last a lifetime. In short, this music contains much valuable material, if it is properly treated.

In time I wrote various grand concertos and trios in this manner, which I clothed in Italian dress, with divers adagios and allegros.   [1]

DUTIES AS A COURT AND CHAPEL MUSICIAN

Until now [his appointment at Eisenach in 1708], I could have been compared to the cook who has many pots on the stove but serves from only one at a time. But now I was to serve everything at once—to show my knowledge of various instruments and my ability with voice and pen. The original intention at Eisenach was to install only an instrumental ensemble, the members of which were chosen by Herr Pantaleon Hebenstreit, whom I can never praise enough, and to whom I was assigned as concertmaster. I had to play the violin and other instruments both at table and in the chamber, while Hebenstreit bore the title of director. He also fiddled in the chamber and was heard on his admirable cembalon.† But after His Grace, the Duke, had found pleasure in some church cantatas that I had sung

---

* A portable organ consisting typically of one to two reed stops.

† Hebenstreit (1667–1750) was famous throughout Europe as the developer and leading virtuoso of a type of hammered dulcimer that became known as the pantaleon.

alone, a chapel was started, and I was ordered to contract for the necessary singers, who had also to double as violinists. Upon their arrival I was appointed conductor, at the same time continuing my former duties. I must say that this chapel, largely arranged in the French manner, surpassed even the Paris opera orchestra, which I had recently heard and which has a great reputation.

At this point I must call attention to Herr Hebenstreit's violinistic skill, which certainly placed him among masters of the first rank. Whenever we were to perform a concerto together, I used to lock myself up a few days before. Fiddle in hand, shirtsleeve rolled up on my left arm, to which I applied nerve-strengthening salves, I acted as my own teacher so that I might in some measure equal his power. And lo, it did help me to improve considerably. Since I composed everything for all the performances (save a few contributions by him), one can easily imagine how much I must have written.   [2]

Jean Philippe Rameau
1683–1764

The public knew Rameau as a composer and organist, while to musicians he was most famous as a theorist. His innovations, which include the classification of all inversions of a chord as a single chord, became the basis for the theory of tonal harmony. During Rameau's life both his music and ideas met with divided opinion. In the war of words between the partisans of French and Italian styles, he took the French side, placing himself at odds with Rousseau and the Encyclopédistes, who claimed to find his music unintelligible and lacking in melody.

From Le Nouveau système de musique théorique, *1726*

COMPOSITION

The moment when one is composing music is not the time to recall the rules that might hold our genius in bondage. We must have recourse to the rules only when our genius and our ear seem to deny what we are seeking.   [1]

We may note that the semiskilled generally use a chord because it is familiar to them or pleases them, but the expert uses it only to the extent that he feels its power.   [2]

We all have our habitual "modulations" into which we lapse when we lack the knowledge that might divert us from them to good purpose. We are accustomed to go through a mode in a certain fashion, to pass to the other, etc. However, all expressions are not alike, the connection between one phrase and another is not always the same, their qualities do not always have the same power, etc.   [3]

TASTE

It is often by seeing and hearing musical works (operas and other good musical compositions), rather than by rules, that taste is formed.   [4]

From Observations sur notre instinct pour la musique et sur son principe, *1734*

Harmony

To enjoy the effects of music fully, we must completely lose ourselves in it; to judge it, we must relate it to the source through which we are affected by it. This source is nature. Nature endows us with the feeling that moves us in all our musical experiences; we might call her gift *instinct*. Let us allow instinct to inform our judgments, let us see what mysteries it unfolds to us before we pronounce our verdicts, and if there are still men sufficiently self-assured to dare make judgments on their own authority, there is reason to hope that none will be found weak enough to listen to them.

A mind preoccupied while listening to music is never free enough to judge it. For instance, if we think to attribute the essential beauty of this art to changes from high to low, from fast to slow, soft to loud—means that do give variety to sounds—we will judge everything according to this prejudice, without considering how weak these means are, or what scant merit there is in making use of them; we will fail to perceive that they are foreign to harmony, which is the sole basis of music and the true source of its glorious effects.

A truly sensitive spirit must judge quite differently! If the spirit is not moved by the power of the expression, by the vivid colors of which the harmonist alone is capable, then it is not absolutely satisfied. The spirit may, of course, lend itself to whatever may entertain it, but it must evaluate things in proportion to the impact the given experience exerts.

Harmony alone can stir the emotions. It is the one source from which melody directly emanates, and draws its power. Contrasts between high and low, etc., make only superficial modifications in a melody; they add almost nothing. . . .

If the imitation of noise and motion is not used as frequently in our music as in Italian music, it is because with us the main object is feeling. Feeling has no predetermined rhythms, and consequently cannot be everywhere reduced to a regular measure without losing that verity which is its charm. The musical expression of the physical lies in beat and rhythm; that which touches the emotions comes, on the contrary, from harmony and its inflections, a fact we must carefully weigh before deciding what should carry the balance.

The comic genre almost never aims to express emotion and consequently is the one genre that lends itself to those cadenced rhythms by which we do honor to Italian music. We do not always notice, however, how our own musicians have made felicitous use of them. Our enjoyment of the few attempts that the delicacy of French taste has permitted our composers to risk has proved how easily we can excel in this genre.   [5]

Habits and Inclinations

Whether a novice or the most experienced person in music, the moment one sings an improvisation, one ordinarily places the first tone in the middle register of the voice and then continues up, even though the voice range above or below this first tone is about equal; this is completely consistent with the resonance of any sounding body, from which all emanating overtones are above its fundamental tone, which one thinks one is hearing alone.

On the other hand, inexperienced as one may be, one hardly ever fails, when improvising on an instrument, immediately to play, ever ascending, the perfect chord made up of the overtones [harmonics] of the sounding body, the major form of which is always preferred to the minor, unless the latter is suggested by some reminiscence.   [6]

Often we think we hear in music only what exists in the words, or in the interpretation we wish to give them. We try to subject music to forced inflections, but that is not the way to be able to judge it. On the contrary, we must not think but let ourselves be carried away by the feeling that the music inspires; without our thinking at all, this feeling will become the basis of our judgment. As for reason, everybody possesses it nowadays; we have just discovered it in the bosom of nature itself. We have even proved that instinct constantly recalls it to us, both in our actions and in our speech. When reason and instinct are reconciled, there will be no higher appeal.
                                                                                            [7]

RHYTHM

From Code de musique pratique, 1760

Of all the elements united in the performance of music, rhythm is the one most natural to us, as it is equally natural to all animals. If this is so, why then do we accuse so many people of lacking an ear for rhythm?

If rhythm consists only in the regularity of movement, let us examine both the movements of animals and our own, such as walking or moving some part of the body. Where reflection or will do not affect them, the movements will always be regular. But if we wish to make someone follow a prescribed rhythm, in which case his mind is preoccupied with a rhythm unfamiliar to him, where thinking, in other words, destroys the natural functioning, should we be surprised that he seems insensitive to it?

Wait until that person completely gets the knack of subjecting the movement to the beat, and we will no longer find him rebellious. Or, let us allow him to prescribe for himself a repeated movement of the hand without thinking about it; let us make him perform something that is familiar to him based on this movement, be it music or dance step, each note or step corresponding to each movement, and soon we will see that we were mistaken about him.   [8]

Johann Sebastian Bach
1685–1750

Bach left behind only a modest number of written documents, and nearly all of them are of an official or quotidian nature. Nevertheless, he was perfectly articulate on musical matters when he needed to be. A number of his statements were recorded by pupils and friends; several of these are included here. Birnbaum's letter, a rebuttal of a letter from J. A. Scheibe criticizing Bach, appears to be a direct reflection of Bach's own views and may have been written with his participation.

From "Short but Most Necessary Draft for a Well-Appointed Church Music, with Certain Modest Reflections on the Decline of Same," memorandum to the town council of Leipzig, August 23, 1730

VOCAL AND INSTRUMENTAL FORCES

A well-appointed church music requires vocalists and instrumentalists.

The vocalists here are made up of the pupils of the Thomas-Schule, being of four kinds, namely, sopranos, altos, tenors, and basses.

In order that the choruses of church pieces may be performed as is fitting, the vocalists must in turn be divided into 2 sorts, namely, concertists and ripienists [soloists and chorus].

The concertists are ordinarily 4 in number; sometimes also 5, 6, 7, even 8; that is, if one wishes to perform music for two choirs.

The instrumentalists are also divided into various kinds, namely, violinists [a term that here includes all other string players], oboists, flutists, trumpeters, and drummers.

The number of resident students of the Thomas-Schule is 55. These 55 are divided into 4 choirs, for the 4 churches in which they must perform partly concerted music with instruments, partly motets, and partly chorales. In the 3 churches, St. Thomas's, St. Nicholas's, and the New Church, the pupils must all be musical. The Peters-Kirche receives the remainder, namely, those who do not understand music and can barely sing a chorale.

Every musical choir should contain at least 3 sopranos, 3 altos, 3 tenors, and as many basses, so that even if one happens to fall ill (as very often happens, particularly at this time of year, as the prescriptions written by the school physician for the apothecary must show) at least a double-chorus motet may be sung. (N.B. Though it would be still better if the classes were such that one could have 4 singers on each part and thus could perform every chorus with 16 persons.) This makes in all 36 persons who must understand music. {1}

STUDENTS AS CHORISTERS

Moreover, it cannot remain unmentioned that the fact that so many poorly equipped boys, and boys not at all talented for music, have been accepted [into the school] to date has necessarily caused the music to decline and deteriorate. For it is easy to see that a boy who knows nothing of music, and who cannot indeed even form a whole step in his throat, can have no natural musical talent and consequently can never be used for the musical service. And that those who do bring a few precepts with them when they come to school are not ready to be used immediately, as is required. For there is no time to instruct such pupils first for years, until they are ready to be used, but on the contrary: as soon as they are accepted they are assigned to the various choirs, and they must at least be sure of *measure* and *pitch* in order to be of use in divine service. Now, if each year some of those who have accomplished something in music leave the school and their places are taken by others who either are not yet ready to be used or have no ability whatsoever, it is easy to understand that the chorus must decline.

Now, however, that the state of music is quite different from what it was, since our artistry has increased very much, tastes have changed astonishingly, and accordingly the former style of music no longer seems to please our ears, and considerable help is therefore all the more needed to choose and appoint such musicians as will satisfy the present musical taste, master the new kinds of music, and thus be in a position to do justice to the composer and his work—now, the meagre compensation [for chorus members], which should have been rather increased than diminished, has been withdrawn entirely. It is, anyhow, somewhat strange that German musicians are expected to be capable of performing at once and *ex tempore* all kinds of music, whether it come from Italy or France, England or Poland, just as may be done, say, by those virtuosos for whom the music is written and who have studied it long beforehand, indeed, know it almost by heart, and who, be it noted, receive good salaries besides, so that their work and industry thus is richly rewarded; while on the other hand, this is not taken into consideration, but they [German musicians] are left to look out for their own wants, so that many a one, for worry about his bread, cannot think of improving—let alone distinguishing—himself. To illustrate this statement with an example one need only go to Dresden and see how the musicians there are paid by His Royal Majesty; it cannot fail, since the musicians are relieved of all concern for their living, free from chagrin, and obliged each to master but a single instrument: it must be something choice and excellent to hear. The conclusion is accordingly easy to draw, that with the stopping of the compensation the powers are taken from me to bring the music into a better state.

In conclusion, I find it necessary to append the enumeration of the present students, to indicate the musical skill of each *in musicis*. . . . Total: 17 usable, 20 not yet usable, and 17 unfit.

Joh. Seb. Bach *Director Musices*   [2]

MELODY AND COUNTERPOINT

From J. A. Birnbaum's Impartial Comments on a Questionable Passage in the Sixth Number of "Der Critische Musicus," *1738*

Birnbaum: Now the idea that the melody must always be in the upper voice and that the constant collaboration of the other voices is a fault is one for which I have been able to find no sufficient grounds. Rather is it the exact opposite that flows from the very nature of music. For music consists of harmony, and harmony becomes far more complete if all the voices collaborate to form it.   [3]

ACADEMICISM

From a letter of F. W. Marpurg to "Herr Legationsrath Mattheson," February 9, 1760

Marpurg: I myself once heard him, when during my stay in Leipzig I was discussing with him certain matters concerning the fugue, pronounce the works of an old and hard-working contrapuntist "dry and wooden," and certain fugues by a more modern and no less great contrapuntist—that is, in the form in which they are arranged for clavier—"pedantic"; the first because the composer stuck continuously to his principal subject, without any change; and the second because, at least in the fugues under discussion, he had not shown enough fire to reanimate the theme by interludes.   [4]

SILBERMANN'S FORTEPIANOS

From texts by J. F. Agricola published in Jacob Adlung's Musica mechanica organoedi, 1768

Agricola: One of them was seen and played by the late kapellmeister Mr. Johann Sebastian Bach. He had played, indeed admired, its tone; but he had complained that it was too weak in the high register, and that the action was too hard to play. This had been taken greatly amiss by Mr. Silbermann. . . . And yet his conscience told him Mr. Bach was not wrong. He therefore decided—greatly to his credit, be it said—not to deliver any more of these instruments, but instead to think all the harder about how to eliminate the faults Mr. Bach had observed. He worked for many years on this. . . . Finally, when Mr. Silbermann had really achieved many improvements, notably in respect to the action, he sold one again to the court of the Prince of Rudolstadt. Shortly thereafter His Majesty the King of Prussia had one of these instruments ordered, and when it met with His Majesty's Most Gracious approval, he had several more ordered from Mr. Silbermann. Mr. Silbermann had also had the laudable ambition to show one of these instruments of his later workmanship to the late Kapellmeister Bach and have it examined by him; and he had received, in turn, complete approval from him.   [5]

TRYING OUT AN ORGAN

From a letter of C. P. E. Bach to J. N. Forkel, c. 1774

C. P. E. Bach: The first thing he would do in trying out an organ was this: he would say, in jest, "Above all I must know whether the organ has good lungs," and, to find out, he would draw out every speaking stop and play in the fullest and richest possible texture. At this the organ builders would often grow quite pale with fright.   [6]

From J. N. Forkel's
On Johann Sebastian Bach's Life, Genius, and Works, *1802*

TEACHING COMPOSITION

Forkel: In all these [lessons in harmony and fugue], and other exercises in composition, he rigorously kept his pupils:

(1) To compose entirely from the mind, without an instrument. Those who wished to do otherwise he called, in ridicule, "knights of the keyboard";

(2) To pay constant attention to the consistency of each single part, in and of itself, as well as to its relation to the parts connected and concurrent with it. No part, not even a middle part, was allowed to break off before it had entirely said what it had to say. Every note was required to have a connection with the preceding: did any one appear of which it was not apparent whence it came, nor whither it tended, it was instantly banished as suspicious. [7]

TALENT AND INDUSTRY

Forkel: When he was sometimes asked how he had contrived to master the art to such a high degree, he generally answered: "I was obliged to be industrious; whoever is equally industrious will succeed equally well." [8]

Benedetto Marcello
1686–1739

Lawyer, politician, musician, and poet, Marcello was surely among the most gifted minds of his generation in Italy. He composed a number of oratorios and other sacred works, as well as secular songs and chamber music. He did not compose any operas, although as opera was a subject of much conversation among the intellectuals of his time, it is not surprising that he would have written a book about it—a satire, aimed particularly at Venetian opera.

From Il teatro alla moda,* *1720*

INSTRUCTIONS FOR LIBRETTISTS

A writer of operatic librettos, if he wishes to be modern, must not have read the Greek and Latin classic authors, nor should he do so in the future. After all, the old Greeks and Romans never read modern writers.

---

* The full title translates as, "Theater à la mode, or, A sure and easy method for effectively composing and performing Italian operas in the modern manner, in which is given useful and necessary advice to poets, composers, musicians of either sex, impresarios, instrumentalists, engineers, painters, decorators, comedians, tailors, pages, extras, prompters, copyists, the protectors and mothers of female virtuosi, and other persons belonging to the theater."

Nor should he have the slightest knowledge of Italian meter and verse. At most he might possibly admit he "had somewhere heard" that verses must consist of seven or eleven syllables. This amply suffices, and he can then suit his fancy by making verses of three, five, nine, thirteen, or even fifteen syllables. He should, on the other hand, boast that he has had thorough schooling in mathematics, painting, chemistry, medicine, law, etc., and should then confess that his genius so strongly compelled him to it that he just *had* to become a poet. Yet he need not have the slightest acquaintance with the various rules concerning correct accentuation or the making of good rhymes. He need not have any command of poetical language. Mythology and history can be closed books to him. To make up for this, as frequently as possible he will employ in his works technical terms from the above-named sciences, or from others, though they may have no relation whatsoever to the world of Poetry. He should call Dante, Petrarch, and Ariosto obscure, clumsy, and dull poets whose works, accordingly, he should never, or only very seldom, use as examples. Instead, the modern librettist should acquire a large collection of contemporary writings; from these he should borrow sentiments, thoughts, and entire verses. This sort of theft he should refer to as "laudable imitation."

Before the librettist begins writing, he should ask the impresario for a detailed list of the number and kind of stage sets and decorations he wishes to see employed. The librettist will then incorporate all these into his drama. He should always be on the alert for elaborate scenes such as sacrifices, sumptuous banquets, supernatural apparitions, or other spectacles. In connection with these, the librettist will consult with the theater engineer to discover how many dialogues, monologues, and arias will be needed to pad each scene of this type, so that all technical problems of staging can be worked out without haste. The disintegration of the drama as an entity and the intense boredom of the audience are without importance compared to these considerations.

He should write the entire opera without preconceived plan, but rather proceed verse by verse. For if the audience never understands the plot, it can be counted on to be attentive to the very end. One thing any able modern librettist must strive for: he must frequently have all characters of the piece on the stage at the same time, even though no one knows why. One by one, they may then leave the stage, singing the usual canzonetta.

The librettist should not worry about the ability of the performers, but much more about whether the impresario has at his disposal a good bear or lion, an able nightingale, genuine-looking bolts of lightning, earthquakes, storms, etc.

For the finale of his opera he should write a magnificent scene with more elaborate effects, so that the audience will not walk out before the work is half over. He should conclude with the customary chorus in praise of the sun, moon, or impresario.   [1]

INSTRUCTIONS FOR COMPOSERS

The modern composer should know no rules of composition aside from some vague generalities. He need not understand numerical proportions in relation to music, the advantages of contrary motion, or the disadvantages of tritones or hexachords with the B natural. He need not know how many modes there are, or how to distinguish them, or how they are divided, or what their characteristics are. Instead, in this connection he might declare that there are only two modes, namely major and minor; the former with the major third and the latter with the minor third. He need not digress to point out what the ancients understood by a major and minor tone. . . .

Before he actually starts to write the music, the composer should call upon all female singers in the company and offer to include anything they might care to have, such as arias without a bass in the accompaniment, *furlanette,* rigadoons, etc., with the violins, the bear, and the extras accompanying in unison.

He must not permit himself to read the entire libretto, which might confuse him. Instead, he should compose it verse by verse and immediately insist that all arias be rewritten [by the librettist]. This is the only way he will be able to utilize every melody that has popped into his head during the summer. If the words to these arias again fail to fit the notes properly—this commonly happens—he will continue to harass the librettist until the latter satisfies him completely.

All arias should have an instrumental accompaniment and care should be taken to have every part move in exactly the same note values, whether eighths, sixteenths, or thirty-seconds. Noise is what counts in modern music, not harmonious sound, which would consist mainly of diverse note values and the interchange of tied and accented notes. To avoid this true kind of harmony, the modern composer should employ nothing more daring than a four-three suspension, and that only in the cadence. If this seems to him a bit old-fashioned, he can make up for it by finishing the piece with all instruments playing in unison.

He must not forget that happy and sad arias should alternate throughout the opera, from beginning to end, regardless of any meaning of text, music, or stage action.

If nouns such as "father," "empire," "love," "arena," "kingdom," "beauty," "courage," "heart," appear in the aria, the modern composer should write long coloraturas over them. This applies also to "no," "without," "already," and other adverbs. This serves to introduce a little change from the old custom of using coloratura passages only over words expressing motion or emotion, for instance, "torment," "sorrow," "song," "fly," "fall." . . .

He should lend his services to the impresario for very little, mindful that thousands of *scudi* must be paid to famous singers. He should be satisfied with less pay than the least of them, though he should not tolerate the injustice of receiving less than the theater bear or the extras.   [2]

CHAPTER THREE

Carl Philipp Emanuel Bach

Christoph Willibald Gluck

Franz Joseph Haydn

Wolfgang Amadè Mozart

Carl Philipp Emanuel Bach
1714–1788

During the late eighteenth century the name "Bach" by itself usually referred to Carl Philipp Emanuel rather than to his father. It was C. P. E. Bach who definitively established the sonata form that was to prove so useful to generations of composers. He also helped develop an "intimately expressive" style of piano writing that profoundly influenced Haydn and Beethoven. Even so, he was a staunch defender of his father's music, which most musicians of his day found hopelessly outmoded. Scholars and performers still refer to his treatise on keyboard playing.

From Essay on the True Art
of Playing Keyboard Instruments, *1753/62*

EMBELLISHMENTS

No one disputes the need for embellishments. This is evident from the great numbers of them to be found everywhere. They are, in fact, indispensable. Consider their many uses: they connect and enliven tones and impart stress and accent; they make music pleasing and command our close attention. Expression is heightened by them; let a piece be sad, joyful, or otherwise, and they will lend fitting assistance. Embellishments provide opportunities for fine performance as well as much of its subject matter. They improve mediocre compositions. Without them the best melody is empty and ineffective, the clearest content clouded.

In view of their many commendable services, it is unfortunate that there are also poor embellishments and that good ones are sometimes used too frequently and ineptly.

Because of this, it has always been better for composers to specify the proper embellishments unmistakably, instead of leaving their selection to the whims of tasteless performers.

In justice to the French, it must be said that they notate their ornaments with painstaking accuracy. So do the masters of the keyboard in Germany, without embellishing to excess. Who knows but that our moderation with respect to both the number and kind of ornaments is the influence that has led the French to abandon their earlier practice of decorating almost every note, to the detriment of clarity and noble simplicity? [1]

PERFORMANCE

Keyboard players whose chief asset is mere technique are clearly at a disadvantage. A performer may have the most agile fingers, be competent at single and double trills, master the art of fingering, read skillfully at sight regardless of key, and transpose extemporaneously without the slightest difficulty; he may play tenths, even twelfths, or runs, cross hands in every conceivable manner, and excel in other related matters; yet he may be something less than a clear, pleasing, or stirring keyboard player. More often than not, one meets technicians, nimble players by profession, who possess all these qualifications and indeed astound us with their prowess without ever touching our sensibilities. They overwhelm our hearing without satisfying it and stun the mind without moving it. In writing this, I do not wish to discredit the praiseworthy skill of reading at sight. A commendable ability, I urge its practice on everyone. A mere technician, however, can lay no claim to the rewards of those who gently move the ear rather than the eye, the heart rather than the ear, and lead it where they will.

———— ⚑ ————

In order to arrive at an understanding of the true content and feeling of a piece and, in the absence of indications, to decide on the correct manner of performance, be it slurred, detached, or whatnot, and further, to learn the precautions that must be heeded in introducing ornaments, it is advisable that every opportunity be seized to listen to soloists and ensembles. This is all the more true as these details of beauty often depend on extraneous factors. The volume and time value of ornaments must be determined by the feeling to be achieved. In order to avoid vagueness, rests as well as notes must be given their exact value at fermatas and cadences. Yet purposeful violations of the beat are often exceptionally beautiful. However, a distinction in their use must be observed: in solo performance and in ensembles made up of only a few understanding players, manipulations are permissible that affect the tempo itself; here, the group will be less apt to go astray than to become attentive to and adopt the change; but in large ensembles made up of motley players, the manipulations must be addressed to the bar alone without touching on the broader pace. . . .

To learn the essentials of good performance, it is advisable to listen to accomplished musicians. Above all, lose no opportunity to hear artistic singing. In so doing, the keyboard player will learn to think in terms of song. Indeed, it is a good practice to sing instrumental melodies in order to reach an understanding of their correct performance. This way of learning is of far greater value than reading voluminous tomes or listening to learned discourses. In the latter one finds such terms as Nature, Taste, Song, and Melody, although their authors are often incapable of putting together as many as two natural, tasteful, singing, melodic tones, for these authors dispense their alms and endowments with completely infelicitous arbitrariness.

A musician cannot move others unless he too is moved. He must feel all the emotions that he hopes to arouse in his audience, for the revealing of his own humor will stimulate a like mood in the listener. In languishing, sad passages the performer must languish and grow sad. Thus will the expression of the piece be more clearly perceived by the audience.* Here, however, the error of a sluggish, dragging performance, caused by an excess of emotion and melancholy, must be avoided. Similarly, in lively, joyous passages, the executant must again put himself into the appropriate mood. Constantly varying the passions, he will barely quiet one before he rouses another. Above all, he must discharge this office in a piece that is highly expressive by nature, whether it be by him or by someone else.

* This sentence is a footnote added to the edition of 1787.

In the latter case, he must make certain that he assumes the emotion that the composer intended in writing it. It is principally in improvisations or fantasias that the keyboard player can best master the feelings of his audience.

Those who maintain that all this can be accomplished without gesture will retract their words when, owing to their own insensibility, they find themselves obliged to sit like statues before their instruments. Ugly grimaces are, of course, inappropriate and harmful; but suitable expressions help the listener to understand our meaning. Those opposed to this stand are often incapable of doing justice, despite their technique, to their own otherwise worthy compositions. Unable to bring out the content of their own works, they remain ignorant of it. But let someone else play these, a person of delicate, sensitive insight, who knows the meaning of a good performance, and the composer will learn, to his astonishment, that there is more in his music than he had ever known or believed. Good performance can, in fact, improve and gain praise for even an average composition.

It can be seen from the many emotions that music portrays that the accomplished musician must have special endowments and be capable of employing them wisely. He must carefully appraise his audience, its attitude toward the expressive content of his program, the recital hall itself, and other additional factors. Nature has wisely provided music with every kind of appeal so that all might share in its enjoyment. It thus becomes the duty of the performer to satisfy, to the best of his ability, every last kind of listener. [2]

ACCOMPANIMENT

The fewer the parts in a piece, the finer must be its accompaniment. Hence, a solo or an aria provides the best opportunity to judge an accompanist. He must take great pains to catch, in his accompaniment, all the nuances of the principal part. Indeed, it is difficult to say whether accompanist or soloist deserves greater credit. The latter may have taken a long time to prepare his piece, which, after the present fashion, he himself must compose. Nevertheless, he cannot count on the applause of his audience, for it is only through a good accompaniment that his performance will be brought to life. [3]

From Autobiography, *1773*

COMPOSING ON COMMISSION

Having been obliged to compose most of my works for particular individuals and for the public, I have been placed under more restraint in these works than in the few pieces I have written for my own pleasure. Indeed, sometimes I have been compelled to follow very ludicrous instructions; still, it is possible that these far from agreeable suggestions may have inspired my creative imagination with a variety of ideas that otherwise probably never would have occurred to me. [4]

CRITICISM

How seldom do we meet with a proper amount of sympathy, knowledge, honesty, and courage in a critic—four qualities they ought, in any event, to possess to some extent. It is sad indeed for the world of music that criticism, in so many respects so useful, should often be the occupation of persons in no way endowed with these qualities. [5]

Christoph Willibald Gluck
1714–1787

Gluck's feel for the theater was already apparent with the success of his first opera in 1741. Four years later he traveled to London, where two of his works were presented in an effort to compete with Handel. Over the next decade his operas were taken up throughout Europe.

The operatic reforms of Gluck and the librettist Calzabigi grew out of the intellectual climate of the time, with its interests in Nature and Reason, although they were the first to convert these popular ideas into a plan of action. Not everyone approved. In Paris, a bitter rivalry arose between the partisans of Gluck and those of Niccolò Piccinni; the rivalry did not, however, extend to the composers themselves.

AN APPROACH TO THE REFORM OF OPERA

From the dedication of Alceste to Duke Leopold of Tuscany, 1769

Your Royal Highness: When I undertook to compose music for *Alceste,* I proposed to abolish entirely all those abuses introduced by the injudicious vanity of singers or by the excessive complaisance of conductors, abuses that have so long disfigured the Italian opera and made it the most ridiculous and tiresome of all entertainments, instead of the most splendid and beautiful. My purpose was to restrict music to its true office, that of ministering to the expression of the poetry and to the situations of the plot, without interrupting the action or smothering it by superfluous ornamentation. I thought the music should accomplish what brilliancy of color and a skillfully adapted contrast of light and shade achieve in a correct and well-designed drawing, by animating the figures without distorting their contours. I wished, therefore, not to arrest an actor in the most exciting moment of his dialogue by making him wait for a wearisome *ritornello* nor, in the midst of half-uttered words, to detain him on a favorite note, whether this aimed to display his fine voice and flexibility in some long passage, or to make him pause till the orchestra gave him time to take breath for a cadenza. I did not feel I should hurry rapidly over the second part of an aria, possibly the most impassioned and important of all, in order to be able to repeat regularly four times over the words of the first part, thus making the aria end where in all probability the sense did not end, and all this for the convenience of the singer, to enable him to vary a passage according to his caprice. In short, I have striven to banish the abuses against which reason and good sense have so long protested in vain.

My idea was that the overture should prepare the spectators for the plot and give some indication of its nature; that the concerted instruments should be regulated according to the interest and passion of the drama; and that in a dialogue there should be no excessive gap between aria and recitative, lest the meaning of a passage be perverted or the force and warmth of the action implausibly interrupted.

Furthermore, I believed that my most strenuous efforts should be directed towards the search for a noble simplicity, thus avoiding a parade of difficulty at the expense of clarity. I did not consider a mere display of novelty to be valuable, unless it was to be suggested naturally by the situation and the expression, and on this point there is not a rule in composition that I would not have gladly sacrificed in favor of the effect produced.

Such are my principles. Fortunately, the libretto was wonderfully adapted to my purpose; the celebrated author, Calzabigi, having imagined a new dramatic plan, replaced flowery descriptions, superfluous similes, and cold sententious morality with the language of the heart, strong passions, interesting situations, and an ever-varying spectacle.   [1]

THE IMPORTANCE OF DETAILS

From the dedication of Paride ed Elena *to the duke of Braganza,*
October 30, 1770

Almost imperceptible differences distinguish Raphael from the common herd of painters, and the slightest alteration in an outline, which would in no way destroy the likeness in a caricature, can entirely disfigure the portrait of a lovely woman. By changing very little in the expression of my aria *Che farò senza Euridice,* it might be turned into a saltarello for puppets. A note more or less sustained, a neglected *rinforzo* carelessly omitted either in the music or in a vocal passage, an appoggiatura out of place, a shake, a passage, a run can easily ruin a whole scene in such an opera, whereas such things do not harm, or may even improve, the common run of operas.

Therefore, the presence of the composer at the performance of this class of music is as indispensable, so to speak, as the presence of the sun to works of nature. He is its absolute soul and life, and without him all is confusion and darkness. But we must be prepared for such obstacles so long as there are people in the world who consider themselves authorized to judge the fine arts, because they have the privilege of possessing eyes and ears, no matter what the quality of these may be. . . .

When truth is sought, it must be varied in accordance with the subject we have to work out, and the greatest beauties of melody and harmony become defects and imperfections when used out of place.   [2]

EXPRESSIVITY

From a letter to the poet and critic Jean-François de la Harpe, October 1777

It is impossible for me, Sir, to resist the very judicious observations you have just made upon my operas in your *Journal de littérature* of the fifth of this month; I find nothing, absolutely nothing, to object against them.

Until now I had been so simple as to believe that music was like the other arts in that all passions fell within its province and that it should give no less pleasure by expressing the heat of one enraged or the cry of one in grief than by rendering the sighs of a lover.

I believed this maxim to be true in music as in poetry. I had persuaded myself that song, colored through and through by the sentiments it was required to express, must change with them and take as many different accents as they had different shades; in short, that the voice, the instruments, all sounds, even pauses, should be directed toward a single aim, that of expression, and that the union of words and singing should be so close that the poem would seem to be fitted to the music no less than the music to the song.

These were not my only errors. It appeared to me that the French language was lightly accented and had no fixed quantities like the Italian. I had been struck by another difference between the singers of the two nations. While I found the voices of the former to be softer and more pliant, the latter seemed to me to bring more vigor and action to their performance: I had concluded from this that the Italian style of singing was unsuitable for French voices. Thereafter, in looking through the scores of old operas, despite the trills, cadenzas, and other defects with which their airs seemed to me to be overloaded, I found in them sufficient real beauty to convince me that the French had their own resources to draw upon.

Those, sir, were my ideas before I read your observations. But light immediately dispelled the darkness; I was confounded at perceiving that you had learned more about my art in a few hours of reflection than I myself after practicing it for forty years. You prove to me, sir, that the man of letters can speak on any subject. I am now fully convinced that the music of the Italian masters is music *par excellence*, that it alone is music, that singing, if it is to please, must be regular and periodic, and that even in disordered moments, when the character who is singing, moved by a variety of passions, passes in succession from one to another, the composer must always preserve the same style.

I agree with you that of all my compositions, *Orfeo* alone is tolerable. I sincerely beseech the god of taste to forgive me for deafening my hearers with my other operas; the number of performances they have received and the applause the public has been good enough to bestow upon them do not prevent me from seeing that they are pitiful. I am so convinced of this that I wish to rewrite them, and as I perceive you to be in favor of tender airs, I shall place in the mouth of the angry Achilles a song so touching and so sweet that the whole audience will be moved to tears.

As for *Armide*, I shall take good care not to leave the poem as it is at present, for as you so justly observe, *Quinault's operas, though full of beauties, are designed in a manner very little suited to music; they are very fine poems, but very bad operas*: so even if they should become very bad poems, the only question being to make fine operas after your manner, I implore you to make me acquainted with some versifier who can take *Armide* in hand and fit every scene with two airs. We shall agree together about the quantity and meter of the lines; so long as they have their full number of syllables I shall not concern myself with the rest. For my part, I am working at the music, from which it goes without saying I shall scrupulously banish all noisy instruments, such as the timpani and the trumpet; in my orchestra I wish only oboes, flutes, French horns, and violins to be heard—with mutes, of course. All that will then remain will be to fit the words to the tunes, which will not be difficult, as we shall have taken our measurements beforehand.

The role of Armide will thus no longer be a *monotonous and wearisome bawling*, she will no longer be a *Medea, a sorceress*, but *an enchantress*; I am resolved that in her despair she shall sing you an air so *regular*, so *periodic*, that any fashionable young lady with the vapors shall be able to hear it without the least irritation of her nerves.   [3]

Franz Joseph Haydn
1732–1809

Haydn composed prolifically in nearly every genre of his time. During his many years in service to the Esterházy family he was obligated to present as many as two operas and two formal concerts weekly. He taught Mozart and Beethoven and remained a major influence on them. Haydn did not actually "invent" the symphony or the string quartet, but he may be said to have brought them to their earliest perfection. Certainly, in his hands music first gained the tremendous scale of artistic ambition that was to mark its next hundred years.

C. P. E. BACH'S *PRUSSIAN SONATAS*

From Georg August Griesinger's
Biographische Notizen über Joseph Haydn, *1809*

I could not tear myself away from my clavier until I had played them all through, and whoever knows me thoroughly will find that I owe a great deal to Emanuel Bach, that I understood and eagerly studied him; Emanuel Bach himself at one time complimented me on this score.   [1]

MOZART

From a letter from Leopold Mozart to his daughter
Maria Anna ("Nannerl"), February 14, 1785

Leopold Mozart: On Saturday evening we had Herr Joseph Haydn and the two Barons Tindi with us. . . . Herr Haydn said to me, "I tell you, calling God to witness and speaking as a man of honor, that your son is the greatest composer I know, either personally or by repute! He has taste and, in addition, the most complete understanding of composition."   [2]

From a letter to Franz Roth,* Esterház, December 1, 1787

You wish me to write an *opera buffa* for you. Most willingly, if you wish to have a vocal composition for yourself alone. But if it is with a view to producing it on the stage in Prague, I cannot comply with your wish, for all my operas are too closely

---

* Superintendent of supplies in Prague and a music patron.

connected with our personal circle [Prince Esterházy's court in Hungary]. Thus they could never produce the proper effect, which I have carefully worked out to accord with the locality. It would be a different were I to have the privilege of composing a new opera for your theater. But even then I would run grave risks, for scarcely any man could stand beside the great Mozart.

I only wish I could instill in every friend of music, and in great men in particular, the depth of musical sympathy and profound appreciation of Mozart's inimitable music that I myself feel and enjoy. Then nations would vie with each other to possess such a jewel within their frontiers. Prague ought to strive to retain this precious man, but also to remunerate him; for without suitable remuneration, the history of a great genius is sad indeed and gives little encouragement to posterity to exert itself further. It is on this account that so many promising geniuses are lost. It enrages me to think that the unparalleled Mozart is not yet engaged by some imperial or royal court! Forgive my intemperance, but I love the man so dearly.   [3]

From a letter to Johann Michael Puchberg, London, January 1792

Because of his [Mozart's] death, I was for some time quite beside myself and could not believe that Providence could have required the presence of this indispensable man in the other world so soon. I only regret that he did not have a chance to convince the still benighted English of the things I preach to them daily.   [4]

BEETHOVEN

From a letter to the Elector of Cologne, Vienna, November 23, 1793

I take the liberty of sending to Your Electoral Highness various musical pieces, namely, a quintet, a partita in eight parts, an oboe concerto, variations for the pianoforte, and a fugue, composed by my dear pupil Beethoven, who has been graciously entrusted to me. I flatter myself that these pieces will be kindly received by Your Electoral Highness as worthy proof of his industry outside his regular studies. On the strength of these pieces, connoisseurs and amateurs must own without bias that Beethoven will one day take his place as one of the greatest composers in Europe, and I shall be proud to call myself his master. I only wish that he may still remain with me a while longer.   [5]

COMPOSING

From Griesinger's Biographische Notizen

I would sit down [at the piano] and begin to improvise, whether my spirits were sad or happy, serious or playful. Once I had captured an idea, I strove with all my might to develop and sustain it in conformity with the rules of art. In this way I tried to help myself, and this is where so many of our newer composers fall short: they string one little piece onto another and break off when they have scarcely started. Nothing remains in one's heart after one has listened to such compositions.   [6]

I was never a quick writer and always composed with care and diligence. Such works are lasting, however, and the connoisseur knows this immediately from the score. When Cherubini would look over some of my manuscripts, he would always recognize those passages that deserved special marks of distinction.   [7]

There was no one near me [at Esterháza] to confuse or torment me, thus I was obliged to be original.   [8]

Wolfgang Amadè Mozart
1756–1791

Mozart's letters—most of them to his father Leopold, himself a composer—reveal a man aware of not only his talents but of his limitations, intolerant of shoddiness and pretension, and not beyond playing a joke. Above all they reveal a man sensitive to matters of musical and human import, from the lofty to the almost unprintable. He had an abiding interest in music of the past, but also kept abreast of new developments, as his letter about Stein's forte-pianos shows.

From a letter to his father, Augsburg, October 17/18, 1777
STEIN'S PIANOFORTES

This time I must start off with [Johann August] Stein's pianofortes. Before I had encountered any of Stein's work, Späth's claviers had been my favorites. Now, however, I prefer Stein's, for they damp so much better than the Regensburg instruments. When I strike a key hard, I can leave my finger on it or I can raise it, but the sound stops the instant I have produced it. I can strike the keys any way I like, but the tone is always the same. It never jars, it never grows stronger or weaker or entirely vanishes; in a word, it is always even. True, he does not sell such a pianoforte for less than three hundred gulden, but the sweat and diligence he lavishes on his instruments is priceless. His instruments have a particular advantage over others in that they are made with an escapement action. Only one maker in a hundred bothers with this. But without an escapement action it is impossible for a pianoforte to avoid jangling or vibrating. When you play the keys, the hammers fall down again the instant they have struck the strings, whether you hold the keys down or release them. When he has finished making such a clavier— as he told me himself—he sits down and has a go at all sorts of passages and runs and jumps, and then he polishes and labors away until it can do everything. He works for the benefit of music alone, and not on his own account; otherwise, he'd be done with his work in no time. He often says: "If I myself were not such an ardent lover of music and could play nothing on the clavier, I would have lost patience with my work long ago. But I'm very much a lover of instruments that will not let their players down, and that are durable." And durable his claviers certainly are. He guarantees that his sounding board will neither break nor split. When he has finished making one, he leaves it exposed to the open air, to the rain, the snow, the sun's heat, and all manner of tortures, so that it finally cracks. Then he is able to glue in wedges, so that it becomes very strong and solid. He's thrilled when a sounding board cracks; it's his assurance that nothing more can happen to it. In fact, he often cuts into it himself, then glues it back together and, in doing so, strengthens it. [1]

THE ORGAN

When I told him [Stein] how much I would like to play the instrument he had built, since the organ was my great love, he was quite astonished and said: "What? A man like you, a great master of the clavier, wants to play on an instrument that allows no gentleness, no expression, no *piano*, no *forte*, nothing the same sound forever?" "None of that matters," I responded. "To my eyes and ears, the organ is the king of instruments." [2]

RUBATO

From a letter to his father, Augsburg, October 23, 1777

They simply cannot understand that, in tempo rubato, my left hand plays independently of my right. When they play, the left hand always matches. [3]

SIGHTREADING

From a letter to his father, Mannheim, January 17, 1778

By the way, before dinner, he [Abbé Vogler] had raced through my concerto at sight (the one the daughter of the house plays—composed for Countess Lutzow [the Piano Concerto in C, K. 426]). The first movement went *prestissimo*, the *andante* went *allegro* and the rondo even more *prestissimo*. Most of the time he played a different bass from what was written, and sometimes he invented entirely different harmonies and melodies. What else would you expect at that speed? The eyes cannot read the music, nor can the hands grasp it. Well, what's supposed to be the good of that? As far as I'm concerned, sightreading of that type is the same as shitting. The listeners (that is, those who are worthy of the name) can say nothing except that they have *seen* music and piano playing. They hear, think, and feel as little during the performance as the performer himself. Well, you can easily imagine how unbearable it was, since I couldn't bring myself to tell him, *"Much too fast!"* Anyway, it is much easier to play a piece faster than slower. In the more taxing passages you can leave out a few notes and nobody will be the wiser. But is that beautiful? In the confusion, one can change the right and left hands without anyone seeing or hearing it; but is that beautiful?

Where, then, lies the art of playing *a prima vista*? In playing the piece at the proper tempo and in playing all the notes, appoggiaturas, etc., and with the appropriate expression and taste, all just as it is written, so that one might believe the performer had written it himself. [4]

Opera

From a letter to his father, February 28, 1778

I love it when an aria fits a singer as perfectly as a well-tailored suit of clothes.   [5]

Vibrato

From a letter to his father, Paris, June 12, 1778

The human voice trembles naturally by itself, just enough to sound beautiful. That is the nature of the voice, and we imitate this effect not only on our wind instruments, but on the strings—and even on the clavier. As soon as one oversteps the bounds, however, it is no longer beautiful, because it is contrary to nature.   [6]

The Melodrama

From a letter to his father, Mannheim, November 12, 1778

[I] have always wanted to write a drama of this kind. I cannot remember whether I told you anything about this type of drama the first time I was here. On that occasion I saw a piece of this kind performed twice and was absolutely delighted. Indeed, nothing has ever surprised me so much, for I had always imagined that such a piece would be quite ineffective! You know, of course, that there is no singing in it, only recitation, to which the music is a sort of obbligato accompaniment to a recitative. Now and then the words are spoken while the music goes on, and this produces the finest possible effect. . . . Well, imagine my joy at having to compose just the kind of work I have so much desired. Do you know what I think? I think that most operatic recitatives should be treated in this way and only sung occasionally, when the words *can be perfectly expressed by the music*.   [7]

Tempo

From a letter to his sister, Vienna, April 20, 1782

If a fugue is not played slowly, the ear cannot clearly distinguish the theme when it comes in and consequently the effect is entirely missed.   [8]

From a letter to his father, Vienna, August 7, 1782

The first *allegro* [of the "Haffner" Symphony] must be played with great fire, the last—as fast as possible.   [9]

Publishing Music

From a letter to his father, Vienna, February 20, 1784

Now I must ask you about a subject of which I know and understand absolutely nothing. If you print something at your own expense, what can you do in order to make sure you won't be cheated by the printer? For the printer can keep as many copies as he wants, and therefore swindle you. You'd have to keep a constant watch over these people, which, in your case, was not possible when you had your book printed* because you were in Salzburg and the book was printed in Augsburg. I would frankly prefer never to sell my works to a printer again, but to have them engraved or printed by subscription at my own expense instead, as most people do, and to make a good profit for myself. I'm not worried about finding subscribers: I've already received subscription offers from Paris and Warsaw.   [10]

PRACTICING

From a letter to his father, Vienna, April 28, 1784

When I played to him [Georg Friedrich Richter], he stared all the time at my fingers and kept on saying, "Good God! How hard I work and sweat—and yet win no applause—and to you, my friend, it is all child's play." "Yes," I replied, "I too had to work hard, so as not to have to work hard any longer."   [11]

OTHER COMPOSERS

From a letter to his father, Paris, July 9, 1778

Incidentally, I do not make acquaintances . . . among other composers. I know my job and they know theirs, and that's good enough.   [12]

From a letter to his father, Vienna, April 10, 1782

I go every Sunday at twelve o'clock to the Baron van Swieten, where nothing is played but Handel and Bach. I am collecting at the moment the fugues of Bach—not only of Sebastian but also of Emanuel and Friedemann. I am also collecting Handel's and should like to have the six I mentioned.   [13]

From a letter to his father, Mannheim, October 14, 1777

It [a flute concerto by F. H. Graf] is not at all pleasing to the ear, not a bit natural. He often plunges into a new key far too brusquely and it is all quite devoid of charm. When it was over, I praised him very highly, for he really deserves it. The poor fellow must have taken a great deal of trouble over it and he must have studied hard enough.   [14]

HAYDN

Undated remark in G. N. Nissen's biography, 1828

I learned from Haydn how to write quartets. No one else can do everything—be flirtatious and be unsettling, move to laughter and move to tears—as well as Joseph Haydn.   [15]

---

* *Versuch einer gründlichen Violinschule* (Treatise on the basic principles of violin playing), 1756.

CLEMENTI'S PIANO SONATAS

From a letter to his father, Vienna, June 7, 1783

Everyone who plays or hears these compositions will sense their insignificance. Except for those passages in sixths and octaves, there is nothing that is exceptional or that stands out. Therefore I beg my sister not to fret too much over these passages, so that she won't spoil her steady, even touch, and so that her hand may not lose its natural lightness, flexibility, and fluid quickness. For what would be gained in the end? Were she to play sixths and octaves with the utmost speed (something nobody can do, not even Clementi), she would produce no more than a dreadful hacking. Clementi is a charlatan, like all Italians. He marks *presto* on a sonata or even *prestissimo* and *alla breve*, then plays it himself *allegro* in ¾ time. I know, because I've heard him myself. What he does play well are the passages in thirds; but he sweated over them day and night in London. Aside from that he has nothing to offer, not the slightest presentation or taste, let alone feeling. [16]

THE ABDUCTION FROM THE SERAGLIO

Letter to his father, Vienna, September 26, 1781

It occurred to me you might be amused if I were to give you an idea of what the opera is like. It originally began with a monologue; I then asked Herr Stephanie* to make a little arietta out of it and to turn the couple's chatter after Osmin's song into a duet. As we have given the part of Osmin to Herr Fischer, who really has a superb bass voice (in spite of the fact that the Archbishop† told me he sang too low for a bass, and that I assured him he would sing higher next time!), one must make the most of his presence, especially as he is so popular here. In the original libretto, though, Osmin had only this one short song; otherwise nothing except for his part in the trio and the finale. He therefore has been given an aria in act 1 and will have another in act 2. I have explained my idea for the aria to Stephanie; in fact, most of the music for it was already finished before Stephanie knew anything about it. I send you just the beginning and the end of it; they ought to make a good impression. Osmin's anger becomes comical by having Turkish-style music for the accompaniment. I have worked out the aria so that it allows Fischer's beautiful low notes to shine through—our Salzburg Midas‡ notwithstanding. It's true that the passage "Drum beim Barte des Propheten" is in the same tempo, but it has faster notes. Moreover, as Osmin's anger increases, it brings on the allegro assai (which is in a totally different tempo and in a different key), right when you think the aria is nearly over. The contrast is bound to make an effect. For just as some-

---

* Gottlieb Stephanie, Jr. (1741–1800), revised the libretto of the *Abduction* from the original of C. F. Bretzner (1748–1807).

† Archbishop Hieronymus Colloredo, Mozart's principal employer from 1772 through 1781, whom the composer did not feel to be appreciative of his talents.

‡ Colloredo.

one in this type of blind rage forgets himself, overstepping the bounds of order and propriety, so must the music forget itself. Still, passions, whether violent or not, must never be expressed to the point of appearing disgusting; and music, even in the most dire situations, must never insult the ear; but rather must remain just what it is: *music*. Therefore I have gone from F (the key of the aria) not into a remote key, but a related one. And yet rather than its nearest relative, D minor, I have chosen the more distant A minor. Now for Belmonte's aria in A major, "O wie ängstlich, o wie feurig"—can you guess how I have written it? His throbbing heart so full of love is depicted by violins playing in octaves. It is the favorite aria of those who have heard it, and it's my favorite too. I wrote it especially for Adamberger's voice. You sense the trembling, the swaying; you see how his swelling breast rises (indicated by a crescendo); you hear the whispering and the sighing (which I have rendered using the first violins, with mutes, playing in unison with a flute).

The Janissary chorus is everything a Janissary chorus ought to be—short, lively, and geared to Viennese tastes. I have sacrificed something of Constanze's aria, "Trennung war mein banges Los und nun schwimmt mein Aug' in Thränen," to the fluid larynx of Mlle Cavalieri. I've attempted to give as much expression to Constanze's feelings of separation and sadness as Italian bravura will allow. The "Hui" I have changed to "schnell," so that it now runs "Doch wie schnell schwand meine Freude," etc. I just don't know what our German poets are thinking. If they don't understand theater, or in this case opera, they should at least know better than to let their characters talk as if they were calling the hogs. *Hui*, sow!

Now for the trio at the end of act 1. Pedrillo has passed off his master as an architect, so that he can meet Constanze in the garden. Pasha Selim has taken him into his service. Osmin, the steward, has no inkling of this. He is an impertinent, ill-mannered lout, the sworn enemy of anyone he doesn't know; so naturally he will not let them go into the garden. The first part is very short and, because the text lends itself, is written for three voices, to fairly successful effect. Then the major key begins immediately, *pianissimo* (it must go very fast), and it winds up with a whole lot of noise, which is all one really needs for the end of an act. The louder the better, and the shorter the better, so that there is no time for the audience to lose the impulse to applaud.

I give you only fourteen bars of the overture, which is very short and alternates between *forte* and *piano*, with Turkish music coming in at the *fortes*. The overture modulates through a number of keys, and while it is being played I doubt anyone could doze off even if he had missed an entire night's sleep. Now comes my dilemma: I finished the first act more than three weeks ago, as well as one aria in act 2 and the drunken duet (*per i signori viennesi* and consisting entirely of my Turkish tattoo). But I can't go any further because the plot is being completely changed around, and at my own request to boot. There is a charming quintet, or rather finale, at the beginning of act 3, but I would rather see it at the end of act 2. In order to bring this off I'll have to make considerable changes. In fact an entirely new plot must be introduced—and Stephanie is already drowning in other projects. So I must be rather patient. Everyone abuses Stephanie. Possibly he is being friendly only to my face. But he's putting the libretto in order for me—and what's more, just the way I want it—so I ask nothing more of him.   [17]

From a letter to his father, Vienna, October 13, 1781

Now, about the libretto to the opera: you are quite right, of course, about Stephanie's work. Still, the poetry is well suited to Osmin's ignorant, crass, and malicious nature. I know full well that the verse isn't the best, but it goes so perfectly with the musical ideas that were already running through my head that I could hardly help liking it. And I'm willing to bet that when it's performed, people will hardly notice whatever might be wrong with the verse. As for the poetry that already existed [before Stephanie took over as librettist], I can't really complain. Belmonte's aria "O wie ängstlich" could hardly have been written better for setting to music. Except for "Hui" and "Kummer ruht in meinem Schoss," the aria isn't bad, especially the first part. And after all, in opera the poetry must be the obedient daughter of the music. Why are Italian comic operas so popular everywhere despite their horrendous libretti—even in Paris, as I myself have witnessed? Because in Italian comic operas, the music reigns supreme, and you forget about everything else. An opera is all the more pleasing when its plot is carefully worked out, and when the words are written for the sake of the music rather than in slavish compliance with the miserable demands of rhyme (which, heaven knows, adds nothing to a theatrical performance of any type, and even detracts). Words, even entire verses, written purely to accommodate rhyme can spoil the composer's whole idea. Yes, verses are the most indispensable ingredient for music, but rhymes for their own sake are the most damaging. Those lofty people who prefer the pedantic approach will always come to nothing—along with their music. The ideal situation is when a good composer, one who understands the dramatic aspect and is himself capable of contributing to it, joins together with that rare bird, a capable poet. Then you need not fear even the applause of the ignorant. For me, poets are about like trumpeters, with all their tricks of the trade. If we composers actually stuck to our rules (which worked perfectly well back when no one knew any better), our music would be as weak as their libretti.
                                                                                        [18]

PIANO CONCERTOS K. 413, 414, 415

From a letter to his father, Vienna, December 28, 1782

These concertos lie somewhere between too easy and too difficult; they are brilliant, pleasing to the ear, and natural without being shallow. There are passages here and there that only a connoisseur can truly appreciate, but that a layperson also can enjoy without even knowing why.

——————— ♪ ———————

In order to garner applause with this happy medium—for true perfection in all things is no longer known or prized—you must write music that is either so sim-

ple a coachman could sing it, or so unintelligible that audiences like it simply because no sane person could understand it. [19]

LAST LETTERS

From a letter to his wife, October 7–8, 1791

I have just come home from the opera; it was as full as ever.—The duetto *Mann
und Weib,* etc., and the *Glöckchenspiel* in act 1 were encored as usual—so was the
boys' trio in act 2—but what pleases me most is the quiet approval!—one can see
clearly that this opera is steadily increasing in popularity. . . .

The most curious thing about it is that on the very evening when my new opera
was performed for the first time amid so much applause, that same evening at
Prague *Tito* was performed, for the last time, also with extraordinary success—
every item was applauded.

From a letter to his wife, October 8–9, 1791

I went onto the stage for Papageno's aria with the *Glöckchenspiel* because today I
felt an impulse to play it myself. I played a joke on Schikaneder [Papageno]: where
he has a pause, I played an arpeggio—he started—looked offstage and saw me.
When the second pause came, I did nothing—so he waited and would not go on.
I guessed what he was thinking and played another chord—whereat he hit the
Glöckchenspiel and said *hold your tongue*—at which everybody laughed—I think this
joke made many people notice for the first time that he does not play the instrument himself. [20]

CHAPTER FOUR

Ludwig van Beethoven

Louis Spohr

Carl Maria von Weber

Gioacchino Rossini

Franz Schubert

Ludwig van Beethoven
1770–1827

The florid encomiums that Beethoven inspired from many musicians stand in contrast to his own terse and practical words. The self-assurance and fierceness of his music may also be found in his writings, but the sense of the heroic is usually vitiated by an atmosphere of alienation and despair.

In 1802 Beethoven's growing deafness reached a crisis, and he was moved to write his will, the so-called Heiligenstadt Testament. He did not die, but lived almost twenty-five years more, battling a host of physical ailments and personal misfortunes and never wholly abandoning the hope that his deafness might be cured.

CRITICS

From a letter to Breitkopf & Härtel, Vienna, April 22, 1801

Advise your reviewer to show more intelligence and discretion, especially with regard to the products of younger authors, for these reviews could easily discourage men who might otherwise do better work. As for myself, it is true that I am far from having attained such perfection as would exempt me from all criticism, yet at first your reviewer's outcry against me was humiliating. Then, by dint of comparing myself with others, I found it scarcely affected me; I remained quite unmoved and thought, they do not understand it. I was able to remain all the more calm when I observed how, elsewhere, your reviewer extolled men of minor importance who indeed, among the better artists here, are almost lost, decent and hardworking as they may be. [1]

TRANSCRIPTIONS

From a letter to Breitkopf & Härtel, Vienna, July 13, 1802

With respect to transcriptions and arrangements, I am now sincerely pleased that you refused them. The unnatural fury that possesses us to transplant even things written for the piano to string instruments, instruments so entirely opposed to each other, should certainly come to an end. It is my firm opinion that only Mozart could translate his own works from the piano to other instruments—Haydn likewise—and without wishing to join company with these two great men, I believe that it is also true of my piano sonatas. The fact that whole passages must be omitted or changed is an additional difficulty, and this great stumbling block can be overcome only by the master himself or at least by one who has no less skill and inventiveness. I have transformed only one of my sonatas [Op. 14, No. 1] into a quartet for string instruments, because I was asked most urgently to do so, and I know for certain that this is a feat others will imitate at their peril. [2]

MUSIC AND MONEY

From a letter to Franz Anton Hoffmeister, Vienna, c. January 15, 1801

There should be a single Art Exchange in the world, to which the artist would simply send his works and be given in return as much as he needs. As it is, one has to be half a merchant on top of everything else, and how badly one goes about it. [3]

From a draft of a contract, c. February 1809

It must be the aim and aspiration of every true artist to place himself in a position in which, undisturbed by other duties or by economic considerations . . . he can devote himself to the composition of larger works and present these to the public upon their completion. Meanwhile, he must also bear in mind his old age and endeavor to make adequate provision for that period of his life. [4]

COMPOSITION

From a letter to George Thomson, Vienna, February 19, 1813

I am not in the habit of altering my compositions once they are finished. I have never done this, for I hold firmly that the slightest change alters the character of the composition. [5]

From a letter to Friedrich Treitschke, Vienna, April 1814

The cursed concert that I was partly forced into by my bad [financial] situation has set me back with the opera [*Fidelio*, third version]. The cantata, too, that I wanted to perform there has robbed me of five or six days. Now everything has to be done at once. I could write something new much faster than add to the old, as I was wont to do. In my instrumental music, too, I always have the whole in my mind; here, however, the whole is to a certain extent divided, and I have to think myself anew into the music. [6]

From Archduke Rudolph's book of instruction, c. 1816

Many maintain that every movement in a minor key must end of necessity in the same mode. *Nego.* On the contrary, I find that precisely the soft scales of the major at the end have a delightful, uncommonly calming effect. Joy follows on sorrow, and sunshine on rain. With this I feel as though I look toward the mild, silver glance of the shining evening star. [7]

From a letter to Archduke Rudolph, Vienna, July 1, 1823

I hope that Your Imperial Highness will continue especially to practice writing down your ideas straightaway at the piano; for this purpose, there should be a small table beside the piano. In this way the imagination is strengthened, and one also learns to pin down the remotest ideas at once. It is likewise necessary to write without a piano. Nor should it pain but rather please Your Imperial Highness to find yourself absorbed in this art, at times to elaborate a simple melody, a chorale with simple and again with more varied figurations in counterpoint, and so on, to more difficult exercises. We develop gradually the capacity to represent exactly what we wish to represent, what we feel within us, which is a need characteristic of all superior persons. [8]

From a written conversation with Louis Schlosser (1822 or 1823)

I carry my thoughts about with me for a long time, often for a very long time, before writing them down. I can rely on my memory for this and can be sure that, once I have grasped a theme, I shall not forget it even years later. I change many things, discard others, and try again and again until I am satisfied; then, in my head, I begin to elaborate the work in its breadth, its narrowness, its height, its depth, and because I am aware of what I want to do, the underlying idea never deserts me. It rises, it grows, I hear and see the image in front of me from every angle, as if it had been cast [like a sculpture], and only the labor of writing it down remains, a labor that need not take long, but varies according to the time at my disposal, since I very often work on several things at the same time. Yet I can always be sure that I shall not confuse one with another. You may ask me where I obtain my ideas. I cannot answer this with any certainty: they come unbidden, spontaneously or unspontaneously. I may grasp them with my hands in the open air, while walking in the woods, in the stillness of night, at early morning. Stimulated by those moods that poets turn into words, I turn my ideas into tones, which resound, roar, and rage until at last they stand before me in the form of notes. [9]

PIANO PEDAGOGY

From a letter to Carl Czerny, Vienna, 1817

With regard to his [your pupil's] playing: When he is with you, I beg you to wait until he is using the right fingers, keeping the right time and playing the notes more or less correctly, and only then to criticize his rendering. Also, once he has got so far, do not interrupt his playing because of small mistakes but point these out only when he has finished the piece. Although I have given few lessons, I have always followed this method, for it soon forms musicians, and this, after all, is one of the foremost aims of art and is less tiring both for master and pupil. [10]

TEMPO MARKINGS AND THE METRONOME

Letter to Ignaz von Mosel, Vienna, 1817

I am delighted to know that you share my opinion of those headings, inherited from times of musical barbarism, by which we describe the tempo of a movement.

What, for example, can be more absurd than *allegro*, which, once and for all, means "cheerful"? How far removed we often are from this meaning! How often a piece of music expresses the very opposite of its heading! . . . We would do well to dispense with headings. The words that describe the character of the piece are a very different matter. These we could not give up; whereas the tempo is really no more than the body, these refer rather to the spirit of the piece. I have often thought of giving up these absurd terms *allegro, andante, adagio, presto*. Maelzel's metronome gives us an excellent opportunity to do so. I give you my word, in my future compositions I shall not use them.

It is an altogether different question whether, by doing so, we shall encourage the general use of a metronome, necessary as it is; I hardly think so. But I do not doubt for a moment that we shall be decried as violators of tradition. If this would serve to further our cause, it would still be preferable to being accused of feudalism. I therefore think that it would be best, especially for our countries where music has become a national need and every village schoolmaster must demand the use of a metronome, if Maelzel attempted to dispose of a certain number of metronomes by subscription, at higher prices; and as soon as this number covers his expenses, he will be able to offer the rest of the metronomes required for the national need at so cheap a price that we can surely expect the most general and extensive use of the instrument. It goes without saying that certain persons should take a prominent part in this enterprise, to arouse enthusiasm. As far as I am concerned, you can definitely count on me and with pleasure I await the part you will assign me in the undertaking. [11]

THE ORGAN

From a written conversation with Karl Gottlieb Freudenberg,
organist in Breslau, c. 1825

I, too, played the organ frequently in my youth, but my nerves could not withstand the power of this gigantic instrument. I should place an organist who is master of his instrument at the very head of all virtuosi. [12]

J. S. BACH

From a letter to Franz Anton Hoffmeister, Vienna, c. January 15, 1801

Your intention to publish the works of Sebastian Bach rejoices my heart, which is full of admiration for the great art of this father of harmony, and I hope that your plan will soon be realized. I hope that I myself shall be able to do something for you here, as soon as we hear golden peace has been declared and as soon as you are ready to collect subscriptions for these works. [13]

C. P. E. BACH

From a letter to Breitkopf & Härtel, Vienna, July 26, 1809

I have only a few of Emanuel Bach's piano works, and yet some of them must yield to every true artist not only the most lofty pleasure but instruction too. [14]

MOZART

Remark to Carl Czerny, no date

He had a fine but choppy way of playing, no *ligato*.   [15]

PIANO WORKS

From a sketch book, June 2, 1804

Finale more and more simple, likewise all my piano music. God knows why my piano music still and always makes the worst impression on me, especially when it is badly played.   [16]

SYMPHONY NO. 6

Notes on the Pastoral *Symphony, 1807*

It is left to the listener to discover the situation. *Sinfonia caracteristica* or a reminiscence of country life. Every kind of painting loses by being carried too far in instrumental music. *Sinfonia pastorella.* Anyone who has the faintest idea of country life will not need many descriptive titles to be able to imagine for himself what the author intends. Even without a description one will be able to recognize it all, for it is sentiments rather than a painting in sounds.   [17]

FIDELIO

From a statement to Georg August Griesinger, c. 1824

My *Fidelio* was not understood by the public, but I know that it will yet be valued; nevertheless, although I know what *Fidelio* is worth, I know just as clearly that the symphony is my true element. When sounds stir within me, I always hear the full orchestra; I know what to expect of instrumentalists, who are capable of almost everything, but with vocal compositions I must always keep asking myself: can this be sung?   [18]

THE HEILIGENSTADT TESTAMENT

Beethoven's will, written at Heiligenstadt, October 6, 1802

For my brothers Carl and [Johann] Beethoven.

You, who hold me to be hostile, stubborn, or misanthropic, how unjustly you treat me; you know nothing of the hidden reasons that make me appear so. My heart and my soul have, since childhood, inclined toward benevolence; I have even stood ready to perform great deeds. But only consider that for six years now I have been afflicted with an incurable condition, made all the worse by inept physicians, year after year deceived by hopes of improvement, only to be forced in the end to confront the prospect of a lasting disability, the healing of which may take years or may prove altogether impossible. Although born with a fiery, impulsive temperament

and partial to the distractions of social contact, I have been compelled to isolate myself and to spend my days in solitude. If I ever, at times, tried to ignore all this, how
harshly was I driven back by the wretched effects of my poor hearing, and yet how
incapable I was of saying to others: speak up, shout, for I am deaf. Alas, how could
I possibly admit to an impairment of the one sense that should be more perfect in
me than in others, a sense I once possessed in its highest form, a form as perfect as
others in my profession have ever possessed—no, I cannot do it, and therefore you
must forgive me when, though I would happily enjoy your company, you see me
withdraw from you. My affliction is doubly hard to bear in that it causes my behavior to be misunderstood. For me there can be no recreation in the company of
others, in intelligent conversation, in the sharing of ideas. Solitary, I venture only
as much social contact as is absolutely necessary; I am forced to live as an exile.
When I do approach the company of others, I feel a flush of terror, sparked by the
fear of circumstances that might cause my condition to be noticed. So has it been
for me during this past half-year in the country as well. When my physician quite
reasonably ordered me to conserve my hearing as much as possible, he really only
encouraged my natural inclination, although, tormented by the desire for compan-
ionship, I have occasionally disregarded his orders. But what a humiliation when
someone standing next to me heard the sound of a flute in the distance while I heard
nothing; or someone heard a shepherd singing and again I heard nothing. Such experiences brought me close to despair. It would have taken very little for me to have
ended my life—nothing but art held me back. It seemed impossible to me that I
should abandon the world until I had brought forth all that I felt I could. Thus did
I endure this wretched existence—truly wretched. So sensitive is my constitution
that a relatively slight change can plunge me from the heights into the most miserable of conditions. Patience—so they say—should now become my guide. Patience I have, and I hope that my resolve will hold until the implacable Fates choose
to sever the thread. Perhaps my condition will improve, perhaps not. I am compelled, at the early age of twenty-eight, to become a philosopher; this is no easy
matter, and more difficult for the artist than for anyone. Divine God, you witness
here my innermost being; you understand it, and you know that love for humankind and the desire to do good reside within it. O men, when one day you read
this, consider how you have wronged me, and let he who is unhappy take some
comfort in finding another like himself—one who, in spite of all of nature's obstacles, did everything within his power to be admitted into the ranks of worthy artists
and people. You, my brothers Carl and [Johann], upon my death, if Professor
Schmidt is still alive, ask him in my name to describe my affliction, and let him add
this document to the report of my illness, so that, as far as possible, the world may
be reconciled with me after I am gone. At the same time I hereby declare you both
to be the heirs of my little estate (if I may call it that). Divide it fairly, and live in
harmony and help each other. What harm you have done me, as you know, has long
since been forgiven. To you, brother Carl, I give special thanks for the devotion you
have shown me in recent times. My wish is that you may lead a better and more
carefree life than mine. Recommend virtue to your children; that alone, and not
money, leads us to happiness. I speak from experience: it was virtue that sustained
me even in my misery. After that I thank my art that I did not end my life by suicide. Farewell; love one another. I give thanks to all my friends, but especially

Prince Lichnowsky and Professor Schmidt. I wish for the instruments given to me by Prince L. to be preserved by one of you; yet allow no quarrel to arise between you on this account. However, if it is more useful for you to sell them, then by all means do so. How much it pleases me to think that even in death I may be able to help you. And so it is done. With joy do I hasten to my death. Should it come before I have fully achieved my artistic mission, then, in spite of the miserable circumstances of my life, it will have come too soon, and I will wish it might have come later. Even so I will be content, for will it not free me from a state of endless suffering? Come when thou wouldst, I go in bravery to meet thee. Farewell, and do not wholly forget me when I am gone. This much I deserve of you, having thought of you often in life with the purpose of making you happy; be ye so.

Ludwig van Beethoven

(Added to the last page)
Heiligenstadt on October 10, 1802, thus do I take leave of you—and sadly so. Yes, the fond hope—that I brought here with me—of being cured at least to a certain extent—I must wholly abandon, like the autumn leaves that fall and wither; so is it for me—that my hope is withered. Almost as I was when I came here—do I leave again. Even the great courage—that often in the beautiful summer days inspired me—has now vanished. O Providence—let me be granted a single day of pure joy—for so long now has the inner resonance of true joy been estranged from me— oh when—oh when, divine one, will I once again know its feeling in the temple of nature and among humankind—never?—no—that would be too hard.   [19]

Louis Spohr
1784–1859

Spohr was among the most famous German musicians of his time. His technique of using symbolic melodies and his blurring of recitative and aria presaged Wagner. An innovator rather than a revolutionary, he lived to see himself overtaken by a younger generation of Romantics who respected his craftsmanship but found his aesthetic dated and provincial.

Spohr's famous account of the mostly deaf Beethoven conducting the Seventh Symphony describes the work's premiere in Vienna on December 8, 1813, a concert in which Spohr and his orchestra participated.

From the composer's autobiography (an abridged version of his unfinished
Memoirs, *published posthumously)*

THE RUSSIAN IMPERIAL HORN BAND

In the first concert, the orchestra consisted of thirty-six violins, twenty basses, and a double set of wind instruments. In addition to these, the choruses were supported by forty hornists from the imperial orchestra, each of whom had only one single note to blow. . . .

Between the first and second parts of this concert, the Imperial hornists executed an overture by Gluck with a rapidity and exactness that would have been difficult for stringed instruments; how much the more so, then, for hornists each of whom blew only one tone. . . . But as may be imagined, the *adagio* of the overture made a greater effect than the *allegro*, for it is always somewhat unnatural to perform such rapid passages with these living organ pipes, and one could not help thinking of the thrashings that must have been inflicted.   [1]

BEETHOVEN IN 1813

Although I had heard much of his conducting, yet it surprised me greatly. Beethoven was wont to give the signs of expression to his orchestra by all manner of extraordinary motions of his body. Whenever a *sforzando* occurred, he flung his arms wide, previously crossed upon his breast. At a *piano,* he bent down, and all the lower in proportion to the softness of tone he wished to achieve. Then when a crescendo came, he would raise himself again by degrees, and upon the commencement of the *forte,* would spring bolt upright. To increase the *forte* yet more, he would sometimes shout at the orchestra, without being aware of it.

It was easy to see that the poor deaf maestro could no longer hear the *pianos* of his own music. This was particularly remarkable in a passage in the second part of the first *allegro* of the symphony (No. 7). At that part there are two holds in quick succession, the second of which is *pianissimo.* This Beethoven had probably overlooked, for he again began to give the time before the orchestra had executed this second hold. Without knowing it, therefore, he was already from ten to twelve bars in advance of the orchestra when it began the *pianissimo.* Beethoven, to signify this in his own way, had crept completely under the desk. Upon the ensuing crescendo, he again made his appearance, raising himself continually and then springing up high at the moment when, according to his calculations, the *forte* should have begun. As this did not take place, he looked around him in dismay, stared with astonishment at the orchestra, which was still playing *pianissimo,* and only recovered himself when at length the long-expected *forte* began, and was finally audible to himself.

Up to this time, there had been no falling off in Beethoven's creative powers. But as of this moment, owing to his constantly increasing deafness, he could no longer hear any music, and that must of necessity have had a prejudicial effect upon his creative imagination. His constant endeavor to be original and to open new paths could no longer, as formerly, be saved from error by the guidance of the ear. Was it, then, to be wondered at that his works became more and more eccentric, disconnected, and incomprehensible? It is true that there are people who imagine they can understand them, and in their pleasure at that claim, rank them far above his earlier masterpieces. But I am not of their number and freely confess that I have never been able to relish the last works of Beethoven. Yes, I must even reckon the much admired Ninth Symphony among these, the three first movements of which seem to me, despite some solitary flashes of genius, worse than all the eight previous symphonies. The fourth movement is, in my opinion, so monstrous and tasteless and, in its grasp of Schiller's *Ode,* so trivial that I cannot understand how a genius like Beethoven could have written it. I find in it another proof of what I had already noted in Vienna, that Beethoven was wanting in aesthetic feeling and in a sense of the beautiful.

As Beethoven had already stopped playing both in public and at private parties at the time I met him, I had but one opportunity to hear him when I came informally to the rehearsal of a new trio (D major, ¾ time) at Beethoven's house. It was by no means enjoyable, for the pianoforte was woefully out of tune in the first place; this, however, troubled Beethoven little, since he could not hear it. Secondly, of the former so greatly admired excellence of the virtuoso scarcely anything was left, in consequence of his total deafness. In the *fortes*, the poor deaf man hammered upon the keys in such a way that entire groups of notes were inaudible, so that one lost all sense of the subject unless the eye followed the score at the same time. I felt moved with the deepest sorrow at so harsh a destiny. It is a sad misfortune for anyone to be deaf. How, then, could a musician endure it without despair? Beethoven's almost continual melancholy was no longer a riddle to me.   [2]

FIRST USE OF THE BATON IN LONDON, 1820

It was still the custom in London at that time, when symphonies and overtures were performed, for the pianist to have the score before him, not exactly to conduct from it but rather to read after and to play in with the orchestra at pleasure, which often produced a very bad effect. The real conductor was the first violin, who gave the tempi and, every now and then when the orchestra began to falter, gave the beat with his bow. Thus a large orchestra, standing so far apart from each other as the members of the Philharmonic, could not possibly be exactly together, and despite the excellence of individual members, the ensemble was much worse than we are accustomed to in Germany. I had therefore resolved that, when my turn came to direct, I would try to remedy this defective system. Fortunately at the morning rehearsal on the day I was to conduct the concert, Mr. Ries* took his place at the piano and readily assented to relinquish the score and to remain wholly excluded from all participation in the performance. I then took my stand with the score at a separate music desk in front of the orchestra, drew my directing baton from my coat pocket, and gave the signal to begin. Quite alarmed at such a novel procedure, some of the directors wished to protest against it, but when I besought them to grant me at least one trial, they quieted down. The symphonies and overtures that were to be rehearsed were well known to me, and I had already directed their performance in Germany. Therefore, I could not only give the tempi in a very decisive manner, but could indicate all their entries to the wind instruments and horns, which gave them a confidence they had not known hitherto. I also felt free to stop when the execution did not satisfy me and, in a polite but earnest manner, to remark upon the manner of execution, which remarks Mr. Ries interpreted at my request to the orchestra. Incited thereby to more than usual attention, and given assurance by the conductor's clearly visible manner of marking time, they played with a spirit and correctness such as they had never been heard to achieve until then. The orchestra, surprised and inspired by the result, immediately expressed its collective assent to the new

* Ferdinand Ries (1784–1838), noted German pianist, composer, and conductor, who lived in London 1814–24.

mode of conducting after the first part of the symphony and thereby overruled all further opposition on the part of the directors. . . .

The triumph of the baton as a time giver was decisive, and no conductor was seen seated at the piano anymore during the performance of symphonies and overtures. [3]

Carl Maria von Weber
1786–1826

Weber composed his first opera at twelve and became a professional conductor at eighteen. With Der Freischütz, *produced in 1821, Weber is credited with launching not only German opera but German national music. The claim is a simplification, but it is not hard to see why* Freischütz *had so profound an effect on his contemporaries.*

Weber's evident talent as a writer was encouraged by his membership in Der Harmonische Verein, a group of artists around Germany whose reports to one another became one of the foundations of professional music criticism.

CRITICISM

From a review of Francesco Morlacchi's oratorio Isacco, *1817*

Most listeners criticize a work uncharitably or harshly merely because they do not measure it by the standards according to which it was written, or they do not view it from the standpoint from which the composer can see it by virtue of his talent, culture, and the conviction and purpose stemming from them.

Ordinarily a German work is as alien and uncomfortable to the Italian mind as an Italian work to the German. Artistic training and familiarity breed in each man a preference and love for the outstanding qualities of his own idiom. In any climate, however, complete truth vanquishes all criticism, which must ultimately bow before one single truth.

Criticism is desirable and truly helpful when, looking kindly through the composer's eyes, it directs him and unravels his secrets, thereby revealing him to himself, since in every human being there exists a pardonable natural bias in favor of his own horizons and capabilities.

It is indeed worthy of praise and recognition when a person, educated according to the artistic tenets and needs of one country, realizes that these do not suffice everywhere. This is already a great step in the right direction, and we must only beware lest we mistake the form for the thing itself. [1]

RHYTHM IN SINGING

From an article on the metronome markings to Euryanthe, *1824*

The most difficult problem of all is to unite voice and instruments so they blend in the rhythmic motion of a piece and the instruments support and enhance the voice in its emotional expression, for voices and instruments are by their very nature opposed to each other. Because of breathing and articulation, singing calls for a certain fluctuation in the measure that may be compared to the uniform beating of waves against a shore. Instruments (particularly strings) divide the time into sharp segments comparable to the swinging of a pendulum. Truth of expression demands the blending of these contrasting characteristics. The beat should not be a tyrannical restriction or the driving of a mill hammer. On the contrary, it should be to music what the pulse beat is to the life of man. There is no slow tempo in which passages that demand a faster movement do not occur and thereby prevent the feeling of dragging. Conversely, there is no *presto* that does not call for the slower execution of certain passages, so that the expression will not be marred by overzealousness.

In heaven's name, however, let no singer feel himself entitled, because of the above remarks, to that maniacal kind of execution that capriciously distorts every measure, making the listener suffer unbearably, as he might on seeing an acrobat forcibly dislocating all his joints. Pressing forward or holding back in tempo must never give the feeling of jerkiness, jolting, or any violence whatsoever. This may occur in a period or a phrase here and there, but only in a musical-poetic significance, depending on the vehemence of expression. . . . These [interpretative insights] are to be found in the sensitive human breast alone, and if they are lacking there, then neither the metronome, which can only prevent gross blunders, nor our highly inadequate markings will help. (There is so much to be said on the subject of markings that I might be tempted to develop it further were I not warned by frustrating experience.) I consider them superfluous, useless, and, I fear, easily misconstrued. Let them remain, but to be used only with caution.   [2]

MUSIC AND MONEY

From a letter to his wife, London, March 12, 1826

At half past ten I drove to Lord Hertford's. Heavens, what a vast assembly! A magnificent room, 500–600 people there, all of the greatest brilliance. Almost the entire Italian opera company, including Veluti, the celebrated Puzzi, and a double bass player, the no less celebrated Dragonetti. Some finales were sung, etc., but not a soul listened. The shrieking and jabbering of this throng of humanity was atrocious. While I played they tried to get a little quiet, and circa 100 people gathered round, displaying the greatest interest. But what they can have heard, God alone knows, for I myself heard very little of it. Meanwhile I thought hard about my 30 guineas, and so was perfectly patient. At last, about 2 o'clock, they went in to supper, whereupon I took my leave.   [3]

BEETHOVEN

From a letter to Hans Georg Nägeli, May 21, 1810
(in response to Nägeli's remark that one of Weber's works
reminded him of Beethoven)

In the first place, I hate everything that bears the stamp of imitation; secondly, my views differ far too much from those of Beethoven ever to come into contact with him. The fiery, almost incredible inventive faculty that inspires him is attended by so many complications in the arrangement of his ideas that it is only his earlier compositions that interest me; the later ones appear to me a confused chaos, an unintelligible struggle after novelty from which occasionally heavenly flashes of genius dart forth, showing how great he might be if he chose to control his luxuriant fancy.   [4]

ROSSINI

From a letter, 1820

Who would not gladly listen to Rossini's lively flights of fancy, to the piquant titillation of his melodies? But who could be so blind as to attribute to him dramatic truth?   [5]

Gioacchino Rossini
1792–1868

Rossini is famous for composing thirty-eight operas (counting revised versions) in his first thirty-eight years, then living the next four decades without writing another. He did not entirely stop composing: his Stabat Mater *and* Petite messe solennelle *were written during these years, along with many smaller pieces. Since his own day, Rossini's reputation has rested on only a few works, above all* The Barber of Seville. *Rossini's description of his laziness in writing overtures is ironic, considering that several of the overtures he mentions are better known than the operas they introduce.*

THE STATE OF MUSIC

Letter to Leopoldo Cicognara, February 12, 1817

Here are my ideas on the present state of music. Ever since the five notes were added to the harpsichord,* I have maintained that a dire revolution was brewing in our art, which at that time had reached perfection; for experience has shown that when we wish perforce to achieve the best, we fall into the worst. Haydn had already begun to corrupt purity of taste by introducing strange chords, artificial passages, and daring novelties into his compositions, but he still preserved a sublimity and traditional beauty that would seem to excuse his deviations.

But after him Cramer and finally Beethoven, with their compositions lacking in unity and natural flow and full of arbitrary oddities, corrupted taste in instrumental music completely. And now, for the simple and majestic styles of Sarti, Paisiello, and Cimarosa, Mayr has substituted in the theater his own ingenious but vicious harmonies in which the main melody is strangled in deference to the new

* Rossini apparently refers to the extension of the keyboard from four and a half to five octaves that took place after 1750.

German school wherein all the young composers have set out to write theater music.

Many of our singers born outside of Italy have renounced purity of musical taste, which never found roots beyond the confines of Italy, and have adopted the impure style of foreigners to please the capitals of Europe. They have then returned, bringing back and spreading here the germs of bad taste.

Warblings, leaps, trills, jumps, abuses of semitones, clusters of notes, these characterize the singing that now prevails. Therefore meter, the essential part of music, without which melody is incomprehensible and harmony falls into disorder, is ignored and violated by singers. They astound rather than move the public, and whereas in the good old days players sought to make their instruments sing, now our singers endeavor to handle their voices as if they were instruments. The populace, meantime applauding such bad style, makes of music what the Jesuits made of poetry and oratory when they preferred Lucan to Virgil, Seneca to Cicero.

These are my ideas on the current state of music, and I confess to you that I have little hope of seeing this divine art emerge from the corruption in which it is submerged without the total overthrow of existing social institutions, and as you see, the remedy might then be worse than the disease.   [1]

REQUIREMENTS OF AN OPERA SINGER

From a letter to Ferdinando Guidicini, Bologna, February 12, 1851

I want to thank you for your kind note in which you ask me a question about music. The question is one of expression rather than of substance, however, and I shall therefore dispose of it briefly. I shall say that, in order to fulfill his part well, the good singer must be only an able *interpreter* of the composer's ideas, seeking to express them with all his skill and investing them with the brilliance inherent in them. In addition, players need only be faithful *executants* of the score as written. But not infrequently it happens that this execution is distorted, often spoiling the ideas of the composer, robbing them of that simplicity of expression which they should have.

The French use the phrase *créer un rôle.* This is French conceit, which is characteristic of those singers who perform a leading role in a new opera for the first time and wish to indicate that they are setting an example that is to be followed by other singers who may be called upon to perform the same part. Here again the word *to create* seems hardly appropriate, since *to create* means to *extract from nothing.* The singer, on the other hand, certainly works on something, that is to say, on poetry and on music that are not of his creation.   [2]

RAMEAU

From a letter to Mme Stephen de la Madeleine, Passy, September 4, 1862

When you ask me to support the raising of a statue to our immortal Rameau, it is, as we say, "an invitation to a wedding." Believe me, I am an ardent admirer of this illustrious man. He rendered such great services to musical art that one would have to be totally ignorant of them not to grasp eagerly at the only way of honoring him. The dramatic productions, the delightful harpsichord compositions, which I have always had performed at my home by their best interpreter, Mme Tardieu, have been and will be the object of my constant admiration and pleasure. *Fiat lux,* I say. Let the statue be raised!

In associating myself with your noble impulse, I send you the expression of my gratitude. [3]

VERDI

Remark to Guglielmo De Sanctis, 1862

I like very much [his] almost savage nature, not to mention his great power of expressing his passions. [4]

Remark to Giovanni Dupré, Florence, 1847

Verdi is a composer whose character is melancholy and serious; his sadness reflects his true nature. I esteem him greatly. [5]

THE BEST TIME TO COMPOSE AN OVERTURE

From a letter, addressee and date unknown

Wait until the evening before opening night. Nothing primes inspiration more than necessity, whether it be the presence of a copyist waiting for your work or the prodding of an impresario tearing his hair. In my time, all the impresarios in Italy were bald at thirty.

I composed the overture to *Otello* in a little room in the Barbaja palace wherein the baldest and fiercest of directors had forcibly locked me with a lone plate of spaghetti and the threat that I would not be allowed to leave the room alive until I had written the last note.

I wrote the overture to *La Gazza Ladra* the day of its opening, in the theater itself, where I was imprisoned by the director and under the surveillance of four stagehands who were instructed to throw my original text out the window, page by page, to the copyists waiting below to transcribe it. In default of pages, they were ordered to throw *me* out the window.

I did better with *The Barber.* I did not compose an overture, but selected for it one that was meant for a semi-serious opera called *Elisabetta.* The public was completely satisfied.

I composed the overture to *Conte Ory* while fishing, with my feet in the water, and in company of Signor Agnado, who talked of Spanish finance. The overture for *William Tell* was composed under more or less similar circumstances. And as for *Mosè,* I did not write one. [6]

MIXED VOICES IN THE CHURCH

Letter to Franz Liszt, Passy, June 23, 1865

I am answering, by return mail, your precious letter of the 17th, which proves to me that time and distance have not weakened your affection for the old man of

Pesaro. I am writing you in my native language, that being the best suited to bring out and express the feelings of my heart. I began to love and admire you in Vienna in 1822, a recollection so dear to me! The succeeding years have only increased my affection for you. Your determination to enter on an ecclesiastical career has not surprised me. Rather has it inspired me. Oh, my dearest Abbé Liszt, allow me to offer my sincere felicitations on the *holy* road you have taken, which assures you the best possible future. However, I am sure that you will not abandon music, in which God has so richly endowed you that the harmony of Heaven will ever be your best escort on this earth.

Apropos of music, I do not know if you have heard that I composed a *Messa di Gloria* [the *Petite messe solennelle*] in four parts, which was performed at the palace of my friend, Count Pillet-Will. This Mass was sung by gifted artists of both sexes and accompanied by two pianos and a harmonium. The foremost Parisian composers (among them my poor colleague Meyerbeer, then still alive) praised it most highly, beyond its deserts. They would like to have me orchestrate it in order to perform it in some Paris cathedral. I am loath to undertake such a work, having put all my scant musical knowledge into this composition and having worked on it with true religious devotion. There exists, I have been told, a *fatal* bull promulgated by a former pope that *prohibits* the mingling of the two sexes in the church. Could I ever consent to hearing my poor notes sung out of tune by boy sopranos rather than by women who were educated ad hoc for sacred music and who, with their pure, well-pitched voices would represent (musically speaking) heavenly angels? If it were given me to live in the Vatican as you do, I would throw myself at the feet of my adored Pius IX to plead for the grace of a *new* bull permitting women to sing in church together with men. Such a step would give new life to sacred music, which is now in total decay. It is my feeling that His Holiness, who, I know, loves music and is not ignorant of my name, would acquire new glory in Paradise by issuing such a bull, and Catholics of every land would bless him for this act of justice (since both sexes mingle in church attendance) and true harmonic sensibility. Our holy religion, though some wretches would like to trample it underfoot, will always remain at its most sublime, and music will ever be a great aid to the devout.

As a courageous priest, dear friend, unite with me and let us try to obtain from His Holiness a grace that must lie doubly close to your heart, as a servant of God and as a musician. I realize that I have imposed on you with this lengthy letter. I shall therefore close by blessing you and telling you that no one loves you more than do I.   [7]

Franz Schubert
1797–1828

Schubert was a capable pianist and singer, but his music making was largely limited to informal "Schubertiades" with his friends; he was the first great composer who was not also well known as a performer. For a living he taught in his father's school and later as a private tutor. Eventually his reputation as a composer, along with the generosity of friends and patrons, freed him from the hated work of teaching. The depth and sophistication of his music are nowhere matched in his few writings, but the sensitivity of character is much the same.

MOZART

From a diary entry dated June 13, 1816

All my life I shall remember this fine, clear, lovely day. I shall hear softly, as from a distance, the magic strains of Mozart's music. . . . In the dark places of this life they point to that clear-shining and distant future in which our whole hope lies. O Mozart, immortal Mozart, how many, how infinitely many inspiring suggestions of a finer, better life have you left in our souls!   [1]

SALIERI'S FIFTIETH VIENNA ANNIVERSARY

From a diary entry dated June 16, 1816

It must be fine and inspiring for a musician to have all his pupils gathered about him, to see how each strives to give of his best in honor of the master's jubilee, to hear in all their compositions the simple expressions of nature, free from all that eccentricity which tends to govern most composers nowadays, and for which we are indebted—almost wholly—to one of our greatest German musicians.* That eccentricity confuses and confounds, without distinguishing between them, tragic and comic, sacred and profane, pleasant and unpleasant, heroic strains and mere noise; it engenders in people not love but madness; it rouses them to scornful laughter instead of lifting up their thoughts to God. To have banned these extravagances from the circle of his pupils, and to have kept them, instead, at the pure source of nature must be the greatest satisfaction to a musician who, following in Gluck's steps, seeks his inspiration in nature alone, despite the unnatural influences of the present day.

After fifty years spent in Vienna and nearly as long in the emperor's service, Herr Salieri celebrated his jubilee, received in recognition from His Majesty a gold medal, and held a big gathering of his pupils of both sexes.   [2]

---

* A reference to Beethoven. In slighting the composer, Schubert is taking a position espoused by Salieri and popular in some circles at the time. Soon afterward Schubert was to reverse himself and become a staunch admirer.

ROSSINI

From a letter to Anselm Hüttenbrunner, Vienna, May 19, 1819

Rossini's *Otello* was given here a short time ago. Except for Radichi it was all very well done. It is a far better, that is to say, a far more characteristic, opera than *Tancredi*. His extraordinary creative genius is undeniable. The orchestration is at times highly original, and the vocal parts too, except for the usual Italian *galopades* and several reminiscences of *Tancredi*.   [3]

From a letter to his father and stepmother, Steyr, July 25, 1825

PUBLISHERS, ADMIRERS, CRITICS, PIANISTS

In Steyreck we stayed with Countess Weissenwolf, who is a great admirer of my humble self, possesses everything I have written, and sings many of the things very prettily, too. The Walter Scott songs made such a good impression on her that she made it clear she would be by no means displeased were I to dedicate them to her. But in connection with these, I mean to break with the usual publishing procedure, which brings in so little profit. I feel that these songs, bearing as they do the celebrated name of Scott, are likely to arouse more curiosity and—if I add the English text—should make my name better known in England, too. If only honest dealing were possible with . . . publishers; but the wise and beneficent regulations of our government have taken good care that the artist remain the eternal slave of these miserable money-grubbers.

With regard to the letter from Milder, I am very pleased about the good reception accorded to "Suleika," although I wish I could have had a look at the critique myself to see if there were anything to be learned from it. A review, however favorable, can be at the same time ridiculous, if the critic lacks reasonable intelligence, as is not seldom the case.

I have come across my compositions all over Upper Austria, but especially at St. Florian and at Kremsmünster, where, assisted by an excellent pianist, I gave a very successful recital of my Variations and Marches for four hands. The Variations from my new sonata for two hands* met with special enthusiasm. These I played alone, and not unsuccessfully, for several people assured me that under my fingers the keys were transformed into singing voices—which, if it be true, pleases me very much, as I cannot abide that cursed hacking of the instrument to which even first-class pianists are addicted; it pleases neither the ear nor the heart.   [4]

DEVOTION IN MUSIC

My new songs to Walter Scott's *Lady of the Lake* made a particularly good impression. Everybody was astounded at the piety I expressed in a hymn to the Holy Virgin, and which, it would seem, moves everyone's soul and puts people into a devout frame of mind. I believe this arises from the fact that I never force myself

---

* Probably the Sonata in A Minor, D. 845, which Schubert had completed that May.

into a devout mood, and never compose such hymns or prayers except when I am unconsciously inspired by Her. Then, however, it is generally real, true devotion.

[5]

THE OP. 100 PIANO TRIO

From a letter to the publisher H. A. Probst, August 1, 1828

This work is to be dedicated to nobody, save those who find pleasure in it. That is the most profitable dedication. [6]

CHAPTER FIVE

Hector Berlioz

Mikhail Glinka

Felix Mendelssohn

Frédéric Chopin

Robert Schumann

Franz Liszt

Richard Wagner

Giuseppe Verdi

Hector Berlioz

1803–1869

With Berlioz came the era of self-conscious Romanticism, epitomized by his Symphonie fantastique *(1830), which the composer described as an episode in the life of a "young musician of morbid sensibilities." A lack of formal musical training precluded a concert career
for Berlioz, although once his reputation as a composer was established he did appear as a
conductor of his own works. As a writer he was gifted and prolific, publishing essays, reviews, and memoirs from 1833 until his death and becoming the first true composer-critic.*

From Mémoires, 1870

PIANISM AND COMPOSITION

My father did not wish me to learn the piano, otherwise I should doubtless have
swelled the ranks of the innumerable army of famous pianists.

He had no intention of making an artist of me; and I daresay he thought that
if I learned the piano I should devote myself too passionately to it and become
more absorbed in music than he wished or intended me to be. I have often felt the
want of this accomplishment, as it might have been of the greatest use to me; but
when I consider the appalling number of miserable musical platitudes to which
the piano has given birth, which would never have seen the light had their authors
been limited to pen and paper, I feel grateful for the happy chance that forced me
to compose freely and in silence, and has thus delivered me from the tyranny of
the fingers, so dangerous to thought, and from the fascination that the ordinary
sonorities always exercise on a composer, more or less. Many amateurs have pitied
me for this deprivation, but that does not affect me much.   [1]

INSTRUMENTATION

There is another most important course wanting in all modern conservatories that
to my mind is becoming more essential every day, namely, one for instrumentation.
That branch of the composer's art has been so greatly developed of late years as to
have attracted the attention both of the critics and the public. It has, however, also
served only too often to mask the poverty of a composer's ideas, to ape real energy,
to counterfeit the power of inspiration, and even in the hands of really able and meritorious writers it has become a pretext for incalculable abuses, monstrous exaggerations, and ridiculous nonsense. It is easy to imagine to what excesses the example
of such masters has beguiled their followers. But these very excesses prove the regular and irregular use now made of instrumentation, a blind use in general, and
when not led by chance, guided by the most pitiable routine. For it does not follow
that, because most composers make more use of instruments than did their predecessors, they are better acquainted with the force, character, and action of each
member of the instrumental family, and the various ties of sympathy uniting them.
Far from this, many illustrious composers are still quite ignorant of the most ele-

mentary part of the science, namely, the *compass* of many of the instruments. One composer, to my certain knowledge, knew nothing of that of the flute. Of that of the brasses in general and trombones in particular they have but a very vague idea; and accordingly you may remark in most modern as in ancient scores, the prudent reserve with which their authors confine themselves to the middle range of those instruments, avoiding with equal care either extremity of the scale. Instrumentation in the present day therefore is like a fashionable foreign language, which many people affect to speak without having learned it, and therefore speak without properly understanding it, and with a great many barbarisms.

Such a class, or course, in conservatories, besides being useful to composition students, would be of great service to those who are called on to become conductors.   [2]

COMPOSERS AND CONDUCTING

It is generally supposed that every composer is a born conductor, that is to say, that he knows the art of conducting without having to learn it. Beethoven was an illustrious example of the fallacy of this opinion, and one might name a host of other masters whose compositions are held in general esteem, but who, the moment they take up the baton, neither mark time nor nuance, and would indeed literally bring the musicians to grief if the latter did not quickly perceive the inexperience of their leader and make up their minds to pay no attention to his whirling arms. There are two distinct parts in the work of a conductor: the first and easiest consists simply in conducting the performance of a work already known to the players and that, to use a phrase in vogue at the theaters, has been mounted beforehand. The second consists in directing the study of a work unknown to the performers, clearly setting forth the author's conception and rendering it salient and distinct, obtaining from the band that fidelity, unity, and expression without which there can be no real music and, the technical difficulties once overcome, identifying the players with himself, exciting them by his own zeal, animating them with his own enthusiasm, in short, imparting to them his own inspiration.

But to do this, there is one more art indispensable to the conductor besides the elementary knowledge acquired by study and practice and those qualities of feeling and instinct that are the gift of nature alone, the absence or presence of which makes the conductor either the composer's best interpreter or his most formidable enemy. This indispensable art is that of *reading the score.*

He who employs a simplified score, or a simple first violin part, as is often done in our day especially in France, cannot detect half the mistakes in the performance and, if he does point out a fault, exposes himself to some such answer as this from the musician addressed: "What do you know about it? You have not got my part"—one of the least of the inconveniences arising from this deplorable system.   [3]

CHORAL SINGING

Where one ordinary voice is detestable, fifty ordinary voices may be ravishing. A soulless singer paralyzes the most powerful effects of the best composer and renders them ridiculous; on the other hand, the average warmth of feeling that always resides in a really musical multitude brings out the inner flame of the work, and now it lives, whereas a single frigid virtuoso would have killed it.   [4]

CRITICS

From Les Grotesques de la musique, 1859

Poor devils! Where do they come from? At what age are they sent to the slaughterhouse? What is done with their bones? Where do such animals pasture in the daytime? Do they have females, and young? How many of them have handled the brush before being reduced to the broom?   [5]

From Mémoires

PALESTRINA

A musician finds the same interest in this music of the past, handed down to us unchanged in style or form, as a painter does in the frescoes of Pompeii. Far from regretting the absence of the trumpets and big drums, which have been introduced by the Italian composers of the day to such excess that both dancers and singers think no effect can be produced without them, we must confess that the Sistine Chapel was the only place in Italy where we felt safe from that deplorable innovation, and from the artillery of the manufacturers of *cavatinas.* We grant that the pope's thirty-two singers, though producing no effect and in fact wholly inaudible in the largest church in the world, suffice for the performance of Palestrina's works in the confined space of the pontifical chapel; we grant that the pure, calm harmony tends to a certain kind of reverie that is not without charm. But the charm is due to the harmonies themselves and is wholly independent of the so-called genius of the composers, if, indeed, you can dignify by that name musicians who spent their lives compiling successions of chords like those which constitute a portion of the *Improperia* of Palestrina:

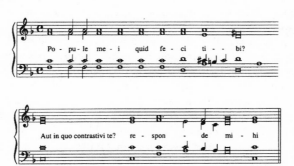

It is quite possible that the musician who wrote these four-part psalms, in which there is neither *melody* nor *rhythm,* and in which the *harmony* is confined to *perfect chords* with a few *suspensions,* may have had some taste and a certain amount of scientific knowledge; but genius—the idea is too absurd! . . .

Beauty and truth of expression gain nothing by the difficulties that the composer may have had to overcome in producing them, any more than his work would have increased in value, had he been suffering physical pain while he was writing it. If Palestrina had lost his hands and been forced to write with his feet, that fact would in no way have enhanced the value of his works or increased their religious merit. . . .

Some gloomy autumn day, when the dreary north wind is howling, read *Ossian* to the accompaniment of the weird moans of an Aeolian harp hung in the leafless branches of a tree, and you will experience a feeling of intense sadness, an infinite yearning for another state of existence and intense disgust with the present—in fact, a regular attack of the "blue devils" and a longing for suicide. This is a much more definite effect than that produced by the music of the Sistine Chapel, and yet no one ever thought of ranking the makers of Aeolian harps among the great composers.   [6]

A PERFORMANCE OF BACH'S *ST. MATTHEW PASSION*

Originally from a letter to Desmarest, Berlin, 1843

I was invited by the director to a performance of Sebastian Bach's *Passion*. That celebrated work, with which you are no doubt familiar, is written for two choirs and two orchestras. The singers, at least three hundred, were arranged upon the steps of a large amphitheater, exactly like that in the chemistry lecture room at the Jardin des Plantes; a space of three or four feet separated the two choirs. The two orchestras, neither of them large, accompany the voices from the highest steps behind the chorus, and are consequently somewhat distant from the conductor, who is placed below, in front, and close beside the piano. I ought to call it a clavecin, for it has almost the tone of the wretched instruments of that name used in Bach's time. I do not know if such choice is made designedly, but I have remarked in all singing schools, in the lobbies of theaters, and in fact everywhere, that the piano intended to accompany the voice is always the most detestable that can be found. The one that Mendelssohn used at Leipzig in the Gewandhaus concert hall is the only exception.

You will want to know what the piano-clavecin can be doing *during the performance* of a work in which the composer has not employed that instrument at all! Well, it accompanies along with the orchestra, and probably serves to keep the first rows of the chorus in tune, since they are supposed not to be able to hear the orchestra properly in the ensemble passages *tutti*, as it is too far back of them. At any rate, this is the custom. The constant strumming of the chords on this bad piano produces a wearisome effect by spreading a thick layer of monotony over the whole, but that is doubtless one reason for not giving it up. An old custom is so sacred when it is bad!

The singers sit while they are silent and rise to sing. I think there is really an advantage for the proper emission of the voice in singing while standing up; but it is unfortunate that the singers should weary of this posture and want to sit down as soon as each has finished, for in a work like Bach's, where the two choirs not only carry on dialogues but are also interrupted every instant by solo recitatives, it follows that one side is always rising and another sitting down, and in the long run this series of ups and downs becomes rather absurd. Besides, it takes away all unexpectedness from certain entries of the choir, because the audience perceives in advance the direction from which the sound will come before it is uttered. I should prefer that the choristers be always seated if they cannot remain standing throughout. But this "impossibility" is among those which vanish instantaneously if the director knows how to say *I will* or *I will not*.

Be this as it may, there was something very imposing in the performance of these vocal masses; the first tutti of the two choruses took away my breath, as I did not expect such a powerful burst of harmony. It must, however, be admitted that one wearies of this fine sonority far more quickly than of that of the orchestra, the timbres of voices being less varied than those of instruments. This is easily understood; there are only four kinds of voice, while the number of different instruments is upwards of thirty. . . .

Whoever is familiar with our musical customs in Paris must witness, in order to believe, the attention, respect, and even reverence with which German audiences listen to such a composition. Everyone follows the words in the book with his eyes; not a movement among the audience, not a murmur of praise or blame, not a sound of applause; they are at divine service, they are hearing the gospel sung, and they listen in silence, not to the concert but to the service. And really such music ought thus to be listened to. They adore Bach and believe in him, without supposing for a moment that his divinity could ever be called into question. A heretic would horrify them; he is forbidden even to speak of him. God is God and Bach is Bach.   [7]

GLUCK

Of all the ancient composers, Gluck, has, I believe, the least to fear from the incessant revolutions of art. He sacrificed nothing either to the caprices of singers, the exigencies of fashion, or to the inveterate routine with which he had to contend on his arrival in France after his protracted struggles with the Italian theaters. . . .

With less conviction or less firmness, it is probable that, despite his natural genius, his degenerate works would not have long survived those of his mediocre rivals now completely forgotten. But truth of expression, purity of style, and grandeur of form belong to all time. Gluck's fine passages will always be fine. Victor Hugo is right: the heart never grows old.   [8]

MOZART'S OPERAS

I have stated that, when I went up for my first examination at the conservatory, I was wholly absorbed in the study of dramatic music of the grand school; I should have said of lyrical tragedy, and it was owing to this that my admiration for Mozart was then so lukewarm. Only Gluck and Spontini could excite me. And this was the reason for my tepid regard for the composer of *Don Giovanni*. *Don Giovanni* and *Figaro* were the two Mozart works most often played in Paris; but they were always given in Italian, by Italians, at the Italian opera house; that alone was sufficient to prejudice me against them. Their great defect in my eyes was that they seemed to belong to the ultramontane school. Another, more legitimate objection was a passage in the part of Donna Anna that shocked me greatly, where Mozart had inserted a wretched vocalization that is a blot on his brilliant work. It occurs in the *allegro* of the soprano aria in the second act, "Non mi dir," a song of intense melancholy in which all the poetry of love is voiced in lamentation and tears, and yet it is made to wind up with such a ridiculous, unseemly phrase that one wonders how the same man could have written both. Donna Anna seems suddenly to have dried her tears and broken out into coarse buffoonery. The words of the passage are *Forse un giorno il cielo ancora senira-a-a-a* (here comes an incredible run, in execrable taste) *pietà di me*. A truly singular form of expression for a noble, outraged woman, to *hope that heaven will one day take pity on her!* . . . I found it difficult to forgive Mozart for this enormity. I now feel I would shed my life's blood if I could thereby erase that shameful page and others of the same kind which disfigure some of his work. [9]

The Young Wagner

As for the young kapellmeister Richard Wagner, who lived for some time in Paris without managing to make himself known except by some articles in the *Gazette musicale,* his authority was exercised for the first time in assisting me with my rehearsals, which he did with both zeal and goodwill. The ceremony of his installation took place the day after my arrival, and when I met him he was in all the intoxication of a very natural delight. After having endured untold privations in France and all the mortifications attendant on obscurity, Wagner, on his return to Saxony, had the boldness to undertake and the good fortune to carry out the composition of both words and music of an opera in five acts, *Rienzi*. It had a brilliant success at Dresden, and was soon followed by *The Flying Dutchman,* an opera in three acts, of which he likewise wrote both words and music. Whatever opinion one may have about the merit of these works, it must be admitted that there are very few men capable of twice accomplishing successfully this double task. It was more than sufficient proof of capacity to attract both attention and interest. . . .

I was much struck by the sombre coloring of *The Flying Dutchman,* and by certain stormy effects perfectly appropriate to the subject; but I also remarked an abuse of the tremolo, the more to be regretted in that it had already struck me in *Rienzi,* and because it implied a certain indolence of mind in the author, against which he is not sufficiently on guard. Of all orchestral effects, the sustained tremolo is the most monotonous; it calls for no inventive power on the part of the composer, unless accompanied by some striking idea either above or below it. [10]

Johann Strauss the Elder

And then there is Strauss, conducting his fine orchestra; and when the new waltzes he writes expressly for each fashionable ball turn out successful, the dancers stop to applaud him, the ladies approach the platform and throw him bouquets, and he is recalled at the end of the waltz. Thus there is no jealousy between dancing and music; each shares with the other in its pleasure and success. This is only fair, for Strauss is an artist. The influence he has already exercised over musical feeling throughout Europe in introducing cross-rhythms into waltzes is not sufficiently recognized. So piquant is the effect that the dancers themselves have already sought to imitate it by creating the *deux-temps* waltz, although the music itself has kept the triple rhythm. If, outside Germany, the public at large can be induced to understand the singular charm frequently resulting from contrary rhythms, it will be entirely owing to Strauss. Beethoven's marvels in this style are too far above them and act at present only upon exceptional hearers; Strauss has addressed himself to the masses, and his numerous imitators have been forced, by imitation, to second and support him. [11]

SELF-EVALUATION

Generally speaking, my style is very bold, but it has not the slightest tendency to subvert any of the constituent elements of art. On the contrary, it is my endeavor to add to their number. I never dreamed of making music *without melody*, as so many in France are stupid enough to say. Such a school now exists in Germany, and I detest it. It is easy to see that, without confining myself to a short air for the theme of a piece, as the great masters often do, I have always taken care that my compositions be melodically rich. The value of the melodies, their distinction, novelty, and charm, may of course be disputed. It is not for me to give an estimate of them; but to deny their existence is unfair and absurd. As they are often on a very large scale, however, an immature or unappreciative mind cannot properly distinguish their forms; or they may be joined to other secondary melodies, which are invisible to that class of mind; and lastly, such melodies are so unlike the little absurdities to which that term is applied by the lower stratum of the musical world that it finds it impossible to give the same name to both.

The prevailing characteristics of my music are passionate expression, intense ardor, rhythmic animation, and unexpected turns. When I say passionate expression, I mean an expression determined to strengthen or underscore the inner meaning of its subject, even when that subject is the contrary of passion, and when the feeling to be expressed is but gentle and tender, or even profoundly calm. This is the sort of expression that has been in *L'Enfance du Christ*, the "Ciel" scene in *The Damnation of Faust* and in the "Sanctus" of the Requiem. [12]

Mikhail Glinka
1804–1857

Glinka was a musical amateur, haphazardly trained as an instrumentalist and largely self-taught as a composer. His output was modest, and only his two finished operas, A Life for the Czar *(1836) and* Ruslan and Ludmila *(1842), have endured. Nevertheless, he has long been regarded as the father of Russian music. Although he was not the reformer or revolutionary that later followers have made him out to be, the reputation is well earned.*

JOHN FIELD'S PLAYING

From a note, undated

Although I did not hear him very often, I still recall his playing, at once gentle and forceful and marked by an admirable precision. It was as if he did not strike the keyboard, but that his fingers, like great drops of rain, poured over the keys as pearls on velvet. I do not share—and here I believe myself in accord with all those who, loving music sincerely, might have heard Field play—I do not share the opinion of Liszt, who told me one day that he found the master's playing "endormi." No, Field's playing was not sleepy; on the contrary, it was often daring, temperamental, unpredictable. It was just that he was careful not to lower his art to the level of charlatanism; pounding the ivories in the style of present-day fashionable pianists was never his ideal. [1]

LISZT'S PLAYING

From a note, 1842

Despite the general blind enthusiasm that I, too, partly shared, I can now render a complete account of the impressions that Liszt's playing made on me. He played Chopin mazurkas, nocturnes, and études, the entire brilliant modern school in particular, very beautifully, if somewhat *à la française*, that is to say, with exaggerations of nuance. His Bach, all of whose *Well-Tempered Clavier* he knew practically by heart, and his Beethoven sonatas were, to my taste, not so satisfying. In classical music his playing had no real dignity; there was something "bangy" about his touch. In his performance of Hummel's Septet one felt the carelessness of the grand seigneur. Hummel himself played the work incomparably better and more simply. On the whole, I would not place the entire manner in which Liszt handled the piano, from the point of view of external finish, in the same class with the playing of Field, Charles Mayer, or even Thalberg, particularly in scale passages. [2]

RUSSIAN SONG

From his memoir, 1854

We inhabitants of the north feel differently. Life's experiences touch us either not at all or sink deep into our souls. With us, it is either mad boisterousness or bitter tears. Even love, that wondrous emotion which brightens the entire universe, is always bound up in us with a certain sadness. There is no doubt that our melancholy Russian songs are children of the north that we have, perhaps, taken over from the east. The songs of the orientals are just as melancholy, even in carefree Andalusia. [3]

BERLIOZ

From a letter to Nestor Koukolnik, Paris, April 15, 1845

In the realm of fantasy, no one has such colossal invention, and his musical combinations possess, among all their other merits, the quality of true novelty. Breadth in ensemble, abundance of detail, a compact harmonic tissue, powerful and until now unheard-of orchestration are the attributes of Berlioz's music. In the drama, carried away by his fantastic temperament, he is out of his element, lacks natural-ness, and gets on the wrong track. Among his pieces that I have heard, here are those I prefer: the overture to *The Francs-Juges,* the Queen Mab scherzo from *Romeo and Juliet,* the "March of the Pilgrims" from *Childe Harold [Harold in Italy],* and the "Dies irae" and "Tuba mirum" from the Requiem. All these pages have produced an indescribable impression on me. At the moment, I have at home several unpub-lished manuscripts by Berlioz, which I am studying with unmixed pleasure. [4]

Felix Mendelssohn
1809–1847

Mendelssohn received his first music lessons from his mother and was soon studying with the noted teacher Karl Friedrich Zelter. His Octet and the Midsummer Night's Dream *over-ture, composed when he was sixteen and seventeen, are often hailed as the greatest manifes-tations of youthful genius in music history. In 1829 he helped kindle a new appreciation for Bach with a centenary performance of the* St. Matthew Passion. *Mendelssohn's affection for his sister Fanny and his high regard of her talent are well documented, although his at-titude toward her nascent professionalism is obviously unsympathetic by present standards.*

SCHOLARLY VERSUS "PEOPLE'S" MUSIC

Letter to Carl Friedrich Zelter, Munich, June 22, 1830

The organist [in Weimar] offered me the choice of hearing something "scholarly" or something for "the people" (because he said that, for people in general, one must compose only easy and bad music). I asked him for something scholarly, but it was not much to be proud of; he modulated around enough to make one giddy, but nothing unusual came of it; he made a number of entries, but no fugue was forth-coming. When my turn came to play to him, I started with the D Minor Toccata of Sebastian [Bach] and remarked that this was both scholarly and something for "the people" too, at least for some of them; but mind, hardly had I begun to play when the superintendent dispatched his valet upstairs with the message that this playing must stop right away because it was a weekday and he could not study with that much noise going on. . . .

Here, in Munich, the musicians behave exactly like that organist; they believe that good music may be considered a heaven-sent gift, but in the abstract only, for as soon as they sit down to play, they produce the stupidest, silliest stuff im-aginable, and when people do not like it they pretend that is because it is still too highbrow. Even the best pianists have no idea that Mozart and Haydn also com-posed for the piano; they have only the vaguest notions of Beethoven and consider the music of Kalkbrenner, Field, and Hummel classical and scholarly. On the other hand, having played myself several times, I found the audience so receptive and open-minded that I was doubly vexed by these frivolities. Recently, at a soirée given by a countess who is supposed to be a leader of fashion, I had an outburst. The young ladies, quite able to perform adequate pieces very nicely, tried to break their fingers with juggler's tricks and rope dancer's feats by Herz. When I was asked to play, I thought: "Well, if you get bored, it serves you right," and started right out with the C-sharp Minor Sonata of Beethoven. When I finished, I noticed that the impression had been enormous; the ladies were weeping, the gentlemen hotly discussing the importance of the work. I had to write down a number of Beethoven sonatas for the female pianists who wanted to study them. Next morning the countess summoned her piano teacher and asked him for an edition of good, really good, music by Mozart, Beethoven, and Weber. This story went around Munich, and the good-natured musicians were very pleased that I had set myself up as a preacher in the desert.   [1]

MUSIC IN ROME

From a letter to his family, Rome, January 1831

There can be no question of a performance here. The orchestras are unbelievably bad; there is a real dearth of musicians, and of the right feeling. Each of the few violinists strikes up in his own way, all beginning or coming in at different times, the wind instruments are tuned too high or too low and add flourishes to their accompaniments such as we are used to hearing from street musicians, but scarcely as good; the general effect is a real caterwauling—and this with pieces they know. . . .

The evening before last a theater that Torlonia has fitted up and is to manage opened with a new opera by Pacini.* There was a tremendous crush; the boxes full of the most elegant people; young Torlonia appeared in the stage box and was much applauded, together with his mother, the old duchess. People called out, "Bravo, Torlonia, grazie, grazie." Opposite him was Jérôme, in his court dress, with bemedaled chest; in the next box a Countess Samoilov, etc. Above the orchestra is a picture of Time, pointing to a dial that slowly moves round, enough to make one melancholy. Then Pacini took his seat at the piano and received an ovation. He had not written an overture; the opera began with a chorus, during which a tuned anvil was beaten in time to the music. The corsair appeared, sang his aria, and was applauded, at which the corsair, up on the stage, and the maestro, down in the orchestra, both bowed (by the way, the pirate sings contralto and is called Mme Mariani). Many other pieces followed, and the thing grew tedious. The audience thought so too, and when Pacini's great finale rang out, the pit rose to their feet, began talking in loud voices and laughing, and turned their backs on the stage. Mme Samoilov swooned away in her box and had to be carried out. Pacini vanished from the piano, and amid considerable tumult the act drop was lowered. Next came the great Bluebeard ballet, and then the last act of the opera. Having once started, they hissed the whole ballet from beginning to end, and accompanied the second act of the opera, likewise, with hisses and laughter. At the end they called for Torlonia, but he did

---

* Giovanni Pacini (1796–1867) composed some eighty operas between 1831 and 1867, as well as numerous other works, and founded a music school in northern Italy.

not come. That is a sober account of a first night and theater opening in Rome. I had expected it to be great fun, and came away in low spirits. If the music had caused a *furore* I would have been vexed, for it is sorry stuff, quite beneath criticism. But it vexes me, too, that they should suddenly turn their backs on Pacini, their great favorite, whom they wanted to crown on the Capitol, ape his tunes, and sing parodies of them; and it shows what a low opinion the public has of such music. On another occasion they carried him home shoulder-high—that is no amends. They would not behave like that with Boieldieu in France—simply from a sense of propriety, apart from any feeling for art.   [2]

THE PARIS CONSERVATORY ORCHESTRA

From a letter to Zelter, Paris, February 15, 1832

The musicians themselves delight in Beethoven's great symphonies—they have made themselves thoroughly familiar with them and are happy to have mastered the difficulties. Some of them, including Habeneck himself, undoubtedly have a perfectly genuine love of Beethoven; but as for the others, who are the loudest in their enthusiasm, I do not believe a word they say about it; for they make this an excuse for decrying the other masters—declaring Haydn was merely a fashionable composer, Mozart an ordinary sort of fellow; and such narrow-minded enthusiasm cannot be sincere. If they really felt what Beethoven meant, they would also realize what Haydn was, and feel small; but not a bit of it, they go briskly ahead with their criticism. Beethoven is uncommonly popular with the concert public, as well, because they believe that only the connoisseur can appreciate him; but only a small minority really enjoy him, and I cannot abide the disdainful attitude toward Haydn and Mozart; it infuriates me.   [3]

"THE REAL HANDEL"

From a letter to the publisher N. Simrock, Berlin, July 10, 1838

Surely it would now be worth some publisher's while to have the *original* scores of a few of Handel's principal oratorios engraved in Germany? It would have to be done by subscription, but I should think a good deal of money could be raised, since not one of those scores so far exists in this country. It had occurred to me that if that were done I might add the organ accompaniment; but in that case it would have to be printed in smaller notes in a different color, so that (1) anyone who wished would have Handel, complete and pure, (2) my organ accompaniment would be there for anyone who wanted it and had an organ, and (3) there could be an appendix giving the organ accompaniment arranged for clarinets, bassoons, and other present-day wind instruments, to be used where there is no organ. In that way any orchestra that plays oratorios could use these scores, and we would at last have the real Handel in Germany instead of one who has first been baptized in Moselle water* and drenched through and through with it.   [4]

---

* A reference to the distorted editions of Handel by Ignaz von Mosel that were popular at the time.

A PLEA FOR NEW MUSIC

From a letter to Ferdinand Hiller, Berlin, July 15, 1838

You will have heard that I was at Cologne for the festival. It all went well; the organ was splendidly effective in Handel and still more so in Bach—it was some newly discovered music of his, which you don't yet know, with an imposing double chorus. But despite this the interest one feels in something new and untried was lacking, to my mind at least. I like it so much when there is that kind of uncertainty that leaves room for me and the public to have an opinion. In Beethoven, Handel, and Bach one knows beforehand what is coming and always must come, and a great deal more besides. You are quite right in saying that it is better in Italy, where people have new music every year, and must also have a new opinion every year. If only music and opinion were a little better!   [5]

THE MEANING OF MUSIC

From a letter to Marc-André Souchay,* Berlin, October 15, 1842

There is so much talk about music, and yet so little is said. For my part, I believe that words do not suffice for such a purpose, and if I found they did suffice I would finally have nothing more to do with music. People often complain that music is too ambiguous, that what they should be thinking as they hear it is unclear, whereas everyone understands words. With me it is exactly the reverse, and not only with regard to an entire speech but also with individual words. These, too, seem to me so ambiguous, so vague, so easily misunderstood in comparison to genuine music, which fills the soul with a thousand things better than words. The thoughts that are expressed to me by music that I love are not too indefinite to be put into words, but on the contrary, too definite. And so I find in every effort to express such thoughts that something is right but, at the same time, that something is lacking in all of them. . . . If you ask me what I was thinking of when I wrote it, I would say: just the song as it stands. And if I happen to have had certain words in mind for one or another of these songs, I would never want to tell them to anyone, because the same words never mean the same things to different people. Only the song can say the same thing, can arouse the same feelings in one person as in another, a feeling that is not expressed, however, by the same words.   [6]

ROSSINI

Letter to his mother and his sister Rebecca, Frankfurt, July 14, 1836

Early yesterday I went to see him [Ferdinand Hiller], and whom should I find sitting there? Rossini, big, fat, and in the sunniest frame of mind.† I really know few

---

* Souchay had asked Mendelssohn the meanings of some of his *Songs without Words.*

† Rossini had written the last of his operas seven years earlier and by this time was composing only intermittently.

men who can be so amusing and witty as he, when he chooses; he kept us laughing the whole time. I promised that the Cecilia Association would sing the B Minor Mass for him and several other works of Sebastian Bach. It will be quite too much fun to see Rossini obliged to admire Bach. He thinks, however, "different countries, different customs," and is resolved to howl with the wolves. He says he is fascinated by Germany, and when he once gets the list of wines at the Rhine Hotel in the evening, the waiter is obliged to show him the way to his room, or he could never manage to find it. He tells the most laughable tales about Paris and all the musicians there, as well as about himself and his compositions, and how he entertains the deepest respect for all the men of the present day—so that you might really believe him, if you had no eyes to see his clever face. Intellect, animation, and wit sparkle in all his features and in every word, and whoever does not consider him a genius ought to hear him expatiating in this way, in order to change his opinion.   [7]

BERLIOZ

From a letter to his mother, Rome, March 15, 1831

But now you shall hear about Berlioz and his music. He makes me sad, because he is really a cultured, agreeable man and yet composes so very badly.

The day after tomorrow he is going back to Paris. He seems terribly in love, and this has been the inspiration for a symphony that he calls *Episode de la vie d'un artiste.* When it was performed, two thousand copies of explanatory notes were distributed. In them he says that the composer has imagined the theme of the first movement as depicting a charming young lady who has fascinated the artist, and that his rage, jealousy, tenderness, and tears are pictured in it. The second movement describes a ball where everything seems empty to him because she is missing. The third is called *scène aux champs;* the cowherds play a *ranz de vaches,* the instruments imitating the rustle of the leaves (all this in the printed program). Fear and hope are mixed in the artist's soul. Before the fourth movement (so continues the program), the artist, having poisoned himself with opium but misjudged the quantity, instead of dying has the most horrible visions. The fourth movement is just such a vision where he is present at his own execution; it is called *marche au supplice.* The fifth and last is called *songe d'une nuit,* in which he sees the witches dancing on the Blocksberg, his beloved among them. At the same time he hears the distorted cantus firmus of the "Dies irae," to which the witches are dancing.

How utterly loathsome all this is to me, I don't have to tell you. To see one's most cherished ideas debased and expressed in perverted caricatures would enrage anyone. And yet this is only the program. The execution is still more miserable: nowhere a spark, no warmth, utter foolishness, contrived passion represented through every possible exaggerated orchestral means: four timpani, two pianos for four hands, which are supposed to imitate bells, two harps, many big drums, violins divided into eight parts, two parts for the double basses, which play solo passages, and all these means (to which I would not object if they were properly employed) used to express nothing but indifferent drivel, mere grunting, shouting, screaming back and forth. And when you see the composer himself, that friendly, quiet, meditative person, calmly and assuredly going his way, never for a moment in doubt of his vocation, unable to listen to any outside voice, since he wishes to follow only his inner inspiration, when you see how keenly and correctly he evaluates and recognizes everything, yet is in complete darkness about himself—it is unspeakably dreadful, and I cannot express how deeply the sight of him depresses me. I have not been able to work for two days.   [8]

LISZT

From a letter to his mother, Leipzig, March 30, 1840

There has been a tremendous coming and going in the last few weeks. Liszt was here for a fortnight and caused a hullabaloo, in the good and bad sense. I think he is basically a good, warm-hearted man and a splendid artist. . . . I have never seen a musician whose feeling for music filled him to the very fingertips and flowed directly out from them, as it does with Liszt; and with this directness and his immense technique and practice he would leave all others far behind were it not that, for all that, original ideas are still the most important thing; and these nature appears—so far at least—to have denied him, so that in this respect most of the other great virtuosi equal or even surpass him.   [9]

THE NIBELUNGEN POEM AS A POSSIBLE OPERA SUBJECT

From a letter to his sister Fanny, Leipzig, November 14, 1840

Do you know that your suggestion as to the "Nibelungen" seems most interesting to me? It has been constantly in my head ever since, and I mean to spend my first day of leisure reading the poem, for I have forgotten the details and can only recall the outlines and the general coloring, which seem to me gloriously dramatic. Will you kindly give me your more specific ideas on the subject? Evidently the poem is more present in your memory than in mine. I scarcely remember what your allusion to the "sinking into the Rhine" refers to. Could you point out to me the various passages that struck you as particularly dramatic when the idea first occurred to you? And above all, say something more definite on the subject; the whole tone, the pictorial qualities, and the characteristic features impress my imagination strongly.   [10]

FANNY MENDELSSOHN HENSEL

Letter to his mother, Frankfurt, June 2, 1837

You write to me about Fanny's new compositions, and say that I ought to persuade her to publish them. Your praise is, however, quite unnecessary to make me heartily rejoice in them, or think them charming and admirable; for I know by whom they are written. I hope, too, I need not say that, if she does resolve to publish anything, I will do all in my power to obtain every facility for her, and to relieve her, so far as I can, from all trouble that can possibly be spared her. But to *persuade* her to publish anything I cannot, because this is contrary to my views and to my convictions. We have often formerly discussed the subject, and I still remain exactly of the same opinion. I consider the publication of a work as a serious matter (at least it ought to be so), for I maintain that no one should publish unless he is resolved to appear as an author for the rest of his life. For this purpose, however, a *succession* of works is indispensable, one after another. Nothing but annoyance is to be looked for from publishing, where one or two works alone are in question; or it becomes what is called a "manuscript for private circulation," which I also dislike; and from my knowledge of Fanny I should say she has neither inclination nor vocation for authorship. She is too much all that a woman ought to be for this. She regulates her house and thinks neither of the public nor of the musical world, nor even of music at all, until her first duties are fulfilled. Publishing would only disturb her in these, and I cannot say that I approve of it. I will not, therefore, persuade her to this step: forgive me for saying so. If she resolves to publish, either from her own impulse or to please Hensel [her husband], I am, as I said before, quite ready to assist her so far as I can; but to encourage her in what I do not consider right is something I cannot do. [11]

Frédéric Chopin
1810–1849

Chopin moved to Paris from his native Poland at the age of twenty-one, already a veteran pianist and composer. Although he inspired no group of disciples, his discovery of new possibilities for pianism opened the door for Liszt and others, and his audacious harmonies were a point of departure for Wagner. His letters, witty and sharply observant though they are, rarely deal with musical matters—hence the inclusion here of several remarks recorded by the artist Eugène Delacroix.

MUSIC IN VIENNA, 1830

From a letter to his family, Vienna, Wednesday before Christmas, 1830

Among the numerous pleasures of Vienna, the hotel evenings are famous. During supper, Strauss or Lanner plays waltzes; they are the local Świeszewskis.* After every waltz, they get huge applause; if they play a quodlibet, or jumble of opera, song, and dance, the hearers are so overjoyed that they don't know what to do with themselves. It shows the corrupt taste of the Viennese public. [1]

From a letter to Jan Matuszynski, Vienna, December 26, 1830

As for Thalberg, he plays excellently, but he's not my man. Younger than I, he pleases the ladies, makes potpourris from *The Dumb Girl*,† gets his piano effects by means of the pedal, not the hand, takes tenths as easily as I do octaves—has dia-

---

* A family based in Warsaw and known during Chopin's time and later as musicians and composers of dance music.

† *The Dumb Girl of Portici*, a popular opera by Daniel-François-Esprit Auber (1782–1871).

mond shirt studs—does not admire Moscheles; so don't be surprised that only the tutti of my concerto pleased him.   [2]

MUSIC IN PARIS, 1831: KALKBRENNER AND MEYERBEER

From a letter to Tytus Wojciechowski, Paris, December 12, 1831

Paris is whatever you choose: you can amuse yourself, be bored, laugh, cry, do anything you like and nobody looks at you, because thousands of others are doing the same, and everyone goes his own way. I don't know where there can be so many pianists as in Paris, so many asses and so many virtuosi. . . . I have met Rossini, Cherubini, Baillot, etc., also Kalkbrenner. You would not believe how curious I was about Herz, Liszt, Hiller, etc. They are all zero beside Kalkbrenner. I confess that I have played like Herz, but would wish to play like Kalkbrenner. If Paganini is perfection, Kalkbrenner is his equal, but in quite another style. It is hard to describe to you his calm, his enchanting touch, his incomparable evenness, and the mastery that is displayed in every note; he is a giant walking over Herz and Czerny and all, and over me. What can I do about it? When I was introduced, he asked me to play something. I should have liked to hear him first; but knowing how Herz plays, I put my pride in my pocket and sat down. I astonished Kalkbrenner, who at once asked me, was I not a pupil of Field, because I have Cramer's method and Field's touch. (That delighted me.) I was still more pleased when Kalkbrenner, sitting down to the piano and wanting to do his best before me, made a mistake and had to break off! But you should have heard it when he started again; I had not dreamed of anything like it. Since then we meet daily; either he comes to me or I go to him; and on closer acquaintance he has made me an offer: that I study with him for three years, and he will make something really—really out of me. I answered that I know how much I lack, but that I cannot exploit him, and three years is too long. But he convinced me that I can play admirably when I am in the mood, and badly when I am not, a thing that never happens to him. After close examination, he told me that I have no school, that I am on an excellent road, but can slip off the track. He says that after his death, or when he finally stops playing, there will be no representative of the great pianoforte school, and that, even if I wish it, I cannot build up a new school without knowing the old, in a word, that I am not a perfected machine and that this hampers the flow of my thoughts. He concedes that I have a mark in composition, and that it would be a pity not to become what I have the promise of being—and so on, and so on.

———— ♪ ————

I don't know whether there has ever been such magnificence in a theater, whether it has ever before achieved the pomp of the new five-act opera, *Robert le Diable,* by Meyerbeer, who wrote *Il Crociato.* It is a masterpiece of the new school, in which devils (huge choirs) sing through speaking-trumpets, and souls rise from graves (but not as in *The Charlatan,** just in groups of fifty or sixty). There is a diorama in the thea-

* Opera by Karol Kurpinsky (1785–1857), a popular composer in Poland at the time and an early exponent of a national style. He conducted at Chopin's first public concerts in Warsaw.

ter against which, at the end, you see the interior of a church, a whole church, at Christmas or Easter, lighted up, with monks, and all the congregation on the benches, and censers—there is even the organ, the sound of which, onstage, is enchanting and amazing (incidentally, it nearly drowns out the orchestra); nothing of the sort could be put on anywhere else. Meyerbeer has immortalized himself.   [3]

MUSIC IN ENGLAND, 1848

From a letter to Woijech Grzymala, London, May 13, 1848

Their orchestra resembles their roast beef and their turtle soup; it is strong, it is famous ... but that is all.   [4]

From a letter to Woijech Grzymala, London, October 21, 1848

Art here means painting, sculpture, and architecture. Music is not an art, and is not called art; if you say "an artist," an Englishman understands the word as meaning a painter, architect, or sculptor. Music is a profession, not an art, and no one speaks or writes of any musician as an artist, for in their language and customs it is something else; it is a *profession*. Ask any Englishman, and he will tell you so, and Neukomm assured me of it, too. No doubt it is the fault of the musicians, but try to correct such things! These queer folk play for the sake of beauty, but to teach them *decent* things is a joke; Lady————, one of the most highly regarded great ladies here in whose castle I spent a few days, is considered a great musician. One day, after my piano playing, and after various songs by other Scottish ladies, they brought a kind of accordion, and she began with the utmost gravity to play on it the most atrocious tunes. How about that? Every creature here seems to have a screw loose. Another lady, showing me her album, said to me: "La reine a regardé dedans et j'ai été à côté d'elle." A third, that she is "la treizième cousine de Marie Stuart." Another sang a French-English romance, standing up for the sake of originality, and accompanying herself on the piano: J'aie aiiemaiie (j'ai aimé!!!). The princess of Parma told me that one lady whistled for her to a guitar accompaniment. Those who know my compositions ask me—"Jouez-moi votre second soupir—j'aime beaucoup vos cloches." And every observation ends with, "leik water," meaning that it flows like water. I have not yet played to any Englishwoman without her saying to me, "Leik water!!!" They all look at their hands, and play the wrong notes with much feeling. Eccentric people, God help them.   [5]

From Eugène Delacroix's journal

HAYDN AND MOZART

February 21, 1847

Delacroix: [We heard a] quartet by Haydn, one of the last he wrote. Chopin tells me that experience gives to it that perfection which we admire in it. Mozart, he added, did not need experience; science, with him, was always on the level of inspiration.   [6]

BEETHOVEN, MOZART, BERLIOZ

April 7, 1849

Delacroix: As [Chopin] said to me, "Where [Beethoven] is obscure and seems lacking in unity, the cause is not to be sought in what people look upon as a rather wild originality, the thing they honor him for; the reason is that he turns his back on eternal principles; Mozart never. Each of the parts has its own movement, which, while still according with the others, keeps on with its own song and follows it perfectly; there is your counterpoint, 'punto contrapunto.'" He told me that the custom was to learn the harmonies before coming to counterpoint, that is to say, the succession of notes that leads to the harmonies. The harmonies in the music of Berlioz are laid on as a veneer; he fills in the intervals as best he can.   [7]

SONORITY

May 16, 1857

Delacroix: That dear, gentle Chopin used always to get indignant against the school that attributes part of the charm of music to sonority.   [8]

Robert Schumann
1810–1856

In his lifetime Schumann was as famous for his music journalism as his compositions. He sometimes spoke through the fictional characters of Florestan, Eusebius, and Master Raro: the extrovert, the introvert, and the voice of moderation. His involvement in founding the Neue Zeitschrift für Musik *in 1834 inaugurated a decade of activity as an editor and writer.*

In 1840 Schumann married the pianist and composer Clara Wieck, against the wishes of her father, one of Schumann's teachers and a co-founder of the Neue Zeitschrift. *Possibly Friedrich Wieck sensed the beginnings of the mental dysfunction that was to lead to the insanity of Schumann's final years.*

Except where noted, all texts are drawn from the collected writings.

ITALIAN MUSIC

From a letter to Friedrich Wieck, Heidelberg, November 6, 1829

I declare you can have no notion of Italian music until you have heard it under the Italian skies that called it into being. . . . In the Leipzig concert room I sometimes experienced a thrill of awe in the presence of the genius of music, but Italy has taught me to love it. Only once in my whole life have I had an impression of the actual presence of God, of gazing reverently and unrebuked into His face; this was at Milan, as I listened to Pasta—and Rossini! Do not smile, dear master, for I speak seriously. But this was my sole musical treat in Italy. Their music is, in the ordinary way, hardly fit to listen to. You have no conception of the sort of slapdash facility with which they reel off everything.   [1]

DECIDING TO BECOME A COMPOSER

From a letter to his mother, Heidelberg, July 30, 1830 (5 A.M.)

My life has been for twenty years one long struggle between poetry and prose, or, let us say, music and law. My aims were as high in practical life as in art. I hoped to find scope for my energies and my powers of overcoming difficulties in a wide sphere of work. But what prospects are there, particularly in Saxony, for an ordinary plebeian, who has neither interest nor fortune, nor any real love for pettifogging legal details? At Leipzig I never troubled myself about my career, but dreamed and pottered away my time without any tangible results; here I have worked better, but my stay in both places has only tended to strengthen my leaning toward art. Now I stand at the crossroads, trembling before the question, Whither? My own instinct points to art, and I believe it to be the right road, but it has always seemed to me—you will not be hurt if I whisper it lovingly—that you rather barred my way in that direction. I quite see your excellent motherly reasons, known to both of us as "a precarious future" and "an uncertain livelihood." But let us look a little further. A man can know no greater torment than to look forward to an unhappy, empty, and lifeless future of his own planning; but neither is it easy for him to choose a profession directly opposed to that for which he was destined from his youth. Such a change means patience, confidence, and a rapid training. My fancy is young and sheds its halo over the artistic life; I have also arrived at the certainty that, given a good teacher and six years' steady, hard work, I shall be able to hold my own against any pianist, for pianoforte-playing is merely a matter of mechanical perfection. I have, besides, an occasional flight of fancy, and what is perhaps a real inspiration to compose. This brings me to the question—which shall I choose? I can make my mark in only one or the other. I tell myself that if I give my whole mind to a thing I am bound to succeed, dear Mother, in the end, through steady application. Thus the battle within rages more fiercely than ever. Sometimes I am foolhardy and confident in my own tenacity; at others, doubtful, when I think of the immense stretch of road before me, which I might by this time have covered. As for Thibaut, he has long been advising me to take up music. I should be very glad if you would write to him, and I know he would be pleased. He went to Rome some time ago, so I shall not have another chance of seeing him.

If I keep to law it certainly means spending another winter here to attend Thibaut's lectures on the Pandects, which no law student can afford to miss. If I decide on music, I must as certainly leave here and return to Leipzig. I should be quite glad to study under Wieck, who knows me, and can gauge my capabilities. Later on I should want a year in Vienna and, if possible, lessons from Moscheles. And now, dear Mother, one request, which you will perhaps be glad to fulfil. *Will you yourself write to Wieck at Leipzig, and ask him plainly what he thinks of me and my scheme?**

---

* Schumann's mother did write to Wieck; he responded that, with training and perseverance, Schumann might well become a successful pianist.

Please let me have a speedy reply, telling me your decision, so I can hasten my departure from Heidelberg, loath as I am to leave this paradise, my many friends, and my bright dreams. Enclose this letter in your own to Wieck, if you like. In any case the matter must be settled by Michaelmas; then I will work, vigorously and without regrets, at my chosen profession.

You will admit that this is the most important letter I have ever written, or am likely to write. I hope you will not mind doing what I ask. Please answer as soon as possible; there is no time to be lost. Farewell, my dear Mother, and do not be anxious. It is a clear case of "Heaven helps those who help themselves," you see.   [2]

FUGUE

From a letter to Friedrich Wieck, Leipzig, January 11, 1832

I shall never agree with Dorn, who is bent on persuading me that a fugue is the whole of music. How very differently people are constituted! Yet I admit that the theoretical studies have done me good; for where I was once content to transfer to paper the impulse of the moment, I now stand critically aside to watch the play of my inspiration, pausing now and again to take my bearings. I wonder if you ever passed through this kind of a haze yourself. There are, as I think, some who, like Mozart, never experience it; others, like Hummel, steer their way through; others, again, like Schubert, never come out of it; while some can even laugh at it with Beethoven.   [3]

MUSIC AS EXPRESSION

From a letter to his mother, Leipzig, August 9, 1832

Music is to me the perfect expression of the soul, while to some it is a mere intoxication of the sense of hearing, and to others an arithmetical problem, and treated as such. You are quite right to insist that every man should aim at contributing to the commonweal; but let me add, he must not sink to the common level. Climbing brings us to the top of the ladder. I have no desire to be understood by the common herd.   [4]

CHARACTERISTICS OF THE KEYS

Based on an article contributed to a general dictionary, 1834

A great deal has been said on both sides; the truth, as usual, lies in the middle. With as little truth can we say that this or that feeling, in order to be correctly expressed in music, must be translated in but one especial key (anger, for example, in C-sharp minor), as that we can agree with Zelter, who declares that any feeling may be expressed in any key. The analysis of this question was already commenced in the past century; the poet Schubart especially professed to have found in some keys the characteristic expression of some feelings. Though a great deal of poetic tenderness is to be found in his characterization, though he was the first to define the great differences that exist between the major and minor scales, there is too much small description, epithet, and specification in his work—though this would be well enough were it all correctly applied. For instance, he calls E minor a girl dressed in white, with a rose-coloured breastknot! In G minor he finds discontent, discomfort, worrying anxiety about an unsuccessful plan, ill-tempered gnawing at the bit. Now compare this idea with Mozart's Symphony in G Minor—that floating Grecian grace!—or Moscheles's Concerto in G Minor! No one will deny that a composition, transposed from its original key into another, produces a different effect, or that this alteration is produced by a difference in the character of the keys: only try the "Désir" waltz in A major, or the "Bridal Chorus" in B major!* The new key seems contradictory to the feeling; the normal state of mind that every composition awakens is carried into a foreign sphere. The process by which the composer selects this or that principal key for the expression of his feelings is as little explainable as the creative process of genius itself, which chooses a certain form as the vehicle in which to enclose a thought with certainty. The composer will select the right key with no more reflection than the painter employs in choosing his colors. [5]

GERMAN OPERA

From a letter to C. Kossmaly, Leipzig, September 1, 1842

What, in the way of music, do you think I pray for night and morning? German opera. There is an unworked mine! But neither must the symphony be forgotten. [6]

ADVICE TO A YOUNG COMPOSER

From a letter to Ludwig Meinardus, Dresden, September 3, 1846

I have been thinking about you a great deal, have read your letter many times, and was pleased with the youthful spirit, as well as with the many clear, practical views expressed in it. All things considered, I should like to call your attention to one or two points before you come to a decision. I was once in a position similar to yours, had to do with an anxious mother, and to fight local prejudices in a small town. At the critical moment, fairly favorable outside circumstances came to my help; things fell out as they were bound to do. I became a musician, and my mother was happy in my happiness. But for those favorable outside circumstances, who knows what would have become of me, or whether I should have defeated the fate to which talent without means so often falls a prey? I cannot say how sorry I am to have to draw your attention precisely to that passage in your letter where you write to me so frankly and confidingly about your circumstances. You yourself thought the matter of sufficient importance to tell me, and you were right.

---

* The "Désir" waltz, attributed at that time to Beethoven but in fact a conflation of Schubert's *Trauer-Walzer* and Himmel's *Favorite-Walzer,* is in A-flat major. The "Bridal Chorus," from Weber's *Freischütz,* is in C major.

Will your courage carry you through the long time that must elapse before there is even a possibility of an assured position for you? Will not the thousand deprivations and humiliations rob you of your youthful strength and creative faculty? In this respect, it seems to me, you have far overestimated your own powers. You would have much to catch up, many things to learn that young musicians of your age have left far behind them long ago. You would certainly have to face a stern discipline. That you might eventually become a good, possibly a great, composer, I can believe from the talent shown in your compositions. But no voice reaches us from the future, for which we have no guarantee.

My advice, then, is this: keep your love for art; practice yourself in composition as much as possible; hold fast to the great models and masters, especially to Bach, Mozart, and Beethoven, not forgetting the present in which you live. But before you decide to follow the career on which your heart is set, subject yourself to the severest self-examination, and if you find you are not strong enough to defy its troubles and dangers, then seek a firm foundation, which you can always adorn with the pictures of your fancy and with those of your most loved artists. That you should keep a kindly recollection of me would please me as your whole letter has done. Let me hear of your work from time to time. Write to me presently about your immediate decisions, and tell me whether you agree with anything in my letter.   [7]

RECOMMENDATIONS FOR PRESERVING THE MUSIC OF THE PAST

From a letter to Franz Brendel,* Dresden, August 8, 1847

First, then, I think it desirable that a section should detach itself from the convention *to consider the protection of classical music against modern adaptations*.

The duties of this section would be to obtain information of all such publications—that is, of all new editions of old compositions of importance; to see how far the original was left untouched, or whether unwarranted alterations had been made; and finally to report on the result of their labors at the next (as I hope) annual meeting of the convention.

I should then like to propose that another section be formed for *the research and restoration of corrupted passages in classical works*, in the sense in which I dealt with it in my essay "On Some Presumably Corrected Passages in the Works of Bach, Mozart, and Beethoven" [*Neue Zeitschrift für Musik* 15:149].

This section would, like the first, be required to search out and collect the necessary material to lay before the next meeting. The result would be some interesting and thoroughly practical debates.

The section given up to minute inquiry would render a very great service, for instance, by looking into Mozart's Requiem, about which the grossest misconceptions are still current, for the existing version is not merely corrupt but, except for certain numbers, spurious.   [8]

---

* Franz Brendel (1811–68) was the manager of the *Neue Zeitschrift für Musik* from 1845. Schumann's letter refers to founding of a Universal German Society of Musicians, whose first meeting was August 13 and 14, 1847. Brendel read the letter to the convention.

FLORESTAN AND EUSEBIUS

From Schumann's verses to Clara

Eusebius's mildness, Florestan's ire—
I can give thee, at will, my tears or my fire,
For my soul by turns two spirits possess—
The spirits of joy and of bitterness.

From a letter to Heinrich Dorn, September 14, 1836

Florestan and Eusebius form my dual nature; I should like to melt them into the perfect man, Raro. [9]

READING SCORES IN CONCERTS

As Eusebius observed a young student of music diligently following a rehearsal of Beethoven's Eighth Symphony, score in hand, he remarked: *"There* is a good musician!"—"By no means," said Florestan. "He is a good musician who understands the music without the score, and the score without the music. The ear should not need the eye, the eye should not need the (outer) ear."—"A lofty standard," concluded Master Raro, "but how I agree with you, Florestan!" [10]

APHORISMS

Composer-Virtuosos

Experience has proven that the composer is not usually the finest and most interesting performer of his own works, especially of his newest, last created, which he cannot yet be expected to master from an objective point of view. It is more difficult for a man to discover his own ideal within his own heart than in that of another. *Eusebius* [11]

Critics

Music induces nightingales to sing, pug dogs to yelp.

They mince the timber of the lofty oak into sawdust.

Like the Athenians, they declare war by means of sheep-bleating. [12]

The Artist's Rewards (Reaction to "a Symphony by N.," 1833)

How deeply moved I feel when an artist—whose development cannot be called unsolid or unnatural, receives nothing from the public for the sleepless nights he has devoted to his labor, destroying, rebuilding, despairing, here and there encouraged by a flash of genius—receives nothing, not even appreciation of the youthful faults he has escaped from! How I felt for him as he stood there, excited, sorrowful, restless, hoping for one encouraging voice! *Florestan* [13]

Dilettantism

Beware, Eusebius, of despising the better kind of dilettantism, so inseparable from artist life. The saying, "No artist, no connoisseur," can only be regarded as a half

truth; for we cannot point to any period in which art has really blossomed without reciprocal action between these classes. *Raro* [14]

People say, "It pleased," or "It did not please." As if there were nothing higher
than the art of *pleasing* the public! [15]

The Prerequisites of Art

Consider how many circumstances must favorably unite before the beautiful, in
all its honor and glory, can appear! We need (1) lofty, deep intention, and great
ideality; (2) enthusiasm in description; (3) technical power and harmonic facility
closely combined; (4) an inward need of giving and receiving, a momentarily favorable mood both in artist and listener; (5) a fortunate combination of outward
circumstances; (6) a sympathy of impressions, feelings, views; a reflection of artistic joy in the eyes of others. Is not such a combination a happy cast, with six
dice, of six times six? *Eusebius* [16]

Beethoven versus Herz

There is a difference when Beethoven writes chromatic scales and when Herz does
it. [17]

THE USE OF TITLES

Titles for pieces of music, since they again have come into favor in our day, have
been censured here and there, and it has been said that "good music needs no sign-
post." Certainly not, but neither does a title rob it of its value; and the composer,
in adding one, at least prevents a complete misunderstanding of the character of
his music. If the poet is licensed to explain the whole meaning of his poem by its
title, why may not the composer do likewise? What is important is that such a
verbal heading should be significant and apt. It may be considered the test of the
general level of the composer's education. [18]

YOUNG ARTISTS AND ANTAGONISM

As soon as young artists meet with antagonists, they regard it as a sign of their
force of talent, and they esteem the greatness of this [talent] in exact proportion
to the perversity of these. [19]

COMEDY IN MUSIC

Half-educated people are generally unable to discover more than the expression of
grief and joy, and perhaps melancholy, in music without words; they are deaf to
the finer shades of passion—anger, revenge, satisfaction, quietude, etc. On this account, it is difficult for them to understand such great masters as Schubert and
Beethoven, who have translated almost every possible condition of life into the
speech of tones. I have fancied, in certain "Moments musicales" of Schubert's, that
I could perceive a sort of Philister-like vexation in them, as though he were un-

able to meet his tailor's accounts. And Eusebius declares that when he hears one of his marches, he sees the whole Austrian national guard pass before him, preceded by their bagpipers, and carrying sausages and hams on the points of their bayonets. But this is really too subjective a fancy! *Florestan*   [20]

"Away with Musical Journals"

It should be the highest endeavour of a just critic to render himself wholly unnecessary (as many try to become); the best discourse on music is silence. What stupid ideas are those of music journalists regarding their own importance! They imagine themselves the idols of artists, yet without artists they would starve. Away with musical journals! No matter how high criticism aspires, it is but the poor manure of works to come; and God's blessed sun will accomplish the work far better. *Florestan*   [21]

Rules and Maxims for Young Musicians (1848)

If anyone places a composition with which you are unacquainted before you, in order that you should play it, read it over first.

Do not be led astray by the applause bestowed on great virtuosos. The applause of an artist should be dearer to you than that of the masses.

Lose no opportunity of playing music, duos, trios, etc., with others. This will make your playing broader and more flowing. Accompany singers often.

Lose no opportunity of practicing the organ; there is no instrument that so quickly revenges itself on anything unclear or impure in composition or playing as the organ.

"Melody" is the amateur's war cry, and certainly music without melody is no music. Therefore you must understand what amateurs fancy the word means: anything easily, rhythmically pleasing. But there are melodies of a very different stamp, and every time you open Bach, Beethoven, Mozart, etc., they will smile out at you in a thousand different ways; you will soon weary, if you know these, of the faded monotony of modern Italian opera melodies.   [22]

The cultivation of the ear is of the greatest importance. Endeavor, in good time, to distinguish tones and keys. The bell, the windowpane, the cuckoo—seek to discover what tones they produce.

You must practice scales and other finger exercises industriously. However, there are people who think they may achieve great ends by doing this alone; up to an advanced age, they practice mechanical exercises for many hours daily. That is as reasonable as trying to recite the alphabet faster and faster every day. Find a better use for your time.

It is not enough that your fingers know your pieces; you should be able to hum them to yourself, away from the pianoforte. Sharpen your powers of imagination so that you may be able to remember correctly not only the melody of a composition but its proper harmonies as well. [23]

As you grow older, converse more with scores than with virtuosi. [24]

BACH

From a letter to G. A. Keferstein, Leipzig, January 31, 1840*

Mozart and Haydn knew Bach only through extracts. The effect he might have had on their productive powers, had they known him in all his greatness, is inconceivable. On the other hand, modern music, with its intricacies, its poetry and humor, has its origin chiefly in Bach. Mendelssohn, Bennett, Chopin, Hiller, all the so-called Romanticists (speaking of Germans only), stand much nearer to Bach than to Mozart in their music. They know Bach thoroughly, one and all. I myself make my daily confession to this high priest with a view to purifying and strengthening my musical nature. Then, again, Kuhnau must not be placed on a line with Bach, however estimable and delightful he may be. Had Bach written nothing but the *Well-Tempered Clavier*, he would still be worth a hundred of Kuhnau. In fact, I consider Bach to be quite unapproachable, immeasurable by ordinary standards. [25]

DOMENICO SCARLATTI

Scarlatti possesses many excellent qualities that distinguish him from his contemporaries. The order of the ideas—armored, as it were—such as we find in Bach, is missing; he is much less substantial, more ephemeral, rhapsodic. One has difficulty in always following his music, because he quickly knots and then unties again the musical threads. Compared to that of his contemporaries, his style is brief, pleasing, and piquant. His works certainly take an important place in piano literature—by continuing much that was new at the time; by the many-sided use they made of the instrument; and in particular by a more independent use of the left hand—but we confess that much in this music no longer pleases us nor ought to please us. [26]

BEETHOVEN'S FOUR OVERTURES TO *FIDELIO*

It should be written in golden letters that last Thursday the Leipzig Orchestra performed—*the four overtures to* Fidelio, *one after another*. Thanks to you, Viennese of 1805, that the first did not please you and that Beethoven in divine rage therefore poured forth the three others. If he ever appeared powerful to me, he did so on that evening, when, better than ever, we were able to listen to him, forming, rejecting,

---

* Keferstein (1799–1861) was a pastor, a writer on music, and the dedicatee (as "K. Stein") of some of Schumann's songs.

altering in his own workshop, and glowing with inspiration. He was most gigantic in his second start. The first overture was not effective; stop! thought he, the second shall rob you of all thought—and so he set himself to work anew and allowed the thrilling drama to pass before him, again singing the joys and sorrows of his heroine. This second overture is demonic in its boldness—even bolder, in certain details, than the third, the well-known great one in C major. But it did not satisfy him; he laid this one aside also, merely retaining certain passages from which, already more certain and conscious, he formed the third. Afterward there followed the lighter and more popular one in E major, which is generally heard in the theater as the prelude.

Such is the great four-overture work. Formed after the manner of nature, we first find in it the roots from which, in the second, the giant trunk arises, stretching its arms right and left, and finally completed by its leafy crown. *Florestan* [27]

WEBER

From a letter to Clara Wieck, Leipzig, May 10, 1840

Weber must have been one of the most refined and intellectual of musicians. [28]

From a review of Euryanthe, *September 23, 1847*

We raved over this as we had not done about anything for a long time. This music is too little known and appreciated. It is heart's blood, the noblest that he had; and this opera certainly cost him a part of his life—but he is also immortal because of it. It is a chain of sparkling jewels from beginning to end—all brilliant and flawless. How splendid the characterization of certain figures, such as Eglantine and Euryanthe—and how the instruments sound! They speak to us from the innermost depths. [29]

BERLIOZ

Berlioz, though he sometimes behaves himself like an Indian fakir, and slays men at the very altar, means it just as honestly as does Haydn when he offers a cherry blossom with his modest air. [30]

From a review of the Symphonie fantastique, *1835*

Berlioz does not try to be pleasing and elegant; what he hates, he grasps fiercely by the hair; what he loves, he almost crushes in his fervor.

——— ♪ ———

Though Berlioz neglects details and sacrifices them to the whole, he understands finely worked-out artistic detail very well. He does not squeeze out his themes to the last drop, nor does he sour our pleasure in a good idea by tiresome thematic treatment, as do many others. In fact, he indicates that he might have worked things out more rigorously, had he so chosen and had it been fitting—sketches in the concise, sparkling manner of Beethoven. He often expresses his loveliest thoughts only once, *en passant,* as it were.

If I were to reproach Berlioz, it would be for his neglected middle parts; but they meet with a peculiar obstacle, such as we seldom remark in any other composer. His melodies are distinguished by such intensity of almost every tone that, like some old folk songs, they will scarcely bear any harmonic accompaniment; indeed, they would even lose fullness of tone through it. On this account, Berlioz generally harmonizes them with a sustained ground bass or with the chords of the surrounding upper and lower fifths. To be sure, his melodies are not to be listened to with the ears alone, else they will remain unheeded by those who do not know how to round them out from within, that is to say, not with half a voice but wholeheartedly. For those who do, however, they will take on a significance that appears to root itself ever deeper the oftener they repeat them.

Born a virtuoso in respect to the orchestra, Berlioz demands inordinate things both of the individual executants and of the ensemble—more than did Beethoven, more than all others. But it is not greater technical proficiency that he asks of the instrumentalist. He demands sympathy, study, love. The individual must subordinate himself to serve the whole, and this in turn must subject itself to the will of the leader. [31]

MEYERBEER AND *LES HUGUENOTS*

What is the impression left behind it by *Les Huguenots*? That we have seen criminals executed and flighty ladies exposed to view. Reflect on the whole, and what does it amount to? In the first act we have an orgy of many men, with—oh, refinement!—only one woman, but veiled; in the second, an orgy of bathing women and, among them, a man scratched up with the nails to please Parisians, with bandaged eyes; in the third, we have a mixture of the licentious and the sanctimonious; slaughter spreads in the fourth; and in the fifth we have carnage in a church. Riot, murder, prayer, and nothing more, does *Les Huguenots* contain; in vain we seek one pure, lasting idea, one spark of Christian feeling in it. Meyerbeer nails a heart on the outside of a skin, and says, "Look! there it is, to be grasped with hands." All is made up, all appearance and hypocrisy. . . .

I do not blame the use of every means in the right place; but we must not exclaim "Glorious!" when a dozen of drums, trumpets, and ophicleides are heard at a little distance, in unison with a hundred singing men. One Meyerbeerian refinement I must mention here. He knows the public too well not to know that an excess of noise stupefies at last. How cleverly he goes to work then! After such explosions as that mentioned above, he gives us whole arias with the accompaniment of a single instrument, as if he means to say, "Behold what I can do with but small means! Look, Germans, look!" [32]

SCHUBERT

If fertility be a distinctive mark of genius, then Franz Schubert is a genius of the highest order. Not much over thirty when he died, he wrote in such abundance that but half of his compositions have as yet been published; another part will soon follow, while a still greater part will never, or not for a long time, be given to the public. Among his first-mentioned works his songs obtained the quickest and widest popularity; gradually he would have set all German literature to music; he would have been the man for Telemann, who claimed that "a good composer should be able to set public notices to music." . . .

There was a time when I was loath to mention Schubert, and would only at night speak of him to the trees and stars. Who of us does not rave at some time? Enraptured with this new mind, whose wealth seemed to me boundless and incommensurable, deaf to everything that could bear witness against him, I thought of nothing but of him. With increasing years, with increasing demands, the circle of our favorites grows smaller and smaller. The cause of this is in ourselves as well as in them. Who is the master of whom one holds the same opinion all one's life? Experiences that youth has not yet achieved are necessary to the evaluation of Bach; it even underestimates Mozart's greatness. Mere musical studies are not enough to enable us to understand Beethoven, just as in certain years he inspires us with one work rather than with another. It is certain that equal ages exert a reciprocal attraction upon each other, that youthful enthusiasm is best understood by youth, and the power of the mature master by the full-grown man. So Schubert will always remain the favorite of youth. He gives what youth desires—an overflowing heart, daring thoughts, and swift deeds; he tells them what they most love, romantic stories of knights, maidens, and adventures; he intermingles a little wit and humor, but not so much that the basic softness of the mood is thereby troubled. Moreover, he gives wings to the performer's own imagination like no other composer save Beethoven. His easily followed peculiarities tempt one to imitate them; we would like to carry out a thousand ideas suggested by him. Thus it is that he has a great future.   [33]

SCHUBERT'S NINTH SYMPHONY

From a letter to Clara Wieck, Leipzig, December 11, 1839

Oh, Clara, I have been in paradise today! They played at the rehearsal a symphony of Franz Schubert's. How I wish you had been there, for I cannot describe it to you. The instruments all sing like remarkably intelligent human voices, and the scoring is worthy of Beethoven. Then the length, the divine length, of it! It is a whole four-volume novel, longer than the choral symphony. I was supremely happy, and had nothing left to wish for, except that you were my wife and that I could write such symphonies myself.   [34]

From a review

We must grant that he possessed an extraordinary talent, in attaining to such peculiar treatment of separate instruments, such mastery of orchestral masses—they often seem to converse like human voices and choruses—although he scarcely heard any of his own instrumental works performed during his life. Save in some of Beethoven's works, I have not elsewhere observed so striking and deceptive a resemblance to the voice in the treatment of instruments; Meyerbeer, in his treatment of the human voice, attains precisely the opposite effect. Another proof of the genuine, manly inspiration of this symphony is its complete independence of the Beethoven symphonies. And how correct, how prudent in judgment, Schubert's genius displays itself here! As if conscious of his own more modest powers, he avoids imitating the grotesque forms, the bold proportions that meet us in Beethoven's later works; he gives us a creation of the most graceful form possible, which, in spite of its novel intricacies, never strays far from the happy medium, but always returns again to the central point. [35]

MENDELSSOHN

From a letter to his sister-in-law Theresa Schumann, Leipzig, April 1, 1836

Mendelssohn . . . is a god among men. [36]

From a letter to Simonin de Sire, Vienna, March 15, 1839

Mendelssohn I consider the first musician of the day; I doff my hat to him as my superior. He plays with everything, especially with the grouping of instruments in the orchestra, but with such ease, delicacy, and art, with such mastery throughout. [William Sterndale] Bennett follows in his steps. The two of them are like angels at the pianoforte, as unaffected as children. Thalberg is only important as a virtuoso. He has, in my opinion, no invention except in technique. [37]

From a review of Mendelssohn's Preludes and Fugues for the Pianoforte, Op. 35

A hot-headed fellow (now in Paris) has defined the meaning of *Fugue* to be "a composition in which one voice rushes out before the other (*fuga a fugere*), and the listener first of all"; on which account he always began to talk loud, and often to scold, at concerts, whenever he met with a fugue. Really he did not understand anything about it, and resembled the fox in the fable—i.e., he could not write one himself, however much he secretly wished to do so. Those who can—finished students of music, cantors, and others—describe it quite differently. According to these, Beethoven never did or could write fugues; even Bach has taken liberties with them, at which we must shrug our shoulders; Marpurg is the only guide; and so on. Others, again, think otherwise; I, for instance, who can luxuriate for hours in Bach's, Handel's, and Beethoven's fugues; and I had thought that only poor, watery, insipid, patchwork things in comparison could be written today, until these by Mendelssohn dissipated such ideas. . . .

Whether reviewers find this out or not, it is certain that the composer did not write them for pastime, but rather to call the attention of pianoforte players to this masterly old form once more, and to accustom them to it again; while he has chosen the right way to succeed in this, by avoiding all useless imitations and small artificialities, allowing the melody of the cantilena to predominate, and holding fast to the Bach form. Whether the latter, however, might not be advantageously transformed without losing the true fugue character is a question many will endeavor to answer. Beethoven shook at that foundation; but he was too largely occupied elsewhere, too busily occupied on high, building the cupolas of so many other cathedrals, to find time for laying the foundations of a new fugue form. Reicha also made an effort, but his creative powers lagged far behind his goodwill; yet his often peculiar ideas are not to be overlooked. However, the best fugue will always be that which the public takes for—a Strauss waltz; in other words, where the artistic root work, like that of a flower, is so beautifully concealed that we perceive only the flowers. [38]

CHOPIN

Review of Variations on "Là ci darem," Op. 2, December 7, 1831

Eusebius entered, not long ago. You know his pale face, and the ironic smile with which he awakens expectation. I sat with Florestan at the pianoforte. Florestan is, as you know, one of those rare musical minds that foresee, as it were, coming, novel, or extraordinary things. But he encountered a surprise today. With the words, "Off with your hats, gentlemen—a genius!" Eusebius laid down a piece of music. We were not allowed to see the title page. I turned over the leaves vacantly; the veiled enjoyment of music that one does not hear has something magical in it. And besides this, it seems to me that every composer presents a different character of note forms to the eye; Beethoven looks very different from Mozart, on paper; the difference resembles that between Jean Paul's and Goethe's prose. But here it seemed as if strange eyes were glancing up at me—flower eyes, basilisk eyes, peacock's eyes, maiden's eyes; in many places it looked yet brighter—I thought I saw Mozart's "Là ci darem la mano" wound through a hundred chords, Leporello seemed to wink at me, and Don Juan hurried past in his white mantle. "Now play it," said Florestan. Eusebius consented; and in the recess of a window we listened. Eusbius played as though he were inspired, and led forward countless forms, filled with the liveliest, warmest life; it seemed that the inspiration of the moment gave to his fingers a power beyond the ordinary measure of their cunning. It is true that Florestan's whole applause was expressed in nothing more than a happy smile, and the remark that the variations might have been written by Beethoven or Franz Schubert, had either of these been a pianoforte virtuoso; but how surprised he was, when, turning to the title page, he read, "'Là ci darem la mano,' varie pour le pianoforte par Frédéric Chopin, Oeuvre 2," and with what astonishment we both cried out, "An Opus 2!" How our faces glowed as we wondered, exclaiming, "That is something reasonable once more—Chopin—I never heard of the name—who can he be?—in any case a genius—is not that Zerlina's smile?—and Leporello"—etc., etc. I could not describe the scene. Heated with wine, Chopin, and our own enthusiasm, we went to Master Raro, who, with a smile, and displaying but little curiosity for Opus 2, said, "Bring me the Chopin! I know you and your newfangled enthusiasm!" We promised to bring it the next day. Eusebius soon bade us good night; I remained a short time with Master Raro; Florestan, who had been for some time without a habitation, hurried through the moonlit streets to my house. At midnight I found him lying on the sofa with his eyes closed. "Chopin's variations," he began as if in a dream, "are constantly running through my head; the whole is dramatic and Chopin-like; the introduction is so self-concentrated—do you remember Leporello's springs, in thirds?—that seems to me somewhat unfitted to the whole: but the theme—why did he write it in B flat?—The variations, the finale, the *adagio*, these are indeed something; genius burns through every measure. Naturally, dear Julius, Don Juan, Zerlina, Leporello, and Masetto are the dramatis personae; Zerlina's answer in the theme has a sufficiently enamoured character; the first variation expresses a kind of coquettish courteousness—the Spanish grandee flirts amiably with the peasant girl in it. This leads of itself into the second, which is at once comic, confidential, disputatious, as though two lovers were chasing each other and laughing more than usual about it. How all this is changed in the third! It is filled with moonshine and fairy magic; Masetto keeps at a distance, swearing audibly, without making any effect on Don Juan. And now the fourth, what do you think of that? Eusebius played it altogether correctly—how boldly, how wantonly it springs forward to meet the man, though the adagio (it seems quite natural to me that Chopin repeats the first part) is in B-flat minor, as it should be, for in its commencement it presents a moral warning to Don Juan. It is at once mischievous and beautiful that Leporello listens behind the hedge, laughing and jesting, that oboes and clarinets enchantingly allure, and that the B-flat major, in full bloom, correctly designates the first kiss of love. But all this is nothing compared to the last—have you any more wine, Julius?—that is the whole of Mozart's finale, popping champagne corks, ringing glasses! Leporello's voice between, the grasping, torturing demons, the fleeing Don Juan—and then the end, which beautifully soothes and closes all." Florestan concluded by saying that he had never experienced feelings similar to those awakened by this finale, except in Switzerland. When the evening sunlight of a beautiful day gradually creeps up toward the highest peaks, and when the last beam vanishes, there comes a moment when we think we see the white alpine giants close their eyes. We feel that we have beheld a heavenly apparition. "And now awake to new dreams, Julius, and sleep!"—"Dear Florestan," I answered, "these confidential feelings are perhaps praiseworthy, although somewhat subjective; but as deeply as yourself I bend before Chopin's spontaneous genius, his lofty aim, his mastership!"—and after that we fell asleep. *Julius*   [39]

From a review of Chopin's Two Nocturnes Op. 37, Ballade Op. 38, and Waltz Op. 42

Chopin might now publish anything without his name; one would nevertheless immediately recognize him. This remark includes praise and blame; praise for his gifts; blame for his endeavor. He possesses such remarkable original power that, whenever it displays itself, it is impossible for a moment to be uncertain as to its source; and he adds to this an abundance of novel forms that compel our admiration for both their tenderness and boldness. But, though ever new and inventive in the outward forms of his compositions, he remains in special instrumental effects intrinsically the same, and we almost fear that he will not rise any higher than he has already risen. And although this is high enough to render his name immortal in the history of modern art, he limits himself to the narrow sphere of piano music, whereas with his powers he might climb to far greater heights, whence to exercise an immense influence on the general development of our art. Let us, however, be content. He has already created so much that is beautiful, continues to give us so much, that we ought to be satisfied, for we should certainly congratulate any artist who has accomplished merely half as much as he. . . . We know how Chopin formerly comported himself, as though overstrewn with spangles, gold trinkets, and pearls. He has altered and grown older; he still loves jewelry, but of a more distinguished kind, through which the loftiness of poetry gleams all the lovelier. Indeed, one must grant him taste, and of the finest, though of a kind not meant for specialists of thoroughbass on the lookout for consecutive fifths and infuriated by every one they detect. Yet they might learn much from Chopin, above all, how to write fifths. We must direct attention to the ballade as a most remarkable work. Chopin has already written one composition of the same name [in G minor]—one of his wildest and most original compositions; the new one is different—as a work of art inferior to the first, but equally fantastic and inventive. Its impassioned episodes seem to have been inserted afterward. I recollect very well that when Chopin played the ballade here, it ended in F major; now it closes in A minor. At that time he also mentioned that certain poems of Mickiewicz had suggested his ballade to him. On the other hand, a poet might easily be inspired to find words to his music; it stirs one profoundly. The waltz finally is, like his earlier ones, a salon piece of the noblest sort; if it were played for dancers, Florestan thinks at least half of the ladies should be young countesses. And he is right, for Chopin's waltz is thoroughly aristocratic.   [40]

LISZT AS PERFORMER (1840)

The whole audience greeted his appearance with an enthusiastic storm of applause, and then he began to play. I had heard him before; but an artist is a different person in the presence of the public compared with what he appears in the presence of a few. The fine open space, the glitter of light, the elegantly dressed audience— all this elevates the frame of mind in giver and receiver. And now the demon's power began to awake; he first played with the public as if to try it, then gave it something more profound, until every single member was enveloped in his art; and then the whole mass began to rise and fall precisely as he willed it. I have never found any artist, except Paganini, to possess in so high a degree as Liszt this power of subjecting, elevating, and leading the public.   [41]

Still fatigued with his journey and from his frequent playing in recent concerts, Liszt arrived in the morning, and went at once to the rehearsal, so that he had little time to himself before the concert hour. It was impossible for him to take any rest. I would not leave this unmentioned: a man is not a god; and the visible effort with which Liszt played on that evening was but a natural consequence of what had preceded the concert. With the most friendly intentions, he had selected three pieces by composers residing here—Mendelssohn, Hiller, and myself; Mendelssohn's latest concerto, études by Hiller, and several numbers from an early work of mine, entitled *Carnaval* [Op. 9, 1833–35]. To the astonishment of many timid virtuosos, I must state that Liszt played these compositions almost at sight. He had had a slight former acquaintance with the études and *Carnaval*, but he had never seen Mendelssohn's concerto until a few days before the concert. He was, however, so continually occupied that he had been unable to find time, at such short notice, for private study. He met my doubt as to whether such rhapsodical sketches as mine of carnival life would make any impression on a general public with the decided assurance that he hoped they would. And yet I think he was mistaken. . . . Though certain traits in it may please certain persons, its musical moods change too rapidly to be easily followed by a general public that does not care to be roused anew every moment. . . .

Everybody wondered where he found the strength to repeat half of the *Hexameron*, and then his own galop, to the delight of the enraptured public. How much I hoped that he would give us some of Chopin's compositions, which he plays incomparably, with the deepest sympathy! But in his own room he amiably plays anything that is asked from him. How often have I thus listened to him in admiration and astonishment! [42]

From a letter to Clara Wieck, {Leipzig}, March 18, 1840

I have at last had a chance of hearing Liszt's wonderful playing, which alternates between a fine frenzy and the utmost delicacy. But his world is not mine, Clärchen. Art, as we know it—you when you play, I when I compose—has an intimate charm that is worth more to me than all Liszt's splendor and tinsel! [43]

LISZT AS COMPOSER

I sincerely believe that had Liszt, with his eminently musical nature, devoted the same time to composition and to himself that he has given to his instrument and to [transcribing] the works of others, he would have become a very remarkable composer. What may yet be expected from him we can only conjecture. To win favor, he must, above all things, return to simplicity and cheerfulness . . . must subject his compositions to a process the reverse of the usual one—must simplify rather than render them more weighty. [44]

WAGNER AND *TANNHÄUSER*

From a letter to Mendelssohn, Dresden, October 22, 1845

What, indeed, does the world in general (many so-called musicians included) understand of pure harmony? There is Wagner, who has just finished another opera. He is certainly a clever fellow, full of crazy ideas and audacious to a degree. Society still raves over *Rienzi*. Yet he cannot write or think out four consecutive bars of beautiful, or even of good, music. All these young musicians are weak in harmony, in the art of four-part writing. How can enduring work be produced in that way? And now we can see the whole score in print, [parallel] fifths, octaves, and all. It is too late now to alter and scratch out, however much he may wish it. The music is no fraction better than *Rienzi*, but duller and more unnatural, if anything. If one says anything of the sort it is always put down to envy, and that is why I only say it to you, knowing you have long been of the same opinion.   [45]

From another letter to Mendelssohn soon afterward (November 12)

I may have a chance of talking to you about Tannhäuser soon. I must take back one or two things I said after reading the score. It makes quite a different effect on the stage. Much of it impressed me deeply.   [46]

From a letter to C. von Bruyck,* Düsseldorf, May 8, 1853

I was much interested in what you said about Wagner. He is, to put it concisely, not a good musician. He has no sense of form or euphony. You must not, however, judge by pianoforte arrangements of his scores. Many parts of his operas could not fail to stir you deeply if you heard them on the stage. If his genius does not send out rays of pure sunlight, it exercises at times a mysterious charm over the senses. Yet, I repeat, the music, considered quite apart from the setting, is inferior—often quite amateurish, meaningless, and repugnant; and it is a sign of decadence in art when such music is ranked with the masterpieces of German drama. But enough—the future will pronounce the verdict.   [47]

BRAHMS

From Schumann's last article, "New Roads," 1853

Many new and significant talents have arisen; a new power in music seems to announce itself; the intimation has been proven true by many aspiring artists of the last years, even though their work may be known only in comparatively limited circles. To me, who followed the progress of these chosen ones with the greatest sympathy, it seemed that under these circumstances a musician must inevitably appear, called to give expression to his times in ideal fashion; a musician who would reveal his mastery not in a gradual evolution but one who, like Athena, would spring fully armed from the head of Zeus. And such a one *has* appeared; a young man over whose cradle graces and heroes have stood watch. His name is Johannes Brahms, and he comes from Hamburg, where he as been working in quiet obscurity, though instructed in the most difficult statutes of his art by an excellent and enthusiastically devoted teacher [Eduard Marxsen]. A well-known and honored master recently recommended him to me. Even outwardly he bore the signs that proclaimed, "This is a chosen one." Sitting at the piano, he began to disclose wonderful regions to us. We were drawn into ever more enchanting spheres. Besides, he is a performer of genius who can make of the piano an orchestra of lamenting and loudly jubilant voices. Here were sonatas—veiled symphonies rather; songs, the poetry of which

---

* Bruyck (1828–1902) was a composer and writer on music in Vienna.

would be understood even without words, although a profound vocal melody runs through them all; single piano pieces, some of them turbulent in spirit while graceful in form; again sonatas for violin and piano, string quartets, every work so different from the others that each seemed to stream from its own individual source. And then it was as though, like a rushing torrent, they were all united by him into a single waterfall, the cascades of which were overarched by a peaceful rainbow while butterflies played about its borders and it was accompanied by the voices of nightingales. Should he direct his magic wand where the massed power in chorus and orchestra may lend him their force, we can look forward to even more wondrous glimpses of the secret world of spirits. May the highest genius strengthen him to this end! Since he possesses yet another facet of genius—modesty—we may surmise that it will come to pass. His fellow musicians hail him on his first steps into a world where perhaps wounds await him. But there will be also palms and laurels. In him we welcome a strong champion.   [48]

ABEGG VARIATIONS, OP. 1

From a letter to his mother, Leipzig, September 21, 1831

The fact is, I shall shortly become the father of a fine, healthy infant, whom I should like to see christened before I leave Leipzig. The child will make its appearance at Probst's. How I hope you will understand its child's message of youth and life! If you did but know the first joys of authorship! Being engaged can be nothing in comparison. What hopes and prophetic visions fill my soul's heaven! The Doge of Venice, as he wedded the sea, was not prouder than I, as I celebrate my nuptials with the great world within whose vast range the artist may roam or rest at will. Is it not a consoling thought that this first leaf of my fancy that flutters into ether may find its way to some sore heart, bringing balm to soothe its pain and heal its wound?   [49]

SCENES FROM CHILDHOOD, OP. 15

From a letter to Heinrich Dorn, Leipzig, September 5, 1839

I have seldom met with anything so clumsy as Rellstab's criticism of my *Kinderszenen*. He seems to think I called up in my imagination a screaming child and fit the notes to it. It is just the other way about, but I will not deny that a vision of children's heads haunted me as I wrote. The inscriptions arose, of course, afterward, and are really nothing more than tiny hints about the interpretation and conception.   [50]

Franz Liszt
1811–1886

Hungarian by birth, Liszt was thoroughly Germanic in culture. His reputation as a composer rests on a tiny fraction of an immense and varied output. As a harmonist, he anticipated twentieth-century developments; as a pianist, he essentially created the high virtuosic technique; as a colleague he was generous, securing performances and publication for others; as a writer, he produced volumes of essays and reviews. In character he was a man of opposites: the devout "abbé" who was also the father of three children by another man's wife, the charismatic and calculating showman whose passion for music was nonetheless authentic.

CONDUCTING MODERN MUSIC

From "A Letter on Conducting," 1853

The works for which I openly confess my admiration and predilection are for the most part those which the more or less famous conductors—especially the so-called *tüchtige Kapellmeister* [efficient bandleaders]—have rarely honored with their personal favor and have as rarely performed. To my way of thinking, these works, beginning with those commonly identified as belonging to the *last period* of Beethoven—excused until not so long ago by Beethoven's deafness and mental derangement—exact from performers and conductors an *advance* that is being carried out at the moment—though it is far from being realized everywhere—in the accentuation, rhythm, manner of phrasing and declamation of certain passages, and in bringing out light and shade: in a word, an *advance* in the style of performance itself. It establishes between players and conductor a different kind of bond from that which is cemented by the imperturbable beating of time. Often the vulgar maintenance of the beat and of each bass note of the measure | 1, 2, 3, 4, | 1, 2, 3, 4, | clashes with both sense and expression. There, as elsewhere, *the letter kills the spirit,* and to this I could never subscribe, however plausible might be the hypocritically impartial attacks to which I am exposed.   [1]

THE STANDING OF THE MODERN MUSICIAN

From "On Beethoven's Music to Egmont," 1854

In our time we have not yet ceased viewing musicians as rare, curious phenomena, half-angels, half-donkeys, who bring heavenly songs to mortals, but who, at the same time, in their day-to-day life, are to be treated in the most ambiguous manner or with the most unambiguous scorn. We are *beginning* to recognize them now as people who, along with the rest of humanity, must comply with the moral duty of developing their minds and acquiring for themselves a general and varied culture; we agree that among them are some who are as skillful with words as with notes.   [2]

THE GYPSY ORCHESTRA

From Des Bohémiens et de leur musique en Hongrie, 1859

The entire instrumental ensemble in a gypsy orchestra serves practically only to double the harmony, mark the rhythm, and provide the accompaniment. Flutes, clarinets, a few brass instruments, a violoncello, contrabass, and numerous violins—these are the usual instruments. The violins and cimbalom are given the main parts; they carry the grand roles in the musical arrangement to be played off, like the *primo uomo* and *prima donna* in the old Italian opera. They are, in the musical jargon of civilized *Bohême,* the "stars" of the band.

The first violin spins out all the twists of fancy and moods of the virtuoso, whose technique often in no way resembles ours. The cimbalomist must follow this course, provide a rhythm for it, set off the accelerations and ritards, the strength or slackening of the beat. With the dexterity and agility of a juggler, he races the little wooden mallets across the brass and steel strings, which in this primitive design take the place of the complicated piano mechanism we set in motion by means of ivory, mother-of-pearl, and tortoiseshell keys.

The cimbalom player, like the first violinist, has the right to develop certain passages and to improvise endless variations at his pleasure. . . . He forces the others to surround, assist, yes, even to follow him blindly, whether he fancies a funeral hymn or a mad lively song. Now and then a good violoncello or clarinet will compete with them and claim the right of uninhibited improvisation. Several such virtuosi have even created a name for themselves in this genre, but they remain exceptions.   [3]

HOLIDAY SYNAGOGUE SERVICE IN VIENNA

From Die Israeliten, *no date*

Only once have we had the awesome experience of seeing and hearing what can happen in Jewish art when, in new art forms created by their Oriental genius, the Israelites pour out the full splendor of their fantasies and dreams, the full intensity of their feelings and stifled passions, and reveal the glow of that burning fire which they most often cautiously cover with ashes that it may seem cold to us.

In Vienna we were acquainted with the famous tenor Sulzer, who, as cantor of the synagogue, had acquired a distinguished reputation among a circle of true connoisseurs. . . . To hear him we went to the synagogue where he both directs and assumes the chief role in the music.

Rarely have we been so deeply stirred, so affected that our spirit surrendered unresistingly to sympathy and devotion as on that evening when, in the light of a thousand candles like stars on a far horizon, a strange chorus of muffled, hollow voices resounded about us. Every breast seemed a dungeon, from the depths of which an inscrutable being strove to break forth in order to glorify, in the midst of sorrow and slavery, the God of the Covenant, to cry to Him with devout and steadfast faith that He one day deliver them from this endless imprisonment, lead them from this despised ground, from these strange rivers, from this new Babylon, the great whore, and unite them again with incomparable glory in their own realm before which the nations tremble.   [4]

BEETHOVEN

From a letter to Wilhelm von Lenz,* Weimar, December 2, 1852

To us musicians the work of Beethoven parallels the pillars of smoke and fire that led the Israelites through the desert, a pillar of smoke to lead us by day, and a pillar of fire to light the night, so that we may march ahead both day and night. His darkness and his light equally trace for us the road we must follow; both the one and the other are a perpetual commandment, an infallible revelation. If it were up to me to categorize the diverse states of thought of the great master as manifested in his sonatas, symphonies, quartets, I should hardly stop at the division into *three styles* generally adopted today, and which you have followed, but . . . would frankly weigh the big question that is the crux of criticism and musical aesthetics to the point where Beethoven has led us: that is, how much traditional, conventional form necessarily determines organization of thought.

The solution of this question, as it is derived from Beethoven's works, would lead me to divide his works, not into three styles or periods *(style* and *period* being here only corollary, subordinate terms, of vague and equivocal significance), but very logically into two categories: one in which the traditional and conventional form contains and rules thought, and the other in which thought recreates and fashions a form and style appropriate to its needs and inspiration. Undoubtedly, in proceeding thus, we shall encounter head-on those perennial problems of *authority* and *freedom.* But why should that frighten us? In the liberal arts, fortunately, they entail none of the dangers and disasters that their fluctuations occasion in the political and social world, for in the realm of the beautiful, genius alone is the authority, dualism disappears, and the concepts of authority and liberty are restored to their original identity. Manzoni, in defining genius as "a greater borrowing from God," has eloquently expressed this truth.   [5]

From "On Beethoven's Music to Egmont"

When the time approaches that decrees a thoroughgoing change in art, induces the impulse for its greater progress, and with hitherto unsuspected vigor and drive propels it onto new paths, the important moment announces itself generally through prophetic signs.

The world, however, seldom suspects the prophetic meaning of such signs when first revealed. . . . Only when the sun of a new day already stands high in the heavens does the world recognize that the scattered rays that, like the dawn, announced the light of a new morning all emerge from one and the same focal point.

A performance the other day of Goethe's *Egmont* with Beethoven's music aroused such thoughts in us. In *Egmont* we discover one of the first examples in

---

* Author of *Beethoven et ses trois styles,* 1852.

modern times of the great composer drawing his inspiration directly from the work of a great poet. As insecure and unsteady as Beethoven's steps may appear to us in this, his first attempt, so in his own time were they brave and significant.

[6]

SCHUBERT

From a letter to Professor S. Lebert, Villa d'Este, December 2, 1868

Our pianists have scarcely an inkling of the wonderful treasures to be discovered among Schubert's piano compositions. For the most part they run through them *en passant*, noticing that here and there will be found repetitions, tedious passages, or signs of what appears to be carelessness . . . and they put them aside. Schubert himself is partly to blame, of course, for the very inadequate attention paid to his excellent piano compositions. He was too overwhelmingly productive, he wrote without pause, mingling the insignificant and the important, the noble and the mediocre, ignoring criticism and going wherever his wings carried him. He lived in music like a bird in the air, singing like an angel all the time.

Oh, ever-flowing, ever-loving genius! Beloved hero of the paradise of youth! Harmony, freshness, strength, sweetness, reverie, passion, tranquillity, tears, and flames pour from the depths and heights of your heart; and we almost overlook your supreme mastery, so much are we bewitched by your natural charm! [7]

MENDELSSOHN'S MUSIC TO *A MIDSUMMER NIGHT'S DREAM*

From an essay of same title, 1854

Mendelssohn, with a sure touch, fixed upon those passages in the play that music might strengthen and spice, thus heightening the charm of the whole. He allowed his art a precisely measured share in the piece. His overture is an organic blending of heterogeneous elements, with its piquant originality, symmetry, and pleasing sound, its grace and freshness that rise to the heights of the poetry itself. One need only recall the chords at the start and finish! Do they not resemble gently lowering and lifting eyelids that frame a gracious dream world of the loveliest contrasts? In these contrasts the elements of the sentimental, the fantastic, and the comic meet, each masterly characterized and yet intertwined by delicate strands of beauty! [8]

CHOPIN

From "Friedrich Chopin," 1850

To him we owe the extension of chords, broken as well as unbroken, and ornamented chord figures, chromatic and enharmonic progressions of which his works offer such astounding examples; little groups of passing tones that are scattered over the melodic figure like brightly shimmering dewdrops. He lent to this sort of embellishment, the prototype of which could be found only in the *fiorituras* of the great old Italian school of singing, the unexpected and the richly varied, which reach beyond the capacity of the human voice. Until then these ornaments had been merely slavishly copied as monotonous and stereotyped trimmings on the piano. He discovered those remarkable harmonic progressions by means of which he impressed a serious character on pieces of music whose unimpressive themes did not seem to *demand* profound significance. Chopin did not content himself merely with a framework within which he could plan his sketches with complete freedom. At times it pleased him to establish his thoughts in classical forms. He wrote concertos and sonatas. Yet in these we readily discover more purposefulness than inspiration. His inspirations were powerful, fantastic, impulsive; his forms could be naught but free. [9]

BERLIOZ'S *ROMEO AND JULIET*

From a letter to Gustav Schmidt,* Weimar, March 6, 1853

By this morning's mail I am sending you the score and parts of Berlioz's symphony *Romeo and Juliet,* together with two pairs of antique cymbals, which you will need for "Queen Mab." I think you will find it expedient to have the complete title of the second part printed in the program just as it appears on Berlioz's score: "Deuxième partie—Roméo seul—Concert et Bal. Grande Fête chez Capulet." Also, I think it would not be at all amiss if you were to have the German text of the story of Queen Mab—or better still, the quotation from Shakespeare—printed as a program note. Again I urge you to rehearse the string and wind sections separately. "Queen Mab," especially, is a difficult piece. When I conduct it, I like occasionally to use Beethoven's method of beating four measures as four quarters, as if it were in $\frac{4}{4}$ time (*ritmo di quattro battute,* as in the scherzo of the Ninth Symphony), thus securing more repose without affecting your precision in any way. Try it sometime; I think you will agree that I am right. I advise you to keep the antique cymbals near your stand—and as a rule, Berlioz prefers to have the fermatas *very* long. [10]

Richard Wagner

1813–1883

Wagner claimed to begrudge the hours his writings cost him, though he produced enough to fill sixteen volumes. His essays reveal the philosophical (and psychological) environment from which his operas sprang—a world where all is viewed from the standpoint of Art, while Art is defined by the composer's personal vision. Admirers and detractors alike have responded to the polemical in Wagner's works, making him a figure of enduring controversy. The article "Judaism in Music" exemplifies one facet of this controversy, with scholars still in disagreement as to the meaning, importance, originating circumstances, and emotional authenticity of Wagner's most notorious foray into print.

---

* Schmidt (1816–82) was conductor of the opera orchestra in Frankfurt am Main from 1851 to 1861.

THE ROLES OF MUSIC AND POETRY IN OPERA

From Opera and Drama, *1851*

The musical basis of opera was, as we know, nothing other than the *aria;* this aria, again, was merely the folk song as rendered by the art singer before the world of rank and quality, but with its word poem left out and replaced by the product of the art poet commissioned to that end. The conversion of the folk tune into the operatic aria was primarily the work of that art singer, whose concern was no longer for the right delivery of the tune, but for the exhibition of his vocal dexterity. It was he who parceled out the resting points he needed, the alternation of more lively with more placid phrasing, the passages where, free from any rhythmic or melodic curb, he might bring his skill to bear as it pleased him best. The composer merely furnished the singer, the poet in his turn the composer, with the material for their virtuosity.

The natural relation of the artistic factors of drama was, at bottom, as yet not quite upheaved: it was merely distorted, inasmuch as the performer, the most necessary condition for drama's possibility, represented but one solitary talent—that of absolute song-dexterity—and nowise all the conjoint faculties of artistic man. This one distortion of the character of the performer, however, sufficed to bring about an ultimate perversion of the natural relation of those factors: to the absolute preferment of the musician before the poet. Had that singer been a true, sound, and whole dramatic performer, then would the composer have come necessarily into his proper relation with the poet; the latter would then have firmly spoken out the dramatic aim, the measure for all else, and ruled its realizing. But the man who stood nearest that singer was the composer—the composer, who merely helped the singer to attain his aim, while this aim, cut loose from every vestige of dramatic, nay even poetic bearing, was nothing other, through and through, than to show off his own specific song-dexterity. . . .

Into the dramatic cantata, to satisfy the luxurious craving of these eminent sirs for change in their amusements, there was dovetailed next the ballet. Dance and dance tune, borrowed just as waywardly from the folk dance and its tune as was the operatic aria from the folk song, joined forces with the singer, in all the sterile immiscibility of unnatural things; while it naturally became the poet's task, midst such a heaping-up of inwardly incongruous matter, to bind the samples of the diverse art dexterities laid before him into some kind of patchwork harmony. Thus, with the poet's aid, an ever more obviously imperative dramatic cohesion was thrust on *that* which, in its actual self, was crying for no cohesion whatever; so that the aim of drama, forced on by outward want, was merely lodged, by no means housed. Song tune and dance tune stood side by side in fullest, chillest loneliness, for exhibition of the agility of singer or of dancer; and only in that which was to make shift to bind them—to wit, the musically recited dialogue—did the poet ply his lowly calling, did the drama peep out here and there.

Neither was recitative itself, by any means, some new invention proceeding from a genuine urgence of opera toward the drama. Long before this mode of intoning was introduced into opera, the Christian Church had used it in her services for the recitation of biblical passages. The banal singsong of these recitals, with its more listlessly melodic than rhetorically expressive incidence of tone, had been early fixed by ritualistic prescript into an arid semblance of speech, but without its reality; and this it was that, merely molded and varied by musical caprice, passed over into the opera. So that, what with aria, dance tune, and recitative, the whole apparatus of musical drama—unchanged in essence down to our very latest opera—was settled once for all. Further, the dramatic ground plans laid beneath this apparatus soon won a kindred stereotyped persistence. Mostly taken from an entirely misconstrued Greek mythology, they formed a theatric scaffolding from which all capability of rousing warmth of human interest was altogether absent, but which, on the other hand, possessed the merit of lending itself to the good pleasure of every composer in his turn; in effect, the majority of these texts were composed over and over again by the most diverse of musicians.

The so famous revolution of Gluck, which has come to the ears of many igno-ramuses as a complete reversal of the views previously current as to opera's essence, in truth consisted merely in this: the musical composer revolted against the wil-fulness of the singer. The composer, who, next to the singer, had drawn the spe-cial notice of the public to himself—since it was *he* who provided the singer with fresh supplies of stuff for his dexterity—felt his province encroached upon by the operations of the latter; he busied himself to shape the stuff according to his own inventive fancy and thus secure that *his* work also and perchance at last *only* his work, might catch the ear of the audience. To reach his ambitious goal, two ways stood open to the composer: either, by use of all the musical aids already at his dis-posal or others yet to be discovered, to unfold the purely sensuous contents of the aria to their highest, rankest pitch; or—and this is the more earnest path, with which we are concerned at present—to put shackles on a capricious execution of that aria by endeavoring to give the tune, before its execution, an expression an-swering to the underlying word text. . . . Gluck was not the first who indited feel-ing airs, nor his singers the first who delivered them with fit expression. But he *bespoke with consciousness and conviction* the fitness and necessity of an expression an-swering to the text substratum, in aria and recitative; this makes him the depar-ture point of a thorough change in the quondam situation of the artistic factors of opera toward one another. Henceforth the scepter of opera passes definitely over to the composer: the singer becomes the *agent of the composer's aim,* and this aim is con-sciously declared to be the matching of the dramatic contents of the text substra-tum with a true and suitable expression. Thus, a halt was cried only to the unbe-coming, heartless vanity of the singing virtuoso, but all the rest of opera's unnatural organism remained unaltered. Fenced off each from each, aria, recita-tive, and dance piece stand side by side, as unaccommodated in the operas of Gluck as before him, and as, with scarcely an exception, they still stand today.

In the situation of the *poet* toward the composer not one jot was altered; rather had the composer grown more dictatorial, since, with his declared consciousness of a higher mission—made good against the virtuoso singer—he set to work with more deliberate zeal at the arrangement of opera's framework. To the poet it never occurred to meddle with these arrangements; he could not so much as dream of music, to which the opera had owed its origin, in any other form than those narrow, close-ruled forms he found set down before him, as binding even upon the musician himself. . . .

It was Gluck's successors who first bethought them to draw profit from their situation for the actual widening of the forms at hand. These followers, among whom we must class the composers of Italian and French descent who wrote for the Paris opera stage at the close of the past and beginning of the present century, gave to their vocal pieces not only more warmth and straightforwardness of expression but also a more extended formal basis. The traditional divisions of the aria, though still substantially preserved, were given a wider play of motive; modulations and connecting phrases were drawn into the sphere of expression; the recitative joined on to the aria more smoothly and less waywardly and, as a necessary mode of expression, stepped into that aria itself. Another notable expansion was given to the aria in that, obedient to the dramatic need, more than *one* person now shared in its delivery, and thus the essential monody of earlier opera was beneficially lost. Pieces such as duets and terzets were indeed known long before; but the fact that two or three people sang in one piece had not made the slightest essential difference in the character of the aria: once started, this had remained exactly the same in melodic plan and insistence on the tonality—which bore no reference to any individual expression but solely to a general, specifically musical mood—and not a jot of it was really altered, no matter whether delivered as a monologue or duet, excepting at the utmost quite materialistic details: namely, its musical phrases were either sung alternately by different voices, or in concert through the harmonic device of combining two, three, or more voices at once. To apply that specifically musical factor in such a way that it should be susceptible of a lively change of individual expression was the object and the work of these composers, as shown in their handling of the so-called *dramatic musical ensemble.* The essential musical substance of this ensemble was still, indeed, composed of aria, recitative, and dance tune; only, when once a vocal expression in accord with the text substratum had been recognized as a becoming claim to make on aria and recitative, the truthfulness of such expression must logically be extended to everything else in the text that betrayed a particle of dramatic coherence. From the honest endeavor to observe this logical consistency arose that broadening of the older musical forms in opera which we meet in the serious operas of Cherubini, Méhul, and Spontini. We may say that in these works there is fulfilled all that Gluck desired, or could desire; nay, in them is once for all attained the acme of all natural, i.e., in the *best* sense, consequential evolution on the original lines of opera.

———— ‹ ————

Now how did the poet respond to all this? . . . With all the maturing of opera's musical form, with all the development of its innate owers of expression, the position of the poet had not altered in the slightest. He still remained the platform dresser for the altogether independent experiments of the composer. . . . Since, then, the poet felt constrained to put trite and meaningless phrases in the mouths of his heroes, even the best will in the world could not have enabled him either to infuse a real character into persons who talked like that, or to stamp the sum total of their actions with the seal of full dramatic truth. His drama was forever a mere *make-be-lieve* of drama; to pursue a *real dramatic aim* to its legitimate conclusions could not so much as occur to him. Therefore, strictly speaking, he only translated drama into the language of opera, and, as a matter of fact, mostly adapted long-familiar dramas already played to death upon the acting stage, as was notably the case in Paris with the tragedies of the Théâtre Français. The dramatic aim, thus bare within and hollow, passed manifestly over into the mere intentions of the composer; from him was awaited that which the poet gave up from the first. To him alone—to the composer—must it therefore fall to clothe this inner void and nullity of the whole, so soon as ever he perceived it; and thus he found himself saddled with the unnatural task of . . . imagining and calling into life . . . of virtually penning the drama, of making his music not merely its expression but its *content;* and yet this content, by the very nature of things, was to be none other than the drama's self!

It is here that the predicate "dramatic" most palpably begins to work a strange confusion in men's notions of the nature of music. Music, as an art of *expression,* can in its utmost wealth of such expression be nothing more than *true;* it has, conformably therewith, to concern itself only with *what* it should express. In opera this is unmistakably the feeling of the characters conversing on the stage, and a music that fulfills this task with the most convincing effect is all that it ever can be. . . . With all its perverse efforts, music, or at least effective music, has actually remained naught other than expression. But from those efforts to make it in itself a content—and the content of a drama, forsooth—has issued what we must recognize as the consequential downfall of opera and an open demonstration of the radical un-nature of that genre of art.   [1]

A VISIT TO ENGLAND, 1855

From a letter to Franz Liszt, London, May 16, 1855

I live here like one of the lost souls in hell. I never thought that I could sink again so low. The misery I feel in having to live in these disgusting surroundings is beyond description, and I now realize that it was a sin, a crime, to accept this invitation to London, which in the luckiest case must have led me far away from my real path. I need not expatiate to you upon my actual situation. It is the consistent outgrowth of the greatest inconsistency I ever committed. I am compelled to conduct an English concert program right down to the end; that says everything. I have got into the middle of a slough of conventionalities and customs, in which I stick up to the ears, without being able to lead into it the least drop of pure water for my recreation. "Sir, we are not accustomed to this"—that is the eternal echo I hear. Neither can the orchestra recompense me. It consists almost exclusively of Englishmen, that is, clever machines that cannot be got into the right swing; handicraft and business kill everything. Then there is the public, which, I am assured, is very favorably inclined toward me, but can never be got out of itself, which accepts the most emotional and the most tedious things without ever showing that it has received a real impression. And, in addition to this, the ridiculous Mendelssohn worship!   [2]

MUSIC AND MONEY

From a letter to Franz Liszt, Weimar, October 3, 1855

If the New York people should ever make up their minds to offer me a considerable sum, I should be in the most awful dilemma. If I refused I should have to conceal it from all men, for everyone would charge me in my position with recklessness. Ten years ago I might have undertaken such a thing, but to have to walk in such byways now in order to live would be too hard—now, when I am fit only to do, and to devote myself to, that which is strictly my business. I should never finish the *Nibelungen* in my life. Good gracious! such sums as I might *earn* in America people ought to *give* me, without asking anything in return beyond what I am actually doing, and which is the best that I can do. Besides this, I am much better adapted to spend 60,000 francs in six months than to "earn" it. The latter I cannot do at all, for it is not my business to "earn money," but it is the business of my admirers to give me as much money as I want, to do my work in a cheerful mood.   [3]

JUDAISM IN MUSIC; MENDELSSOHN

From "Judaism in Music," 1850/1869*

We have no need to first substantiate the be-Jewing of modern art; it springs to the eye, and thrusts upon the senses, of itself. Much too far afield, again, should we have to fare, did we undertake to explain this phenomenon by a demonstration of the character of our art history itself. But if emancipation from the yoke of Judaism appears to us the greatest of necessities, we must hold it weighty above all to prove our forces for this war of liberation. Now we shall never win these forces from an abstract definition of that phenomenon per se, but only from an accurate acquaintance with the nature of that involuntary feeling of ours that utters itself as an instinctive repugnance against the Jew's prime essence. Through it, through this unconquerable feeling—if we avow it quite without ado—must there become plain to us *what* we hate in that essence; what we then know definitely, we can make head against; nay, through his very laying bare, may we even hope to rout the demon from the field, whereon he has only been able to maintain his stand beneath the shelter of a twilight darkness—a darkness we good-natured Humanists ourselves have cast upon him, to make his look less loathsome.

The Jew—who, as everyone knows, has a God all to himself—in ordinary life strikes us primarily by his outward appearance, which, no matter to what European nationality we belong, has something disagreeably foreign to that nationality: instinctively we wish to have nothing in common with a man who looks like that. . . . This is of great weight: a man whose appearance we must hold unfitted

---

* "Das Judenthum in Musik" was originally published, under a pseudonym, in the *Neue Zeitschrift für Musik* in 1850. It was revised and published as a pamphlet in Leipzig in 1869. The excerpts here are based on the 1869 edition.

for artistic treatment—not merely in this or that personality, but according to his kind in general—neither can we hold him capable of any sort of artistic utterance of his essence.

By far more weighty, nay, of quite decisive weight for our inquiry, is the effect the Jew produces on us through his *speech;* and this is the essential point at which to sound the Jewish influence on music. The Jew speaks the language of the nation in whose midst he dwells from generation to generation, but he speaks it always as an alien. . . . Our whole European art and civilization . . . have remained to the Jew a foreign tongue; for, just as he has taken no part in the evolution of the one, so has he taken none in that of the other; but at most the homeless wight has been a cold, nay more, a hostile looker-on. In this speech, this art, the Jew can only after-speak and after-patch—not truly make a poem of his words, an artwork of his doings.

In particular does the purely physical aspect of the Jewish mode of speech repel us. Throughout an intercourse of two millennia with European nations, culture has not succeeded in breaking the remarkable stubbornness of the Jewish *naturel* as regards the peculiarities of Semitic pronunciation. The first thing that strikes our ear as quite outlandish and unpleasant, in the Jew's production of the voice sounds, is a creaking, squeaking, buzzing snuffle. . . . If we hear a Jew speak, we are unconsciously offended by the entire want of purely human expression in his discourse: the cold indifference of its peculiar "blubber" never by any chance rises to the ardor of a higher, heartfelt passion. If, on the other hand, we find *ourselves* driven to this more heated expression, in converse with a Jew, he will always shuffle off, since he is incapable of replying in kind. Never does the Jew excite himself in mutual interchange of feelings with us, but—so far as we are concerned—only in the altogether special egoistic interest of his vanity or profit. . . .

Now, if the aforesaid qualities of his dialect make the Jew almost incapable of giving artistic enunciation to his feelings and beholdings through *talk,* for such an enunciation through *song* his aptitude must needs be infinitely smaller. Song is just talk aroused to highest passion: music is the speech of passion. All that worked repellently upon us in his outward appearance and his speech makes us take to our heels at last in his song, providing we are not held prisoners by the very ridicule of this phenomenon. Very naturally, in song—the vividest and most indisputable expression of the personal emotional being—the peculiarity of the Jewish nature attains for us its climax of distastefulness; and on any natural hypothesis, we might hold the Jew adapted for every sphere of art excepting that whose basis lies in song.

The true poet, no matter in what branch of art, still gains his stimulus from nothing but a faithful, loving contemplation of instinctive life, of that life which only greets his sight amid the folk. Now, where is the cultured Jew to find this folk? Not, surely, on the soil of that society in which he plays his artist role? If he has any connection at all with this society, it is merely with that offshoot of it, entirely loosened from the real, the healthy stem; but this connection is entirely loveless, and this lovelessness must ever become more obvious to him, if for sake of foodstuff for his art he clambers down to that society's foundations: not only does he here find everything more strange and unintelligible, but the instinctive ill will of the folk confronts him here in all its wounding nakedness, since—unlike its fellow in the richer classes—it here is neither weakened down nor broken by reckonings of advantage and regard for certain mutual interests.

———— ⚹ ————

Just as words and constructions are hurled together in this [the Jewish] jargon with wondrous inexpressiveness, so does the Jew musician hurl together the diverse forms and styles of every age and every master. Packed side by side, we find the formal idiosyncrasies of all the schools, in motleyest chaos. As in these productions the sole concern is talking at all hazards, and not the object that might make that talk worth doing, so this clatter can only be made at all inciting to the ear by its offering at each instant a new summons to attention, through a change of outer expressive means. Inner agitation, genuine passion, each finds its own peculiar language at the instant when, struggling for an understanding, it girds itself for utterance: the Jew, already characterized by us in this regard, has no true passion, and least of all a passion that might thrust him on to art creation. But where this passion is not forthcoming, *there* neither is any calm: true, noble calm is nothing else than passion mollified through resignation. Where the calm has not been ushered in by passion, we perceive naught but sluggishness: the opposite of sluggishness, however, is nothing but that prickling unrest which we observe in Jewish musical works from one end to the other, saving where it makes place for that soulless, feelingless inertia. What issues from the Jews' attempts at making art must necessarily therefore bear the attributes of coldness and indifference, even to triviality and absurdity; and in the history of modern music we can but class the Judaic period as that of final unproductivity, of stability gone to ruin.

By what example will this all grow clearer to us—ay, well-nigh what other single case could make us so alive to it—as the works of a musician of Jewish birth whom nature had endowed with specific musical gifts as very few before him ? All that offered itself to our gaze, in the inquiry into our antipathy against the Jewish nature; all the contradictoriness of this nature, both in itself and as touching us; all its inability, while outside our footing, to have intercourse with us upon that footing, nay, even to form a wish to further develop the things that had sprung from out our soil: all these are intensified to a positively tragic conflict in the nature, life, and art career of the early-taken Felix Mendelssohn-Bartholdy. He has shown us that a Jew may have the amplest store of specific talents, may own the finest and most varied culture, the highest and the tenderest sense of honor—yet without all these pre-eminences helping him, were it but one single time, to call forth in us that deep, that heart-searching effect which we await from art because we know her capable thereof, because we have felt it many a time and oft, so soon as once a hero of our art has, so to say, but opened his mouth to speak to us. To professional critics, who haply have reached a like consciousness with ourselves hereon, it may be left to prove by specimens of Mendelssohn's art products our statement of this indubitably certain thing; by way of illustrating our general impression, let us here be content with the fact that, in hearing a tone piece of this composer's, we have only been able to feel engrossed where nothing beyond our more or less amusement-craving fantasy was roused through the presentation, stringing together, and entanglement of the most elegant, the smoothest, and most polished figures—as in the kaleidoscope's changeful play of form and color—but never where those figures were meant to take the shape of deep and stalwart feelings of the human heart.

So long as the separate art of music had a real organic life need in it, down to the epochs of Mozart and Beethoven, there was nowhere to be found a Jewish composer: it was impossible for an element entirely foreign to that living organism to take part in the formative stages of that life. Only when a body's inner death is manifest do outside elements win the power of lodgment in it—yet merely to destroy it. Then indeed that body's flesh dissolves into a swarming colony of insect life: but who, in looking on that body's self, would hold it still for living? The spirit—that is, the *life*—has fled from out that body, has sped to kindred other bodies; and this is all that makes out life. In genuine life alone can we, too, find again the ghost of art, and not within its worm-befretted carcass.

I said above that the Jews had brought forth no true poet. We here must give a moment's mention, then, to Heinrich Heine. At the time when Goethe and Schiller sang among us, we certainly knew nothing of a poetizing Jew: at the time, however, when our poetry became a lie, when every possible thing might flourish from the wholly unpoetic element of our life, but no true poet—then was it the office of a highly gifted poet-Jew to bare with fascinating taunts that lie, that bottomless aridity and jesuitical hypocrisy of our versifying, which still would give itself the airs of true poesis. His famous musical congeners, too, he mercilessly lashed for their pretense to pass as artists; no make-believe could hold its ground before him: by the remorseless demon of denial of all that seemed worth denying was he driven on without a rest, through all the mirage of our modern self-deception, till he reached the point where in turn he duped himself into a poet, and was rewarded by his versified lies being set to music by our own composers. He was the conscience of Judaism, just as Judaism is the evil conscience of our modern civilization.   [4]

Giuseppe Verdi
1813–1901

Verdi's best-known operas have been part of the repertoire since his own time, a reflection not only of their musical quality—something critics and musical professionals were slow to acknowledge—but of their emotional resonance and their social sensibilities. Seldom has a composer's output been so democratic in spirit while remaining so thoroughly aristocratic in character. Verdi left no body of essays or reviews, but in his hundreds of letters he speaks with an affecting directness, even when irony colors his words.

OPERA

From a letter to the librettist Salvatore Cammarano, Paris, November 23, 1848

I know you are rehearsing *Macbeth* [the first version], and since it is an opera that interests me more than all the others, you will permit me to say a few words about it. They gave the role of Lady Macbeth to Tadolini, and I am very surprised that she consented to do the part. You know how much I admire Tadolini, and she knows it herself; but in our common interest I think we should stop and consider. Tadolini has too great qualities for this role! Perhaps you think that a contradiction! Tadolini's appearance is good and beautiful, and I would like Lady Macbeth twisted and ugly. Tadolini sings to perfection, and I don't wish Lady Macbeth really to sing at all. Tadolini has a marvelous, brilliant, clear, powerful voice, and for Lady Macbeth I should like a raw, choked, hollow voice. Tadolini's voice has something angelic. Lady Macbeth's voice should have something devilish. Pass on these reflections to the management and Maestro Mercadante: more than anyone else, he will approve my ideas. Pass them on to Tadolini herself, and then do what you think best, according to your lights.   [1]

From a letter to Cesare De Sanctis, Busseto, March 12, 1853

I adore *Faust,* but I shouldn't like to treat it. I've studied it a thousand times, but I don't find Faust's character musical—musical (understand me well) in the way I feel music.   [2]

From a letter to Cesare De Sanctis, Sant' Agata, April 22, 1853

My long experience has confirmed me in the beliefs I've always held concerning dramatic effect, though in my youth I didn't have the courage to put them wholly into practice. (For instance, ten years ago I wouldn't have risked composing *Rigoletto*.) To me our opera nowadays sins in the direction of too great monotony, so much so that I should refuse to write on such subjects as *Nabucco*, [*I due*] *Foscari,* etc. They offer extremely interesting dramatic situations, but they lack variety. They have but one burden to their song; elevated, if you like, but always the same.

To be more explicit: Tasso's work may be better, but I prefer Ariosto a thousand times. For the same reason I prefer Shakespeare to all other dramatists, including the Greeks. As far as dramatic effectiveness is concerned, it seems to me that the best material I have yet put to music (I'm not speaking of literary or poetic worth) is *Rigoletto.* It has the most powerful dramatic situations, it has variety, vitality, pathos; all the dramatic developments result from the frivolous, licentious character of the Duke. Hence Rigoletto's fears, Gilda's passion, etc., which give rise to many dramatic situations, including the scene of the quartet, which, so far as effect is concerned, will always be one of the finest our theater can boast. Many operas have been written on *Ruy Blas,* eliminating the character of Don Cesare. But if I were to put that subject to music, I should be attracted above all by the contrast which that most original character produces. Now you will have understood what my feelings and thoughts are, and since I know I'm writing to a man

of sincere, frank character, I take the liberty of telling you that though the subjects you propose are eminently dramatic, I don't find in them all the variety my
crazy brain desires. You say that you can insert in *Sordello* some festivity, a ban-
quet, or even a tournament, but even so the characters would still produce the
same impression of gravity and austerity.   [3]

From a letter to Antonio Somma, Paris, May 17, 1854

I would be willing to set even a newspaper or a letter, etc., to music, but in the
theater the public will stand for anything except boredom.   [4]

From a letter to Leon Escudier, Genoa, June 11, 1867

Two things will always be wanting at the [Paris] Opéra—rhythm and enthusiasm.
They may do many things well, but they will never exhibit the fire that transports
and carries one away, or at any rate not until they teach singing better at the Conservatoire. . . . But it is also a little the fault of you French, putting stumbling
blocks in the ways of your artists with your *bon goût, comme il faut,* etc. . . . You
should leave the arts in complete liberty and tolerate defects in matters of inspiration. If you terrify the man of genius with your wretched measured criticism, he
will never let himself go, and you will rob him of his naturalness and enthusiasm.
But if you are content as things are, and if the Opéra likes losing several hundred
thousand francs and eight or ten months' time in producing an opera, then go on
doing it—I don't mind.   [5]

From a letter to Giulio Ricordi, Sant' Agata, July 10, 1871

So-called vocal perfection concerns me little; I like to have roles sung as I wish,
but I am unable to provide the voice, the soul, that certain something which
should be called the spark—it is usually described by the Italian phrase "to have
the Devil on your back."   [6]

From a letter to Clarina Maffei, Sant' Agata, October 20, 1876

It may be a good thing to copy reality; but to invent reality is much, much better.
   These three words, "to invent reality," may look like a contradiction, but ask
Papa [Shakespeare]! Falstaff he may have found as he was, but he can hardly have
found a villain as villainous as Iago, and never, never such angels as Cordelia, Im-
ogene, Desdemona, etc., etc. And yet they are so very real! It's a fine thing to imitate reality, but it is photography, not painting.   [7]

Letter to Clarina Maffei, April 20, 1878

We are all working, without meaning to, for the downfall of our theater. Perhaps I
myself, perhaps you and the others, are at it, too. And if I wanted to say something
that sounds foolish, I should say that the Italian Quartet Societies were the first

cause; and that a more recent cause was the success of the performances (not the works) given by the Scala orchestra in Paris. I've said it—don't stone me! To give all the reasons would take up too much time. But why, in the name of all that's holy, must we do German art if we are living in Italy? Twelve or fifteen years ago I was elected president of a concert society, I don't remember whether in Milan or elsewhere. I refused, and I asked: "Why not form a society for vocal music? That's alive in Italy—the rest is an art for Germans." Perhaps that sounded as foolish then as it does now; but a society for vocal music that would let us hear Palestrina, the best of his contemporaries, Marcello, and such people, would have preserved for us our love of song, as it is expressed in opera. Now everything is supposed to be based on orchestration, on harmony. The alpha and omega is Beethoven's Ninth Symphony, marvelous in the first three movements, very badly set in the last. No one will ever approach the sublimity of the first movement, but it will be an easy task to write as badly for voices as is done in the last movement. And supported by the authority of Beethoven, they will all shout: "That's the way to do it ... "

Never mind! Let them go on as they have begun. It may even be better; but it's a "better" that undoubtedly means the end of opera. Art belongs to all nations—nobody believes that more firmly than I. But it is practiced by individuals; and since the Germans have other artistic methods than we have, their art is basically different from ours. We cannot compose like the Germans, or at least we ought not to; nor they like us. Let the Germans assimilate our artistic substance, as Haydn and Mozart did in their time; yet they are predominantly symphonic musicians. And it is perfectly proper for Rossini to have taken over certain formal elements from Mozart; he is still a melodist for all that. But if we let fashion, love of innovation, and an alleged scientific spirit tempt us to surrender the native quality of our own art, the free natural certainty of our work and perception, our bright golden light, then we are simply being stupid and senseless.   [8]

From a letter to Giuseppe Piroli, Genoa, February 2, 1883

Our music differs from German music. Their symphonies can live in halls; their chamber music can live in the home. Our music, I say, resides principally in the theater. Now the theaters can no longer exist without government subsidy.   [9]

THE AUTHORITY OF THE COMPOSER

From a contract with Ricordi Publishers, Florence, May 20, 1847

In order to prevent changes that theaters make in musical works, it is forbidden to insert anything into the above-mentioned score, to make cuts, raise or lower a key, or in general make any alteration that would entail the slightest change in instrumentation, on pain of 1000 francs fine, which I shall demand of you for every theater where a change is made in the score.   [10]

From a letter to Giulio Ricordi, Genoa, April 11, 1871

As to conductors' inspiration . . . and to "creative activity in every performance" . . . this is a principle that inevitably leads to the baroque and untrue. It is precisely the path that led music to the baroque and untrue at the end of the last century and in the first years of this, when singers made bold to "create" (as the French say) their parts and in consequence made a complete hash and contradiction of sense out of them. No; I want only one single creator, and I shall be quite satisfied if they perform simply and exactly what he has written. The trouble is that they do not confine themselves to what he has written. I often read in the papers about effects that the composer never could have thought of, but for my part, I have never found such a thing. I understand everything you say about Mariani;* we are all agreed on his merit. But it is not a question of a single person, were he ever so eminent; it is a question of art itself. I deny that either singers or conductors can "create" or work creatively—this, as I have always said, is a conception that leads to the abyss. . . . Shall I give you an example? You spoke to me recently in praise of an effect that Mariani achieved in the overture to *La Forza del Destino* by having the brass enter fortissimo on G [bar 168]. Now then, I disapprove of this effect. These brasses, intended to be *mezza voce*, could not express anything but the Friar's song. Mariani's fortissimo completely changes the character of the passage and turns it into a warlike fanfare. It has nothing to do with the subject of the drama, in which all warlike matters are mere episodes. And there we are again on the path to the baroque and untrue.   [11]

MUSICAL EDUCATION

From a letter to Giuseppe Piroli, Genoa, February 20, 1871

In view of the musical conditions and tendencies of our day, the guiding principles that should be adopted by a commission for the reorganization of musical instruction are, in my opinion, as follows:

For young composers I should wish a long and thorough course of counterpoint in all its ramifications. Study of old music, both sacred and profane. But it must be kept in mind that not all old music is beautiful, either, and therefore it is necessary to choose.

No study of the moderns! Many people will think this strange. But today, when I hear and see so many works put together the way a bad tailor puts clothes together on a standard model, I cannot budge in my opinions. I know, of course, that many modern works could be cited that are as good as the old, but what of that?

When a young man has gone through a severe course of training, when he has achieved his own style, then, if he sees fit, he can study these works, and he will no longer be in danger of turning into a mere imitator. It may be objected: "But who will teach him instrumentation? Who will teach him the theoretical aspects of composition?"—His own head and heart, if he has any.

For singers, I should want a broad knowledge of music, exercises in voice production, long courses in solfège, as in the past, exercises in clear diction both in speaking and singing. Then, without having any finishing master teach him embellishments or style, let the young man, who by now is solidly grounded in music and has a practiced, subtle voice, sing with his own feelings as his only guide. The

* Angelo Mariani (1822–73), an Italian conductor, introduced *Lohengrin* to Italy at Bologna, 1871.

result will not be singing according to any specific school, but according to inspiration. The artist will be an individuality; he will be *himself;* or better yet, he will be the character he has to portray in the opera.

I need not add that these musical studies should be combined with a broad literary education.   [12]

THE STATE OF MUSIC

From a letter to Opprandino Arrivabene, Sant' Agata, July 14, 1875

I cannot tell you how we shall escape from this musical maelstrom. One man wants to equal Bellini in melody, another to rival Meyerbeer in harmony. I would not wish one or the other; and I wish that every young man when he begins to write music would not concern himself with being a melodist, a harmonist, a realist, an idealist or a futurist or any other such devilish pedantic things. Melody and harmony should be simply tools in the hands of the artist, with which he creates music; and if a day comes when people stop talking about the German school, the Italian school, the past, the future, etc., etc., then art will perhaps come into its own. Another present-day trouble is that all the operas produced by these young men are the fruit of fear. No one lets himself go in writing; when these young fellows begin to compose, they do it with the overriding idea that they must not offend the public and that they must win the good graces of the critics.

You will tell me I owe my success to my amalgamation of the two schools. I never gave it a thought. Anyhow, that is an old story, which others have repeated for some time past!   [13]

From a letter to Opprandino Arrivabene, February 12, 1884

Good music has always been a rarity, at all periods, and now it is almost an impossibility. Why? you may ask. . . . Because too much music is composed; because people think too hard; because they stare into the darkness and ignore the sunshine! Because we have exaggerated the minor details! Because what we do is *big*, not great! The *big* leads to the petty and the baroque! That's where we stand.   [14]

PALESTRINA

From a letter to Giuseppe Gallignani, Milan, November 15, 1891

I am particularly glad for the performance of Palestrina's music: he is the real king of sacred music, and the Eternal Father of Italian music.

Palestrina cannot compete with the bold harmonic innovations of modern music, but if he were better known and studied, we would write in a more Italian spirit, and we would be better patriots (in music, I mean).   [15]

ROSSINI AND BELLINI

From a letter to Camille Bellaigue, Milan, May 2, 1898

I can't help thinking that, for abundance of real musical ideas, for comic verve, and truthful declamation, the *Barber of Seville* is the finest *opera buffa* in existence.

Like you, I admire *William Tell,* but how many other magnificent, sublime things are in various of Rossini's other operas.

Bellini is weak instrumentally and harmonically, it's true; but he is rich in feeling and in a certain personal melancholy, which is completely his own. Even in his less well known operas like *La Straniera* and *Il Pirata,* there are long, long, long spun-out melodies, like nothing that had been written before.   [16]

BERLIOZ

From a letter to Opprandino Arrivabene, June 5, 1882

Berlioz was a poor, sick man who raged at everyone, was bitter and malicious. He was greatly and subtly gifted. He had a real feeling for instrumentation, anticipated Wagner in many instrumental effects. (The Wagnerites won't admit it, but it is true.) He had no moderation. He lacked the calm and what I may call the balance that produces complete works of art. He always went to extremes, even when he was doing admirable things.   [17]

WAGNER

From a letter to Giulio Ricordi, February 14, 1883

Sad, sad, sad.

Wagner is dead!

When I read the news yesterday, I may truly say that I was completely crushed. Let us not discuss it. It is a great personality that has disappeared. A name that leaves a mighty imprint on the history of art.   [18]

GOUNOD

From a letter to Opprandino Arrivabene, Sant' Agata, October 14, 1878

I know little about Gounod's success. But we mustn't delude ourselves. We must consider men as they are. Gounod is a great musician, a great talent, who composes excellent chamber and instrumental music in a manner all his own. But he isn't an artist of dramatic fiber. *Faust* itself, though successful, has become small in his hands. *Romeo and Juliet* and this *Poliuto* will be the same. In a word, he always does the intimate piece well; but his treatment of situations is weak and his characterization is bad.   [19]

PUCCINI

From a letter to Opprandino Arrivabene, June 10, 1884

I have heard the composer Puccini well spoken of. I have seen a letter, too, reporting all kinds of good things about him. He follows the new tendencies, which is only natural, but he keeps strictly to melody, and that is neither new nor old. But it seems that he is predominantly a symphonist; no harm in that. Only here one must be careful. Opera is opera, symphony, symphony; I don't think it is a good idea to insert a symphonic piece into an opera just for the pleasure of letting the orchestra cut loose once in a while. [20]

SELF-EVALUATION

From a letter to Signor Filippi, March 4, 1869

Please don't think that when I speak of *my extreme musical ignorance* I'm merely indulging in a little *blague*. It's the truth, pure and simple. In my home there is almost no music; I've never gone to a music library, or to a publisher, to look at a piece of music; I keep up with a few of the best operas of our day, not by studying them, but only by hearing them now and then in the theater. In all this I have a purpose that you will understand. So I repeat to you: of all past or present composers, I am the least erudite. Let's understand each other—I tell you again that this is no *blague* with me: I'm talking about *erudition,* not about musical *knowledge.* I should be lying if I denied that in my youth I studied long and hard. That is why my hand is strong enough to shape the sounds as I want them, and sure enough for me generally to succeed in making the effect I have in mind. And when I write something that doesn't conform to the rules, I do it because, in that case, the strict rule doesn't give me what I need, and because I don't really believe that all the rules that have been taught up to now are good. The schoolbooks of counterpoint must be revised. [21]

CHAPTER SIX

Edouard Lalo

Bedřich Smetana

Johannes Brahms

Alexander Borodin

César Cui

Camille Saint-Saëns

Edouard Lalo
1823–1892

Lalo is remembered primarily for his Symphonie espagnole *for violin and orchestra, premiered in 1875 with Pablo de Sarasate as soloist. He built his reputation with chamber and orchestral works, many of them virtuoso or character pieces. With larger forms he was less fortunate, although his* Le Roi d'Ys *(1875–81) was a success when the Opéra-Comique mounted it in 1888 and is still well known in France.*

TITLES OF COMPOSITIONS
From a letter to Otto Goldschmidt, Paris, August 20, 1879*

I absolutely reject the title Suite for my last piece [*Concerto russo*]; the Suites of Massenet, Godard, Guiraud, Ries, Raff, Hoffman, Holstein, etc., etc., have made the word repellent to me; it's a worn-out tag, one must find another. Artistically, a title means nothing and the work itself is everything; this is an absolute principle; but *commercially,* a tainted, discredited title is never a good thing. I kept the title *Symphonie espagnole* contrary to and in spite of everybody, first, because it conveyed my thought—that is to say, a violin solo soaring above the rigid *form* of an old symphony—and then because the title was less banal than those that were proposed to me. The cries and criticisms have died or will die down; the title will remain, and in a letter of congratulation Bülow wrote me that this *happy* title placed the piece beyond all the others.

Another example: that shapeless thing which calls itself the Second Concerto of Bruch (a concerto that has no first movement, that begins with the second, passes through an intermezzo in recitative form, and concludes with a poor finale) raised a clamor among the scholastics. Strictly, it is nothing but a suite, but Bruch kept the title, and did quite well *commercially;* it is classed as a concerto, and violinists who play the magnificent First Concerto want to play the Second. With this title, it is given as the main number in a program; with the *real* title, Suite, another concerto would have to be given first. So you see, *commercially* a title is of great importance. [1]

BRAHMS
From a letter to Pablo de Sarasate, Paris, August 28, 1878

My dear friend: I am writing you today in a state of inexpressible stupefaction! The cause is the Second Symphony, in D, of Brahms. I read it yesterday morning and heard it the same day at the Concert Populaire. So this is the gentleman some place

---

* German pianist, conductor, and composer (1829–1907) who was Jenny Lind's accompanist and husband and also toured with Sarasate.

above, and others at the side of, Schumann!! Schumann, the great poet, powerful, inspired, whose every note is *individual,* and the composer of the Second Symphony in D judged on the same scale! It is grotesque!

Brahms is an inferior spirit whose pickax has probed every nook of counterpoint and modern harmony. This is his only recommendation. He is not a born musician; his inventiveness is always insignificant and imitative; in his latest symphony, the imitativeness is especially flagrant. I have conscientiously followed his chamber music work: It holds up because it is based on deep study, but as for invention, it is faltering, and one senses that here is a man who looks right and left for what he cannot find within himself. Furthermore, on the pretext of increasing the sonorities, he abuses unison writing unbearably. (Beethoven knew enough about harmony to be aware of unisons, but his power over sonority needed no such ridiculous means to achieve it.) And lastly, the piano quintet: There is in the ensemble of this work an explosive quality that gives one the hope that the composer has definitely found his groove. Alas! the works that follow flounder in a quagmire of exercises and are absolutely insignificant from the point of view of invention. . . .

I met Saint-Saëns that same evening, and his opinion of the symphony was identical.   [2]

Bedřich Smetana
1824–1884

In spite of his talents as a violinist and pianist and the sponsorship of Liszt in publishing his Op. 1, Smetana for years had to rely on teaching for his income. Several sojourns in Göteborg, Sweden, where he could also conduct and play, offered some respite. Only at forty-one, with The Brandenburgers in Bohemia, *did he emerge as the great Czech nationalist composer. In his final decade Smetana was deaf, ill, and often depressed, yet he composed with undiminished powers, finishing* Má vlast *and writing two string quartets and three operas.*

From Ernst Rychnowsky's biography, 1924

ABSOLUTE MUSIC

Absolute music is impossible for me in any genre.

My compositions do not belong to the realm of absolute music, where one can get along well enough with musical signs and a metronome.   [1]

OLD FORMS

I am no enemy of old forms in old music, but I am against imitating them today. I came to the conclusion myself—no one pointed it out to me—that hitherto existing forms are finished.   [2]

OPERA

I am no friend of overtures. On first hearing, when they are entirely unfamiliar, the audience cannot even understand them. Here the overture is nothing but a game of tones. I was pressed into writing my overtures, those to *The Kiss* and *The Secret,* for example, by several friends. My overtures do not please me. I have written none to my serious operas, just a short introduction to the first scene. In the case of *Libuše,* it was different. Its festive character demanded a rather long prelude. But also in comic operas, an overture belongs only when one can write a grand allegro, as in *The Bartered Bride.*   [3]

MUSIC IN SWEDEN

From a letter to Liszt, Göteborg, April 10, 1857

Following Dreyschock's advice that I move to Sweden, namely to Göteborg, I arrived here in mid-October of last year. The result of two concerts was the repeated invitation by the musical contingent that I take up permanent residence. Economically I am in a much better position than in Prague, as I am literally inundated with lessons; but musically I am completely isolated, not only because of a dearth of musical communication, but also because of a lack of direction. The people here are still solidly fixed in an antediluvian artistic point of view. Mozart is their idol, though he is not really understood, Beethoven is feared, Mendelssohn declared unpalatable, and the moderns are unknown. I performed Schumann's works here for the first time. . . .

So you see, my honored friend, here I am effective as I could never have been in Prague, and since I have found fertile soil for good works, I can hope to give a most gratifying direction to art in a short time. Besides, I have introduced Wagner, Schumann, and yourself to smaller circles and found what I was looking for, receptivity. The Göteborg inhabitants, left to themselves until now, did not know what art is all about. They are mainly wealthy merchants who *carry on* (if I might use the expression) this very superfluous art insofar as it affords them a bit of passing entertainment. Yet now they are really demanding more, and my energy, as well as my ruthless promotion of contemporary masters, seems to please them. Next season I hope to achieve even better and greater results.   [4]

Johannes Brahms
1833–1897

The composer that later generations have acclaimed for his richness of expression and unerring taste is one that many contemporaries found to be dry, artificial, and grotesque. In the face of such criticisms Brahms remained blasé and good humored. His interest in earlier music is manifest not only in his compositional style, but also in his transcriptions, his choice of variation themes, and his editions, which range from Schubert to Couperin. He was a life-

long admirer of Clara Wieck Schumann; persuasive evidence that they were ever more than friends has yet to materialize.

INSPIRATION

From a letter to Clara Schumann, Hannover, February 22, 1856

It always saddens me to think that after all I am not yet a proper musician; still, I have more aptitude for the calling than probably many of the younger generation. It gets knocked out of me. Boys should be allowed to indulge in jolly music; the serious kind comes of its own accord, although the lovesick does not. How lucky is the man who, like Mozart and others, goes to the tavern of an evening and writes some fresh music. For he lives while he is creating, though he does what he likes.   [1]

VARIATIONS

From a letter to Joseph Joachim, Düsseldorf, June 1856

At times I reflect on the variation form and I come to the conclusion that variations should be kept purer, more strict.

The older composers adhered strictly to the bass of their theme—the bass is the actual theme—throughout.

Beethoven varies his melody, harmony, and rhythm so beautifully.

However, I am sometimes inclined to think that the moderns (we both!) rummage about too much with the theme. We anxiously hang on to the melody, but don't treat it freely. We create nothing new out of it; we merely overload it, and hence the melody is rendered unrecognizable.   [2]

COLLECTED EDITIONS

From a letter to Eduard Hanslick, Vienna, May 1884

You know it has always been my heart's desire that the so-called collected works of our masters should not be published so "collectively," but be made available completely, yet singly, in good copies in our larger libraries. You know how zealously I have sought to become acquainted with their unprinted works. But I do not want to own all the printed works of even some of our most beloved masters. I find it neither fitting nor healthy that amateurs or young artists be misled into overloading their libraries or their brains with "collected works" and into confusing their sense of values.

Our Haydn has not yet had the honor of a complete edition. A truly complete edition of his works would be as impossible as it would be impractical. Yet how desirable would be a manuscript collection of the same and a number of facsimiles for public libraries. How little is done to bring out new editions of certain works that it would be so desirable to study and circulate—for example, old vocal music of every genre. You will perhaps say that they are never made use of. But they should be; and no doubt they are being used more and more.   [3]

BACH'S CHACONNE*

From a letter to Clara Schumann, Pörtschach, June 1877

The Chaconne is, in my opinion, one of the most wonderful and most incomprehensible pieces of music. Using the technique adapted to a small instrument, the man writes a whole world of the deepest thoughts and most powerful feelings. If I could picture myself writing, or even conceiving, such a piece, I am sure that the extreme excitement and emotional tension would have driven me mad. If one has no supremely great violinist at hand, the most exquisite of joys is probably simply to let the Chaconne ring in one's mind. But the piece certainly inspires one to occupy oneself with it somehow. One does not always want to hear music actually played, and in any case Joachim is not always there, so one tries it otherwise. But whether I try it with an orchestra or piano, the pleasure is always spoiled for me. There is only one way in which I can secure undiluted joy from the piece, though on a small and only approximate scale, and that is when I play it with the left hand alone. . . . The same difficulty, the nature of the technique, the rendering of the arpeggios, everything conspires to make me feel like a violinist.

You try it yourself. I wrote it only for you. But do not overstrain your hand; it requires so much resonance and strength. Play it for a while *mezza voce*. Also make the fingering easy and convenient. If it does not exert you too much—which is what I am afraid of—you ought to get great fun out of it.   [4]

BEETHOVEN

From the 1884 letter to Hanslick

Dear friend: You went away and left me a treasure without having looked it over yourself. Hence, I must write you a few words of thanks so that you may know just how valuable a treasure it is. There is no doubt whatsoever that in it the two cantatas Beethoven wrote in Bonn—on the death of Joseph II and the accession of Leopold II—have been discovered. Thus we now have two large-scale works for chorus and orchestra from a period in which no compositions to which we could attach any particular significance existed, as far as we knew. If they did not bear the date (February 1790), we would guess them to be of a later period, since we know nothing of that period! However, even if there were no name on the title page, there would still be no doubt concerning the composer—throughout it is altogether Beethoven! Here is the beautiful, noble pathos, the great sensitivity and imagination, the power as well as violence of expression, added to the special quality of the voice leading and declamation at which we marvel in his later works!   [5]

From a conversation with Richard Heuberger, 1896

I always find Beethoven's C Minor concerto [the Third Piano Concerto] much smaller and weaker than Mozart's. . . . I realize that Beethoven's new personality

---

* From the Second Partita for Violin Unaccompanied, in D minor, S. 1004. Brahms arranged the piece for piano left hand.

and his new vision, which people recognized in his works, made him the greater composer in their minds. But after fifty years, our views need more perspective. One must be able to distinguish between the charm that comes from newness and the value that is intrinsic to a work. I admit that Beethoven's concerto is more modern, but not more significant!

I also realize that Beethoven's First Symphony made a strong impression on people. That's the nature of a new vision. But the last three Mozart symphonies are far more significant. . . . Yes, the Rasumovsky quartets, the later symphonies—these inhabit a significant new world, one already hinted at in his Second Symphony. But what is much weaker in Beethoven compared to Mozart, and especially compared to Sebastian Bach, is the use of dissonance. Dissonance, true dissonance as Mozart used it, is not to be found in Beethoven. Look at *Idomeneo*. Not only is it a marvel, but as Mozart was still quite young and brash when he wrote it, it was a completely new thing. What marvelous dissonance! What harmony! You couldn't commission great music from Beethoven since he created only lesser works on commission—his more conventional pieces, his variations and the like. When Haydn or Mozart wrote on commission, it was the same as their other works. [6]

MENDELSSOHN, BERLIOZ, CHERUBINI

From a conversation with Heuberger, 1892

People cannot understand that an accomplished master has no use for potpourri. Mendelssohn could find nothing to like in Berlioz, and people hold it against him. It's the same with Cherubini. . . . They hold it against him because he—who towered over Berlioz—made a few comic remarks about that dilettante! [7]

SCHUMANN

Letter to Heinrich von Herzogenberg, Vienna, October, 1886

I think you and Joachim will derive considerable pleasure and interest from the enclosed.

It is an exact compilation of the printed score and the original concept of Schumann's D Minor Symphony,* modestly and, I think, unjustly described by the composer in his introduction as a rough sketch. You are, of course, familiar with the state of affairs, which is quite simple.

Schumann was so upset by a first rehearsal, which went off badly, that he subsequently orchestrated the symphony afresh at Düsseldorf, where he was used to a bad and incomplete orchestra.

The original scoring has always delighted me. It is a real pleasure to see anything so bright and spontaneous expressed with corresponding ease and grace. It reminds me (without comparing it in other respects) of Mozart's G Minor, the au-

---

* The original version of this work (1841) was the second symphony Schumann composed; the revised version (1851) appeared as the Fourth Symphony.

tograph of which I also possess. Everything is so absolutely natural that you cannot imagine it differently; there are no harsh colors, no forced effects, and so on. On the other hand, you will no doubt agree that one's enjoyment of the revised form is not unmixed; eye and ear seem to contradict each other. [8]

From a conversation with Heuberger, 1894

Often the most beautiful things in Schumann are, as they are written, scarcely playable. That makes them all the more fantastic! [9]

DIE MEISTERSINGER

From a letter to Clara Schumann, Vienna, March 20, 1870

Die Meistersinger had to be put on the program five times and taken off again, and now the repeat performances are causing just as much bother. This alone is enough to prevent the public from working up any enthusiasm, and a certain amount of "go" is necessary for that. I think the public is much less interested than I expected. I am not enthusiastic, either, about this work or about Wagner in general, but I listen as attentively as possible—and as often—as I can stand it. I confess it provokes one to discussion. But I am glad it is not necessary to say all that I feel about it plainly and aloud, etc. This I do know: In everything else I attempt, I step on the heels of my predecessors, who embarrass me. But Wagner would not hinder me at all from proceeding with the greatest pleasure to the writing of an opera. [10]

Alexander Borodin
1833–1887

Borodin's extraordinary musical accomplishments were largely the result of talent alone, his musical education having been almost nonexistent. By profession he was a medical chemist, with an academic career. He composed only sporadically, leaving a small number of works, many of them incomplete. Balakirev he saw as a mentor, and was hurt and puzzled when Balakirev abandoned the "Mighty Handful" in a fever of mysticism and piety. The visit with Liszt took place while Borodin was on a trip to inspect German university laboratories.

LISZT'S PIANO CLASSES

From a letter to his wife, Jena, July 12, 1877

Liszt never assigns any pieces to his students; he allows them freedom of choice. However, he gives them general advice in order to avoid their being stopped after a few measures with a remark of this kind:
"What odd taste to play such an ineptitude!"

He pays little attention to technique, to fingering, but concerns himself primarily with interpretation and expression. But, except in rare cases, his students possess excellent techniques, although they stem from very different schools.

Above all Liszt impressed me with his personality.   [1]

BALAKIREV

From a letter to his wife, October 24–25, 1871

I don't understand why Balakirev turns away so stubbornly from our circle and obviously avoids any encounter with us. I fear that his mind is not quite in order, but perhaps it's only his conceit gnawing at him. He is so despotic by nature that he demands complete subordination to his wishes, even in the most trifling matters. It doesn't seem possible for him to understand and acknowledge freedom and equality. He cannot endure the slightest opposition to his tastes, even to his whims. He wants to impose his yoke upon everyone and everything. Yet he is quite aware that we all have already grown up, that we stand firmly on our feet, and no longer require braces. This evidently irks him. . . .

There may also be a reason for his estrangement in his curious and unexpected switch to pietism of the most fanatic and most naïve sort. For instance, Mili doesn't miss a single morning mass, breaks a piece from his holy wafer, fervently crosses himself before each church, etc. It's quite possible that, in these circumstances, it's unpleasant for him to meet people who are unsympathetic to all this; he may even be afraid of the tactless and coarse barrage of reproaches from Vladimir Stasov,* who, whenever he meets him, starts forthwith "demonstrating" to him that all this is nonsense, that he "cannot understand" how an intelligent man like Mili, and so on, and so on. Moreover, most of the reproaches concern his apathy to musical matters, especially during the last year. . . . Modinka [Musorgsky] is offended by Mili's unjust, high-handed remarks about *Boris,* expressed tactlessly and sharply in the presence of people who on no account ought to have heard them. Korsinka [Rimsky-Korsakov] resents his indifference to *Pskovityanka* and is pained by Mili's behavior.

Cui also is indignant about Mili's apathy and his lack of interest in what happens in our musical circle. Before, Mili used to be concerned with the slightest novelty, even in embryo. There is no denying that the abyss between him and us grows wider and wider. This is terribly painful and pitiful. Painful chiefly because the victim of all this will be Mili himself. The other members of the circle now live more peacefully than ever before. Modinka and Korsinka particularly, since they began to share a room, have both greatly developed. They are diametrically opposed in musical qualities and methods; one seems to complement the other. Their influence on each other has been extremely helpful. Modeste has improved the recitative and declamatory sides of Korsinka, who has, in his turn, wiped out Modeste's tendency toward awkward originality, and has smoothed all his rough harmonic edges, his pretentiousness in orchestration, his lack of logic in the construction of musical form—in short, he has made Modeste's things incomparably more musical. And in

---

* Art and music critic; more under César Cui.

all the relations within our circle there's not a shadow of envy, conceit, or selfishness; each is made sincerely happy by the smallest success of another. . . . Mili alone shuns this *family* equality. [2]

LISZT ON BORODIN'S FIRST SYMPHONY

From the 1877 letter to his wife

He [Liszt] told me that he had presented my modulations as models to his students. Pointing out several, he remarked that nothing similar could be found in Beethoven, Bach, or anywhere else, for that matter, and that despite its novelty and originality, the work could not be caviled with since it was so polished, definitive, and full of attractive qualities. He regarded the first movement very highly; its pedal points, particularly the one on C, pleased him enormously.

He said nothing special about the other movements, but gave me some practical advice in case I were to publish a second piano version, namely, to write certain passages an octave higher or lower to facilitate reading. [3]

César Cui
1835–1918

With Balakirev, Cui founded the "Mighty Handful," the group named and championed by the art and music critic Vladimir Stasov (the other members were Borodin, Rimsky-Korsakov, and Musorgsky). Cui was a military man, rising to the rank of general and becoming a military academy professor. He was also an active music critic; by the time he drafted the credo of the Mighty Handful, he had been writing for newspapers in St. Petersburg for fifteen years, and would continue for another twenty.

RUSSIAN FOLK MUSIC

From an article in the Revue et gazette musicale, *Paris, 1878–79*

One of the principal elements in the structure of Russian song is the complete freedom of rhythm, carried to the point of caprice. Not only may the musical phrases be composed of an unequal number of measures, but even in the same song the rhythm of the measures may change several times. Here is an example:

This song starts with two measures of $\frac{5}{4}$, followed by three measures of $\frac{3}{4}$, and the motive finishes with one measure of $\frac{4}{4}$. One finds measures of seven beats as well as five; yet, in spite of the daring of such license, the musical phrase never loses its naturalness, for it adapts itself perfectly to the text; everything turns out correctly pronounced and accented. The Russian people have ever felt the need to subordinate the music to the prosodic exigencies of the text—an indication of real superiority of artistic instinct. These changing rhythms are, above all, *right,* since they are supremely expressive. At the same time, they utterly exclude the impression of banality and monotony that sometimes results from the prolonged use of a uniform and overworked rhythm. . . .

Couldn't the composer in quest of new effects, tired of the uniformity of our harmonic and melodic constructions, exploit this fertile mine? Must not the new, in a certain measure, come out of the old, and isn't there the germ of flourishing youth in what we call decay? More than once have the potent masters had recourse to the old modes; let us cite only Beethoven, who, in his Quartet Op. 132 wrote an *adagio* in the Lydian mode; it is one of the most admirable productions in musical art.

The Russian folk song imperiously demands an original harmonization and a very special art of modulation. First, it is rare to come on a song the melody of which can be treated entirely in one of the two modes, major or minor; most often, even if it spans but a few measures, it passes from the minor to its relative major and vice versa. These changes, generally unexpected, are almost always of a striking and sympathetic effect.

Here again is a happy example of a modulation from the major to the minor, by descending one tone:

There are also cases where the harmony of a single chord remains stationary throughout an entire song, which lends it an overall quality of vague melancholy, a complexion of deliberate monotony.

Russian folk tunes are ordinarily confined within a very restricted note span, only rarely exceeding the interval of a fifth or sixth. And the older the song, the smaller its compass. The theme is always short; some are limited to two measures, but these measures are repeated as many times as the scope of the text demands.   [1]

THE CREDO OF THE "MIGHTY HANDFUL"

From an article in the Revue et gazette musicale, *Paris, 1878–79*

The new Russian school has undertaken to bring to light certain principles of the highest importance, the first of which is the following: *Dramatic music must always have an intrinsic worth, as absolute music, independent of the text.* This principle has been too long neglected; even today it is far from being strictly observed. Because composers have been mainly preoccupied with pure melody and vocal virtuosity— guarantees of success—the most astounding and naïve banalities have been justified and accepted. What would have been discarded with justifiable disdain in a symphonic composition found its way naturally into opera. In this business, the Italians are masters beyond compare. Content with facile successes, based on florid passages and on high B flats and C sharps, keeping step with and sustaining the public's bad taste, they not only resort to using the most banal themes, but they parade these horrors in all their nakedness, never so much as attempting to mitigate them with even slightly elegant harmonies. The best among these musicians either repeat each other or repeat themselves, in style, themes, and harmonies. In this way they have managed to make their operas a series of degenerate twins that bear a distressing resemblance to each other. To be convinced, one has merely to glance at the thirty-odd Italian operas of Rossini, at the seventy and more of Donizetti.* Both offer two or three typical works, of which the rest of their output is only a more or less feeble and pallid reproduction. And even in their masterpieces, what commonplaces, what insignificant and stale pages!

In the case of a great number of non-Italian composers, the results are just about the same: they write too much, too often they speculate on the fortunate abilities of the performers, on the beautiful and irresistible effect of the decor, on the ever-certain charm of the ballet scenes. Would Meyerbeer himself, one of the greatest dramatic composers, not gain a great deal if he suppressed the princesses and queens with their roulades in his operas?

The new Russian school envisages the question from an absolutely different point of view. According to its principles, nothing must deflect opera music from being in itself *true and beautiful music;* everything that is most seductive in musical art must relate to it; the charm of harmony, the science of counterpoint, polyphony, and orchestral color must be equal. . . .

Vocal music must be in perfect agreement with the sense of the words. Again a clear and simple truth, good to repeat, and the application of which is all too frequently neglected. The text does not serve exclusively to facilitate vocal gymnastics; if such were its object, a text could be chosen at random and joined to no matter what music. Since texts vary, since each has its particular meaning, it is absolutely necessary that the musical part be intelligently adapted to it. . . .

---

* Donizetti actually wrote sixty-two operas.

The Russian school does not treat the question of poetry lightly; the musicians who represent this school resort, by preference, to the productions of the great poets. They seek out art in the subject itself, and aspire, with their chosen text, to give birth to a new creation that should be a work of art in two senses, the poetic and musical.

For music as well as for libretto, *the structure of the scenes composing an opera must depend entirely on the relation of the characters, and on the general movement of the play.* Here is an elementary logic that the greatest composers sometimes overlook. In how many operas one finds that a chorus or ensemble ignores the meaning of the words, wastes an enormous amount of time onstage singing some *corriam* or *fuggiam,* before they finally stir a step. Or, and here we have an embarrassment of riches, there is a catastrophe, some grave dramatic disaster; this is the signal for the cast to line up before the footlights, with the chorus ranged in rows at their heels, and break into a long piece with broad and slow movements; when this is finished, the applause and recalls done with, the catastrophe resumes its course. . . .

Furthermore, the new Russian school is striving musically to project the character and type of the dramatis personae as clearly as possible, to model each phrase of a role to an individual and not a general pattern, and lastly, to portray truthfully the historical epoch of the drama, and to depict the local color, the descriptive as well as the picturesque aspects of the action in its poetic as well as exact sense.

Doubtless all these principles have considerable affinity with Wagnerian ideas; but the methods of attaining the same end differ essentially between the two schools. Wagner concentrates all his musical interest on the orchestra, to the point of granting only secondary importance to the vocal part. . . . On the contrary, the Russian musicians reserve musical supremacy, all the important phrases of the score (with rare exceptions) for the singers. For them the singers are the true interpreters of the musical ideas of the composer. In this one clearly sees that the new Russian school derives from Glinka and Dargomijsky.*   [2]

WAGNER

From a letter to Nikolai Rimsky-Korsakov, March 9, 1863

Wagner is a man devoid of all talent. His melodies, where they are found at all, are in worse taste than Verdi and Flotow and more sour than the stalest Mendelssohn. All this is covered up with a thick layer of rot. His orchestration is decorative but coarse. The violins squeal throughout on the highest notes and throw the listener into a state of extreme nervousness.   [3]

TCHAIKOVSKY AND *EUGENE ONEGIN*

From a review in the St. Petersburg News, November 5, 1884

There are people who constantly complain about their fate and tell with especial fervor all about their maladies. In his music, Tchaikovsky also complains about his

---

* Alexander Dargomijsky (1813–69) is best known for his 1872 opera, *The Stone Guest.*

fate and talks about his maladies. The overture to his opera *Eugene Onegin* begins with a whimper. . . . The whimpers continue in the form of a duet. . . . Lensky's aria in the duel scene is pitiful diatonic whining. . . . The duel itself produces a comical impression because of the ridiculous position of the opponents. . . . As an opera, *Eugene Onegin* is stillborn and absolutely incompetent.   {4}

RACHMANINOFF'S FIRST SYMPHONY

From a review in the St. Petersburg News, *March 16, 1897*

If there were a conservatory in hell, and if one of its talented students were to compose a symphony based on the story of the seven plagues of Egypt, and if he had written one similar to Rachmaninoff's, he would have brilliantly accomplished his task and would have delighted the inhabitants of hell.   {5}

Camille Saint-Saëns
1835–1921

During his long life Saint-Saëns was widely known as a virtuoso on the organ and piano, impressing with feats of improvisation and sight-reading as much as technique. While his music initially received more attention in Germany, by the era of Debussy he was considered the embodiment of the older, conservatory-centered French tradition. He also wrote poetry and plays and produced a great many essays and articles, not only on music but on various cultural, historical, and scientific topics.

THE PARIS CONSERVATORY

From Portraits et souvenirs, *1899*

I loved its antiquity, the utter absence of any modern note, its atmosphere of other days. I loved that absurd court with the wailing notes of sopranos and tenors, the rattling of pianos, the blasts of trumpets and trombones, the arpeggios of clarinets, all uniting to form that ultra-polyphony which some of our composers have tried to attain—but without success.   [1]

EMBELLISHMENTS

From Au courant de la vie, *1914*

Nowadays music is written pretty nearly as it should be executed; in the old days it was otherwise, and conventional signs were used, which had to be translated. Performing old music as it is written is comparable to spelling a foreign language one does not know how to pronounce. The greatest difficulty, apparently, is the appoggiatura, which is no longer in use in our time. Everybody interprets it in his own fashion according to his taste: now, this is not a matter of taste, but of erudition. It is not a question of knowing what one prefers, but what the composers intended to write.   [2]

OVERCOLORATION IN MUSIC

From a letter to Camille Bellaigue, Cairo, January 30, 1907

In my opinion, the desire to push works of art beyond the realm of art means simply to drive them into the realm of folly. Richard Strauss is in the process of showing us the road.   [3]

HANDEL

From a letter to Camille Bellaigue, Las Palmas, January 23, 1897

I have studied Handel considerably and, besides, having had the good fortune of browsing in the Queen's Library at Buckingham Palace, I was curious to see what the contemporaries and the predecessors of the great master wrote, and to discover why and in what way he had eclipsed them. I finally came to the odd conclusion that he had achieved his astonishing popularity through his use of the picturesque and the descriptive, something new and unheard-of at the time. Others besides him possessed the sovereign gift of writing choruses, handling fugues. What he added was color, that modern element which we no longer notice, for good and sufficient reasons.

Here it cannot be a question of the exotic. Take a look at *Alexander's Feast, Israel in Egypt* and particularly *L'Allegro ed il penseroso* with his point of view in mind, and try to forget all that has been done since. At every turn you will find the pursuit of the picturesque, the effects of imitation. It is real and very intense for the milieu in which it was produced, and where it seems to have been unknown up to then.   [4]

BACH AND MOZART

From a letter to Camille Bellaigue, Cairo, February 4, 1907

What gives Sebastian Bach and Mozart a place apart is that these two great expressive composers never sacrificed form to expression. As high as their expression may soar, their musical form remains supreme and all-sufficient.   [5]

THE WAGNER LITERATURE

From an early draft of the article "L'illusion wagnerienne,"
Revue de Paris, *1899*

For forty years and more, newspaper and magazine articles, brochures and books have been accumulating on Richard Wagner, his works, and his theories; for twenty-five years they have been swarming in every language. A library could be built with them. And each day appear still new articles, new brochures, and new books. One would think that after all of Wagner's own writings and the illuminating tract by Liszt on *Tannhäuser* and *Lohengrin* there would be little left to say about the theories, let alone anything else. Such an excess is really amazing.

But there is something still more surprising.

So long as these studies limit themselves to analysis of the works, all is well, except that it is perforce ever the same thing, and it is hard to see the need for the perpetual reiteration; but as soon as they approach the core of the question and venture into the heart of things, as soon as they try to explain wherein the new art differs *essentially* from the old, why music drama must be mythological, how the old and new art are separated by an insuperable abyss, and other similar questions, a thick fog descends on their style; their words conflict, become strange and incoherent, they talk gibberish, and finally sheer nonsense. Observe that though there are some madmen and imbeciles among these commentators, there are others, on the contrary, whose names are synonymous with intelligence and talent, yet they do not escape this fatal tendency.   [6]

DEBUSSY

From a letter to Maurice Emmanuel, August 4, 1920

The *Prelude to the Afternoon of a Faun* has pretty sonority, but one does not find in it the least musical idea, properly speaking; it resembles a piece of music as the palette used by an artist in his work resembles a picture. Debussy did not create a style; he cultivated an absence of style, logic, and common sense.   [7]

CHAPTER SEVEN

Georges Bizet

Modest Musorgsky

Piotr Ilyich Tchaikovsky

Antonín Dvořák

Edvard Grieg

Nikolai Rimsky-Korsakov

Gabriel Fauré

Georges Bizet

1838–1875

Bizet entered the Paris Conservatory at the age of eight. His teachers there included Jacques Halévy, whose daughter he later married. In 1857 he won the Prix de Rome, but instead of composing the customary mass he wrote a two-act Italian opera. Had he lived to forty, Bizet would have seen Carmen *produced internationally to great acclaim. Instead he died during the first run, just as he attained the height of his powers and without ever knowing whether* Carmen *would survive its indifferent first reception.*

GENIUS

From a letter to Hector Gruyer, Rome, December 31, 1858

There are two kinds of genius: natural genius and rational genius. Though I admire the latter immensely, I will not hide the fact that the former has all my sympathies. Yes, I have the courage to prefer Raphael to Michelangelo, Mozart to Beethoven, and Rossini to Meyerbeer, which is equivalent to saying that if I had heard Rubini, I would have preferred him to Duprez.* I do not place the one group in second rank in order to put the other in first; that would be absurd. It is just a matter of taste. One sort of idea exerts a stronger attraction on me than the other. When I see the *Last Judgment,* when I hear the *Eroica* or the fourth act of *The Huguenots,* I am moved and surprised, and my eyes, ears, and intelligence are inadequate to admire them enough. But when I hear *The Marriage of Figaro* or the second act of *William Tell,* I am altogether happy, I experience a feeling of well-being, a complete satisfaction, I forget everything. Ah, how fortunate are they who thus are gifted!   [1]

FACILITY IN ART

From a letter to his mother, Rome, January 22, 1859

Facility in art is almost indispensable, yet only when the man and the artist are mature does it cease to be a threat. I don't want to do anything that is merely stylish; I want to have ideas before beginning a piece.   [2]

THE MELODIC GIFT

From a letter to his mother, Rome, March 19, 1859

You attribute the series of failures of which our better composers have been the victims for several years to the weakness of their libretti. You are right, but there is another reason: these composers haven't a complete talent. Some—Massé, for example—lack style, a broad conception. Others—David (Félicien), I suppose—lack musical experience and understanding, soul. Even the strongest lack the one means

---

* Rubini and Duprez were famous tenors.

the composer must have to make himself comprehensible to the public today: the melodic gift, which is quite wrongly called the "idea." One can be a great artist without having it, but then one must renounce money and popular success. But one may also be a superior person and possess this precious gift, witness Rossini. Rossini is the greatest of all because he has, like Mozart, all the qualities: loftiness, style and finally . . . the melodic sense. I am utterly convinced of what I am telling you, and that is why I have hope. I know my business well, I orchestrate very well, I am never ordinary, and I have finally discovered this eagerly sought open-sesame. I have a dozen good melodies in my opera [*The Pearl Fishers*], real ones, rhythmic and easily remembered, and yet I have made no concessions in my taste. I would like you to hear it all. You would see that I have already found a little of what I lacked so completely. Next year I shall try for real melodic line in grand opera. That is much more difficult, but it is already something to have found it in *opéra comique*.   [3]

ITALIAN MUSIC

From a letter to Paul Lacombe, March 11, 1867

I lived in Italy for three years and wanted no part of the country's disreputable way of life, though I was taken with the temperament of some of its composers. Moreover, my sensuous nature allowed itself to be carried away by this music, at once facile, lazy, amorous, sensual, and passionate. I am by conviction, heart, and soul German. But sometimes I lose myself in low artistic places. And I must confess to you in a whisper that I get infinite pleasure from it. In a word, I love Italian music as one loves a mistress, but she must be charming. And when we have cited two thirds of *Norma,* four pieces from *Puritani,* three from *Somnambula,* two acts of *Rigoletto,* an act of *Trovatore,* and just about half of *Traviata*—add *Don Pasquale*—we can throw the rest away anywhere you please. As for Rossini, he has his *William Tell*—his sun—*Count Ory,* the *Barber,* and one act of *Otello*—his planets. Because of these we may pardon the terrible *Semiramide* and all his other sins.   [4]

VARIOUS COMPOSERS

From a letter to Paul Lacombe, December, 1867

I place Beethoven above the greatest, the most famous. The Choral Symphony is for me the culminating point of our art. . . . Neither Mozart with his divine form, nor Weber with his powerful, colossal originality, nor Meyerbeer with his thundering dramatic genius can, in my opinion, dispute the crown of this Titan, this Prometheus of music. He is overwhelming.

Only one man knew how to compose quasi-improvised music, or at least, what seems such. That is Chopin. Here is a charming personality, strange, unique, inimitable.

To my mind, the repeating of expositions has become old-fashioned; most of Beethoven's and Mendelssohn's symphonies (and of course, Mozart's) would gain by being performed without repeats.   [5]

VERDI

From a letter to his mother, Rome, February 19, 1859

Verdi is a man of great talent who lacks the essential quality that makes the great masters: style. But he has bursts of marvelous passion. His passion is brutal, it is true, but it is better to be impassioned in this way than not at all. His music is at times exasperating, but it is never boring. In short, I do not understand the fanatics or the detractors he has excited. In my opinion, he merits neither the one nor the other.   [6]

WAGNER'S *RIENZI*

From a letter to Edmond Galabert, April, 1869

Yesterday I attended the dress rehearsal of *Rienzi* at the Théâtre Lyrique. It began at 8 o'clock and finished at 2. Eighty musicians in the orchestra, thirty on the stage, a hundred and thirty in the chorus, a hundred and fifty supers. A badly constructed piece. A single role—Rienzi. A racket that cannot be described; a jumble of Italian motives; a bizarre and bad style; music of decadence rather than of the future. Wretched numbers! Admirable numbers! All in all, an astounding work, terrifically *alive*: a grandeur, an Olympian breath! Genius, immoderate, disorderly, but genius! Will it be a success? I don't know! The hall was filled, and no claque! Prodigious effects! Disastrous effects! Enthusiastic cries! Then half-hour gloomy silences! Some maintained: "It's bad Verdi!," others: "It's good Wagner!" It is sublime! It's frightful! It's mediocre! It isn't bad! The audience is perplexed! It is very amusing. Few people have the courage to persist in their hatred of Wagner.   [7]

From a letter to his mother-in-law, Mme Halévy, May 29, 1871

WAGNER

It is the fate of great geniuses to be misunderstood by their contemporaries. Wagner is no friend of mine, and I am fairly indifferent to him, yet I cannot forget the immeasurable enjoyment I owe to this original genius. The charm of his music is inexpressible. Here are voluptuousness, tenderness, love.

If I played you some of it for a week, you would become passionately fond of it. Moreover, the Germans, who, alas, are just as good as we are musically, have understood that Wagner is one of their most solid pillars. This man is the nineteenth-century German spirit incarnate.

You know very well how painful disdain can be to a great artist. Fortunately for Wagner, he is endowed with such insolent conceit that criticism can't touch his heart—admitting that he has a heart, which I doubt.

I will not go so far as you and I will not pronounce Beethoven's name alongside Wagner's. Beethoven is not a man, he is a god, like Shakespeare, like Homer, like Michelangelo! Well, take the most intelligent audience and play the greatest pages our art possesses for them—the Choral Symphony. They will understand nothing, absolutely nothing. We have had this experience; we repeat it every year with the same result. It is only that Beethoven is fifty years dead and it is the fashion to find his music beautiful.

Judge for yourself, forgetting everything that you have heard said, forgetting the foolish and malicious articles and the most spiteful book published by Wagner [a book belittling the French and French music], and you will see. It is not the music of the future—that means nothing—but it is, as you have said so well, the music of all times. . . .

Of course, in spite of my admiration, if I thought I were imitating Wagner, I would never write another note. A fool imitates. It is better to do inferior work of one's own than to copy someone else's. And besides, the more beautiful the model, the more ridiculous the imitation. Michelangelo, Shakespeare, and Beethoven have been imitated. Heaven knows what horrors this rage for imitation has thrust on us.

[8]

TALENT VERSUS IDEAS

In art (music, painting, above all, sculpture) as in letters, what makes success is talent, and not ideas. The public (and I speak of intelligent people, the rest don't count: that's my democracy for you)—the public understands the idea *later.* To achieve this *later,* the artist's talent must manifest itself in an agreeable form and so ease the road for the public, not repel it from the outset.

Thus Auber, who had so much talent and few ideas, was almost always understood, while Berlioz, who had genius but no talent at all, was almost never understood.

[9]

Modest Musorgsky
1839–1881

Musorgsky held a series of government jobs, improvising and composing in his spare time and leaving many of his works unfinished. While he turned to Balakirev and Rimsky-Korsakov more than once for training in traditional techniques, his originality lay in a different direction. Most of Musorgsky's published scores have come to us through other hands; some debate still lingers as to how much help his music may have needed (see Rimsky-Korsakov on the subject). Beyond debate is the fact that his innovations in harmony and orchestration had a profound impact on twentieth-century composers.

GERMANS AND RUSSIANS

From a letter to Rimsky-Korsakov, Shilovo, August 15, 1868

Brief, symphonic development, technically understood, is developed by the German, just as his philosophy is. The German, when he thinks, first theorizes at length, and then proves. Our Russian brother proves first, and then amuses himself with theory.

[1]

From a letter to Alexandra and Nadezhda Purgold,
Petrograd, June 20, 1870

The greatest German geniuses, Beethoven, Weber, and Schumann (each in his own way), were poor vocal composers. . . . The Germans sing as they speak, but they speak *à faire tonner le gosier,* but when they compose for singing, then they do not think of the *gosier,* forcibly cramming human thought into the frame of a preconceived musical phrase. As a people they are theoretical in music, too, and at every other step fall into abstraction.   [2]

TECHNIQUE

From a letter to Vladimir Stasov, Petrograd, July 13, 1872

Maybe I'm afraid of technique, because I'm poor at it? However, there are some who will stand up for me in art, and in this respect as well. For example, I cannot bear it when a hostess serves a good pie she has prepared and, while we are eating, says: "A million *puds* of butter, five hundred eggs, a whole bed of cabbages, 150¼ fish ..." You are eating the pie and it tastes good, then you hear all about the kitchen, and at once you can imagine the cook, always dirty, a chopped-off chicken head lying on a bench, gutted fish on another . . . . and well, the pie grows less tasty. There is in ripe artistic productions that side of chaste purity that, when touched by dirty paws, grows loathsome.

In truth, until the artist musician rids himself of his diapers, his braces, straps, so long will the *symphonic* priests rule, setting up their Talmud "of the 1st and 2nd editions," as the alpha and omega in the life of art. The little brains sense that their Talmud cannot be used in living art; where there are people and life, there is no place for prejudiced paragraphs and articles. And so they cry: "Drama, the stage, they cramp us—give us space!" And here they go giving free rein to their brains: "The world of sounds is unlimited!" Yes, but their brains are limited, so what use is this sound of worlds, or rather world of sounds! One gets as much space when lying on "the lawn and following the flight of the heavenly clouds": there's a fleecy lamb, there's an old granddad, here's simply nothing at all, then suddenly, a Prussian soldier. I can't blame Polonius for agreeing with Hamlet about the clouds. The esteemed cloud is very changeable and in the wave of the hand may turn from a camel to, perhaps, a Laroche.* It isn't the symphonies I object to, but symphonists—incorrigible conservatives. So do not tell me why our musicians chatter more often about technique than about aims and historical tasks—because this *derives from that.*   [3]

MUSICAL GIANTS

From a letter to Stasov, St. Petersburg, October 18, 1872

In poetry there are two giants: coarse Homer and refined Shakespeare. In music there are two giants: the thinker Beethoven and the superthinker Berlioz. When

---

* Music critic in St. Petersburg.

around these four we gather all their generals and aides-de-camp, we have a pleasant company; but what has this company of subalterns achieved? Skipping and dancing along in the paths marked out by the giants—but to dare to "go very far ahead," this is terrifying! [4]

OPERA

From a letter to Arseni Golenishchev-Kutuzov, Tsarskoye-Selo, August 15, 1877

Pushkin wrote *Boris* [*Godunov*] in dramatic form, but not for the stage; Gogol wrote "The Fair at Sorochintzi" in the form of a story—and, of course, not for the stage. But both giants with their creative power projected so subtly the contours of scenic action that all one has to do is to apply the colors. But woe to him whose whim it is to use Pushkin or Gogol for his only text. . . . As only the *genuine, sensitive* nature of an artist can create in the realm of the word, the musician must maintain a very "polite" attitude toward the creation, in order to penetrate into its very substance, into the very *essence* of that which the musician intends to embody in musical form. The genuine, *truly artistic* cannot be anything but capricious, because *independently* it cannot easily be embodied in another artistic form, because it is *independent* and demands profound study and sacred love. But when artistic kinship between workers in different fields of art does work out—it's a fine adventure! [5]

THE MARRIAGE

From a letter to Ludmila Shestakova, {Shilovo}, July 30, {1868}

This is what I would like: my stage people should speak like living people; but besides this, their character and power of intonation, supported by the orchestra, which forms the musical pattern of their speech, must achieve their aim directly; that is, my music must be an artistic reproduction of human speech in all its finest shades; that is, the sounds of human speech, as the external manifestations of thought and feeling, must, without exaggeration or violence, become true, accurate *music*—that is, artistic, highly artistic. That is the ideal toward which I strive ...

Now I am working on Gogol's *The Marriage*. The success of Gogol's speech depends on the actor, on his true intonation. I want to give Gogol his place and the actor his also; in other words, I want to speak musically as the characters of Gogol would wish to speak, and in such a way that no one could say it in any other way. In *The Marriage* I am crossing the Rubicon. This is living prose in music. The scorn of musician-poets for common human speech, stripped of all heroic robes, will not be found here; instead there is reverence toward the language of mankind; this is a reproduction of simple human speech. [6]

SELF-EVALUATION

Prepared for Riemann's Musik-Lexikon, June 1880

Musorgsky cannot be classed with any existing group of musicians, either by the character of his compositions or by his musical views. The formula of his artistic *profession de foi* may be explained by his view, as a composer, of the task of art: art is a means of communicating with people, not an aim in itself. This guiding principle has defined the whole of his creative activity. Proceeding from the conviction that human speech is strictly controlled by musical laws (Virchow, Gervinus*), he considers the task of musical art to be the reproduction in musical sounds not merely of the mood of a feeling, but chiefly of the mood of human speech. Acknowledging that in the realm of art only artist-reformers such as Palestrina, Bach, Gluck, Beethoven, Berlioz, and Liszt have created the laws of art, he considers these laws as not immutable but liable to change and progress, like the entire spiritual world of man. [7]

Piotr Ilyich Tchaikovsky
1840–1893

Tchaikovsky began a career in civil service, then quit at twenty-three to attend Anton Rubinstein's music school in St. Petersburg. Within a decade he had acquired an enviable technique and had found his voice. From 1868 to 1874 he wrote frequently as a newspaper reviewer. Beginning in 1876, Tchaikovsky received an income from Nadezhda von Meck, a wealthy widow; she supported him for the next fourteen years, though at his insistence they never met in person.

THE MIGHTY HANDFUL

From a letter to Nadezhda von Meck, San Remo, December 24, 1877†

The young Petersburg composers are very gifted, but they are all impregnated with the most horrible presumptuousness and a purely amateur conviction of their superiority to all other musicians in the universe. The one exception, in latter days, has been Rimsky-Korsakov. He was an "auto-dictator," like the rest, but recently he has undergone a complete change. By nature he is very earnest, honorable, and conscientious. As a young man he dropped into a set that first solemnly assured him he was a genius and then proceeded to convince him that he had no need to study, that academies were destructive to all inspiration and dried up creative activity. At first he believed all this. His earliest compositions bear the stamp of striking ability and a lack of theoretical training. The circle to which he belonged was a mutual admiration society. Each member was striving to imitate the work of another, after proclaiming it as something very wonderful. Consequently the whole set suffered from one-sidedness, lack of individuality, and mannerisms. Rimsky-Korsakov is the only one among them who discovered, five years ago, that

---

* Musorgsky probably encountered the views of the scientist Rudolf Virchow and the Shakespeare scholar Georg Gervinus in Chernyshevsky's novel *What Is to Be Done?*

† Tchaikovsky dated his letters according to the Julian calendar then in use in Russia. At the time of these letters the Julian calendar was twelve days behind our Gregorian calendar.

the doctrines preached by this circle had no sound basis, that their mockery of the schools and the classical masters, their denial of authority and of the masterpieces, was nothing but ignorance. I possess a letter dating from this time that moved me very deeply. Rimsky-Korsakov was overcome by despair when he realized how many unprofitable years he had wasted, and that he was following a road that led nowhere. He began to study with such zeal that the theory of the schools soon became to him an indispensable atmosphere. During one summer he completed innumerable exercises in counterpoint and sixty-four fugues, ten of which he sent me for inspection. From contempt for the schools, Rimsky-Korsakov suddenly went over to the cult of musical technique. Shortly after this, his symphony and also his quartet appeared. Both works are full of obscurities and—as you will justly observe—bear the stamp of dry pedantry. At present he appears to be passing through a crisis, and it is hard to predict how it will end. Either he will turn out a great master, or be lost in contrapuntal intricacies.

Cui is a gifted amateur. His music is not original, but graceful and elegant; it is too coquettish, "made up"— so to speak. At first it pleases, but soon satiates us. That is because Cui's specialty is not music but fortification, about which he has to give a number of lectures in the various military schools in St. Petersburg. He himself once told me he could compose only by picking out his melodies and harmonies as he sat at the piano. When he hit upon some pretty idea, he worked it up in every detail, and this process was very lengthy, so that his opera, *Ratcliff,* for instance, took him ten years to complete. But, as I have said, we cannot deny that he has talent of a kind—and at least taste and instinct.

Borodin—age fifty—Professor of Chemistry at the Academy of Medicine, also possesses talent, a very great talent, which, however, has come to nothing for want of instruction, and because blind fate has led him into the science laboratories instead of a vital musical existence. He has less taste than Cui, and his technique is so poor that he cannot write a bar without assistance.

With regard to Musorgsky, as you very justly remark, he is "used up." His gifts are perhaps the most remarkable of all, but his nature is narrow, and he has no aspirations toward self-perfection. He has been too easily led astray by the absurd theories of his set and the belief in his own genius. Besides which, his nature is not of the finest quality; he likes what is coarse, unpolished, and ugly. He is the exact opposite of the distinguished and elegant Cui.

Musorgsky plays with his lack of polish; he even seems proud of his want of skill, writing just as it comes to him, believing blindly in the infallibility of his genius. As a matter of fact, his very original talent flashes forth now and then.

Balakirev is the greatest personality of the entire circle. But he lapsed into silence before he accomplished much. He possesses a wonderful talent, which various fatal hindrances have helped to extinguish. After having proclaimed his agnosticism rather widely, he suddenly became "pious." Now he spends all his time in church, fasts, kisses the relics—and does very little else. In spite of his great gifts, he has done a great deal of harm. For instance, it was he who ruined Korsakov's early career by assuring him he had no need to study. He is the inventor of all the theories of this remarkable circle, which unites so many undeveloped, falsely developed, or prematurely decayed talents.

These are my frank opinions of these gentlemen. What a sad phenomenon! So many talents from which—with the exception of Rimsky-Korsakov—we can scarcely hope for anything serious. But this is always our case in Russia: vast forces that are impeded by the fatal shadow of a Plevna from taking the open field and fighting as they should. But all the same, these forces exist. This Musorgsky, with all his ugliness, speaks a new idiom. Beautiful it may not be, but it is new. We may reasonably hope that Russia will one day produce a whole school of strong men who will open up new paths of art. [1]

From a letter to his brother Modest, Moscow, October 20, 1874

I have studied *Boris Godunov* and *The Demon* thoroughly. Musorgsky's music I send to the devil; it is the most vulgar and vile parody on music. There are charming bits in *The Demon* but a lot of ballast. [2]

BERLIOZ

From a letter to his brother Anatoli, Paris, February 12, 1879

Last night I had the most enjoyable artistic experience. I heard the whole of *The Damnation of Faust*, which is one of the miracles of art. Several times I had to suppress my sobs. The devil only knows what a curious man Berlioz is. On the whole his musical nature does not attract me, and I cannot agree with the ugliness of some of his harmonies and modulations, but sometimes he reaches extraordinary heights. [3]

WAGNER AND THE *RING*

From a letter to his brother Modest, Vienna, August 8, 1876

Maybe the *Ring* is a great composition, but I have never heard anything so boring and so drawn out as this. A collection of the most complicated harmonies, the singing parts colorless, unending dialogues; a hellish darkness in the theater, lack of interest and poetry in the subject—all this is excessively tiring to the nerves. And this is what Wagner's reform is leading to? Up to now one tried to charm people by music, now one tortures and exhausts them. There are, of course, beautiful parts, but the whole thing together bores me to death. [4]

From a letter to Nadezhda von Meck, Vienna, November 26, 1877

What a Don Quixote is Wagner! He expends all his strength in pursuing the impossible, and all the time, if he would but follow the natural bent of his extraordinary gift, he might evoke a whole world of musical beauties. In my opinion Wagner is a symphonist by nature. . . . I will prove to you by one example how far the symphonic prevails over the operatic style in his operas. You have probably heard his celebrated "Ride of the Valkyries"? What a great and marvelous picture! How we actually seem to see these fierce heroines flying on their magic steeds amid thunder and lightning! In the concert room this piece makes an extraordinary impression. On the stage, in view of the cardboard rocks, the canvas clouds, and the soldiers running about awkwardly in the background . . . the music loses all power of expression. Here the stage does not enhance the effect, but acts rather like a wet blanket.   [5]

BRAHMS

From a letter to Nadezhda von Meck, Rome, February 18, 1880

The [Violin] Concerto of Brahms does not please me better than any of his other works. He is certainly a great musician, even a master, but his mastery overwhelms his inspiration. So many preparations and circumlocutions for something that ought to come and charm us at once—and nothing does come but boredom. His music is not warmed by any genuine emotion. It lacks poetry, but makes great pretensions to profundity. These depths contain nothing; they are void. Take the opening of the concerto, for instance. It is an introduction, a preparation for some-thing fine; an admirable pedestal for a statue; but the statue is lacking, we only get a second pedestal piled upon the first. I do not know whether I have properly expressed the thoughts, or rather feelings, Brahms's music awakens in me. I mean to say that he never expresses anything, or when he does, he fails to express it fully. His music is made up of fragments of some indefinable *something*, skillfully welded together. The design lacks definite contour, color, life.

But I must simply confess that, independent of any definite reproach, Brahms, as a musical personality, is antipathetic to me. I cannot abide him. Whatever he does—I remain unmoved and cold. It is a purely instinctive feeling.   [6]

From a letter to his brother Modest, Hamburg, February 28, 1889

Brahms stayed an extra day to hear my [Fifth] Symphony and was very kind. We had lunch together after the rehearsal and quite a few drinks. He is very sympa-thetic and I like his honesty and open-mindedness. Neither he nor the players liked the finale, which I also think rather horrible.   [7]

BIZET AND *CARMEN*

From a letter to his brother Modest, Simaki, July 18, 1880

To refresh myself last night I played *Carmen* from beginning to end and all my wonder and love for this wonderful opera flared up again. I even mapped out in my mind an article in which *Carmen,* in spite of its modest pretensions to be only an *opéra comique* and not grand opera, is shown as really one of—if not the most—prominent lyric-dramatic creations of our time. Under the influence of this idea I even wrote a few words to Nadezhda Filaretovna [von Meck], which are the es-sence of my imagined article. So as not to tire myself by a new version of my thoughts, I am going to copy them into my letter to you, which I have not yet posted. I want you to know my opinion. As to the article, I shall never write it. I have too little of skill or knowledge—both of which Laroche has got in plenty. A pity in a way, for I am ready to swear on oath that in a few years *Carmen* will be looked upon as a perfect *chef d'oeuvre*. Here is what I have written to Nadezhda Filaretovna:

"In my opinion *Carmen* is an absolute *chef d'oeuvre,* i.e., a work that is very much the reflection of the musical taste and aspiration of a whole epoch. It seems to me that the epoch we live in differs from its predecessor by reason of this characteristic trait—that composers pursue (what Mozart, Beethoven, and Schubert never did) pretty, piquant, musical effects. What, for example, is the new Russian school if not a cult of spicy harmonizations, original orchestral combinations, and all sorts of superficial effects? The musical idea has been pushed into the background. It has become not the aim but only the means, that is, the reason for the invention of this or that combination of sounds. This purely intellectual process of musical reasoning makes contemporary music, however amusing, witty, curious, and even 'delectable' (an expression invented by and most characteristic of the new Russian school), at the same time cold, not warmed by real inspiration. But suddenly a Frenchman appears (whom I can really call a genius) whose piquancy and spiciness do not result from ingenuity but flow in an unhindered stream, to flatter your hearing, to excite, and to touch you at the same time. As if he means to say, 'You do not want anything grand, mighty, and strong, but prettiness—here it is!' He has, indeed, given us an example of the element that is called pretty—*le joli.* Bizet is an artist who, in spite of paying tribute to the decadent taste of this century, is full of sincere feeling and inspiration."

That is the newspaper article chatter, which will give you an idea of what I think. But I don't have the guts to write a proper article. I would have to prove that not only the Russian school but Wagner and Liszt are also pursuing prettiness and "delectability," and that the last of the Mohicans of the Golden Age of Music were Mendelssohn, Chopin, Schumann, and Glinka; but in their music, too, you can see a move away from the great and beautiful to the "delectable." In brief, I have not enough of what it takes to write a proper article. [8]

COMPOSITION AND INSTRUMENTATION

From a letter to his brother-in-law Lev Davydov, Moscow,
May 19, 1877

When I am composing an opera it means that (1) I must not see a soul during certain hours of the day, and know that no one can see or hear me; I have a habit, when composing, of singing very loud, and the thought that someone could hear me disturbs me very much. (2) A grand piano is at my disposal near me, i.e., in my bedroom—without which I cannot write, at least not peacefully and easily. [9]

From a letter to Nadezhda von Meck, Clarens, March 5, 1878

You ask how I manage my instrumentation. I never compose in the abstract; that is to say, the musical thought never appears otherwise than in a suitable external form. In this way I invent the musical idea and the instrumentation simultaneously. Thus I thought out the scherzo of our symphony [Fourth Symphony] at the moment of its composition—exactly as you heard it. It is inconceivable except as pizzicato. Were it played with the bow, it would lose all its charm and be a mere body without a soul.

As regards the Russian element in my works, I may tell you that not infrequently I begin a composition with the intention of introducing some folk melody into it. Sometimes it comes of its own accord, unbidden (as in the finale of our symphony). As to this national element in my work, its affinity with the folk songs in some of my melodies and harmonies comes from my having spent my childhood in the country, and, from my earliest years, having been filled with the characteristic beauty of our Russian folk music. I am passionately fond of the national element in all its varied expressions. In short, I am Russian in the fullest sense of the word.   [10]

From a letter to Nadezhda von Meck, Kamenka, June 24, 1878

You want to know my methods of composing. . . . It is very difficult to give a satisfactory answer to your question, because the circumstances under which a new work comes into the world vary considerably in each case.

(1) Works I compose on my own initiative—that is to say, from an invincible inward impulse.

(2) Works that are inspired by external circumstances: the wish of a friend, or publisher, and *commissioned* works.

Here I should add that experience has taught me that the intrinsic value of a work has nothing to do with its place in one or the other of these categories. It frequently happens that a composition that owes its existence to external influences proves very successful, while one that proceeds entirely from my own initiative may, for various indirect reasons, turn out far less well. These indirect circumstances, upon which depends the mood in which a work is written, are of the greatest importance. During the actual time of creative activity, complete quiet is absolutely necessary to the artist. In this sense every work of art, even a musical composition, is *objective.* Those who imagine that a creative artist can, through the medium of his art, express his feelings at the moment when he is *moved,* make the greatest mistake. Emotions, sad or joyful, can be expressed only *retrospectively,* so to speak. Without any special reason for rejoicing, I may be moved by the most cheerful creative mood, and vice versa, a work composed in the happiest surroundings may be touched with dark and gloomy colors.

In a word, an artist lives a double life: an everyday human life and an artistic life, and the two do not always go hand in hand.

In any case, it is absolutely necessary for a composer to shake off all the cares of daily existence, at least for a time, and give himself up entirely to his art-life. Works belonging to the first category do not require the least effort of will. It is only necessary to obey our inward promptings, and if our material life does not crush our artistic life under its weight of depressing circumstances, the work progresses with inconceivable rapidity. Everything else is forgotten, the soul throbs with an incomprehensible and indescribable excitement, so that, almost before we can follow this swift flight of inspiration, time passes literally unreckoned and unobserved.

There is something *somnambulistic* about this condition. *On ne s'entend pas vivre.* It is impossible to describe such moments. Everything that flows from one's pen, or merely passes through one's brain (for such moments often come at a time when writing is an impossibility) under these circumstances is *invariably good,* and if no external obstacle comes to hinder the creative glow, the result will be an artist's best and most perfect work. Unfortunately, such external hindrances are inevitable. A duty has to be performed, dinner is announced, a letter arrives, and so on. This is the reason why there exist so few compositions that are of equal quality throughout. Hence the *joints, patches, inequalities, and discrepancies.*

For the works in my second category, it is necessary to *get into the mood.* To do so, we are often obliged to fight indolence and disinclination. Besides this, there are many other fortuitous circumstances. Sometimes the victory is easily gained. At other times inspiration eludes us and cannot be recaptured. I consider it, however, the *duty* of an artist not to be conquered by circumstances. He must not wait. Inspiration is a guest who does not care to visit those who are indolent.

Now I will try to describe my actual procedure in composition.

I usually write my sketches on the first piece of paper to hand. I jot them down in the most abbreviated form. A melody never stands alone, but invariably with the harmonies that belong to it. These two elements of music, together with the rhythm, must never be separated; every melodic idea brings its own inevitable harmony and its suitable rhythm. If the harmony is very intricate, I set down in the sketch a few details on the working out of the parts; when the harmony is quite simple, I put in only the bass, or a figured bass, and sometimes not even this. If the sketch is intended for an orchestral work, the ideas appear ready-colored by some special instrumental combination. The original plan or instrumentation often undergoes some modification.

The text must *never* be written after the music, for if music is written to given words only, these words invoke a suitable musical expression. It is quite possible to fit words to a short melody, but in treating a serious work such adaptation is not permissible. It is equally impossible to compose a symphonic work and afterward to attach to it a program, since every episode of the chosen program should evoke its corresponding musical presentation. This stage of composition—the sketch—is remarkably pleasant and interesting. It brings an indescribable delight, accompanied, however, by a kind of unrest and nervous agitation. Sleep is disturbed and meals forgotten. Nevertheless, the development of the project proceeds tranquilly. The instrumentation of a work that is completely thought out and matured is a most enjoyable task.

The same does not apply to the bare sketch of a work for pianoforte or voice, or little pieces in general, which are sometimes very tiresome.

You ask: Do I confine myself to established forms? Yes and no. Some compositions imply the use of traditional forms, but only as regards their general features, the sequence of the movements. The details permit of considerable freedom of treatment, if the development of the ideas requires it.

You ask me about melodies built on the notes of the harmony. I can assure you, and prove it by many examples, that it is quite possible, by means of rhythm and the transposition of the notes, to evolve millions of new and beautiful melodic combinations. But this applies only to homophonic music. With polyphonic music such a method of building up a melody would interfere with the independence of the parts. In the music of Beethoven, Weber, Schumann, Mendelssohn, and especially Wagner, we frequently find melodies that consist of the notes of the common chord; a gifted musician will always be able to invent a new and interesting fanfare.   [11]

From a letter to Nadezhda von Meck, Kamenka, June 25, 1878

Yesterday, when I wrote you about my methods of composing, I did not sufficiently enter into that phase related to the working out of the sketch. This phase is of primary importance. What has been set down in a moment of ardor must now be critically examined, improved, extended, or condensed, as the form requires. Sometimes one must do oneself violence, must sternly and pitilessly take part against oneself, before one can mercilessly erase things thought out with love and enthusiasm. I cannot complain of poverty of imagination, or lack of inventive power; but on the other hand, I have always suffered from my want of skill in the management of form. Only after strenuous labor have I at last succeeded in making the form of my compositions correspond, more or less, with their contents. Formerly I was careless and did not give sufficient attention to the critical overhauling of my sketches. Consequently my "seams" showed, there was no organic union between my individual episodes. This was a very serious defect, and I only improved gradually as time went on; but the form of my works will never be *exemplary,* because, although I can modify, I cannot radically alter the essential qualities of my musical temperament.   [12]

TEACHING AT THE MOSCOW CONSERVATORY

From a letter to his brother Anatoli, Moscow, September 18, 1878*

I feel like a visitor at the Conservatory; it has become so alien to me that I do not get angry or boil over anymore as I used to do during classes, but have a numb disgust for my male and female pupils and their work. The professors with their servile attitude to Rubinstein, with their petty quarrels and trivial interests, seem to be some sort of foreigners with whom I have nothing in common. I come to the Conservatory only to give lessons, leave at once after them, and try not to meet or speak to anyone. When I hear someone say, "Hello!" or "See who is here!" I disappear around the next corner as fast as I can.   [13]

THE GERMAN PREMIERE OF ONEGIN

From a letter to his nephew Vladimir Davydov, Hamburg, January 7, 1892

The only rehearsal took place yesterday and the performance was today. The opera had been perfectly rehearsed and quite nicely produced, but because of the changes

---

* Tchaikovsky resigned his teaching post later the same year.

in the recitatives that result from the use of the German text I could not help making mistakes, and in spite of everyone trying to persuade me I refused to conduct for fear of spoiling everything. Besides, the German conductor is not second-rate but quite a genius and is longing to conduct the first night. I heard him direct a wonderful performance of *Tannhäuser*. . . . His name is Mahler.   [14]

GENESIS OF THE SIXTH SYMPHONY

From a letter to Vladimir Davydov, Klin, February 11, 1893

I want to tell you about the excellent state of mind I'm in so far as my works are concerned. You know that I destroyed the symphony I had composed and partly orchestrated in the autumn. And a good thing too! There was nothing of interest in it—an empty play of sounds, without inspiration. Now, on my journey, the idea of a new symphony came to me, this time one with a program, but a program that will be a riddle to everyone. Let them try to solve it. . . . The program of this symphony is completely saturated with myself and quite often during my journey I cried profusely. Having returned, I have settled down to write the sketches and the work is going so intensely, so fast, that the first movement was ready in less than four days, and the others have taken shape in my head.   [15]

Antonín Dvořák
1841–1904

In 1892 Dvořák came to the United States to direct a new conservatory in New York City. While in the U.S., he sought out African American and Native American folk musics and made a conscious effort to absorb their influence. The effect on Dvořák's own music was modest—his style was already established and his folk sources were limited. But through example and advice he helped inspire an entire school of "nativist" composers and inaugurated a debate on the identity of American music that continued for decades.

DVOŘÁK'S MISSION IN AMERICA

From a letter to Mr. and Mrs. Josef Hlávka, Boston, November 27, 1892

The Americans expect great things of me and the main thing is, so they say, to show them to the promised land and kingdom of a new and independent art, in short, to create a national music. If the small Czech nation can have such musicians, they say, why could not they, too, when their country and people is so immense.   [1]

MUSIC IN AMERICA

From an article in Harper's Magazine, *February 1895*

The two American traits which must impress the foreign observer, I find, are the unbounded patriotism and capacity for enthusiasm of most Americans. Unlike the more diffident inhabitants of other countries, who do not "wear their hearts upon their sleeves," the citizens of America are always patriotic, and no occasion seems to be too serious or too slight for them to give expression to this feeling. Thus nothing better pleases the average American, especially the American youth, than to be able to say that this or that building, this or that new patent appliance, is the finest or the grandest in the world. This, of course, is due to that other trait—enthusiasm. The enthusiasm of most Americans for all things new is apparently without limit. It is the essence of what is called "push"—American push. Every day I meet with this quality in my pupils. They are unwilling to stop at anything. In the matters relating to their art they are inquisitive to a degree that they want to go to the bottom of all things at once. It is as if a boy wished to dive before he could swim.

At first, when my American pupils were new to me, this trait annoyed me, and I wished them to give more attention to the one matter in hand rather than to everything at once. But now I like it, for I have come to the conclusion that this youthful enthusiasm and eagerness to take up everything is the best promise for music in America. The same opinion, I remember, was expressed by the director of the conservatory in Berlin,* who, from his experience with American students of music, predicted that America within twenty or thirty years would become the first musical country.

Only when the people in general, however, begin to take as lively an interest in music and art as they now take in more material matters will the arts come into their own. Let the enthusiasm of the people once be excited, and patriotic gifts and bequests must surely follow.

It is a matter of surprise to me that all this has not come long ago. When I see how much is done in every other field by public-spirited men in America—how schools, universities, libraries, museums, hospitals, and parks spring up out of the ground and are maintained by generous gifts—I can only marvel that so little has been done for music.

——— ♪ ———

Art, of course, must always go a-begging, but why should this country alone, which is so justly famed for the generosity and public spirit of its citizens, close its door to the poor beggar? In the Old World this is not so. Since the days of Palestrina . . . princes and prelates have vied with each other in extending a generous hand to music. Since the days of Pope Gregory the Church has made music one of her own chosen arts. In Germany and Austria, princes like Esterházy, Lobkowitz, and Harrach, who supported Haydn and Beethoven, or the king of Bavaria, who did so much for Wagner, with many others, have helped create a demand for good music, which has since become universal, while in France all governments, be they monarchies, empires, or republics, have done their best to carry on the noble work that was begun by Louis XIV. Even the little republic of Switzerland annually sets aside a budget for the furtherance of music, literature, and the arts. . . .

* Probably the violinist Joseph Joachim (1831–1907), from 1868 the director of the Hochschule für Ausübende Tonkunst.

The great American republic alone, in its national government as well as in the several governments of the States, suffers art and music to go without encouragement. Trades and commerce are protected, funds are voted away for the unemployed, schools and colleges are endowed, but music must go unaided, and be content if she can get the support of a few private individuals. . . .

Not long ago a young man came to me and showed me his compositions. His talent seemed so promising that I at once offered him a scholarship in our school, but he sorrowfully confessed that he could not afford to become my pupil because he had to earn his living by keeping books in Brooklyn. Even if he came just two afternoons in the week, or on Saturday afternoon only, he said, he would lose his employment, on which he and others had to depend. I urged him to arrange the matter with his employer, but he only received the answer: "If you want to play, you can't keep books. You will have to drop one or the other." He dropped his music.

Our musical conservatory in Prague was founded but three generations ago, when a few nobles and patrons of music subscribed five thousand florins which was then the annual cost of maintaining the school. Yet that little school flourished and grew, so that now more than sixfold that amount is annually expended. Only lately a school for organ music has been added to the conservatory, so that the organists of our churches can learn to play their instruments at home, without having to go to other cities. Thus a school benefits the community in which it is. . . .

If a school of art can grow so in a country of but six million inhabitants, what much brighter prospects should it not have in a land of seventy millions? The important thing is to make a beginning, and in this the State should set an example.

They tell me that this cannot be done. I ask, why can't it be done? If the old commonwealths of Greece and Italy, and the modern republics of France and Switzerland, have been able to do this, why cannot America follow their example? The money certainly is not lacking. Constantly we see great sums of money spent for the material pleasures of the few, which, if devoted to the purposes of art, might give pleasure to thousands. If schools, art museums and libraries can be maintained at the public expense, why should not musical conservatories and playhouses? The function of the drama, with or without music, is not only to amuse, but to elevate and instruct while giving pleasure. Is it not in the interest of the State that this should be done in the most approved manner, so as to benefit all of the citizens? Let the owners of private playhouses give their performances for diversion only, let those who may, import singers who sing in foreign tongues, but let there be at least one intelligent power that will see to it that the people can hear and see what is best, and what can be understood by them, no matter how small the demand.

That such a system of performing classic plays and operas pleases the people was shown by the attitude of the populace in Prague. There the people collected money and raised subscriptions for over fifty years to build a national playhouse. In 1880 they at last had a sufficient amount and the "National Theatre" was accordingly built. It had scarcely been built when it was burned to the ground. But the people were not to be discouraged. Everybody helped, and before a fortnight was over more than a million had been collected, and the house was at once built up again, more magnificent than it was before.

In answer to such arguments I am told that there is no popular demand for good music in America. That is not so. Every concert in New York, Boston, Philadelphia, Chicago, or Washington, and most other cities, no doubt, disproves such a statement. American concert halls are as well filled as those of Europe, and, as a rule, the listeners—to judge them by their attentive conduct and subsequent expression of pleasure—are not a whit less appreciative. . . .

In a sense, of course, it is true that there is less of a demand for music in America than in certain other countries. Our common folk in Bohemia know this. When they come here, they leave their fiddles and other instruments at home, and none of the itinerant musicians with whom our country abounds would ever think of trying their luck over here. Occasionally, when I have met one of my countrymen whom I knew to be musical in this city of New York or in the West, and have asked him why he did not become a professional musician, I have usually received the answer, "Oh, music is not wanted in this land." This I can scarcely believe. Music is wanted wherever good people are, as the German poet has sung. It only rests with the leaders of the people to make a right beginning.

When this beginning is made, and when those who have musical talent find it worth their while to stay in America and to study and exercise their art as the business of their life, the music of America will soon become more national in its character.

———— ♪ ————

A while ago I suggested that inspiration for truly national music might be derived from the Negro melodies or Indian chants. I was led to take this view partly by the fact that the so-called plantation songs are indeed the most striking and appealing melodies that have yet been found on this side of the water, but largely by the observation that this seems to be recognized, though often unconsciously, by most Americans. All races have their distinctively national songs, which they at once recognize as their own, even if they have never heard them before. . . .

Undoubtedly the germs for the best in music lie hidden among all the races that are commingled in this great country. The music of the people is like a rare and lovely flower growing amidst encroaching weeds. Thousands pass it, while others trample it under foot, and thus the chances are that it will perish before it is seen by the one discriminating spirit who will prize it above all else. The fact that no one has as yet arisen to make the most of it does not prove that nothing is there.

Not so many years ago Slavic music was not known to the men of other races. A few men like Chopin, Glinka, Moniuszko, Smetana, Rubinstein, and Tchaikovsky, with a few others, were able to create a Slavic school of music. Chopin alone caused the music of Poland to be known and prized by all lovers of music. Smetana did the same for Bohemians. Such national music, I repeat, is not created out of nothing. It is discovered and clothed in new beauty, just as the myths and the legends of a people are brought to light and crystallized in undying verse by the master poets. All that is needed is a delicate ear, a retentive memory, and the power to weld the fragments of former ages together in one harmonious whole. . . . The music of the people, sooner or later, will command attention and creep into the books of composers.

An American reporter once told me that the most valuable talent a journalist could possess was a "nose for news." Just so the musician must prick his ear for music. Nothing must be too low or too insignificant for the musician. When he walks he should listen to every whistling boy, every street singer or blind organ-grinder. I myself am often so fascinated by these people that I can scarcely tear myself away, for every now and then I catch a strain or hear the fragments of a recurring melodic theme that sound like the voice of the people. These things are worth preserving, and no one should be above making a lavish use of all such suggestions. It is a sign of barrenness, indeed, when such characteristic bits of music exist and are not heeded by the learned musicians of the age.   [2]

WAGNER

Remark to his student Josef Michl, 1893

You can talk a great deal about Wagner and you can criticize a great deal, too—but he is undefeatable. What Wagner did nobody did before him and nobody can take away from him. Music will go its way, will pass Wagner by, but Wagner will remain, just like the statue of that poet from whom they still learn at school today—Homer. And such a Homer was Wagner!   [3]

BRAHMS

From a letter to the publisher Simrock, October 10, 1883

What a heart and mind the man has! You know how reserved he is as regards his creative work even towards his dearest friends, but he has never been so with me. My wish to hear something from his new symphony [the Third] he granted at once and played the first and last movements. . . . What lovely melodies are there! It is pure love, and on hearing it your heart melts within you!   [4]

HIS "AMERICAN" WORKS

From a letter to Dr. Emil Kozánek, New York, April 12, 1893

I have not much work at school so that I have enough time for my own work and am now just finishing my E minor symphony [*From the New World*]. I take great pleasure in it and it will differ very considerably from my others. Well, the *influence* of America must be felt by everyone who has any "nose" at all.   [5]

From a letter to Dr. Kozánek, Spillville, Iowa, September 19, 1893

I hear that the papers at home are writing as if I wished to stay here in America for good! Oh no, never! [But] I am very well off here, God be praised, I am in good health and am working well and I know that, as for my new symphony, the F major string quartet and the quintet (composed here in Spillville)—I should never have written these works "just so" if I hadn't seen America.   [6]

Edvard Grieg
1843–1907

After studies at the Leipzig Conservatory and with Niels Gade in Copenhagen, Grieg turned his skills toward the development of a folk-based Norwegian art music. An international career as composer and performer was launched when, at twenty-five, he was the soloist in the premiere of his piano concerto. He became a national figure in Norway, achieving success in songs, chamber works, and a modest number of symphonic pieces.

MOZART AND WAGNER

From an article in the Century Magazine, *November 1897*

"What kind of face would Bach, Handel, Haydn, and Mozart make after hearing an opera by Wagner?" asks an English writer. I shall not attempt to answer for the first three, but it is safe to say that Mozart—the universal genius whose mind was free from Philistinism and one-sidedness, would not only open his eyes wide, but would be as delighted as a child with all the new acquisitions in the departments of drama and orchestra. In this light must Mozart be viewed. . . . Where he is greatest, he embraces all times.

In Bach, Beethoven, and Wagner we admire principally the depth and energy of the human mind; in Mozart, the divine instinct. His highest inspirations seem untouched by human labor. Unlike the masters cited, no trace of struggle remains in the forms in which he molded his material. Mozart has the childish, happy, Aladdin nature which overcomes all difficulties as in play. He creates like a god, without pain. . . .

When we compare Mozart and Wagner, the truth of the proverb that "extremes meet" forces itself upon us. That these two masters represented the "extremes" is easily understood by any lover of music, but it may perhaps be necessary to indicate where they "meet." Truly Weber may be regarded as Wagner's predecessor; but if Gluck is named, and not improperly, as the man on whose shoulders Wagner stands, then we must not forget how much he owes to Mozart. For the greatness of Mozart lies in the fact that his influence in the dramatic part of music extends to our time. I have in mind, for example, the developed recitative where Mozart more and more trod paths which it remained for Wagner to develop in his dialogue still further for the modern music drama. Certain recitatives of Donna Anna and Elvira in *Don Giovanni* are the originals after which our whole conception of the recitative has been molded.   [1]

SCHUMANN AND MENDELSSOHN

From an article in the Century Magazine, *January 1894*

The influence Schumann's art has exercised and is exercising in modern music cannot be overestimated. In conjunction with Chopin and Liszt, he dominates at this time the whole literature of the piano, while the piano compositions of his great contemporary Mendelssohn, which were once exalted at Schumann's expense, would seem to be vanishing from the concert program. . . . In orchestral compositions Mendelssohn still maintains his position, while Schumann has taken a place at his side as his equal. I say his equal, for surely no significance can be attached to the circumstance that a certain part of the younger generation (Wagnerians chiefly) have fallen into the habit of treating Schumann, as an orchestral composer, *de haut en bas*. These enthusiasts, equipped with an excess of self-esteem, and holding it to be their duty to level everything which, according to their opinion, interferes with the free view of the Bayreuth master, venture to shrug their shoulders at Schumann's instrumentation, to deny his symphonic sense, to attack the structure of his periods and his plastic faculty. They do not even hesitate to characterize his entire orchestral composition as a failure; and in order to justify this indictment, they propound the frank declaration that his orchestral works are only instrumentalized piano music. The fact that Schumann did not occupy himself with Mendelssohn's formally piquant effects, and was not an orchestral virtuoso in the style of Wagner, is turned upside-down in the effort totally to deny him both the plastic sense and the faculty of instrumentation. At the same time they refrain from recognizing all the ideal advantages that primarily make Schumann the world-conquering force he has now virtually become. . . .

Much is whispered in corners about the attitude of Schumann and Mendelssohn toward each other. One thing is, however, likely to impress the unprejudiced observer as curious, viz., that Schumann's writings furnish numerous and striking evidences of his boundless admiration for Mendelssohn, while the latter in his many letters does not once mention Schumann or his art. This cannot be due to accident. Whether Mendelssohn was really silent, or whether the editor of his letters, out of regard for his memory, has chosen to omit all references to Schumann, is of slight consequence. This, however, is beyond dispute: his silence speaks, and we of posterity have the right to draw the clue to a judgment of the opinions which the two masters entertained of each other. Of petty envy on Mendelssohn's part there can be no suspicion. He was of too pure and noble a character to be animated by such a sentiment; and, moreover, his fame was too great and too well established in comparison with Schumann's. But his horizon was too contracted to enable him to see Schumann as the man he was. How perfectly comprehensible! He had his forte in clear delineation, in classical harmony; and where Schumann fell short of his requirements in this respect, his honesty forbade him to feign a recognition he could not candidly grant.   [2]

SCHUMANN'S SONGS

From an article in the Century Magazine, *January 1894*

If there is anything at all that Schumann has written which has become, and has deserved to become, world literature, it is surely his songs. All civilized nations have made them their own. And there is probably in our own day scarcely a youth interested in music to whom they are not, in one way or another, interwoven with his most intimate ideals. Schumann is the *poet,* contrasting in this respect with his greatest successor, Brahms, who is primarily *musician,* even in his songs.

It cannot be maintained that Schumann was the first to accord a conspicuous role to the accompaniment of his songs. Schubert had anticipated him as no other of his predecessors had done, in making the piano depict the mood. But what Schubert began, Schumann further developed; woe to the singer who tries to render Schumann without keeping a close watch over what the piano is doing, even to the minutest shades of sound. I have no faith in a renderer of Schumann's songs who lacks appreciation of the fact that the piano has fully as great a claim upon interest and study as the voice of the singer. Nay, I would venture to assert that, up to a certain point, he who cannot play Schumann, cannot sing him either. In his treatment of the piano, Schumann was, furthermore, the first who, in a modern spirit, utilized the relation between song and accompaniment which Wagner has later developed to a degree that fully proves what importance he attached to it. I refer to the carrying of the melody by the piano, or the orchestra, while the voice is engaged in the recitative. Heaven preserve me, however, from insinuating that Wagner consciously could have received an impulse from Schumann! A dyed-in-the-wool Wagnerian would, of course, regard even a hint of such a possibility as an outrageous want of respect for the master of Bayreuth which would amount almost to an insult. But, for all that, it is a fact that contemporaries influence each other whether they want to or not. That is one of nature's eternal laws, to which we are all subject. [3]

Nikolai Rimsky-Korsakov
1844–1908

A naval officer by profession, Rimsky-Korsakov also taught at the conservatory in St. Petersburg. His musical style grew out of Glinka's. In orchestration he looked to Berlioz, eventually becoming such a master that his orchestration textbook was widely used in Russia and the West. With Glazunov he spent much effort bringing the scores of Musorgsky, Borodin, and others into line with accepted practice, diluting their originality but gaining them exposure.

FORMAL STUDY

From a letter to Semyon Kruglikov, November 9, 1880

One can learn by oneself; sometimes one needs advice, but one has also to learn, that is, one must not neglect harmony and counterpoint and the development of a good technique and a clean leading subject. All of us, myself and Borodin and Balakirev, but especially Cui and Musorgsky, neglected this. I consider that I caught myself in time and made myself get down to work. Owing to such deficiencies in technique Balakirev writes little; Borodin, with difficulty; Cui, sloppily; Musorgsky, messily and often nonsensically; and all this constitutes the very regrettable specialty of the Russian school. [1]

ORCHESTRATION

From the preface to Principles of Orchestration, *1896–1908*

It is a great mistake to say: this composer scores well, or that composition is well orchestrated, for orchestration is *part of the very soul of the work*. A work is thought out in terms of the orchestra, certain tone colors being inseparable from it in the mind of its creator and native to it from the hour of its birth. Could the essence of Wagner's music be divorced from its orchestration? One might as well say that a picture is well *drawn* in colors.

More than one classical and modern composer has lacked the capacity to orchestrate with imagination and power; the secret of color has remained outside the range of his creative faculty. Does it follow that these composers do not *know how* to orchestrate? Many among them have had greater knowledge of the subject than the mere colorist. Was Brahms ignorant of orchestration? And yet nowhere in his works do we find evidence of brilliant tone or picturesque fancy. The truth is that his thoughts did not turn toward color; his mind did not exact it.

The power of subtle orchestration is a secret impossible to transmit, and the composer who possesses this secret should value it highly and never debase it to the level of a mere collection of formulas learned by heart. . . .

As a starting point I lay down the following fundamental axioms:

I. *In the orchestra there is no such thing as ugly quality of tone.*

II. *Orchestral writing should be easy to play;* a composer's work stands the best chance when the parts are well written.

III. *A work should be written for the size of orchestra that is to perform it,* not for some imaginary body; many composers persist in doing so, introducing brass instruments in unusual keys upon which the music is impracticable because it is not played in the key the composer intends.

It is difficult to devise any method of learning orchestration without a master. As a general rule it is best to advance by degrees from the simplest scoring to the most complicated.

The student will probably pass through the following phases: (1) The phase during which he puts his entire faith in percussion instruments, believing that beauty of sound emanates entirely from this branch of the orchestra—this is the earliest stage; (2) The phase when he acquires a passion for the harp, using it in every possible chord; (3) The phase during which he adores the woodwinds and horns, using stopped notes in conjunction with strings, muted or pizzicato; (4) The more advanced period, when he has come to recognize that the string group is the richest and most expressive of all.

When the student works alone, he must try to avoid the pitfalls of the first three phases. The best plan is to study full scores and listen to an orchestra, score in hand. But it is difficult to decide what music should be studied and heard. Music of all ages, certainly, but principally the fairly modern. This music will teach the student how to score; classical music will prove of negative value to him. Weber, Mendelssohn, Meyerbeer *(The Prophet)*, Berlioz, Glinka, Wagner, Liszt, and modern French and Russian composers—these will prove his best guides. It is useless for a Berlioz or a Gevaert to quote examples from the works of Gluck. The musical idiom is too old-fashioned and strange to modern ears; such examples are of no further use today. The same may be said of Mozart and of Haydn, the father of modern orchestration.

The gigantic figure of Beethoven stands apart. His music abounds in countless leonine leaps of orchestral imagination, but his technique, viewed in detail, remains much inferior to his titanic conception. The use of the trumpets, standing out above the rest of the orchestra, the difficult and unhappy intervals he gives to the horns, the distinctive features of the string parts and his often highly colored manner of employing the woodwinds are features that will cause the student of Beethoven to stumble upon a thousand and one points of contradiction.

It is a mistake to think that the beginner will light upon no simple and instructive examples in modern music, in Wagner and others. On the contrary, clearer, and better examples are to be found among modern composers than in what is called the range of classical music.   [2]

MUSORGSKY

Undated statement in Gerald Abraham's biography, 1945

If Musorgsky's compositions are fated to last unfaded for fifty years after his death, then an archaeologically exact edition can be used. In the meantime what was needed was an edition for performance, for practical artistic purposes, for the making known of his great talent, not for the study of his personality and artistic transgressions.   [3]

WAGNER AND *SIEGFRIED*

From a letter, 1901

I have been ardently reading the score of *Siegfried*. As always, after a long interval, Wagner's music repelled me. I am outraged by his various aural aberrations, which surpass the limit of the harmonically feasible. Cacophony and nonsense are scattered in *Siegfried* all over the score. What terrible harm Wagner did by interspersing his pages of genius with harmonic and modulatory outrages to which both young and old are gradually becoming accustomed and which have procreated d'Indy and Richard Strauss!   [4]

Gabriel Fauré
1845–1924

Taking the disciplined technique of his teacher Saint-Saëns, Fauré fashioned a personal style whose balance and taste did not preclude a wide range of expressive possibilities. He succeeded Saint-Saëns as organist of the Madeleine in Paris and taught composition at the Conservatoire, where his students included Maurice Ravel, Georges Enesco, and Nadia Boulanger. For fifteen years starting in 1905 he was the conservatory's director. During this same period he wrote reviews for Le Figaro, *which reveal a breadth of perceptiveness and appreciation.*

MOZART

From a review, June 1, 1909

Mozart's music is particularly difficult to perform. His admirable clarity exacts absolute cleanness; the slightest incorrectness in it stands out like black on white. As I heard Saint-Saëns say lately: "It is music in which all the notes must be heard." Essentially simple, natural, it demands a simple, natural expression as well; in other words, that to which its interpreters, even the best-intentioned, have least accustomed us. [1]

CARMEN

From a review, December 24, 1904

That Merimée's novelette, transported onto the stage of the Favart Theatre in 1875, could have surprised and disconcerted the public, that it should have seemed scarcely to conform to the traditions of the *opéra comique* is understandable. What is not understandable is that Bizet's music, so utterly clear, so sincere, so colorful, sensitive, and charming should not have conquered the public from the outset; dramatic eloquence of such pathos, so vigorous and direct, should immediately have moved the audience.

This music had to achieve the extraordinary reputation it acquired abroad, before our ears, our spirits, and our hearts finally opened to it. It was necessary for time to intervene here.

Fortunately, time could accomplish its task of justice without the admirable qualities in Bizet's score being altered an iota. The youth, joy, passion, and life that it contains remain as overflowing as they are unalterable. And the indifference and hostility of yesteryear have given way to the most brilliant, most universal favor.

This does not mean, however, that the lesson has proved profitable. The injustice of which Bizet was victim will crop up anew along the road of other artists, until the end of time. [2]

RELIGIOUS MUSIC: FRANCK AND GOUNOD

From an article, 1922

What music is religious? What music is not? To try to resolve the question is quite hazardous, since no matter how deeply sincere a musician's religious feeling may be, it is through his personal taste that he expresses it and not according to rules one can fix. Every classification in this field of ideas has always seemed arbitrary to me. Can one maintain, for example, that among those religious compositions of César Franck that reach the loftiest heights (up to the very quiver of angels' wings), there might not be a few that, because of their very smoothness, are not absolutely free of sensuality? On the other hand, doesn't that child voice which soars alone to sing Gloria in excelsis Deo in the *Messe solennelle* of Gounod create an effect of exquisite purity? And because the text of the Agnus Dei inspired him to accents of ineffable tenderness, can one say that Gounod profaned the text? I cite these two musicians because the religious style of the one has so often been contrasted with the religious style of the other, and because I am trying to show that in the realm of truly musical and beautiful works, it is almost impossible to draw a line of demarcation between those that are religious and those that "savor of heresy."   [3]

PUCCINI

From a review, December 29, 1906

Puccini is the most famous of the musicians who today represent the Italian school; he is one of the most gifted, certainly the best equipped and the most experienced. Though he translates moving situations by means one may find too uniform, though accents, emphatic and often wanting in invention, take too important a place in his works, on the other hand, he excels in scenes of movement; his verve, his taste for harmonic and orchestral quests, his manner of adorning the most slender ideas with charming details, present a feast of pleasure to the listener.   [4]

SALOME

From a review, May 9, 1907

The novelty that primarily distinguishes the score of *Salome* is that Mr. Richard Strauss carries over into it the particular aesthetic his symphonic poems embody; that is, the principles of musical description and analysis forced to their extreme limits. *Salome* is a symphonic poem with vocal parts added. Here there is not a character whose physical individuality, whose morality (or immorality), whose thoughts and acts are not minutely translated, almost to the point of naïveté. Atmosphere and color are portrayed in their finest nuances, all by means of mediocre themes, it is true, but developed, worked, interwoven with such marvelous skill that their intrinsic interest is exceeded by the magic of an orchestral technique of real genius, until these themes—mediocre, as I said—end by acquiring character, power, and almost emotion.

This cleverness, this prodigious facility, has its drawbacks. The instability of the music, the fleeting changes of orchestral effects, always new, always arresting, scarcely absorbed before replaced by others, end by creating a perpetual dazzle that tires not only the spirit, but—does this seem absurd?—even the eyes. Besides, is it because of the particularly brutal character of the subject, or is it solely to shock that Mr. Strauss has introduced so many cruel dissonances that defy all explanation? Is it to parallel Good and Evil, which run side by side in the drama, that he has juxtaposed the least reconcilable tonalities in his music? It will be said that his bewitching orchestra makes everything permissible, which is often true; I could not help thinking so in suffering certain terrible discords, while Salome, kissing the lips of the beheaded prophet says: "There is a bitter taste on thy mouth."

Nevertheless, as far as I am concerned, these criticisms do not denote weaknesses, but only musical means with which I cannot sympathize, in a work vigorously conceived, executed with skill and virtuosity of the first order, and which contains some very impressive pages: for example, the first appearance of Jochanaan from the cistern, Salome's dance—a veritable little drama within a big drama—the extraordinary and comic discussion of the five Jews, and especially the final scene, one of genuine beauty.   [5]

CHAPTER EIGHT

Leoš Janáček

Giacomo Puccini

Hugo Wolf

Gustav Mahler

Frederick Delius

Claude Debussy

Richard Strauss

Carl Nielsen

Ferruccio Busoni

Erik Satie

Leoš Janáček
1854–1928

Janáček spent most of his life in the Moravian city of Brno, where he founded an organ school and led it for almost forty years. He had a deep interest in folk music and in the "melodies" of Czech speech, which he transcribed in musical notation. In 1917 Janáček developed an infatuation for Kamila Stösslová, a married woman thirty-eight years his junior. Over the last eleven years of his life he sent her some seven hundred letters. Through most of this time Stösslová remained aloof, the bewildered inspiration for a sheaf of remarkable works.

THE MUSICALLY GIFTED

From an article in Moravská orlice, *Brno, July 1903*

To the musically gifted, music is the most fitting expression, and the most effective impulse of the energy of intellectual life. That is why I think that the foundation of musical talent lies at the very root of intellectual life, in the physiological faculties of man. Music cheers him, saddens him, makes him weep. To get to hear music he recognizes no barriers in long journeys, spares no time or money: he would rather starve.

A tune springs to his mind and he cannot for the life of him get rid of it! It accompanies him everywhere, grows inside him. It is like a little canopy over his soul that does not let a foreign word through.

He will analyze by ear and faithfully interpret what for others is a chaos of sound. He will play out what he has heard, even without a teacher.

His whole body bears witness to his feeling for every tone: this is the artistic temperament that makes *conductors* and spirited virtuosi. . . .

A snippet of a note, once heard, does not vanish as fast for a musically gifted man as for an ordinary man. It shines within him for a long time and is easily regenerated and strengthened.

All of this—regardless of how long it takes to become aware of the note—explains in particular the mutual *penetration of notes,* their adhesion in a chord, their fusion in a key. Only under such conditions is it possible by education to reach rich harmonic and modulatory thought.

Each note of a tune awakens a retinue of notes that at once announces itself by a chord and is arranged according to the notes' meaning and importance: this is *a gift for harmonization.*

Even a child, if musically gifted, will be able to play an accompaniment to a familiar tune.

I regard this gift for harmonization as the chief proof of a genuine musical talent. It must be ascertained before anyone devotes himself to music as a profession.

FOLK MUSIC

From the essay Moravian Folk Songs from the Musical Point of View,
Prague, 1901

The proof that folk songs originated from words lies in the special character of their rhythm. There is no possibility of dividing them into barlines. The rhythm of folk songs, unbelievably rich in variety, can be put into order only by the words. It is impossible to compose a melody and then add words. In Moravian folk songs, the unusual rhythm makes this especially impossible. Each beat in our songs is reasonable and convincing. Each rhythm is timed and accentuated and the whole song sublimated even from the metric point of view. In every note of each song there is, as I see it, a fragment of an idea. If you leave out a single note from the melody, you perceive that it has become incomplete and has ceased to make sense. . . .

Folk songs are as beautiful as the language from which they spring and are dependent on the locality in which they are sung, on the time at which they are sung, on the occasion, and mood in which they are sung. These various circumstances change the melody and rhythm of the songs. Among the people, there are no singers who would use the songs on occasions when they are not apt; that is to say, in sympathy with the human heart and the human spirit. For this reason, many songs are sung only very rarely. But fortunately, among the people, there are a great number of singers who preserve the songs in their memories.   [2]

From a speech, London, May 3, 1926

In folk song, there is the whole man: body, soul, landscape, all of it, all. He who grows from folk song, grows into a whole man. . . . If I took a Czech, or an English, French, or any other folk song and did not know that it is a Czech, an English, or a French song, I could not tell what belongs to whom. Folk song has one spirit, because it possesses the pure man, with God's own culture, and not the one grafted on him. Therefore I think that if our art music can grow out of this folk source, all of us will embrace each other in these products of art music. It will be common to all of us: it will unite us. Folk song can bind the nation—indeed nations—can bind all of mankind into one spirit, one kind of happiness, one kind of bliss. This is why I was so pleased when, suddenly, I heard an English folk song. At once I was close to the English soul; at once I was its friend.   [3]

SPEECH MELODIES

From an article in Hlídka, *Brno, 1905*

The melodic curves of speech are an expression of the complete organism and of all phases of its spiritual activities. They demonstrate whether a man is stupid or intelligent, sleepy or awake, tired or alert. They tell us whether he is a child or an old man, whether it is morning or evening, light or darkness, heat or frost, and disclose whether a person is alone or in company. The art of dramatic writing is to compose a melodic curve that will, as if by magic, reveal immediately a human being in one definite phase of his existence.   [4]

From an article in Literární svět, Prague, March 8, 1928

For me, music as it comes out of the instruments, from the repertoire, whether it is by Beethoven or anyone else, has little truth in it. Perhaps it was like this, strange as it seemed, that whenever someone spoke to me, I may have not grasped the words, but I grasped the rise and fall of the notes! At once I knew what the person was like: I knew how he or she felt, whether he or she was lying, whether he or she was upset. As the person talked to me in a conventional conversation, I knew, I *heard* that, inside himself, the person perhaps wept. Sounds, the intonation of human speech, indeed of every living being, have had for me the deepest truth. And you see—this was my *need in life*. The whole body has to work—it is something different from just working the keys.

I have been collecting speech melodies since 1879; I have an enormous collection. You see, these speech melodies are windows into peoples' souls—and what I would like to emphasize is this: for *dramatic music* they are of great importance.   [5]

"MORAVANY! MORAWAAN!"

From an article in Lidové noviny, Brno, April 1918*

f Mo - ra - va - ny! Mo - ra - waan!

In the heading, I envisage a Czech name in its Czech version next to its German one.

That was how the guard called out the name of the railway station on 18 August 1917.

How the different "spirit" of both languages shone through here. Our version is ranged in the notes of a warm triad D flat–F–A flat. The German version cut harshly and roughly in the same triad, with a dissonance of a seventh; it has crushed the third syllable and torn off the last one; it has ground into grumbling the sweetness of the first two. In the Czech version you hear a song that winds along in equal lengths within a rainbow of colors; o-a-a-y.

The guard, breathless, rushed along the train.

Somewhere from the end of the snake formed by the train, through the noise of the station, only the musical tag of the name shouted by the guard still reaches me.   [6]

---

* The article was written immediately after the dress rehearsal for the first performance of his opera *Jenufa* in Vienna. Janáček was shaken by hearing German words sung to melodies he had imbued with Czeck inflections.

QUOTATIONS IN CONVERSATION

From an essay in Lidové noviny, *Brno, October 1924*

When, during a conversation, we quote the words of someone else, we are halfway to a theatrical performance.

We quote the words in such a way as to bring alive, before our eyes, a particular person known to us.

We even quote the speed of speech, a thin little voice or a coarse one; a singsong tone, a nasal intonation, or a snuffling voice. We might quote an angry expression, a reproachful look, or a look of unctuous tenderness. And we quote even the tonal register of the speech and its melodic rise and fall.

In that moment it is as if our acquaintance comes alive within us, whether he or she is far away or nearby, alive or already passed away.

There are many examples in life—and I have plenty of evidence.   [7]

CHORDS

From an essay in Listy hudební matice, *Prague, 1924/5*

By the analysis and elimination of affects—the source from which the chord is born, whose rippling waves it carries forth, through which it is revealed, through which it shines, rings out, changes, grows, and dies away—through this I learn the reason for the chord's existence.

For me, a chord is a being come alive: a blood-stained flower of the musical art. I know when I write it that pain grips my heart; that the heart moans, wails, falls hard on the ground, crushes, is fragmented by the mist, hardens into granite. What do I care for the borrowed attributes *beautiful* or *ugly*!

In a flash of life, the chord's essence corresponds to my being.

Even the tame look of a chick, the searching eye of a hawk, an ardent kiss, a handshake grown cool, even the dreaming, pale blue of the forget-me-not, even the burning fire of the wild poppy, evoke a chord within me.   [8]

INSPIRATION

From answers to a questionnaire in Národní listy, *Prague, December 1921*

An idea, when it arises, acknowledges neither spare time nor time that is tied down. It wakes you from sleep, slows or quickens your step during a walk. You stop and stare, in thought—it lifts you above your immediate surroundings.

As the idea grows, you lose yourself.

When it becomes clear, you hold fast to it, you do not allow it to be smothered, you cherish it for hours in the noise and hum of the streets.

Does the idea ask whether I have spare time or not?

I am its victim everywhere, all the time.

When the work is done, only the horizon of the thought changes.

I reach into every phenomenon's region of sound: even a stone that cracks in the heat or the frost.

With curiosity, I follow through in my consciousness and in the consciousness of others the mint of phonetic phenomena, misted over with complications.   [9]

TRUTH IN MUSIC

From a letter to Kamila Stösslová, Brno, May 18, 1925

They have produced my *Cunning Little Vixen* [in Prague] but not as I would have wished. . . . I had been looking forward to it for months, yet it did not come off as I had expected. One thing is certain; you cannot persuade anyone with art. It is like beating an eiderdown with your fist; it merely bulges somewhere else. They applaud everything. And yet there is only one truth in music. A truth everyone is after but only a few have attained.   [10]

BEETHOVEN

Contribution to an article about a Beethoven symposium held in March 1927

When I was twenty-five years old, I had Beethoven's *Missa solemnis* at my fingertips. I conducted it in Brno on April 2, 1879. But to tell the truth, Beethoven's works left me cold; they never took me out of myself. They never carried me to a world of ecstasy. I came to know them too well, too soon. But this was also the reason why they had such possesion of my soul. In their broad flow I could feel the power of the firmament, see the sun bathing the clouds in melody and banishing the shadows; and over all this, the moon pouring out her loneliness. But what of it—I want to be in direct contact with the clouds, I want to feast my eyes on the blue of the sky, I want to gather the sun's rays into my hands, I want to plunge myself in shadow, I want to pour out my longings to the full: all directly.

In the choir of the Leipzig Conservatoire, I was made [a] first bass, Reinecke was the conductor of Beethoven's *Missa solemnis*—it was toward the end of that same year, 1879. But I escaped from the choir, failed to attend rehearsals, and avoided the performance of the work.   [11]

SMETANA

From a Smetana memorial volume, 1908/9

My memory of Smetana resembles a picture of the way that children imagine God—in the clouds. It was at the Zofín concert, in what was, for Smetana, the fateful year of 1874. I was standing near the orchestra. The performance had just come to an end and the deafening storm of applause came together in one exclamation: "Smetana!" All of a sudden so many people shimmered past and shoved that the air all but darkened. They led the ailing composer up the staircase. Only his face imprinted itself onto my soul. I still have it clearly in my mind: however, always as through murmuring and mist. Certainly my eyes absorbed only him— to all else I was deaf and blind.   [12]

Article for the centenary of Smetana's birth, March 1924

There are paths where you know whom you will meet.
I pass by them all, except the one on which Smetana's creative mind advanced.

His creative mind appears to me to be more *vigorous*—
No wonder that its music follows the bleat of bagpipes,
it follows the song of the lark in flight,
it toys with the smugglers' whistle.
But its music clings also to the rumble behind the stove,
it tunes itself to the thumping on the door and the creaking of the hinge,
it follows the lash of the flails, the silver zigzag of the lightning,
it trembles with the daybreak of the sun's rays,
gathers up the pale shine of the moon.
It hastens in the shimmer and rush of Vltava's waves.
Where has it not stopped in all these parts!

It is more *Czech*—
The tones of the flute rock the first wavelets of the Vltava, gathering up on their way the flowers of the meadows and the shadows of the woods. Near the steep Vysehrad, visions of the past are brought alive by the sound of the harp.

With a clash of arms, the clusters of chords fill *Šárka,* open up the bowels of the Blaník: they rise with the strength of Tábor. The rhythms in the music of Vašek, of the marriage broker, the little bagpiper, of Kalina, Malina, and so on grow out of their characters: and Smetana's other rhythms are as if their beds were made on Czech native soil. *The Czechness of the music lies where it is almost possible to measure it.* Music will have its share of Czechness, as will the character of the people, the region, and the land where they live.

His creative mind is *softer, more tender*—
Smetana's music found in every phenomenon a spot
where there would be fire, wailing,
Longing,
joy,
angry pressure,
prophecy—all through song.
Through song he makes Mařenka and Vendulka tender, makes even Libuše and Přemysl tender; even the Devil, the people and their region. Thus, with this broad emotional embrace, Smetana's work becomes *national*.

It is more *cosmopolitan*—
He knew the tonal language of the West, of Liszt, of Richard Wagner. In his music, the accumulated tradition of styles also surged forward; the reforming aims glimmered there.

It is not the structuring of his works, but the refraction of light and color and the echo within, the sprouting into hundreds of wonderful motifs linked together, that dazzles.

He is *powerful*—

Each of his works reaches both the horizon and the firmament of its subject.

Impossible to get higher, to make a broader sweep.

It would be foolish to want another *Bartered Bride,* another *Má vlast.* Where he stands with his work there is no room for anyone else. But he casts no smothering shadow. Every composition can grow alongside him, freely and with the same verve.

In his early works, his music is embodied only in notes.

In Smetana's late works, it seems that the music can be grasped by sight and touch.

The ground is not hard enough for him,
> the gale not fierce enough,
>> the lightning not dazzling enough,
>>> the storm not sufficiently deafening,
>>>> the sun not red-hot,

no phenomenon is mysterious enough: he favors everything with his music.

This is where the philosophy of Smetana's music begins. Matter is a multifarious substance; it is the ray of light or a musical note in the expression of grief, in merrymaking, in the form of thought. The exploitation of this *materialism,* this cleaving in thought of man to man, of age to age, is the power of evolution in Smetana's music. This materialism is almost tangible within the work of its creator. The shining light of Bedřich Smetana will stay among us always.   [13]

DVOŘÁK

From an article in Hudební listy, Brno, January 1, 1888

I am convinced that Mr. Dvořák's scores are masterly studies in counterpoint. He is not satisfied with the mere harmonization of a single melody in a clear and interesting way; he combines two, three, or even five varying themes. I could compare his scores to a good picture: a single idea recurring in many groups of scattered figures, each face bearing its own particular characteristics. Similarly, the pages of Dvořák's scores are filled with interesting figures that unite to produce a great harmonic thought, without, however, a single one resembling another. A musician grows attached to Dvořák's scores. What is most important, Dvořák never leaves his figures perpetually in one voice; hardly has one of them claimed our interest than another rises up for notice. We are kept in constant excitement.   [14]

From an article in Hudební revue, 1911

Do you know what it is like when someone takes your words out of your mouth before you speak them? This is how I always felt in Dvořák's company. I can interchange his personality with his work. He has taken his melodies from my heart. Nothing on earth can sever such a bond. . . .

Like a lightning flash, one moment enlightened me for all time as to the secret of his creativity. He had no expression harsh enough for Škroup's "Where is my homeland"—he would have composed a new Czech anthem —and yet in a short time he composes, on Škroup's themes, music for *Kajetán Tyl*! Irritated, he leafs through Berlioz's Requiem, and next thing the publication of his Requiem is announced. I see him with Liszt's *St. Elizabeth,* and in a short time London is listening to Dvořák's *St. Ludmila.*

Only a great composer is able to retrace the steps of his great predecessors. Did the same feelings of exasperation kindle the creation of his other, his chamber works—and if so which, and how deeply? [15]

BERG

From an article in Literární svět, *Prague, March 8, 1928*

Let us mention Berg's *Wozzeck.* Injustice—what an injustice! They wrong *Wozzeck.* They have wronged Berg terribly. He is a dramatist of astonishing importance, of deep truth. Speak out! Let him speak out! Today, he is distraught. He suffers. As if stopped in his tracks. Not another note.* And each of his notes has been dipped in blood. [16]

THE EXCURSIONS OF MR. BROUČEK

From a letter to Kamila Stösslová, Brno, March 12, 1920

So do you know what that Brouček is?

A quite ordinary fellow; he gripes at the whole world and drowns his whole life in a glass of beer. He's not up to anything good on earth.

You ask: "So why did you choose such a person for an opera?"

Because I wanted everyone to be disgusted by him, for him to be a laughing-stock, a warning!

The Russians also have such a "spineless" man; he's called Oblomov.† Really, every second Russian was an Oblomov—and where did that lead them! A terrible revolution is cleansing it now with rivers of blood.

That's why I expose Brouček—as a warning. There are also many, many *Broučeks* on all sides in our nation!

The stomach alone is everything to them.

So my dear *Brouček* gets drunk again, somewhere on Hradcany he falls asleep and has a dream: He's flying to the moon!

There he lands. Oh, horrors! The people there feed only on the scent of flowers. They give Brouček only flowers to smell. And now a female Moon-being falls in love with him there! Bloodless, a body like gauze.

Well, more about it next time. [17]

---

* Janáček exaggerates here; Berg had recently finished the *Lyric Suite* and was beginning work on *Lulu.*

† The apathetic protagonist of an 1859 novel by Goncharov.

RESPONSE TO A BIOGRAPHICAL SKETCH

Letter to Jan Mikota, Brno, April 18, 1926*

I read your story about myself in the train. My worst enemy could not have done it better.

1. First of all, I presume I am a Czech composer and not only a *Moravian* one as they nowadays like to pretend in Prague.

2. I was Professor of Composition for the master class of the Conservatoire in Prague and not in Brno.

3. I am a Doctor of Philosophy of the Masaryk University in Brno, and not of the Charles University in Prague.

4. After having studied the musical side of the language, I am certain that all melodic and rhythmic mysteries of music in general are to be explained solely from rhythmic and melodic points of view on the basis of the melodic curves of speech. No one can become an opera composer who has not studied living speech. I wish that this could be understood once and for all. I have studied this and am therefore able to compose dramatic music—that is to say, opera.

5. Is it therefore understood that this attitude is detrimental to my instrumental works? Therefore the Quartet is bad, *Youth,* the Violin Sonata, the Concertino—all that London has chosen is therefore bad?

6. I proclaimed freedom in harmonic progressions long before Debussy, and really do not need French impressionism.

Please see that all this is put right immediately. That is why I am writing to you at once tonight.   [18]

Giacomo Puccini
1858–1924

As a child, Puccini was indifferent to music. But with four generations of composers on his father's side, the family demanded there be a fifth. Eventually his interest was kindled, and his progress from then on was rapid. In his work habits Puccini was methodical, searching for a new libretto as soon as he had finished the last project, although it was not uncommon for him to change his mind and discard a new subject as quickly as he had embraced it.

PELLÉAS ET MÉLISANDE

From a letter to the publisher Giulio Ricordi, Paris, November 15, 1906

Debussy's *Pelléas et Mélisande* has extraordinary harmonic qualities and the most delicate instrumental effects. It is very interesting, in spite of its coloring, which is somber and unrelieved, like a Franciscan's habit.   [1]

---

* Mikota's sketch of Janáček had appeared in the Riemann-Einstein *Musik-lexikon.*

SALOME

From a letter to Giulio Ricordi, Naples, February 2, 1908

Last night I was able to go to the premiere of *Salome,* conducted by Strauss, and sung (?) by Bellincioni, whose dancing is marvelous. It was a success . . . but there must be many who doubt the verdict. The playing of the orchestra was like a badly mixed Russian salad. But the composer was there, and everybody says that it was perfect.

At the rehearsals, when Strauss was trying to work up his orchestra to a rough and tempestuous kind of execution, he said: "Gentlemen, this is not a question of music, but of a menagerie. Make a noise! Blow into your instruments!" What do you think of that?   [2]

THE RITE OF SPRING

From a letter to Tito Ricordi, Paris, no date

I went to hear *The Rite of Spring*: the choreography is ridiculous, the music sheer cacophony. There is some originality, however, and a certain amount of talent. But taken altogether, it might be the creation of a madman. The public hissed, laughed—and applauded.   [3]

LA BOHÈME

From a letter to Giulio Ricordi, Torre del Lago, September 7, 1894

There is no doubt about its being an original work! And such a one! The last act is most beautiful. So is that of the Quartier Latin, but very difficult. . . . It would be a good thing if you would glance through it, too, and rid it of certain extravagances that are really quite unessential. For example: "The horse is the king of animals," and "Rivers are wines made of water," and many other such lines which Illica [the librettist] loves like his own sons (if he had any). What must be shortened—and very much—is the second act, at the Barrière d'Enfer. This, in my opinion, is the weak act. Shall I be proved wrong? All the better! But the one I think particularly successful is the last. The death of Mimi, with all that leads up to it, is very moving.   [4]

From letter to Giulio Ricordi, no date

You will have the copy of act 4 at hand. Will you be so good as to open it at the point where they give Mimi the muff? Don't you think it rather poor at the moment of her death? Just an extra phrase, a word of affection to Rodolfo, would be enough. No doubt it is a fancy of mine, but when this girl, for whom I have worked so hard, dies, I should like her to leave the world less for herself and a little more for him who loved her.   [5]

TOSCA

From a letter to Giulio Ricordi, Torre del Lago, October 12, 1899

Your letter was an extraordinary surprise to me! I am still under the unpleasant impression. Nevertheless I am quite convinced that if you read the act [3] through again, you will change your opinion! This is not vanity on my part. It is the conviction of having colored to the best of my ability the drama that was before me. You know how scrupulous I am in interpreting the situation or the words and all that is of importance, before putting anything down on paper. The detail of my having used a fragment of *Edgar* can be criticized by you and the few who can recognize it, and may be taken as a labor-saving device, if you like. As it stands, if one rids oneself of the idea that it belongs to another work, if one wipes out *Edgar*, act 4, it seems to me full of the poetry that emanates from the words. Oh, I am sure of this, and you will be convinced when you hear it in its place, in the theater. As for its being fragmentary, I wanted it so. It cannot be a uniform and tranquil situation such as one connects with other love duets. Tosca's thoughts continually return to the necessity of a well-acted fall on Mario's part and a natural bearing in face of the firing squad. [6]

MADAMA BUTTERFLY

From a letter to Giulio Ricordi, Torre del Lago, no date

I have had a visit today from Mme Ohyama, wife of the Japanese ambassador. She told me a great many interesting things and sang some native songs to me. She has promised to send me some native Japanese music. I sketched the story of the libretto for her, and she liked it, especially as just such a story as Butterfly's is known to her as having happened in real life. [7]

THE GIRL OF THE GOLDEN WEST

From a letter to Tito Ricordi, New York, February 18, 1907

The world is expecting an opera from me, and it is high time it were ready. We've had enough now of *Bohème, Butterfly,* and Co.! Even I am sick of them! But I really am greatly worried! I am tormented not for myself alone, but for you, for Signor Giulio, and for the house of Ricordi, to whom I wish to give and must give an opera that is sure to be good.

Here, too, I have been on the lookout for subjects, but there is nothing possible, or rather, complete enough. I have found some good ideas in Belasco, but nothing definite, solid, or complete.

The "West" attracts me as a background, but in all the plays I have seen, I have found only some scenes here and there that are good. There is never a clear, simple line of development; just a hodgepodge and sometimes in very bad taste and very *vieux jeu*. [8]

From a letter to Giulio Ricordi, Boscolungo, no date

The *Girl* promises to become a second *Bohème*, but more vigorous, more daring, and on an altogether larger scale. I have in mind a magnificent scenario, a clearing in the great Californian forest, with some colossal trees. But we shall need eight or ten horses on the stage. [9]

From a letter to Sybil Seligman, Torre del Lago, July 12, 1907

Have you any means of obtaining, in America or in London itself, some early American music and some modern music too? I'm writing on my own account, but I need as much as possible in order to *get the atmosphere.*   [10]

TURANDOT

From a letter to Giuseppe Adami, no date

If I touch the piano, my hands get covered with dust. My desk is piled up with letters—there isn't a trace of music. Music? Useless, if I have no libretto. I have the great weakness of being able to write only when my puppet executioners are moving on the scene. If only I could be a purely symphonic writer! I should then at least cheat time—and my public. But that was not for me. I was born so many years ago—oh, so many, too many, almost a century—and Almighty God touched me with His little finger and said: "Write for the theater—mind, only for the theater." And I have obeyed the supreme command. Had He marked me out for some other task perhaps I should not be, as now, without material.   [11]

From a letter to Adami, Torre del Lago, November 10, 1920

I am afraid *Turandot* will never be finished. It is impossible to work like this. When fever abates, it ends by disappearing, and without fever there is no creation; because emotional art is a kind of malady, an exceptional state of mind, over-excitation of every fiber and every atom of one's being, and so on, ad aeternam.

For me the libretto is nothing to trifle with. It is not a question of finishing it. It is a question of giving life that will endure to a thing that must be alive before it can be born, and so on till we make a masterpiece.*   [12]

Hugo Wolf
1860–1903

During his three years as a critic for the Salonblatt *in Vienna, Wolf earned himself many enemies with his insightful but bitter writing. As a composer he had operatic ambitions, which he pursued without much success, although his gift of lyricism made him an outstanding lieder composer. Toward the end of his relatively short life he went insane; at one point he believed he had been made director of the Vienna Opera and was dismissing Mahler as conductor. The passages here are all from reviews in the* Salonblatt.

* As it happened, Puccini did not live to complete *Turandot*. The opera was finished by Franco Alfano (1875–1954), who added the last scene.

MODERN CHAMBER AND SYMPHONIC MUSIC (1884)

It is the adroit manipulation of technique, not the need to express a musical thought, that induces our modern composers to write chamber music. Hence their adagios—that type of movement in which Beethoven's heart expands into an immeasurable world, a world which encloses within itself every human heart, so that all may share in the superhuman raptures one heart alone cannot bear— hence their *adagios* are dull, artificial, tortured, and their poverty of thought with its mask of boredom grimaces at us over and over again through no matter what clever piquancy. The modern composer still feels himself most secure in the scherzo and the finale. He need merely be a clever contrapuntalist, need merely juggle the voices gaily to give himself the air of actually accomplishing something. Intricate inversions, strettos according to the rules, perhaps a witty fugato, or even a fugue! This fills the public with fear and respect. Two, three, or four themes when all else fails—piled one on another, torn asunder, attacked again, and hunted down afresh—a small skirmish, but without the thunder of cannon, without battle cries, with little powder, but with all the more flashing cavalry charges, a troupe of make-believe gypsies, Czardas, etc. Truly a charming hash and quite amusing! But for a time at least, the boredom that has crept up on us while we were hearing the *adagios* is banished, and therefore we find the chamber music of modern composers (*andantes* and *adagios* excepted) still bearable.   [1]

OPERA IN ITALY (1884)

In Italy, where only Italian music is fostered, one may be delighted with the grotesque operatic singing style, with the exaggerated gestures of the singers. There it pays less to sing beautifully than effectively, just as the gestures do not so much underline the word as the melodic line. So an Italian singer will sing the news of a shocking occurrence with unparalleled calm, as long as no high B or C looms before him, whereas the most casual circumstance, provided the singer's throat has been adequately considered by the composer, can throw him into an excitement and mobility that, in terms of vocal effects, falls more or less into the farcical. The most arrant scoundrel in the most horrible revenge aria bowls over the Italian rabble no less than the most sentimental lover in his tenderest lyrical outpourings. The high notes are the deciding factor. The Italian *eo ipso* does not bother about the action onstage; even the single musical numbers and recitatives exist for him only insofar as the vocal wrinkles in them have been duly taken care of. The singer wishes to roar or whisper, and the public wishes to be roared at or fluted to. These people understand one another, and therefore any intimacy between singer and audience, be it ever so vulgar, need not astonish us. Thus, for instance, the slain victim of an onstage duel, resurrected through the miracle of applause, takes the arm of his deadly foe, steps before the footlights, and together they politely thank the audience. Thereupon, immediately after the interjected peace, he madly attacks his newly won friend just as quickly, and as happily slays him; whereupon the mutual lovemaking between the singer and the audience begins anew, to last as long as it amuses both.   [2]

VISITING AND RESIDENT CONDUCTORS (1884)

To the piano virtuoso it is of no moment whether he plays on a Bösendorfer, Blüthner, Bechstein, or a Steinway, as long as the instrument itself is good. Also it is a matter of indifference to X if Y played on it the day before, etc. In this respect the orchestra is quite different. The latter gets used to its conductor in time, refractory as it might be at the start. It is a wild horse, which resists bridle and rider at first, but finally accustoms itself to both. Let a strange rider mount it, and though the reins be handled precisely as by the original rider, you will see a sorry picture. The relation between the orchestra and its conductor is exactly the same. Tradition is mighty. Habit is perhaps the strongest of all passions.   [3]

HAYDN'S *CREATION* (NOVEMBER 15, 1885)

The Creation of Haydn! What a devout, childlike spirit speaks from the heavenly clear tones of Haydn's muse! What naturalness, simplicity, what perception and sensitivity! What a great artist Haydn is: listening to his works, one is not struck by their ingenuity, and yet what an abundance of ingenious forms surround his graceful tone pictures! His extraordinarily fine artistic sense is evidenced especially in what has been assiduously exercised of late, but at the same time has fallen into disrepute—tone painting. In fact, we should shudder to think of a subject like *The Creation* or *The Seasons,* which give so much opportunity for tone painting, being handled or, more aptly, mishandled by a modern composer. We would not, for sheer imagery, get to hear any music. Should a modern composer wish to illustrate Chaos musically, we should certainly find no triad there, unless it were an occasional augmented one; but in all probability the duty would fall to open fifths, to defray the musical costs of such a presentation.   [4]

FAUST AS HANDLED BY BERLIOZ AND OTHERS (MARCH 1886)

Berlioz was incapable of creating an organic work of art, congruent in form and content, like the two compositions of Wagner and Liszt (the *Faust* Overture and *Faust* Symphony). His *Faust* is a fragmentary mosaic, a building without plan, full of the most beautiful detail but without a conscious aim. The Faust theme, in its purely human features an inexhaustible spring of artistic ideals, disintegrates with Berlioz into the idle play of arbitrary fancies, which, though admirable in themselves and full of genius, shatter the poetic intention and do not allow complete enjoyment of the whole work. This reproach applies also to Schumann's *Faust.* An inner instability is common to both, and if Schumann's *Faust* follows with finer feeling Goethe's original, Berlioz's work surpasses it in musical content. But whatever one may think of Berlioz's conception of the Faust idea, one thing is certain— that almost every number in this work invites our most ardent admiration.   [5]

BRAHMS'S THIRD SYMPHONY (1884)

As a symphony of Herr Dr. Johannes Brahms, it is to some extent a capable, meritorious work; as a symphony of a second Beethoven it is a complete failure, since one must ask of a second Beethoven all that which is lacking in a Dr. Johannes Brahms—originality. Brahms is the epigone of Schumann and Mendelssohn and as such exercises about as much influence on the course of the history of art as the late Robert Volkmann; that is, he has for the history of art just as *little* importance as Volkmann, which is to say *no* influence at all. He (Brahms) is a proficient musician who knows his counterpoint, to whom occur ideas now and then good, occasionally excellent, now and then bad, here and there familiar, and frequently no ideas at all. . . .

Schumann, Chopin, Berlioz, Liszt, the leaders of the revolutionary movement in music since Beethoven (in which period Schumann himself hoped for a Messiah and in the person of—Brahms!) have passed by our symphonist without trace. He was, or pretended to be, blind, as the eyes of astonished mankind opened and overflowed before the radiant genius of Wagner, as Wagner, like Napoleon, borne on the waves of the Revolution, led them into new channels by his despotic power, created order, and performed deeds that will live on eternally in the memory of mankind. But the man who has written three symphonies and apparently intends to allow a further six to follow these three cannot be affected by such a phenomenon, for he is only a relic from primeval ages and no vital part of the great stream of time.   [6]

BRAHMS'S FOURTH SYMPHONY (1886)

Conspicuous is the crab-like progress in Brahms's output. It has, to be sure, never reached beyond the level of mediocrity, but such nothingness, emptiness, and obsequiousness as prevails throughout the E minor symphony has not appeared in any previous work of Brahms in so alarming a manner. The art of composing without ideas has decidedly found in Brahms its worthiest representative. Just like the good Lord, Brahms understands the trick of making something out of nothing.   [7]

BRUCKNER (DECEMBER 28, 1884)

I mentioned Mr. Bruckner before as a titan at battle with the gods. Truthfully I could scarcely think of a more suitable metaphor with which to describe the peculiarities of this composer. Praise as well as blame are equally divided in this description. . . . An extraordinary artistic natural power, freshness, and naïveté at war with musical consciousness, intelligence out of step with the educational heights achieved by our time, these are the principal characteristics in the creative work of this artist, which unfortunately find themselves in conflict with one another. Had the composer been able to reconcile these conflicts, he would doubtless have grown into one of what Liszt terms the "all-embracing great." The lack of intelligence is what makes the Bruckner symphonies, for all their originality, greatness, strength, fantasy, and invention, so hard for us to understand. Everywhere will, colossal strivings, but no gratification, no artistic resolution. From this stems the formlessness of his works, the apparent exaggeration of his expression. Bruckner wrestles bravely with the idea, but hasn't the courage to place it foremost, and thus to write with a clear consciousness. Thus he wavers, half in Beethoven, half in the new discoveries, as in Liszt's symphonic poems, where they have found their most complete expression, sending out roots between the two, without being able to decide on either. That is his misfortune. Nevertheless, I do not hesitate to designate the symphonies of Bruckner as the most significant symphonic creations that have been written since Beethoven. [8]

Gustav Mahler
1860–1911

Born in Bohemia and trained in Vienna, Mahler held a series of conducting posts around Europe before returning to Vienna in 1897 to lead the Opera. In 1907 he moved to New York, first to direct the Metropolitan Opera, later the Philharmonic. Audiences cheered, but not the trustees, who thought him too autocratic. Mahler's symphonies struck his contemporaries as dissonant and overlong, but within fifty years of his death they had become some of the most highly prized works in the repertory.

PROGRAM NOTES

From a letter to an unknown addressee, May 15, 1894

Please accept my thanks for your kind offer. However, it is hardly my intention to confuse the audience at a musical performance with technical remarks—and in my opinion it amounts to nothing else when one stuffs a "program booklet" into the audience's hands, thereby forcing it to see rather than to hear!

Certainly I consider it necessary that the web of motives be clear to every listener. But do you really believe that in a modern work the singling out of several themes is sufficient for this? One must achieve the cognition and recognition of a musical work through exhaustive study, and the more profound a work, the harder it is, and the longer its study takes. At a first performance, however, the principal thing is to give oneself with pleasure or displeasure to the work, to allow the human-poetic in general to affect one, and if one then feels drawn to it, to occupy oneself with it more thoroughly. How does one do when one meets a person who is certainly much more profound and better than his work? Where is the program booklet here? Here also it means sedulously cultivating him and zealously studying him. Of course, he grows and changes, whereas the work always remains the same. But at some point or other, comparisons always limp. [1]

From a letter to Max Kalbeck, Meiernigg, undated

Beginning with Beethoven there exists no modern music that hasn't its inner program. But no music is worth anything when the listener has to be instructed as to what is experienced in it—in other words, what he is expected to experience. And so again: *pereat*—every program! One must bring along one's ears and heart and, not least, surrender willingly to the rhapsodist. A bit of mystery always remains— even for the creator!   [2]

From a letter to Max Marschalk,* Hamburg, March 26, 1896

For myself I know that so long as I can sum up my experience in words, I can certainly not create music about it. My need to express myself in music symphonically begins precisely where dark feelings hold sway, at the gate that leads into the "other world," the world in which things no longer are divided by time and space.

So, just as I find it insipid to invent music to a program, so I view it as unsatisfactory and unfruitful to wish to give a program to a piece of music. That does not alter the fact that the motive for a musical picture is certainly an experience of the author's, indeed an actual one, which might after all be concrete enough to be clothed in words. We stand now—of this I am certain—at the great crossroads that divides forever the diverging paths of symphonic and dramatic music so easily visible to the eye of him who is clear about the direction of music. Even now, should you hold up a Beethoven symphony against the tone pictures of Wagner, you will easily recognize the essence of the difference between them. Indeed, Wagner made the means of expression of symphonic music his own, just as now the symphonist fully qualified in, and completely conscious of, his medium, will take over from the wealth of expression that music gained through Wagner's efforts. In this sense, all the arts, yes, even art and nature, hang together. However, this has not been thought about enough as yet, because up to now not enough perspective has been gained on the subject. I have not concocted this "system" and then adapted my creation to it either; but only after writing several symphonies (with real birth pangs), and forever coming up against the same misunderstandings and questions, did I finally—for me at least—gain this insight into things.

In spite of everything, it is therefore good that at the beginning, when my style is still foreign to him, the listener be provided with a few signposts and milestones along his journey, or shall we say: a map of the stars to comprehend the night sky with its shining worlds. But such an exposition cannot offer more. A person must fasten upon something he knows, or he gets lost. Consequently I shall be grateful to you if you publish your essay. I like it better than anything else that has been said of me up to now.   [3]

ADVICE TO A COMPOSER

From a letter to Max Marschalk, Hamburg, April 12, 1896

You still go in primarily for "tone and color"! It is the fault of all gifted beginners who create today. I could show you similar things in my own development. Mood music is a dangerous foundation. Believe me, it [composition] rests principally on

* Critic, teacher, and composer (1863–1940), who had written program notes for Mahler's First Symphony.

the old tried and true: Themes, clear and plastic, distinctly recognizable in every transformation and further development; then a varied and, above all, arresting execution through the logical development of the inner idea, and conversely, through the genuine contrasting of themes pitted one against another. . . .

You must get rid of the pianist in you. This is no orchestral movement; it is conceived for piano and then fairly slavishly translated in the spirit of that instrument for orchestra. . . .

I have suffered from this also. We of today all proceed from the piano, whereas the old masters stem from the violin and the voice. . . .

You frequently carry through long stretches in the same rhythm and even with the same orchestration. This makes for monotony. Change and contrast! This is and remains the secret of effectiveness! In this manner even blockheads manage for a time to hide lack of content. [4]

COMPOSING FOR THEATER AND CONCERT HALL

From a letter to the musicologist Guido Adler, New York, January 1, 1910

The technique of the theater is altogether different, and I am convinced that a host of my inadequacies in instrumentation up to now rests on the fact that I am accustomed to listening under the completely different acoustical conditions of the theater. [5]

TEMPO IN CONDUCTING

From a statement, no date

A tempo is correct when everything can still be heard. When a figure can no longer be understood because the tones run into one another, then the tempo is too fast.

In a *presto* the extreme limit of distinctness is the correct tempo; beyond this it loses its effectiveness. [6]

STRAUSS AND *SALOME*

From a letter to Alma Mahler, Dresden, December 19, 1901

I had a serious talk with Strauss in Berlin and tried to show him the blind alley he had got into. Unfortunately, he could not quite follow what I meant. He's a charming fellow, and I'm touched by his attitude toward me. And yet I can mean nothing to him—for whereas I see over his head, he sees only up to my knees. [7]

From a letter to Alma Mahler, Salzburg, July 16, 1906

Strauss is now also here, and especially charming, as he always is when we are alone together. However, his nature will always remain foreign to me. His manner of thinking and feeling is worlds apart from mine. I wonder if we two will ever meet on the same planet.   [8]

From a letter to Alma Mahler, Berlin, January 14, 1907

Salome, then, yesterday. The impression it made was stronger than ever and I am firmly convinced that it is one of the greatest masterpieces of our time. I cannot make out the drift of it, and can only surmise that it is the voice of the "earth spirit" speaking from the heart of genius, a spirit that does not indeed make a dwelling place for itself to suit human taste but in accordance with its own unfathomable needs. Perhaps in time I shall gain a clearer understanding of this "cocoon" it has spun for itself.   [9]

TOSCA

From a letter to Alma Mahler, Lvov, 1903

Last night there was my visit to the Opera; *Tosca*, as I told you. An excellent production in every way; quite an eye-opener, for a provincial town in Austria. But as for the work itself! Act 1, papal pageantry with continual chiming of bells (specially imported from Italy). Act 2. A man tortured; horrible cries. Another stabbed with a sharp bread knife. Act 3. More of the magnificent tintinnabulations and a view over all Rome from a citadel. Followed by an entirely fresh onset of bell ringing. A man shot by a firing squad.

I got up before the shooting and went out. Needless to say, a masterpiece. Nowadays any bungler orchestrates to perfection.   [10]

BRAHMS AND BRUCKNER

From a letter to Alma Mahler, Meiernigg, 1904

I have now gone through practically all of Brahms. Well, I must say, he is really a little man with a narrow chest. Heavens, when one has at the same time been buffeted by the blast from Richard Wagner's lungs! How Brahms in his poverty must economize in order to get along! Whereby I do not mean to insult him. Where he gets stuck—you will be astonished when I say this to you—is in his so-called developments. Only in the rarest cases does he know what to do with his frequently lovely themes. Only Beethoven and Wagner *knew.*

After I had gone through all of Brahms, I turned again to Bruckner. Singularly average people! The former remained "in the crucible" too long, the latter must now be poured into it. Now I am on Beethoven. There are only *he* and *Richard*— and otherwise nothing!   [11]

SIBELIUS

From a letter to Alma Mahler, Helsinki, February 2, 1907

I heard some pieces of Sibelius at the concert too—the Finnish national composer who makes a great stir not only here but throughout the world of music. In one of them, the most hackneyed clichés were served up, with harmonizations in the "Nordic" style, as a national dish. "Pui Kaiki!"*

This is always the way with these national geniuses. It is the same in Russia and Sweden, not to mention Italy—all those harlots and their *souteneurs*.   [12]

SCHOENBERG

Remark to Schoenberg, 1905

I have conducted the most difficult scores of Wagner; I have written complicated music myself in scores of up to thirty staves and more; yet here is a score [First String Quartet] of not more than four staves, and I am unable to read them.   [13]

Remark recorded by Alma Mahler following a performance of the Chamber Symphony No. 1, c. 1907

I don't understand his music, but he's young and perhaps he's right. I am old and I daresay my ear is not sensitive enough.   [14]

GENESIS OF THE SECOND SYMPHONY

Letter to the conductor Anton Seidl, Hamburg, February 17, 1897

You have given me great joy and a powerful stimulation with your kind and thoughtful letter. It is curious how, in a certain sense, you have clarified me to my-self. You have quite decisively characterized my aims, in contrast to those of Strauss. You say correctly that my "music finally arrives at its program as a last ideal elucidation, whereas in Strauss the program is present as a given curriculum." I believe that with this you have particularly hit on the great enigmas of our time, and have at the same time pointedly expressed the either-or. When I conceive a large musical structure, I always come to the point where I must bring in the word as the bearer of my musical idea. Something similar must have happened to Bee-thoven in his Ninth, only his own time could not yet furnish him with the mate-rial suitable for this.

For basically the Schiller poem is not capable of formulating the fantastic that he had in mind. Incidentally, I recall that Richard Wagner at some point expresses this quite plainly. In the last movement of my second symphony it so happened to me that I actually searched through the entire world literature back to the Bible to find the redeeming word—and finally was forced to lend words myself to my feelings and thoughts.

How I got the inspiration for this is profoundly significant for the nature of ar-tistic creation.

For a long time I turned over in my mind the inclusion of a chorus in the last movement, and only the fear that this might be considered a superficial imitation

* "Phooey."

of Beethoven made me hesitate again and again. At this time Bülow died, and I was present at his memorial. The mood in which I sat there and thought of him who had passed away was exactly the spirit of the work I was then mulling over. Then the chorus from the organ loft intoned the Klopstock chorale "Resurrection"! This struck me like a flash of lightning, and everything appeared quite clear and distinct within me! The creator waits for this flash; this is the "holy conception"!

What I experienced at that moment, I had now to create in sound. And yet, had I not already borne this work within me, how could I have had such an experience? After all, thousands sat with me in the church at that moment! So it always is with me: only when I experience, do I compose—only when I compose, do I experience! I know that you understand me without my elaborating on this any further. A musician's nature can hardly be expressed in words. It would be easier to explain how he is different from others. What it is, however, perhaps he least of all would be able to explain. It is the same with his goals, too. Like a somnambulist he wanders toward them—he doesn't know which road he is following (it may skirt dizzy abysses), but he walks toward the distant light, whether this be the eternally shining stars or an enticing will-o'-the-wisp.   [15]

SECOND AND FOURTH SYMPHONIES

From a letter to Alma Mahler, Dresden, December 19, 1901

How I wish you could be here for the C Minor. The piano score gives no idea of it. And it is so important you should know it—for my Fourth will mean nothing to you.—It again is all humor—"naïve," as you would say; just what you can so far understand least in me—and what in any case only the fewest of the few will ever understand to all futurity.   [16]

THIRD SYMPHONY

From a letter to Bruno Walter, Steinbach am Attersee, July 2, 1896

I hope that a few weeks will see the entire Third happily completed. . . . I have no doubt that our friends, the critics, appointed or self-appointed, will once again suffer from dizziness, but those who enjoy the pleasant strolls I offer will find them fun. The whole thing is, of course, tainted with my deplorable sense of humor and "often takes the opportunity to submit to my dreary taste for dreary noise." The players frequently "do not pay the least attention to one another, and my entire gloomy and brutal nature is nakedly exposed." It is well known that I cannot do without trivialities.   [17]

From a letter to Anna Bahr-Mildenburg, Steinbach am Attersee, July 18, 1896

But I have surely written you that I am at work on a large composition. You cannot believe how this claims one's entire being, and how one is often so deep in it that for the outer world one is as if dead. Try to conceive a work so vast that in it the entire world is mirrored—one is, so to speak, only an instrument on which the whole universe plays. (I have explained this to you often, and you must accept it, if you really wish to understand me. Everyone who wishes to live with me must learn this. In such moments I no longer belong to myself.) . . . These are fearful birth pains the creator of such a work suffers, and before all this organizes itself, builds itself up, and ferments in his brain, it must be preceded by much preoccupation, engrossment with self, a being dead to the outer world. My symphony will be something the world has not as yet heard! In it all nature becomes a voice and reveals profound mysteries as one has perhaps surmised only in dreams. I tell you that at certain points I become uneasy, and it seems to me as if I myself had not done it at all. If only I can fulfill everything as I project it to myself!   [18]

FIRST PERFORMANCE OF THE FIFTH SYMPHONY

From a letter to Alma Mahler, Cologne, October 16, 1904

[The first rehearsal] went off tolerably well. The scherzo is the very devil of a movement. I see it is in for a peck of troubles! Conductors for the next fifty years will all take it too fast and make nonsense of it; and the public—Oh, heavens, what are they to make of this chaos of which new worlds are forever being engendered, only to crumble in ruin the moment after? What are they to say to this primeval music, this foaming, roaring, raging sea of sound, to these dancing stars, to these breathtaking, iridescent, and flashing breakers? What has a flock of sheep to say but "baaa!" to the Brüdersphären-Wettgesang? How blessed, how blessed a tailor to be! Oh, that I had been born a commercial traveler* and engaged as baritone at the Opera! Oh that I might give my symphony its first performance fifty years after my death!

Now I'm going for a walk along the Rhine—the only man in all Cologne who will quietly go his way after the premiere without pronouncing me a monster. Oh, that I were "quite the mama, quite the papa!"†   [19]

Frederick Delius
1862–1934

German by heritage and English by birth, Delius lived most of his life in the small French town of Grez-sur-Loing. He is often grouped with the English pastoralists, though in fact he found their music weak and retrograde; his subtle and eccentric originality springs from a very different aesthetic. At the same time he was no modernist, but rather an exponent of a moderate progressivism whose place in music history remains poorly defined. In his letters Delius often wrote quickly, voicing firmly held views in spontaneous language marked by personal usages.

---

* Alma Mahler identifies this as a reference to a singer named Demuth.

† A reference to Strauss's *Sinfonia domestica*.

THE STATE OF ENGLISH MUSIC

From a letter to Ethel Smyth, Grez-sur-Loing, February 17, 1909

Music now is exactly in the same stale state as painting was in France at the time of Manet, Turner etc. I say in France, as painting has scarcely begun in England and music hardly. Handel paralysed music in England for generations and they have not yet quite got over him.

As far as I can judge, the English race is lacking in emotion, the essential part of music. Conventionalism and respectability did it, and they live and think and work in cut and dried forms. That is why they love the formalists in music so much, and do not understand the colorists in any art whatever.

Still I believe the coming generation may cast off this spell and express something human ...   [1]

ART AND REVOLUTION

From a letter to Granville Bantock, Grez-sur-Loing, March 16, 1909

In art there never was evolution—it was always revolution against an existing accepted art—which everyone had already got accustomed to—The danger of custom is enormous "Habitude" it destroys all keener perception & sensitiveness.   [2]

SYSTEMS OF COMPOSITION

From a letter to Philip Heseltine, Grez-sur-Loing, December 4, 1911*

I do not believe in any music constructed knowingly on any Harmonic Scheme whatsoever. All the people who write about the Harmonic system or try to invent other systems quarter tones etc. Dont seem to have anything to say on Music— Systems are put together from the compositions of inspired musicians Harmony is only a means of expression which is gradually developing—I dont believe in learning Harmony or counterpoint. . . .

It is of no importance whether you write at the piano or not—As long as you *feel* you want to Express some emotion—*music is nothing else.*   [3]

From a letter to Philip Heseltine, Biarritz, July 3, 1918

COMPOSING

You ask me about the mental processes of my own work. I dont believe in the possibility of conceiving an entire work in all its details instantaniously—Especially one in several movements—I, myself, am entirely at a loss to explain how I compose—I know only that at first I conceive a work suddenly—thro' a feeling—the work appears to me instantaniously as a whole, but as a feeling—The working out of the whole work in detail is then easy as long as I have the feeling—the emotion—

* Heseltine (1894–1930) composed under the pen name Peter Warlock.

it becomes difficult as the emotion becomes less keen; sometimes I am obliged to put the work aside for months—sometimes years—& take it up again, having almost, or entirely, forgotten it, in order to bring back my first feeling.   [4]

THE POWER OF THE INDIVIDUAL

You see an individual or genius is always dangerous—The bourgeois feels it instinctively—He feels that an individual is going to alter his tastes & habits—& the individual does alter them—that is why the new has such a lot of enemies, especially in old countries—America is a better country for a genius than either France or England or Italy—In America they have no very old preconceived ideas & welcome something new even if they dont understand it—It, at least, amuses them.   [5]

THE STATE OF MUSIC

From "At the Crossroads," The Sackbut, September 1920

How does music stand today? Is the world full of men of as much importance as Bach and Beethoven, Chopin and Wagner? If we are to believe some of the composers themselves, or rather, their trumpeters and tub-thumpers, we have amongst us not the equals but the superiors, the *superseders* even, of the old masters. After a thousand years of evolution, music is just beginning to become articulate! Already some music publishers have put up electric signs and others have had recourse to their literary equivalent. The average man of the present day is so accustomed to having his mind made up for him by advertisements, posters and illuminated signs at every street corner, that he comes to believe implicitly anything he reads often enough on the hoardings. If this is the case with patent medicines, it is also the case with art, and we find that propaganda and advertisement carry all before them.

This is an age of anarchy in art; there is no authority, no standard, no sense of proportion. Anybody can do anything and call it "art" in the certain expectation of making a crowd of idiots stand and stare at him in gaping astonishment and admiration. . . .

Great men must be denied and great achievements scoffed at in order that the little ones may become conspicuous. There must be a complete transvaluation of values. Art has been "serious" too long; now let us play the fool, in season and out of season, let us deny everything, turn all our values upside down.   [6]

THE FUTURE OF OPERA

From an interview with G. M. Stevensen Reece, 1919

The future of opera generally as an art form? Length and cumbrousness, in my opinion, will be the first features to disappear, and that is the end towards which I am working—brevity and conciseness. Long dialogues and wearisome narrations must go, and will be replaced by short, strong emotional impressions given in a series of terse scenes. Ninety minutes to two hours is long enough for any opera, and by reducing intervals, as I have done in my own work, to three minutes instead of the usual half-hour necessitated by ponderous realistic decoration, this limit can be easily preserved.

Every word must be cleanly heard, and the construction of the work itself should obviate any need of explanation. Suggestion will replace masses of detail in opera, as in modern painting. By these methods I believe it will be possible for opera to become the supreme vehicle for the expression of the finest and subtlest psychological ideas, and we shall achieve "opera without tears"—other than those, that is to say, of pleasant emotion and genuine thankfulness. [7]

Claude Debussy
1862–1918

Ridiculed and slandered by all manner of musical eminences, Debussy in his writings responded with wisdom, sophistication, and humor—albeit a humor that could be insolent and barbed. Most of his reviews and essays were written between 1901 and 1914, the same years in which Pelléas et Mélisande *and* La Mer *were being introduced to the world and roundly condemned by critics. In 1921 a number of Debussy's reviews were collected and published as the now-classic* Monsieur Croche, the Dilettante Hater, *named for the imaginary figure who serves as Debussy's alter ego in many of the reviews.*

MODERN OPERA

From a letter to André Poniatowski, Paris, February 1893

How fortunate you are, occupying yourself with railways and living among numbers, for thus you are spared the melancholy spectacle furnished to those who love art by those who call themselves its modern representatives. We've just had a *Werther* by Massenet, in which one finds a remarkable talent for satisfying the craving of the dilettante mind for all that is poetically lacking and lyrically cheap! Everything about it contributes to this mediocrity, and as well to this appalling habit of taking something which in itself is perfectly fine and subverting its spirit with light, facile sentimentalities: there's *Faust* eviscerated by Gounod, or *Hamlet* turned upside-down by Monsieur Ambroise Thomas. We punish those who put their efforts into forging banknotes, but we think nothing of these others who are truly forgers as well, and who likewise are doing it for the money. I would quite understand the author who put a notice on his works: "It is prohibited to park your music anywhere in this book." [1]

ADVICE TO YOUNGER COMPOSERS

From a letter to Charles Levadé, Bichain, September 4, 1903

Ultimately you will learn orchestration better by listening to the sound of the leaves as they are stirred by the wind than by consulting treatises, in which the instruments take on the feeling of anatomical specimens, and which in any case are mediocre when it comes to discussing the innumerable ways of blending the instruments with each other.

Your question on the subject of orchestral forces is a delicate one. Who can assure you that the standard scoring will be right for everything you want to do? Anyway, here it is: 3 flutes, 2 oboes, 1 cor anglais, 2 clarinets, 3 bassoons, 4 horns, 3 trumpets, 3 trombones, 1 tuba, 2 harps. . . .

But believe me, don't limit yourself in advance with a system or a formula ... by the tenth measure you won't know what to do with it ... Don't ever fear that you haven't got enough instruments! And above all remember that the brass are very delicate and not instruments of carnage! Only in the most extreme circumstances should a trombone blare. . . . Look at Wagner, so much the victim of his own system; even with his quartet of tubas and his trumpets of every type, what comes of it is none the richer ... And in spite of Berlioz, Charpentier, Ganne, and Puccini, you must never believe that the triangle is an expressive instrument! [2]

From a letter to his stepson Raoul Bardac, Paris, February 24–25, 1906

From your description your daily schedule sounds wonderful, with idle hours, so it seems to me, judiciously distributed. You are right ... it's important to let your brain marinate in the sun. Observe the flowers, look at snapshots—while your gray matter is still open to stimulation.

Collect impressions. Don't be in a hurry to write them down. Because music has this over painting: it can bring together variations of color and light within a single image. This is a truth very much overlooked, for all its simplicity ... forget about music completely, from time to time. It was an idiot who decreed that you had to write a lot in order to learn how to write. [3]

METRONOME MARKINGS

From a letter to Jacques Durand, Pourville, October 9, 1915

You know my opinion of metronome markings: they are right for a single measure, like "roses, which exist but for a morning," only, there are "those" who don't hear music and who, because of this, use the markings to hear it even less! [4]

JAVANESE MUSIC

From a letter to Pierre Louÿs, Paris, January 22, 1895

But my dear good fellow! Remember the music of Java [at the Universal Exhibition in 1889], which contained every nuance, even the ones we no longer have names for. There tonic and dominant had become empty shadows of use only to stupid children. [5]

HUNGARIAN GYPSY MUSIC

From a letter to the impresario Barczy and his wife, December 19, 1910

I received the Hungarian music and I thank you for it, but how far it is from the impression made on me by [the Gypsy violinist] Radics! . . . It is like a beautiful butterfly under glass! The wings have remained brilliant, but they no longer stir, and their rich colors are tarnished. Is it possible that you, being Hungarians, cannot be judges of its true value? It is so familiar to you that you no longer see in it the artistic importance, so complete and so profound, that it has.

Besides, just see what it becomes in the interpretation Liszt gives it! For all his genius, he domesticates it. . . . It loses its freedom and this feeling of boundlessness that characterizes it.

In listening to Radics, one's surroundings vanish ... One inhales the forest air and hears the rush of streams; and it is also the melancholy intimacy of a heart that aches and laughs, almost in the same instant. . . .

In my opinion, one must never tamper with this music. One would even have to defend it, as much as possible, from the ineptness of the "professionals." For that reason ... respect your gypsies all the more. May they no longer be the simple entertainers who are brought in to add interest to a fair, or to encourage the drinking of champagne! In truth, this music is as beautiful as your old embroideries, your laces ... why then do you not have the same respect for them, the same love?

Your young musicians could gain from being inspired by them, not by copying but in trying to transpose their freedom, their gift for evocation, pathos, and rhythm. Wagner's teachings were bad for much music and many countries ...

One must not use the folk music of one's country except as a base, never as a procedure. That is especially true of yours ... Love it as passionately as you want to, but do not dress it up in school uniforms, do not give it eyeglasses with golden rims!   [6]

PALESTRINA

From a letter to André Poniatowski, Paris, February 1893

These last few days I have taken some consolation in a very beautiful musical experience: at Saint-Gervais, a church where an intelligent priest has gotten the idea to revive some of the ancient and beautiful sacred music. They sang a Palestrina mass, for unaccompanied voices. It was marvelously beautiful; this music, although written in a severe style, gives the effect of total whiteness, and emotion is not represented (as it has been in more recent times) by cries but by melodic arabesques, which create their effect through contour, and through their interweaving, which produces something that strikes you as unique: harmony that is made of melodies!   [7]

RAMEAU

From a letter to Louis Laloy, Paris, September 10, 1906

I am delighted with your enthusiasm for Rameau; he deserves it, for all of that music that ought to have saved us from the lying grandiloquence of a Gluck, from the showy metaphysics of a Wagner, from the false mystique of the old Belgian angel,* whom we have so ineptly adapted to a mode of understanding that is its exact antithesis—neglecting, like children crazed with vanity—the perfect taste, the strict elegance which constitute the absolute beauty of Rameau's music. . . .

And, unfortunately, if we seem to be coming round to him, it is only in a spirit of vanity, because we are almost incapable of feeling what we have lost by having listened to it so poorly. [8]

MOZART

From a letter to the publisher Jacques Durand, Paris, February 15, 1916

It is correct to say that, nowadays, the symphonies of Mozart are played badly because one feels obliged to overstress the nuances. [9]

BEETHOVEN'S OP. 130 STRING QUARTET

From a letter to Pierre Louÿs, Paris, February 23, 1895

Beethoven's fourteenth quartet is without a question one long practical joke, in spite of what these young metaphysicians say in *L'Art et la vie*. People should stop lumbering us with old furniture that hasn't even retained its period smell. [10]

BEETHOVEN AND THE SYMPHONY

From Monsieur Croche, the Dilettante Hater

A fog of verbiage and criticism surrounds the Ninth Symphony. It is amazing that it has not been finally buried under the mass of prose it has provoked. Wagner intended to complete the orchestration. Others fancied that they could explain and illustrate the theme by means of pictures. If we admit to a mystery in this symphony, we might clear it up; but is it worthwhile? There was not an ounce of literature in Beethoven, not at any rate in the accepted sense of the word. He had a great love of music, representing to him, as it did, the joy and passion piteously absent from his private life. Perhaps we ought in the *Choral* Symphony to look for nothing more than a magnificent gesture of musical pride. A little notebook with over two hundred different renderings of the dominant theme in the finale of this symphony shows how persistently Beethoven pursued his search and how entirely musical his guiding motive was; Schiller's lines can have only been used for their appeal to the ear. Beethoven determined that his leading idea should be essentially self-developing and, while it is of extraordinary beauty in itself, it becomes sublime because of its perfect response to his purpose. It is the most triumphant example of the molding of an idea to the preconceived form; at each leap forward there is a new delight, without either effort or appearance of repetition; the magical blossoming, so to speak, of a tree whose leaves burst forth simultaneously. Nothing is superfluous in this stupendous work, not even the *andante*, declared by modern aestheticism to be overlong; is it not a subtly conceived pause between the

---

* Evidently a reference to Franck.

persistent rhythm of the scherzo and the instrumental flood that rolls the voices irresistibly onward to the glory of the finale?

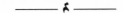

It seems to me that the proof of the futility of the symphony has been established since Beethoven. Indeed, Schumann and Mendelssohn did no more than respectfully repeat the same forms with less power. The Ninth Symphony, nonetheless, was a demonstration of genius, a sublime desire to augment and liberate the usual forms by giving them the harmonious proportions of a fresco.

Beethoven's real teaching, then, was not to preserve the old forms, still less to follow in his early steps. We must throw wide the windows to the open sky; they seem to me to have only just escaped being closed forever. The fact that here and there a genius succeeds in this form is but a poor excuse for the laborious and stilted compositions we are accustomed to call symphonies.

The young Russian school has endeavored to give new life to the symphony by borrowing ideas from popular melodies; it has succeeded in cutting brilliant gems; but are not the themes entirely disproportionate to the developments into which they have been forced? Yet the fashion for popular airs has spread quickly throughout the musical world: from east to west the tiniest villages have been ransacked, and simple tunes, plucked from the mouths of hoary peasants, find themselves, to their consternation, trimmed with harmonic frills. This gives them an appearance of pathetic discomfort, but a lordly counterpoint ordains that they shall forget their peaceful origin.

A symphony is usually built up on a melody heard by the composer as a child. The first section is the customary presentation of a theme on which the composer proposes to work; then begins the necessary dismemberment; the second section seems to take place in an experimental laboratory; the third section cheers up a little in a quite childish way, interspersed with deeply sentimental phrases during which the melody recedes, as is more seemly; but it reappears and the dismemberment goes on; the professional gentlemen, obviously interested, mop their brows and the audience calls for the composer. But the composer does not appear. He is engaged in listening modestly to the voice of tradition, which prevents him, it seems to me, from hearing the voice that speaks within him. [11]

WEBER

From Monsieur Croche

His work had a sort of dreamy melancholy, characteristic of his time, though never marred by the crude German moonlight in which nearly all his contemporaries were bathed. . . .

He was the master of every known means of interpreting the fantastic through music. Even in our own days, rich as they are in the science of orchestration, few have surpassed him. If he attached too much importance to the flourish and the coloratura we must not forget that he married a singer. [12]

BERLIOZ

From Monsieur Croche

The work of Berlioz, through his preoccupation with color and incident, became at once a subject for artists; one might even say without irony that Berlioz has always been the favorite musician of those who do not know much about music.   [13]

CHOPIN'S PEDALING

From a letter to Jacques Durand, Pourville, September 1, 1915

Saint-Saëns's notions about pedaling in Chopin* are not—despite my respect for his great age—entirely right, as I have very detailed memories of what Mme Manté de Fleurville told me. He (Chopin) felt one should practice without pedal and, except in very rare instances, should not hold it down.† This is, really, the art of turning the pedal into a kind of *breathing,* which I observed in Liszt's playing when I had the opportunity to hear him once, in Rome. Saint-Saëns appears to forget that pianists are poor musicians, for the most part, and cut up music into unequal pieces, like a chicken.

The plain truth is, perhaps, that abusing the pedal is only a means of disguising weaknesses in technique, and that making a lot of noise is a way to drown out the music you are slaughtering. Theoretically, we should be able to find a way of indicating this "breathing" pedal graphically. . . . It can't be impossible.   [14]

LISZT

From Monsieur Croche

The undeniable beauty of Liszt's works arises, I believe, from the fact that his love of music excluded every other kind of emotion. If sometimes he gets on easy terms with it and frankly takes it on his knee, this is surely no worse than the stilted manner of those who behave as though they were being introduced to it for the first time; very polite, but rather dull. Liszt's genius is often disordered and feverish, but that is better than rigid perfection, even in white gloves.   [15]

FRANCK AND WAGNER

From Monsieur Croche

César Franck is allied to the great masters for whom tones have an exact meaning within their own sphere; they use them with precision and without ever exacting from them more than is explicit in them. Here lies all the difference between the impure art of Wagner, with its peculiar beauty and seduction, and the art of

---

* I had conveyed to Debussy some of Saint-Saëns's thoughts on the use of the pedal in Chopin. [Durand]

† When performing. [Durand]

Franck, which renders service to music without expecting any return. What he takes from life he restores to art with a modesty that is almost selfless. When Wagner takes from life he conquers it, places his foot on its neck, and forces it to shriek the name of Wagner louder than the trumpets of Fame.   [16]

WAGNER AND *PARSIFAL*

From Monsieur Croche

Wagner's art can never completely die. It will suffer that inevitable decay, the cruel brand of time on all beautiful things; yet noble ruins must remain, in the shadow of which our grandchildren will brood over the past splendor of this man who, had he been a little more human, would have been altogether great.

In *Parsifal,* the final effort of a genius that compels our homage, Wagner tried to drive his music on a looser rein and let it breathe more freely. We have no longer the distraught breathlessness that characterizes Tristan's morbid passion or Isolde's wild screams of frenzy; nor yet the grandiloquent commentary on the inhumanity of Wotan. Nowhere in Wagner's music is a more serene beauty attained than in the prelude to the third act of *Parsifal* and in the entire Good Friday episode, although it must be admitted that Wagner's peculiar conception of human nature is also shown in the attitude of certain characters in this drama. Look at Amfortas, that melancholy Knight of the Grail, who whines like a shop girl and whimpers like a baby. Good heavens! A Knight of the Grail, a king's son, would plunge his spear into his own body rather than parade a guilty wound in doleful melodies for three acts! As for Kundry, that ancient rose of hell, she has furnished much copy for Wagnerian literature; I confess I have but little affection for such a sentimental draggle-tail. Klingsor is the finest character in *Parsifal:* a quondam Knight of the Grail, sent packing from the Holy Place because of his too-pronounced views on chastity. His bitter hatred is amazing; he knows the worth of men and scornfully weighs the strength of their vows of chastity in the balance. From this it is quite obvious that this crafty magician, this old jailbird, is not merely the only human character but the only moral character in this drama, in which the falsest moral and religious ideas are set forth, ideas of which the youthful Parsifal is the heroic and insipid champion.

Here, in short, is a Christian drama in which nobody is willing to sacrifice himself, though sacrifice is one of the highest of the Christian virtues! . . .

The above remarks apply only to the poet, whom we are accustomed to admire in Wagner, and have nothing to do with the musical beauty of the opera, which is supreme. It is incomparable and bewildering, splendid and strong. *Parsifal* is one of the loveliest monuments of sound ever raised to the serene glory of music.   [17]

From responses to a questionnaire
from the Mercure de France, *1903*

Wagner, if one may express oneself with some of the grandiloquence that belongs to him, was a beautiful sunset that was mistaken for a dawn.   [18]

GOUNOD

From Monsieur Croche

Although Gounod may lack the sweeping harmony that we could wish for him, he deserves our praise for having evaded the domination of the genius of Wagner. . . .

Gounod, with all his faults, is needed. To begin with, he is cultured; he knows Palestrina and draws upon Bach. His respect for tradition is discriminating enough for him not to be swept away by Gluck, another rather indeterminate foreign influence. It is rather Mozart for whom he asks the affection of young people, which is proof of great disinterestedness. His relations with Mendelssohn were more obvious, since it is to him that he owes his method, so convenient when the flow of inspiration fails, of developing the melody step by step. . . . Let it be stated once again that a name lives in the memory of men for various though not necessarily weighty reasons. One of the best means of achieving this is to stir the emotions of the majority of one's contemporaries. Of that no one will deny Gounod made generous use. [19]

MUSORGSKY

From Monsieur Croche

No one has given utterance to the best within us in tones more gentle or profound: he is unique, and will remain so, because his art is spontaneous and free from arid formulas. Never has a more refined sensibility been conveyed by such simple means; it is like the art of an enquiring savage discovering music step by step through his emotions. [20]

STRAUSS

From Monsieur Croche

This piece [*Till Eulenspiegel*] might almost be called "an hour of original music in a lunatic asylum." . . . One wants either to shout with laughter or to shriek with pain. . . . Meanwhile, there is no gainsaying that genius is shown at times in this work, above all in the amazing orchestral assurance, the mad rhythm that sweeps us along from beginning to end and forces us to share in all the hero's merry pranks. [21]

From a letter to Gabriel Astruc, Paris, May 23, 1907

I did not hear *Salome* until last Friday. It's difficult to feel anything other than enthusiasm for this work, which is obviously a masterpiece ... a phenomenon almost as rare as the appearance of a comet. [22]

RAVEL

From a letter to Louis Laloy, Paris, March 8, 1907

I agree with you that Ravel is extraordinarily gifted, but what annoys me is the attitude he adopts of being a "conjurer," or rather a fakir casting spells and making flowers burst out of chairs. . . The trouble is, a conjuring trick always has to have a buildup, and after you've seen it once you're no longer astonished.   [23]

STRAVINSKY

From a letter to Jacques Durand, Paris, July 6, 1910

[*The Firebird*] is not a perfect piece, but from certain aspects it is nevertheless very fine, for here the music is not the docile servant of the dance. And at times you hear altogether unusual combinations of rhythms!   [24]

From a letter to Robert Godet, Paris, January 4, 1916

I've recently seen Stravinsky ... He says: my *Firebird*, my *Sacre*, like a child saying: my top, my hoop. And that's exactly what he is: a spoiled child who, on occasion, gives music a tweak on the nose. He's also a young savage who wears loud ties, and kisses the ladies' hands while stepping on their feet. When old, he'll be unbearable, that is to say, he won't be able to bear any kind of music; but, for the moment, he's incredible.

He professes a great friendship for me, because I've helped him climb a height from which he can hurl grenades, which don't all explode. But, as I say, he's incredible.   [25]

PELLÉAS ET MÉLISANDE

From a letter to Ernest Chausson, Paris, October 2, 1893

I was too quick to cry victory over *Pelléas et Mélisande*, for after one of those long nights that bears counsel, I had to admit to myself that this wouldn't do. It was like the duet of any Mr. So-and-so, or anybody else; and, especially, the ghost of old Klingsor—alias R. Wagner—appeared at the detour of a measure, so I tore everything up and began anew in search of a bit more personal stamp in phrasing, and made an effort to be as much Pelléas as Mélisande. I went in search of music behind all the veils it accumulates, even for its most ardent devotees! I came back from there with something that might please you. As for the others, it's all the same to me—I even helped myself, rather spontaneously, to a means that to me seems rare enough—to silence, that is (don't laugh) as an agent of expression— and perhaps the only way to emphasize the emotion of a phrase. For, if Wagner made use of it, it seems to me it was in a totally dramatic way, a little in imitation of other dreams.   [26]

Letter to the violinist Eugène Ysaÿe, October 13, 1896

I was most touched by your kind letter and your friendly anxiety for *Pélleas et Mélisande.* The poor little creatures are so difficult to introduce into the world, for with a godfather like you the world doesn't want to have anything to do with them.

Now I must humbly tell you why I am not of your opinion about a partial performance of *Pelléas*. First, if this work has any merit, it is in the connection be-tween the drama and the music. It is quite obvious that at a concert performance this connection would disappear, and no one could be blamed for seeing nothing in the "silences" with which this work is starred. Moreover, as the simplicity of the work gains significance only on the stage, at a concert performance they would throw in my face the American wealth of Wagner, and I'd be like some poor fel-low who couldn't afford to pay for the "contrabass tubas"! In my opinion Pelléas and Mélisande must be given *as they are,* and then it will be a matter of taking them or leaving them, and if we have to fight, it will be worthwhile.   [27]

IMAGES

From a letter to Jacques Durand, Pourville, September 3, 1907

The music of this piece has this about it: it is elusive, and consequently cannot be handled like a robust symphony that walks on all fours (sometimes on threes, but walks nevertheless).

Besides, I am more and more convinced that music is not, in essence, a thing that can be cast into a traditional and fixed form. It is made up of colors and rhythms.

The rest is a lot of humbug invented by frigid imbeciles riding the backs of the Masters, who have almost always written music of their own time.

Bach alone divined eternal truth.

In any case, music is a very young art, from the point of technique as well as knowledge.   [28]

OBSERVATIONS

From a letter to André Poniatowski, Paris, February 1893

But music, don't you know, is a dream from which the veils have been lifted. It's not even the expression of a feeling, it's the feeling itself.   [29]

From a letter to Ernest Chausson, Paris, September 3, 1893

Music should really be a hermetic science, guarded by texts that require such a lengthy and difficult interpretation that the hordes of people who use music as casually as one uses a handkerchief would become discouraged instead of making efforts to disseminate art to the public; I propose the foundation of a "Society of Musical Esotericism."   [30]

From a letter to Pierre Louÿs, Paris, August 20, 1894

No one's ever really pointed out how few chords there are in any given century! Im-possible to count how often since Gluck people have died to the chord of the sixth and now, from Manon to Isolde, they do it to the diminished seventh! And as for that idiotic thing called the perfect triad, it's only a habit, like going to a café!   [31]

From a letter to Jacques Durand, Paris, March 21, 1917

It is curious how two "parasitic" measures can demolish the most solidly built edifice. This is just what has happened to me, and nothing can prevent it, neither long experience nor the most beautiful talent! It is instinct only—as old as the world—that can save you!   [32]

Richard Strauss
1864–1949

Strauss wrote his first song at five and composed prolifically for the next eighty years. His music was widely played, and he was also known as a conductor; by the time he was twenty, premieres of his symphonies had been given on both sides of the Atlantic and he had earned his first conducting post. Strauss remained in Germany through 1945, but his relationship with the Nazi government was one of mutual mistrust. His choice of Stefan Zweig as a librettist for Die schweigsame Frau *was seen as an act of defiance, though in the main Strauss's attitude toward politics was one of studied obtuseness. This attitude is evident in the 1935 letter to Zweig—a letter that, distasteful as it may be, did not go nearly far enough for the Nazis, who learned of the letter when a Gestapo agent intercepted it.*

From Betrachtungen und Erinnerungen *(1949), Strauss's collected essays*

TEN GOLDEN RULES FOR YOUNG CONDUCTORS

Inscribed in the album of a young conductor, c. 1925

1. Bear in mind that you are not making music for your own pleasure, but for the pleasure of your audience.

2. You must not perspire while conducting; only the public must get warm.

3. Direct *Salomé* and *Elektra* as if they had been written by Mendelssohn: fairy music.

4. Never encourage the brass, except with a curt glance, in order to give an important entrance cue.

5. On the contrary, never let the horns and woodwinds out of your sight; if you can hear them at all, they are too loud.

6. If you think that the brass is not blowing loud enough, mute it by a couple of degrees.

7. It is not enough that you yourself understand the singer's every word, which you know from memory; the public must be able to follow without effort. If the audience does not understand the text, it falls asleep.

8. Always accompany the singer so that he can sing without strain.

9. When you think that you have reached the most extreme *prestissimo*, take the tempo again as fast.*

---

* Might I alter the above today (1948): take the tempo half as fast. (For Mozart conductors!) [Strauss]

10. If you bear all this cheerfully in mind, you, with your beautiful talent and great knowledge, will ever be the untroubled delight of your listeners.   [1]

COMPOSING (1929)

It is simply not true that one can compose "everything," insofar as one understands "composing" as the translation of an expression of feeling or perception into the symbolic language of music. At the same time, it is just as true that one can paint in tones and sounds, particularly motives expressing action, but there always remains the imminent danger of relying too much on the music and falling into the trap of a boring imitation of nature. In this case, though the music be done with ever so much spirit and technical know-how, it will always remain second-rate music.

———— ♪ ————

It lies perhaps in the nature of the times that our successors, our "younger generation," our "moderns," can no longer view my dramatic and symphonic works as a valid expression of that which permitted me to live in them musically and as a human being, but which no longer holds any musical or artistic problems for me, though these are just beginning for the "younger generation." We are all children of our time, and can never leap beyond its shadow.   [2]

THE CONDUCTOR'S EQUIPMENT

Preface to An Orchestra Player on Conducting *by Hans Diestel, 1931*

When, as Royal Musical Director at the Munich Court Theater during the years 1886–89, I conducted my first opera (there were so many nice things in those days, what with unlimited subventions and singers without contractual vacations), my sixty-five-year-old father still sat in fabulous loyalty to duty an hour before curtain time in his accustomed chair of forty-five years as first horn, and was nervous not only about his own ticklish solos in *Così fan tutte*, but also lest the "green" baton of his unrouted *filius* on the podium reveal any weaknesses.

Somewhat disdainfully the old Lachner partisan and enemy of Bülow remarked: "Oh, you conductors, you flatter yourselves about the miracle of your authority! When a man takes over—the way he ascends the podium, opens the score, before he has lifted his baton—we already know whether he is master or we are."

Setting up these words as a motto, so to speak, for their work, I should like to admonish my colleagues of the podium: Don't be too proud of your three recalls after the third *Leonore* Overture! There below in the pit, among the first violins, there to the rear among the horns, or all the way at the other end among the drums, sit Argus-eyed watchers, who follow your quarters and eighths with critical glances, who groan when you "flail about" the *alla breves* from *Tristan* in four-four time "under their very noses," when you celebrate the "Scene at the Brook" or the second variation in the *adagio* of the Ninth with twelve precisely beat-out eighths. They rebel, when you continuously scream down to them "pst" and "*piano*, gentlemen" during the performance, while your right hand unceasingly conducts *forte*. They blink when, at the beginning of the rehearsal, you warn, "The woods are not in tune," and then you yourself cannot say which instrument is too sharp or too flat. While the big chief believes that they are hanging on his baton, they are faithfully playing on, without glancing at him as he misses a beat; they chalk every wrong tempo to his "individual conception," when he conducts a symphony, perhaps for the first time, which they have played a hundred times before under better conductors. . . .

In short, the tales of conductors tripped up by members of the orchestra could fill volumes! And yet, this malicious horde which dawdles about in a chronic *mezzo forte*, which maintains no precision in recitative chords when the right man is not sitting at the helm, with what enthusiasm do these musicians—so often tortured by unskillful bungling at rehearsal, dead tired from giving lessons—with what devotion even, do they rehearse when they have confidence in their director, if he doesn't harass them uselessly. How they follow his slightest gesture throughout the evening (particularly if he has made them a present of one rehearsal), if his right hand, in full control of conducting technique, is capable of conveying his intentions to the minutest degree, if his eye, at once stern and benevolent, watches over their playing, and his left hand does not clench itself into a fist at *fortissimos*, and he doesn't unnecessarily pester them at *pianos*.   [3]

TIMELY NOTES ON MUSIC EDUCATION (1933)

Music is a language the layman believes he understands better than Turkish, for instance, because its few characters are more quickly learned than those of the Koran, and because the naïve ear can retain a simple eight-bar melody more easily and fancies it better sounding than a Chinese sentence. Every child from the age of two on learns his mother tongue easily and by imitation. When he leaves primary school, he can read every book. Through daily comparison the eye has already trained itself to the point where a twelve-year-old student at the Pinakothek [art museum in Munich] can differentiate a Madonna from a St. Sebastian, and by dint of diligent reading does not take the signature of a Ruisdael for a Corot, or a Titian for a Rembrandt. But has he thereby a true understanding of wherein a real work of art differs from the most ordinary, tawdry work done in cheap and gaudy colors? Can he ascertain why a Sans Souci picture by Menzel is better painting than a Versailles *Coronation* by Anton von Werner? Though he experience the same deep, pious awe on entering the St. Stefan cathedral in Vienna as he does on hearing the Kyrie from the Bach B Minor Mass, though he sink into a pleasant, comfortable mood in which his fantasy allows him to glimpse ineffable visions, will he, without further ado, be able to recognize and enjoy that Gothic dome, the *Meistersinger* score, in its full significance as an art work? Since he at least knows the language, since he has eyes in his head, the *Wallenstein* trilogy or the Sistine Madonna will at any rate offer him more aesthetic enjoyment than one of the last Beethoven quartets, the brittle sound of which does not even arouse in him the same pleasant sensation as listening to the magnificently orchestrated *Lohengrin* Prelude with its instinctively thrilling, grandiose climax. Every layman, on listening to a Schiller poem, knows at least what he has heard. With a Mozart quartet, this is simply not the case.

Our humanistic culture still bases itself on disciplines, the study of which was an indispensable condition of higher intellectual learning before the invention of our music. It is today still burdened with unessential studies of higher mathematics, rudiments of chemistry and physics, which we can certainly leave to those in the universities and technical schools who wish to dedicate themselves to these professions. The study of music in our high schools, till now altogether neglected, is a requisite of higher general education. This means the study of at least harmony, form, counterpoint up to the understanding of a Bach fugue, the study of scores to the full comprehension of the contrapuntal soul struggle in the third act of *Tristan,* the architecture and thematic development of a Beethoven symphonic movement, the symphonic construction of an act of the *Nibelungen Ring.*   [4]

MELODIC INSPIRATION (1940)

Mozart's melodies, his G Minor String Quintet, Beethoven's symphonies, sonatas, quartets (the A-flat-major *adagio* from the E-flat-Major Quartet, Op. 127), Schubert's songs, the second and third acts of *Tristan* (to mention just a few outstanding examples) are symbols that reveal the most exalted truths of the soul, which are not "invented," but are "lent in a dream" to those favored with them. Whence they come, nobody knows, not even their creator, the unconscious instrument of the world spirit. The melodic idea, coming straight out of the ether, which suddenly overtakes me, which appears without any material stimulus or psychic emotion—the latter is also frequently a direct cause, as I myself have experienced it in excitement of a quite different, not necessarily artistic order—emerges from the imagination, immediate, unconscious, without benefit of the intelligence. It is the greatest of divine gifts, not to be compared with any other.

Poetic inspiration can still have a connection with the intelligence, because it must externalize itself through words—melodic inspiration is the absolute revelation of final mysteries.

It has been my own experience in creative activity that a motive or a two- to four-measure melodic phrase occurs to me suddenly. I put it down on paper and immediately extend it to an eight, sixteen, or thirty-two bar phrase, which naturally does not remain unaltered, but after a shorter or longer "maturing" is gradually worked out into its definitive form, which holds its own against even the most severe, blasé self-criticism. This work now proceeds at a rate that depends primarily on my awaiting the moment at which my imagination is capable and ready to serve me further. But this readiness is mostly evoked and promoted by considerable leisure, after lengthy reflection, also through inner excitement (also anger and indignation). These mental processes pertain not only to innate talent but also to self-criticism and self-development. "Genius is industry," Goethe is supposed to have said. But industry and the desire to work are inborn, not merely acquired.

Only where content and form are clothed in the highest perfection, as among our truly great, is finished art achieved. Our music scholars—I speak of the two principal names, Friedrich von Hausegger *(Music As Expression)* and Eduard Hanslick *(Music As Form in Tonal Motion)*—made formulations that have since been considered as inimical opposites. This is wrong. They are the two aspects of music, which mutually complement each other. The points of departure of our contemporary music are of various kinds. "Form in tonal motion" has its source truly in the dance, "music as expression" in the cry of pain, in the necessity to give artistic form to religious prayer (Gregorian chant, Palestrina masses, and the chorales of J. S. Bach). At the same time, proceeding from Monteverdi, the recitative developed, then flowed into the aria and with it into contemporary opera.

We may designate as "form in tonal motion" most of the Bach and Handel instrumental works, in the slow movements of which deeper feeling struggles for expression, a feeling that later speaks to our hearts directly with form-perfected logic in all gradations of emotion in the works of Haydn, Mozart, Beethoven, and Schubert. The so-called sonata form, which, from Haydn to the late Beethoven, fused itself with the emotional content of the works, was not achieved again by any of the descendants of these heroes, Brahms or Bruckner, for instance, in whose compositions, excellent in themselves, the sonata form has become a conventional formula in the midst of which one often painfully senses arbitrary music making, whereas one stands with eyes and ears open in delight before a Haydn quartet.

These instrumental works of the classicists may also be termed "forms in tonal motion," but they are, however, no longer rhythmically moving tonal play as in Bach and Handel, but happy or impassioned, vital expressions of noblest spirituality. In the variation form still popular today, and of late frequently dull (in my *Don Quixote* carried *ad absurdum* and tragicomically travestied), is found united all the passagework invented and constantly enriched by the classicists. Finally, Richard Wagner combined all kinds of rich passagework with the most evocative melodies to serve dramatic expression. *Tristan, The Ring, Meistersinger,* and *Parsifal* constitute the peak toward which all species of "form in tonal motion" and "musical expression" strive. In Wagner, music reached its greatest capacity for expression.   [5]

MOZART (1944)

It has become the custom to treat this most sublime of all tonal masters as a "rococo artist," to represent his work as the epitome of the ornamental and the playful. Though it is correct to say that he was one who solved all "problems" before they were even posed, that in him passion is divested of everything earthly and seems to be viewed from a bird's-eye perspective, it is equally true that his work contains—even when transfigured, spiritualized, and liberated from reality—all phases of human experience from the monumental, dark grandeur of the Commandant's scene in *Don Giovanni* to the daintiness of the Zerlina arias, the heavenly frivolities of *Figaro,* and the deliberate ironies of *Così fan tutte.*

With less amplitude, but with no less abundance, the entire gamut of human feeling is expressed in his nondramatic creations. To set up a uniform Mozart style for the reproduction of this infinitely fine and richly organized soul-picture is as foolish as it is superficial.   [6]

From letters to Hugo von Hofmannsthal

Operas and Librettos

Garmisch, July 28, 1916

I share your view completely that the prelude to *Ariadne* takes precisely the new path that must be followed, and I myself incline toward realistic comedy with genuine, interesting people, be it of lyric content as *Rosenkavalier* with its superb Marschallin, or burlesque, a parody of the Offenbach type. But to alter the style of *Die Frau ohne Schatten* to the one toward which you are so sympathetic, and toward which we must both steer, is absolutely wrong. This has nothing to do with the music or text; this lies in the material itself, in its romanticism, in its symbolism. One cannot inject red corpuscles into figures like the King, the Queen, and the Nurse as one can into a Marschallin, an Octavian, or an Ochs. I may rack my brain endlessly, and I am tormenting myself no end, what with sifting and more sifting, but my heart is only half in it, and since my head must accomplish the greater half of the work, there must remain a breath of academic frigidity in it (what my wife so aptly calls "music crocheting"), which no bellows can fan into a real fire.   [7]

Garmisch, early September, 1916

Your cry of distress against "music making" à la Wagner has pierced my heart and has thrown open the door onto a completely new landscape, so that, guided by *Ariadne*, and particularly by its prelude, I hope to betake myself completely into the realm of un-Wagnerian theater, into opera of the heart and humanity. I see my way clearly before me, and I thank you for having prodded me, but for me to achieve this, you must create the necessary librettos, librettos à la *Black Domino*, *Maurer und Schlosser*, *Wildschütz*, *Zar und Zimmermann*, *Teufels Anteil*, à la Offenbach, but they must be filled with Hofmannsthalish people instead of puppets. An amusing, interesting plot, be it clothed in dialogue, arias, duets, ensembles, vitalized with real composable people like the Marschallin, Ochs, or Batak! In whatever form you wish! I promise you that I have now definitely stripped myself of the Wagnerian musical armor.   [8]

Munich, July 17, 1917

Today I want to express my strongest doubts concerning the melodrama form. It is the most awkward, most stupid art form that I know. Since every kind of musical exercise in the melodrama form must be limited to the veriest minimum, as otherwise the text is understood even less than in opera, it offers the musician the least rewarding of tasks and as a consequence, a very frugal aural feast to the public.   [9]

Garmisch, October 10, 1923

Everything that you have indicated with the word "spoken" I should like—for the present—to have really spoken. I find the so-called Mozartean "secco recitative" (with piano accompaniment) a not too happy art form, and am again beginning more and more to prefer dialogue between set pieces, which gain a freshness thereby. First, the purely spoken word is better understood, and precisely in such realistic dialogue as in the first Aithra scenes, the sung notes obliterate the characteristic cadence. I have the feeling that the solo scene between Helena and Aithra that you read to me will be more effective if much of it is spoken, and undue length will be avoided. [10]

MUSIC AND RACE

From a letter to Stefan Zweig, June 17, 1935

Your letter of the 15th drives me to despair! This Jewish obstinacy! It's enough to make anyone anti-Semitic! The pride of race, the feeling of solidarity—it gives even me a sense of difference! Do you imagine I've ever been influenced in any transaction by the idea that I'm a Teuton (perhaps, *qui le sait*)? Do you imagine that Mozart wrote consciously "Aryan" music? So far as I am concerned, people fall into two categories, those who have talent and those who have not; and so far as I am concerned the general public exists only from the moment it forms an audience. Whether the audience consists of Chinese, Upper Bavarians, New Zealanders, or Berliners is all the same to me, provided they've paid the full price for their seats. . . . Who told you I had gone so far politically? Because I took a concert for Bruno Walter? I did that for the sake of the orchestra—because I stepped into the gap for the other "non-Aryan," Toscanini? I did that for the sake of Bayreuth. That has nothing to do with politics. It doesn't matter to me how the news-rags interpret it, and you shouldn't bother about that either. That I go through the motions of being president of the Reichsmusikkammer? That's in order to do good and safeguard against greater evils. Simply from a sense of artistic duty. . . . So be a good fellow, forget Moses and the other Apostles for a few weeks and just work at your two-act libretto. [11]

Carl Nielsen
1865–1931

Nielsen studied the violin, cornet, and trombone, taught himself piano, and later took up conducting. As he matured, the Romanticism of his earlier works gave way to a judicious and personal blend of the pre-Romantic and the Modern. The modest fame Nielsen enjoyed in life grew steadily after his death; by his centennial he was widely recognized as Denmark's most significant composer. The slender volume Living Music *is Nielsen's only substantial contribution to the literature.*

From Living Music, *1925*

KNOWLEDGE AND INSPIRATION

It is interesting that though knowledge and culture can never for a moment conceal poverty of spirit, it is music that of all the arts requires the strictest discipline and will least tolerate superficiality. The most exacting studies there must be; but they must have been made *beforehand*. The man who composes with an effort had better not; but he who produces music without ever having toiled should do the same. Many believe in the catchphrase that knowledge and scholarship are detrimental to simplicity, and that, at all costs, they must preserve their souls from the poison of learning and the prose of labor. But it is an undisputed fact that the composers who have written the happiest, sprightliest works have passed through the hardest school (e.g., Mozart). Nor will music submit to affectation. Music devoid of originality is redundant and therefore affected. But ideas on this point are nearly always turned upside down.   [1]

IMAGINATION VERSUS EMOTION

Most musicians have got caught in the great flypapers that were put up for them in their youth. You see them struggling with their back legs to get free, but the sticky stuff is too strong, and in the end they lie down on their side and eat and live on what they would rather escape from.

Let them lie. For although one might help to release them, so much of the stuff would adhere that their footprints would always bear the mark of it. This glue is dangerous indeed. It is made up of the following ingredients: imagination, emotion, pathos, profundity, and the like. No room, you see, for grace, gaiety, and humor! And since "imagination" to most people means the same thing as "emotion," it will be seen that everything turns in the same direction. In other words, all is stagnation—there is no movement at all, no conflict. When all is of one direction, one sex, what can you expect but sterility, emptiness? Here, perhaps, we have the explanation of why the works of music in the "grand manner" that at present dominate the world's opera houses and concert halls go in for such pathetic and crudely emotional posturing; it is simply because, fundamentally, they lack the stuff of conflict that gives vigor and vitality, that knows itself and has no need to shout louder that it has the strength and energy for. The weak always shout loudest.   [2]

TRENDS

It is right that the historian should indicate the summits of achievements in art (the poetry, architecture, and sculpture of ancient Greece, sixteenth- and eighteenth-century music, Renaissance painting, etc.); but in a sense this is of little use to us. The claims of life are stronger than the sublimest art; and even were we to agree that we had achieved the best and most beautiful it is possible to achieve, we should be impelled in the end, thirsting as we do more for life and experience than for perfection, to cry out: "Give us something else; give us something new; for Heaven's sake give us something bad, so long as we feel we are alive and active and not just passive admirers of tradition!" . . .

There was a time in music, not long ago, when the pursuit of originality led to monster orchestras. Imagine the incredible naïveté of trying to get a greater effect with bigger orchestras! It was not more than fifteen to twenty years ago, and there are composers still living who took part in the movement. But of course the limit was soon reached. Orchestras of one, two, three, and four hundred players were the cry, and the mass display culminated with a thousand at a concert, I think, in Vienna. And what then? That was as far as it could go; and clear-headed people outside the profession—not conductors and musicians—began to react in speech and print. A new and equally absurd cry went up, this time for small orchestras at any price. Wind ensembles with one stringed instrument, harp duets with a percussion instrument, and so forth. While citing the old masters, their advocates overlooked the essential point that they wrote for the orchestras they had at hand or were commissioned to write for. . . .

Are we to return to something old, then? By no means. We should cease to reckon with either old or new. But woe to the musician who fails alike to learn and love the good things in the old masters and to watch and be ready for the new that may come in a totally different form from what we expected.   [3]

RESTS

For what is . . . a rest? It is really a continuation of the music; a cloth draped over a plastic figure, concealing part of it. We cannot see the figure under the draping, but we know from the exposed part that it is there; and we feel the organic connection between what we see and what we do not. . . .

The rests, then, are just as important as the notes. Often, they are far more expressive and appealing to the imagination. For this reason one could wish that many modern composers would confine themselves to rests—but perhaps that is too much to ask.   [4]

MOZART

There is still a residuum of music lovers who regard all that Mozart ever wrote as equally inspired. An old-fashioned, cultured, and nice sort of people who meet together and, perhaps, celebrate Mozart's birthday over a cup of tea. These nice people will then play the slightest of his sonatas and symphonies for one or two performers, and are happy every time they are *not* surprised. Of these Mozart worshippers there are not many, and they do neither good nor harm, for they can have no influence on the younger generation. Then there are the musical people whom I would call the conventionally orthodox. They do not really care for Mozart and prefer to pass him by, though with a reverent raising of the hat and an apologetic bow. There are many of these, especially among singers, players, conductors, and composers. Finally, among younger musicians, there are a few who realize that for anyone wishing to study music in all its aspects, there is no escaping Mozart. The fact is, Mozart is extraordinarily severe, logical, and consistent in his scoring and modulation, yet, at the same time, freer and less constrained in form than any of the classical masters who have employed the difficult sonata form so favoured by composers since Philipp Emanuel Bach—the form on which the symphony is based.

———— ⸙ ————

From Beethoven one learns to build up an *allegro* movement with its two subjects and development. But it is remarkable how this master—the greatest lyrical composer—is regular, often even wooden and rigid, in form. One turns to Mozart and marvels at the liberties he takes. He relaxes all restraints and says everything that strikes his fancy in the most convincing and natural manner possible. Ideas that at first seem irrelevant prove to be essential. A carefree theme bobs up next to a grave one; one idea is barely expressed before the next presses in. Yet the whole thing moves forward with such assurance and order that never for a moment do we get confused or lose the thread.

As a dramatist, Mozart introduced something new when he made his characters real, live people. He felt this himself. In a letter to his father, dated September 1781, one discerns his pleasure at the variety of moods he has got into Belmonte's aria in *Seraglio;* and his fine observations on the relationship of music to text are worth a good deal more than Gluck's long prefaces. In fact, it was Mozart who brought about the *musical*-dramatic advancement for which Gluck has been given the credit. But he wrote no prefaces proclaiming a revolution, a proclamation for the credulous, unmusical "musical historians" to perpetuate right down to our own time.

It follows from what I have said that Mozart's music is extraordinarily difficult to understand fully, and it is still more difficult to play. We need not only deep and sincere sympathy with his art, but a well-matured mind, if we are to render his works at all well. It is an offense against Mozart and against the young student of music, therefore, for a teacher to set his pupil to play Mozart's sonatas and quartets as soon as he has acquired a modicum of technique. It is barbarous, in fact, and will only spoil the pupil's desire to study Mozart subsequently. How can we expect young people to appreciate the exquisitely alternating moods of this music, or feel the beauty of an art that expresses itself with such restraint and in so strangely spiritual a manner! What youth wants, above all else, is something it can grasp, something it can lay hold on with both hands. But the content of Mozart's music is the least tangible, and so it is better to let the young musician get his fingers into Chopin and Liszt than choke the life out of Mozart. . . . I know few musicians who can play Mozart's music satisfactorily; most of them "stylize" his works in a manner altogether intolerable.   [5]

WAGNER

From a diary entry, 1893

Wagner's characters undertake too little; they only talk. They talk about what has happened, what is happening, and what is going to happen. Yet nothing happens at all. These human beings cannot act, and Wagner neither. As a dramatic poet he is nothing and as a dramatic composer almost nothing; as soon as he tries to express life and passionate emotions they become tawdry. As a lyric poet he is great, but with lyrics one does not construct a drama; they melt away.   [6]

Ferruccio Busoni
1866–1924

A prodigy at the piano who matured into one of the great virtuosos of his time, Busoni was also a self-styled musical intellectual. His music draws on both sides of his talent, indulging an almost philosophical brand of experimentalism while making fierce demands on technique. Audiences have tended to find Busoni's music more curious than satisfying, and he remains better known for his grandiose piano transcriptions of Bach than for his own works.

From Sketch of a New Esthetic of Music, *1906*

THE POTENTIALS OF MUSIC

Architecture, sculpture, poetry, and painting are old and mature arts; their conceptions are established and their objects assured; they have found the way through uncounted centuries, and, like the planets, describe their regular orbits.*

Music, compared with them, is a child that has learned to walk, but must still be led. It is a virgin art, without experience in life or suffering.

It is all unconscious as yet of what garb is becoming, of its own advantages, its unawakened capacities. [1]

FORM AND FREEDOM

Such lust of liberation filled Beethoven, the romantic revolutionary, that he ascended one short step on the way leading music back to its loftier self:—a short step in the great task, a wide step in his own path. He did not quite reach absolute music, but in certain moments he divined it, as in the introduction to the fugue of the Sonata for Hammerclavier. Indeed, all composers have drawn nearest the true nature of music in preparatory and intermediary passages (preludes and transitions), where they felt at liberty to disregard symmetrical proportions and unconsciously drew free breath. Even a Schumann (of so much lower stature) is seized, in such passages, by some feeling of the boundlessness of this pan-art (recall the transition to the last movement of the D Minor Symphony); and the same may be asserted of Brahms in the introduction to the finale of his First Symphony.

But the moment they cross the threshold of the *Principal Subject,* their attitude becomes stiff and conventional, like that of a man entering some bureau of high officialdom. [2]

MUSICAL LAWS

The creator should take over no traditional law in blind belief, which would make him view his own creative endeavor, from the outset, as an exception contrasting with that law. For his individual case he should seek out and formulate a fitting indi-

---

* Nonetheless, in these arts, taste and individuality can and will unceasingly find refreshment and rejuvenation. [Busoni]

vidual law, which, after the first complete realization, he should annul, that he himself may not be drawn into repetitions when his next work shall be in the making.

The function of the creative artist consists in making laws, not in following laws ready made. He who follows such laws ceases to be a creator.

Creative power may be the more readily recognized, the more it shakes itself loose from tradition. But an intentional avoidance of the rules cannot masquerade as creative power, and still less engender it.   [3]

KEYS AND SCALES

We have divided the octave into twelve equidistant degrees, because we had to manage somehow, and have constructed our instruments in such a way that we can never get in above or below or between them. Keyboard instruments, in particular, have so thoroughly schooled our ears that we are no longer capable of hearing anything else—incapable of hearing except through this impure medium. Yet Nature created an *infinite gradation—infinite!* who still knows it nowadays? . . .

We teach twenty-four keys, twelve times the two series of seven, but, in point of fact, we have at our command only two, the major and the minor key. . . .

To each of these a definite character has been attributed; we have learned and have taught that they should be heard as contrasts, and they have gradually acquired the significance of symbols: Major and Minor, *Maggiore e Minore,* Contentment and Discontent, Joy and Sorrow, Light and Shade. The harmonic symbols have fenced in the expression of music, from Bach to Wagner and yet further on until today and the day after tomorrow.* Minor is employed with the same intention, and has the same effect upon us now, as two hundred years ago. Nowadays it is no longer possible to "compose" a funeral march, for it already exists, once for all. Even the least-informed nonprofessional knows what to expect when a funeral march—whichever you please—is to be played. Even the layman can anticipate the difference between a symphony in major and one in minor.   [4]

NOTATION AND IMPROVISATION

Notation, the writing out of compositions, is primarily an ingenious expedient for catching an inspiration, with the purpose of exploiting it later. But notation is to improvisation as the portrait to the living model. It is for the interpreter to *resolve the rigidity of the signs* into the primitive emotion.   [5]

RESTS

That which, within our present-day music, most nearly approaches the essential nature of the art is the rest and the hold (pause). Consummate players, improvisers, know how to employ these instruments of expression in loftier and ampler measure. The tense silence between two movements—*in itself music*, in this environment—leaves wider scope for divination than the more determinate, but therefore less elastic, sound.   [6]

---

* This was written in 1906. The intervening ten years have somewhat helped to educate our ear. [Busoni (note added in the second German edition)]

THE PIANO

Respect the pianoforte! Its disadvantages are evident, decided, and unquestionable: the lack of sustained tone, and the pitiless, unyielding adjustment of the inalterable semitone scale.

But its advantages and prerogatives approach the marvelous.

It gives a single man command over something complete; in its potentialities from softest to loudest in one and the same register, it excels all other instruments. The trumpet can blare, but not sigh; contrariwise the flute; the pianoforte can do both. Its range embraces the highest and deepest practicable tones. Respect the pianoforte! . . .

And the pianoforte has one possession wholly peculiar to itself, an inimitable device, a photograph of the sky, a ray of moonlight—the pedal.   [7]

TRANSCRIPTIONS

From a letter to his wife, Berlin, July 22, 1913

Transcription occupies an important place in the literature of the piano, and looked at from the right point of view, every important piano piece is the reduction of a big thought to a practical instrument. But transcription has become an independent art, no matter whether the starting point of a composition is original or unoriginal. Bach, Beethoven, Liszt, and Brahms were evidently all of the opinion that there is artistic value concealed in a pure transcription, for they all cultivated the art themselves, seriously and lovingly. In fact, the art of transcription has made it possible for the piano to take possession of the entire literature of music. Much that is inartistic, however, has got mixed up with this branch of the art. And it was because of the cheap, superficial estimation made of it by certain men, who had to hide their nakedness with a mantle of "being serious," that it sank to what was considered a low level.   [8]

BEETHOVEN

From a letter to Egon Petri, 1916

The Latin attitude to art, with its cool serenity and its insistence on outward form, is what refreshes me. It was only through Beethoven that music acquired that growling and frowning expression which was natural enough to him, but which perhaps ought to have remained his lonely path alone. Why are you in such a bad temper, one would often like to ask, especially in the second period[?]   [9]

STRAUSS

From a letter to his wife, Rochester, New York, March 21, 1904

Strauss is a person of decided talent and has rich gifts. Polyphony and movement are necessary elements to him.

An admirable facility for making things complicated and spreading out what is small. Strauss seems to write out the principal voices, then the principal middle voice, and afterward cram everything there is still room for in between. One can go on and on with that, but he does not stop in time. He does not understand the mastery of the unfinished. [10]

AN EARLY RECORDING SESSION

From a letter to his wife, London, November 20, 1919

From the first day I have been as depressed as if I were expecting to have an operation. To do it is stupid and a strain. Here is an example of what happens: They wanted the *Faust* waltz (which lasts a good ten minutes) *but it was only to take four minutes!* That meant quickly cutting, patching, and improvising, so that there should still be some sense left in it; watching the pedal (because it sounds bad); thinking of certain notes that had to be stronger or weaker in order to please this devilish machine; not letting oneself go for fear of inaccuracies and being conscious the whole time that every note was going to be there for eternity; how can there be any question of inspiration, freedom, swing, or poetry? Enough that yesterday, for nine pieces of four minutes each (half an hour in all), I worked for three and a half hours! Two of these pieces I played four or five times. Having to think so quickly at the same time was a severe effort. In the end, I felt the effects in my arms; after that, I had to sit for a photograph and sign the discs. At last it was finished. [11]

Erik Satie
1866–1925

After a long period at the Paris Conservatory, Satie became a cabaret pianist, in which context he first wrote music of an individual stamp. His eccentric charm earned him many musical friends, though his music itself, with its insistence on the significance of the trivial and with its innovations born of a suspicion of technique, received little notice until Satie was "discovered" by Ravel around 1911, and later by Jean Cocteau. Satie was an influence on Debussy, Milhaud, Poulenc, and others, although his elevation to the status of cult figure did not occur until the 1960s, when he came to be seen as a precursor of the conceptual artist.

INTELLIGENCE AND MUSICALITY AMONG THE ANIMALS

From Memoires d'un amnésique, *1914*

Few animals benefit from human instruction. The dog, the mule, the horse, the donkey, the parrot, and a few others are the only animals to receive a semblance of education. And yet, can you call it education? Compare this instruction, if you please, to that given the young human undergraduate by the universities, and you will see it is worthless, it can neither broaden the knowledge nor facilitate the learning the animal might have acquired through his own labors, by his own devotion. But musically? Horses have learned to dance; spiders have remained under a piano throughout an entire concert—a long concert organized for them by a respected master. So what? So nothing. Now and then we are told about the musicality of the starling, the melodic memory of the crow, the harmonic ingenuity of the owl who accompanies himself by tapping his stomach—a purely artificial contrivance and polyphonically meager.

As for the perennially cited nightingale, his musical knowledge makes his most ignorant auditors shrug. Not only is his voice not placed, but he has absolutely no knowledge of clefs, tonality, modality, or measure. Perhaps he is gifted? Possibly, almost certainly. But it can be stated flatly that his artistic culture does not equal his natural gifts, and that the voice of which he is so inordinately proud is nothing but an inferior useless instrument. [1]

PROGRESS AND ITS ENEMIES

From notes published in L'Humanité, October 11, 1919

In order to combat "advanced" ideas in politics or in art, all means are justified—especially underhand means. "New" artists—those who "change something"—have always suffered attacks from their enemies who wage war on the newness of trends—and visions—which they cannot understand.

In art as in politics: Jaurès* was attacked in the same way as Manet, Berlioz, Wagner, Picasso, Verlaine, and so many others. That is always "starting up" again and it is always the same people who resist progress in all its shapes and forms: the upholders of the "status quo," the good folk who *know what they like."* [2]

CRITICS

From a lecture, February 1918

Last year I gave several lectures on "Intelligence and Musicality among animals." . . .

Today, I am going to speak to you about "Intelligence and Musicality among Critics." . . .

The subject is much the same, with some modifications, of course.

———— 𝄢 ————

There are three sorts of critics: those of importance, those of less importance, those of no importance at all. The two latter kinds don't exist: all critics are important.

———— 𝄢 ————

An artist can be imitated; the critic is inimitable and invaluable. How could anyone imitate a critic? I ask myself. However, it would not be very interesting, not interesting at all: we have the original, that's enough for us.

———— 𝄢 ————

* Jean-Léon Jaurès (1859–1914) was a progressive journalist and politician who was assassinated in a Paris café.

A critic's brain is a department store, a big department store. You can find every-thing there: artificial limbs, scientific instruments, bedding, art supplies, travel rugs, a wide selection of furniture. French and foreign writing paper, articles for smokers, gloves, umbrellas, woolen goods, hats, sporting goods, canes, optical prod-ucts, perfumes, etc. The critic knows everything, sees everything, says everything, hears everything, touches everything, moves everything, eats everything, confuses everything, and thinks none the less of it. What a man! Let us tell ourselves that!

———— ♪ ————

They have no passions at all, none. Always calm, they never think of anything but their duty of correcting the poor world's faults and earning a good living—so as to buy tobacco, quite simply.   [3]

APHORISMS

From an unpublished note, c. 1920

Jazz speaks to us of its suffering and we don't give a damn. That's why it's beau-tiful, real ...   [4]

From Pierre-Daniel Templier's biography, 1932

Like money, [the piano] pleases only those who touch it.   [5]

All great artists are amateurs.   [6]

The musician is perhaps the most modest of all animals, but he is also the proud-est. It is he who invented the sublime art of ruining poetry.   [7]

The exercise of an art demands that we live in a state of the most absolute renun-ciation.   [8]

Although our information is incorrect, we do not vouch for it.   [9]

DEBUSSY

From a journal entry, c. 1920

When all is said and done, *ce bon* Debussy was something else again than all the others put together.   [10]

From an article on Debussy, 1923

When I first met Debussy, he was full of Musorgsky and was very deliberately seeking a way that wasn't very easy for him to find. In this problem I was well in advance of him. I was not weighed down with the Prix de Rome, or any other prize, for I am a man like Adam (of Paradise) who never won any prizes—a lazy fellow, no doubt.

At that time I was writing *Le Fils des étoiles* to a libretto by Joseph Péladan, and I explained to Debussy that a Frenchman had to free himself from the Wagnerian adventure, which wasn't the answer to our national aspirations. I also pointed out that I was in no way anti-Wagnerian, but that we should have a music of our own—if possible without any *sauerkraut.*

Why could we not use the means that Claude Monet, Cézanne, Toulouse-Lautrec, and others had made known? Why could we not transpose these means into music? Nothing simpler. [11]

RAVEL

From a letter to his brother Conrad, Arcueil, April 11, 1911

Ravel . . . occupies a considerable place in modern music. I knew him as a child and have always taken an interest in his work. I confess to my shame—that I didn't think him capable of publicly acknowledging that he owes me a lot. I was very moved by it. [12]

From a letter to Georges Jean-Aubry, Arcueil, November 19, 1919

I love Ravel deeply, but his art leaves me cold, alas! [13]

From a note published in Le Coq, May 1920

Ravel refuses the Legion of Honor, but all his music accepts it. [14]

STRAVINSKY

From "Propositions Proposed about Igor Stravinsky," Feuilles libres, 1922

For us scurvy troublemakers, Igor Stravinsky is one of the most remarkable geniuses ever to have existed in music. The lucidity of his mind has set us free; his fighting strength has won us rights that we can never lose again. That is a fact.

His penetrating power is sharper than that of Debussy and cannot be blunted; it is too finely tempered. Stravinsky has so many different methods, such a sense of inventiveness, that one can only be amazed. [15]

From the manuscript of an article for Vanity Fair, 1923

One of the characteristics of Stravinsky's music is its "transparency of sound." This quality is always to be found in the works of pure masters, who never allow "leftovers" to be heard in their music—leftovers that you will meet all the time in the "musical material" of the Impressionist composers, and even of certain Romantics, alas! . . .

Where Stravinsky reveals to us the utter richness of his musical power is in his use of "dissonance." Here he declares himself and plunges us into a vast intellectual ecstasy. What a superb magician!

For him, "dissonance" means "increased pressure," and through it he "leans" on the sensibility of the appreciative listener. The "dissonance" is in no way harsh; it takes place "in the wings," all shimmering, but always with a function.   [16]

STUDY WITH D'INDY

From a letter to his brother Conrad, 1910

In 1905 I began to study with d'Indy. I was tired of being reproached for an ignorance that I believed myself in truth to be guilty of, since competent people had pointed to it in my works.

At the end of three years' hard work, I received from the Schola Cantorum a diploma in counterpoint, signed by my excellent teacher, who is certainly the best and most learned man in the world. So there I was, in 1908, holding a degree conferring on me the right to call myself contrapuntist. Very proud of my newly acquired knowledge, I began to compose. My first composition of this kind was a Chorale and Fugue for four hands. I've often been insulted in the course of my sad existence, but never before had I been so despised. Why on earth had I gone to d'Indy? The things I had written before had such charm, such depth! And now? What nonsense! What dullness!

Thereupon, "the young ones" organized an anti-d'Indy movement and decided to play the Sarabandes, Le Fils des étoiles, etc., the same works which were once considered the fruits of my great ignorance—quite wrongly, according to the same "young ones."   [17]

SELF-OBSERVATIONS

From an article by E. Demets in the Bulletin des Editions musicales, Paris, 1913

My sense of humor recalls that of Cromwell. I also owe much to Christopher Columbus; for American wit has sometimes tapped me on the shoulder and I have been pleased to feel its ironical and icy bite.   [18]

Before I compose a piece, I walk round it several times, accompanied by myself.
    [19]

From a note published in Le Coq, June 1920

There is no school of Satie. Satieism could never exist. I would oppose it.   [20]

YOUTH AND EXPERIENCE

From Rollo Myers's biography, 1948

I have always trusted youth. And so far I have not been disappointed. Our epoch is favorable to youth. But let them beware—their youth will expose them to attack. One need not be very astute to notice that people of a certain age always talk about their "experience" ... It is very good of them ... But one ought, all the same, to be sure that they have really had any worthwhile experience ... Human memory is very short—is one not accustomed, whenever the weather behaves erratically, to hear people say: "There's been nothing like this within living memory"? I'm quite ready to believe them. But don't let them talk to me too much about their "experience." . . . I know them only too well. And so these young men will be blamed because they are young. I wrote my Sarabandes at the age of twenty-one, in 1887; the *Gymnopédies* when I was twenty-two, in 1888. These are the only works that my detractors—those over the age of fifty, of course—admire. To be logical, they ought to like the works of my maturity. They don't.   [21]

CHAPTER NINE

Ralph Vaughan Williams

Max Reger

Sergei Rachmaninoff

Arnold Schoenberg

Charles Ives

Maurice Ravel

Manuel de Falla

Ralph Vaughan Williams
1872–1958

Vaughan Williams's musical training included three degrees from Cambridge and studies with Max Bruch in Leipzig. Still not entirely satisfied, he went to Paris in 1908 to study orchestration with Ravel, who was a few years his junior. His music shows many influences, including Impressionism, folk song, Tudor composers, and Anglican liturgical music. Stylistically his music is more varied (and often more vigorous) than his most popular pieces suggest. His book National Music *derives from a series of lectures given at Bryn Mawr College in 1932.*

From National Music, *1934*

SHOULD MUSIC BE NATIONAL?

Whistler used to say that it was as ridiculous to talk about national art as national chemistry. In saying this he failed to see the difference between art and science. Science is the pure pursuit of knowledge and thus knows no boundaries. Art, and especially the art of music, uses knowledge as a means to the evocation of personal experience in terms which will be intelligible to and command the sympathy of others. These others must clearly be primarily those who by race, tradition, and cultural experience are the nearest to him; in fact those of his own nation, or other kind of homogeneous community. But unfortunately for the art of music some misguided thinker . . . has described music as the "universal language." It is not even true that music has a universal vocabulary, but even if it were so, it is the use of the vocabulary that counts and no one supposes that French and English are the same language because they happen to use twenty-five out of twenty-six of the letters of their alphabet in common. In the same way, in spite of the fact that they have a musical alphabet in common, nobody could mistake Wagner for Verdi, or Debussy for Richard Strauss. And, similarly, in spite of wide divergencies of personal style, there is a common factor in the music, say, of Schumann and Weber. And this common factor is nationality.

———— ♪ ————

One of the three great composers of the world (personally I believe the greatest) was Johann Sebastian Bach. Here, you may say, is the universal musician if ever there was one; yet no one could be more local, in his origin, his life work, and his fame for nearly a hundred years after his death, than Bach. He was to outward appearance no more than one of a fraternity of town organists and "town pipers" whose business it was to provide the necessary music for the great occasions in church and city. He never left his native country, seldom even his own city of Leipzig. "World movements" in art were then unheard of; moreover, it was the tradition of his own country which inspired him. True, he studied eagerly all the music of foreign composers that came his way in order to improve his craft. But is not the work of Bach built up on two great foundations, the organ music of his Teutonic predecessors and the popular hymn tunes of his own people?   [1]

NATIONALISM AND MUSICAL STANDARDS

I doubt if there is [an] absolute standard of goodness. I think it will vary with the occasion on which it is performed, with the period at which it was composed and with the nationality of those that listen to it. Let us take examples of each of these—firstly, with regard to the occasion. The Venusberg music from *Tannhäuser* is good music when it comes at the right dramatic moment in the opera; but it is bad music when it is played on an organ in church. I am sorry to have to tell you that this is not an imaginary experience. A waltz of Johann Strauss is good music in its proper place as an accompaniment to dancing and festivity, but it would be bad music if it were interpolated in the middle of the *St. Matthew Passion*. And may we not even say that Bach's *B Minor Mass* would be bad music if it were played in a restaurant as an accompaniment to eating and drinking?

Secondly, does not the standard of goodness vary with time? What was good for the fifteenth century is not necessarily good for the twentieth. Surely each new generation requires something different to satisfy its different ideals. Of course there is some music that seems to defy the ravages of time and to speak a new message to each successive generation. But even the greatest music is not eternal. We can still appreciate Bach and Handel or even Palestrina, but Dufay and Dunstable have little more than an historical interest for us now. But they were great men in their day and perhaps the time will come when Bach, Handel, Beethoven, and Wagner will drop out and have no message left for us. Sometimes, of course, the clock goes round full circle and the twentieth century comprehends what had ceased to have any meaning for the nineteenth. This is the case with the modern revival of Bach after nearly one hundred and fifty years of neglect, or the modern appreciation of Elizabethan madrigals. There may be many composers who have something genuine to say to us for a short time, and for that short time their music may be surely classed as good. We all know that when an idiom is new we cannot detect the difference between the really original mind and the mere imitator. But when the idiom passes into the realm of everyday commonplace, then and then only we can tell the true from the false. For example, any student at a music school can now reproduce the tricks of Debussy's style, and therefore it is now, and only now, that we can discover whether Debussy had something genuine to say or whether, when the secret of his style becomes common property, the message of which that style was the vehicle will disappear.

Then there is the question of place. Is music that is good music for one country or one community necessarily good music for another? It is true that the great monuments of music, the *Missa Papae Marcelli,* or the *St. Matthew Passion,* or the Ninth Symphony or *Die Meistersinger*, have a worldwide appeal, but first they must appeal to the people, and in the circumstances where they were created. It is because Palestrina and Verdi are essentially Italian and because Bach, Beethoven, and Wagner are essentially German that their message transcends their frontiers. And even so, the *St. Matthew Passion,* much as it is loved and admired in other countries, must mean much more to the German, who recognizes in it the consummation of all that he learned from childhood in the great traditional chorales which are his special inheritance. Beethoven has a universal meaning, but to the German, who finds in it that same spirit exemplified in its more homely form in those Volkslieder which he learned in his childhood, he must have a specialized meaning.

——— ⁂ ———

I think there is no work of art which represents the spirit of a nation more surely than *Die Meistersinger* of Richard Wagner. Here is no plaything with local color, but the raising to its highest power all that is best in the national consciousness of his own country. This is universal art in truth, universal because it is so intensely national.   [2]

GENIUS

The great men of music close periods; they do not inaugurate them. The pioneer work, the finding of new paths, is left to smaller men. We can trace the musical genealogy of Beethoven, starting right back from Philipp Emanuel Bach, through Haydn and Mozart, with even such smaller fry as Cimarosa and Cherubini to lay the foundations of the edifice. Is not the mighty river of Wagner but a confluence of the smaller streams of Weber, Marschner, and Liszt?

I would define genius as the right man in the right place at the right time. We know, of course, too many instances of the time being ripe and the place being vacant and no man to fill it. But we shall never know of the numbers of "mute and inglorious Miltons" who failed because the place and time were not ready for them. Was not Purcell a genius born before his time? Was not Sullivan a jewel in the wrong setting?   [3]

BEETHOVEN

From Musical Autobiography, *1952*

To this day the Beethoven idiom repels me, but I hope that I have at last learnt to see the greatness that lies behind the idiom I dislike, and at the same time to see an occasional weakness behind the Bach idiom I love.   [4]

STRAVINSKY

From National Music

At one time he will toy with jazz, at another time with Bach and Beethoven seen through a distorted mirror. Or he will amuse himself by adding piquant "wrong notes" to the complacent beauty of Pergolesi. This seems to be not the work of a serious composer, but rather that of the too clever craftsman, one might almost say, the feats of the precocious child.   [5]

Max Reger
1873–1916

Reger was a professor of composition, a concert organist, and a pianist and conductor who toured internationally with his compositions. He admired Brahms and shared his Classical sympathies, but also appreciated Wagner and Strauss. From 1911 to 1914 he was director of the Meiningen Court orchestra, enjoying a correspondence with Duke Georg II, who welcomed Reger's efforts to return the orchestra to the heights it had achieved under Hans von Bülow.

TEMPO, COLOR, AND DYNAMICS

Letter to Georg II of Sachsen-Meiningen, Meiningen, January 7, 1912

The tempo of a piece is determined not only by the directions of the composer but also by its harmonic and polyphonic content, by the hall in which it is played, and by the principle of utmost clarity. Thus, for example, one can never take an organ fugue as fast in a church as in a concert hall, since the peculiar acoustical conditions in every church might otherwise create noise and chaos. Brahms is so polyphonic that the greatest care must be taken not to drown out important middle voices, thereby suppressing the most beautiful passages.

Besides—now I am committing a sacrilege, but I believe I may receive absolution considering my well-known admiration for Brahms—besides, Brahms too often indicates tempi that are too fast. The inwardly stimulated creator is often misled by his excitement into prescribing overfast tempi. I know from my own experience that I have indicated tempi which I have later taken much more slowly myself! Thus it is impossible to take the first movement of Brahms's Fourth Symphony at the tempo he marks it without making a complete hash of it. Particularly Brahms! Only too often did he orchestrate so that the most important passages lie in the "weak" ranges of certain instruments so that it is impossible to bring them out. Naturally such passages do not sound—and Brahms is condemned by detractors as "hard to understand," "confused"! We must make many, many changes, we must make ruthless alterations in some voices in order to fulfill Brahms's true intent. Brahms's treatment of horns is sometimes untenable. He gives passages to bassoons that can only be conceived in the horns. The bassoons blow for dear life and the result is a horrible squeak. Give the identical passages to the horns and they "sound" immediately. Brahms tended to write for horns "conservatively," yet his harmony is sensitive, modern. Hence the dichotomy between "sound" and intent.   [1]

FREE CREATION

From a letter to Ella Kerndl, Weiden, October 1, 1900

Creation must be completely free. Every fetter one imposes on oneself by taking into account playability or public taste leads to disaster. By this I do not mean that every immature conservatory student should sit down and compose nonsensically. These young gentlemen should first learn something solid. [2]

CRITICS

From a letter to Rudolph Louis, February 1906

I am sitting in the smallest room in the house. I have your review in front of me. Soon it will be behind me. [3]

BRAHMS

From a letter to Adalbert Lindner, Wiesbaden, April 6, 1894

Brahms is the greatest composer since Beethoven, but he also has his mannerisms: Phrygian thirds, Dorian sixths, etc. In the treatment of the piano he stands alone. In his hands, a piano piece takes on a completely orchestral color. To be sure, he makes no use of passages, chromatic scales, etc., but he makes up for it through a pure polyphony and the noblest of melodic lines, which is often designated by denigrators as "disregard for sensuous sound." But one must first immerse oneself in the highly expressive power of his melodic line. He is not obvious; he loves to shroud the beauties of his works with a veil, and one becomes aware of these beauties only after a thorough knowledge of the work. True, his music is somewhat incomprehensible to the average audience; nevertheless, Brahms has carried his art so far that all really discerning musicians must come to consider him as the greatest living composer, if they are not to be considered unknowledgeable. His three symphonies (D major, F major, and C minor) place him as a symphonist in a direct line after Beethoven, and he has enriched us considerably with his chamber music and songs. [4]

Sergei Rachmaninoff
1873–1943

Rachmaninoff's popularity with audiences and his dismissal by the musical establishment—both long-standing traditions—share the same misapprehension of the music, seeing it as merely showy and sentimental rather than the work of a cognizant and incisive mind. Born to Russian gentry, Rachmaninoff was forced to leave the country with the 1917 revolution. He lived first in Europe and later in America, settling in Beverly Hills.

Rachmaninoff was the last true composer-virtuoso, earning his living as a touring and recording artist as well as through conducting and composing. His recordings show him to be a pianist of almost unimaginable agility, by common consent one of the greatest of the twentieth century.

From Oskar von Riesemann's Rachmaninoff's Recollections, *1934*

RIMSKY-KORSAKOV

In Rimsky-Korsakov's scores there is never the slightest doubt about the "meteorological" picture the music is meant to convey. When there is a snowstorm, the flakes seem to dance and drift from the woodwinds and the soundholes of the violins; when the sun is high, all instruments shine with an almost fiery glare; when there is water, the waves ripple and splash audibly through the orchestra, and this effect is not achieved by the comparatively cheap means of a harp glissando; the sound is cool and glassy when he describes a calm winter night with a glittering starlit sky. He was a great master of orchestral sound-painting, and one can still learn from him. It seems strange that a man who handled the secrets of the orchestra in so masterly a fashion, down to the smallest detail, should be so helpless as a conductor. "Conducting is a black art," he says in his book *Chronicles of My Musical Life.* Unfortunately, this thought was not exclusively his own, but presented itself to the audience as he stood at the conductor's desk.   {1}

MAHLER AS CONDUCTOR

The [first] performance of my Third Concerto took place in New York, under the direction of Damrosch. Immediately afterward I repeated it in New York, but under Gustav Mahler.

At that time Mahler was the only conductor whom I considered worthy to be classed with Nikisch. He touched my composer's heart straight away by devoting himself to my concerto until the accompaniment, which is rather complicated, had been practiced to the point of perfection, although he had already gone through another long rehearsal. According to Mahler, every detail of the score was important—an attitude that is unfortunately rare among conductors. . . .

I still remember an incident that is characteristic of him. Mahler was an unusually strict disciplinarian. This I consider an essential quality for a successful conductor. We had reached a difficult violin passage in the third movement that involves some rather awkward bowing. Suddenly Mahler, who had conducted this passage *a tempo*, tapped his desk:

"Stop! Don't pay any attention to the difficult bowing marked in your parts . . . Play the passage like this," and he indicated a different method of bowing. After he had made the first violins play the passage over alone three times, the man sitting next to the leader put down his violin:

"I can't play the passage with this kind of bowing."

Mahler (quite unruffled): "What kind of bowing would you like to use?"

"As it is marked in the score."

Mahler turned toward the leader with an interrogative look, and when he found the latter was of the same opinion he tapped the desk again:

"Please play as is written!"

This incident was a definite rebuff for the conductor, especially as the excellent leader of the Moscow Philharmonic Orchestra had pointed out to me this disputed method of bowing as the only possible way of playing the passage. I was curious to see how Mahler would react to this little scene. He was most dignified. Soon afterward he wanted the double basses to tone down their playing of a passage. He interrupted the orchestra and turned to the players:

"I would beg the gentlemen to make more of a diminuendo in this passage," then, addressing the argumentative neighbor of the leader with a hardly perceptible smile:

"I hope you don't object."

Forty-five minutes later Mahler announced:

"Now we will repeat the first movement."

My heart froze within me. I expected a dreadful row, or at least a heated protest from the orchestra. This would certainly have happened in any other orchestra, but here I did not notice a single sign of displeasure. The musicians played the first movement with a keen or perhaps even closer application than the previous time. At last we had finished. I went up to the conductor's desk, and together we examined the score. The musicians in the back seats began quietly to pack up their instruments and to disappear. Mahler blew up:

"What is the meaning of this?"

The leader: "It is after half-past one, Master."

"That makes no difference! As long as I am sitting, no musician has a right to get up!"

At the beginning of the rehearsal Mahler had practiced Berlioz's Symphony *La Vie d'un artiste* [*Symphonie fantastique*]. He conducted it magnificently, especially the passage called "Procession to the High Court," where he obtained a crescendo of the brass instruments such as I have never before heard achieved in this passage: The windows shook. The very walls seemed to vibrate.   [2]

CHAUFFEUR AND CONDUCTOR

A good conductor ought to be a good chauffeur; the qualities that make the one also make the other. They are concentration, an incessant control of attention, and presence of mind: the conductor only has to add a little sense of music.   [3]

THE FAILURE OF THE FIRST SYMPHONY

I do not wish to belittle the terrible failure of my symphony in St. Petersburg. According to my present conviction this fate was not undeserved. It is true that the performance was beneath contempt and the work in parts unrecognizable, but, apart from this, its deficiencies were revealed to me with a dreadful distinctness even during the first rehearsal. Something within me snapped. All my self-confidence broke down, and the artistic satisfaction that I had looked forward to was never realized. The work made a very bad impression, too, on the St. Petersburg musicians who were present. "Forgive me, but I do not find this music at all agreeable," said Rimsky-Korsakov to me in his dry and unsparing manner at a rehearsal. And I, utterly disillusioned, knew that he was right, and that this harsh judgment was not only due to the general embitterment against Moscow. I "listened in" to my own work. I found the orchestration abominable, but I knew that the music also was not up to much. There are serious illnesses and deadly blows from fate that entirely change a man's character. This was the effect of my own symphony on myself. When the indescribable torture of this performance had at last come to an end, I was a different man.   [4]

SELF-EVALUATION

I have never been quite able to make up my mind as to which was my true calling— that of a composer, pianist, or conductor. These doubts assail me to this day. There are times when I consider myself nothing but a composer; others when I believe myself capable only of playing the piano. Today, when the greater part of my life is over, I am constantly troubled by the misgiving that, in venturing into too many fields, I may have failed to make the best use of my life. In the old Russian phrase, I have "hunted three hares." Can I be sure that I have killed one of them?   [5]

CREDO

From an interview with David Ewen, Etude, December 1941

Composing is as essential a part of my being as breathing or eating; it is one of the necessary functions of living. My constant desire to compose music is actually the urge within me to give tonal expression to my feelings, just as I speak to give ut- terance to my thoughts. That, I believe, is the function that music should serve in the life of every composer; any other function it may fill is purely incidental.

I have no sympathy with the composer who produces works according to pre- conceived formulas or theories. Or with the composer who writes in a certain style because it is the fashion to do so. Great music has never been produced in that way—and I dare say it never will. . . .

Study the masterpieces of every great composer, and you will find every aspect of the composer's personality and background in his music. Time may change the technique of music, but it can never alter its mission.

From all of this you can gather that I have no warm feeling for music that is ex- perimental—your so-called "modern music," whatever that may mean. For, after all, is not the music of composers like Sibelius and Glazunov *modern* music, even though it is written in a more traditional manner? I myself could never care to write in a radical vein that disregards the laws of tonality or harmony. Nor could I learn to love such music, if I listened to it a thousand times. And I say again and again that music must first and foremost be loved; it must come from the heart and must be directed to the heart. Otherwise, it cannot hope to be lasting, inde- structible art.

Yet, I must add, I can respect the artistic aim of a composer if he arrives at the so-called modern idiom after an intense period of preparation. Stravinsky, after all, did not compose *Le Sacre du printemps* until he had had an intensive period of study with a master like Rimsky-Korsakov, and until he had composed a classical sym- phony and other works in the classic forms. Otherwise, *Le Sacre du printemps*—for all its boldness—would not have possessed such solid musical merits in the form of imaginative harmonies and energetic rhythms. Such composers know what they are doing when they break a law; they know what to react against, because they have had experience in the classical forms and style. Having mastered the rules, they know which can be violated and which should be obeyed. But, I am sorry to say, I have found too often that young composers plunge into the writing of experimental music with their school lessons only half learned. Too much radical music is sheer sham, for this very reason: its composer sets about revolutionizing the laws of music before he learned them himself. Whatever a composer's goal as an artist may be, he can never dispense with a thorough technical training; a complete scholastic training is indispensable, even with all the talent in the world. . . .

And there is always this possibility: if you insist upon becoming intimately acquainted with the old world before venturing upon a new one, you may very well discover that there is room enough for you in the former—that there is no need for you to seek new paths. I frequently have the feeling, in listening to the radical works of many younger men, that they go in all directions, harmonically and contrapuntally, in their music, because they are not sufficiently well instructed in the old methods to make them pliable tools for their ideas. It is my own pet belief that, if you have something important to say, you don't need a new language in which to say it. The old language is sufficiently rich and resourceful. The young composers make the mistake of believing that you achieve originality through *technique*. Actually, the only originality worth achieving is that which comes from *substance*. A composer can use all the accepted tools of composition and produce a work far different in style and subject matter from any ever produced, because he has put into music his own personality and experiences.   [6]

Arnold Schoenberg
1874–1951

Schoenberg's music and influence were controversial from the first. Vituperative criticism of works such as Pierrot lunaire *(1912) eventually led Schoenberg to help organize a Society for Private Musical Performances, from whose performances critics were excluded. The twelve-tone or serial method of composition he arrived at only gradually; the accepted date of its first use in an entire composition is 1924, with the Op. 25 Suite for Piano. While Schoenberg lost no opportunity to promote his views and accomplishments, he himself was undogmatic in his use of serialism and condemned attempts to view it as either an autonomous or automatic method for generating music.*

TEACHING

From a letter to Karl Weiner, Vienna, March 19, 1910

I do not force anyone to compose in the modern manner if he does not feel in a modern way; but he will learn to understand classical music more throughly than he would if taught by the dyed-in-the-wool academicians. On the other hand: anyone who wants to study modern music will learn from me all that can be learned: based on a solid classical foundation, right up to the latest achievements in our art. . . .

All that might be brought up against me, I think, is that I write a kind of music that does not appeal to those who do not understand anything about it. On the other hand, it must be admitted that it does appeal to those who do understand it. (This is really what the whole thing comes to.) And also that my example leads young people to compose in a similar manner. This objection will not hold water at all. First of all, I do not in fact have this effect on my pupils and do not even wish to have it. In that objectionable sense I influence only those who are inclined that way from the start, whereas those who are constitutionally immune to my art (= untalented) remain so and develop the way they would have developed in any case. Only, they will know a bit more. Secondly, it will not be possible to prevent the young and gifted from emulating my style. *For in ten years every talented composer* will be writing this way,* regardless of whether he has learned it directly from me or only from my works. [1]

FORM AND EXPRESSION

From a letter to the artist Wassily Kandinsky, Vienna, January 24, 1911

Every formal procedure that aspires to traditional effects is not completely free from conscious motivation. But art belongs to the *unconscious*! One must express *oneself*! Express oneself *directly*! Not one's taste, or one's upbringing, or one's intelligence, knowledge, or skill. Not all these *acquired* characteristics, but that which is *inborn, instinctive*. And all form making, all *conscious* form making, is connected with some kind of mathematics, or geometry, or with the golden section or suchlike. But only unconscious form making, which sets up the equation "form = outward shape," really creates forms; that alone brings forth prototypes that are imitated by unoriginal people and become "formulas." But whoever is capable of listening to himself, recognizing his own instincts, and also engrossing himself reflectively in every problem, will not need such crutches. One does not need to be a pioneer to create in this way, only a man who takes himself seriously—and thereby takes seriously that which is the true task of humanity in every intellectual or artistic field: to recognize, and to express what one has recognized!!! This is my belief! [2]

STYLE AND CONTENT

From a letter to Kandinsky, Berlin, September 28, 1913

Style is important only when everything else is present! And even then it is still not important, since we do not like Beethoven because of his style, which was new

---

* This was still fourteen years before the Suite Op. 25, and four years before his first proto-serial works.

at the time, but because of his content, which is always new. Naturally, for someone who otherwise hears nothing in a work, a modern style is a convenient means of establishing a relation with the author. But that doesn't give me much joy. I would like people to take notice of *what* I say, not how I say it. Only when people have perceived the former will they realize the latter is inimitable.   [3]

CUTS

From a letter to Alexander Zemlinsky,* Vienna, March 20, 1918

Cutting isn't the way to improve a work. Brevity and succinctness are a matter of *exposition*. In this case [Schoenberg's *Pelleas und Melisande*] the details are not conceived compactly; it is all long-winded. If I cut some such details, the other long-winded ones remain, and it remains a work of long-winded exposition. It will not take so long to play, but it *will not really be shorter*! A work that has been shortened by cutting may very well give the impression of being an excessively long work (because of the exposition) that is too short in various places (where it has been cut).   [4]

"ATONALISM"

From a letter to Alban Berg, Zandvoort, January 25, 1921

I share your opinion regarding "atonal." There is no such thing in music. You know my opinion about "labeling." Otherwise I would prefer "polytonal." . . . "Expressionism," too, is just a name and only serves the same purpose that a trade name does for manufactured goods. "Globin," the superior shoe polish. What's the point of saying something basically unessential when what's essential is never recognized until fifty years later and then one realizes that it was basically the same old thing[?]   [5]

From a letter to Kandinsky, Traunkirchen, July 20, 1922

These atonalists! Damn it all, I did my composing without any "ism" in mind. What has it got to do with me?   [6]

REHEARSALS

From a letter to Paul Scheinpflug, Traunkirchen, July 29, 1922

In my view it is no proof of skill to manage with few rehearsals, since it is always done at the cost of the work. What is a proof of skill is to have the material for many rehearsals, to go on being dissatisfied with oneself and the others, always

---

* The composer and conductor Zemlinsky (1871–1942) had earlier given Schoenberg lessons in compositional technique. Since 1901 Schoenberg had been married to Zemlinsky's sister Mathilde.

finding a way of improving something more, not being able to bring oneself to present a thing until one has brought it as close to perfection as possible.   [7]

A DEFINITION OF MUSIC

From a letter to Walter E. Koons,* New York, {April 1934}

Music is a simultaneous and a successive-ness of tones and tone-combinations, which are so organized that its impression on the ear is agreeable, and its impression on the intelligence is comprehensible, and that these impressions have the power to influence occult parts of our soul and of our sentimental spheres and that this influence makes us live in a dreamland of fulfilled desires, or in a dreamed hell of ... etc., etc., ...   [8]

ART VERSUS SCIENCE

From a letter to Ernst Krenek, Los Angeles, December 1/12, 1939

American young people's intelligence is certainly remarkable. I am endeavoring to direct this intelligence into the right channels. They are extremely good at getting hold of principles, but then want to apply them too much "on principle." And in art that's wrong. What distinguishes art from science is: that here there should not be principles of the kind one has to use on principle: that the one "narrowly" defines what must be left "wide open"; that musical logic does not answer to "if—, then—," but enjoys making use of the possibilities excluded by if-then.   [9]

ADVICE TO A YOUNG COMPOSER

From a letter to Sgt. Lester Trimble,† {Los Angeles, early 1940s}

I see you are aiming at a contemporary American style in some of these compositions. This is of course perfectly all right. It is your task, all of you young American talents, to create a style of your own, and it is every single man's duty to contribute as much as possible to this goal.

On the other hand there are two points on account of which I would advocate that everybody should become perfectly acquainted with the achievements of the masters of the past, with the development of the musical language up to our times. Firstly: after some time most of these national characteristics fade and only the idea remains. Secondly: it would be too great a loss, if this technique, produced by centuries, be abandoned and a new technique started at the point where the European started long, long ago.

This is why I recommend you to study the masterworks.   [10]

---

* Koons, a music supervisor at NBC, had written to many well-known figures and asked for their definitions of music. Schoenberg's response is in his own English.

† Trimble (1920–86) studied with Milhaud and Copland and became a noted composer, critic, editor, and teacher. Schoenberg wrote to him in English.

"A REAL COMPOSER"

From a letter to Andrew J. Twa, Los Angeles, July 29, 1944

A real composer is not one who plays first on the piano and writes down what he has played.

A real composer conceives his ideas, his entire music, in his mind, in his imagination, and he does not need an instrument. [11]

THE COMPOSITION WITH TWELVE TONES

From an essay of same title, 1950

Form in the arts, and especially in music, aims primarily at comprehensibility. The relaxation which a satisfied listener experiences when he can follow an idea, its development, and the reasons for such development are closely related, psychologically speaking, to a feeling of beauty. Thus, artistic value demands comprehensibility, not only for intellectual but also for emotional satisfaction. However, the creator's *idea* has to be presented, whatever the *mood* he is impelled to evoke.

Composition with twelve tones has no other aim than comprehensibility. In view of certain events in recent musical history, this might seem astonishing, for works written in this style have failed to gain understanding in spite of the new medium of organization. Thus, should one forget that contemporaries are not final judges but are generally overruled by history, one might consider this method doomed. But though it seems to increase the listener's difficulties, it compensates for this deficiency by penalizing the composer. For composing thus does not become easier, but rather ten times more difficult. Only the better-prepared composer can compose for the better-prepared music lover.

The method of composing with twelve tones grew out of necessity.

In the last hundred years the concept of harmony has changed tremendously through the development of chromaticism. The idea that one basic tone, the root, dominated the construction of chords and regulated their succession—the concept of *tonality*—had to develop first into the concept of *extended tonality*. Very soon it became doubtful whether such a root still remained the center to which every harmony and harmonic succession must be referred. Furthermore, it became doubtful whether a tonic appearing at the beginning, at the end, or at any other point really had a constructive meaning. Richard Wagner's harmony had promoted a change in the logic and constructive power of harmony. One of its consequences was the so-called impressionistic use of harmonies, especially practiced by Debussy. His harmonies, without constructive meaning, often served the coloristic purpose of expressing moods and pictures. Moods and pictures, though extramusical, thus became constructive elements, incorporated in the musical functions; they produced a sort of emotional comprehensibility. In this way, tonality was already dethroned in practice, if not in theory. This alone would perhaps not have caused a radical change in compositional technique. However, such a change became necessary when there occurred simultaneously a development that ended in what I call the *emancipation of the dissonance*.

The ear had gradually become acquainted with a great number of dissonances and so had lost the fear of their "sense-interrupting" effect. One no longer expected preparations of Wagner's dissonances or resolutions of Strauss's discords; one was not disturbed by Debussy's nonfunctional harmonies, or by the harsh counterpoint of later composers. This state of affairs led to a freer use of dissonances comparable to classic composers' treatment of diminished seventh chords, which could precede and follow any other harmony, consonant or dissonant, as if there were no dissonance at all.

What distinguishes dissonances from consonances is not a greater or lesser degree of beauty, but a greater or lesser degree of *comprehensibility*. In my *Harmonielehre* I presented the theory that dissonant tones appear later among the overtones, for which reason the ear is less intimately acquainted with them. This phenomenon does not justify such sharply contradictory terms as *concord* and *discord*. Closer acquaintance with the more remote consonances—the dissonances, that is—gradually eliminated the difficulty of comprehension and finally admitted not only the emancipation of dominant and other seventh chords, diminished sevenths, and augmented triads, but also the emancipation of Wagner's, Strauss's, Musorgsky's, Debussy's, Mahler's, Puccini's, and Reger's more remote dissonances.

The term *emancipation of the dissonance* refers to its comprehensibility, which is considered equivalent to the consonance's comprehensibility. A style based on this premise treats dissonances like consonances and renounces a tonal center. By avoiding the establishment of a key, modulation is excluded, since modulation means leaving an established tonality and establishing *another* tonality.

The first compositions in this new style were written by me around 1908 and, soon afterward, by my pupils Anton von Webern and Alban Berg. From the very beginning such compositions differed from all preceding music, not only harmonically but also melodically, thematically, and motivically. But the foremost characteristics of these *in statu nascendi* were their extreme expressiveness and their extraordinary brevity. At that time, neither I nor my pupils were conscious of the reasons for these features. Later I discovered that our sense of form was right when it forced us to counterbalance extreme emotionality with extraordinary shortness. Thus, subconsciously, consequences were drawn from an innovation that, like every innovation, destroys while it produces. New colorful harmony was offered, but much was lost.

Formerly the harmony had served not only as a source of beauty but, more important, as a means of distinguishing the features of the form. For instance, only a consonance was considered suitable for an ending. Establishing functions demanded different successions of harmonies than roving functions; a bridge, a transition, demanded other successions than a codetta; harmonic variation could be executed intelligently and logically only with due consideration of the fundamental meaning of the harmonies. Fulfillment of all these functions—comparable to the effect of punctuation in the construction of sentences, of subdivision into paragraphs, and of fusion into chapters—could scarcely be assured with chords whose constructive values had not as yet been explored. Hence, it seemed at first impossible to compose pieces of complicated organization or of great length.

A little later I discovered how to construct larger forms by following a text or a poem. The difference in size and shape of its parts and the change in character and mood were mirrored in the shape and size of the composition, in its dynamics and tempo, figuration and accentuation, instrumentation and orchestration. Thus the parts were differentiated as clearly as they had formerly been by the tonal and structural functions of harmony.

Formerly the use of the fundamental harmony had been theoretically regulated through recognition of the effects of root progressions. This practice had grown into a subconsciously functioning *sense of form* that gave a real composer an almost somnambulistic sense of security in creating, with utmost precision, the most delicate distinctions of formal elements.

Whether one calls oneself conservative or revolutionary, whether one composes in a conventional or progressive manner, whether one tries to imitate old styles or is destined to express new ideas—whether one is a good composer or not—one must be convinced of the infallibility of one's own fantasy and one must believe in one's own inspiration. Nevertheless, the desire for a conscious control of the new means and forms will arise in every artist's mind; and he will wish to know *consciously* the laws and rules that govern the forms he has conceived "as in a dream." Strongly convincing as this dream may have been, the conviction that these new sounds obey the laws of nature and of our manner of thinking, the conviction that order, logic, comprehensibility, and form cannot be present without obedience to such laws, forces the composer along the road to exploration. He must find, if not laws or rules, at least ways to justify the dissonant character of these harmonies and their successions.

After many unsuccessful attempts during a period of approximately twelve years, I laid the foundations for a new procedure in musical construction that seemed fitted to replace those structural differentiations provided formerly by tonal harmonies.

I called this procedure *Method of Composing with Twelve Tones That Are Related Only with One Another.*

This method consists primarily of the constant and exclusive use of a set of twelve different tones. This means, of course, that no tone is repeated within the series and that it uses all twelve tones in the chromatic scale, though in a different order. It is in no way identical with the chromatic scale.*

The above example shows that such a basic set consists of various intervals. It should never be called a scale, although it is invented to substitute for some of

---

* Curiously and wrongly, most people speak of the "system" of the chromatic scale. Mine is no system but only a method, which means a *modus* of applying regularly a preconceived formula. A *method can, but need not,* be one of the consequences of a system. I am also not the inventor of the chromatic scale; somebody else must have occupied himself with this task long ago. [Schoenberg]

the unifying and formative advantages of scale and tonality. The scale is the source of many figurations, parts of melodies and melodies themselves, ascending and descending passages, and even broken chords. In approximately the same manner the tones of the basic set produce similar elements. Of course, cadences produced by the distinction between principal and subsidiary harmonies will scarcely be derived from the basic set. But something different and more important is derived from it with a regularity comparable to the regularity and logic of the earlier harmony; the association of tones into harmonies and their successions is regulated by the order of these tones. The basic set functions in the manner of a motive. This explains why such a basic set has to be invented anew for every piece. It has to be the first creative thought. It does not make much difference whether or not the set appears in the composition at once like a theme or a melody, whether or not it is characterized as such by features of rhythm, phrasing, construction, character, etc. Why such a set should consist of twelve different tones, why none of these tones should be repeated too soon, why, accordingly, only one set should be used in one composition—the answers to all these questions came to me gradually.

Discussing such problems in my *Harmonielehre,* I recommended the avoidance of octave doublings. To double is to emphasize, and an emphasized tone could be interpreted as a root, or even as a tonic; the consequences of such an interpretation must be avoided. Even a slight reminiscence of the former tonal harmony would be disturbing, because it would create false expectations of consequences and continuations. The use of a tonic is deceiving if it is not based on *all* the relationship of tonality.

The use of more than one set was excluded because in every following set one or more tones would have been repeated too soon. Again there would arise the danger of interpreting the repeated tone as a tonic. Besides, the effect of unity would be lessened.

Justified already by historical development, the method of composing with twelve tones is also not without esthetic and theoretical support. On the contrary, it is just this support that advances it from a mere technical device to the rank and importance of a scientific theory.

Music is not merely another kind of amusement, but a musical poet's, a musical thinker's representation of musical ideas; these musical ideas must correspond to the laws of human logic; they are a part of what man can apperceive, reason, and express. Proceeding from these assumptions, I arrived at the following conclusions:

The two-or-more-dimensional space in which musical ideas are presented is a unit. Though the elements of these ideas appear separate and independent to the eye and the ear, they reveal their true meaning only through their cooperation, even as no single word alone can express a thought without relation to other words. All that happens at any point of this musical space has more than a local effect. It functions not only in its own place, but also in all other directions and planes, and is not without influence even at remote points. For instance, the effect of progressive rhythmic subdivision, through what I call "the tendency of the shortest notes" to multiply themselves, can be observed in every classic composition.

A musical idea, accordingly, though consisting of melody, rhythm, and harmony, is neither the one nor the other alone, but all three together. The elements of a musical idea are partly incorporated in the horizontal plane as successive sounds, and partly in the vertical plane as simultaneous sounds. The mutual relation of tones regulates the succession of intervals as well as their association into harmonies; the rhythm regulates the succession of tones as well as the succession of harmonies and organizes phrasing. And this explains why a basic set of twelve tones can be used in either dimension, as a whole or in parts.

The basic set is used in diverse mirror forms. The composers of the last century had not employed such mirror forms as much as the masters of contrapuntal times; at least, they seldom did so consciously. . . .

The last century considered such a procedure cerebral and thus inconsistent with the dignity of genius. The very fact that there exist classical examples proves the foolishness of such an opinion. But the validity of this form of thinking is also demonstrated by the previously stated law of the unity of musical space, best formulated as follows: *the unity of musical space demands an absolute and unitary perception.* In this space, as in Swedenborg's heaven (described in Balzac's *Seraphita*) there is no absolute down, no right or left, forward or backward. Every musical configuration, every movement of tones has to be comprehended primarily as a mutual relation of sounds, of oscillatory vibrations, appearing at different places and times. To the imaginative and creative faculty, relations in the material sphere are as independent from directions or planes as material objects are, in their sphere, to our perceptive faculties. Just as our mind always recognizes, for instance a knife, a bottle, or a watch, regardless of its position, and can reproduce it in the imagination in every possible position, even so a musical creator's mind can operate subconsciously with a row of tones regardless of their direction, regardless of the way in which a mirror might show the mutual relations, which remain a given quantity.

The introduction of my method of composing with twelve tones does not facilitate composing; on the contrary, it makes it more difficult. Modernist-minded beginners often think they should try it before having acquired the necessary technical equipment. This is a great mistake. The restrictions imposed on a composer by the obligation to use only one set in a composition are so severe that they can be overcome only by an imagination that has survived a tremendous number of adventures. Nothing is given by this method, but much is taken away.

It has been mentioned that for every new composition a special set of twelve tones has to be invented. Sometimes a set will not fit every condition an experienced composer can foresee, especially in those ideal cases where the set appears at once in the form, character, and phrasing of a theme. Rectification in the order of tones may then become necessary.

In the first works in which I employed this method, I was not yet convinced that the exclusive use of one set would not result in monotony. Would it allow the creation of a sufficient number of characteristically differentiated themes, phrases, motives, sentences, and other forms? At this time I used complicated devices to assure variety. But soon I discovered that my fear was unfounded; I could even base a whole opera, *Moses and Aron,* solely on one set; and I found that, on the contrary, the more familiar I became with this set the more easily I could draw themes from it. Thus, the truth of my first predictions had received splendid proof. One has to follow the basic set; nevertheless, one composes as freely as before.

In every composition preceding the method of composing with twelve tones, all the thematic and harmonic material is primarily derived from three sources: the tonality; the *basic motive,* which in turn is a derivative of the tonality; and the rhythm, which is included in the basic motive. A composer's whole thinking was bound to remain in an intelligible manner around the central root. A composition that failed to obey these demands was considered "amateurish," but a composition that adhered to it rigorously was never called "cerebral." On the contrary, the capacity to obey the principle instinctively was considered a natural condition of a talent.

The time will come when the ability to draw thematic material from a basic set of twelve tones will be an unconditional prerequisite for obtaining admission into the composition class of a conservatory.

The possibility of . . . canons and imitations, and even fugues and fugatos, has been overestimated by analysts of this style. Of course, for a beginner it might be as difficult to avoid octave doubling here as it is difficult for poor composers to avoid parallel octaves in the "tonal" style. But while a "tonal" composer still has to lead his parts into consonances or catalogued dissonances, a composer with twelve independent tones apparently possesses the kind of freedom that many would characterize by saying, "Everything is allowed." "Everything" has always been allowed to two kinds of artists: to masters on the one hand, and to ignoramuses on the other. However, the meaning of composing in imitative style here is not the same as it is in counterpoint. It is only one of the ways of adding a coherent accompaniment, or subordinate voices, to the main theme, whose character it thus helps to express more intensively.   [12]

MAHLER

Letter to Gustav Mahler, December 12, 1904

My dear Director,

I must not speak as a musician to a musician if I am to give any idea of the incredible impression your symphony [the Fifth] made on me: I can speak only as one human being to another. For I saw your very soul, naked, stark naked. It was revealed to me as a stretch of wild and secret country, with eerie chasms and abysses neighbored by sunlit, smiling meadows, haunts of idyllic repose. I felt it as an event of nature, which after scourging us with its terrors puts a rainbow in the sky. What does it matter that what I was told afterward of your "program" did not seem to correspond altogether with what I had felt? Whether I am a good or a bad indicator of the feelings an experience arouses in me is not the point. Must I have a correct understanding of what I have lived and felt? And I believe I felt your symphony. I shared in the battling for illusion; I suffered the pangs of disillusionment; I saw the forces of evil and good wrestling with each other; I saw a man in torment struggling toward inward harmony; I divined a personality, a drama, and *truthfulness*, the most uncompromising truthfulness.

I had to let myself go. Forgive me. I cannot feel by halves. With me it is one thing or the other! [13]

Remark, no date, reported in Willi Reich's biography of Alban Berg

If you are in a position to observe the way Mahler ties his tie, you can learn more counterpoint from this than you can in three years at the conservatory. [14]

From a letter to Winfried Zillig, Los Angeles, December 1, 1948

The orchestra's liking my Five Pieces for Orchestra is a very great piece of progress, and the fact that they went along with Mahler, even though very reluctantly, is also very important as a step toward establishing Mahler's art. What most seems to set Mahler back is that faint reminiscence of popular tunes. I am quite convinced, though, that in fifty years' time these popular tunes would, in the nature of things, be entirely unknown or long forgotten, if [ever known] at all, and only then will people see the greatness of the experience behind them. [15]

STRAUSS

From a letter to an unknown correspondent, Berlin, April 22, 1914

I regret that I am unable to accept your invitation to write something for Richard Strauss's fiftieth birthday.

In a letter to Frau Mahler (in connection with the Mahler Memorial Fund) Herr Strauss wrote about me as follows:

"The only person who can help poor Schönberg now is a psychiatrist . . ."

"I think he'd do better to shovel snow instead of scribbling on music paper . . ."

It seems to me that the opinion I myself and indeed everyone else who knows these remarks is bound to have of Herr Strauss as a man (for here is envy of a "competitor") and as an artist (for the expressions he uses are as banal as a cheap song) is not suitable for general publication in honor of his fiftieth birthday. I have no intention of damaging Herr Strauss "morally." . . . He is no longer of the slightest artistic interest to me, and whatever I may once have learned from him, I am thankful to say I misunderstood. [16]

CHARLES IVES

Undated note (probably c. 1945) found among Schoenberg's papers

There is a great Man living in this country—a composer. He has solved the problem how to preserve one's self and to learn.

He responds to negligence by contempt.

He is not forced to accept praise or blame.

His name is Ives. [17]

WEBERN

From the foreword to Webern's Six Bagatelles for String Quartet, June 1924

While the brevity of these pieces is their eloquent advocate, such brevity stands equally in need of advocacy. Think what self-denial it takes to cut a long story so short. A glance can always be spun out into a poem, a sigh into a novel. But to convey a novel through a single gesture, or felicity by a single catch of the breath: such concentration exists only when emotional self-indulgence is correspondingly absent. [18]

BERG AS A STUDENT

From a letter to the publisher Emil Hertzka, Vienna, January 5, 1910

One [student] (Alban Berg) is an extraordinarily gifted composer. But the state he was in when he came to me was such that his imagination apparently could not work on anything but lieder. Even the piano accompaniments to them were song-like in style. He was absolutely incapable of writing an instrumental movement or inventing an instrumental theme. You can hardly imagine the lengths I went to in order to remove this defect in his talent. As a rule teachers are absolutely incapable of doing this, because they do not even see where the problem lies, and the result is composers who can think only in terms of a single instrument. (Robert Schumann is a typical example.) I removed this defect and am convinced that in time Berg will actually become very good at instrumentation. [19]

GERSHWIN

From Merle Armitage's George Gershwin, 1938

Many musicians do not consider George Gershwin a serious composer. But they should understand that, serious or not, he is a composer, that is, a man who lives in music and expresses everything, serious or not, sound or superficial, by means of music, because it is his native language. There are a number of composers, serious (as they believe) or not (as I know), who learned to add notes together. But they are only serious on account of a perfect lack of humor and soul.

It seems to me that this difference alone is sufficient to justify calling the one a composer, but the other none. An artist is to me like an apple tree. When the time comes, whether it wants to or not, it bursts into bloom and starts to produce apples. And as an apple tree neither knows nor asks about the value experts of the market will attribute to its product, so a real composer does not ask whether his products will please the experts of serious arts. He only feels he has to say something and says it.

It seems to me beyond doubt that Gershwin was an innovator. What he has done with rhythm, harmony, and melody is not merely style. It is fundamentally different from the mannerism of many a serious composer. Such mannerism is based on artificial presumptions, which are gained by speculation and are conclusions drawn from the fashions and aims current among contemporary composers at certain times. Such a style is a superficial union of devices applied to a minimum of ideas, without any inner reason or cause. Such music could be taken to pieces and put together in a different way, and the result would be the same nothingness expressed by another mannerism. One could not do this with Gershwin's music. His melodies are not products of a combination, nor of a mechanical union, but they are units and could therefore not be taken to pieces. Melody, harmony, and rhythm are not welded together, but cast. [20]

RESPONSE TO A FILM PROPOSAL

From a letter to Emil Hertzka, {Berlin, 1913}

You ask what are the artistic terms on which my *Glückliche Hand* might be reproduced cinematographically. There is little I can say at the moment about details, which will arise only during the work of adaptation. But in general I can say as follows:

I. *No change is to be made in the music!*

II. If *I* find it necessary to make improvements in the text, I shall make them myself, and nobody else, whoever it may be, shall have the right to require them of me.

III. As many rehearsals as I think necessary! This cannot be estimated in advance. Rehearsals must go on until it goes as well as *Pierrot lunaire.**

IV. Performances may be given only with performers approved by me, and if possible with the original ensemble. . . .

V. Performances may be given only with a (full) orchestra rehearsed and directed by me or my trusted deputies, or (if these mechanical organs turn out to be as good as I hope) with an organ (e.g., Aeolian [player] organ). Further, in large cities it must always be an orchestra. . . .

VI. What I think about the sets is this: the basic unreality of the events, which is inherent in the words, is something that they should be able to bring out even better in the filming (nasty idea that it is!). For me this is one of the main reasons for considering it. For instance, in the film, if the goblet suddenly vanishes as if it had never been there, just as if it had simply been forgotten, that is quite different from the way it is on the stage, where it has to be removed by some device. And there are a thousand things besides that may be easily done in this medium, whereas the stage's resources are very limited. My foremost wish is therefore for something the opposite of what the cinema generally aspires to. I want:

The utmost unreality!

The whole thing should have the effect (not of a dream) but of chords. Of music. It must never suggest symbols, or meaning, or thoughts, but simply the play of colors and forms. Just as music never drags a meaning around with it, at least not in the form in which it manifests itself, even though meaning is inherent in its nature, so too this should simply be like sounds for the eye, and so far as I am concerned everyone is free to think or feel something similar to what he thinks or feels while hearing music. [21]

---

* The premiere of *Pierrot* in Berlin the previous year had required forty rehearsals.

PIANO CONCERTO, *ODE TO NAPOLEON, VARIATIONS ON A RECITATIVE*

From a letter to René Leibowitz, Los Angeles, July 4, 1947

It was not my purpose to write dissonant music, but to include dissonance in a logical manner without reference to the treatment of the classics: because such a treatment is impossible. I do not know where in the Piano Concerto a tonality is expressed. It is true that the *Ode* at the end sounds like E flat. I don't know why I did it. Maybe I was wrong, but at present you cannot make me feel this.

The organ piece represents my "French and English Suites," or, if you want, my *Meistersinger* quintet, my *Tristan* duet, my Beethoven and Mozart fugues (who were homophonic-melodic composers): my pieces in Old Style, like the Hungarian influence in Brahms. In other words, as I have stated often, almost every composer in a new style has a longing back to the old style (with Beethoven, fugues). The harmony of the Organ Variations fills out the gap between my chamber symphonies and the "dissonant" music. There are many unused possibilities to be found therein.   [22]

UNDERSTANDING OF HIS MUSIC

From a letter to Hans Rosbaud, Los Angeles, May 12, 1947

Understanding of my music *still* goes on suffering from the fact that the musicians do not regard me as a normal, common-or-garden composer who expresses his more or less good and new themes and melodies in a not entirely inadequate musical language—but as a modern dissonant twelve-note experimenter.

But there is nothing I long for more intensely (if for anything) than to be taken for a better sort of Tchaikovsky—for heaven's sake: a bit better, but really that's all. Or if anything more, then that people should know my tunes and whistle them.   [23]

From a letter to K. Aram, Los Angeles, November 15, 1947

I am quite conscious of the fact that a full understanding of my works can not be expected before some decades. The minds of the musicians and of the audiences have to mature ere they can comprehend my music. I know this, I have personally renounced an early success, and I know that—success or not—it is my historic duty to write what my destiny orders me to write.   [24]

Charles Ives
1874–1954

Although Ives's background and formal musical education were solidly mainstream, as a composer he was an outsider. His interest in innovation stemmed from musical experiments designed by his father, a cornetist and bandmaster in Danbury, Connecticut. Balancing this experimentalism was a deep nostalgia for preindustrial New England, a nostalgia compounded by the early death of his father while Ives was still in college. Working in artistic solitude, Ives fused these two passions into music of originality and unexpected beauty. By the time he began to be recognized in the 1930s, he had long since stopped composing and had retired from the insurance firm where he had made his career. Ives's Essays Before a Sonata *were written as a companion to his* Concord Sonata. *Most of the material in the posthumously published* Memos *was written in the 1920s and 1930s.*

From Essays Before a Sonata, *1920*

SUBSTANCE AND MANNER

In such an abstruse art as music, it is easy for one to point to this as substance and to that as manner. Some will hold, and it is undeniable—in fact quite obvious— that manner has a great deal to do with the beauty of substance, and that to make a too arbitrary division or distinction between them, is to interfere, to some extent, with an art's beauty and unity. There is a great deal of truth in this too. But on the other hand, beauty in music is too often confused with something that lets the ears lie back in an easy chair. Many sounds that we are used to do not bother us, and for that reason, we are inclined to call them beautiful. Frequently—possibly almost invariably—analytical and impersonal tests will show, we believe, that when a new or unfamiliar work is accepted as beautiful on its first hearing, its fundamental quality is one that tends to put the mind to sleep. A narcotic is not always unnecessary, but it is seldom a basis of progress, that is, wholesome evolution in any creative experience. This kind of progress has a great deal to do with beauty, at least in its deeper emotional interests, if not in its moral values.   [1]

MUSICAL TRUTH

The man "born down to Babbitt's Corners" may find a deep appeal in the simple but acute "Gospel Hymns of the New England camp meetin'" of a generation or so ago. He finds in them—some of them—a vigor, a depth of feeling, a natural-soil rhythm, a sincerity, emphatic but inartistic, which, in spite of a vociferous sentimentality, carries him nearer the "Christ of the people" than does the *Te Deum* of the greatest cathedral. These tunes have, for him, a truer ring than many of those groove-made, even-measured, monotonous, non-rhythmed, indoor-smelling, priest-taught, academic, English or neo-English hymns (and anthems), well-written, well-harmonized things, well-voice-led, well-counterpointed, well-corrected, and well-O.K.'d by well-corrected Mus. Bac. R.F.O.G.'s—personified sounds, correct and inevitable to sight and hearing—in a word, those proper forms of stained-glass beauty, which our over-drilled mechanisms, boy choirs, are limited to. But if the Yankee can reflect the fervency with which "his gospels" were sung—the fervency of "Aunt Sarah" who scrubbed her life away for her brother's ten orphans, the fervency with which this woman, after a fourteen-hour workday on the farm, would hitch up and drive five miles, through the mud and rain to "prayer meetin'," her one articulate outlet for the fullness of her unselfish soul— if he can reflect the fervency of such a spirit, he may find there a local color that will do all the world good. If his music can but catch that "spirit" by being a part with itself, it will come somewhere near his ideal—and it will be American, too, perhaps nearer so than that of the devotee of Indian or Negro melody. In other words, if local color, national color, any color, is a true pigment of the universal color, it is a divine quality; it is a part of substance in art, not of manner.   [2]

RAGTIME

Someone is quoted as saying that "ragtime is the true American music." Anyone will admit that it is one of the many true, natural, and, nowadays, conventional means of expression. It is an idiom, perhaps a "set or series of colloquialisms" similar to those that have added through centuries and through natural means, some beauty to all languages. . . . To examine ragtime rhythms and the syncopations of Schumann or of Brahms seems to the writer to show how much alike they are not. Ragtime, as we hear it, is, of course, more (but not much more) than a natural dogma of shifted accents, or a mixture of shifted and minus accents. It is something like wearing a derby hat on the back of the head, a shuffling lilt of a happy soul just out of a Baptist Church in old Alabama. Ragtime has its possibilities. But it does not "represent the American nation" any more than some fine old senators represent it. Perhaps we know it now as an ore before it has been refined into a product. It may be one of nature's ways of giving art raw material. Time will throw its vices away and weld its virtues into the fabric of our music. It has its uses as the cruet on the boardinghouse table has, but to make a meal of tomato ketchup and horse-radish, to plant a whole farm with sunflowers, even to put a sunflower into every bouquet, would be calling nature something worse than a politician.   [3]

MEANING IN MUSIC

A child knows a "strain of joy" from one of sorrow. Those a little older know the dignified from the frivolous—the Spring Song from the season in which the "melancholy days have come" (though is there not a glorious hope in autumn!). But where is the definite expression of late-spring against early-summer, of happiness against optimism? A painter paints a sunset—can he paint the setting sun?

    In some century to come, when the school children will whistle popular tunes in quarter-tones, when the diatonic scale will be as obsolete as the pentatonic is now, perhaps then these borderland experiences may be both easily expressed and readily recognized. But maybe music was not intended to satisfy the curious definiteness of man. Maybe it is better to hope that music may always be a transcendental language in the most extravagant sense. Possibly the power of literally distinguishing these "shades of abstraction"—these attributes paralleled by "artistic intuition" (call them what you will)—is ever to be denied man for the same reason that the beginning and end of a circle are to be denied.   [4]

MUSIC AND SOUND

A MS. score is brought to a concertmaster—he may be a violinist—he is kindly disposed, he looks it over, and casually fastens on a passage: "That's bad for the fiddles—it doesn't hang just right—write it like this, they will play it better." But that one phrase is the germ of the whole thing. "Never mind, it will fit the hand better this way—it will sound better." My God! What has sound got to do with music! The waiter brings the only fresh egg he has, but the man at breakfast sends it back because it doesn't fit his eggcup. Why can't music go out in the same way it comes in to a man, without having to crawl over a fence of sounds, thoraxes, catguts, wire, wood, and brass? . . . That music must be heard is not essential— what it *sounds* like may not be what it *is*.   [5]

TONALITY

How quarter-tones will affect tonality, how they will help work out satisfactory polytonal and atonal systems, involves so many considerations that I won't venture to say much about it. . . . But it strikes me that a great deal depends on whether or not satisfactory scales can be developed. If they can, listeners in future generations may enjoy or curse, as the case may be, tonalities a little longer. But quarter-tones or no quarter-tones, why tonality as such should be thrown out for good, I can't see. Why it should be always present, I can't see. It depends, it seems to me, a good deal—as clothes depend on the thermometer—on what one is trying to do, and on the state of mind, the time of day or other accidents of life.   [6]

SONGS

From the "Postface" to 114 *Songs, 1922*

A song has a few rights, the same as other ordinary citizens. If it feels like walking along the left-hand side of the street, passing the door of physiology or sitting on the curb, why not let it? If it feels like kicking over an ash can, a poet's castle, or the prosodic law, will you stop it? Must it always be a polite triad, a "breve gaudium," a ribbon to match the voice? Should it not be free at times from the dominion of the thorax, the diaphragm, the ear, and other points of interest? If it wants to beat around in the valley, to throw stones up the pyramids, or to sleep in the park, should it not have some immunity from a Nemesis, a Rameses, or a policeman? Should it not have a chance to sing to itself, if it can sing?—to enjoy itself without making a bow, if it can't make a bow?—to swim around in any ocean, if it can swim, without having to swallow "hook and bait," or being sunk by an operatic greyhound? If it happens to feel like trying to fly where humans cannot fly, to sing what cannot be sung, to walk in a cave on all fours, or to tighten up its girth in blind hope and faith and try to scale mountains that are not, who shall stop it?

—In short, must a song
   always be a song! [7]

From Memos

MUSICAL PEDIGREES

Some nice people, whenever they hear the words "Gospel Hymns" or "Stephen Foster," say "Mercy Me!," and a little high-brow smile creeps over their brow—"Can't you get something better than that in a symphony?" The same nice people, when they go to a properly dressed symphony concert under proper auspices, led by a name with foreign hair, and hear Dvořák's *New World Symphony,* in which they are told this famous passage was from a negro spiritual, then think that it must be quite proper, even artistic, and say "How delightful!" But when someone proves to them that the Gospel Hymns are fundamentally responsible for the negro spirituals, they say, "Ain't it awful!" "You don't really mean that!"—"Why, only to think!"—"Do tell!"—"I tell you, you don't ever hear Gospel Hymns even mentioned up there to the New England Conservatory." [8]

Many American composers, I believe, have been interested in working things out for themselves to a great extent, but it seems to be the general opinion that, unless a man has studied most of his life in a European conservatory, he has no right (and does not know how) to throw anything at an audience, good or bad. [9]

MUSIC AND MONEY

I might add one more matter, as some ask me about [it] and apparently don't get it all right:—why and how a man who apparently likes music so much goes into business. Two things:—(1) As a boy [I was] partially ashamed of it—an entirely wrong attitude, but it was strong—most boys in American country towns, I think, felt the same. When other boys, Monday A.M. on vacation, were out driving grocery carts, or doing chores, or playing ball, I felt all wrong to stay in and play piano. And there may be something in it. Hasn't music always been too much an emasculated art? Mozart etc. helped.

(2) Father felt that a man could keep his music-interest stronger, cleaner, bigger, and freer, if he didn't try to make a living out of it. Assuming a man lived by himself and with no dependents, no one to feed but himself, and willing to live as simply as Thoreau—[he] might write music that no one would play, publish, listen to, or buy. But—if he has a nice wife and some nice children, how can he let the children starve on his dissonances—answer that, Eddy! So he has to weaken (and as a man he should weaken for his children), but his music (some of it) more than weakens—it goes "ta ta" for money—bad for him, bad for music, but good for his boys!! [10]

Music's Possibilities

That a symphony, sonata, or jig—that all nice music should end where it started, on the Doh key, is no more a natural law than that all men should die in the same town and street number in which they were born. . . .

The more one studies and listens and tries to find out all he can in various ways, technically, mathematically, acoustically, and aurally, [the more] he begins to feel (and more than that, actually know and sense) that the world of tonal vibrations, in its relation to the physiological structure of the human ear, has unthought of (because untried) possibilities for man to know and grow by—greater and more transcendent than what has too easily and thoughtlessly [been] called a natural law! Just a few months' study of what can be found in the tables of acoustical vibrations—pure, tempered, differences of over tones, beats, etc.—as found in Helmholtz et al—and it will be realized that nature's laws are greater than a mere plagal cadence.   [11]

From Essays Before a Sonata

Beethoven and Strauss

Strauss remembers, Beethoven dreams.   [12]

Brahms's Orchestration

Some accuse Brahms's orchestration of being muddy. This may be a good name for a first impression of it. But if it should seem less so, he might not be saying what he thought. The mud may be a form of sincerity which demands that the heart be translated, rather than handed around through the pit. A clearer scoring might have lowered the thought.   [13]

From Memos

Influence of His Father

One thing I am certain of is that, if I have done anything good in music, it was, first, because of my father, and second, because of my wife. . . .

What my father did for me was not only in his teaching, on the technical side, etc., but in his influence, his personality, character, and open-mindedness, and his remarkable understanding of the ways of a boy's heart and mind. He had a remarkable talent for music and for the nature of music and sound, and also a philosophy of music that was unusual. Besides starting my music lessons when I was five years old, and keeping me at music in many ways until he died, with the best teaching that a boy could have, Father knew (and filled me up with) Bach and the best of the classical music, and the study of harmony and counterpoint etc., and musical history. Above all this, he kept my interest and encouraged open-mindedness in all matters that needed it in any way.

For instance, he thought that man as a rule didn't use the faculties that the Creator had given him hard enough. I couldn't have been over ten years old when he would occasionally have us sing, for instance, a tune like *The Swanee River* in the key of E-flat, but play the accompaniment in the key of C. This was to stretch our ears and strengthen our musical minds, so that they could learn to use and translate things that might be used and translated (in the art of music) more than they had been. In this instance, I don't think he had the possibility of polytonality in composition in mind, as much as to encourage the use of the ears—and for them and the mind to think for themselves and be more independent—in other words, not to be too dependent upon customs and habits. (He even let me try out "two keys to once," as an Interlude in an organ piece, *Variations on America,* but didn't let me do it much, as it made the boys laugh.)   {14}

Also as a boy I had heard and become somewhat familiar with tone-divisions other than the half-tone. . . . In testing or experimenting in the divisions of tone, father tried:

  1) the slide cornet,
  2) glasses for very small intervals,
  3) tuned piano in actual partials (as well as he could by ear—no acousticon),
  4) new scales without octaves (glasses),
  5) also violin strings stretched over a clothes press and let down with weights.
                                                                            {15}

When I went to New Haven, and took the courses with Professor Horatio W. Parker [at Yale University], in connection with the regular academic courses, I felt more and more what a remarkable background and start Father had given me in music. Parker was a composer and widely known, and Father was not a composer and little known—but from every other standpoint I should say that Father was by far the greater man. Parker was a bright man, a good technician, but apparently willing to be limited by what Rheinberger et al and the German tradition had taught him. After the first two or three weeks in Freshman year, I didn't bother him with any of the experimental ideas that father had been willing for me to think about, discuss, and try out.   {16}

Father used to say, "If you know how to write a fugue the right way *well*, then I'm willing to have you try the wrong way—*well*."   {17}

Maurice Ravel
1875–1937

Never less than a gentleman, Ravel could be vigorous and unyielding when writing in defense of his artistic principles. His essays and reviews also evince the ironic detachment and dry wit that are evident in his music. These latter qualities he shared with Debussy, along with an affinity for the coloristic that was to become the defining characteristic of Impressionism. It is not accurate to say, however, that he imitated Debussy. Ravel's works are more classical in their basic design and are sometimes more elaborate harmonically. In his piano music certain techniques actually anticipate Debussy.

NATIONALISM

Letter to the Committee of the National League for the Defense of French Music, Paris, June 7, 1916

Gentlemen: An enforced rest finally allows me to acknowledge receipt of the announcement and statutes of the National League for the Defense of French Music, which reached me quite late. I hope you will excuse my having been unable to write you sooner; my various transfers and my adventurous service have left me scarcely any leisure. Excuse me also for being unable to subscribe to your statutes; a careful reading of them and of your announcement prevents my doing so.

Naturally, I can only laud your "fixed idea of the triumph of the Fatherland," which has also pursued me ever since the opening of hostilities. Consequently I fully approve the "need for action" out of which the National League was born. This need for action has been so strong in me that it forced me to quit civilian life when I was not obliged to.

Where I cannot follow you is where you state the principle that "the role of musical art is economic and social." I have never considered either music or the other arts in that light.

I gladly concede you the "moving pictures," the "gramophone records," the "popular song writers." All these have only a distant relation to musical art. I even grant you the "Viennese operettas," which are, however, more musical and of more careful workmanship than similar products of our own. This material does come under the domain of the "economic."

But I do not believe that "for the safeguarding of our artistic national patrimony" it is necessary to "prohibit the public performance in France of those contemporary German and Austrian works that do not lie within the public domain." If it "cannot be a question of repudiating, for us and for future generations, the classics, which constitute one of the immortal monuments of humanity," it should be even less a question of "removing from us, for a long time" interesting works, destined, perhaps, in their turn, to constitute monuments, and from the performing of which we might draw useful lessons.

It might even prove dangerous for French composers systematically to ignore the output of their foreign colleagues, and thus to form a sort of nationalistic group. Our musical art, so rich at the present time, would not be long in degenerating and immuring itself in commonplace formulas.

It matters little to me that Mr. Schoenberg, for example, is an Austrian. He is nonetheless a musician of great worth, whose very interesting experiments have had a happy influence on certain Allied composers, including our own. Moreover, I am delighted that Messieurs Bartók, Kodály, and their disciples are Hungarian and manifest it in their works with so much relish.

In Germany, aside from Richard Strauss, we hardly see other than second-rate composers, whose equivalents it would be easy to find without crossing our frontiers. But it is possible that shortly some young artists will appear there whom it would be interesting to know here.

On the other hand, I do not think it necessary that all French music be made to predominate in France, or be spread abroad, no matter what its worth.

So you see, gentlemen, that my opinion differs from yours on so many levels that I cannot permit myself the honor of being considered one of you.

I hope, nevertheless, to continue to "act as a Frenchman," and to "count myself among those who mean never to forget that they are Frenchmen." [1]

WEBER

Remark to Hélène Jourdan-Morhange, no date

No more fertile spring ever fed German Romanticism! At a time when Italianism invaded music, Weber dammed that fashionable wave with experiments one might compare to Goethe's, and drew from the folk essence the freshness that was to give his lieder a new form. Sensibility and drama were to become the warp and woof of music, if one might so express it. [2]

CHOPIN

From an essay, 1910

Rien de plus haïssable qu'une musique sans arrière-pensée.
Nothing is more detestable than music without hidden meaning.
—Frédéric Chopin

Profound statement, this, and too little understood. It is true that Chopin proclaimed it constantly in his work. But did anyone understand? Yes, in retrospect; myriads of underlying meanings were unveiled later! Up to that time music addressed itself to the emotions. It was then shifted to the understanding, but understanding did not know what to do with it.

Music for musicians, that is the true interpretation of Chopin's idea. Not for the professionals, by God, but for the musician, the creator, the dilettante. You must be sensitive to rhythm, melody, harmony, to the atmosphere which sounds create, to be thrilled with the linking together of two chords, as with the harmony of two colors. The most important element in all the arts is content. The rest flows from it.

Architecture! What a futile comparison! There are rules for making a building "stand up." There is none for constructing modulations. Yes; only one: Inspiration!

The architects trace vast lines. They establish all the modulations in advance ... Inverted themes ... Retrograde canons ... Light and dark modulations. That means nothing to you? Nor to me, for that matter. It doesn't always seem coherent to you, despite all the effort? Then you are really not in the business.

Having something to say, that is what is missing in all this: the hidden meaning of Chopin.

His contribution is striking in the polonaises; before him the polonaise was a festival march, solemn, brilliant, completely exterior. Look at Weber, Moniuszko, etc. Of Chopin's, only one (A major, Op. 40) is in the traditional style. But how superior in inspiration, in harmonic richness, to all those of his contemporaries. The *Grande Polonaise* in E-flat with its heroic vehemence, its splendid driving middle section, is already of another caliber. Often he introduces into these dances a dolorous, poignant element, until then unknown (C minor, Op. 26).

At times this tragic sentiment reaches the sublime (*Polonaise-Fantasie* in A-flat, Op. 61), to such a degree that one may discover in it a complete epic. The sincerity of the expression, grief or heroism, saves it from the bombastic.

The sagacity of the critics has busied itself even with the nocturnes and the impromptus. It is a property of all true music to evoke, incidentally, feelings, landscapes, characters.   [3]

LISZT'S *LES IDÉALS*

From a concert review, 1912

Of Liszt's entire output, what faults in this work matter to us? Aren't there virtues enough in this tumultuous, seething, vast, and magnificent chaos of musical matter from which several generations of illustrious composers drew?

To be truthful: it is in a great measure to these faults that Wagner owes his declamatory vehemence; Strauss, his overenthusiasm; Franck, his tedious loftiness; the Russian school, its sometimes gaudy picturesqueness; the contemporary French school, the excessive coquetry of its harmonic grace. But do not these so dissimilar authors owe the best of their qualities to the truly prodigious musical generosity of their grand precursor? Can one not recognize in this frequently awkward, ever abundant form the embryo of the ingenious, limpid, and easy development of Saint-Saëns? And his dazzling orchestra, of a sonority at once powerful and light—what a considerable influence it exercised on the most openly avowed of Liszt's adversaries!   [4]

FRANCK AND BRAHMS

From an essay, 1912

In art it is not possible to practice mere craftsmanship in the strict sense of the word. Inspiration plays an unlimited part in the elegance of construction of the well-marked divisions of a work. Mere determination to produce something is necessarily fruitless. This is most clearly demonstrated in most of the work of Brahms. This can be confirmed by the D Major Symphony [No. 2] recently played at the Lamoureux concerts. The thoughts are those of intimate and tender musicality. While the melodic contours and the rhythms are very individual, they are closely related to those of Schubert and Schumann. They hardly appear before their pace becomes heavy and laborious. It seems as though the composer is ceaselessly plagued by the desire to do as Beethoven did. But the charming essence of his inspiration is not compatible with that of those broad, fiery, almost disorderly developments that spring directly from Beethoven's themes, or, more properly, gush forth from his inspiration. Brahms acquired his craft by study, something his predecessor Schubert lacked by nature. He did not merely discover it in himself.

Must one ascribe the disillusion one feels at each rehearing of César Franck's symphony to similar causes? There is no doubt of it, even though the two symphonies are very dissimilar in their thematic values and in their embodiment. Yet their shortcomings have the same sources, the same disproportion between ideas and execution. In Brahms: clear and direct inspiration, sometimes lively, sometimes melancholy, scholarly broad speech, difficult and well-developed working out of an idea. In Franck: melody of a cultivated and cheerful spirit, daring harmonies of especial richness, but a devastating poverty in form. . . .

It is no wonder that in Germany, as in France, use has been made of these two composers in the struggle against Wagnerian influence, because their imperfections arouse an impression of coldness and tedium. The overpowering spontaneity of the man who summed up the entire treasury of sentiment of the nineteenth century must have alarmed those very musicians who were the first to succumb to his powerful magic. Even today, when we hear the Venusberg music, which is one of the most typical works of Wagnerian art, one grasps, after this explosion of passionate joys and pains, after this wild inundation of heathen vitality, how necessary a peaceful and even determined retreat had become.   [5]

PRÉLUDE À L'APRÈS-MIDI D'UN FAUN

Remark to Jacques de Zogheb, a neighbor in Montfort-l'Amaury, no date

On hearing this work I really understood what music is.   [6]

SCHOENBERG AND ATONALITY

From a public statement, Houston, April 1928

We have often heard or read that atonality is a blind alley leading nowhere, but I do not accept the validity of this opinion; because, while as a system it may be so, it certainly cannot as an influence. In fact, the influence of Schoenberg may be overwhelming on his followers, but the significance of his art is to be identified with influences of a more subtle kind—not the system, but the aesthetic, of his art. I am quite conscious of the fact that my *Chansons madécasses* are in no way Schoenbergian, but I do not know whether I ever should have been able to write them had Schoenberg never written.   [7]

SELF-CRITICISM

From a concert review, 1912

By the irony of chance, the first work which I must review happens to be my *Pavane pour une infante défunte*. I feel no embarrassment in discussing it; it is old enough for time to allow the composer to relinquish it to the critic. From such a distance I no longer see its good qualities. But alas! I see all too clearly its faults: the too flagrant influence of Chabrier, and the rather poor form. The remarkable interpretation of this incomplete and unventuresome work contributed much, I think, to its success.   [8]

VIOLIN SONATA

From H. H. Stuckenschmidt's biography

In the writing of the Sonata for Violin and Piano, two fundamentally incompatible instruments, I assumed the task, far from bringing their differences into equilibrium, of emphasizing their irreconciliability through their independence.

[9]

MIROIRS

From Ravel's autobiography, 1938

The *Miroirs* of 1905 are a collection of piano pieces that mark a decided turn in the development of my harmony, so that musicians had to revise the views they had previously been accustomed to hold about my style. The first written and, in my view, the most typical in the collection is the second piece in the album, *Oiseaux tristes*. These are birds lost in the mazes of an extremely dark forest during the hottest hours of summer.

[10]

PIANO TRIO

Remark to Maurice Delage, no date

My Trio is finished. I only need the themes for it.

[11]

BOLÉRO

Material sent by Ravel to M. D. Calvocoressi and published in the London Daily Telegraph, July 16, 1931

I am particularly desirous that there should be no misunderstanding as to my *Boléro*. It is an experiment in a very special and limited direction and should not be suspected of aiming at achieving anything different from, or anything more than, what it actually does achieve. Before the first performance, I issued a warning to the effect that what I had written was a piece lasting seventeen minutes and consisting wholly of orchestral tissue without music—of one long, very gradual *crescendo*. There are no contrasts, and there is practically no invention except in the plan and manner of the execution. The themes are impersonal folk tunes of the usual Spanish-Arabian kind. Whatever may have been said to the contrary, the orchestral treatment is simple and straightforward throughout, without the slightest attempt at virtuosity. In this respect, no greater contrast could be imagined than that between the *Boléro* and *L'Enfant et les sortilèges,* in which I freely resort to all manners of orchestral virtuosity.

It is perhaps because of these peculiarities that composers do not like the *Boléro*. From their point of view they are quite right. I have done exactly what I set out to do, and it is for the listeners to take it or leave it.

[12]

Remark to Arthur Honegger, no date

I have written only one masterpiece. That is the *Boléro*. Unfortunately, it contains no music. [13]

GOALS AND BELIEFS

Ravel's aesthetic creed, as written down by Roland-Manuel
and approved by Ravel, no date

I have never felt the need to formulate the principles of my aesthetic creed, either for myself or for others. If I were obliged to do so, I would crave permission to adopt the simple explanations that Mozart has given. He was content to say that music can do, dare, and describe anything, provided only that it gives joy and, once and for all, remains music.

At times people have been pleased to ascribe to me contradictory intentions regarding falsehood in art and the dangers of frankness. The fact is that I refuse, absolutely and unequivocally, to confuse the conscience of the artist, which is one thing, with honesty in art, which is another. The latter is of no value unless the former helps it to become manifest. Good conscience requires that we develop into good craftsmen. Therefore, my aim is technical perfection. I can strive for it unceasingly because I know I can never attain it. The important thing is to come ever closer to it. No doubt art can produce other effects. But, in my view, the artist should have no other goal. [14]

Remark to Jacques de Zogheb, no date

Basically, the only love affair I ever had was with music. [15]

Manuel de Falla
1876–1946

After seven years of study in Paris, Falla returned to Spain and quickly became known as its leading nationalist composer. Falla's earlier studies with Felipe Pedrell had included Spanish folk music, in particular cante jondo *("deep song"), the flamenco of the Gypsies. While* cante jondo *is the basis for modern flamenco, its remarkable variety of scales, ornaments, and rhythmic subtleties has been reduced to a few established formulas. The original flamenco art, hardly recognizable next to its commercial counterpart, is now virtually extinct. Falla's essay appeared in a booklet for a* cante jondo *festival he organized in 1922.*

From an essay, 1922

THE MUSICAL ELEMENTS OF *CANTE JONDO*

The essential elements of *cante jondo* present the following analogies with some of the songs of India and other Oriental countries:

First: Enharmony as a modulating means. The word *modulating* does not have its modern significance in this case. We designate as modulation the simple passing from one tonality to another like it [i.e., with the same scale structure]. . . . But the primitive Indian systems and their derivatives do not consider invariable the places in which the smaller intervals (in our tempered scale, semitones) occur in the melodic series (the scales), believing rather that the occurrence of these smaller intervals, destructive of similarity of scale movement, must obey the rising and falling of the voice demanded by the expression of the word sung. . . . Only three of the tones that formed the scale were invariable; moreover, each of the tones susceptible to alteration was divided and subdivided, the results in certain cases being that notes of attack and resolution of some fragments of a phrase were altered, which is exactly what we encounter in *cante jondo.*

Let us add to this the frequent practice, both in Indian songs and in ours, of vocal *portamento,* or the way of handling the voice so as to produce the infinite gradations of pitch lying between two conjunct or disjunct tones.

Second: We recognize as a characteristic of *cante jondo* the use of a melodic compass rarely exceeding the limits of a sixth. It is clear that this sixth is not made up merely of nine semitones, as in our tempered scale, but that through the use of enharmony, the number of sounds the singer emits is augmented considerably.

Third: The reiterated and almost obsessive use of the same note often accompanied by its higher or lower appoggiatura. This procedure is characteristic of certain forms of incantation and even of those mumbo-jumbos that we might call prehistoric, and that give rise to the belief . . . that song is anterior to the other forms of language. For this reason it has been possible in certain songs of the group we are studying, especially the *siguiriya,* to destroy all sensation of metrical rhythm, producing the impression of sung prose, when in reality the literary text is verse.

Fourth: Though gypsy melody is rich in ornamental passages, these, just as in primitive Oriental songs, are employed at certain times as elaborations or outbursts suggested by the emotional power of the text. They are to be considered, for the most part, more as extended vocal inflections than as ornamental passages, even though they take on the appearance of ornaments when they are translated into the geometrical intervals of the tempered scale.

Fifth: The sounds and cries with which our people inspire and excite their singers and players also have their origin in that which is still observed in analogous cases in races of Oriental origin.

Let no one think, however, that the *siguiriya* and its derivatives are simply songs transplanted from the Orient to the Occident. Here we have, on the contrary, a grafting, or better, a sharing of origins, which was certainly not revealed at a single given moment, but which follows, as we said before, the accumulation of folk history evolved in our peninsula.

INFLUENCE OF *CANTE JONDO* ON EUROPEAN COMPOSERS

Though the songs and dances of other nations have been equally utilized in universal music, this use is almost always reduced to the simple application of their characteristic rhythms. . . .

Our natural music, on the contrary, has not only been the source of inspiration for many of the most illustrious modern foreign composers, but has served to enrich their means of musical expression, revealing to them certain great musical values systematically disregarded by the composers of the so-called classic period. And that is the reason that the moderns (we call those authors modern who date from after the middle of last century) did not limit themselves to taking one element only from our music, but all, absolutely all elements that go to form it, always provided they lent themselves to the tempered scale and the usual notation. . . .

Here are some facts that confirm our thesis.

In the *Cancionero musical español,* its eminent author, Felipe Pedrell, says, referring to Michael Ivanovitch Glinka and his long sojourn in Spain:

"One of the delights of the great Russian composer was to listen for hours on end while [Francisco] Rodriguez Murciano* improvised variations to the accompaniments of *rondeñas, fandangos, jotas aragonesas,* etc., which he noted down with careful persistence, struggling to transcribe them for piano or orchestra.

Glinka's struggles were fruitless; defeated, but hypnotized, he turned back to his companion, listening to him draw from his strings a shower of rhythms, modalities, flourishes, rebellious and refractory to all notation."

As admirable as was the art with which Rodriguez Murciano translated the songs and dances of Spain on his guitar, this signified no more than an instrumental interpretation. It is obvious that Glinka would not have lost opportunities to enrich his notebooks with an approximation (in the majority of cases it could not have been more) not only of dances and songs gathered directly from the people, but also of its guitar, drumstick, drum, and handclapping accompaniments, so much the more since all this vibrated very intensely in the milieu in which he lived and from which he did not separate himself during his long stay in Spain. Since the *cante jondo* songs were those most cultivated in that epoch (1849), they were the ones that exercised the greatest influence on the Russian composers. Given the affinity existing between the group of our songs referred to above and the other no less important group of the Russians, the comprehension and assimilation of our songs by those composers must have been effected in the most natural and spontaneous way. . . .

Not only Russia was influenced by the music of our country; another great musical nation later followed its example, and that nation was France, in the person of Claude Debussy. Though not a few French composers preceded him along this road, their intentions reduced themselves to making music *a la española* (in the Spanish manner), and even Bizet in his admirable *Carmen* seems not to have aimed at anything more.

These musicians, from the most middling to the most eminent, contented themselves with the material—in how many cases how inauthentic!—furnished them by this or that collection of songs and dances, which offered no guarantee of its national authenticity other than that of listing authors with Spanish names. And since these names unfortunately did not always coincide with that of the artists meriting such a title, the document often lacked any validity.

It is clear that such a procedure could not satisfy a man like Debussy. His music

---

* A popular guitarist of the time.

is not written *a la española* but *en español* [in Spanish], or rather *en andaluz,* since it is our *cante jondo,* in its most authentic form, that gave origin not only to his consciously Spanish works but also to certain musical values in other of his works not intended to be Spanish. We are referring to the frequent use of certain modes, cadences, chord connection, rhythms, and even melodic turns that reveal an obvious relation to our natural music.

And yet the great French composer was never in Spain, except for a few hours spent in San Sebastian to see a bull fight. . . .

The knowledge he acquired of Andalusian music was due to the frequency with which he attended the performances of *cante* and *baile jondo* given in Paris by singers, players, and dancers from Seville and Granada at the last two universal expositions held there.

Ravel is also one of those who have not been content to write music *a la española.* . . . The part of his work in which is revealed, now expressly, now unconsciously, the Andalusian musical idiom, proves in an unequivocal manner to what point Ravel assimilated the purest essence of this idiom. Obviously, in this case as well as in those previously enumerated, it has been translated into the style peculiar to each author. [1]

CHAPTER TEN

Ernest Bloch

Béla Bartók

Igor Stravinsky

Zoltán Kodály

Anton Webern

Alban Berg

Edgard Varèse

Ernest Bloch
1880–1959

Bloch experimented with a wide range of techniques over his long life, including serialism and quarter tones, but his idiom was always rooted in tonality. Born in Switzerland, he studied violin and composition in Belgium, Germany, and France, then returned to Switzerland for a time before emigrating to the United States in 1924. At about this time his music began to express a feeling of identity with his Jewish heritage. The works from this period, particularly Schelomo, *subtitled "Hebrew rhapsody for cello and orchestra," have remained his enduring contributions to the repertoire.*

THE STATE OF MUSIC; WAGNERISM AND "DEBUSSYSME"

From *"Man and Music,"* Seven Arts, *March 1917*

Only that art can live which is an active manifestation of the life of the people. It must be a necessary and essential portion of that life, and not a luxury. It must have its roots deep within the soil that brings it forth. Needless to say, it cannot be the direct output of crowds; but, however indirectly, they must have contributed to its substance. A work of art is the soul of a race speaking through the voice of the prophet in whom it has become incarnate. Art is the outlet of the mystical, emotional needs of the human spirit; it is created rather by instinct than by intelligence; rather by intuition than by will. Primitive and elemental races have had marvellous arts; and there have been periods of superior civilization, sterile in this form of expression; particularly those in which the practical and intellectual elements have been dominant. Indeed, it would seem as if certain social states, like certain individual conditions, give forth an atmosphere that is hostile to art and exclude it. And it is a proper question whether a society, primarily utilitarian like our own, is of a sort to foster art. For art is a completely disinterested function; it is free of all practical compromise and deaf to the law of supply and demand.

In certain epochs of history broad truths, social, political or religious, have set up wide currents of thought and feeling that have swept man along in a unity of action and of faith. In such times, art has been one with life and its expression has stood for humanity. Egypt, Greece, the Middle Ages, the Renaissance knew such an art. It seems to me that the latest example of one of these collective states of soul in music was Richard Wagner: for in him we find incarnate the future dream and development of his race. But since Wagner's time no great conception, no great conviction has fertilized mankind. On the other hand, the critical instinct has developed, the positive sciences have reigned; industrialism and the vulgarization of art, heightened communication and interchange of ideas have foisted on our consciousness a febrile mixture of thought and feeling. We find the most hostile theories living side by side. The old convictions are shattered, and new ideas are not strong enough to become convictions. Everywhere there is chaos. And art indeed has been the mirror of our uncertainties. It is significant to find, in a single epoch, the flourishing of works and styles so varied and so opposed: Reger to Strauss; Mahler to Schoenberg; Saint-Saëns to d'Indy or Debussy; Puccini to Dukas. Our arts tend more and more toward an individualistic, non-representative and non-racial expression. Nor is the factitious renaissance of national arts which manifested itself before the war to be taken seriously. The ardor of these prophets was an affair of the will, of the intellect. Their influence on the real domain of art is negligible.

There can be no doubt, for instance, that a great artist like Claude Debussy stands for the best and purest traditions of the French. But chiefly he is representative aesthetically and in form. The essence of his inspiration has little in common with the present state of France. He stands far less for France than a Rabelais, a Montaigne, a Voltaire, a Balzac, a Flaubert. He represents in reality only a small part of his country.*

Debussy represents the goal of the pre-Raphaelite doctrines propounded by the symbolist poets and painters of France. Above all, he represents Claude Debussy. And it is precisely in this fact that his immense value lies: his personality, his special individuality.

Unfortunately, this is not what musicians have sought in him. Quite the contrary, they appreciate and emulate the exterior part of his work, which is of importance only because of what it expresses; so that the fate of Debussy has been the usual one. First, he was ignored. Now, he is understood and admired only through his superficial and trivial qualities. An army of imitators, of second-hand manufacturers, pounced on the technique of Claude Debussy. And through their ironical activities that which was the peculiar asset of a peculiar personality becomes a debased tongue; musicians who have nothing in common with Debussy now think that they must use his words. And criticism which seems perennially unable to distinguish the true work from the pastiche exalts with the same adjectives the authentic expression and the sickening imitation.

Of course, the language of Debussy has become vulgarized and denatured; false usage has emptied it of its native color. It has become a mechanical procedure, without power and without soul. And the consequence, as with Wagner, has been a constant musical depreciation. For the ears of these moderns Debussy is already "vieux jeu." Debussy has had to be outbidden. From one tonal exaggeration to another, we have been hurried along until our ears have become actually perverse and incapable of savoring the clean and fresh beauty of old masterpieces. Our appetite increases for still hotter spices, for still wilder complexities.

First, the Wagnerians created "Wagnerism," a narrow doctrine that declared itself the absolute truth; then the admirers of Debussy forged their "Debussysme," a doctrine equally narrow and equally intolerant of the past. And now comes a new aesthetic—that of the *bored ones!* It is based exclusively upon technical considerations. With the charge of rhetoric it denies most of the superb eras of musical history, as if its own rhetoric were better; and it succeeds utterly in confounding the

---

* Perhaps it is unjust to seek this manifestation of France in her music. Here poets and novelists, painters and sculptors are certainly more typical. Each race has its arts of predilection. [Bloch]

means of art with its end. Its cry is for novelty, and still more novelty. This frenzied search for originality has led to cubism, futurism, all those tendencies which above everything are creations of reason and not of feeling.

Here is a new criterion; and all our musicians, artists, critics, are touched by it in some degree. When I say that they are not free, I mean that an intellectual barrier exists between their emotion and their work—a sort of sensory perversion that twists their thoughts, inhibits their inspiration, and warps their taste. They are forever thinking of the development of their art, not as the corollary of a logical growth of thought, not as a spontaneous expression of life, but as a thing-in-itself, apart from life. And the truth is that they neither understand nor are they interested in anything so much as the elaboration of their technique. [1]

ON HIS HEBREW MUSIC

From a program note, 1933

I do not propose nor do I want to attempt the reconstruction of Hebrew music, nor do I base my work on more or less authentic melodies. I am not an archeologist; I believe that the most important thing is to write good and sincere music. It is rather the Hebrew spirit that interests me, the complex, ardent, restless spirit I feel pulsating throughout the Bible, the freshness and ingenuousness of the Patriarchs, the violence of the books of the Prophets, the fierce love of the Hebrews for justice, the despair in the book of Ecclesiastes, the sorrow and grandeur of the book of Job, the sensuality of the Song of Songs. All this resides in us, all this resides in me, is the best part of me. And this is what I try to feel within me and to translate into my music: the holy fervor of the race which is latent in our soul. [2]

Béla Bartók
1881–1945

In his musical background—childhood lessons, a formal education, and an interest in regional folk music—Bartók had all the makings of a nationalist composer, but talent and an intense curiosity carried him well beyond nationalism and established him as one of the major figures of early Modernism. His project to collect Hungarian folk music became an important early model for ethnomusicological field research; it was also to furnish him with one of the central elements of his mature style. Beginning in 1905, Bartók and Kodály recorded thousands of examples of Magyar, Slovak, Transylvanian, Romanian, and other folk songs and dances using a modified portable phonograph. In 1913 Bartók made a similar trip to North Africa. He subsequently transcribed and published many of the themes, some in his own arrangements.

Bartók's early works show the influence of Liszt, whom he admired, though he had reservations about the spurious nature of the Hungarian influences in Liszt's music. As contemporary accounts and a modest number of recordings attest, Bartók was an exceptional pianist. He concertized fairly widely, playing primarily his own music.

RACE PURITY IN MUSIC

From an essay in Modern Music, *1942*

In the present period of controversy over racial problems, it may be timely to examine the question: Is racial impurity favorable to folk (i.e., peasant) music or not? (I apply the word racial here to the music itself, and not to the individuals creating, preserving, or performing the music.) . . .

From the beginning I have been amazed by the extraordinary wealth of melody types existing in the territory under investigation in Eastern Europe. As I pursued my research, my amazement increased. In view of the comparatively small size of the countries—numbering forty to fifty million people—the variety in folk music is really marvelous! It is still more remarkable when compared with the peasant music of other more or less remote regions, for instance North Africa, where the Arab peasant music presents so much less variety.

What can be the reason for this wealth? . . . Comparison of the folk music of these peoples made it clear that there was a continuous give-and-take of melodies, a constant crossing and recrossing that had persisted through centuries.

I must now stress a very important fact. This give-and-take is not so simple as many of us might believe. When a folk melody passes the language frontier of a people, sooner or later it will be subjected to certain changes determined by environment, and especially by difference of language. The greater dissimilarity between the accents, inflections, metrical conditions, syllabic structure, and so on of two languages, the greater the changes that fortunately may occur in the "emigrated" melody. I say "fortunately" because this phenomenon itself engenders a further increase in the number of types and subtypes.

I have used the term "crossing and recrossing." Now, the "recrossing" generally takes place this way. A Hungarian melody is taken over, let us say, by the Slovakians and "Slovakized"; this Slovakized form may then be retaken by the Hungarians and so "re-Magyarized." But—and again I say, fortunately,—this re-Magyarized form will be different from the original Hungarian. . . .

Contact with foreign material not only results in an exchange of melodies, but—and this is still more important—it gives an impulse to the development of new styles. At the same time, the more or less ancient styles are generally well preserved, too, which still further enhances the richness of the music. . . .

It is obvious that if there remains any hope for the survival of folk music in the near or distant future (a rather doubtful outcome considering the rapid intrusion of higher civilization into the more remote parts of the world), an artificial erection of Chinese walls to separate peoples from each other bodes no good for its development. A complete separation from foreign influence means stagnation; well-assimilated foreign impulses offer possibilities of enrichment. [1]

THE SIGNIFICANCE OF FOLK MUSIC TO MODERN MUSIC

From an essay in Uj Idok, *1931*

At the beginning of the twentieth century there was a turning point in the history of modern music.

The excesses of the romanticists began to be unbearable for many. There were composers who felt: "This road does not lead us anywhere; there is no other solution but a complete break with the nineteenth century."

Invaluable help was given this change (or let us rather call it rejuvenation) by a kind of peasant music unknown till then.

The right type of peasant music is most varied and perfect in its forms. Its expressive power is amazing, and at the same time it is void of all sentimentality and superfluous ornaments. It is simple, sometimes primitive, but never silly. It is the ideal starting point for a musical renaissance, and a composer in search of new ways cannot be led by a better master. What is the best way for a composer to reap the full benefits of his studies in peasant music? It is to assimilate the idiom of peasant music so completely that he is able to forget all about it and use it as his musical mother tongue.

In order to achieve this, Hungarian composers went into the country and made their collections there. It may be that the Russian Stravinsky and the Spaniard Falla did not go on journeys of collection and mainly drew their material from the collections of others, but they, too, I feel sure, must not only have availed themselves of books and museums but have studied the living music of their countries.

In my opinion, the effects of peasant music cannot be deep and permanent unless this music is studied in the country as part of a life shared with the peasants. It is not enough to study it as it is stored up in museums. It is the character of peasant music, indescribable in words, that must find its way into our music. It must be pervaded by the very atmosphere of peasant culture. Peasant motifs (or imitations of such motifs) will only lend our music some new ornaments: nothing more.

Some twenty to twenty-five years ago well-disposed people often marveled at our enthusiasm. How was it possible, they asked, that trained musicians, fit to give concerts, took upon themselves the "subaltern" task of going into the country and studying the music of the people on the spot. What a pity, they said, that this task was not carried out by people unsuitable for a higher type of musical work. Many thought our perseverence in our work was due to some crazy idea that had got hold of us. Little did they know how much this work meant to us. We went into the country and obtained firsthand knowledge of a music that opened up new ways to us.

The question is, what are the ways in which peasant music is taken over and becomes transmuted into modern music?

We may, for instance, take over a peasant melody unchanged or only slightly varied, write an accompaniment to it and possibly some opening and concluding phrases. This kind of work would show a certain analogy with Bach's treatment of chorales.

Two main types can be distinguished among works of this character.

In the one case, accompaniment and introductory and concluding phrases are of secondary importance; they serve only as an ornamental setting for the precious stone: the peasant melody.

It is the other way round in the second case: the melody serves only as a "motto," while that which is built round it is of real importance.

All shades of transition are possible between these two extremes, and sometimes it is not even possible to decide which of the elements is predominant in any given case. But in every case it is of the greatest importance that the musical qualities of the setting should be derived from the musical qualities of the melody, from such characteristics as are contained in it openly or covertly, so that melody and all additions create the impression of complete unity. . . .

It may sound odd, but I do not hesitate to say that the simpler the melody the more complex and strange may be the harmonization and accompaniment that go well with it. Let us, for instance, take a melody that moves on two successive notes only (there are many such melodies in Arab peasant music). It is obvious that we are much freer in the invention of an accompaniment than in the case of a melody of a more complex character. These primitive melodies, moreover, show no trace of the stereotyped joining of triads. That again means greater freedom for us in the treatment of the melody. It allows us to bring out the melody most clearly by building round it harmonies of the widest range varying along different keynotes. I might almost say that the traces of polytonality in modern Hungarian music and in Stravinsky's music are to be explained by this possibility.

Similarly, the strange turnings of melodies in our Eastern European peasant music showed us new ways of harmonization. For instance, the new chord of the seventh, which we use as a concord, may be traced back to the fact that in our folk melodies of a pentatonic character the seventh appears as an interval of equal importance with the third and the fifth. We so often heard these intervals treated equally in the succession that it was only natural to give them equal importance when used simultaneously. We sounded the four notes together in a setting that made us feel it was not necessary to break them up. In other words: the four notes were made to form a concord.

The frequent use of the intervals of the fourth in our old melodies suggested to us the use of chords built of fourths. Here again what we heard in succession we tried to build up in a simultaneous chord.

Another method by which peasant music becomes transmuted into modern music is the following: The composer does not make use of a real peasant melody but invents his own imitation of such melodies. There is no true difference between this method and the one described above. . . .

There is yet a third way in which the influence of peasant music can be traced in a composer's work. Neither peasant melodies nor imitations of peasant melodies can be found in his music, but it is pervaded by the atmosphere of peasant music. In this case we may say, he has completely absorbed the idiom of peasant music, which has become his musical mother tongue. . . .

In Hungarian music the best example of this kind can be found in Kodály's work. It is enough to mention the *Psalmus hungaricus,* which would not have been written without Hungarian peasant music. (Neither, of course, would it have been written without Kodály.)

Many people think it a comparatively easy task to write a composition around folk tunes. A lesser achievement, at least, than a composition on "original" themes. Because, they think, the composer is freed of part of the work: the invention of themes.

This way of thinking is completely erroneous. To handle folk tunes is one of the most difficult tasks; equally difficult, if not more so, than to write a major original composition. If we keep in mind that borrowing a tune means being bound by its individual peculiarity, we shall understand one part of the difficulty. Another is created by the special character of folk tune. We must penetrate into it, feel it, and bring out its sharp contours by the appropriate setting. The composition around a folk tune must be done in a "propitious hour" or, as is generally said, it must be a work of inspiration just as much as any other composition. . . .

We know that Shakespeare borrowed the plots of his plays from many sources. Does that prove that his brain was barren and that he had to go to his neighbors, begging for themes? Did he hide his incompetence? Molière's case is even worse. He borrowed not only the themes for his plays but also part of the construction, and sometimes took over from his source expressions and whole lines unchanged.

We know that Handel adapted a work by Stradella in one of his oratorios. His adaptation is so masterly, so far surpassing the original in beauty, that we forget all about Stradella. . . .

The work of Bach is a summing up of the music of some hundred-odd years before him. His musical material consists of themes and motives used by his predecessors. We can trace in Bach's music motifs and phrases that were also used by Frescobaldi and many others among Bach's predecessors. Is this plagiarism? By no means. For an artist it is not only right to have his roots in the art of some former time, it is a necessity.

Well, in our case it is peasant music that contains our roots.

The conception that attributes so much importance to the invention of a theme originated in the nineteenth century. It is a romantic conception that values originality above all.

From what has been said above, it must have become clear that it is no sign of "barrenness" or "incompetence" if a composer bases his music on folk music instead of taking Brahms and Schumann as his models.

Let us consider how it is possible to reconcile music based on folk music with the modern movement of atonality, or music on twelve tones.

Let us say frankly that this is not possible. Why not? Because folk tunes are always tonal. Atonal folk music is completely inconceivable. Consequently, music on twelve tones cannot be based on folk music. . . .

There exists another conception of modern music that seems exactly the opposite of the former.

There are people who believe that nothing more is needed to bring about the full bloom in a nation's music than to steep oneself in folk music and to transplant its motives into established musical forms.

This opinion is founded on the same mistaken conception as the one discussed above. It stresses the all-importance of themes and forgets about the art of formation that alone can make something out of these themes. This process of moulding is part of the composer's work, which proves his creative talent.

And thus we may say: folk music will become a source of inspiration for a country's music only if the transplantation of its motifs is the work of a great creative talent. In the hands of incompetent composers neither folk music nor any other musical material will ever attain significance. . . .

Folk music will have an immense, transforming influence on music in countries with little or no musical tradition. Most countries of southern and eastern Europe, Hungary, too, are in this position.   [2]

LISZT

From an address to the Hungarian Academy, 1936

Every composer, even the greatest, must start from something that already exists, perhaps one kind of thing, perhaps several related ones. From this, one composer—the innovator—gradually reaches new points, from which it is hardly possible to remember the starting point; another composer—the great traditionalist—develops what already exists to a stage never foreseen, and into a unity never imagined. Liszt, however, did not start from any one point, nor fuse together in his own works several related things; he submitted himself to the influence of the most diverse, contradictory, and almost irreconcilable elements.

Let us look at these influences one by one. Of his contemporaries, we feel the influence of Chopin to a very great degree, chiefly in certain kinds of piano works. The imprint of the bel canto style of the Italians of the previous century is plainly to be seen in every work, and it is hardly necessary to mention that he was subject to the influence of the Hungarian so-called gypsy music. He also allowed himself to be influenced by the utterly different, popular, half-folk music of Italy, as his works connected with Italy clearly show. Nor was he untouched by the equivalent Spanish popular music, witness the "Spanish Rhapsody." There is also in manuscript a very little known "Wallachian Rhapsody." Later, chiefly in his religious music, Gregorian influences become apparent. His relationship to Wagner is not easy to make out. A separate study, based on chronological data, would be necessary to show which of the elements in Liszt that might be called "Wagnerian" owed their origin to Liszt, and which to Wagner. Probably Wagner had much to thank Liszt for, but on the other hand, in Liszt's later works, such as the last symphonic poem, we may expect to find a certain amount of Wagner's influence. It is, however, quite apparent, and significant, that apart from Wagner's we can hardly find another trace of German influence, whether of folk music or art music, in Liszt's work.

How did Liszt fit these contradictory elements into a unified structure? First of all, it must be said that whatever Liszt touched . . . became unmistakably his own. Still more important, however, is the fact that he mixed with these foreign elements so many more that were genuinely drawn from himself that there is no work in which we can doubt the greatness of his creative power. We can say that he was eclectic in the best sense of the word; one who took from all foreign sources, but gave still more himself.

However, there are certain elements that go together ill; for instance, Gregorian music and Italian aria. Such things could not be fused into unity even with all Liszt's art. To quote only one example, there is the *Totentanz* for piano and orchestra. This composition, which is simply a set of variations on the Gregorian melody "Dies irae," is startlingly harsh from beginning to end. But what do we find in the middle section? A variation hardly eight bars long, of almost Italianate emotionalism. Here Liszt obviously intended to relieve the overwhelming austerity and darkness with a ray of hope. The work as a whole always has a profound effect upon me, but this short section sticks out so from the unified style of the rest that I have never been able to feel that it is appropriate. In many of Liszt's works we find similar little outbursts breaking up the unity of style.

In the end, however, this is not so important; this fleeting disturbance of the unity is merely external and is dwarfed into insignificance beside the wealth of power and beauty that forms the essence of the work. But the general public obviously finds it an insurmountable obstacle; they do not perceive nor understand the beauty, and they miss the compensation of dazzling brilliance, which hardly exists in such works as the *Totentanz*, so they drop the whole work. Another cause, or at least I imagine so, is that tendency to prolixity in Liszt's greater works. This is not the Schubertian "heavenly length," which we forgive without hesitation for the sake of the youthfully exuberant and astonishingly beautiful ideas. In Liszt's greater works there are certain sequential repetitions of long sections, in the relative major or minor key, for instance, that we today, perhaps because we are used to the faster tempo of life in general, do not always feel to be necessary. But this again is not an essential point. The essence of these works we must find in the new ideas. . . .

One could draw attention to the bold harmonic turns, the innumerable modulatory digressions, such as the juxtaposition, without any transition at all, of the two keys most distant from each other, and to many other points that would require the use of too many technical terms. But all these are mere details. What is more important is the absolutely new imaginative conception that manifests itself in the chief works (the Piano Sonata and the two outer movements of the *Faust* Symphony, for instance) by reason of which these works rank among the outstanding musical creations of the nineteenth century. Formally, too, though he did not break with tradition completely, Liszt created much that was new. Thus one finds in him, in the E-flat Major Piano Concerto, for instance, the first perfect realization of cyclic sonata form, with common themes treated on variation principles. After Liszt's time this solution of formal problems came to acquire more and more importance. It was Liszt who, after Berlioz, developed the symphonic poem further, and we may say that the musical form that arose from the juxtaposition of the *lassú* (slow) and the *friss* (fast) was Liszt's innovation, though he was in fact led to it by the usual order of Hungarian folk and semifolk dances.

His piano technique was at first derived from Chopin's and from that of various less significant composers, but in his maturity it was transformed into something new and individual. He brought his own artistic and expressive medium to such a pitch of perfection that he covered every possible development, in consequence of which his successors in this field could hardly do anything and were forced to turn in other directions. As an innovator in instrumentation, with his absolutely individual orchestral technique, he stands beside the other two great orchestrators of the nineteenth century, Berlioz and Wagner.

From one part of his piano music it seems as if he were intentionally seeking to satisfy public taste. Of course even in these, down to the tiniest details, his great creative artistry is apparent. But from the point of view of content, these brilliant pieces have not half so much to offer us as the other piano works, particularly those from his maturity, which are absolutely free from bombast and frills. . . . For the sake of truth, I must stress that the rhapsodies, particularly the Hungarian ones, are perfect creations of their own kind. The material that Liszt uses in them could not be treated with greater artistry and beauty. The value of the material itself is quite another question, and this is obviously one reason why the general value of the works is slight, and their popularity great.   [3]

DEBUSSY

Remark to Serge Moreux, Paris, Spring 1939

Debussy's great service to music was to reawaken among all musicians an awareness of harmony and its possibilities. In that, he was just as important as Beethoven, who revealed to us the meaning of progressive form, and as Bach, who showed us the transcendent significance of counterpoint.   [4]

KODÁLY

From an article in Nyugat, 1921

Kodály is one of the most outstanding composers of our day. His art, like mine, has twin roots: it has sprung from Hungarian peasant music and modern French music. But though our art has grown from this common soil, our works from the very beginning have been completely different (it is sheer injustice or ignorance to declare that Kodály is an "imitator").   [5]

STRAVINSKY'S USE OF FOLK THEMES

From the Uj Idok essay

Stravinsky never mentions the sources of his themes. . . . What he has judged suitable for his purpose has become through this very use his intellectual property. . . . In maintaining that the question of the origin of a theme is completely unimportant from the artist's point of view, Stravinsky is right. The question of origins can be interesting only from the point of view of musical documentation.

Lacking any data, I am unable to tell which themes of Stravinsky's from his so-called Russian period are his own inventions and which are borrowed from folk music. This much is certain, that if among the thematic material of Stravinsky's there are some of his own invention (and who can doubt that there are), these are the most faithful and clever imitations of folk songs. It is also notable that during his Russian period, from Le Sacre du printemps onward, he seldom uses melodies of a closed form consisting of three or four lines, but short motives of two or three bars and repeats them "a la ostinato." These recurring primitive motifs are very characteristic of Russian music of a certain category. This type of construction occurs in some of our old music for wind instruments and also in Arab peasant dances. . . .

The steady repetition of primitive motifs creates an air of strange feverish excitement even in folk music where it occurs. The effect is increased a hundredfold if a master of Stravinsky's supreme skill and his precise knowledge of dynamic effects employs these rapidly chasing sets of motifs.   [6]

Igor Stravinsky
1882–1971

That Stravinsky possessed a shrewd musical intellect and an instinctive grasp of culture is beyond dispute, but the extent of his contribution to many of the texts and statements issued under his name remains uncertain. Both the Chronicle of My Life *and the* Poetics of Music *were produced with co-authors or editors. Cloudier still is the situation with the books written by or with his assistant, Robert Craft. Both Craft and Stravinsky acknowledged that Craft substantially edited and expanded the composer's thoughts. While some have asserted that Craft's role was more that of author than co-author, the content and viewpoint of many of the remarks, as well as their sharpness, suggest an authenticity of meaning if not always of word.*

RADIO, RECORDINGS, AND THE LISTENER

From Chronicle of My Life, *1935*

In the domain of music the importance and influence of its dissemination by mechanical means, such as the record and the radio—those redoubtable triumphs of modern science, which will probably undergo still further development—make them worthy of the closest investigation. The facilities they offer to composers and executants alike for reaching great numbers of listeners, and the opportunities they give those listeners to acquaint themselves with works they have not heard, are obviously indisputable advantages. But one must not overlook the fact that such advantages are attended by serious danger. In Johann Sebastian Bach's day, he had to walk ten miles to a neighboring town to hear Buxtehude play his works.* Today anyone, living no matter where, has only to turn a knob or put on a record to hear what he likes. Indeed, it is in just this incredible facility, this lack of necessity for any effort, that the evil of this so-called progress lies. For in music, more than in any other branch of art, understanding is given only to those who make an active effort. Passive receptivity is not enough. To listen to certain combinations of sound and automatically become accustomed to them does not necessarily imply that they have been heard and understood. For one can listen without hearing, just as one can look without seeing. The absence of active effort and the liking acquired for this facility make for laziness. The radio has got rid of the necessity that existed in Bach's day for getting out of one's armchair. Nor are listeners any longer impelled to play themselves, or to spend time on learning an instrument in order to acquire a knowledge of musical literature. The radio and the gramophone do all that. [1]

---

* The oft-repeated story to which Stravinsky refers is not entirely correct. The distance from Arnstadt to Lübeck is 212 miles, and based on chronology and other factors it is doubtful that Bach made the journey on foot.

From Poetics of Music, *1939*

CONSONANCE AND DISSONANCE

Consonance, says the dictionary, is the combination of several tones into a harmonic unit. Dissonance results from the deranging of this harmony by the addition of tones foreign to it. One must admit that all this is not clear. Ever since it appeared in our vocabulary, the word dissonance has carried with it a certain odor of sinfulness.

Let us light our lantern: in textbook language, dissonance is an element of transition, a complex or interval of tones that is not complete in itself and that must be resolved to the ear's satisfaction into a perfect consonance.

But just as the eye completes the lines of a drawing that the painter has knowingly left incomplete, just so the ear may be called upon to complete and cooperate in the resolution of a chord that has not actually been realized in the work. Dissonance, in this instance, plays the part of an allusion.

Either case applies to a style where the use of dissonance demands a resolution. But nothing forces us to be looking constantly for satisfaction that resides only in repose. For more than a century, music has provided repeated examples of a style in which dissonance has emancipated itself. It is no longer tied down to its former function. Having become an entity in itself, dissonance often neither prepares nor anticipates anything. Dissonance is thus no more an agent of disorder than consonance is a guarantee of stability. The music of yesterday and of today unhesitatingly unites parallel dissonant chords that thereby lose their functional value, and our ear quite naturally accepts their juxtaposition.

Of course, the instruction and education of the public have not kept pace with the evolution of technique. The use of dissonance, for ears ill prepared to accept it, has not failed to confuse and enfeeble the listener's response until the dissonant is no longer distinguished from the consonant.

We thus no longer find ourselves in the framework of classic tonality, in the scholastic sense of the word. It is not we who have created this state of affairs, and it is not our fault if we find ourselves confronted with a new logic of music that would have appeared unthinkable to the masters of the past. And this new logic has opened our eyes to riches whose existence we never suspected.

Having reached this point, we must obey, not new idols, but the external necessity of affirming the axis of our music, and we must recognize the existence of certain poles of attraction. Diatonic tonality is only one means of orienting music toward these poles. The function of tonality is completely subordinated to the force of attraction of the pole of sonority. All music is nothing more than a succession of impulses that converge toward a definite point of repose. That is as true of Gregorian chant as it is of a Bach fugue, as true of Brahms's music as it is of Debussy's.

This general law of attraction is satisfied in only a limited way by the traditional diatonic system, for that system possesses no absolute value. [2]

TONALITY AND ATONALITY

The superannuated system of classic tonality, which has served as the basis for musical constructions of compelling interest, has had the authority of law among musicians for only a short period of time—a period much shorter than is usually imagined, extending only from the middle of the seventeenth century to the middle of the nineteenth. From the moment when chords no longer serve to fulfill merely the functions assigned to them by the interplay of tones but, instead, throw off all constraint to become new entities free of all ties—from that moment, one may say that the process is completed: the diatonic system has lived out its life cycle. The work of the Renaissance polyphonists had not yet entered into this system, and we have seen that the music of our times abides by it no longer. A parallel progression of ninth chords would suffice as proof. It was here that the gates opened upon what has been labeled with the abusive term *atonality*.

The expression is fashionable. But that doesn't mean that it is very clear. And I should like to know just what those persons who use the term mean by it. The negating prefix *a-* indicates a state of indifference in regard to the term, negating without entirely renouncing it. Understood in this way, the word *atonality* hardly corresponds to what those who use it have in mind. If it were said that my music is atonal, that would be tantamount to saying that I had become deaf to tonality. Now, it well may be that I remain for a considerable time within the bounds of the strict order of tonality, even though I may quite consciously break up this order for the purposes of establishing a new one. In that case I am not atonal, but antitonal. I am not trying to argue pointlessly over words but essentially to discover what we deny and what we affirm. [3]

CACOPHONY

Our vanguard elite, sworn perpetually to outdo itself, expects and requires that music should satisfy the taste for absurd cacophony.

I say *cacophony* without fear of being classed with the conventional *pompiers,* the *laudatores temporis acti.* And in using the word, I am certain I am not in the least reversing myself. My position in this regard is exactly the same as it was at the time when I composed the *Rite,* and when people saw fit to call me a revolutionary. Today, just as in the past, I am on my guard against counterfeit money and take care not to accept it for the true coin of the realm. Cacophony means bad sound, counterfeit merchandise, uncoordinated music that will not stand up under serious criticism. Whatever opinion one may hold about the music of Arnold Schoenberg (to take as example a composer evolving along lines essentially different from mine, both aesthetically and technically), whose works have frequently given rise to violent reactions or ironic smiles—it is impossible for a self-respecting mind equipped with genuine musical culture not to feel that the composer of *Pierrot lunaire* is fully aware of what he is doing and that he is not trying to deceive anyone. He adopted the musical system that suited his needs, and within this system he is perfectly consistent with himself, perfectly coherent. One cannot dismiss music that one dislikes by labeling it cacophony.

Equally degrading is the vanity of snobs who boast of an embarrassing familiarity with the world of the incomprehensible, and who delightedly confess that they find themselves in good company. It is not music they seek, but rather the effect of shock, the sensation that befuddles understanding.

So I confess that I am completely insensitive to the prestige of revolution. All the noise it may make will not call forth the slightest echo in me. For revolution is one thing, innovation another. And even innovation, when not presented in an excessive form, is not always recognized by its contemporaries.   [4]

TRADITION

It is culture that brings out the full value of taste and gives it a chance to prove its worth simply by its application. The artist imposes a culture upon himself and ends by imposing it upon others. That is how tradition becomes established.

Tradition is entirely different from habit, even from an excellent habit, since habit is by definition an unconscious acquisition and tends to become mechanical, whereas tradition results from a conscious and deliberate acceptance. A real tradition is not the relic of a past that is irretrievably gone; it is a living force that animates and informs the present. In this sense the paradox that banteringly maintains that everything that is not tradition is plagiarism is true. . . .

Far from implying the repetition of what has been, tradition presupposes the reality of what endures. It appears as an heirloom, a heritage that one receives on condition of making it bear fruit before passing it on to one's descendants.

Brahms was born sixty years after Beethoven. From the one to the other, and from every aspect, the distance between them is great; they do not dress the same way, but Brahms follows the tradition of Beethoven without borrowing one of his habiliments. For the borrowing of a method has nothing to do with observing a tradition. "A method is replaced; a tradition is carried forward in order to produce something new." Tradition thus assures the continuity of creation. The example that I have just cited does not constitute an exception but is one proof out of a hundred of a constant law. This sense of tradition that is a natural need must not be confused with the desire the composer feels to affirm the kinship he finds across the centuries with some master of the past.   [5]

MODERNISM AND ACADEMICISM

What is modern is what is representative of its own time and what must be in keeping with and within the grasp of its own time. Sometimes artists are reproached for being too modern or not modern enough. One might just as well reproach the times with not being sufficiently modern or with being too modern. A recent popular poll showed that, to all appearances, Beethoven is the composer most in demand in the United States. On that basis one can say that Beethoven is very modern and that a composer of such manifest importance as Paul Hindemith is not modern at all, since the list of winners does not even mention his name.

In itself, the term *modernism* implies neither praise nor blame and involves no obligation whatsoever. This is precisely its weakness. The word eludes us, hiding under any application of it one wishes to make. True, it is said that one must live in one's own time. The advice is superfluous; how could one do otherwise? Even if I wanted to relive the past, the most energetic strivings of my misguided will would be futile.

It follows that everyone has taken advantage of the pliability of this vacuous term by trying to give it form and color. But, again, what do we understand by the term *modernism*? In the past the term was never used, was even unknown. Yet our predecessors were no more stupid than we are. Was the term a real discovery? We have shown that it was nothing of the sort. Might it not rather be a sign of a decadence in morality and taste? Here I strongly believe we must answer in the affirmative. . . .

The term *modernism* is all the more offensive in that it is usually coupled with another whose meaning is perfectly clear: I speak of *academicism*.

A work is called academic when it is composed strictly according to the precepts of the conservatory. It follows that academicism considered as a scholastic exercise based on imitation is in itself something very useful and even indispensable to beginners who train themselves by studying models. It likewise follows that academicism should find no place outside the conservatory, and that those who make an ideal of academicism when they have already completed their studies produce stiffly correct works that are bloodless and dry.

Contemporary writers on music have acquired the habit of measuring everything in terms of modernism, that is to say in terms of a nonexistent scale, and promptly consign to the category of "academic"—which they regard as the opposite of modern—all that is not in keeping with the extravagances that in their eyes constitute the thrice-distilled quintessence of modernism. To these critics, whatever appears discordant and confused is automatically relegated to the pigeonhole of modernism. Whatever they cannot help finding clear and well ordered, and devoid of ambiguity that might give them an opening, is promptly relegated in its turn to the pigeonhole of academicism. Now, we can make use of academic forms without running the risk of becoming academic ourselves. The person who is loath to borrow these forms when he has need of them clearly betrays his weakness. How many times have I noticed this strange incomprehension on the part of those who believe themselves good judges of music and its future! What makes this all the more difficult to understand is the fact that these same critics admit as natural and legitimate the borrowing of old popular or religious melodies harmonized in ways incompatible with their essence. They are not at all shocked by the ridiculous device of the leitmotiv and let themselves be inveigled into musical tours conducted by the Cook Agency of Bayreuth. They believe themselves up to the minute when they applaud the very introductory measures of a symphony employing exotic scales, obsolete instruments, and methods that were created for entirely different purposes. Terrified at the thought of showing themselves for what they are, they go after poor academicism tooth and nail, for they feel the same horror of forms consecrated by long use that their favorite composers feel, who are afraid to touch them. [6]

MUSIC AND EXPRESSION

From Chronicle of My Life

I consider that music, by its very nature, is essentially powerless to *express* anything at all, whether a feeling, an attitude of mind, a psychological mood, a phenomenon of nature, etc. . . . *Expression* has never been an inherent property of music. That is by no means the purpose of its existence. If, as is nearly always the case, music appears to express something, this is only an illusion and not a reality. It is simply an additional attribute that, by tacit and inveterate agreement, we have lent it, thrust upon it, as a label, a convention—in short, an aspect that, unconsciously or by force of habit, we have often come to confuse with its essential being. [7]

From books written with Robert Craft:
Conversations with Igor Stravinsky, *1957;* Memories and Commentaries, *1958/9;* Expositions and Developments, *1960*

That over-publicized bit about expression (or non-expression) was simply a way of saying that music is supra-personal and super-real and as such beyond verbal meanings and verbal descriptions. It was aimed against the notion that a piece of music is in reality a transcendental idea "expressed in terms of" music, with the *reductio ad absurdum* implication that exact sets of correlatives must exist between a composer's feelings and his notation. It was offhand and annoyingly incomplete, but even the stupider critics could have seen that it did not deny musical expressivity, but only the validity of a type of verbal statement about musical expressivity. I stand by the remark, incidentally, though today I would put it the other way around: music expresses itself.

A composer's work *is* the embodiment of his feelings and, of course, it may be considered as expressing or symbolizing them—though consciousness of this step does not concern the composer. More important is the fact that the composition is something entirely new *beyond* what can be called the composer's feelings. . . . A new piece of music *is* a new reality.

On another level, of course, a piece of music may be "beautiful," "religious," "poetic," "sweet," or as many other expletives as listeners can be found to utter them. All right. But when someone asserts that a composer "seeks to express" an emotion for which the someone then provides a verbal description, that is to debase words *and* music. [8]

COMPOSING

The composer works through a perceptual, not a conceptual, process. He perceives, he selects, he combines, and he is not in the least aware at what point meanings of a different sort and significance grow into his work. All he knows or cares about is his apprehension of the contour of the form, for the form is everything. He can say nothing whatever about meanings. [9]

PERFORMING WORKS IN THE ORIGINAL LANGUAGE

Let librettos and texts be published in translation, let synopses and arguments of plots be distributed in advance, let imaginations be appealed to, but do not change the sound and the stress of the words that have been composed to precisely certain music at precisely certain places. [10]

The presentation of works in their original language is a sign of rich culture in my opinion. And, musically speaking, Babel is a blessing. [11]

ADVICE TO YOUNG COMPOSERS

A composer is or isn't; he cannot learn to acquire the gift that makes him one, and whether he has it or not, in either case, he will not need anything I can tell him. The composer will know that he is one if composition creates exact appetites in him, and if in satisfying them he is aware of their exact limits. Similarly, he will know he is not one if he has only a "desire to compose" or "wish to express himself in music." These appetites determine weight and size. They are more than manifestations of personality, are in fact indispensable. "Experiment" means something in the sciences; it means nothing at all in musical composition. No good musical composition could be merely "experimental"; it is music or it isn't; it must be heard and judged as any other. [12]

AMERICAN MUSIC

I hope I am wrong, but I fear that in some ways the American composer is more isolated today [1957] than he was in 1925. He has at present a strong tendency to say: "We'll leave all of that *avant-garde* stuff to Europe and develop our own musical style, an American style." The result of having already done that is now clear in the way the "Intellectual advanced stuff" (some of it, that is, for at least ninety-nine per cent of all *avant-garde* products are transparent puerilities) is embarrassing everybody; compared to Webern, for example, most of our simple homespun "American style" is fatuous in expression and in technique the vilest cliché. In the phrase "American Music," "American" not only robs emphasis from "music" but it asks for lower standards. Of course, good music that has grown up here will be American. [13]

SOME PERSONAL DEFINITIONS

Genius: A "pathetic" term strictly; or, in literature, a propaganda word used by people who do not deserve rational opposition. I detest it literarily and cannot read it in descriptive works without pain. If it doesn't already appear in the *Dictionnaire des idées reçues,** it should be put there with, as its automatic responses, "Michelangelo" and "Beethoven." [14]

Sincerity: A *sine qua non* that at the same time guarantees nothing. Most artists are sincere anyway and most art is bad—though of course some insincere art (sincerely insincere) is quite good. [15]

Good instrumentation: When you are unaware that it *is* instrumentation. The word is a gloss. It pretends that one composes music and then orchestrates it. This is true, in fact, in the one sense that the only composers who can be orchestrators are those

---

* Flaubert's satire of intellectual complacency.

who write piano music which they transcribe for orchestra; and this might still be the practice of a good many composers, judging from the number of times I have been asked my opinion as to which instruments I think best for passages the composers play on the piano. . . . It is not, generally, a good sign when the first thing we remark about a work is its instrumentation; and the composers we remark it of— Berlioz, Rimsky-Korsakov, Ravel—are not the best composers.   [16]

Technique: The whole man. We learn how to use it but we cannot acquire it in the first place; or, perhaps I should say that we are born with the ability to acquire it. At present it has come to mean the opposite of "heart," though, of course, "heart" is technique too. A single blot on a paper by my friend Eugene Berman I instantly recognize as a Berman blot. What have I recognized—a style or a technique? Are they the same signature of the whole man? Stendhal (in the Roman Promenades) believed that style is "the manner that each one has of saying the same thing." But, obviously, no one says the same thing because the saying is also the thing. A technique or a style for saying something original does not exist *a priori,* it is created by the original saying itself. We sometimes say of a composer that he lacks technique. We say of Schumann, for example, that he did not have enough orchestral technique. But we do not believe that more technique would change the composer. "Thought" is not one thing and "technique" another, namely, the ability to transfer, "express" or develop thoughts. We cannot say "the technique of Bach" (I never say it), yet in every sense he had more of it than anyone; our extraneous meaning becomes ridiculous when we try to imagine the separation of Bach's musical substance and the making of it. Technique is not a teachable science, neither is it learning, nor scholarship, nor even the knowledge of how to do something. It is creation, and, being creation, it is new every time. There are other legitimate uses of the word, of course. Painters have watercolor and gouache techniques, for example, and there are technological meanings; we have techniques of bridge-building and even "techniques for civilization." In these senses one may talk of composing techniques—the writing of an academic fugue. But in my sense, the original composer is still his own and only technique.   [17]

APHORISMS

Academies are formed by bad artists who wish to distinguish themselves by subsequently electing a few good ones.   [18]

Academicism results when the reasons for the rule change, but not the rule.   [19]

I can define sense of humor in music only by example, and my perfect example would be Schumann's *The Poet Speaks.*   [20]

Lent and oratorios, they deserve each other.   [21]

JAZZ

Jazz is a different fraternity altogether, a wholly different kind of music making. It has nothing to do with composed music and when it seeks to be influenced by contemporary music it isn't jazz and it isn't good. Improvisation has its own time world, necessarily a loose and large one since only in an imprecisely limited time could real improvisation be worked up to; the stage has to be set, and there must be heat. The percussion and bass (not the piano; that instrument is too hybrid and besides, most of the players have just discovered Debussy) function as a central heating system. They must keep the temperature "cool," not cool. It is a kind of masturbation that never arrives anywhere (of course) but which supplies the "artificial" genesis the art requires. The point of interest is instrumental virtuosity, instrumental personality, not melody, not harmony, and certainly not rhythm. Rhythm doesn't exist really because no rhythmic proportion or relaxation exists. Instead of rhythm there is "beat." The players beat all the time merely to keep up and to know which side of the beat they are on. The ideas are instrumental, or, rather, they aren't ideas because they come after, come from the instruments. . . .

Has jazz influenced me? Jazz patterns and, especially, jazz instrumental combinations did influence me forty years ago, of course, but not the idea of jazz. As I say, that is another world. I don't follow it but I respect it. It can be an art of very touching dignity as it is in the New Orleans jazz funerals. And, at its rare best, it is certainly the best musical entertainment in the U.S.   {22}

CRITICS

They are not even equipped to judge one's grammar. They do not see how a musical phrase is constructed, do not know how music is written; they are incompetent in the technique of the contemporary musical language. Critics misinform the public and delay comprehension. Because of critics many valuable things come too late. Also, how often we read criticisms of first performances of new music—in which the critic praises or blames (but usually praises) performance. Performances are of something; they do not exist in the abstract, apart from the music they purport to perform. How can the critic know whether a piece of music he does not know is well or ill performed?   {23}

From an interview in the Evening Standard, London, October 29, 1969

I had another dream the other day about music critics. They were small and rodent-like with padlocked ears, as if they had stepped out of a painting by Goya.   {24}

MUSIC APPRECIATION

From an interview in the New York Times Magazine, September 27, 1964

The trouble with music appreciation in general is that people are taught to have too much respect for music; they should be taught to love it instead.   {25}

BEETHOVEN

From Chronicle of My Life

In our early youth we were surfeited by his works, his famous *Weltschmerz* being forced upon us at the same time, together with the "tragedy" and all the commonplaces voiced for more than a century about this composer, who must be recognized as one of the world's greatest musical geniuses.

Like many other musicians, I was disgusted by this intellectual and sentimental attitude, which has little to do with serious musical appreciation. This deplorable pedagogy did not fail in its result. It alienated me from Beethoven for many years.

Cured and matured by age, I could now approach him objectively so that he wore a different aspect for me. Above all I recognized in him the indisputable monarch of the instrument. It is the instrument that inspires his thought and determines its substance. The relations of a composer to his sound medium may be of two kinds. Some, for example, compose music *for* the piano; others compose *piano music*. Beethoven is clearly in the second category. In all his immense pianistic work, it is the "instrumental" side that is characteristic of him and makes him infinitely precious to me. It is the giant instrumentalist that predominates in him, and it is thanks to that quality that he cannot fail to reach any ear that is open to music. . . .

It is in the quality of his musical method and not in the nature of his ideas that his true greatness lies.

It is time that this was recognized, and that Beethoven was rescued from the unjustifiable monopoly of the "intellectuals" and left to those who seek nothing in music but music. It is, however, also time—and this is perhaps even more urgent—to protect him from the stupid drivel of fools who think it up-to-date to giggle as they amuse themselves by running him down. Let them beware; dates pass quickly.   [26]

From the Craft/Stravinsky books

HANDEL

Handel's inventions are exterior; he can draw from inexhaustible reservoirs of *allegros* and *largos*, but he cannot pursue a musical idea through an intensifying degree of development.   [27]

HAYDN

Of all the musicians of his age Haydn was the most aware, I think, that to be perfectly symmetrical is to be perfectly dead.   [28]

GLINKA

Glinka was the Russian musical hero of my childhood. He was always *sans reproche* and this is the way I still think of him. His music is minor, of course, but he is not; all music in Russia stems from him.   [29]

STRAUSS AND HIS OPERAS

I would like to admit all Strauss operas to whichever purgatory punishes triumphant banality. Their musical substance is cheap and poor; it cannot interest a musician today. That now so ascendant *Ariadne*? I cannot bear Strauss's six-four chords: *Ariadne* makes me want to scream. . . .

I watched him at rehearsals and I admired the way he conducted. His manner to the orchestra was not admirable, however, and the musicians heartily detested him; but every corrective remark he made was exact: his ears and his musicianship were impregnable. [30]

SCRIABIN

As a pupil of Taneyev, Scriabin was better grounded in counterpoint and harmony than most of the Russians—very much better equipped in these respects than, say, Prokofiev, whose gifts were perhaps more brilliant. His own ground was derived in part from Liszt, which was natural for the age. I had nothing against Liszt, but I did not like Scriabin's way of continually arguing a Chopin-Liszt line as against a German tradition. I have elsewhere described his shock when I expressed my admiration for Schubert. The marvelous Schubert F minor Fantasia for piano four-hands was for Scriabin *la musique pour les jeunes demoiselles.* But most of his musical opinions were no better than that. [31]

Note *in the Sketchbook for* Renard, *1916*

I sometimes think taste does not matter, but then I listen to Scriabin. [32]

From the Craft/Stravinsky books

RACHMANINOFF

Some people achieve a kind of immortality just by the totality with which they do or do not possess some quality or characteristic. Rachmaninoff's immortalizing totality was his scowl. He was a six-and-a-half-foot-tall scowl. [33]

IVES

The danger now is to think of Ives as a mere historical phenomenon, "The Great Anticipator." He is certainly more than that, but nevertheless his anticipations continue to astonish me. Consider, for example, the *Soliloquy, or a Study in 7ths and Other Things* [probably composed in 1907]. The vocal line of this little song *looks* like Webern's *Drei Volkstexte,* albeit the Ives was composed a decade and more before the Webern. The retrogrades are of the sort Berg was concerned with in the *Kammerkonzert* and *Der Wein,* though the *Soliloquy* was composed a decade and more before the Berg pieces. The rhythmic devices such as "4 in the time of 5" are generally thought to be the discoveries of the so-called post-Webern generation, but Ives anticipates this generation by four decades. The interval idea itself, the idea of the aphoristic statement, and the piano style all point in the direction of later and more accepted composers, too, and the use of rotation and of tone clusters (see also the song *Majority*) suggest developments of the 1950's. But Ives had already transgressed the "limits of tonality" more than a decade before Schoenberg, had written music exploiting polytonality almost two decades before *Petrushka*, and had experimented with poly-orchestral groups a half-century before Stockhausen. Ives lived in rural New England, however, where Donaueschingens and Darmstadts do not exist, and where the "authoritative musical opinion" of the day could not encourage music such as his. The result of this natal accident was that he was not performed and did not develop as he might have developed, though, to be fair, Arnold Schoenberg was the only living musician who would have understood him, and he was thousands of miles and almost as many cultures away. Ives was an original man, a gifted man, a courageous man. Let us honor him through his works.   [34]

WEBERN

He is like a village priest in that his world does not extend beyond his village—indeed, he makes my world seem a million miles away. His manners and address are also both *villageoises* and—priestly. He contains no word of technical jargon (to Berg: "art must be simple") and no aesthetics ("I don't understand what 'classic' and 'romantic' mean"). He is infinitely patient and, of course, he takes infinite pains but composing is entirely natural to him. He does not have a rebellious heart—indeed, he accepts without criticism the musical tradition to which he was born—nor has he any conception of himself as a radical composer; he was what he was wholly apart from the so-called *Zeitgeist*. This Webern will embarrass "Webernists." They will blush for their master's "naïveté" and "provincialism." They will cover his nakedness and look the other way. And this turning away will coincide, too, with a reaction against his music (in favor of Berg's; I hear everywhere now that Webern's series are too symmetrical, that his music makes one too conscious of twelves, that *la structure sérielle chez Berg est plus cachée;* for me, however, Berg's music, compared with Webern's, is like an old woman about whom one says "how beautiful she must have been when she was young"). Webern was too original—i.e., too purely himself. Of course the entire world had to imitate him, of course it would fail, of course it will blame Webern. No matter, though. The desperate contrivance of most of the music now being charged to his name can neither diminish his strength nor stale his perfection. He is a perpetual Pentecost for all who believe in music.   [35]

BOULEZ'S *PLI SELON PLI*

From an unfinished interview, Spring 1971

Am I the only listener who finds *Pli selon pli* pretty monotonous and monotonously pretty?   [36]

RELATIONSHIP WITH THE PIANO

From Chronicle of My Life

I should like to quote a remark of Rimsky-Korsakov's that he made when I became his pupil. I asked him whether I was right in always composing at the piano. "Some compose at the piano," he replied, "and some without a piano. As for you, you will compose at the piano." As a matter of fact, I do compose at the piano and I do not regret it. I go further; I think it is a thousand times better to compose in

direct contact with the physical medium of sound than to work in the abstract medium provided by one's imagination.   [37]

From the Craft/Stravinsky books

I could not have made a career as a pianist—ability apart—because of the lack of
what I call "the performer's memory." I believe that composers and painters mem-
orize selectively, whereas performers must be able to take in "the whole thing as
it is," like a camera; I believe, in fact, that a composer's first memory impression
is already a composition. But I have no idea whether other composer-performers
complain of this difficulty. . . .

I have already told how at the first performance of [the Piano Concerto] I was
obliged to ask the conductor to remind me of the theme of the second movement.
. . . Another time, while playing the same concerto, I suffered a lapse of memory
because I was suddenly obsessed by the idea that the audience was a collection of
dolls in a huge panopticon. Still another time, my memory froze because I suddenly noticed the reflection of my fingers in the glossy wood at the edge of the
keyboard. . . .

Whether or not I am a pianist, however, the instrument itself is the center of
my life and the fulcrum of all my musical discoveries. Each note that I write is
tried on it, and every relationship of notes is taken apart and heard on it again and
again. The process is like slow motion, or those greatly reduced-in-speed recordings of bird calls.   [38]

COMPOSING THE RITE OF SPRING

I was guided by no system whatever in *Le Sacre du printemps.* When I think of the
other composers of that time who interest me—Berg, who is synthetic (in the best
sense), Webern, who is analytic, and Schoenberg, who is both—how much more
theoretical their music seems than *Le Sacre;** and these composers were supported
by a great tradition, whereas very little immediate tradition lies behind *Le Sacre
du printemps.* I had only my ear to help me. I heard and I wrote what I heard. I am
the vessel through which *Le Sacre* passed.   [39]

FIRST PERFORMANCE OF THE RITE (MAY 29, 1913)

Mild protests against the music could be heard from the very beginning of the performance. Then, when the curtain opened on the group of knock-kneed and long-
braided Lolitas jumping up and down (Danse des adolescents), the storm broke.
Cries of "Ta gueule" ["Shut up"] came from behind me. I heard Florent Schmitt
shout "Taisez-vous garces du seizième"; the "garces" of the sixteenth arrondisse-
ment were, of course, the most elegant ladies in Paris. The uproar continued, how-

---

* At the time Stravinsky composed *The Rite* (1911–13), Berg and Webern had written only their
earliest works and Schoenberg was still more than a decade away from formulating the system of
serialism.

ever, and a few minutes later I left the hall in a rage; I was sitting on the right near the orchestra, and I remember slamming the door. I have never again been that angry. The music was so familiar to me; I loved it, and I could not understand why people who had not yet heard it wanted to protest in advance. I arrived in a fury backstage, where I saw Diaghilev flicking the house lights in a last effort to quiet the hall. For the rest of the performance I stood in the wings behind Nijinsky holding the tails of his *frac,* while he stood on a chair shouting numbers to the dancers, like a coxswain. [40]

I was sitting in the fourth or fifth row on the right and the image of Monteux's back is more vivid in my mind today than the picture of the stage. He stood there apparently impervious and as nerveless as a crocodile. It is still almost incredible to me that he actually brought the orchestra through to the end. I left my seat when the heavy noises began—light noise had started from the very beginning—and went backstage behind Nijinsky in the right wing. Nijinsky stood on a chair, just out of view of the audience, shouting numbers to the dancers. I wondered what on earth these numbers had to do with the music for there are no "thirteens" and "seventeens" in the metrical scheme of the score. From what I heard of the musical performance it was not bad. Sixteen full rehearsals had given the orchestra at least some security. After the "performance" we were excited, angry, disgusted, and—happy. I went with Diaghilev and Nijinsky to a restaurant. So far from weeping and reciting Pushkin in the Bois de Boulogne as the legend is, Diaghilev's only comment was: "Exactly what I wanted." He certainly looked contented. No one could have been quicker to understand the publicity value and he immediately understood the good thing that had happened in that respect. [41]

THE RITE AND DISNEY'S FANTASIA

In 1938 I received a request from the Disney office in America for permission to use *Le Sacre* in a cartoon film. The request was accompanied by a gentle warning that if permission were withheld the music would be used anyway. *(Le Sacre,* being "Russian," was not copyrighted in the United States.) The owners of the film wished to show it abroad, however (i.e., in Berne copyright countries), and they therefore offered me $5,000, a sum I was obliged to accept (though, in fact, the percentages of a dozen esurient intermediaries quickly reduced it to a fraction of that). I saw the film with George Balanchine in a Hollywood studio at Christmas time 1939. I remember someone offering me a score and, when I said I had my own, the someone saying, "But it is all changed." It was indeed. The instrumentation had been improved by such stunts as having the horns play their glissandi an octave higher in the Danse de la Terre. The order of the pieces had been shuffled, and the most difficult of them eliminated—though this did not save the musical performance, which was execrable. [42]

Zoltán Kodály
1882–1967

From the early 1900s until his death, Kodály undertook a vast project of collecting and publishing Hungarian folk songs. By the 1950s the number of pieces catalogued had reached 100,000. Like his colleague Bartók, he made extensive use of folk tunes and influences, although his music remained more traditional in character. For many decades Kodály was at the Academy of Music in Budapest, teaching in nearly every musical subject. In the 1930s he began developing the materials and compositions for the choral-based teaching method for children that bears his name.

NEW MUSIC FOR OLD

From an Article in Modern Music, 1925

To the Hungarian composer, a knowledge of his native music offers greater inspiration than do the German, French or Italian songs to composers of these nationalities. In all countries of an older cultural tradition, the substance of folk music has long since been absorbed into the masterpieces. Great artists have always been huge reservoirs of racial power. Bach is a condensation of German music such as no other nation has. The German student who knows his Bach need not concern himself long with folk songs.

This is not our situation. Our only tradition is folk music. And though it cannot replace Bach, it may yet produce a great interpreter. Our folk music is not that of a crude unlettered class. It is, or has been until very recently, the music of the whole nation. Elsewhere in Europe, great music flourished at the courts, or under the protection of rich communities. In Hungary no foreign dynasty ever encouraged the idea of a national culture. The aristocracy cherished only foreign art. During the centuries of continuous fighting, the middle classes and the peasantry, left entirely to their own resources, had no opportunity to create a great art themselves. This was a period of flowering of folk art. Later, when the middle classes "elevated" themselves sufficiently to do homage to foreign ideas, when they were denationalized and mixed with foreign immigrants, the old music became the exclusive treasure of the peasantry.

Certain modern Hungarian works apparently have created the impression abroad of a musical revolution. They are more accurately to be described as conservative. Our intention has been not to break with the past, but to renew and strengthen the links by recreating the atmosphere of the ancient, forgotten melodies, by erecting new structures from their scattered stones. These old songs are our heirlooms; their creators, long since silent, are our true ancestors.

It is but natural that our new works should be markedly different from any other music. Those who find in the German classical style the single mold of real music—and there are many such—unconsciously accept the mother tongue of Germanic-Italian folk music, on which it is based, as the only orthodox foundation for music. It is necessary to decide at the outset for or against the right to existence of other musical idioms, before further considering modern Hungarian music. Much that is strange in it can be traced back to the peculiarities of the old songs. . . .

From the foreigner our music exacts an effort both in interest and understanding. It is only after mastering its idiom that he can discover therein the portrait of the nation, and can respond to its expressive power and heroic emotional force.

[1]

BARTÓK THE FOLKLORIST

From an article in La Revue musicale, *1952*

I want to devote my life at all times, at all costs, and in every sphere to but one cause: the welfare of the Hungarian nation, the welfare of my Hungarian fatherland.
—Bartók, 1903

Three periods may be distinguished in the evolution of Bartók's collections of folk songs. In the first his transcriptions are sketchy; even the transcription of those sections recorded on the phonograph is defective (*Ethnograpia,* 1908). Later, in revising them, he included details down to the slightest ornaments. He made a new revision of his entire collection from 1934 to 1940, while working three times a week on the preparation of the Academy's large collection of folk songs. On the one hand, his knowledge of Arab, Romanian, and other songs, and on the other, the use of earphones, revealed to him details heretofore undiscovered. His transcriptions represent the ultimate limits to be attained by the human ear without the aid of instruments. Beyond that, there is only sound photography. . . .

The largest part of Bartók's work will endure. Every period in the history of science is generally characterized by the fact that it brings new inventions, modifications in relation to the results achieved by preceding periods. Thanks to his good sense, Bartók succeeded in steering clear of all romantic theories. His principal aim was the most exact reproduction and interpretation of his material. Here, then, is no theory, but life, and a guarantee of permanence even if the theories based on this work collapse with time like a house of cards. He also had ideas about certain relationships among the folk songs of diverse nations, but he developed them with many reservations, mindful that truth can be attained only from clear evidence. Whoever swerves from the path of reality is irrevocably lost in the emptiness of illusions. . . .

When in the future we are acquainted with all of his work, we will know better how to appreciate the universal importance of him who, from his youth, believed only in serving his own country. [2]

Anton Webern
1883–1945

After writing a few works in the prevailing post-Romantic manner, Webern began to study with Schoenberg. As his abilities grew, his appetite for atonal exploration matched and at times outstripped that of his teacher. By the time Schoenberg had fully developed the concept of serialism, Webern was ready to adapt it to his own ends. Using the serial technique with equal measures of rigor and elegance, he achieved great purity and subtlety of expression. Webern's works are brief and concentrated; his entire output can be listened to in an afternoon.

KNOWLEDGE

Remark to Humphrey Searle, 1939

Don't write music entirely by ear. Your ears will always guide you aright, of course, but you must *know* why one progression is good and another bad. [1]

SCHOENBERG AS TEACHER

From the Symposium Arnold Schoenberg, 1912

The belief in technique as the only means of salvation must be suppressed, the striving toward truth furthered.
—Arnold Schoenberg, "Problems of Art Instruction"

In his essay "Problems of Art Instruction," Arnold Schoenberg himself has presented the most brilliant refutation of all the malicious, envious persecution and slander that backward minds have contrived against him as a teacher.

Never were more penetrating, truer words spoken on the subject. And what Schoenberg expresses therein, every one of his students could and can experience for himself. It is believed that Schoenberg teaches his style and forces his students to adapt themselves to it. This is absolutely untrue.

Schoenberg teaches no style whatsoever; he preaches the use of neither old nor new artistic means. In the same essay he says: "What sense is there in teaching the mastery of the commonplace? The student learns to use something he may not employ if he wishes to be an artist. But the most important thing one cannot give him: the courage and the strength to put himself in a position from which everything he views becomes, through the manner in which he views it, unique."

However, this "most important thing" is what the Schoenberg student learns. Schoenberg demands above all that, in his exercises, the student write not merely any notes whatsoever in order to fill an academic form, but that he complete these exercises out of the necessity for expression.

Hence, he must actually create, even in the most primitive beginnings of musical movement construction. What Schoenberg explains to the student is altogether bound up, then, with the work in hand; he brings in no external dogmas.

Thus Schoenberg educates through actually creating.

He follows the traces of the student's personality with the utmost energy, tries to deepen them, to help them break through, in short, to give the student "the courage and the strength to put himself in a position from which everything he views becomes, through the manner in which he views it, unique."

This is a training toward the most complete honesty with oneself. It affects not only the purely musical aspect, but every other realm of human life as well.

Yes, with Schoenberg one truly learns more than art rules. Whosoever's heart is open is here shown the road to the Good.

However, how can one explain that every one of his students who works independently today composes in a manner that brings the style of his compositions into immediate proximity with the work of Schoenberg? This is the chief reason for the misunderstanding of Schoenberg's teaching mentioned at the start. One cannot explain this. The secret of artistic creation is especially involved in this question.

Who can explain it?

It cannot at all be a question of a mere external appropriation of these artistic means.

What then is it?

Here reigns a necessity, the reasons for which we do not know, but in which we must believe.   [2]

VARIATIONS FOR ORCHESTRA, OP. 30

From a letter to Willi Reich,* May 3, 1941

The first reaction to this score may well be: "There is nothing in it." One looks in vain for the many, many notes one is used to. But this touches upon the most essential point: the basic thing is that here (in my score) a different style is employed. . . . And I believe it is a new style. Its material is ruled by physical laws exactly as were the earlier forms of tonality. It too forms a tonality, but this tonality uses the possibilities offered by the nature of tone in a different manner: it is based on a system in which the twelve separate tones as we know them from Western music are "related to each other," as Schoenberg expressed it. Nevertheless, this new system does not overlook the laws that are inherent in the nature of tone. This would indeed be impossible if what is expressed in tones is still to make sense.   [3]

* Austrian-born Swiss music critic (1898–1980) who studied with Berg and Webern.

Alban Berg
1885–1935

When he first met Schoenberg in 1904 (the result of answering a newspaper ad), Berg was essentially untrained in music. He rapidly absorbed his teacher's knowledge and embraced his avant-garde philosophies. Even so, Berg's musical identity remained distinct. He never entirely abandoned the Romantic lyricism of his youthful songs, and his serial works abound in references to tonality and earlier forms. Berg's Wozzeck *became the most famous Modernist opera and one of the most extensively discussed works of the century, starting from its first performance in 1925. His essay on Schoenberg's music refers not to the serial works but to the earlier String Quartet in D Minor.*

GOALS OF THE SOCIETY FOR PRIVATE MUSICAL PERFORMANCES

From a statement of aims written by Berg and issued over Schoenberg's signature, Vienna, February 16, 1919

The Society was founded in November 1918 for the purpose of enabling Arnold Schoenberg to carry out his plan to give artists and music lovers a real and precise knowledge of modern music.

The attitude of the public toward modern music is affected to an immense degree by the impression of obscurity it receives from this music. Aim, tendency, intention, scope and manner of expression, value, essence, and goal—all are obscure. Most performances of modern music lack clarity; and the public's consciousness of its own needs and wishes is even more lacking in clarity. All modern works are therefore valued, considered, judged, and lauded, or else misjudged, attacked, and rejected, exclusively upon the basis of one effect, which every work yields equally: the effect of obscurity.

This situation can in the long run satisfy no one whose opinion is worthy of consideration, neither the serious composer nor the thoughtful member of an audience. To bring light into this darkness and thus fulfill a justifiable need and desire was one of the motives that led Arnold Schoenberg to found this society.

To attain this goal three things were necessary:

1. Clear, well-rehearsed performances.
2. Frequent repetition.
3. The performances must be removed from the corrupting influence of publicity; that is, they must not be directed toward the winning of competitions and must be unaccompanied by applause or demonstrations of disapproval.

Herein lies the essential difference revealed by a comparison of the society's aims with those of the everyday concert world, from which it is quite distinct in principle. Although it may be possible, in preparing a work for performance, to get along with the strictly limited and always insufficient number of rehearsals hitherto available, for the society the number of rehearsals allotted to works to be performed, for better or worse (usually the latter), will be as many as is necessary for the attainment of the greatest possible clarity and for the fulfillment of all the composer's intentions as revealed in his work. And if the attainment of these minimum requirements for good performance should necessitate more rehearsals than can be affforded (as was the case, for example, with a symphony of Mahler, which received its first performance after twelve four-hour rehearsals and was repeated after two more), then the work concerned should not, and will not, be performed by the society.

In rehearsing new works, the performers will be chosen preferably from among the younger and less well known artists, who place themselves at the society's disposal out of interest in the cause; artists of high-priced reputation will be used only as the music demands and permits; and moreover that kind of virtuosity will be shunned which makes of the work to be performed not the end in itself but merely a means to an end the society does not share—namely, the display of irrelevant virtuosity and individuality and the attainment of a purely personal success. Such things will automatically be rendered impossible by the exclusion (already mentioned) of all demonstrations of applause, disapproval, and thanks. The only success an artist can have here (and the success that should in any event be most important to him) is that of having rendered the work—and thus also its composer—intelligible.

While such thoroughly rehearsed performances are a guarantee that each work will be enabled to make itself rightly understood, an even more effective means to this end is given to the society through the innovation of weekly meetings and by frequent repetitions of every work. . . .

The third condition for the attainment of the aims of the society is that the performances shall be in all respects private; that guests (foreign visitors excepted) shall not be admitted, and that members shall be obligated to abstain from giving any public report of the performances and other activities of the society, and espcially to write or inspire no criticisms, notices, or discussions of them in periodicals.

This rule, that the sessions shall not be publicized, is made necessary by the semi-pedagogic activities of the society and is in harmony with its tendency to benefit musical works solely through good performance and thus simply through the good effect made by the music itself. Propaganda for works and their composers is not the aim of the Society.

For this reason no school shall receive preference and only the worthless shall be excluded; for the rest, all modern music—from that of Mahler and Strauss to the newest, which practically never or, at most, rarely is to be heard—will be performed.   [1]

WHY IS SCHOENBERG'S MUSIC SO HARD TO UNDERSTAND?

From an essay of the same title, 1924

It is not so much so-called atonality, which has by now become the mode of expression of so many contemporaries, that makes Schoenberg's music so difficult to understand; it is rather Schoenberg's musical structure, the abundance of the artistic means everywhere employed in this harmonic style, the application of all compositional possibilities presented by music throughout the centuries—in a word: its immeasurable richness.

Here, too, we find the same diversity in harmony, the same variety of chord progression characterizing the cadence;

here again the melodic line suitable to such harmony, melody that makes the most daring use of the potentialities of the twelve tones;

here, too, the asymmetrical and quite free construction of themes with their never-flagging development of the motive;

here again the art of variation, which in this music is developed thematically as well as harmonically, contrapuntally as well as rhythmically;

here again polyphony permeating the entire work, and unequalled contrapuntal part writing;

finally, here again the diversity of form and differentiation of rhythms of which one can only say that, besides being subject to their own laws, they are also subject to the rules of variation, thematic development, counterpoint, and polyphony. Thereby an art of construction is attained in this field also, which shows how erroneous it is to speak of an "undefined rhythm," especially in Schoenberg's work.

How fundamentally different—viewed from a universal standpoint—the picture of other contemporary composers appears, even when they have broken with the sovereignty of the triad in their harmonic speech. Naturally, the musical means just enumerated are demonstrable in their music also. Never, however, do we find them united in the works of a single personality, as in Schoenberg, but always divided among various groups, schools, movements, nations, and their representatives of a given moment.

One favors the polyphonic method of writing, while reducing thematic development and the art of variation to a minimum; another prefers daring harmony that shrinks from no clash, but in which only a melody line going scarcely beyond homophony has a place—a melody line that is also characterized for the most part by the use of merely two- and four-measure phrases. The "atonality" of one consists in his setting wrong basses to primitively harmonized periods; still others employ two or more (major or minor) keys simultaneously, though the musical procedure within each key often shows a frightening poverty of invention. Some music distinguished by a more richly moving melodic line and unconfined thematic construction suffers from harmonic inertia, which manifests itself in a dearth of harmonic variety, endlessly held chords, endless organ points, and ever-recurring harmonic patterns. I am inclined to say that music so built cannot do without more or less mechanical repetitions, often even primitive sequences. This stands out in rhythmical aspects particularly. Here we find a rhythm, sometimes rigid, sometimes hammered, sometimes dancelike or otherwise lilting, that continues almost to the point of monotony and, among the otherwise reigning poverty, creates an illusion of richness mainly through plentiful changes and dislocations of meter. Such a rhythm, more often than one might believe, furnishes the only element of cohesion in an otherwise inconsequential music. The representatives of this technique of composition are preferably known as "stark rhythmists."

This adherence to such more or less firmly laid-down principles, this one-sidedness that frequently degenerates into mannerism, this complacency, this being modern but not too "ultra" (as it is so neatly termed), helps even "atonal" as well as otherwise "progressively oriented" music toward being accepted and relatively liked. For the most part, even when in one or more respects it poses some difficult problems for the listener, it deviates so little from tradition in every other regard, it often is so consciously "primitive," that thanks precisely to those negative characteristics it can also speak to the ears of the musically uninitiated: in short, it pleases. This, all the more, since the authors of such music, in order to be stylistically pure, must keep in mind only the consequences of their special type of modernity and therefore are not forced to come to terms with all these possibilities combined.

When I say that such an inescapable necessity, which, I repeat, consists in drawing the ultimate consequences from a self-imposed universality, is to be found but once, and that in the compositions of Schoenberg, I believe that this conveys the final and most potent reason for the difficulty of their comprehension. That this lofty necessity is combined with a mastery granted, I might say, to genius alone, also gives one the right, as does everything else I have said about Schoenberg's unequaled knowledge, to assume, nay, to be certain, that here we have the work of a master who—once the "classicists" of our era belong to history—will be one of the very few who will be termed classicists for all time. For he has not only, as Adolf Weissmann in his book *Die Musik in der Weltkrise* (Music in the world crisis) so aptly says, "drawn from German musical culture the final, most daring conclusions"; he has also advanced further than those who, without foundation, searched for new ways and, consciously or unconsciously, more or less denied the art of this musical culture. So that today, on Schoenberg's fiftieth birthday, one can say, without being a prophet, that through the work he has brought to the world up to now, not only the predominance of his own personal art seems assured but, what is more, that of German art for the next fifty years.   [2]

WOZZECK

From "Das Opernproblem," 1928

I never entertained the idea of reforming the artistic structure of the opera with *Wozzeck*. Neither when I started nor when I completed this work did I consider it a model for further operatic efforts, whoever the composer might be. I never assumed or expected that *Wozzeck* should in this sense become the basis of a school.

I wanted to compose good music, to develop musically the contents of Büchner's immortal drama, to translate his poetic language into music; but other than that, when I decided to write an opera, my only intentions, including the technique of composition, were to give the theater what belongs to the theater. In other words, the music was to be so formed as consciously to fulfill its duty of serving the action at every moment. Even more, the music should be prepared to furnish whatever the action needed to be transformed into reality on the stage. It was the function of the composer to solve the problems of an ideal stage director. And at the same time, this aim must not prejudice the development of the music as an absolute, purely musical entity. There was to be no interference by externals with its individual existence.

That these purposes should be accomplished by use of musical forms more or less ancient (considered by critics as one of the most important of my ostensible reforms of the opera) was a natural consequence. For the libretto it was necessary to make a selection from twenty-six loosely constructed, sometimes fragmentary scenes by Büchner. Repetitions that did not lend themselves to musical variations had to be avoided. Finally, the scenes had to be brought together, arranged, and grouped into acts. The problem therefore became, utterly apart from my will, more musical than literary, one to be solved by the laws of musical structure rather than the rules of dramaturgy.

It was impossible to take the fifteen scenes I selected and shape them in different manners so that each would retain its musical coherence and individuality, and at the same time follow the customary method of developing the music along the lines of their literary content. An absolute music, no matter how rich structurally, no matter how aptly it might fit the dramatic events, would, after a number of scenes so composed, inevitably create musical monotony. The effect would become positively boring with a series of a dozen or so formally composed entr'actes, which offered nothing but this type of illustrative music. Boredom, of course, is the last thing one should experience in the theater.

I obeyed the necessity of giving each scene and each accompanying piece of entr'acte music, whether prelude, postlude, connecting link, or interlude, an unmistakable aspect, a rounded and finished character. It was therefore imperative to use every warranted means to create individualizing characteristics on the one hand, and coherence on the other; thus the much-discussed use of old and new musical forms, including those used only in absolute music.

In one sense, the use of these forms in opera, especially to such an extent, was unusual, even new. But certainly, as conscious intention, it is not at all to my credit, as I have already demonstrated, and consequently I can and must reject the claim that I am a reformer of the opera through such innovation. However, I do not wish to depreciate my work through these explanations. Others who do not know it so well can do it much better. I therefore would like to suggest something I consider my particular accomplishment.

No matter how cognizant any particular individual may be of the musical forms contained in the framework of this opera, of the precision and logic with which everything is worked out and the skill manifested in every detail, from the moment the curtain parts until it closes for the last time, there must be no one in the audience who pays any attention to the various fugues, inventions, suites, sonata movements, variations, and passacaglias—no one who heeds anything but the idea of this opera, which by far transcends the personal destiny of Wozzeck. This I believe to be my achievement.   [3]

Edgard Varèse
(1885–1965)

Studies in Berlin with Busoni and exposure to Schoenberg's Pierrot lunaire *and other works set Varèse on his way as an innovator. He was among the first to combine musical and mechanical sounds in compositions, and to write for percussion ensemble. He was fascinated by the musico-acoustic potentials of electronics, and pioneered the concept of "organized sound," in which traditional thematic development was supplanted by a process based on the quality of the sounds themselves. Although he achieved fame as an iconoclast, particularly toward the end of his life, his interest was not revolution but simply the exploration of new modes of music making.*

NEW INSTRUMENTS, NEW MUSIC
From the periodical 391, June 1917

I dream of instruments obedient to my thought and which with their contribution of a whole new world of unsuspected sounds, will lend themselves to the exigencies of my inner rhythm.   [1]

From a lecture at Mary Austin House, Santa Fe, 1936

The emotional impulse that moves a composer to write his scores contains the same element of poetry that incites the scientist to his discoveries. There is solidarity between scientific development and the progress of music. Throwing new light on nature, science permits music to progress—or rather to grow and change with changing times—by revealing to our senses harmonies and sensations before unfelt. On the threshold of beauty science and art collaborate. . . .

When new instruments will allow me to write music as I conceive it, the movement of sound-masses, of shifting planes, will be clearly perceived in my work, taking the place of the linear counterpoint. When these sound-masses collide, the phenomena of penetration or repulsion will seem to occur. Certain transmutations taking place on certain planes will seem to be projected onto other planes, moving at different speeds and at different angles. There will no longer be the old conception of melody or interplay of melodies. The entire work will be a melodic totality. The entire work will flow as a river flows.

We have actually three dimensions in music: horizontal, vertical, and dynamic swelling or decreasing. I shall add a fourth, sound projection—that feeling that sound is leaving us with no hope of being reflected back, a feeling akin to that aroused by beams of light sent forth by a powerful searchlight—for the ear as for the eye, that sense of projection, of a journey into space.

Today with the technical means that exist and are easily adaptable, the differentiation of the various masses and different planes as well as these beams of sound, could be made discernible to the listener by means of certain acoustical arrangements. Moreover, such an acoustical arrangement would permit the delimitation of what I call "zones of intensities." These zones would be differentiated by various timbres or colors and different loudnesses. Through such a physical process these zones would appear of different colors and of different magnitude, in different perspectives for our perception. The role of color or timbre would be completely changed from being incidental, anecdotal, sensual or picturesque; it would become an agent of delineation, like the different colors on a map separating different areas, and an integral part of form. These zones would be felt as isolated, and the hitherto unobtainable non-blending (or at least the sensation of non-blending) would become possible.

In the moving masses you would be conscious of their transmutations when they pass over different layers, when they penetrate certain opacities, or are dilated in certain rarefactions. Moreover, the new musical apparatus I envisage, able to emit sounds of any number of frequencies, will extend the limits of the lowest and highest registers, hence new organizations of the vertical resultants: chords, their arrangements, their spacings—that is, their oxygenation. Not only will the harmonic possibilities of the overtones be revealed in all their splendor, but the use of certain interferences created by the partials will represent an appreciable contribution. The never-before-thought-of use of the inferior resultants and of the differential and additional sounds may also be expected. An entirely new magic of sound!

I am sure that the time will come when the composer, after he has graphically realized his score, will see this score automatically put on a machine that will faithfully transmit the musical content to the listener. As frequencies and new rhythms will have to be indicated on the score, our actual notation will be inadequate. The new notation will probably be seismographic. And here it is curious to note that at the beginning of two eras, the Mediaeval primitive and our own primitive era (for we are at a new primitive stage in music today), we are faced with an identical problem: the problem of finding graphic symbols for the transposition of the composer's thought into sound. At a distance of more than a thousand years we have this analogy: our still primitive electrical instruments find it necessary to abandon staff notation and to use a kind of seismographic writing much like the early ideographic writing originally used for the voice before the development of staff notation. Formerly the curves of the musical line indicated the melodic fluctuations of the voice; today the machine instrument requires precise design indications.   [2]

RULES AND EXPERIMENTATION

From the Santa Fe lecture, 1936

Art's function is not to prove a formula or an esthetic dogma. Our academic rules were taken out of the living works of former masters. As Debussy has said, *works of art make rules but rules do not make works of art*. Art exists only as a medium of expression.   [3]

From a lecture at the University of Southern California, 1939

I should say that in music the "reverent approach" has done a great deal of harm: it has kept would-be appreciators from really appreciating! And it has created the music critic! The very basis of creative work is irreverence! The very basis of creative work is experimentation—bold experimentation. You have only to turn to the revered past for the corroboration of my contention. The links in the chain of tradition are formed by men who have all been revolutionists! To the student of music I should say that the great examples of the past should serve as springboards from which he may leap free, into his own future.

In every domain of art, a work that corresponds to the need of its day carries a message of social and cultural value. Preceding ages show us that changes in art occur because societies and artists have new needs. New aspirations emanate from every epoch. The artist, being always of his own time, is influenced by it and, in turn, is an influence. It is the artist who crystallizes his age—who fixes his age in history. Contrary to general notion, the artist is never ahead of his own time, but is simply the only one who is not way behind.   [4]

From a lecture at Princeton University, 1959

Many of the old masters are my intimate friends—all are respected colleagues. None of them are dead saints—in fact, none of them are dead—and the rules they made for themselves are not sacrosanct and are not everlasting laws. Listening to music by Pérotin, Machaut, Monteverdi, Bach, or Beethoven, we are conscious of living substances; they are "alive in the present." But music written in the manner of another century is the result of culture and, desirable and comfortable as culture may be, an artist should not lie down in it.   [5]

"ORGANIZED SOUND"

From a lecture at Yale University, 1962

First of all, I should like you to consider what I believe is the best definition of music, because it is all-inclusive: "the corporealization of the intelligence that is in sound," as proposed by Hoëne Wronsky.* If you think about it you will realize that, unlike most dictionary definitions, which make use of such subjective terms as beauty, feelings, etc., it covers all music, Eastern or Western, past or present, including the music of our new electronic medium. Although this new music is being gradually accepted, there are still people who, while admitting that it is "interesting," say: "but is it music?" It is a question I am only too familiar with. Until quite recently I used to hear it so often in regard to my own works that, as far back as the twenties, I decided to call my music "organized sound" and myself, not a musician, but "a worker in rhythms, frequencies, and intensities." Indeed, to stubbornly conditioned ears, anything new in music has always been called noise. But after all, what is music but organized noises? And a composer, like all artists, is an organizer of disparate elements. Subjectively, noise is any sound one doesn't like.   [6]

---

* Wronsky (1778–1853), a Polish philosopher and mathematician, created a system of messianism.

CHAPTER ELEVEN

Sergei Prokofiev

Arthur Honegger

Darius Milhaud

William Grant Still

Paul Hindemith

Virgil Thomson

Roger Sessions

Henry Cowell

George Gershwin

Carlos Chávez

Francis Poulenc

Aaron Copland

Ruth Crawford Seeger

Sergei Prokofiev
1891–1953

By his twelfth year, Prokofiev had nearly mastered the piano, was being tutored by Rein-hold Glière, and had finished two operas. In the first works of his maturity he flirted with atonality; here he also revealed his taste for the grotesque and his acid sense of humor. In 1936 he returned to Russia after seventeen years in the West, but soon found himself under pressure from the Soviet government to write music that was less "decadent." He complied, producing a string of propagandistic works, although this was also the period of such mas-terpieces as the Fifth Symphony, Cinderella, *and* Alexander Nevsky.

From Autobiography, *1948*

ENCOUNTERS WITH RACHMANINOFF AND MEDTNER

In 1915 I met Rachmaninoff. He was very pleasant, took my hand in his huge paw, and talked to me in a most friendly fashion. In the autumn he gave a concert dedicated to the memory of Scriabin, in which, among other pieces, he played the Fifth Sonata. When Scriabin played this sonata his music soared into ethereal realms, but with Rachmaninoff every tone, precise and solid, remained entirely earthbound. Great excitement among Scriabin's friends in the audience! The tenor Altschevski, whom we had to hold back by his coattails, cried: "Just wait, I must have this out with him!" I felt that I had to remain objective and replied that, though we were accustomed to the composer's interpretation of the sonata, it was obvious that another presentation was also permissible.

When I entered the greenroom, I remarked quite ingenuously to Rachmaninoff: "And nevertheless, Sergei Vassilievitch, you played very well." Rachmaninoff an-swered with a forced smile: "And did you think that I would play badly?" imme-diately turning his back on me to greet somebody else. And with that our good relations ceased. In addition, there was the fact that he did not like my music; in some curious way it irritated him.

Somewhat later an unfortunate episode occurred with [Nikolay] Medtner. I had hoped that at his concert he would play his great C Major Sonata, in which I was interested. Instead, he chose one of his simpler sonatas for which the composer's interpretation was hardly necessary. I told him that I was disappointed in his choice.

"And the sonata I played?"

"Well, that one is more suitable for home use."

On the basis of this incident as related by Medtner, Rachmaninoff later indig-nantly broadcast the story that Prokofiev divided sonatas into real sonatas and so-natas for home consumption.   [1]

PREMIERE OF THE *SCYTHIAN SUITE*

During the autumn of 1915 I directed my Sinfonietta in its revised version and on January 29, 1916, my *Scythian Suite* at the Siloti Concerts [in St. Petersburg]. After the suite there was an uproar similar to the one following my first appearance in the second concert at Pavlovsk, except that this time the whole of musical Petrograd was assembled. Glazunov, whom I had looked up for the express purpose of inviting him to the concert, flew into a rage and left the hall eight measures before the end because he could no longer listen to the "Dawn" section. . . . The timpanist tore the kettledrum head with his heavy blows, and Siloti promised me that he would send me the mangled piece of leather as a keepsake. In the orchestra itself there were noticeable signs of antagonism. "Just because I have a sick wife and three children, must I be forced to suffer this hell?" grumbled the cellist, while behind him the trombonists blew fearful chords right into his ears. Siloti, in fine fettle, walked up and down the hall, repeating, "Right on the nose, right on the nose!" which was as much as to say that he and Prokofiev had given the public a slap in the face. "A scandal in high society," remarked the critic in the magazine *Music,* not without a certain malicious pleasure.   [2]

ORCHESTRATING *THE GAMBLERS*

I spent the entire summer of 1916 orchestrating, scoring about ten pages a day; in the uncomplicated sections I even did as many as eighteen. My mother chanced to ask [Nikolay] Tcherepnin how many pages a day he could orchestrate. "Sometimes only one chord," he answered, seeking to impress her with his careful workmanship. *"My* son does eighteen pages a day," declared my mother, quite proudly.   [3]

COMPOSING AWAY FROM THE PIANO;
GENESIS OF THE *CLASSICAL SYMPHONY*

I spent the summer of 1917 in complete solitude in the environs of Petrograd; I read Kant and worked hard. I had purposely not had my piano moved to the country because I wanted to try composing without it. Up to now I had generally written at the piano, but I wanted to establish the fact that thematic material worked out without a piano is better. When transferred to the piano it seems at first glance rather strange, but after several tryouts it becomes clear that only in this way and in no other must it be done.

The idea occurred to me to compose an entire symphonic work without the piano. Composed in this fashion, the orchestral colors would of necessity be clearer and cleaner. Thus the plan of a symphony in Haydnesque style originated, since as a result of my studies in Tcherepnin's classes, Haydn's technique had somehow become especially clear to me, and with such intimate understanding it was much easier to plunge into the dangerous flood without a piano. It seemed to me that were he alive today, Haydn, while retaining his own style of composition, would have appropriated something from the modern. Such a symphony I now wanted to compose: a symphony in the classic manner. As it began to take on actual form I named it *Classical Symphony;* first, because it was the simplest thing to call it; second, out of bravado, to stir up a hornet's nest; and finally, in the hope that should the symphony prove itself in time to be truly "classic," it would benefit me considerably.   [4]

Arthur Honegger
1892–1955

*Of Swiss heritage, Honegger was born in France and spent most of his life there. His first
renown came with* Pacific 231 *(1923), a symphonic depiction of a locomotive in action.
More enduring have been some of his vocal works, such as the oratorios* Le Roi David *(final
version 1923) and* Jeanne d'Arc au bûcher *(1935), with their effective sense of drama
and clear yet sophisticated musical language.* Je suis compositeur *(I am a composer) was
written for a series of books called "My Profession."*

From Je suis compositeur, 1951

SURPRISE AND COMPETENCE

Surprise is, on the whole, proof of insecurity, of the fact that the musician does not
know his business. A composer worthy of the name must foresee everything. Once
he does, it is enough for him to verify with his ear what his brain has conceived.
Were I to benefit by the privileges accorded to painters, I would have an orchestra at my disposal to play my rough sketches one after the other. That would be
like taking a perspective at my leisure. Unfortunately, it is impossible. I must wait
for the dress rehearsal. By that time the orchestral material is set, the parts are copied, and any serious corrections entail considerable work. True, there are some
publishers willing to re-engrave entire pages after a first edition. But they are few
and far between, you may be sure! For the rest, one must know how to accept risks.

The most appropriate comparison seems to me to be with the builder of boats
who, at the moment of launching, risks seeing the boat turn over. Luckily, in music
the same accident doesn't offer the same kind of evidence. Many modern scores float
upside down. Very few people are aware of it.   [1]

THE COMPOSER'S INNER EAR

The fact is that, to the lay mind, the act of composing music remains an incomprehensible thing. "When you are composing, do you figure out on the piano what
will make a piece? But if it is a piece for orchestra, how can you play all the instrumental parts at the same time?"

I try to explain that musical construction must first be done in the mind, then
be noted on paper in its large lines.

"But without hearing the notes played?"

"Naturally, since I don't, so to speak, play the piano."

"Then you are obliged to have it played by someone else?"

"No, because composing is a mental operation that takes place in the brain of
the composer. However, I don't claim that to check certain passages at the piano
is not useful, if only as an aid or guide in the linking of certain elements."

When you read a book, you do not have to pronounce the words aloud; they sound in your mind. It is the mind, the thought, that must create the music, and not the fingers wandering at random on the keys. Nevertheless, searching at the piano can be fruitful, especially when the composer is a skillful instrumentalist who gives himself over to improvisation. Schumann condemned this technique, but it is probable that a Chopin or a Liszt practiced it. It can produce excellent results. Thus, chance becomes inspiration, since the first spurt is caught, worked over, improved, made precise by the musical knowledge of the author.   [2]

THE STATE OF MUSIC

What strikes me about [our age] is the haste of reactions, the premature discarding of methods. It took centuries, from Monteverdi to Schoenberg, to arrive at the free use of twelve tones. After this discovery, evolution suddenly became very rapid. We all face a wall; this wall, consisting of all the materials piled up little by little, stands before us today, and everybody is trying to find an opening in it; each one searches for it according to his own intuition.

There are, on the one hand, the champions of Satie's method: they extol the return to simplicity—*sancta simplicitas!*—on the other hand, those who, returning to Schoenberg's researches forty years later, look for an exit by way of atonality, setting up, more arbitrarily still, the twelve-tone system. This system boasts a very narrow codification; the dodecaphonists remind me of convicts who, having broken their chains, voluntarily attach two-hundred-pound balls to their feet in order to run faster. Their dogma is entirely comparable to that of classroom counterpoint, with this difference, that while the aim of counterpoint is merely to facilitate the pen and stimulate invention through its exercise, the serial principles are presented, not as a means, but as an end!

I believe that there is here no possibility of expression for a composer, because his melodic invention is subject to intransigent laws that hinder the free expression of his thought. I am not at all opposed to discipline freely accepted, or even sought out, for artistic ends. But such discipline must have direction and not be arbitrary and despotic.

On the other hand, anarchic freedom, from the point of view of the harmonies resulting from superimposed lines, opens the road to the most dangerous fantasies. Here is what René Leibowitz, the eminent theoretician of the twelve-tone system, says: "It follows that the composer's thinking can finally function in an entirely linear (horizontal) manner, *since no vertical restriction can have any hold on him.* No forbidden dissonances, no fixed harmonic formulas (such as the cadences of model counterpoint, or the harmonic steps in tonal counterpoint); in other words, the composer can give free rein to the invention of his voices, which thus acquire at the same time a total individual freedom and the faculty of superimposing themselves one above the other." And further: "The imminent possibility [exists] for the composer to write in a purely horizontal manner, without any a priori vertical concern."

Evidently the restrictions imposed by the formation of an orthodox "set" are largely compensated for by this freedom. That explains why young people not too well endowed with musical invention have thrown themselves enthusiastically into this technique. However, it must not be forgotten that the listener hears music vertically, and that the most complex contrapuntal combinations lose all interest and acquire an elementary facility when they dispense with all discipline.

Another inconvenience of the twelve-tone system is the suppression of modulation, which offers so many, endlessly renewed, possibilities. "Passing from one region to another," maintains Leibowitz, "is vaguely equivalent to what modulation signifies in the realm of tonal architecture." Finally, I fear the poverty of form, "since one might say that every twelve-tone piece is only a suite of variations on the initial 'set.'"

The aim of conquest is to widen horizons, to abolish frontiers, not to narrow them. The efforts of creators have always been in the direction of liberation from formulas and conventions. But what examples of the reverse all around us! The demagogues have evolved toward an imperialism more autocratic than the one they have destroyed, while the dictators return to demagogy. I am very much afraid that the forced growth of the twelve-tone system—incidentally, we see it on the decline—is producing a reaction toward a too simplified, too rudimentary music. The cure for having swallowed sulfuric acid will be to drink syrup. The ear, fatigued by intervals of the ninth and the seventh, will welcome with delight accordion music and sentimental songs! [3]

Music is dying not of anemia but of plethora. [4]

Darius Milhaud
1892–1974

Milhaud's appetite for novelty was balanced by a firm technique. He traveled widely—to Brazil, the United States, Russia, and throughout Europe—happily observing and absorbing musical influences along the way, urban vernacular traditions in particular. Along with works in most traditional genres, his extensive output includes innovative theater pieces, "furniture music" à la Satie, and two string quartets that can be played simultaneously as an octet. Notes sans musique *was the first of his two autobiographical books.*

From Notes sans musique, *1949*

THE "SIX"

After a concert at the Salle Huyghens [in 1919], at which Bertin sang Louis Durey's *Images à Crusoe* on words by Saint-Léger Léger and the Capelle Quartet played my *Fourth Quartet,* the critic Henri Collet published in *Comoedia* a chronicle entitled "Five Russians and Six Frenchmen." Quite arbitrarily he had chosen six names—Auric, Durey, Honegger, Poulenc, Tailleferre, and my own—merely because we knew each other, were good friends, and had figured on the same programs, quite irrespective of our different temperaments and wholly dissimilar characters. Auric and Poulenc were partisans of Cocteau's ideas, Honegger derived from the German Romantics, and I from Mediterranean lyricism. I fundamentally disapproved of joint declarations of aesthetic doctrines and felt them to be a drag, an unreasonable limitation on the imagination of the artists, who must for each new work find different, often contradictory means of expression. But it was useless to protest. Collet's article excited such worldwide interest that the "Group of Six" was launched, and willy-nilly I formed part of it.

This being so, we decided to give some *Concerts des Six*. The first was devoted to my works; the second to foreign music. The latter program consisted of works by Lord Berners, Casella, Lourié, who was then People's Commissar for the Fine Arts in Soviet Russia, and Schoenberg and Bartók, whose latest works we had been unable to hear owing to the war. Satie was our mascot. He was very popular among us. He was so fond of young people that he said to me one day: "I wish I knew what sort of music will be written by the children who are four years old now." The purity of his art, his horror of all concessions, his contempt for money, and his ruthless attitude toward the critics were a marvelous example for us all.

The formation of the Group of Six helped to draw the bonds of friendship closer among us. For two years we met regularly at my place every Saturday evening. . . . We were not all composers, for our number also included performers . . . painters . . . and writers. . . . The poets would read their poems, and we would play our latest compositions. Some of them, such as Auric's *Adieu New York,* Poulenc's *Cocardes* and my *Boeuf sur le toit* were continually being played. We even used to insist on Poulenc's playing *Cocardes* every Saturday evening; he did so most readily. Out of these meetings, in which a spirit of carefree gaiety reigned, many a fruitful collaboration was to be born; they also determined the character of several works strongly marked by the influence of the music hall.   [1]

BRAZILIAN FOLKLORE

My first contact with Brazilian folklore was very sudden. I arrived in Rio in the middle of the Carnival [of 1917] and immediately sensed the mood of crazy gaiety that possessed the whole town. . . . Six weeks before the Carnival is due to begin, the *cordoes* perambulate the streets on Saturday and Sunday evenings, select a little square and dance to the music of the *violaõ* (a kind of guitar) and a few percussion instruments like the *choucalca* (a kind of round, copper container filled with iron filings and terminating in a rod that is rotated, thus producing a continuous rhythmical sound). One of the dancers' favorite amusements is to improvise words to a tune repeated over and over again. The singer must keep on finding new words, and as soon as his imagination begins to flag, someone else takes his place. The monotony of this neverending chorus and its insistent rhythm end by producing a sort of hypnosis to which the dancers fall victim. . . .

For six weeks the whole populace is passionately given over to singing and dancing; there is always one song that wins more favor than the others, and thereby becomes the "Carnival Song." Thus "Pelo Telefono," the Carnival song for 1917, was to be heard wherever one went, ground out by little orchestras, churned out by pianolas and gramophones, whistled and sung after a fashion in every house—and it haunted us all winter.

I was fascinated by the rhythms of this popular music. There was an imperceptible pause in the syncopation, a careless catch in the breath, a slight hiatus that I found very difficult to grasp. So I bought a lot of maxixes and tangos, and tried to play them with their syncopated rhythms that run from one hand to the other. At last my efforts were rewarded, and I could both play and analyze this typically Brazilian subtlety. One of the best composers of this kind of music, Ernesto Nazareth, used to play the piano at the door of a cinema in the Avenida Rio Branco. His elusive, mournful, liquid way of playing also gave me deeper insight into the Brazilian soul.   [2]

POLYTONALITY

I had undertaken a thoroughgoing study of the problems of polytonality. I had noted—and interpreted for myself—that a little duet by Bach written in canon at the fifth really gave one the impression of two separate keys succeeding one another, and then becoming superimposed and contrasted, though of course the harmonic texture remained tonal. The contemporary composers, Stravinsky or Koechlin, made use of chords containing several tonalities, often handled contrapuntally or used as a pedal. I set to work to examine every possible combination of two keys superimposed and to study the chords thus produced. I also studied the effect of inverting them. I tried every imaginable permutation by varying the mode of the tonalities making up these chords. Then I did the same thing in three keys. What I could not understand was why, though the harmony books dealt with chords and their inversions and the laws governing their sequence, the same thing could not be done for polytonality. I grew familiar with some of these chords. They satisfied my ear more than the normal ones, for a polytonal chord is more subtly sweet and more violently potent.   [3]

MUSIQUE D'AMEUBLEMENT ("FURNITURE MUSIC")

Just as one's field of vision embraces objects and forms, such as the pattern on the wallpaper, the cornice of the ceiling, or the frame of the looking glass, which the eye sees but to which it pays no attention, though they are undoubtedly there, Satie thought that it would be amusing to have music that would not be listened to, *musique d'ameublement* or background music, that would vary like the furniture of the rooms in which it was played. Auric and Poulenc disapproved of this suggestion, but it tickled my fancy so much that I experimented with it, in cooperation with Satie, at a concert given in the Galerie Barbazange [in 1921]. During the program, Marcelle Meyer played music by *Les Six,* and Bertin presented a play by Max Jacob called *Un Figurant au théâtre de Nantes,* which required the services of a trombone. He also sang Stravinsky's *Berceuse du chat* to the accompaniment of three clarinets, so Satie and I scored out music for the instruments used in the course of these various items on the program. In order that the music might seem to come from all sides at once, we posted the clarinets in three different corners of the theater, the pianist in the fourth, and the trombone in a box on the first floor. A program note warned the audience that it was not to pay any more attention to the ritornelles that would be played during the intervals than to the candelabra, the seats, or the balcony. Contrary to our expectations, however, as soon as the music started up, the audience began to stream back to their seats. It was no use for Satie to shout: "Go on talking! Walk about! Don't listen!" They listened without speaking. The whole effect was spoiled—Satie had not bargained on the charm of his own music. Nevertheless, Satie wrote another *ritournelle d'ameublement* for Mrs. Eugene Meyer of Washington, when she asked him, through me, to give her an autograph. But for this *Musique pour un cabinet préfectoral* to have its full meaning, she should have had it recorded and played over and over again, thus forming part of the furniture of her beautiful library, adorning it for the ear in the same way as the still life by Manet adorned it for the eye. In any case, the future was to prove Satie right; nowadays, children and housewives fill their homes with unheeded music, reading and working to the sound of the radio. And in all public places, large stores and restaurants, the customers are drenched in an unending flood of music. In America, every cafeteria is equipped with a sufficient number of machines for each client to be able, for the modest sum of five cents, to furnish his own solitude with music or supply a background for his conversation with his guest. Is this not *musique d'ameublement*— heard, but not listened to?   [4]

JAZZ

It was during this visit to London [in 1920] that I first began to take an interest in jazz. Billy Arnold and his band, straight from New York, were playing in a Hammersmith dance hall.

In his *Coq et l'Arlequin*, Cocteau described the jazz accompaniment to the number by Gaby Deslys at the Casino de Paris in 1918 as a "cataclysm in sound." In the course of frequent visits to Hammersmith, where I sat close to the musicians, I tried to analyze and assimilate what I heard. What a long way we had traveled from the gypsies who, before the war, used to pour their insipid, treacly strains intimately into our ears, or the singers whose questionably tasteful glides were borne up by the wobbly notes of the cimbalom, or the crudity of our bals-musettes with the unsubtle forthrightness of cornet, accordion, and clarinet! The new music was extremely subtle in its use of timbre: the saxophone breaking in, squeezing out the juice of dreams, the trumpet, dramatic or languorous by turns, the clarinet, frequently played in its upper register, the lyrical use of the trombone, glancing slidingly over quartertones in crescendos of volume and pitch, thus intensifying the feeling. The whole, various yet not disparate, was held together by the piano, subtly punctuated by the complex rhythm of the percussion, a kind of inner beat, the vital pulse of the rhythmic life of the music. The constant use of syncopation in the melody was of such contrapuntal freedom that it gave the impression of unregulated improvisation, whereas, in actual fact, it was elaborately rehearsed daily, down to the last detail. I had the idea of using these timbres and rhythms in a work of chamber music, but first I had to penetrate more deeply into the arcana of this new musical form, whose technique still baffled me. The musicians who had already made use of jazz had confined themselves to what were more or less interpretations of dance music. Satie, in the "Rag-time du paquebot" of *Parade*, and Auric, in the fox-trot *Adieu New York*, had made use of an ordinary symphony orchestra, and Stravinsky had written his *Rag-Time* for eleven solo instruments, including a cimbalom.   [5]

THE EFFECTS OF POPULARITY ON JAZZ

I disappointed the American reporters by telling them that I was no longer inter-ested in jazz. It had now [by 1926] become official, and won universal recogni-tion. The Winn School of Popular Music had even published three methods: *How to Play Jazz and the Blues,* in which syncopation was analyzed—I might even say dissected. The various ways of assimilating jazz were taught, as well as jazz style for the piano, and improvisation; its freedom within a rigid rhythmic framework, all the breaks and passing discords, the broken harmonies, arpeggios, trills and or-naments, the variations and cadences that can return ad lib in a sort of highly fan-tastic counterpoint. You could also find instructions on playing the trombone, in-cluding the principal types of glissando and the way to make the sound quiver by a rapid little to-and-fro movement of the slide, and there were clarinet manuals exploiting all the new technical possibilities opened up by jazz. Even in Harlem, the charm had been broken for me. White men, snobs in search of exotic color, sightseers curious to hear Negro music, had penetrated to even the most secluded corners. That is why I gave up going.   [6]

William Grant Still
1895–1978

Still had a varied training that included learning the violin and oboe, attending Oberlin Conservatory, studying composition with Varèse, and working for several years with W. C. Handy. His lifelong ambition was to found an African American tradition of classical music, a goal exemplified in his best-known work, the Afro-American Symphony. *Four other symphonies followed, as well as several operas and ballets, some chamber works, and a wide variety of pictorial and programmatic symphonic works.*

AN AFRO-AMERICAN COMPOSER'S POINT OF VIEW

Statement in Henry Cowell's
American Composers on American Music, *1933*

Melody, in my opinion, is the most important musical element. After melody comes harmony; then form, rhythm, and dynamics. I prefer music that suggests a program to either pure or program music in the strict sense. I find mechanically produced music valuable as a means of study; but even at its best it fails to satisfy me completely. My greatest enjoyment in a musical performance comes through seeing as well as hearing the artist.

The exotic in music is certainly desirable. But if one loses sight of the conven-tional in seeking for strange effects, the results are almost certain to be so extreme as to confound the faculties of the listeners. Still, composers should never confine themselves to materials already invented, and I do not believe that any one tonal-ity is of itself more significant than another.

I am unable to understand how one can rely solely on feeling when composing.

The tongue can utter the letters of the alphabet, but it is the intellect alone that makes it possible to combine them so as to form words. Likewise a fragment of a musical composition may be conceived through inspiration or feeling, but its development lies altogether within the realm of intellect.

Colored people in America have natural and deep-rooted feeling for music, for melody, harmony, and rhythm. Our music possesses exoticism without straining for strangeness. The natural practices in this music open up a new field which can be of value in larger musical works when constructed into organized form by a composer who, having the underlying feeling, develops it through his intellect.   [1]

INFLUENCE AND CONVICTION

From a lecture at UCLA, November 21, 1957

My suggestion is that everyone would profit by being able to know and use various styles if and when he wishes. Then, the innate character of each composition will itself dictate the treatment, the style, and the form the music is going to take. No outsider should presume to tamper with a composer's conviction in that respect. No matter how sensitive and alert we are to outside influences, we should never allow them to throw us off balance. Criticism must be *evaluated* before it's accepted or rejected.

By all means, the young composer should learn from everything and everyone. He should realize that nothing is valueless or totally undesirable. He should listen to all his teachers, study his textbooks, absorb all the musical influences around him—but at the same time, reserve the right to disagree with anything he feels unable to accept.

There is no substitute for keeping an open mind and for analyzing both sides of a question. There is also no substitute for having the courage of one's convictions. No one really wants to be a carbon copy of anyone else, no matter how much he may admire the other person or his work.

I have always felt, when people have asked me to bow to their will, that I may indeed be wrong—but if I *am* wrong, let it be my own mistake, not one I have been led into.   [2]

AMERICAN MUSIC

From an address at the Indiana University Seminar on Black Music, 1969

American music is a composite of all the idioms of all the people comprising this nation, just as most Afro-Americans who are "officially" classed as Negroes are products of the mingling of several bloods. This makes us *individuals*, and that is how we should function, musically and otherwise. My personal feeling is that the avant-garde idiom as it stands is not the idiom of the future, no matter how its adherents try to convince me that I'm unsophisticated to think so. I've watched its deleterious effect on audiences and have noted that the general public, for whom music is supposed to be written, couldn't care less. I would urge young Afro-American composers to think of the avant-garde as a phase, not an end in itself, and if not a phase, a facet of composition.   [3]

MUSICAL BACKGROUND

From the UCLA lecture

Back in the days when America became aware of the blues, I worked with W. C. Handy in his office on Beale Street in Memphis. This certainly would not seem to be an occupation nor a place where anything of real musical value could be gained. Nor would nearby Gayoso Street, which was then a somewhat disreputable section. But in searching for musical experiences that might later help me, I found there an undeniable color and musical atmosphere that stemmed directly from the folk.

Any alert musician could learn something, even in that sordid atmosphere. W. C. Handy listened and learned—and what he learned profited him financially and in other ways in the succeeding years. He, of course, belongs in the popular field of music. But if a popular composer could profit by such contacts with folk music, why couldn't a serious composer? Instead of having a feeling of condescension, I tried to keep my ears open so that I could absorb and make mental notes of things that might be valuable later.

As the years went on, and I went from one commercial job to another, there were always people who tried to make me believe that the commercial field was an end in itself, and who argued that I should not waste my time on what is now often called "longhair" music. In this I disagreed. I felt that I was learning something valuable, not only insofar as I could use it to serve a larger purpose.

The next important step was my study with Edgard Varèse. He might be classed as one of the most extreme of the ultramodernists. He took for himself, and encouraged in others, absolute freedom in composing. Inevitably, while I was studying with him, I began to think as he did and to compose music which was performed; music which was applauded by the avant-garde, such as were found in the International Composers' Guild. As a matter of fact, I was so intrigued by what I learned from Mr. Varèse that I let it get the better of me. I became its servant, not its master. It followed as a matter of course that, after freeing me from the limitation of tradition, it too began to limit me.

It took me a little while to realize that it *was* limiting me, and that the ultramodern style alone (that is to say, in its unmodified form) did not allow me to express myself as I wished. I sought then to develop a style that debarred neither the ultramodern nor the conventional.

Certain people thought this decision was unwise, and tried to persuade me to stay strictly in the ultramodern fold. I didn't do it, but at the same time, the things I learned from Mr. Varèse—let us call them the horizons he opened up to me—have had a profound effect on the music I have written since then. The experience I gained was thus most valuable even though it did not have the result that might have been expected.

After this period, I felt that I wanted for a while to devote myself to writing racial music. And here, because of my own racial background, a great many people decided that I ought to confine myself to that sort of music. In that, too, I disagreed. I was glad to write Negro music then, and I still do it when I feel so inclined, for I have a great love and respect for the idiom. But it has certainly not been the *only* musical idiom to attract me. [4]

Paul Hindemith
1895–1963

After an early period of provocative works—particularly theater pieces—Hindemith tem-
pered his style and became a major figure of Neoclassicism. He wrote prolifically, creating
sonatas for nearly every instrument and advancing the idea of Gebrauchsmusik, *music cre-*
ated with a practical use in mind. Branded as a "cultural Bolshevik" by the Nazis for mu-
sical as well as personal reasons, Hindemith moved to the United States, where he taught
at Yale University from 1940 to 1953. The book A Composer's World *derives from the*
Charles Eliot Norton lectures that Hindemith delivered at Harvard University during the
1950–51 academic year.

From A Composer's World, 1952

EMOTION IN MUSIC

Real feelings need a certain interval of time to develop, reach their climax, and
fade again; reactions to music, however, may change as fast as musical phrases
do; they may spring up in full intensity at any given moment and disappear entirely when the musical pattern that provoked them ends or changes. Thus these
reactions may, within a few instants, skip from the most profound grief to utter
hilarity and on to complacency, without causing any discomfort to the mind experiencing them, as would be the case with a rapid succession of real feelings.
In fact, if it happened with real feelings, we could be sure that it could be only
in the event of slight insanity. The reactions music evokes are not feelings; they
are the images, the memories of feelings. We can compare these memories of
feelings to the memories we have of a country in which we have traveled. The
original journey may have taken several weeks or months, but in conjuring up
in our memory the events of it, we may go through the entire adventure in a
few seconds and still have the sensation of a very complete mental reconstruction of its course. It is the same trick dreams play on us. They, too, compress
the reproductions of events that in reality would need long intervals of time for
their development into fractions of a second, and yet they seem to the dreamer
as real as adventures he has when he is wide awake. In some cases, these dream-
events may even be the "real" life of the individual, while the facts they reflect,
distort, or rearrange are nothing but inconsequential and sober successions of
trifles. . . .

If music did not instigate us to supply memories out of our mental storage
rooms, it would remain meaningless; it would merely have a certain tickling effect on our ears. We cannot keep music from uncovering the memory of former
feelings, and it is not in our power to avoid them, because the only way to
"have"—to *possess*—music, is to connect it with those images, shadows, dreamy reproductions of actual feelings, no matter how realistic and crude or, on the contrary, how denatured, stylized, and sublimated they may be.   [1]

"GOOD" AND "BAD" MUSIC

If all music ever written could only be classified as "good" or "bad," with some pieces perhaps occasionally falling short of either extreme, what would a singer or player do with a composition of the highest quality, viewed objectively, but not serving his personal purposes? Take one of the more florid Gregorian melodies, such as those sung at Easter or Whitsunday, which will doubtless be considered by every musician of some taste the most perfect, convincing one-line compositions ever conceived. Of course, fully to understand their overwhelming linear power, you cannot restrict yourself to just reading or hearing them. You must participate in singing these melodic miracles, if you want to feel how they weld the singing group into a spiritual unit, independent of the individualistic prompting of a conductor, and guided only by the lofty spirit and technical excellence of the structure. Now, imagine that you are forced to sing them by yourself—solo, that is—transplanting those immaculate creations into another environment. Don't you feel as if you were expelled from a community of worthy friends? Has the music not lost its savor and assumed a taste of bitterness instead? And then play these same melodies, which were the precious vessels of highest linear revelations, on a wind instrument, then on a fiddle, and finally on the piano. The quality of the melodic line seems gradually to disappear, greatness turns into inexpressive melismatism, then becomes insipid passage work, and finally ends in ridicule. If . . . perfection remained perfection under all circumstances, how could such a disintegration of values take place merely by altering the means of performance? . . .

We all agree that, in a fugue, the linear arrangement of the musical material must be strongly emphasized, and this is often carried to the highest degree of contrapuntal rigidity. Consequently, any group of instruments that allows this contrapuntal fabric to appear in transparent lucidity should in principle be preferable to all others. Since linear writing for pianos or other keyboard instruments can only be an artificial projection of several independent melodic planes into one single plane, a keyboard fugue played on non-keyed melodic instruments should reveal its linear spirit in a more appropriate and therefore more convincing manner than the original form could ever do. Now play some of the undisputed masterpieces of this species, namely, fugues from Bach's *Well-Tempered Clavier* as string trio or string quartet pieces. You will have a queer and rather disagreeable sensation: compositions which you knew as being great, heavy, and as emanating an impressive spiritual strength, have turned into pleasant miniatures. With the increase in contrapuntal clarity, we have had to accept a deplorable loss of majesty and gravity. Although the supremacy of the piece has remained the same, the pieces have shrunk, despite the improved reproduction , and their structural and spiritual relation to the original keyboard form has become that of a miniature mummified Incan head to its previous animate form. In our fugues we have reduced to almost nothing the heavy technical resistance that a player of polyphonic keyboard music has to overcome, since the string players have produced their isolated lines without noticeable effort. [2]

THE COMPOSER'S EDUCATION

In earlier times composition was hardly taught at all. If a boy was found to be gifted for music, he was given as an apprentice into the care of a practical musician. With him he had to get acquainted with many branches of music. Singing was the foundation of all musical work. Thus singing, mostly in the form of group singing, was one of the most important fields of instruction. The practical knowledge of more or less all instruments was a *sine qua non.* Specialization was almost unknown. Frequently a musician may have been better on the keyboard than with the bow and with woodwinds or brass, but that would not have absolved him from playing as many other instruments as possible. And all this playing was done with one aim in mind: to prepare the musician for collective work; it was always the community that came first. Soloistic training was nothing but a preliminary and preparatory exercise for this purpose. Hand in hand with this daily all-around routine in instrumental training went a solid instruction in the theory of music—not only what we call theory in our modern curricula, namely harmony, counterpoint, and other branches of practical instruction, but true theory, or if you prefer another name, the scientific background of music. . . .

Today, the situation is quite different. . . . In former times one had to be a good musician before he could take up composing, and it was up to history to decide whether or not he was to be regarded as a great creative genius. Nowadays we can be sure to find in most applicants' souls, openly shown or bashfully hidden, the conviction "I feel that I am a great creative genius, therefore people have to take me for an excellent musician." . . .

Do we not know how long an extraordinary musician like Mozart had to struggle till he was able to bend, press, and mold the tonal material into the shape he wanted it? As a boy of five he wrote little compositions, at nine he was as qualified a composer as many others of that period; at twelve he had thoroughly mastered the technique of his time; yet it took him about twenty more years of his short life to write himself free from all restraints, so as to reach that superior technique—not to mention the uninhibited power to reveal his visions in musical forms—which for us is one of the intrinsic qualities of his works. . . .

The most conspicuous misconception in our educational method is that composers can be fabricated by training. If you go through two years of Harmony, one of Counterpoint, fulfill your requirements in Composition I and Composition II, have some courses in Orchestration and Form, throw in some minor courses for credits, and do some so-called "free" work in a post-graduate course, you are inevitably a composer, because you paid for your courses—or somebody else did—and you can expect to get something for your money. We produce composers the democratic way, as we produce congressmen. . . .

It is extremely dishonest to give every student the education that is meant to turn out a Beethoven, while we know that he will never be more than a medium-sized commonplace composer. Would it not be better, more honest, and even more economical, to provide him with an all-round technique of general validity, on which his talents may thrive[?] . . . Trained in this old and renewed system—if the most natural musical activity can be called a system—composers would again be musicians, who could be used in many fields of music equally well; who are useful players, not of one instrument but of several; who sing acceptably, who know how to handle classes, choirs, and orchestras; who have a decent knowledge of theory, and beyond all, who certainly know how to compose. [3]

MODERN MUSIC; SERIALISM

Let us investigate briefly some of those allegedly "modern" achievements. The best known and most frequently mentioned is the so-called twelve-tone technique, or composition in pre-established tone series. The idea is to take the twelve tones of our chromatic scale, select one of its some four hundred million permutations, and use it as the basis for the harmonic (and possibly melodic) structure of a piece. This rule of construction is established arbitrarily and without any reference to basic musical facts. It ignores the validity of harmonic and melodic values derived from mathematical, physical, or psychological experience; it does not take into account the differences in intervallic tensions, the physical relationship of tones, the degree of ease in vocal production, and many other facts of either natural permanence or proven usefulness. Its main "law" is supplemented by other rules of equal arbitrariness, such as: tones must not be repeated; your selected tone series may skip from one stratum of the texture to any other one; you have to use the inversion and other distortions of this series; and so on—all of which can be reduced to the general advice: avoid so far as possible anything that has been written before.

The only segment of our conventional body of theoretical musical knowledge which the dodecaphonists have deigned to admit and which, in fact, alone makes their speculations possible, is the twelve-tone tempered scale. We have already been told of this scale's weakness: because of its basic impurity it can be used only as a supplementary regulative to a tone system containing natural intervals—at least, so long as we want to save our music from total instrumental mechanization and have human voices participate in its execution. True, some kind of a restricted technique of composition can be developed on a foundation of compromise scales and arbitrary working rules, but doubtless the general result will always be one similar to the kind of poetry that is created by pouring written words out of a tumbler without calling in grammar and syntax. A higher tonal organization is not attempted and cannot be achieved, especially if one permits the technical working rules to slip off into the aforementioned set of supplementary statutes which are nothing but stylistic whims, and as such, not subject to any controlling power of general validity. [4]

Virgil Thomson
1896–1989

Born in Kansas City and educated at Harvard, Thomson lived for fifteen years in France, where he studied with Nadia Boulanger and developed a lifelong affinity for French music. He returned to the United States in 1940, writing reviews for the New York Herald Tribune *for the next fourteen years and contributing to various other publications until his death. In spite of his association with Gertrude Stein and Parisian intellectual circles, his music retains a deliberate accessibility and simplicity of material. The passages below that are listed with date only are drawn from Thomson's* Tribune *reviews.*

From The State of Music, *1939*

THE MUSIC CONSUMER AND THE CRITIC

Consumer criticism and consumer applause of music, as of architecture, are often more perspicacious than professional criticism and applause. What one must never forget about them is that the consumer is not a professional. He is an amateur. He makes up in enthusiasm what he lacks of professional authority. His comprehension is intuitive, perfidious, female, stubborn, seldom to be trusted, never to be despised. He has violent loves and rather less violent hatreds. He is too unsure for hatred, leaves that mostly to the professionals. But he does get pretty upset sometimes by music he doesn't understand.

On the whole he is a nice man. He is the waves around our island. And if any musician likes to think of himself as a granite rock against which the sea of public acclaim dashes itself in vain, let him do so. That is a common fantasy. It is a false image of the truth, nevertheless, to group all the people who like listening to music into a composite character, a hydra-headed monster, known as The Public. The Public doesn't exist save as a statistical concept. A given hall- or theaterful of people has its personality, of course, and its own bodily temperature, as every performer knows; but such an audience is just like any other friend to whom one plays a piece. A performance is a flirtation, its aim seduction. The granite-rock pose is a flirting device, nothing more. The artist who is really indifferent to an audience loses that audience. [1]

DISCUSSING MUSIC

Verbal communication about music is impossible except among musicians. Even among them there is no proper vocabulary. There is only technical jargon plus gesture. The layman knows neither convention. . . . If he knows a little of either, communication merely becomes more difficult, because both jargon and sign language have one meaning for the outside world, a dictionary meaning if you like, and five hundred meanings for the insider, hardly one of which is ever the supposed meaning. The musician and his employer are like an Englishman and an American, or like

a Spaniard and an Argentine. They think they are differing over principles and disliking each other intensely, when they are really not communicating at all.   [2]

COMPOSERS AND TEACHING

I sometimes think the worst mischief a composer can get into is teaching. I mean,
as a main source of income. As a supplementary source a little of it doesn't hurt,
is rather good, in fact, for clarifying the mind. A little criticism or music journalism is good too. A lot of either is not so good, because they both get you worried
about other men's music. Whenever the by-products of his musical education become for any length of time the main source of a composer's income, occupational
diseases and deformities set in.   [3]

LISTENING

In my student days I used to go to the Boston Symphony concerts every week. I
found that if I arrived with my conscious mind already at a certain degree of musical saturation, as I often did, the only way I could understand anything the orchestra played was by not listening consciously at all. I would read the program.
. . . The music provided just enough slight-annoyance value (like railway-riding
noises) to keep my attention on the reading. And the reading provided a subject
for conscious attention to play with that enabled me to really hear the music. Occasionally the music would pull me away from the book and make me listen to it
all over me. More often I just read on, paying no attention to the music, and of
course never missing a note of it.   [4]

From reviews

FRENCH RHYTHM

November 14, 1943

What makes French music so French? Basically, I should say it is the rhythm. German musicians and Italian musicians tend to consider rhythm as a series of pulsations. French musicians consider pulsations as a special effect appropriate only to
dance music, and they train their musical young most carefully to avoid them in
other connections. In the Italo-German tradition, as practiced nowadays, the written measure is likely to be considered as a rhythmic unit and the first count of that
measure as a dynamic impulse that sets the whole thing in motion. In French musical thought the measure has nothing to do with motion; it is a metrical unit
purely. . . . Accent is a stress that may occur either regularly or irregularly, but in
any case, it is always written in. It may occur on the first note of a measure, but in
well-written music it will usually appear more frequently in other positions.   [5]

AMERICAN SINGERS AND SONGS

February 16, 1947

Is it any wonder that our American singers are not masters and mistresses of their
art, when the repertory they all learn music through is so incompetently com-

posed? They don't know that English vowel lengths, like Continental ones, are immutable. They don't know that poetic expression, no matter what its subject, falls into four or five styles, or genres rather, and no more. They don't know that lyric poetry does not permit an aggressive mood, that impersonation of the poet by the interpreter is unbecoming to it, that it can be recited or sung but never acted, though the ballad style can, on the contrary, be dramatized up to the hilt.

How can they know these things when the composers of the music that is virtually their whole fare write as if they didn't know them either, and when singing teachers, for lack of a better repertory, give them for study year after year pieces that nobody can vocalize correctly or interpret convincingly because they are incorrectly composed? . . . There are probably not twenty American "art songs" that can be sung in Town Hall with dignity or listened to there without shame. Nor are there five American "art composers" who can be compared, as song writers, for either technical skill or artistic responsibility, with Irving Berlin.   [6]

TOSCANINI AND THE "WOW TECHNIQUE"

May 17, 1942

Toscanini's conducting style, like that of Mendelssohn (if Wagner is to be believed about the latter), is very little dependent on literary culture and historical knowledge. It is disembodied music and disembodied theater. It opens few vistas to the understanding of men and epochs; it produces a temporary, but intense, condition of purely auditory excitement. . . . Like Mendelssohn, he quite shamelessly whips up the tempo and sacrifices clarity and ignores a basic rhythm, just making the music, like his baton, go round and round, if he finds his audience's attention to waver. No piece has to mean anything specific; every piece has to provoke from its hearers a spontaneous vote of acceptance. This is what I call the "wow technique."

[7]

WAGNER

From The State of Music

It is really too bad the movies got born a century late. They would have served as an ideal dramatic medium for Richard Wagner. . . . History has willed it otherwise. Wagner did his heroic job, did it on the opera. It is too late now to do the same job on the movies, because the same battle can't ever be fought twice. His goddesses and heroes are fat theatrical screamers who stand around among cardboard rocks and wander through canvas forests. There is nothing naturalistic or credible about them; they are symbols embedded in concert music.   [8]

From reviews

February 21, 1943

Wagner never learned the elementary rules of thumb that aided Bach and Handel and Haydn and Mozart and even Schubert to estimate the strength of melodic materials. His rhythmic patterns are frequently monotonous too; and he has a weakness for step-wise modulating sequences. [9]

ELGAR

October 11, 1940

I've an idea the Elgar [*Enigma*] *Variations* are mostly a pretext for orchestration, a pretty pretext and a graceful one, but a pretext for fancywork all the same, for that massively frivolous patchwork in pastel shades of which one sees such quantities in any intellectual British suburban dwelling. [10]

MacDowell's Shorter Piano Works

November 5, 1944

MacDowell did not leave his mark on music as a stylist; he left us merely a repertory of unforgettable pieces, all different from one another and all charming. And he left to American composers an example of clear thought and objective workmanship that has been an inspiration to us all. . . .

His music, like that of [Stephen] Foster, is part of every American's culture who has any musical culture. Everybody has played it, loved it, remembered it. . . . To have become, whether by sheer genius for music making, as in Foster's case, or, as in MacDowell's, by the professional exercise of a fully trained gift and by an integrity of attitude unequaled in our musical history, part and parcel of every musical American's musical thought is, in any meaning of the term, it seems to me, immortality. [11]

Debussy

March 28, 1948

His profound originality lies in his concept of formal structure. Where he got it I do not know. It may have come out of Impressionist painting or Symbolist poetry. Certainly there is small precedent for it in music. It remains, nevertheless, his most radical gift to the art.

This formal pattern is a mosaic texture made up of tiny bits and pieces all fitted in together so tightly that they create a continuity. The structural lines of the composition are not harmonic, not in the bass, but rhythmic and melodic. Debussy freed harmony from its rhetorical function, released it wholly to expression. He gave everything to expression, even structure. [12]

Sibelius

October 11, 1940

Twenty years' residence on the European continent has largely spared me Sibelius. Last night's Second Symphony was my first in quite some years. I found it vulgar, self-indulgent, and provincial beyond all description. I realize that there are sincere Sibelius lovers in the world, though I must say I've never met one among educated professional musicians.   [13]

SATIE

January 5, 1941

This writer is in agreement with Darius Milhaud and with some of the other contemporary French composers in placing Satie's work among the major musical values of our century. He has even gone so far in print, nearly twenty years ago, as to parallel the three German B's—Bach, Beethoven, and Brahms—with the three S's of modern music—in descending order of significance, Satie, Schönberg, and Stravinsky. . . .

The Satie musical esthetic is the only twentieth-century musical esthetic in the Western world. Schönberg and his school are Romantics; and their twelve-tone syntax, however intriguing one may find it intellectually, is the purest Romantic chromaticism. Hindemith, however gifted, is a neoclassicist, like Brahms, with ears glued firmly to the past. The same is true of the later Stravinsky and of his satellites. Even *Petrushka* and *The Rite of Spring* are the Wagnerian symphonic theater and the nineteenth-century worship of nationalistic folklore applied to ballet.

Of all the influential composers of our time, and influence even his detractors cannot deny him, Satie is the only one whose works can be enjoyed and appreciated without any knowledge of the history of music. These lack the prestige of traditional modernism, as they lack the prestige of the Romantic tradition itself, a tradition of constant revolution. They are as simple, as straightforward, as devastating as the remarks of a child.

To the uninitiated they sound trifling. To those who love them they are fresh and beautiful and firmly right. And that freshness and rightness have long dominated the musical thought of France. Any attempt to penetrate that musical thought without first penetrating that of Erik Satie is fruitless. Even Debussy is growing less and less comprehensible these days to those who never knew Satie.   [14]

IVES

From an essay in the New York Review of Books, *May 21, 1970*

It has been [this writer's] experience that Ives's work in general, though thoroughly interesting to inspect, frequently comes out sounding less well than it looks on the page. Some of this disappointment comes from musical materials which, although intrinsically interesting for appearing to be both highly spontaneous and highly complex, seem to be only casually felt. . . .

[Ives's songs] seem so aptly related to the words both by sentiment and by a naturalistic declamation (for which he had a gift) that one expects almost any of them, embellished as they so often are by inventive accompaniments, to be a jewel. And yet they do not, will not, as we say, come off. . . . Ives's weakness is seldom in the vocal line, which is musically sensitive even when the poetry is poor, but quite regularly in the piano part, which fails to interweave, harmonically or rhythmically, with the voice.   [15]

From reviews

HINDEMITH

February 9, 1941

Paul Hindemith's music is both mountainous and mouselike. The volume of it is enormous; its expressive content is minute and not easy to catch. . . . It is obviously both competent and serious. It is dogmatic and forceful and honest and completely without charm. . . . It is neither humane nor stylish, though it does have a kind of style, a style rather like that of some ponderously monumental and not wholly incommodious railway station.   [16]

SCHOENBERG

September 10, 1944

It is probably the insufficiencies of Schoenberg's own rhythmic theory that prevent his music from crystallizing into great, hard, beautiful, indissoluble works. Instrumentally they are delicious. Tonally they are the most exciting, the most original, the most modern-sounding music there is. What limits their intelligibility, hamstrings their expressive power, makes them often literally halt in their tracks, is the naïve organization of their pulses, taps, and quantities. Until a rhythmic syntax comparable in sophistication to Schoenberg's tonal one shall have been added to this, his whole method of composition, for all the high intellection and sheer musical genius that have gone into its making, will probably remain a fecund but unsupportable heresy, a strict counterpoint valuable to pedagogy but stiff, opaque, unmalleable, and inexpressive for free composition.   [17]

GERSHWIN AND *PORGY AND BESS*

From an article in Modern Music, November 1935

The *Rhapsody in Blue* remains a quite satisfactory piece. Rhapsodies, however, are not very difficult to write, if one can think up enough tunes. The efforts at a more sustained symphonic development, which the later pieces represent, appear now to be just as tenuous as they have always sounded. One can see through *Porgy* that Gershwin has not and never did have the power of sustained musical development. His invention is abundant, his melodic quality high, although it is inextricably involved with an oversophisticated commercial background. . . . Leaving aside the slips, even, and counting him at his best, that best which is equally well exemplified by *Lady Be Good* or *I've Got Rhythm* or the opening of the *Rhapsody in Blue*, he is still not a very serious composer. . . .

Porgy is nonetheless an interesting example of what can be done by talent in spite of a bad setup. With a libretto that should never have been accepted on a subject that should never have been chosen, a man who should never have attempted it has written a work that has a considerable power. . . .

As for the development, or musical build-up, there simply isn't any. When he gets hold of a good number he plugs it. The rest of the time he just makes up what music he needs as he goes along. Nothing much of interest, little exercises in the jazzo-modernistic style, quite pleasant for the most part but leading nowhere. The scoring is heavy, overrich, and ineffective. Throughout the opera there is, however, a constant stream of lyrical invention and a wealth of harmonic ingenuity.   [18]

THE MASTERPIECE CULT; SHOSTAKOVICH

From a review

June 25, 1944

The enjoyment and understanding of music are dominated in a most curious way by the prestige of the masterpiece. Neither the theater nor the cinema nor poetry nor narrative fiction pays allegiance to its ideal of excellence in the tyrannical way that music does. They recognize no unbridgeable chasm between "great work" and the rest of production. Even the world of art painting, though it is no less a victim than that of music to Appreciation rackets based on the concept of gilt-edged quality, is more penetrable to reason in this regard, since such values, or the pretenses about them advanced by investing collectors and museums, are more easily unmasked as efforts to influence market prices. But music in our time (and in our country) seems to be committed to the idea that first-class work in composition is separable from the rest of music writing by a distinction as radical as that recognized in theology between the elect and the damned. Or at the very least by as rigorous an exclusion from glory as that which formerly marked the difference between Mrs. Astor's Four Hundred and the rest of the human race.

This snobbish definition of excellence is opposed to the classical concept of a Republic of Letters. It reposes, rather, on the theocratic idea that inspiration is less a privilege of the private citizen than of the ordained prophet. Its weakness lies in the fact that music, though it serves most becomingly as religion's handmaiden, is not a religion. Music does not deal in general ideas of morality or salvation. It is an art. It expresses private sentiments through skill and sincerity, both of which last are a privilege, a duty, indeed, of the private citizen, and no monopoly of the prophetically inclined.

In the centuries when artistic skills were watched over by guilds of workmen, a masterpiece was nothing more than a graduation piece, a work that marked the student's advance from apprenticeship to master status. Later the word was used to mean any artist's most accomplished work, the high point of his production. It came thus to represent no corporate judgment, but any consumer's private one. Nowadays most people understand by it a piece differing from the run of repertory by a degree of concentration in its expressivity that establishes a difference of kind. And certain composers (Beethoven was the first of them) are considered to have worked consciously in that vein. The idea that any composer, however gifted and skillful, is merely a masterpiece factory would have been repellent to Bach or Haydn or Handel or Mozart, though Gluck was prone to advertise himself as just that. But all the successors of Beethoven who aspired to his position of authority—

Brahms and Bruckner and Wagner and Mahler and Tchaikovsky—quite consciously imbued their music with the "masterpiece" tone.

This tone is lugubrious, portentous, world-shaking; and length, as well as heavy instrumentation, is essential to it. Its reduction to absurdity is manifest today through the later symphonies of Shostakovich. Advertised frankly and cynically as owing their particular character to a political directive imposed on their author by state disciplinary action, they have been broadcast throughout the United Nations as models of patriotic expression. And yet rarely in the history of music has any composer ever spread his substance so thin. Attention is not even required for their absorption. Only Anton Rubinstein's once popular symphony, *The Ocean,* ever went in for so much water. They may have some value as national advertising, though I am not convinced they do; but their passive acceptance by musicians and music lovers can certainly not be due to their melodic content (inoffensive as this is) or to their workmanship (roughly competent as this is, too.)

What imposes about them is their obvious masterpiece-style one-trackness, their implacable concentration on what they are doing. . . . But that what these pieces are up to in any musical sense, chiefly rehashing bits of Borodin and Mahler, is of much intrinsic musical interest I have yet to hear averred by a musician. And that is the whole trouble with the masterpiece cult. It tends to substitute an impressive manner for specific expression, just as oratory does.   [19]

APHORISMS AND OBSERVATIONS

How infinitely superior in simple effectiveness are our popular composers over our tonier ones. They have no technical drama of composition. They are at ease in their notation.

Our highbrow music, on the other hand, is notoriously ineffective. It is the bane of audiences at home and abroad, in spite of the very best will on everybody's part. (*Modern Music*, January 1932)   [20]

Always beware of ex-composers. Their one aim in life is to discourage the writing of music. (*The State of Music*)   [21]

Writing a review is not giving an examination; it is taking one. (February 21, 1954)   [22]

Ever since I simplified my machinery, I've kept a list of people who I think should've simplified theirs. . . . The basic simplicity applies even to the complex set-ups. I've always thought that Bartók would've been better off if he'd done something like that. (Interview, April 1977)   [23]

Silk-Underwear Music. (Headline for a review of Jascha Heifetz, October 31, 1940)   [24]

Boulez is a German agent. (Interview, April 1977)   [25]

The way to write American music is simple. All you have to do is to be an American and then write any kind of music you wish. (January 25, 1948)   [26]

FOUR SAINTS IN THREE ACTS

From The State of Music

I shall never forget the scandal in the world of modernist music that greeted the appearance in 1927 of Sauget's ballet *La Chatte* and in 1934 of my own opera *Four Saints in Three Acts*. After twenty years of everybody's trying to make music just a little bit louder and more unmitigated than anybody else's, naturally everybody's sounded pretty much alike. When we went them one better and made music that was melodic and harmonious, the fury of the vested interests in modernism flared up like a gas tank. That fury still burns in academic places.   [27]

Roger Sessions
1896–1985

During his lifetime Sessions was widely admired in musical circles but was less well known to the listening public. The reason in both cases was the exactitude of his idiom—an idiom that appears dauntingly complex on first hearing, but eventually resolves itself into an intelligent and severe beauty. Sessions was a respected teacher, holding positions at eight colleges over a career of almost seventy years. His book The Musical Experience of Composer, Performer, Listener *is based on a series of lectures given at the Juilliard School of Music during the summer of 1949.*

THE AMERICAN FUTURE

From a letter to Modern Music, 1940

A certain number of our musicians, together with a not negligible part of our musical press, is demanding with a voice quite reminiscent of various totalitarian phrases which we have heard, that music which shall "express the national feeling," "reflect the American scene," "establish an American Style"—as if these were in any sense measurable or specific quantities, or as if they were in any sense criteria or even basic ingredients of musical quality. We hear frequent statements to the effect that "European music is played out," that "American composers are doing in every way better work than their European contemporaries."

The demand for "national" art is fundamentally a defensive attitude, the reflex action of a pervasive inferiority complex. If American composers tend to think of musical life in terms of competition, it is not merely a quite false analogy taken over from the business world, but a sign of their own self-consciousness that may make them think of musical development in egocentric terms rather than in terms of music itself. If they are self-conscious and hypersensitive with respect to "European" music, it is only to a very small extent because of real or fancied slights that have been dealt them in the name of European tradition; for these would prove largely quite illusory and in any case quite negligible if they had really found themselves and were primarily absorbed in their own creative impulses. But just as the valetudinarian frequently becomes, through excessive preoccupation with his health, the victim of his own hypochondria, the artist who is excessively afraid of "influences" or insistent on the purity of his origins tends to wither from lack of nourishment. A consciously "national" style, in any field, inevitably becomes a picturesque mannerism, a kind of trademark, devoid of significant human content, irremediably outmoded the moment its novelty has gone. . . .

My second cause for concern is that the nationalistic attitude tends to remove composers, through the artificial isolation which they thereby assume, from the realities of their art, since it is indeed to a considerable extent a pretext for escape from those realities. Especially in a country like ours, in which development has been inevitably so rapid, there is always the danger of superficiality; and the establishment of specialized criteria leads all too easily to a neglect of the fundamental requirements of the art. Hence in asking that music be American we almost inevitably neglect to demand that it be music—that it spring from a genuine and mature impulse on the part of the composer and be more than simply a more or less promising attempt. I am not speaking here of technical inadequacy but of the half-baked quality, the undefiniteness, which we so often tend to mistake for vitality. No amount of "technical" proficiency can compensate for a lack of the basic spiritual discipline which alone can produce a mature artist. Composers, to be sure, are born, not made. But once born, they must grow; and far more composers are born than ever come to real fruition. "Talent" and "promise" are exceedingly common, and one need not be unduly impressed by them when they so often remain at that primitive stage. They can never get past that stage unless artists demand of themselves something more than provincialism.

For nationalistic criteria are, in the last analysis, quite unreal. I do not really believe that our advocates of "American" music would be seriously content with a picturesque folklore or with the musical reproduction, either specific or general, of American scenes or landscapes—we are quite adequately supplied with these in our popular music and various other manifestations. A nation is something far greater than that: it is, rather, the sum of a great many efforts towards goals which are essentially human and not parochial. It gains much of its character, no doubt, from the conditions of time and space under which those efforts are made. But it is the efforts and the goals which are really essential. So how on earth can we demand in advance, qualities that can reveal themselves only gradually, in works, the products of clear artistic vision? It is such works that, if and when they come into existence, will reveal America to us, not as the mirror of things already discovered, but as a constantly renewed and fresh experience of the realities which music alone can reveal. It seems to me so clear that this was the real achievement of the great music of the past. Bach and Mozart and Beethoven did not *reflect* Germany, they helped to create it; they brought in each instance new and unexpected, but essential materials to its construction. And only after the picture had really begun to take clear shape, through the influence of their finished work, was it possible to point with some certainty to specifically German characteristics in their art. It is not, moreover, as "German" composers that we value them, but rather we value Germany because of them, as creators of immortal music.   [1]

From The Musical Experience of Composer, Performer, Listener, *1949*

LISTENING TO MUSIC

Composer, performer and listener can, without undue exaggeration, be regarded not only as three types or degrees of relationship to music, but also as three successive stages of specialization. In the beginning, no doubt, the three were one. Music was vocal or instrumental improvisation; and while there were those who did not perform, and who therefore heard music, they were not listeners in our modern sense of the word. They heard the sounds as part of a ritual, a drama, or an epic narrative, and accepted it in its purely incidental or symbolic function, subordinate to the occasion of which it was a part. Music, in and for itself can hardly be said to have existed, and whatever individual character it may have had was essentially irrelevant.

Later, however, as certain patterns became fixed or traditional, the functions of composer and performer began to be differentiated. The composer existed precisely because he had introduced into the raw material of sound and rhythm patterns that became recognizable and therefore capable of repetition—which is only another way of saying that composers began to exist when music began to take shape. The composer began to emerge as a differentiated type exactly at the moment that a bit of musical material took on a form that its producer felt impelled to repeat.

The same event produced the performer in his separate function; the first performer was, in the strictest sense, the first musician who played or sang something that had been played or sung before. His type became more pronounced in the individual who first played or sang music composed by someone other than himself. At both of these points the performer's problems began to emerge, and whether or not he was aware of the fact, his problems and his characteristic solutions and points of view began to appear at the same time.

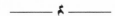

Listening to music, as distinct from reproducing it, is the product of a very late stage in musical sophistication, and it might with reason be maintained that the listener has existed as such only for about three hundred and fifty years. The composers of the Middle Ages and the Renaissance composed their music for church services and for secular occasions, where it was accepted as part of the general background, in much the same manner as were the frescoes decorating the church walls or the sculptures adorning the public buildings. Or else they composed it for amateurs, who had received musical training as a part of general education, and whose relationship with it was that of the performer responding to it through active participation in its production. Even well into the nineteenth century the musical public consisted largely of people whose primary contact with music was through playing or singing in the privacy of their own homes. For them concerts were in a certain sense occasional rituals which they attended as adepts, and they were the better equipped as listeners because of their experience in participating, however humbly and however inadequately, in the actual process of musical production. By the "listener," I do not mean the person who simply hears music, who is present when it is performed and who, in a general way, may either enjoy or dislike it, but who is in no sense a real participant in it. To listen implies rather a real participation, a response, a real sharing in the work of the composer and of the performer, and a greater or less degree of awareness of the individual and specific sense of the music performed. For the listener, in this sense, music is no longer an incident or an adjunct but an independent and self-sufficient medium of expression. His ideal aim is to apprehend to the fullest and most complete possible extent the musical utterance of the composer as the performer delivers it to him.   [2]

THE COMPOSER'S INDICATIONS

Composers have always, I believe, set down in scores everything they considered necessary for the performer's guidance; and the evolution of musical notation, the development of increasing subtlety, has been the result not of an independent effort but of the development of music itself. Certainly this has been true in recent history. If Bach, for instance, was sparing in dynamic indications, this was only partly owing to the fact that he himself was able to supervise the performance of his works and therefore could afford to neglect such matters. Still less, certainly, is it the result, as has sometimes been assumed, of any taboo against so-called expressive performance. One must assume that musicians of Bach's generation and before were as sensitive to the expressive modelling of phrases, to clear and discriminating stressing of accents, to the throwing of contrasts into relief, even to subtle inflections in tempo, as musicians have always been. In a similar sense it is impossible to conceive of composers like Josquin des Près, Orlando di Lasso, even Palestrina, urging their singers to suppress the natural eloquence of vocal inflection in order to achieve the complete neutrality of effect which is sometimes even today demanded as requisite for the performance of this music, and for which the composers of the Renaissance are sometimes held up as models.

Bach frequently, though by no means always, set off his contrasts by dynamic indications of the very simplest type: piano and forte, which always indicate generalized and large-scale contrasts. In the music of later composers, the sharper the essential contrasts on which the music is built, the more carefully the composer indicates and emphasizes these contrasts by nuances of all kinds. The tendency to minute indications runs in the most striking parallel to the development of minute elaboration and sharp contrast in musical detail, and the nuances are in the score, as always, for the purpose of throwing the detail into more drastic relief.

Any composer of the first magnitude may be cited in illustration of this fact. Possibly Beethoven's scores offer as good an illustration as any, since Beethoven stands, as it were, on the peak dividing the eighteenth and the nineteenth centuries and certainly partakes of both. His vast musical designs are not only completely integrated but, far more than those of any composer before him, they are extraordinarily rich in contrast and detail. It is for this reason that he carried the use of so-called expressive nuance so far, and what is amazing, and in itself worth years of study, is the absolute mastery—of one piece with his mastery of the design as a whole, and in fact one aspect of it—with which, by means of the nuances, he illuminates every essential detail of the whole and always in relation to this whole, that is, to the largest line.

To speak of dynamic and rhythmic nuances in this connection as "functional" is not to deny that they are essentially expressive. My intention is rather to demonstrate what is certainly obvious to all mature musicians: the expression, or *espressivo*, or expressivity, is in the music itself from the beginning and is not imposed from without. To perform a piece of music correctly, one plays not only the notes; one plays, in the first place, not so much notes as motifs, phrases, periods, sections, the rhythmic groups or the impulses of which the music is composed. One sets them in the relationship to each other which the composer has indicated. And I firmly believe that a certain type of instrumental instruction which teaches students first to learn notes and then, as it is quaintly put, to "put in the expression," is not only musically but instrumentally false. But what is "*espressivo*," if not the accentuating of contrasts, the throwing of contours into relief? In the music of Beethoven and those who came after him—in fact one may eventually say all the music of the tonal and the post-tonal period—the *espressivo* is in the music itself and nowhere else. It is in the structure of the music and, in the last analysis, is identical with this structure.   [3]

THE PERFORMER'S ROLE

What, then, is the task of the performer? Is it simply fidelity to the composer's text, or is the performer himself a creative artist for whom the music performed is simply a vehicle for the expression of his personality?

Stated thus, the most obvious comment is that it is not "simply" either one of these things, or, in fact, simply anything at all. In what consists "fidelity" to the text? What constitutes "personality"? Let us acknowledge at the outset that fidelity is fidelity, or truth; infidelity is falsehood. Are we to be understood, then, as asking whether or not the performer shall give a true or a false performance of the music? For after all, if the performer plays, let us say, a crescendo where a diminuendo is indicated, he is playing as surely falsely as he would should he sound F sharp where the composer has asked for G.

What makes both of the above questions absurd is the word "simply." For in the first place, fidelity to the composer's text is anything but simple, since the text itself is already very complex. It is complex because the composer has attempted to indicate (I can find no better word) by means of a vastly complex system of symbols the essentials of what I have called a musical gesture. And yet, as I have also tried to imply, a gesture, if it is to be living and genuinely expressive, must be unique; it must go beyond mere mechanical repetition and be invested with fresh energy if it is to live in time. Paradoxically enough, it cannot be really perpetuated in any other way; this is the very condition of its existence and, above all, of its endurance. For the listener—the person who responds to the music, who re-creates it, either internally or externally—will respond to the musical gesture only as long as it strikes him freshly, or as long as he is capable of apprehending it as created anew and not as something mechanically repeated.

The agent of this re-creation is the imagination of the performer, or, if you will, his "personality." It is his task, and I believe his whole task, to apply his imagination to discovering the musical gestures inherent in the composer's text, and then to reproducing them according to his own lights; that is, with fullest participation on his own part. This is only another way of saying that, having discovered as well as he can the composer's intentions, he must then apply himself to the task of reproducing them with the utmost conviction. It seems to me clear and beyond all doubt that both elements—fidelity, not so much to the text as to the music as expressed in the text, and conviction as animated by the musical nature of the performer—are essential. Without fidelity, a performance is false; without conviction, it is lifeless; in other words, it is hardly music. [4]

RECORDINGS

We can listen to a recording and derive a maximum of pleasure from it just as long as it remains to a degree unfamiliar. It ceases to have interest for us, however, the instant we become aware of that fact of literal repetition, of mechanical reproduction, when we know and can anticipate exactly how a given phrase is going to be modelled, exactly how long a given fermata is to be held, exactly what quality of accent or articulation, of acceleration or retard, will occur at a given moment. When the music ceases to be fresh for us in this sense, it ceases to be alive, and we can say in the most real sense that it ceases to be music. [5]

CONTINUITY IN MUSICAL THOUGHT AND FORM

The past is never, as our jargon implies, a fixed quantity; it is in movement. If we regard it clearly, we see it moving toward us, and if we set out to meet it, we find that it sees itself quite differently from the way we see it. Mozart, for his contemporaries, was not the serene classic, the apostle of measure and perfection, that so many of his admirers of the nineteenth century, and even some of those of today, have liked to conjure up. On the contrary, he was for them a painter of intense and even sombre canvases, of large scope and vast design, whom Lorenzo da Ponte is said on one occasion to have coupled in comparison with Dante of the *Inferno*. [6]

UNDERSTANDING CONTEMPORARY MUSIC

The key to the understanding of contemporary music lies in repeated hearing; one must hear it till it sounds familiar, until one begins to notice false notes if they are played. One must make the effort to retain it in one's ear, and one will always find that the accurate memory of sounds heard coincides with the understanding of them. In fact, the power to retain sounds by memory implies that they have been mastered. For the ear by its nature seeks out patterns and relationships, and it is only these patterns that we can remember and that make music significant for us. [7]

From Questions about Music, *1970*

MUSIC AND THE MARKETPLACE

The artist's values are not, and cannot be, those of the market. If one must think of him as writing *for* anyone, the answer is, I would think, clear; he is writing for all who love music, and he may reasonably assume that a decent number of these will come to his music in their own good time. He is not writing for "posterity"—certainly a concept that in our day has taken on some very problematical aspects. If he thinks of his work in terms of the future at all, his main preoccupation may very well be to work in such a manner that he himself, say, twenty-five years later, may regard what he has done without blushing.   [8]

TALENT AND IDEOLOGY

I have been genuinely impressed by music that was to a large extent aleatoric, and have even defended it warmly on occasion. I have also been impressed by music that embodied principles of "total serialization." I have certainly been bored by music of both kinds, and neither of these two ideas—so-called "chance music" and total serialism—seems to me to have any validity as a general principle. But the point I am making is that a composer of authentic talent and imagination, and of course craft, will somehow succeed in achieving results that are genuinely musical, with everything he seriously uses—sometimes almost in spite of himself. He accomplishes this not by dint of effort, but because he cannot do otherwise—because this is the natural shape his ideas will take.   [9]

From a series of interviews with Andrea Olmstead, 1975–77, published in Tempo, *December 1978*

RULES

I think rules are made to be disobeyed. They're made to be disciplined by, but then disregarded. In the interests of a higher morality, so to speak. Rules have a certain coordinating purpose. But they only take you so far. And that purpose, if you have your materials firmly in mind, can be served in independence of the rules.   [10]

ORGANIZATION

It's the *music* that has to be organized, not simply the notes. Because very often people assume that if you can find *some* kind of organization there, whether it has any relation to what you actually hear or experience in hearing, or should think of in hearing, that then you're disposed of the problem. I don't think you've *approached* the problem in those terms. It has to be organized in terms of the musical ideas.   [11]

SCHOENBERG AS A PERSONAL INFLUENCE

From an interview in Soundpieces, *1975*

I always knew some of Schoenberg's music very well, but I was not at all sure that Schoenberg's system, which I didn't fully understand at that time [the 1930s], could fit my needs. I came to it fairly slowly. When I lived in California, I had some very good talks with Schoenberg and found out that our ideas were not very far apart. Soon afterwards, I found myself in favor of it. Then, in Italy, I got to know Luigi Dallapiccola very well; he was also using the twelve-tone system. I said to him one day, "You know, I'm fifty-five years old now and I don't see myself learning a new technique at this age." He understood perfectly well.

It's important to remember that Schoenberg wasn't at all dogmatic about the use of twelve-tone technique. In fact, at one time I told Schoenberg that I thought that he had been misunderstood very much. I especially felt that his twelve-tone system had been misunderstood because it had been over-publicized and somewhat turned into a system of rules and formulas. He looked glum for a minute and said, "Yes, you're quite right; I have to admit that it's partly my fault." Then he suddenly grew more animated and said, "But it's much more the fault of some of my disciples!" Of course I understood that very well; I always felt much closer to Schoenberg than to Webern, because Webern was, or seemed to be, very dogmatic about it, and that's quite contrary to my own nature. This is a technique that one comes to by one's self or one does not. When I actually came to it, I used it very freely—as I still do—because I was writing my own music and not Schoenberg's music at all.   [12]

Henry Cowell
1897–1965

Cowell's place in history owes as much to his ideas and activities as to his compositions. As an adolescent he experimented with "tone clusters" that were played with the fists and forearms, later developing the first system for their organization. His music for modified piano influenced John Cage, among others. Cowell was a tireless advocate for new music—teaching, performing, lecturing, touring, organizing concerts, publishing several books, and founding the New Music Quarterly.

From American Composers on American Music, 1933

NATIONALISM AND AMERICAN MUSIC

Certain music may be called essentially American because it expresses some phase of American life or feeling. Other music may be named American if it contains new materials which are created by an American composer of the American folk.

Nationalism in music has no purpose as an aim in itself. Music happily transcends political and racial boundaries and is good or bad irrespective of the nation in which it was composed. Independence, however, is stronger than imitation. In the hands of great men independence may result in products of permanent value. Imitation cannot be expected to produce such significant achievements.

American composition up to now has been tied to the apron-strings of European tradition. To attain musical independence, more national consciousness is a present necessity for American composers. The result of such an awakening should be the creation of works capable of being accorded international standing.

When this has been accomplished, self-conscious nationalism will no longer be necessary. [1]

IVES

As a beginning toward an analytical understanding of Ives's works, one must take into consideration his point of view. He believes in music as a vehicle of expression, not so much a personal expression of himself, the composer (although this is included also), but a general human expression. He regards a musical composition almost as though it were a living organism, of which the composer gives the germ, the performer adding to its growth by widening the initial concept. For this reason, although there are always certain delicately balanced sounds about which he is very particular, he gives the performer unusual freedom in playing his works. He does not believe in laying down an absolutely rigid pattern for performers to follow, but believes that if the performer is great and adds his creative fire to the composer's in the rendition of the work, new and unexpected beauties will be born and the concept of the work will grow and flourish. This view has made it difficult for Ives to find the best way of writing down his music. There are always passages which he feels may be played in any of several different ways, depending upon who the performer is and how he feels at the moment, without injury to the composition, since the composition is a germ idea which may develop in any of a number of different directions. Therefore, if he writes down one certain way, he fears that the form of the piece will become crystallized, and that players will fail to see the other possibilities. This idea has led him to pay particular attention to the manner of writing down works, and has resulted in a number of characteristic features of his scores. For instance, he gives directions in a certain place for the performer to play very loud if his feelings have been worked up sufficiently; if not, he is to continue playing more softly. Very frequently, also, he gives a choice of measures. When the player comes to a certain place, he chooses between two or three different measures, according to how he feels. The same idea is also carried out in individual notes: there will be very full chords written, with a footnote stating that, if the player wishes, he may leave out certain notes or, if he wishes, he may add still more!

He is not content, like many superficial radicals, with merely tearing down known standards. If Ives finds it necessary to reject an older standard, he never rests until he has created a new structure to take its place. Such creations he has made and still makes in every field of music, and the result is a wonderfully universal, rounded-out whole, not technical, but deliciously and fascinatingly human and charming, and with an emotional but not a sentimental basis. [2]

VARÈSE

One key to a comprehension of Varèse's music is the fact that he is more interested in finding a note that will sound a certain way in a certain instrument and will "sound" in the orchestral fabric than he is in just what position the note occupies in the harmony; except, of course, in so far as its harmonic position will pertain to its "coming out" in the scoring. . . .

Just as harmonic combinations of sound qualities are emphasized above harmony itself by Varèse, one finds that dynamic nuances on the same note, or repeated tones, often take the place of melody. He very frequently does away with melody entirely by having only repeated tones for certain passages. Removing from the listener's ear that which it is accustomed to follow most closely, sometimes almost to the exclusion of everything else, naturally induces a keener awareness of other musical elements such as rhythm and dynamics. Varèse, however, is always careful to supply the ear with subtleties of dynamic change which take the place of melody in certain passages. Owing to his reliance on specific tone-qualities and dynamics for the very essence of his music, there are dynamic markings and directions as to quality applying to nearly every note in Varèse's scores. Sometimes a single note will have a number of signs, as for instance a certain note in the trumpet part of "Octandre" which is marked *sf, diminuendo, p, crescendo, sfff.* I have heard Varèse express great contempt for composers who do not use many expression marks. "They do not know how they wish their music to sound," he says. . . .

Varèse does not ignore melody and harmony, but merely does away with them on occasion. He limits himself almost exclusively to harmonies containing strong dissonances, i.e., minor seconds or ninths, and major sevenths. One may therefore say that he has developed for himself a rule that such dissonant intervals are requisite for the harmonic fabric he desires. To introduce a consonant harmony would remove the sense of implacable, resilient hardness, and create a weak link in the chain; the let-down would be so great that the whole composition might fall to pieces. Varèse's chords are obviously not haphazard, but belong to a special category in which he is careful to have certain general proportions of different sorts of intervals. . . .

There is a dramatic and incisive element about Varèse's music which causes it to stand out on a program, and to "kill" any work standing next to it by brute force. This does not mean that the music is better or worse; but it is unquestionably telling. And if stirring auditors to an almost unendurable irritation be taken into account, then the music can be said to be highly emotional. While he lacks melodic invention and harmonic succession, Varèse is in other respects unique, and deserves the highest place among European composers who have become American.   [3]

George Gershwin
1898–1937

Gershwin's talent proved as unclassifiable as it was immense. He wrote his first hit song at nineteen, and by twenty-six he had his first successful musical, Lady Be Good. *But Gershwin wanted to prove himself in the classical world, and that same year he appeared as the soloist in the premiere of his* Rhapsody in Blue. *The event was a phenomenal success. Even more successful were his songs and musicals, which provided a lavish income. Still he was not universally accepted as a serious composer, and he sought out various experts, including several famed composers, for lessons to improve his technique. Little came of this, but the quality of Gershwin's few concert works and his one opera,* Porgy and Bess, *eventually won out, firmly establishing him as a great composer—though he himself did not live long enough to enjoy the triumph.*

From an article, 1933

AMERICAN AND EUROPEAN RECIPROCAL INFLUENCES

Unquestionably modern musical America has been influenced by modern musical Europe. But it seems to me that modern European composers, in turn, have very largely received their stimulus, their rhythms and impulses from Machine Age America. They have a much older tradition of musical technique which has helped them put into musical terms a little more.clearly the thoughts that originated here. They can express themselves more glibly.

IDEAS AND FEELING

There is only one important thing in music and that is ideas plus feeling. The various tonalities and sound mean nothing unless they grow out of ideas. Not many composers have ideas. Far more of them know how to use strange instruments which do not require ideas. Whoever has inspired ideas will write the great music of our period. We are plowing the ground for that genius who may be alive or may be born today or tomorrow. If he is alive, he is recognized to a certain degree, although it is impossible for the public at large to assimilate real greatness quickly. Take a composer like Bach. In his lifetime, he was recognized as one of the greatest organists in the world, but he was not acclaimed as one of the greatest composers of his time or of all time until generations after his death.

JAZZ

It is difficult to determine what enduring values, aesthetically, jazz has contributed, because jazz is a word which has been used for at least five or six different types of music. It is really a conglomeration of many things. It has a little bit of ragtime, the blues, classicism, and spirituals. Basically, it is a matter of rhythm. Intervals come after rhythm in importance, music intervals which are peculiar to the rhythm. After all, there is nothing new in music. I maintained years ago that there is very little difference in the music of different nations. There is just that little individual touch. One country may prefer a peculiar rhythm or a note like the seventh. This it stresses, and it becomes identified with that nation. In America this preferred rhythm is called jazz. Jazz is music, it uses the same notes that Bach used. When jazz is played in another nation, it is called American. When it is played in another country it sounds false. Jazz is the result of the energy stored up in America. It is a very energetic kind of music, noisy, boisterous and even vulgar. One thing is certain. Jazz has contributed an enduring value to America in the sense that it has expressed ourselves. It is an original American achievement which will endure, not as jazz perhaps, but which will leave its mark on future music in one form or another.

EMOTION

Music is a phenomenon that to me has a very marked effect on the emotions. It can have various effects. It has the power of moving people to all of the various moods. Through the emotions, it can have a cleansing effect on the mind, a disturbing effect, a drowsy effect, an exciting effect. I do not know to what extent it can finally become a part of the people. I do not think music as we know it now is indispensable, although we have music all around us in some form or other. There is music in the wind. People can live more or less satisfactorily without orchestral music, for instance. And who can tell that we would not be better off if we weren't as civilized as we are, if we lacked many of our emotions? But we have them, and we are more or less egotistic about them. We think that they are important and that they make us what we are. We think that we are an improvement over people of other ages who didn't have them. Music has become a very important part of civilization, and one of the main reasons is that one does not need a formal education to appreciate it. Music can be appreciated by a person who can neither read nor write, and it can also be appreciated by people who have the highest form of intelligence. For example, Einstein plays the violin and listens to music. People in the underworld, dope fiends and gun men, invariably are music lovers, or at least they are affected by it. Music is entering into medicine. Music sets up a certain vibration which unquestionably results in a physical reaction. Eventually the proper vibration for every person will be found and utilized. I like to think of music as an emotional science.

RECORDINGS

The composer, in my estimation, has been helped a great deal by the mechanical reproduction of music. Music is written to be heard, and any instrument that tends to help it to be heard more frequently and by greater numbers is advantageous to the person who writes it. . . .

The radio and the phonograph are harmful to the extent that they bastardize music and give currency to a lot of cheap things. They are not harmful to the composer. The more people listen to music, the more they will be able to criticize it and know when it is good. . . .

The composer has to do every bit of his work himself. Handwork can never be replaced in the composition of music. If music ever became machine-made in that sense, it would cease to be an art. [1]

FOLK MUSIC AND CONCERT MUSIC

Statement in American Composers on American Music, *"as set down by Henry Cowell,"* 1933

The great music of the past in other countries has always been built on folk music. This is the strongest source of musical fecundity. America is no exception among the countries. The best music being written today is music that comes from folk-sources. It is not always recognized that America has folk-music; yet it really has not only one but many different folk-musics. It is a vast land, and different sorts of folk-music have sprung up in different parts, all having validity, and all being a possible foundation for development into an art-music. For this reason, I believe that it is possible for a number of distinctive styles to develop in America, all legitimately born of folk song from different localities. Jazz, ragtime, Negro spirituals and blues, Southern mountain songs, country fiddling, and cowboy songs can all be employed in the creation of American art-music, and are actually used by many composers now. These composers are certain to produce something worth while if they have the innate feeling and talent to develop the rich material offered to them. There are also other composers who can be classed as legitimately American who do not make use of folk-music as a base, but who have personally, working in America, developed highly individualized styles and methods. Their new-found materials should be called American, just as an invention is called American if it is made by an American!   [2]

BERG'S *LYRIC SUITE*

Quote in an article in Musical America, *1928*

Although this quartet is dissonant . . . it seems to me that the work has genuine merit. Its conception and treatment are thoroughly modern in the best sense of the word.   [3]

Carlos Chávez
1899–1978

Considered to be Mexico's first composer of international stature, Chávez studied first in Mexico City and later in Europe. In 1928 he founded the Orquestra Sinfónica de México, serving as its conductor for two decades and leading the first Mexican performances of many new works. For several years he also was director of the National Conservatory. Through teaching and commissions he fostered a new generation of composers, while in his own music he showed how the country's profusion of musical traditions might be used to give the cosmopolitan language of Modernism a distinctly Mexican character.

THE MUSIC OF MEXICO

From an essay in American Composers on American Music, *1933*

For many reasons the need of a critical review of the music and the other arts of Mexico is of utmost urgency. A knowledge of our history and of our country will make us really feel ourselves. The greater part of Mexican art has not really become completely Mexican, because Mexican artists have failed to saturate themselves with the life of Mexico in all the multiplicity of its expressions. Regionalism really becomes nationalism when nationalism comes to be in truth the balanced sum of all the regions. The "national style" will be the result of mutual understanding among the many groups of the Mexican people and of the country itself in all its manifestations. In Mexico not only does an almost complete gulf exist between the people of the country and those of the city, but even within the city itself there exist countless groups, more or less cultured, that do not know one another.

Tradition, in its best significance, should be considered as the substance of the conscience of a country throughout its past. Thus considered, tradition is a living fountain of knowledge and of character. There are peoples who have a well-established tradition. The Mexican people is not one of them. It has been impossible here in Mexico to sum up our life because the very factors have been kept apart by a multitude of political causes: The Spanish conquerors triumphed; as rulers in the land they governed, ignoring or denying the culture of the aboriginal element; at the advent of the Republic the racial, social, and intellectual conditions of the Mexicans had reached points of contrast violent in their degree of utter diversity, and to this day no form of proper co-ordination can be attained.

A revolutionary political organization, firmly established and fearlessly carried out, and a program which, bringing together all of the factors of Mexican culture, synthesizes one tradition will undoubtedly, in the end, give us nationality. Then we shall have culture and national arts. We talk much of "nationalism." Is this a symptom that Mexico is endeavoring to define her personality in all its varied aspects—in science, in art, in legislation?

The musicians of Mexico must know our tradition, for until such day as they do, our composers will not write Mexican music and they will go on saying that we have to continue in the European tradition and that the Mexican tradition does not exist. Professional musicians will continue their nine-year courses of composition, teaching our youth the rules of French and German conservatories. They will continue making us believe that music is Bach or Beethoven. They will go on destroying in our youth all its native force, annihilating all expression of the natural qualities peculiar to this race and to this country. Yet the Mexican painters of today have found the Mexican tradition of painting which the academies prior to the Revolution had denied without knowing. . . .

Factually, the music of Mexico may be divided into three great epochs in relation to our general history:

1. The aboriginal culture
2. The *mestizaje*, or phase representing the intermixing of Indian and Spanish
3. The nationalism of the revolution

The first epoch is known by a group so small as to be counted without difficulty; it is ignored by practically the entire public. But in point of force and originality this division is perhaps the most important of all.

Among the ancient Mexicans music was not only an individual expression indispensable to the life of the spirit but a concern of an entire state organization. Institutions for the teaching of music existed and special musical instruction was required in all religious and military schools. The political, social, and religious solemnities, as well as the various public celebrations of a secular character, always centered around music as a basis. . . .

The second epoch is neither well known in its entirety nor in the various phases of its evolution. This epoch may be considered as extending from the Conquest down to the Revolution of 1910. It is rich in the variety of its manifestations, from the country and from the city, and includes the following:

"*Mestizo*" music from the country
 Sonnet (*son*)
 Ballad (*corrido*)
 Song (*canción*)
 Dance music—religious and profane
 Romance or pastoral (*pastorela*)
"*Mestizo*" music of the city
 Compositions of the professional composers
 Concert and chamber music
 Dance music

The third epoch is the present. It may be considered to have begun when, in 1912, Manuel M. Ponce initiated the movement popularizing the Mexican song (*canción Mexicana*) and some of our regional dances, such as the *jarabe*. The very great interest which this movement aroused was undoubtedly due to the conviction of its initiator and to the nationalistic restlessness which at that time, and as a result of the Revolution of 1910, raged in a manner uncontrollable.

At the present time, with new phases of the Revolution begun in 1910 now lived through and past, leaving their very decisive contribution to the cementing of a criterion and a national culture, the musical nationalism of Mexico may definitely launch itself upon a determined course. It should consider itself as the product of balanced *mestizaje*, hybridism, in that the personal expression of the artist is absorbed neither by Europeanism nor by Mexican regionalism. We must recognize our own tradition, temporarily eclipsed. We should saturate ourselves with it, placing ourselves in personal contact with the manifestations of our land, native and mixed (*mestizos*), and this without disavowing the music of Europe, since it signifies human and universal culture, but receiving it in its multiple manifestations from the most remote antiquity, not through the medium of the "didacticism" of the German and French conservatories as has been our custom heretofore. We disdain the professional Mexican music prior to our own epoch, for it is not the fruit of the true Mexican tradition.

In the end we musicians must forge ourselves through work; we must make an art that is for all, not inclosed solely within the four walls of the concert hall. We must tend toward the more spectacular performances of music, theater and ballet, such as the ancient Mexicans were accustomed to enact, such as Greece had, spectacles which epitomize, which forge into one, the soul and the national conscience.

[1]

Francis Poulenc
1899–1963

Among his colleagues in "Les Six," Poulenc was the most classical in outlook and the most urbane in manner. As a young composer he was drawn to the simple means and vernacular immediacy of Satie. He later allowed himself greater richness of texture; after World War II he adopted a more serious cast of mind, but never abandoned the crisp, essentially tonal style that had become his hallmark. The interviews and diary writings excerpted below date from Poulenc's tours of the United States with the baritone Pierre Bernac.

From Feuilles americaines, 1950

TRADITION

We come to the problem of tradition and must deplore the fact that tradition is such a precarious thing. It is really astonishing how, only thirty years after Debussy's death, the exact meaning of his message has been lost. How many of his interpreters, themselves lacking in sensuality, betray Debussy! The word "sensuality" stuns my interviewer. I perceive that this is a term which he is not in the habit of applying to music.

"You undoubtedly mean eroticism?"

"Not necessarily, sensuality sometimes being a more gratuitous form of eroticism."

Then, moving on to a more concrete example, I explain to him that if Toscanini has revealed *La Mer* and Sabata has revealed *Jeux* to the public, it is because, as true Italians not blushing for Puccini (bravo!), they do not understand how we can escape the Massenet aspect of many pages of Debussy. I must add that a conductor, by placing *Jeux* in a refrigerator, and another, placing it in a sterilizer, do more harm to this jewel than silence. [1]

YOUNG AMERICAN COMPOSERS

Heard this afternoon some works by young American composers. Gifted, certainly, lots of health, some technique, drive; but how dangerous are the lessons taken from the great composer-teachers. In Los Angeles the young musicians write like Schoenberg, in Boston like Hindemith. Milhaud alone, to the gratitude of his students, maintains in San Francisco a climate of eclecticism. [2]

MENOTTI'S *THE CONSUL*

What a strange success is *The Consul,* a three-act opera by Menotti! What an astounding instinct for the stage! Menotti has served at once as composer, librettist, and director. From this ensemble results a prodigious cohesion, but one that is not without injury to the music. In my opinion this is a grave defect. In Verdi or Puccini the music is always sovereign. Here not. But what ingenuity, what strength, what power of persuasion! Seized by the drama, an audience of stylish first-nighters forgot, for once, to look one another over, left the theater with eyes red and beating hearts. [3]

THE CHARACTER OF FRENCH MUSIC

Remark to Roland Gelatt, 1950

You will find sobriety and dolor in French music just as in German or Russian. But the French have a keener sense of proportion. We realize that sombreness and good humor are not mutually exclusive. Our composers, too, write profound music, but when they do, it is leavened with that lightness of spirit without which life would be unendurable. [4]

Aaron Copland
1900–1990

Born in Brooklyn to Russian Jewish parents, Copland went to France to study composition and orchestration with Nadia Boulanger from 1920 to 1924. Through the popularity of works like Appalachian Spring, Rodeo, *and* Fanfare for the Common Man, *he became the most visible composer in America during the last half century of his life. Because of this visibility he was often called upon to defend contemporary music to an increasingly alienated public. His responses to this challenge are interesting for their style and their strategic approach as well as for their content—not least because Copland himself was sometimes ambivalent about the music he was being asked to defend.*

MODERN MUSIC

From an article in the New York Times, December 25, 1949

Why must new music be so dissonant?

A satisfactory reply to this troublesome question is exceedingly difficult because of the fact that a dissonance in music is a purely relative thing. What sounds dissonant to you may sound quite mellifluous to me. The whole history of Western music proves that our ear tends to increase its capacity for considering chords pleasurable which in former times were considered painfully discordant. Harmonies thought to be unusual or bizarre in the time of Monteverdi or Wagner are accepted as current usage by later generations of ordinary music lovers. Our period has hastened this historical process, since nowadays any chord, no matter what its degree of dissonance, is considered usable if it sounds "right" to the composer (that is, right for its expressive purpose), and is handled well within its context. If you find yourself rejecting music because it is too dissonant, it probably indicates that your ear is insufficiently accustomed to contemporary musical vocabulary and needs more training—that is, listening. Reading about a dissonant chord doesn't make it sound any sweeter, but repeated hearing certainly does. It is interesting to note in this connection that bebop, the latest jazz manifestation, has been introducing more and more dissonant harmonic textures into popular music, thereby arousing some of the same resistance from the mass public as was encountered by the serious composers in their field.

Is it true that the new composers care little about melody?

No, it definitely is not true. The greater proportion of today's music is melodically conceived, but it must be remembered that conceptions of melodic writing have changed. Here again it is not easy to agree upon a common ground for discussion, since the average person's idea of melody is so limited in scope. A melody is not merely something you can hum. It may be too complex for that, too tortuous or jagged or fragmentary, and in instrumental writing, it may go far beyond the limitations of the human voice. You must broaden your conception of what a melody may be if you want to follow what goes on in the composer's mind.

Part of the difficulty, as it concerns modern melody, may be traced to the harmonic problem. Many listeners become so lost in the web of unfamiliar harmonies that they never manage to hear the tunes that *are* being played. Since most music of serious pretensions deals in simultaneously sounded independent melodies, forming a contrapuntal texture that requires wide-awake listening even if the melodies are conventionally cast, it follows that a similar structure made of more recondite melodic writing will imply even more attentive listening. (Composers—and not only contemporary ones—have sometimes exaggerated in that direction, forgetting that the human ear is limited in absorbent capacity.) In general I would say that the melodies are there, but they may not always be of the immediately recognizable variety.

Is contemporary music supposed to be without sentiment or feeling, cerebral and clever rather than romantic?

A brief paragraph can hardly suffice to deal adequately with so persistent a misconception. If a contemporary composer's work strikes you as cold and intellectual, it may be that you are using standards of comparison that really do not apply. Most music lovers do not appreciate to what an extent they are under the spell of the romantic approach to music. Our audiences have come to identify nineteenth century musical romanticism as analogous to the art itself. Because *it* was, and still remains, so powerful an expression, they tend to forget that great music was written for hundreds of years before the romantics flourished.

It so happens that a considerable proportion of present day music has closer aesthetic ties with that earlier music than it has with the romantics. The way of the uninhibited and personalized warmth and surge of the best of the romanticists is not our way. That may be regrettable from your angle, but it remains a fact nevertheless—unavoidable fact probably, for the romantic movement had reached its apogee by the end of the last century, in any case, and nothing fresh was to be extracted from it.

Even composers found it difficult to break the spell, so it is hardly to be wondered at that the public should have been slow to grasp the full implication of what was happening. The literary world does not expect Gide or Mann or T. S. Eliot to emote with the accents of Victor Hugo or Walter Scott. Why, then, should Bartók or Milhaud be expected to sing with the voice of Schumann or Tchaikovsky? When a contemporary piece seems dry and cerebral to you, when it seems to be giving off little feeling or sentiment, there is a good chance that you are not willing to live in your own epoch, musically speaking. [1]

From a New York Times Magazine review of The Agony of Modern Music, March 13, 1955

The plain fact is that the composer of our century has earned the right to be considered a master of new sonorous images. Because of him music behaves differently, its textures are different—more crowded or more spacious, it sings differently, it rears itself more suddenly and plunges more precipitously. It even stops differently. But it shares with older music the expression of basic human emotions, even though at times it may seem more painful, more nostalgic, more obscure, more hectic, more sarcastic. Whatever else it may be, it is the voice of own age and in that sense it needs no apology.

This is the music we are told nobody likes. But let's take a closer look at "nobody." There is general agreement that new multitudes have come to serious music listening in the past two or three decades. Now we are faced with a situation long familiar in the literary world; namely, the need to differentiate clearly among the various publics available to the writer. No publisher of an author-philosopher like Whitehead would expect him to reach the enormous public of a novelist like Hemingway. Ought we then to say "nobody" reads Whitehead?

In music we have failed to make distinctions among lovers of serious works. Thus the philosophical music of Charles Ives is discussed as if it were meant to appeal to the same audience reached by music of the Khachaturian type. To say that Ives, or any similar composer, has "no audience" is like saying that Whitehead has no audience. He has, through the nature of his work, a smaller but no less enthusiastic audience—and one that in the long view may mean more to the art of music than the "big" audience will. [2]

From an interview in Soundpieces, 1975

People think of music too often as a set kind of art, invented nobody knows quite when. But we composers who work in it all the time are very aware of its belonging to culture as a whole, which tends to change from generation to generation. Man experiences new things, the world becomes different all the time, and music changes along with all those happenings. But the big public always wants to be lulled by it, as a nice, pleasant, consoling, entertaining music that they've become accustomed to. But we composers don't think along those lines. That's where the rub comes, that's where the trouble starts. [3]

From Music and Imagination, 1952

SERIALISM

There is no doubt that Schoenberg and his followers derived great stimulus from this new method. Without the evidence of the music itself one might imagine that all ties with tonal music had been broken. But strangely enough, the classicist in Schoenberg was not to be so easily downed, and so we find him writing string quartets in the customary four movements, each separate movement partaking somewhat of the usual expressive content, and the general outlines recognizably those of a first-movement allegro, a minuet, a slow movement, and a rondo. Alban Berg, even before his adoption of the twelve-tone method, had written his opera *Wozzeck* in such a way that each of the fifteen scenes is based on some normal set form—a passacaglia, a military march, a series of inventions, and so forth. Anton Webern, in many of his works, wrote canons and variations. Other twelve-tone composers followed suit. An extraordinarily paradoxical situation developed: despite the rigorous organization of the twelve tones according to the dictates of the series and its mutations, and despite the adoption at times of the outward semblance of traditional shapes, the effect the music makes in actual performance is often one of near-chaos.

We are faced, then, with two seemingly opposite facts: on the one hand the music is carefully plotted in its every detail; and on the other it undeniably creates an anarchic impression. On the one hand the musical journals of every country are filled with articles explaining the note-for-note logic of Schoenbergian music, accompanied by appropriate graphs, abstracts, and schematized reductions, enormous ingenuity being expended on the tracking down of every last refinement in an unbelievably complex texture. (One gains the impression that it is not the music before which the commentators are lost in admiration so much as the way in which it lends itself to detailed analysis.) But on the other hand, when we return to the concert hall and listen once again to these same compositions we leave with the disturbing memory of a music that borders on chaos.

What are to conclude? Quite simply that these innovators are more revolutionary than they themselves know or are willing to admit. While appearing to have engineered merely a harmonic revolution, and set up a new method of composing in its place, they have in actuality done away with all previous conceptions of the normal flow of music.   [4]

LISTENING

Listening is a talent, and like any other talent or gift, we possess it in varying degrees. I have found among music-lovers a marked tendency to underestimate and mistrust this talent, rather than to overestimate it. The reason for these feelings of inferiority are difficult to determine. Since there is no reliable way of measuring the gift for listening, there is no reliable way of reassuring those who misjudge themselves. I should say that there are two principal requisites for talented listening: first, the ability to open oneself up to musical experience; and secondly, the ability to evaluate critically that experience. Neither of these is possible without a certain native gift. Listening implies an inborn talent of some degree, which, again like any other talent, can be trained and developed. This talent has a certain "purity" about it. We exercise it, so to speak, for ourselves alone; there is nothing to be gained from it in a material sense. Listening is its own reward; there are no prizes to be won, no contests of creative listening. But I hold that person fortunate who has the gift, for there are few pleasures in art greater than the secure sense that one can recognize beauty when one comes upon it.   [5]

Not infrequently I have been moved to tears in the theater; never at music. Why never at music? Because there is something about music that keeps its distance even at the moment that it engulfs us. It is at the same time outside and away from us and inside and part of us. In one sense it dwarfs us, and in another we master it. We are led on and on, and yet in some strange way we never lose control. It is the very nature of music to give us the distillation of sentiments, the essence of experience transfused and heightened and expressed in such fashion that we may contemplate it at the same instant that we are swayed by it. When the gifted listener lends himself to the power of music, he gets both the "event" and the idealization of the "event"; he is inside the "event," so to speak, even though the music keeps what Edward Bullough rightly terms its "psychical distance."

[6]

From self-observation and from observing audience reaction I would be inclined to say that we all listen on an elementary plane of musical consciousness. I was startled to find this curious phrase in Santayana concerning music: "the most abstract of arts," he remarks, "serves the dumbest emotions." Yes, I like this idea that we respond to music from a primal and almost brutish level—dumbly, as it were, for on that level we are firmly grounded.

[7]

From undated journal excerpts published in Copland on Music, *1963*

WRITERS AND MUSIC

The literary man and the art of music: subject for an essay. Ever since I saw Ezra Pound turn pages for George Antheil's concert in the Paris of the twenties, I have puzzled over what music means to the literary man. For one thing, when he takes to it at all, which is none too often, he rarely seems able to hear it for itself alone. It isn't that he sees literal images, as one might suspect, or that he reads into music meanings that aren't there. It's just that he seldom seems *comfortable* with it. In some curious way, it escapes him. . . . When he puts two words together to characterize a musical experience, one of them is almost certain to be wrong.

[8]

THE ORCHESTRAL MUSICIAN

Being the underdog in a feudal setup, he quickly develops a sort of imperturbability, especially as regards music. One can almost say that he flatly refuses to get excited about it. He is being paid to do a job—"Now let's get on with it, and no nonsense about it" is the implied attitude. You cannot play an instrument in an orchestra and admit openly a love for music. The rare symphonic instrumentalist who has managed to retain his original zest for music generally finds some means for expressing it outside his orchestral job. In thirty years of backstage wandering I have never yet caught a musician with a book on music under his arm. As for reading program notes about the pieces he plays, or attending a lecture on the aesthetics of music—all that is unthinkable.

[9]

PAST AND PRESENT

To my mind no one can adequately interpret the classics of the past without hearing them through the ears of the present. To play or conduct Beethoven's *scherzi* in a contemporary spirit, you must feel at home with Stravinskian rhythms. And I can even recommend familiarity with the rhythms of American jazz for those who want to play Couperin. [10]

ELECTRONIC MUSIC

From the Soundpieces *interview*

I've often thought that one of the great drawbacks of electronic music is the fact that it has to be put on tape. You rarely have it produced live. The minute you put a thing on tape, you're stuck with it. . . . On the other hand, naturally, you can produce musical effects not otherwise producible, and that is a great advantage. Those men and women who have worked in the medium are obviously fascinated with it, and I would expect a real contribution to musical art in the end.

Q: Is it this problem of freezing the music that has kept you away from electronic composition?

A: No, I don't have any talent with electricity. I feel lucky if I push a switch and the light goes on. [11]

From a lecture at the University of New Hampshire, 1959

BACH

What strikes me most markedly about Bach's work is the marvelous rightness of it. It is the rightness not merely of a single individual but of a whole musical epoch. [12]

BEETHOVEN

One doesn't need much historical perspective to realize what a shocking experience Beethoven's music must have been for his first listeners. Even today, given the nature of his music, there are times when I simply do not understand how this man's art was "sold" to the big musical public. Obviously he must be saying something that everyone wants to hear. And yet if one listens freshly and closely the odds against acceptance are equally obvious. As sheer sound there is little that is luscious about his music—it gives off a comparatively "dry" sonority. He never seems to flatter an audience, never know or care what they might like. His themes are not particularly lovely or memorable; they are more likely to be expressively apt than beautifully contoured. His general manner is gruff and unceremonious, as if the matter under discussion were much too important to be broached in urbane or diplomatic terms. He adopts a peremptory and hortatory tone, the assumption being, especially in his most forceful work, that you have no choice but to listen. And yet this is precisely what happens: you listen. [13]

LISZT

From Music and Imagination

Think of what Liszt did for the piano. No other composer before him—not even Chopin—better understood how to manipulate the keyboard of the piano so as to produce the most satisfying sound textures ranging from the comparative simplicity of a beautifully spaced accompanimental figure to the shimmering of a delicate cascade of chords. One might argue that this emphasis upon the sound appeal of music weakens its spiritual and ethical qualities. But even so, one cannot deny the role of pioneer to Liszt in this regard, for without his sensuously contrived pieces we would not have had the loveliness of Debussy's or Ravel's textures, and certainly not the languorous piano poems of Alexander Scriabin. Liszt quite simply transformed the piano, bringing out not only its own inherent qualities, but its evocative nature as well: the piano as orchestra, the piano as harp, the piano as cimbalom, the piano as organ, as brass choir, even the percussive piano as we know it may be traced to Liszt's incomparable handling of the instrument.   [14]

VERDI

From the University of New Hampshire lecture

Verdi can be commonplace at times, as everyone knows, but his saving grace is a burning sincerity that carries all before it. There is no bluff here, no guile. On whatever level he composed a no-nonsense quality comes across; all is directly stated, cleanly written with no notes wasted, and marvelously effective. In the end we willingly concede that Verdi's musical materials need not be especially choice in order to be acceptable.   [15]

FAURÉ

From an article in the New York Times, *November 25, 1945*

It is perfectly true that you must listen closely if you would savor the exquisite distinction of Fauré's harmonies or appreciate the long line of a widely spaced melodic arch. His work has little surface originality. Fauré belongs with that small company of musical masters who knew how to extract an original essence from the most ordinary musical materials. To the superficial listener he probably sounds superficial. But those aware of musical refinements cannot help admire the transparent texture, the clarity of thought, the well-shaped proportions. Together they constitute a kind of Fauré magic that is difficult to analyze but lovely to hear.   [16]

RACHMANINOFF

From the University of New Hampshire lecture

Rachmaninoff's characteristic tone is one of self-pity and self-indulgence tinged with a definite melancholia. As a fellow human being I can sympathize with an artist whose distempers produced such music, but as a listener my stomach won't take it. I grant you his technical adroitness, but even here the technique adopted by the composer was old-fashioned in his own day. I also grant his ability to write long and singing melodic lines, but when these are embroidered with figuration, the musical substance is watered down, emptied of significance.   [17]

RAVEL

From Music and Imagination

What a pity that Ravel never wrote a treatise on orchestration! The first precept would have been: no doubling allowed, except in the full orchestral tutti. In other words, discover again the purity of the individual hue. And when you mix your pure colors be sure to mix them with exactitude, for only in that way can you hope to obtain the optimum of delicate or dazzling timbres. An instinctual knowledge of the potentiality of each instrument plus a balanced calculation of their combined effect helps to explain, in part, the orchestral delights of the later Ravel scores. Debussy, by comparison, was less precise in his orchestral workmanship, depending on his personal sensitivity for obtaining subtle balances, and as a consequence his scores need careful adjustment on the part of orchestra and conductor.   [18]

SESSIONS

From a review for Modern Music of a concert in London, 1930

The [First Piano] Sonata . . . is not merely an example of perfected technique; it is music of character. Sessions adopts a "universal" style, a style without any of the earmarks of obvious nationalism, and within this "universality" he is able to express an individuality robust and direct, simple and tender, and of a special sensitivity. Peculiarly characteristic is a certain quiet melancholy one finds in the middle section of the slow movement, a melancholy neither sentimental nor depressing in effect, but lyrical and profound. To perceive this personality, the listener must have an acquaintance with the music; no cursory examination will suffice. To know the work well is to have the firm conviction that Sessions has presented us with a cornerstone upon which to base an American music.   [19]

CHÁVEZ

From American Composers on American Music, 1933

Carlos Chávez is one of the best examples I know of a thoroughly contemporary composer. Without consciously attempting to be "modern," his music indubitably succeeds in belonging to our own age. This is not so merely because he can on occasion contrive intricate rhythms, or because he prefers linear to vertical writing, or because he composes ballets rather than operas. These things alone do not constitute modern music. But Chávez is essentially of our own day because he uses his composer's gift for the expression of objective beauty of universal significance rather than as a mere means of self-expression. Composing to him is a natural function, like eating or sleeping. His music is not a substitute for living but a manifestation of life. [20]

CAGE

From an essay in The New Music Lover's Handbook, 1973

How one reacts to Cage's ideas seems to me largely to depend on one's own personal temperament. Those who envisage art as a bulwark against the irrationality of man's nature, and as a monument to his constructive powers, will have no part of the Cagean aesthetic. But those who enjoy teetering on the edge of chaos will clearly be attracted. [21]

BRITTEN

From an article in Notes, March 1947

I know of no other composer alive today who writes music with such phenomenal flair. Other composers write with facility, but Britten's facility is breath-taking. He combines an absolutely solid technical equipment with a reckless freedom in handling the more complex compositional textures. The whole thing is carried off with an abandon and verve that are irresistible. The resultant music may not always be of the best quality, but it is certainly of a unique quality—for there is no one in contemporary music who is remotely like him. [22]

OBSERVATIONS AND OPINIONS

It is quite evident that there is no further revolution possible in the harmonic sphere, none, at any rate, so long as we confine ourselves to the tempered scale and normal division by half tones. There is no such thing any longer as an inadmissible chord, or melody, or rhythm—given the proper context, of course. Contemporary practice has firmly established that fact. (*Music and Imagination*) [23]

Music is in a continual state of becoming. (*Music and Imagination*) [24]

I don't at all mind actively disliking a piece of contemporary music, but in order to feel happy about it I must consciously understand why I dislike it. Otherwise it remains in my mind as unfinished business. (University of New Hampshire lecture) [25]

I wouldn't want to be thought of as a mere purveyor of Americana . . . nice as that may be from one aspect. There are other things in the world besides Americana that interest me. (*Soundpieces*) [26]

Ruth Crawford Seeger

1901–1953

A love of American folk music led Seeger to publish several collections of folk songs, including two that reflected her interest in young children. Her own compositions, which are few in number, are of a very different nature, rigorously dissonant and often daringly experimental. She was precociously talented and began teaching at the School of Musical Arts in Jacksonville, Florida, while still in her teens. She studied composition with the ethnomusicologist Charles Seeger, whom she later married.

A "CREDO"

From a letter to Edgard Varèse,
Chevy Chase, Maryland, May 29, 1948

One reason I have been late in answering is, that you asked for a kind of "credo." I found that a little hard, for I am still not sure whether the road I have been following the last dozen years is a main road or a detour. I have begun to feel, the past year or two, that it is the latter—a detour, but a very important one to me, during which I have descended from stratosphere onto a solid well-traveled highway, folded my wings and breathed good friendly dust as I traveled along in and out of the thousands of fine traditional folktunes which I have been hearing and singing and transcribing from field-recordings, for books and for pleasure. Until a year or so ago I had felt so at home among this (to me) new found music that I thought maybe this was what I wanted most. I listened to nothing else, and felt somewhat like a ghost when my compositions were spoken of. I answered no letters pertaining to them; requests for scores and biographical data were stuck in drawers. There were, of course, occasional periods during which I returned to composition, as for instance when CBS wanted works for orchestra utilizing folk material for performance on the "School of the Air." . . . But for years the only instrument in the house was a guitar, a modern dulcimer, and a special slow speed phonograph for transcription of folk recordings.

Whether I ever unfold the wings and make a start toward the stratosphere and how much of the dust of the road will still cling to me, is an interesting question, at least to me. If I do, I will probably pull the road up with me.

As for a "credo" typifying my music of the type of [the] String Quartet and Three Songs for Contralto and Orchestra, which ISCM chose for [the] Amsterdam festival back in 1933, I could mention a few points about which I felt strongly. And I still feel strongly about them. I believe when I write more music these elements will be there, or at least striven for:

Clarity of melodic line
Avoidance of rhythmic stickiness
Rhythmic independence between parts
Feeling of tonal and rhythmic center

Experiment with various means of obtaining, at the same time, organic unity and various sorts of dissonance.

As to works which I consider most representative, I am inclined to choose the String Quartet (1931). It is the slow movement of this quartet which was recorded on New Music Recordings, a copy of which Mrs. Varèse says you have. I am sending the score of this quartet, with the third and fourth movements analyzed as to tone, rhythm, form, and dynamics. I would like to mention that the recording was made at rather short notice, and that therefore the counterpoint of the crescendos, mentioned in the analysis, is not well heard on the recording.   {1}

CHAPTER TWELVE

Dmitri Shostakovich

Olivier Messiaen

Elliott Carter

John Cage

Milton Babbitt

Leonard Bernstein

Dmitri Shostakovich
1906–1975

To an extraordinary extent the story of Shostakovich's life is the story of his interactions with the Soviet government, which recognized him as one of the country's greatest artists but feared and mistrusted his independence of mind. He could never be certain how his music would be viewed by the authorities, or what humiliations and punishments might lie in store for him. At the same time, he responded to official pressures with either a sullen indifference or a strictly superficial compliance, inwardly preserving a spirit of resistance. This phenomenon may be observed in his letters, where Shostakovich sometimes makes an obsequious display of respect for a public figure or ideology.

MODESTY AND PRETENSION

From a letter to Isaac Glikman,* Moscow, February 26, 1960

I don't think that either self-deprecation or self-aggrandizement is among the defining qualities of an artist. Of course, "modesty is the best quality of a Bolshevik," as comrade Stalin has taught us. But, after all, Beethoven could have been forgiven if his symphonies had gone to his head. Gretchaninoff could also be forgiven if his *Dobrinya nikititch* went to his head.† But neither one could be forgiven for writing a piece that was amoral, servile, the work of a flunky. I think the oratorio composer‡ will be rewarded, if only because he has joined the ranks of such masters as [the authors] Kotchetov, Sofronov, Simonov, and other distinguished exponents of Socialist Realist art.

There are pretensions and then there are pretensions. But the pretensions and arrogance of a Beethoven (if indeed he was really guilty of such things) are a good deal more forgivable than the pretensions and arrogance of a Bulgarin, the author of [the novel] *Ivan Vyguin*.   [1]

From Solomon Volkov's
Testimony: The Memoirs of Dmitri Shostakovich, *1979*

MUSIC AND MEANING

I am horrified by people who think the commentaries to a symphony are more important than the symphony. What counts with them is a large number of brave words—and the music itself can be pathetic and woebegone. This is real perversion. I don't need brave words on music and I don't think anyone does. We need

---

* Glikman (b. 1911) was a literary critic who taught at the Leningrad Conservatory and was one of Shostakovich's close friends.

† Alexander Gretchaninoff (1864–1956) was best known for his sacred music, written in a conservative tradition. Since 1946 he had been a United States citizen. Shostakovich thought his opera *Dobrinya nikititch* mediocre.

‡ It is not known to whom this refers.

brave music. I don't mean brave in the sense that there will be charts instead of notes, I mean brave because it is truthful. Music in which the composer expresses his thoughts truthfully, and does it in such a way that the greatest possible number of decent citizens in his country and other countries will recognize and accept that music, thereby understanding his country and people. That is the meaning of composing music, as I see it.   [2]

Meaning in music—that must sound very strange for most people. Particularly in the West. It's here in Russia that the question is usually posed: What was the composer trying to say, after all, with this musical work? What was he trying to make clear? The questions are naïve, of course, but despite their naïveté and crudity, they definitely merit being asked. And I would add to them, for instance: Can music attack evil? Can it make man stop and think? Can it cry out and thereby draw man's attention to various vile acts to which he has grown accustomed? To the things he passes without any interest?   [3]

"Why Russian Composers Write So Little"

Borodin's apartment was a madhouse. I'm not exaggerating; this is not a poetic simile, so popular in our times, as in "Our communal apartment is a madhouse." No, Borodin's place was a madhouse without similes or metaphors. He always had a bunch of relatives living with him, or just poor people, or visitors who took sick and even—there were cases—went mad. Borodin fussed over them, treated them, took them to hospitals, and then visited them there.

That's how a Russian composer lives and works. Borodin wrote in snatches. Naturally, there was someone sleeping in every room, on every couch, and on the floors. He didn't want to disturb them with the piano. Rimsky-Korsakov would visit Borodin and ask, "Have you written anything?" Borodin would reply, "I have." And it would turn out to be another letter in defense of women's rights. And the same jokes came up with the orchestration of *Prince Igor.* "Did you transpose that section?" "Yes. From the piano to the desk." And then people wonder why Russian composers write so little.   [4]

Meyerbeer

*From a remark to Isaac Glikman, July 4, 1966**

That's undoubtedly true, but there's so much trash in Meyerbeer! The real geniuses know where their writing has to be good and where they can get away with some mediocrity.   [5]

From Testimony

Wagner and Publicity

I felt differently toward Wagner at different stages of my life. He wrote some pages of genius, and a lot of very good music, and a lot of average music. But Wag-

* Responding to Glikman's assertion that act 4 of *Les Huguenots* was as good as the best moments in Verdi.

ner knew how to peddle his goods. The composer-publicity man is a type I found alien; it is certainly not in the tradition of Russian music. That may be the reason why Russian music is not as popular in the West as it should be. Glinka, our first professional composer, was also the first to say, replying to Meyerbeer, "I do not hawk my own works." And that was so. Not like Meyerbeer.

And then there was Musorgsky, who refused to go to see Liszt despite all his invitations. Liszt planned to give him marvelous publicity, but Musorgsky preferred to remain in Russia and compose. He was not a practical man. . . .

Of the major Russian composers, only two have known how to sell themselves, Stravinsky and Prokofiev. But it's no accident that both are composers of a new era, and in a sense children, even though adoptive ones, of Western culture. Their love and taste for publicity, I feel, keep Stravinsky and Prokofiev from being thoroughly Russian composers. There's some flaw in their personalities, a loss of some very important moral principles. [6]

MAHLER

Studying Mahler changed many things in my tastes as a composer. Mahler and Berg are my favorite composers even today, as opposed to Hindemith, say, or Krenek or Milhaud, whom I liked when I was young but cooled toward rapidly. [7]

GLAZUNOV; RECOLLECTIONS OF LISZT

Glazunov's erudition in music history was outstanding for those days. He knew, as few others did, the wonderful music of the great contrapuntalists of the Flemish and Italian schools. It's only nowadays that everyone is so smart and no one doubts the genius and viability fifteenth- and sixteenth-century music. But in those days, let's be frank, the picture was completely different; that music was hidden beneath seven seals. Even Rimsky-Korsakov felt that music began with Mozart, and Haydn was dubious; Bach was considered a boring composer. What, then, of the pre-Bach period? For my comrades it was nothing but a desert.

——— ᛘ ———

Glazunov was the first to convince me that a composer must make the performers submit to his will and not the other way around. If the composer doesn't need a triple or quadruple complement of brass instruments for his artistic vision, that's one thing. But if he starts thinking about practical matters, economic considerations, that's bad. The composer must orchestrate in the way he conceived his work and not simplify his orchestration to please the performers, Glazunov used to say. And for instance, I still feel that Stravinsky was mistaken in doing new orchestral editions of *Firebird* and *Petrushka,* because these reflected financial, economic, and practical considerations.

Glazunov insisted that composing ballets was beneficial because it developed your technique. Later I learned that he was right about that, as well.

——— ᛘ ———

Glazunov was an admirer of Liszt, whom he had met in Weimar, I believe. Liszt played Beethoven for him. Glazunov liked to tell about the interpretation and juxtapose Liszt's playing to Anton Rubinstein's. Glazunov often referred to Rubinstein when he spoke of piano timbres and quoted him as saying, "You think that the piano is one instrument. It's really a hundred." But in general, he didn't like the way Rubinstein played, and preferred Liszt's manner.

In Glazunov's telling, Liszt's manner differed vastly from what we are used to imagining as such. When we hear the name we usually picture banging and ballyhoo, gloves tossed in the air, and so on. But Glazunov said that Liszt played simply and accurately and transparently. Of course, this was the late Liszt, so to speak, and he wasn't performing on stage but playing at home, where he didn't have to impress assorted women and young ladies.

The sonata in question, as I recall, was Beethoven's C-sharp minor and Glazunov said that Liszt played it steadily and with control and that the tempos were extremely moderate. Liszt revealed all the "inner" voices, which Glazunov liked very much.   [8]

SCRIABIN

[Sollertinsky] shared my opinion that Scriabin knew as much about orchestration as a pig about oranges. Personally, I think all of Scriabin's symphonic poems—the "Divine," and the "Ecstasy," and "Prometheus"—are gibberish.   [9]

STRAVINSKY

From a letter to Isaac Glikman, Moscow, September 9, 1971

I am in perfect agreement with you about Stravinsky's *Conversations*. The only justification for these reflections might be that he said whatever was on his mind at the time and then signed it without any editing, just to be done with it.

He's not the only person to do such things.

I revere Stravinsky the composer.

I have nothing but contempt for Stravinsky the thinker.*   [10]

From Testimony

Stravinsky gave me a lot. It was interesting to listen to him and it was interesting to look at the scores. I liked *Mavra*, I remember, and *L'Histoire du soldat,* particularly the first parts; it's too boring to listen to the work in its entirety. It's fashionable now to speak disparagingly of Stravinsky's opera *The Rake's Progress,* and that's a shame. The work is deeper than a first glance would lead you to believe. But we've become lazy and lack curiosity.

---

* Shostakovich had expressed more than once his admiration for Stravinsky's music. He even had Stravinsky's portrait on his desk in Moscow. But he couldn't stomach Stravinsky's egotism and his disregard for artists who had been persecuted while Stalin was in power. [Glikman]

I have special memories of the *Symphony of Psalms*. I transcribed it for four-hand piano as soon as I got my hands on the score, and showed it to my students. I must note that it has its problems in terms of construction. It's crudely worked out, crudely. The seams show. In that sense the *Symphony in Three Movements* is stronger. In general, Stravinsky often has this problem; his construction sticks out like a scaffolding. There's no flow, no natural bridges. I find it irritating, but on the other hand, this clarity makes it easier for the listener. That must be one of the secrets of Stravinsky's popularity.

I like his violin concerto, and I love his mass—that's marvelous music. Fools think that Stravinsky began composing more poorly toward the end. That's calumny and envy speaking. To my taste, it's just the reverse. It's the early works I like less—for instance, *Le Sacre du printemps*. It's rather crude, so much of it calculated for external effect and lacking substance. I can say the same for *The Firebird*, I really don't like it very much.

Still, Stravinsky is the only composer of our century whom I call great without any doubt. Perhaps he didn't know how to do everything, and not everything that he did is equally good, but the best delights me.   [11]

Stravinsky and I are very different people. I found it difficult to talk to him. We were from different planets.   [12]

PROKOFIEV

I doubt that a final summing up of Prokofiev's music is possible now. The time hasn't come for it yet, I imagine. . . .

So many of his works that I liked once upon a time seem duller now.

A new period seemed to begin in his work just before his death; he seemed to be feeling his way along new paths. Perhaps this music would have been more profound than what we have, but it was only a beginning and we don't know the continuation.   [13]

Prokofiev had the soul of a goose; he always had a chip on his shoulder.   [14]

BRITTEN

From a letter to Isaac Glikman, Zhukovka, August 1, 1963

I've received a recording of Benjamin Britten's *War Requiem*. I've played it repeatedly and I can't get over the genius in this work. It's on the same level as Mahler's *Das Lied von der Erde* and other great works of humanity. When I hear the Britten *War Requiem*, my life becomes more cheerful, more joyful than ever.   [15]

PREMIERE OF THE FIRST SYMPHONY

From a letter to his mother, July 6, 1926

[At the rehearsal] I listened and was in despair: instead of three trumpets there were only two, instead of three timpani, only two, and instead of a grand piano a revolting, rattling old upright. . . . At last it came to the concert. . . . Malko stood at the conductor's desk, and somewhere close at hand some dogs started to bark loudly. They went on barking for an awfully long time, and the longer they went on the louder they got. The public was beside itself with laughter. Malko stood there motionless on stage. At last the dogs stopped barking. Malko started. The trumpet (there were three players at the concert) immediately bungled his first phrase. He was followed by the bassoon playing piles of wrong notes (we stumbled on an exceptionally awful bassoon player here). After about ten bars, the dogs started barking again. And throughout the first movement the dogs often added their solo. The orchestra barely got through the first movement. Then the second movement started. In the first two bars, however much Malko had gone over them at rehearsals, the celli and double basses made a terrible hashup. Then the clarinet started playing slower than the strings. . . .

It was over at last. The applause started, and the composer was called. I didn't want to take a bow, but Malko started clapping in my direction (I was sitting in the front row). It was awkward not to go. So I took a bow, and then another one, and then clambered on to the stage and bowed again. Outwardly it was successful, but of course the audience didn't understand anything and only clapped from inertia. But there was no booing. [16]

BOLT

From a letter to Ivan Sollertinsky, February 1930

Comrade Smirnov has read me the libretto for a ballet, *The New Machine*. Its theme is extremely relevant. There once was a machine. Then it broke down (problem of material decay). Then it was mended (problem of amortization), and at the same time they bought a new one. Then everybody dances around the new machine. Apotheosis. This all takes up three acts. [17]

FIFTH SYMPHONY

From Testimony

I will never believe that there are only idiots everywhere. They must be wearing masks—a survival tactic that permits you to maintain a minimal decency. Now everyone says, "We didn't know, we didn't understand. We believed Stalin. We were tricked, ah, how cruelly we were tricked."

I feel anger at such people. Who was it who didn't understand, who was tricked? An illiterate old milkmaid? The deaf-mute who shined shoes on Ligovsky Prospect? No, they seemed to be educated people—writers, composers, actors. The people who applauded the Fifth Symphony. I'll never believe that a man who understood nothing could feel the Fifth Symphony. Of course they understood, they understood what was happening around them and they understood what the Fifth was about.

And this makes it even harder for me to compose. It must sound odd: it's hard to compose because the audience understands your music. It's probably the other way around in most cases: when they understand it's easier to write. But here everything is back to front, because the larger the audience, the more informers there are.   [18]

I think that it is clear to everyone what happens in the Fifth. The rejoicing is forced, created under threat, as in *Boris Godunov*. It's as if someone were beating you with a stick and saying, "Your business is rejoicing, your business is rejoicing," and you rise, shaky, and go marching off, muttering, "Our business is rejoicing, our business is rejoicing."

What kind of apotheosis is that? You have to be a complete oaf not to hear that.   [19]

SEVENTH SYMPHONY; OTHER SYMPHONIES

Remark to Isaac Glikman, August 1941

I don't know what will become of this piece.

Our brave critics will no doubt charge me with imitating Ravel's *Boléro*. Too bad—this is how I hear war.   [20]

From Testimony

Is a musical concept born consciously or unconsciously? It's difficult to explain. The process of writing a new work is long and complicated. Sometimes you start writing and then change your mind. It doesn't always work the way you thought it would. If it's not working, leave the composition the way it is—and try to avoid your earlier mistakes in he next one. That's my personal point of view, my manner of working. Perhaps it stems from a desire to do as much as possible. When I hear that a composer has eleven versions of one symphony, I think involuntarily, How many new works could he have composed in that time?

No, naturally I sometimes return to an old work; for instance, I made many changes in the score of my opera *Katerina Izmailova*.

I wrote my Seventh Symphony, the "Leningrad," very quickly. I couldn't not write it. War was all around. I had to be with the people, I wanted to create the image of our country at war, capture it in music. From the first days of the war, I sat down at the piano and started work. I worked intensely. I wanted to write about our time, about my contemporaries who spared neither strength nor life in the name of Victory Over the Enemy.

I've heard so much nonsense about the Seventh and Eighth Symphonies. It's amazing how long-lived these stupidities are. I'm astounded sometimes by how lazy people are when it comes to thinking. Everything that was written about those symphonies in the first few days is repeated without any changes to this very day, even though there has been time to do some thinking. After all, the war ended a long time ago, almost thirty years.

Thirty years ago you could say that they were military symphonies, but symphonies are rarely written to order, that is, if they are worthy to be called symphonies.

I do write quickly, it's true, but I think about my music for a comparatively long time, and until it's complete in my head I don't begin setting it down. Of course, I do make mistakes. Say, I imagine that the composition will have one movement, and then I see that it must be continued. That happened with the Seventh, as a matter of fact, and with the Thirteenth. And sometimes it's the reverse. I think that I've started a new symphony, when actually things come to a halt after one movement. That happened with *The Execution of Stepan Razin,* which is now performed as a symphonic poem. . . .

Naturally, fascism is repugnant to me, but not only German fascism; any form of it is repugnant. Nowadays people like to recall the prewar period as an idyllic time, saying that everything was fine until Hitler bothered us. Hitler is a criminal, that's clear, but so is Stalin.

I feel eternal pain for those who were killed by Hitler, but I feel no less pain for those killed on Stalin's orders. I suffer for everyone who was tortured, shot, or starved to death. There were millions of them in our country before the war with Hitler began.

The war brought much new sorrow and much new destruction, but I haven't forgotten the terrible prewar years. That is what all my symphonies, beginning with the Fourth, are about, including the Seventh and Eighth. . . .

The majority of my symphonies are tombstones. Too many of our people died and were buried in places unknown to anyone, not even their relatives. It happened to many of my friends. . . .

I think constantly of those people, and in almost every major work I try to remind others of them.   [21]

EIGHTH SYMPHONY

From a letter to Isaac Glikman, Moscow, December 21, 1949

During my illness (or rather illnesses) I got out the score of one of my compositions. I looked it over from first note to last. I was struck by how good it was. It seemed to me that, having written it, I could feel proud and be at peace. I was overwhelmed at the idea that, of all people, *I* was the composer.   [22]

EIGHTH QUARTET

From a letter to Isaac Glikman, Zhukovka, July 19, 1960

While there [East Germany] I was provided with ideal working conditions. I stayed in the resort town of Görlitz. . . . The good working conditions were fruitful: while I was there, I composed my Eighth Quartet. There was really no point in racking my brains trying to write film music; at the time I just couldn't bring myself to do it. Instead, I wrote this quartet that's ideologically suspect and of no use to anyone. I figured that no one would think of composing a work honoring me after I'm dead, so I'd better do it myself. The title page might read: "Dedicated to the memory of the composer himself." The quartet's main theme is taken from my initials—D. S. C. H. [D, E-flat, C, B, in German nomenclature]. I've also used themes from other works of mine as well as the revolutionary song "Tormented by Grievous Bondage." The earlier themes are from my First and Eighth

Symphonies, the Piano Trio, the [First] Cello Concerto, and from my opera, *Lady Macbeth of Mtsensk*. There's also a nod to Wagner (the funeral music from *Götterdämmerung*) and Tchaikovsky (the second theme from the first movement of the Sixth Symphony). A real crazy quilt! The pseudo-tragedy of this quartet is such that, while I was composing it, the tears just kept streaming down like urine after a half-dozen beers. When I got back home, I tried playing it once or twice [at the piano] and each time I started weeping all over again. But this time, not so much from my pseudo-tragedy, but in amazement of its splendid formal structure. Of course, the self-satisfaction implicit in that will no doubt soon be followed by my intoxication on feelings of self-criticism. [23]

FIFTEENTH QUARTET

From a remark to the violist Fyodor Druzhinin, July 5, 1975

Play [the first movement] so that flies drop dead in mid-air, and the audience starts leaving the hall from sheer boredom. [24]

WORK HABITS

From Testimony

I'll admit that writing doesn't always come, but I'm totally against walking around looking at the sky when you're experiencing a block, waiting for inspiration to strike you. Tchaikovsky and Rimsky-Korsakov didn't like each other and agreed on very few things, but they were of one opinion on this: you had to write constantly. If you can't write a major work, write minor trifles. If you can't write at all, orchestrate something. I think Stravinsky felt the same way. [25]

As a rule, I hear the score and write it down in ink, finished copy—without rough drafts or studies—and I'm not saying this to brag. In the final analysis, everyone composes as best suits him, but I've always seriously warned my students against picking out tunes on the piano. I had a near-fatal case of this disease, improviser's itch, in childhood.

Musorgsky is a tragic example of the dangers of piano composing. Very tragic—while he plinked away, so much great music was never written down! Of the many works about which only stories remain, I am most tormented by the opera *Biron*. What a piece of Russian history! It has villainy and a foreign martinet. He showed parts of it to friends, he did. They tried to talk him into writing it down, but he replied stubbornly, "I've got it firmly in my head." What you have in your head, put down on paper. The head is a fragile vessel. [26]

PHYSICAL AND PSYCHOLOGICAL CONDITIONS

From a letter to Isaac Glikman, Moscow, January 2, 1945

My plans for 1945 are unclear. I'm not writing music because my living conditions are deplorable. From six in the morning to six at night, I'm deprived of two basic needs for human comfort: light and water. The hardest time is from three to six p.m., because it is already dark by then. I can't write by oil lamp. The darkness gets on my nerves. There's apparently no reason to expect the situation to get any better. [27]

From a letter to Isaac Glikman, Moscow, December 12, 1948

Lately I've been worn out. It takes all I have to pull myself together to write the music for the film *Meeting on the Elbe*. I can't see how this score is ever going to get finished. I'm not feeling well physically, which doesn't help the flow of creative energy. . . . Starting last week, or a little before that, I've been suffering a sudden onset of old age, and the aging process has accelerated at an incredible rate. Unfortunately, with this physical aging comes an end to the youthful soul. Or maybe this is all just the result of overwork. I've written, over the last year, quite a few film scores. It keeps me alive but extremely tired. [28]

"MUDDLE INSTEAD OF MUSIC"

Remark to Isaac Glikman, January 29, 1974*

Nowadays, there's nothing so terrifying about the article. For years, it was used to instill fear, to threaten. Stalin got what he wanted. Not only was it forbidden to speak out against this article, but you couldn't even reveal the slightest reservation about it. Anyone who took issue with it was committing a sin against the religion of Stalinism. And a sinner could only be saved by repenting of his sin. As you recall, the authorities called upon me to repent and redeem myself. And I refused. [29]

OBSERVATIONS AND CONVICTIONS

Remark reported in Khentova's Shostakovich

If a composer sets himself the aim of writing purely dodecaphonic music at all costs, then he is artificially limiting himself. But using elements of this system can be fully justified when dictated by the actual compositional concept. [30]

From a letter to the composer and theorist Boleslav Yavorsky, April 16, 1925

I passionately love music. I have dedicated myself completely to music, or it would be more correct to say that I will dedicate myself completely to music. There are no other joys in life apart from music. For me, all of life is music. [31]

---

* This date was the thirty-eighth anniversary of the famous review "Muddle Instead of Music," denouncing Shostakovich and inaugurating a long period of official disfavor. The article appeared directly after Stalin attended a performance of *Lady Macbeth of Mtsensk*.

From a letter to the stage director Nikolai Smolich, October 30, 1930

I am more than ever convinced that in every piece of music theater the music must play the main, and not the supporting role. [32]

From a letter to Isaac Glikman, Miskhor, August 28, 1955

A great piece of music is beautiful regardless of how it is performed. Any prelude or fugue of Bach can be played at any tempo, with or without rhythmic nuances, and it will still be great music. That's how music should be written, so that no one, no matter how philistine, can ruin it. [33]

From an article in the New York Times, *October 25, 1959*

A creative artist works on his next composition because he is not satisfied with his previous one. When he loses a critical attitude toward his own work, he ceases to be an artist. [34]

Olivier Messiaen
1908–1992

From 1930 until his death, Messiaen was organist at Trinity Church in Paris. This was interrupted only during World War II, when for two years Messiaen was held as a prisoner of war in Görlitz. While in the prison camp he composed and gave the premiere of his Quartet for the End of Time. *He was also a dedicated teacher, holding a position at the Paris Conservatory from 1948 on. Viewed as a father figure by postwar avant-garde composers across Europe, Messiaen also continued the long and fairly conservative French tradition of composer-organists, which extended back through his teacher Marcel Dupré to Widor, Fauré, Franck, the Couperins, and even earlier. His defining influences—fascinations with birdsong and Hindu rhythms, a mystical Catholicism—are distinctly personal.*

"THE CHARM OF IMPOSSIBILITIES"
Opening words of Technique of My Musical Language, *1944*

Knowing that music is a language, we shall seek at first to make melody "speak." The melody is a point of departure. May it remain sovereign! And whatever may be the complexities of our rhythms and our harmonies, they shall not draw it along in their wake, but, on the contrary, shall obey it as faithful servants; the harmony especially shall always remain the "true," which exists in a latent state in the melody, has always been the outcome of it. We shall not reject the old rules of harmony and of form; let us remember them constantly, whether to observe them, or to augment them, or to add to them some others still older (those of plainchant and Hindu rhythmics) or more recent (those suggested by Debussy and all contemporary music). One point will attract our attention at the outset: the charm of impossibilities. It is a glistening music we seek, giving to the aural sense voluptuously refined pleasures. At the same time, this music should be able to express some noble sentiments (and especially the most noble of all, the religious sentiments exalted by the theology and the truths of our Catholic faith). This charm, at once voluptuous and contemplative, resides particularly in certain mathematical impossibilities of the modal and rhythmic domains. Modes that cannot be transposed beyond a certain number of transpositions, because one always falls again into the same notes; rhythms that cannot be used in retrograde, because in such a case one finds the same order of values again—these are two striking impossibilities. . . . Immediately one notices the analogy of these two impossibilities and how they complement one another, the rhythms realizing in the horizontal direction (retrogradation) what the modes realize in the vertical direction (transposition). . . . After this relation, there is another between values added to rhythms and notes added to chords. . . . Finally, we superpose our rhythms . . . we also superpose our modes.   [1]

From Claude Samuel's Conversations with Olivier Messiaen, *1967*

RHYTHM AND WESTERN CLASSICAL COMPOSERS

The classics, in the Western sense of the term, were bad rhythmicians, or, rather, composers who knew nothing of rhythm. In Bach's music there are harmonic colors, and extraordinary contrapuntal craftsmanship; it's marvelous and inspired, but there's no rhythm. . . . The explanation is this: in these works an uninterrupted succession of equal note values plunges the listener into a state of beatific satisfaction; nothing thwarts his pulse, breathing, or heartbeats. Thus he is very much at ease, receives no shock, and all this appears to him to be perfectly "rhythmic." . . .

The greatest rhythmician in classical music is certainly Mozart. Mozartian rhythm dons a kinematic aspect, but it belongs above all to the field of accent, deriving from word and speech. With Mozart, one distinguishes between masculine and feminine groups. The first are in a single volley, coming to a dead stop, just like the male body and character; the feminine groups (more supple, like the female body and character) are the more important and characteristic, including a preparatory period called the "anacrusis," a more or less intense apex which is the "accent," and a more or less weak falling back (the "mute" or "flexional ending," formed of one or several note values). Mozart continually used these rhythmic groups, which have so great an importance in his work that, if the exact placing of the accents is not observed, Mozartian music is completely destroyed. This is why so many bad interpretations of Mozart are heard, for most musicians are not sufficiently educated in rhythm to discern the true position of the accents.   [2]

BIRDS

It's probable that in the artistic hierarchy birds are the greatest musicians existing on our planet.

——— ♪ ———

Each species has its own specific song. There again one may distinguish several categories. First, the birds that have an innate song, that is to say that they are born with a certain style and aesthetic, and, as soon as one hears them, one says right away, "That's a blackbird! That's a thrush! That's a nightingale!", just as at a concert of classical music you can say, "That's Mozart! That's Debussy! That's Berlioz!"

On the other hand, some birds haven't this innate song and are obliged to learn it rather painfully from their parents. A very common and virtuosic bird, the finch, has no innate song; young finches work under the direction of their father and generally have much difficulty in arriving at the end of the victorious roulade they compose. It must be acknowledged that it's a difficult song to sing, containing repeated notes, then a roll, slow at first but accelerating wildly and getting louder and louder. This accelerando ends in a victorious codetta, which may descend or ascend, following the regional or dialectical endings. It's extremely difficult to get right, and the young finches may be heard stumbling over the final notes without being able to bring off this rare coda.

The resemblances between one species and another should also be pointed out; thus the willow warbler also has an accelerando on a rolled note, but, instead of having the victorious codetta of the finch, it has a dying fall, slowing and sad, and above all it doesn't learn only a single codetta but ceaselessly invents new ones.

———— ♪ ————

Birds have extraordinary virtuosity no tenor or coloratura soprano could ever equal, for they possess a peculiar vocal organ, a "syrinx," which allows them to perform rolls and very small intervals, and to sing extremely fast. [3]

LITURGICAL MUSIC

From an address at the Conférence de Notre Dame, December 4, 1977

There is only one [liturgical music]: plainsong. Only plainsong possesses all at once the purity, the joy, the lightness necessary for the soul's flight toward Truth. Unfortunately—with the exception of some monks in the monasteries, some great theoreticians like Dom Mocquereau, and some professional musicians who still know how to read it—plainsong is not well known. It is not well known mainly because it is not sung well. And the first mistake committed by our immediate ancestors was its harmonization. Plainsong was written in an epoch where the obstruction of conventional chords, of complexes of sounds, and even of simple instrumental support were unknown. [4]

WAGNER AND A UNIVERSAL MUSICAL LANGUAGE

From a panel discussion, Düsseldorf, December 7, 1968

It seems to me that only one person ever came near to it [a universal musical language]: Richard Wagner, who with his leitmotiv not only, as was long believed, tried to depict objects and ideas, but also created a set of basic symbols that enabled him to speak directly to his public, really to speak, and that without the support of the text, or of actors or decor or costumes—without any kind of assistance, quite simply with the "trick" of the leitmotiv. Whether or not this was successful is not important—but he was the only one who's tried it. Perhaps future searches for a universal language, for a kind of music that can speak, will take this direction, but that is outside the scope of aesthetic considerations. Aesthetics can't be the same for all composers—and furthermore, neither can technique.   [5]

BOULEZ

From Conversations

For me, Pierre Boulez is the greatest musician of his generation and, perhaps, of the half century. He's also the greatest composer of serial music; I'd even say he was the only one. He is, moreover, in a certain sense, my successor in the field of rhythm. Pierre Boulez took from me the idea of rhythmic unease and the idea of rhythmic research, and also the use of certain formulas deriving directly from Greek and Indian rhythms, although in an unavowed manner. Despite this, he is very far from my musical universe.   [6]

INDEPENDENCE AS A COMPOSER

From an address, Amsterdam, June 25, 1971

Freedom is a necessity for artists. By choosing its future, freedom creates a new past, and that's what builds us up. It's that, too, which determines the style of the artist, his characteristics, his signature. . . .

All the same, one has to understand the word "freedom" in its widest sense. The freedom about which I am speaking has nothing to do with fantasy, disorder, revolt, or indifference. It is a constructive freedom, which is arrived at through self-control, respect for others, a sense of wonder of that which is created, meditation on the mystery, and the search for Truth. This wonderful freedom is like a foretaste of the freedom of Heaven.   [7]

From the Düsseldorf panel discussion

COMPOSING USING BIRDSONG

Once the birdsong is written down, the real work begins; that is, it has to be worked into a piece, whether it be for piano, for orchestra, or whatever other instruments. To begin with, one has to have a great number of sketches in order to arrive at an ideal bird, for example, the song thrush—it's one of the loveliest birds and songsters in all Europe. It has a special style, which is distinguished in a somewhat magical way by tripartite repetitions: it sings its stanza three times in a row, and every time, the one differs from the others through a marked rhythm and a "timbre melody." That means that the tone color of each note is different and the rhythms vary with each stanza. The stanza is repeated three times; on the next day there'll be different stanzas, which will also be repeated three times, but then they're gone once and for all, one'll never hear them again. Therefore, one has to put together an ideal song thrush, after having heard hundreds of them, and to know all the possibilities of stanza creation, in order to condense these to a normal solo occupying the correspondingly short space of time. Following the difficulty of the rhythmic and melodic notation, which I try to execute as exactly as possible, comes a further difficulty: the reproduction of timbres. These tone colors are so extraordinary that no musical instrument can reproduce them. One needs combinations of instruments, and still more combinations or complexes of pitches. If I want to reproduce on the piano, let's say, the song of a garden warbler or a song thrush or a nightingale, I need to find a complex of pitches for every melody note. Each note of the melody is furnished with a chord that is intended to reproduce the timbre of that note. If we have an orchestra, not only is each note provided with a chord, but every chord also has a particular function within the orchestral sound, and even the change from one instrument to another helps toward reproducing the required timbre—as you see, it's very complicated work.   [8]

FOUR CONFLICTS

From Music and Color, *1986*

There have been four conflicts in my life as a composer, four eternal conflicts, constantly confirmed and wonderfully magnified by Saint François. The first is that, as a composer-believer, I speak of faith to atheists. How do you expect them to understand me? My second conflict is that I'm an ornithologist and speak of birds to people who live in cities, who have never wakened at four o'clock in the morning to hear the call of birds in the countryside. They see horrible pigeons in the streets and sparrows in the squares, but don't know what bird songs are. One proof among thousands: most critics have said that I've imitated chirping. Only sparrows chirp. . . .

Now here's my third conflict: when hearing sounds, I see colors in my mind's eye.* I announce it to the public, I repeat it to the press, I've explained it to my pupils, but no one believes me. No matter how much I put in my music—harmonies, sound complexes, and orchestration—listeners hear, but they see nothing.

As for my fourth conflict, it's less terrible, but it's based on a formidable misunderstanding: I am a rhythmician, and I'm eager to say so. You'll tell me that all composers should be rhythmicians, but this notion has been so neglected that I've had to add the word "rhythmician" alongside the expression "composer of music." Now, most people think that rhythm and the steady beat of a military march are one and the same, whereas rhythm is in fact an unequal element given to fluctuations, like the waves in the sea, the sound of the wind, or the shape of tree branches.

[9]

SEEING MUSIC AS COLORS

From an interview in Tempo, *March 1979*

Colors are very important to me because I have a gift—it's not my fault, it's just how I am—whenever I hear music, or even if I read music, I see colors. They cor-

---

* Messiaen repeatedly stated that his ability to visualize music was not the result of synethesia, a physical disorder involving the confusion of information from the optic and auditory nerves.

respond to the sounds, rapid colors which turn, mix, combine and move with the sounds. Like the sounds they are high, low, quick, long, strong, weak, etc. The colors do just what the sounds do. They are always changing, but they are marvelous and they reproduce themselves each time one repeats the same sound complex. It's a theory that's a bit complicated, but I'll explain how it works. Take a note, any note, and there is a corresponding color. If you change the note, even by a semitone, it's no longer the same color. With the twelve semitones the color never remains the same. But once you reach the octave, you have the original color again. It recommences with the high octaves and with the low octaves. In the higher octaves, it becomes progressively more diluted with white, and in the lower octaves, it is mixed with black so that it's darker.   [10]

Elliott Carter
b. 1908

Carter did not devote himself to music full time until he was twenty-one. His bachelor's degree was in literature, and he learned sufficient math, physics, and ancient Greek to teach these subjects at the college level. After studies with Nadia Boulanger he returned to the United States in 1935, holding a series of teaching posts and fellowships for the next three decades. Carter's ability to write music that is intricate and virtuosic yet also manifestly expressive has helped to make him one of the most highly respected and frequently performed American composers of his time, both in his own country and abroad. In spite of this renown, he has remained aware of the obstacles facing most contemporary composers—a topic that appears in many of his writings.

THE AMERICAN COMPOSER

From "The Milieu of the American Composer,"
Perspectives of New Music, *1962*

Having to face the continual uncertainty that surrounds his small, financially unprofitable, and but slightly respected artistic efforts, the American composer is almost forced into a position of affirmation if he is to compose at all. Professionally destructive efforts are scarcely meaningful in this situation, although exasperation with the poor quality of our mass entertainment is widespread and sometimes leads to great pessimism and rebellion. Indeed the tendency to adopt positions counter to those accepted in the society in which they live is characteristic of many contemporary artists and intellectuals, especially when faced with the low grade of mass culture. And this position leads the artist to reaffirm the traditions of Europe as a gesture of reaction against his society. A person with this point of view has, therefore, no inclination to turn to the almost nihilistic defiance so understandable among advanced thinkers and artists in Europe today. Nor does the American composer need to deny the value of experiment by holding to an equally nihilistic cultivation of naïveté. It is by carrying on the European tradition and by following the methods of some of its experiments in the different context of his own experience that our composer affirms his identity and the identity of American music.

Thus in America a composer of art music comes face to face with many of the most urgent problems of modern civilization. Living in a situation where routine, custom, and habit no longer insure the continuity of culture but where such culture needs to be continually retested and reaffirmed before a mass public apathetic to these interests, he fights a special kind of adventurous battle. The fact, for instance, that compositional skills are laborious to master well enough to promote the imaginative conceptions of the composer, and that these skills are still being learned at a time when they seem unimportant to a profession which has, under public pressure, been forced to devote its abilities to the performance of works of the past, makes the composer's struggle seem quixotic. Yet this struggle is entered into by more and more young people every year, and this small fraction of a small minority group—the music profession—whose importance is not generally accepted by a large enough part of our citizenry to provide adequate support, forces the profession to meet the very difficult challenge of constantly proving its worth. The fact that this struggle is increasingly carried out under the protection of the universities implies the danger, on the other hand, that music may be assimilated to other university disciplines that deal in historical, semantic, acoustical, or psychological research, and thus be destroyed as a public artistic communication. Once compositions are treated as illustrations or examples of general principles rather than for what they are in themselves they lose a large measure of their significance. On the other hand, so many people are becoming involved with this field that certainly some will constitute part of the future musical public who can influence the less trained members. In any case, the random development of music here, without the imposition of authoritarian and customary attitudes and tastes, will be the prime factor in molding our own music into something of its own, with a freshness, we hope, drawn from these very circumstances; and a quality, not necessarily more simplified or naïve, perhaps the very reverse of this, that exhibits a vivid sense of what it is to communicate through the sound medium itself.

Art music in America has been like a plant, transplanted in a new place that provides a very different environment from the one in which it originally developed. In this new situation, hitherto unrealized qualities inherent in its nature begin to appear, and the special challenge of trying to live and develop under new circumstances may produce a considerable mutation. The plant is sturdy, the environment strange to it, the desire for adaptation great, and the process of adaptation filled with difficulties which at times seem insurmountable and threatening to the life of the plant, yet its will to live and develop is very strong.   [1]

THE COMPOSER AND THE ORCHESTRA

From an essay in Robert Stephan Hines's
The Composer's Point of View, *1970*

Because it is difficult to get multiple performances with American symphony orchestras, since they are interested mainly in *premières*, composers do not write for this medium unless they are commissioned or have the stimulus of a prize contest. There is little satisfaction in a poorly rehearsed *première*. And, under the present rehearsal and performance situations, there are such absurdly small performance and royalty fees that the copying of the parts is seldom repaid except by potboilers. (No performance or royalty fees would be given if a number of us had not fought a bitter battle twenty-five years ago to try to establish what one would have thought was an obvious principle.) Prize contests do not solve the problem any better since the authority of juries is infrequently respected by musicians. . . .

Here is an example of what can happen at a prize contest: My *Holiday Overture* won a prize of $500, publication, and performance by one of the major symphonies, whose conductor was one of the jurors. The score and parts were taken from me, remained in the orchestra's library four years without ever being performed, and were then returned. I had no copy of the parts, and I could not get other performances during this time, for when I tried to withdraw the parts, the possibility of a performance that might take place very soon and which I might lose if the parts were not in the library was held before me. Finally, I sneaked the parts out without the librarian's knowing it, had them photostatted, and returned. From these parts the work got its first performance in Frankfurt, Germany, and later in Berlin with Serge [*sic*] Celibidache conducting. The American orchestra never knew of this. Why it held up the *Holiday Overture* I never learned, but the experience did not add to my desire to deal with American conductors and orchestras.   [2]

From an interview in Andrew Ford's Composer to Composer, *1991*

I feel that the orchestra is a lost cause: it's too expensive and too much trouble. If you write very original music, nowadays the orchestras in America haven't time to rehearse it. They try sometimes, and with a good deal of good will they can raise the thousands of dollars it takes to have the extra rehearsals. And then the public doesn't see why they should have bothered to do it when they hear the music. The two big pieces I've written—the *Concerto for Orchestra* and *A Symphony of Three Orchestras*—have seldom been performed in America and in almost every case not well.   [3]

From Flawed Words and Stubborn Sounds, *1971*

COMPOSITIONAL SYSTEMS AND MUSICAL SENSE

As I see it, there is in every case *first* of all a general desire for communication and only secondly a desire for what I call "making musical sense," which begins to employ a sort of rationalized or ordered system, and does so *only* to achieve the desired communication, which must therefore in every case be the prime and ultimate determinant of any musical system pretending to genuine *musical* rationality.

Now in my opinion a great many of the recent systems are not rational at all in this sense, which, as I see it, is the only possible sense the term can have in music. That is, these systems are perfectly fine as abstract schemata of one kind or another, but are often useless for musical purposes, simply because they don't have any particular relation to the composer's desire to communicate feelings and thoughts of many different kinds, which, as I say, are logically prior to the evolution of any system. This lack of relation to the composer's desire to communicate goes together with the fact that these systems lack any relation to the *listener's* psychology of musical hearing. The so-called "system" of tonal harmony was obviously not invented as a mechanically or arithmetically perfect system on paper—it was invented by constant *musical* experiment over many years by composers attempting to communicate something to intelligent listeners. If tonal harmony had been invented in a purely Pythagorean way, it would have been of extremely limited serviceability from any musical point of view, and that's how I feel about the many kinds of serial systems.

It's obvious that the real order and meaning of music is the one the listener *hears* with his ears. Whatever occult mathematical orders may exist on paper are not necessarily relevant to this in the least. Now it's true that in writing my own works I sometimes try quasi-"geometric" things in order to cut myself off from habitual ways of thinking about particular technical problems and to place myself in, so to speak, new terrain, which forces me to look around and find new kinds of ideas and solutions I might not have thought of otherwise. Nonetheless, if what I come up with by these methods is unsatisfactory from the point of view of what I think is interesting to *hear,* I throw it out without a second thought.   [4]

AUDIENCES

They were—and still are—in the position I was in as a little boy, when it comes to modern music—they aren't able to distinguish very much about any of [it]; they just know new music doesn't sound very much like Brahms, and that's about all, as far as I can see. In fact, I probably should have known better than to try writing works like my First Symphony and *Holiday Overture* in a deliberately restricted idiom—that is, in an effort to produce works that meant something to me as music and yet might, I hoped, be understandable to the general musical public I was trying to reach for a short period after writing *Pocahontas.* I did this out of a natural desire to write something many people could presumably grasp and enjoy easily at a time of social emergency, but I did so without appreciating just how serious was the audience paralysis engendered by this lack of interest in or familiarity with the new in any of its artistic forms. Thus I wrote music which escaped the average listener, despite what seemed to me its directness.   [5]

THE IDEAL LISTENER

The difficulty in much contemporary music is, of course, that most listeners are so unfamiliar with its vocabulary as to be unable to perceive events clearly and make the comparisons—even the initially quasi-subconscious ones—necessary to the development of a sense of musical continuity and, correlatively, of musical expectations on which the work depends for its effect.

Thus, as a serious composer, one has to write for a kind of intelligent and knowledgeable listener one seldom comes across in any number. But that the composer should nonetheless always try to think of the music he is writing, and of the means by which he is trying to achieve his communication, from the point of view of such an ideal listener remains no less paramount a requirement, in my opinion, simply because it seems to me that the real "composer" of any music is the listener who interprets it and makes sense of it—if any sense is to be made of it. And while the listener ideally should be as "good" as the composer, the composer himself, *if* he is to achieve his desired communication, must in every case be his own first ideal *listener*.   [6]

THE "CHARACTER-STRUCTURES" OF INSTRUMENTS

It's always seemed to me that instruments, in a certain sense, offer one materials for composition just by virtue of having, as they always do, built-in "character-structures," so to speak, which can be suggestive of musical possibilities both on the level of sonority and on that of actual musical behavior. If one pays no particular attention to this fact, then one automatically has in mind some other generalized idea of sound and musical character, which particular instruments are made to fit after the fact.

It's obvious, for example, that Stravinsky and Copland work at the piano when they compose and then transfer, in many cases, the percussive character of pianistically based ideas to, say, the orchestra, and that their musical conceptions are to a degree independent of their final instrumental incarnation. This was also the case, I understand, with Ravel, and was invariably true of composers in the Renaissance and much of the Baroque. In these periods the musical language was, so to speak, "indifferent" to the possibilities of differentiation of musical character that are latent in any group of instruments. It's really only with the Classical period that a repertoire of kinds of *écriture* related to the sonorities and technical peculiarities of particular instruments arises. This began to be used in a dramatic way by Mozart, particularly in his piano concertos, where often one instrument is made to "imitate" another by playing a passage of a character usually associated with that other instrument—that is, say, the piano soloist will play a distinctly "horn call" type of figure, which the horns will answer, and so on. In this case the sonorous characteristics and behavioral possibilities of the instruments play a role not only in that they suggest varied and distinct kinds of musical materials, but also in that they become dramatic identities that can be played off against each other in many ways and thus actually help create the musical argument itself.

Now in more recent times there have been contrary attitudes on this question—some composers have attempted to reinstitute a kind of "uniform canon" of musical sonority and behavior to which instruments would then be made to conform. This is true of Hindemith and is markedly the case with Webern after his Op. 20. The serialists of more recent vintage have carried this even further. ("L'Après-midi d'un vibraphone"—with the *o* pronounced Germanically—has lasted now for over fifteen years.) I myself, however, have been interested in pursuing the possibilities of dramatic contrast and interplay offered by the individual character of instruments and have attempted in all my works, at least since my Piano Sonata, to exploit these possibilities in the most vivid ways I could imagine. Of course one might ask whether there could be such a thing as a "totally idiomatic" piece—whether a piece, or a part in a piece, could be written that would employ *only* those kinds of sonority or gesture "peculiar" to the instrument in question—but naturally this cuts out one dramatic possibility, which is to have an instrument play *against* its nature. And of course in any "dialogue," musical or otherwise, there must be areas of overlap and interchange as well as points of convergence. Thus in my music there is a kind of ongoing dialectic of affirming and contradicting the character of the instruments involved, which nonetheless have an organic relation to the character of the musical ideas and to the formal-dramatic conception of the whole work in each case. [7]

ALEATORIC MUSIC

From an interview in Soundpieces, *August 10, 1975*

I feel about aleatoric music in general that it always borders on something very nondescript. Anything that doesn't have a clear-cut intention behind it will, in the end, always produce something which is rather obvious. It will sound like confusion, just a rather simple kind of confusion. My music sounds like confusion, but if you hear it more often it isn't so confused as you think! [8]

ELITISM

From Composer to Composer

We're always being condemned as being elitist in our field, but the entire repertory of classical music was written for an elite. The Beethoven symphonies were not written for the general public of Vienna. [9]

WEBERN

From Flawed Words and Stubborn Sounds

It seems to me that Webern's music is so consistently "sensitive," in a "special" vein, that one can easily have too much of it. In this it's like Fauré—beautiful but very limited. Indeed, I find it extraordinary that it has become the basis of a "school," except perhaps that certain people were fascinated by it because it used to be badly played and seemed intriguingly arcane and chaotic. Actually, it makes a lot of sense when it's played correctly—rather old-fashioned, romantic sense—a kind of condensed and refined Bruckner-sense. [10]

IVES

From a review in Modern Music, *March 1939*

For a good long while now many of us have been puzzled about the musical merits of the *Concord* Sonata and other of Ives's longer pieces. I came to know the sonata in the years when Stravinsky first scandalized America in person and Whiteman gave the Carnegie premiere of the *Rhapsody in Blue.** A keen time with lots of enthusiasm and lots of performances of new music to which I sometimes went with Ives him-

---

* Stravinsky's first tour of the United States, as soloist with the Boston Symphony, was in 1925. Gershwin's *Rhapsody in Blue* was premiered in 1924.

self. Sunday afternoons, after these concerts, a few of us would go . . . to discuss the music in the calm atmosphere of his living-room, a Henry James, old New York interior. They were lively talks; new music was new and very "modern" and Ives was much interested. Often he would poke fun, sit down at the piano to play from memory bits of a piece just heard, like *Daphnis and Chloe* or the *Sacre,* taking off the Ravel major seventh chords and obvious rhythms, or the primitive repeated dissonances of Stravinsky, and calling them "too easy." "Anybody can do that" he would exclaim, playing "My Country 'Tis Of Thee," the right hand in one key and the left in another. His main love, however, was for Bach, Brahms, and Franck, for he found in them spiritual elevation and nobility, which, like many a critic of his generation, he felt contemporary music had simplified away. . . .

During these afternoons we would coax him to try some of his own music, and as he saw we were sincere and not merely polite he would jump to the piano and play. Then the respectable, quiet, Puritan atmosphere was oddly disturbed, a gleam would come into his eyes as fiery excitement seized him, and he would smash out a fragment of *Emerson,* singing loudly and exclaiming with burning enthusiasm. Once the captain of the football team at Yale, he put the same punch into his music. It was a dynamic, staggering experience, which is hard even now to think of clearly. He hated composers who played their works objectively "as if they didn't like them." This strong, wiry Yankee vitality, humor, and transcendental seriousness were very much to our taste and we always came away from Ives full of life's glad new wine and a thousand projects for the future.

———— ♪ ————

In form and esthetic [the *Concord* Sonata] is basically conventional, not unlike the Liszt Sonata, full of the paraphernalia of the overdressy sonata school, cyclical themes, contrapuntal development sections that lead nowhere, constant harmonic movement which does not clarify the form, and dramatic rather than rhythmic effects. Because of the impressionistic intent of most of the music, the conventional form seems to hamper rather than aid, resulting in unnecessary, redundant repetitions of themes, mechanical transitions uncertain in their direction; unconvincing entrances of material; dynamics which have no relation to the progress of the piece. Behind all this confused texture there is a lack of logic which repeated hearings can never clarify, as they do for instance in the works of Bartók or Berg. The rhythms are vague and give no relief to the more expressive sections, and the much touted dissonant harmonies are helter-skelter, without great musical sense or definite progression. The esthetic is naïve, often too naïve to express serious thoughts, frequently depending on quotation of well-known American tunes, with little comment, possibly charming, but certainly trivial. As a whole, the work cannot be said to fill out the broad, elevated design forecast in the composer's prefaces.   [11]

From Flawed Words and Stubborn Sounds

American composers like Ives, Varèse, and Ruggles have interested me partly because of the fact that they don't fall into the frame of taste and esthetics we normally associate with European music. Thus thinking about Ives has been particularly fruitful to me: about how he calls into question matters of style, coherence, and even the integrity, the "seriousness" of serious music—and especially thinking about the whole question of his inclusion of popular songs and hymns, which has been constantly perplexing.* Sometimes, as in the *Concord* Sonata, his music seems like the work of an extraordinarily accomplished and skilled composer, particularly the "Emerson" movement, where all the motivic material is so highly organized and so closely interconnected, as are the harmonic materials. And then there are other pieces that seem to wipe all this aside and do something else. I have the impression that Ives must have known very much what he was doing and thus must have had many different identities as a composer—sometimes to write pieces in a high style and at other times to write sort of angry vaudeville pieces.   [12]

From an article in Vivian Perlis's Charles Ives Remembered, *1974*

A matter which puzzles me still is the question of Ives's revisions of his own scores. I can remember vividly a visit on a late afternoon to his house on East 74th Street, when I was directed to a little top-floor room where Ives sat at a little upright piano with score pages strewn around on the floor and on tables—this must have been around 1929. He was working on, I think, *Three Places in New England,* getting the score ready for performance. A new score was being derived from the older one to which he was adding and changing, turning octaves into sevenths and ninths, and adding dissonant notes. Since then, I have often wondered at exactly what date a lot of the music written early in his life received its last shot of dissonance and polyrhythm. In this case he showed me quite simply how he was improving the score. I got the impression that he might have frequently jacked up the level of dissonance of many works as his tastes changed. While the question no longer seems important, one could wonder whether he was as early a precursor of "modern" music as is sometimes made out.   [13]

From Flawed Words and Stubborn Sounds

VARÈSE

The whole question of "substance" in music is posed radically in the works of Varèse, which seem to rest entirely on the sounds of chords and of the instruments that play them, and on the timbre of percussion. I often wonder how interesting this music will continue to seem years hence, as there seems to be almost no "substance" to it, in the usual sense, beyond these very simple elements. I myself feel that my own music should somehow have substance, because if it doesn't, I myself will soon become tired of it, as I do of other people's music if it doesn't have this. Varèse's music is on the borderline, and I vary greatly in my estimation of it, although I always end up returning to it with admiration.   [14]

---

* In one way Mahler is perplexing for the same reason, partly because some of his works remind one of those old "patriotic symphonies" that were simply potpourris of national and religious anthems. See my review of the premiere of the *Concord* Sonata, *Modern Music* 16, no. 3, pp. 172–76. [Carter]

SESSIONS

Sessions's music has been one long confrontation with the musical materials of our time, first in its late-Romantic and "Impressionist" stage and then in its neo-classic Stravinskyan and Schoenbergian stage. The profound faith in ordered processes of musical thought and expression that go into the making of a work of art as it was conceived by the masters of the eighteenth, nineteenth, and early twentieth centuries, and still is by most of those interested in music, makes Sessions's music very satisfying to follow—full of musical substance and . . . rich in expression and idea.   [15]

COPLAND

Copland has had the opposite problem of development from Sessions—that of dealing with the damage the American publicity machine can easily do to its public figures by constantly drawing attention to irrelevancies and straitjacketing the development of an artist by coarsely typecasting him and then condemning him for not following what is expected of the type. Copland managed to escape from this because his allegiance has really been with his sense of the contemporary and because he has always evolved with the times, despite the obstacles placed in the way of acceptance of the works he has written that transcend the public image concocted for him by publicists.   [16]

STRAVINSKY

From "Igor Stravinsky, 1882–1971,"
Perspectives of New Music, 1971

He took me to his work room, and showed me a large book of blank pages onto which short fragments of musical sketches, roughly torn out of larger sketch-pages, had been pasted. Since the original sketch-pages had been papers of different qualities and colors and the musical fragments (sometimes only two or three notes) had been written on staves that were hand-drawn, often in quite fanciful curves, the scrapbook itself gave a very interesting visual impression. This was the work book for *The Flood,* which I don't think had yet been performed. He proceeded to explain how he chose fragments from his sketches, tore them out, shuffled them in different orders until he found one that satisfied him, and then pasted them down. I was genuinely surprised to learn of such an unexpected way of composing. . . . Naturally, he explained that all the fragments were derived from one chosen piece of material (as was evident). . . .

Some time later, I began to realize that what I saw corresponded to glimpses I had had of this technique in his music elsewhere. The description and quotation of Stravinsky telling how he cut up the final "fugue" of *Orpheus* and inserted fragments of harp figurations characteristic of the work, given in Nicholas Nabokov's *Old Friends and New Music,* as well as in a brilliant lecture by Edward Cone on the *Symphonies for Wind Instruments,* recalled to me how pervasive cross-cutting was in the music. I had not expected to see it so graphically demonstrated.   [17]

NADIA BOULANGER

From a radio lecture, 1960s

The teacher to whom I owe the most, Mlle. Nadia Boulanger, frequently says to her students that a true artist can be recognized by the quality of his refusals, bringing sternly to our attention the critical activity that lies behind all good artistic work. To say that the higher the quality of ideas the artist rejects, the higher the quality of his final accomplishment, however, implies a commitment to an order of values that may be possible only in a unified culture such as that of France. For unless there is some general agreement about grades of quality, it is obviously impossible for different individuals to judge, according to the same standards as the artist, the quality of refusals, or even to agree on the quality of his final accomplishment.   [18]

From Flawed Words and Stubborn Sounds

When Nadia Boulanger put me back on tonic and dominant chords in half-notes, I found to my surprise that I learned all kinds of things I'd never thought of before. Every one of her lessons became very illuminating, as she would point out how the parts could have done this or this. It's such a pleasure to me now to hear certain of the simplest progressions in the music of Bach and realize that there could have been many other voice-leadings, and that the one that has been chosen is especially meaningful coming as and where it does in a particular work. This awareness is extremely hard to communicate to a student, and I don't know whether I would have been in a position to appreciate it if I'd been doing my harmony for the first time with her. In any case, this was very valuable to me as a student composer, for it brought me a full consciousness of the importance of the very smallest details of a musical work and of the way that these can influence the expressive character of the whole.   [19]

ATTITUDES AND INFLUENCES

In considering constant change–process–evolution as music's prime factor, I found myself in direct opposition to the static repetitiveness of much early twentieth-century music, the squared-off articulation of the neoclassics, and indeed much of what is written today in which "first you do this for a while, then you do that." I wanted to mix up the "this" and the "that" and make them interact in other ways than by linear succession. Too, I questioned the inner shape of the "this" and the "that"—of local musical ideas—as well as their degree of linking and non-linking. Musical discourse, it became obvious to me, required as thorough a rethinking as harmony had been subjected to at the beginning of the century.

Now concretely, in the course of thinking about all of this, I once again—after many years' hiatus—took up interest in Indian *talas*, the Arabic *durub*, the "tempi" of Balinese gamelans (especially the accelerating *gangsar* and *rangkep*), and studied newer recordings of African music, that of the Watusi people in particular. At the same time the music of the early *quattrocento*, of Scriabin, and Ives, and the "hypothetical" techniques described in Cowell's *New Musical Resources* also furnished me with many ideas. The result in my own music was, first of all, the way of evolving rhythms and continuities now called "metric modulation," which I worked out during the composition of my Cello Sonata of 1948.* Now while, as I say, my thinking about musical time was stimulated by a consideration of, among other things, different kinds of rhythmic devices found in non-Western music such as I have mentioned, I feel it is important to point out that these devices interested me as suggestions of many syntactical possibilities that would participate in a very rich and varied large-scale rhythmic continuity such as is never found in non-Western music, but is suggested by some aspects of Western classical music, starting with Haydn especially. This aim of mine is something very different from that of many European composers who have been influenced by non-Western music and who have tended to be interested in exotic rhythmic devices as "things in themselves"— as local ideas more or less immediately transposable into a (usually) extremely conventional and uninteresting over-all rhythmic framework derived from the simplest aspects of older Western music and only slightly more varied than that of the exotic music from which the local ideas have been borrowed. As far as I am concerned, on the contrary, what contemporary music needs is not just raw materials of every kind but a way of relating these—of having them evolve during the course of a work in a sharply meaningful way; that is, what is needed is never just a string of "interesting passages," but works whose central interest is constituted by the way everything that happens in them happens as and when it does in relation to everything else. [20]

John Cage
1912–1992

Cage's innovations—born, by his own cheerful admission, of a failure to master various traditional techniques—include the use of chance procedures in composition and the construction of entire pieces from "found" noises, texts, and instruments. In 1952 he wrote his most notorious work, 4' 33", which requires the performer to remain silent throughout. The same year, he presented a theatrical event at Black Mountain College in North Carolina that is considered to have been the first Happening. Cage applied his techniques to writing, film, and art, some-

---

* There is nothing new about metric modulation but the name. To limit brief mention of its derivations to notated Western music: it is implicit in the rhythmic procedures of late fourteenth-century French music, as it is in music of the fifteenth and sixteenth centuries that uses hemiola and other ways of alternating meters, especially duple and triple. From then on, since early sets of variations like those of Byrd and Bull started a tradition of establishing tempo relationships between movements, metric modulation began to relate movements of one piece together, as can be seen in many works of Beethoven, not only in the variations of Op. 111, but in many places where *doppio movimento* and other terms are used to indicate tempo relationships. In fact, at that very time, the metronome was invented, which establishes relationships between all tempi. In our time, Stravinsky, following Satie, perhaps, wrote a few works around 1920 whose movements were closely linked by a very narrow range of tempo relationships, and much later Webern did the same. [Carter]

times in collaboration with such figures as Merce Cunningham and Marcel Duchamp, and attracted a large following outside classical music circles, particularly during the 1960s.

THE USE OF NOISE

The Future of Music: Credo, 1937/58*

I BELIEVE THAT THE USE OF NOISE

Wherever we are, what we hear is mostly noise. When we ignore it, it disturbs us. When we listen to it, we find it fascinating. The sound of a truck at 50 m.p.h. Static between the stations. Rain. We want to capture and control these sounds, to use them, not as sound effects, but as musical instruments. Every film studio has a library of "sound effects" recorded on film. With a film phonograph it is now possible to control the amplitude and frequency of any one of these sounds and to give to it rhythms within or beyond the reach of anyone's imagination. Given four film phonographs, we can compose and perform a quartet for explosive motor, wind, heart beat, and landslide.

TO MAKE MUSIC

If this word, music, is sacred and reserved for eighteenth- and nineteenth-century instruments, we can substitute a more meaningful term: organization of sound.

WILL CONTINUE AND INCREASE UNTIL WE REACH A MUSIC PRODUCED THROUGH THE AID OF ELECTRICAL INSTRUMENTS

Most inventors of electrical musical instruments have attempted to imitate eighteenth- and nineteenth-century instruments, just as early automobile designers copied the carriage. The Novachord and the Solovox are examples of this desire to imitate the past rather than construct the future. When Theremin provided an instrument with genuinely new possibilities, Thereministes did their utmost to make the instrument sound like some old instrument, giving it a sickeningly sweet vibrato, and performing upon it, with difficulty, masterpieces from the past. Although the instrument is capable of a wide variety of sound qualities, obtained by the mere turning of a dial, Thereministes act as censors, giving the public those sounds they think the public will like. We are shielded from new sound experiences.

The special property of electrical instruments will be to provide complete control of the overtone structure of tones (as opposed to noises) and to make these tones available in any frequency, amplitude, and duration.

WHICH WILL MAKE AVAILABLE FOR MUSICAL PURPOSES ANY AND ALL SOUNDS THAT CAN BE HEARD. PHOTO-ELECTRIC, FILM, AND MECHANICAL MEDIUMS FOR THE SYNTHETIC PRODUCTION OF MUSIC

It is now possible for composers to make music directly, without the assistance of intermediary performers. Any design repeated often enough on a sound track is

* First delivered as a lecture in 1937 in Seattle; later published as program note for twenty-five-year retrospective concert in 1958.

audible. 280 circles per second on a sound track will produce one sound, whereas a portrait of Beethoven repeated 50 times per second on a sound track will have not only a different pitch but a different sound quality.

WILL BE EXPLORED. WHEREAS, IN THE PAST, THE POINT OF DISAGREEMENT HAS BEEN BETWEEN DISSONANCE AND CONSONANCE IT WILL BE, IN THE IMMEDIATE FUTURE, BETWEEN NOISE AND SO-CALLED MUSICAL SOUNDS.

THE PRESENT METHODS OF WRITING MUSIC, PRINCIPALLY THOSE WHICH EMPLOY HARMONY AND ITS REFERENCE TO PARTICULAR STEPS IN THE FIELD OF SOUND, WILL BE INADEQUATE FOR THE COMPOSER WHO WILL BE FACED WITH THE ENTIRE FIELD OF SOUND.

The composer (organizer of sound) will not only be faced with the entire field of sound but also with the entire field of time. The "frame" or fraction of a second, following established film technique, will probably be the basic unit in the measurement of time. No rhythm will be beyond the composer's reach.

NEW METHODS WILL BE DISCOVERED, BEARING A DEFINITE RELATION TO SCHOENBERG'S TWELVE-TONE SYSTEM

Schoenberg's method assigns to each material, in a group of equal materials, its function with respect to the group. (Harmony assigned to each material, in a group of unequal materials, its function with respect to the fundamental or most important material in the group.) Schoenberg's method is analogous to modern society, in which the emphasis is on the group and the integration of the individual in the group.

AND PRESENT METHODS OF WRITING PERCUSSION MUSIC

Percussion music is a contemporary transition from keyboard-influenced music to the all-sound music of the future. Any sound is acceptable to the composer of percussion music; he explores the academically forbidden "nonmusical" field of sound insofar as is manually possible.

Methods of writing percussion music have as their goal the rhythmic structure of a composition. As soon as these methods are crystallized into one or several widely accepted methods, the means will exist for group improvisations of unwritten but culturally important music. This has already taken place in Oriental cultures and in hot jazz.

AND ANY OTHER METHODS WHICH ARE FREE FROM THE CONCEPT OF A FUNDAMENTAL TONE. THE PRINCIPLE OF FORM WILL BE OUR ONLY CONSTANT CONNECTION WITH THE PAST. ALTHOUGH THE GREAT FORM OF THE FUTURE WILL NOT BE AS IT WAS IN THE PAST, AT ONE TIME THE FUGUE AND AT ANOTHER THE SONATA, IT WILL BE RELATED TO THESE AS THEY ARE TO EACH OTHER

Before this happens, centers of experimental music must be established. In these centers, the new materials, oscillators, generators, means for amplifying small sounds, film phonographs, etc., available for use. Performances of results. Organization of sound for musical and extramusical purposes (theater, dance, film).

THROUGH THE PRINCIPLE OF ORGANIZATION OR MAN'S COMMON ABILITY TO THINK.

[1]

Structure

From a lecture at Black Mountain College, Summer 1948

In the field of structure, the field of the definition of parts and their relation to a whole, there has been only one new idea since Beethoven. And that new idea can be perceived in the work of Anton Webern and Erik Satie. With Beethoven the parts of a composition were defined by means of harmony. With Satie and Webern they are defined by means of time lengths. The question of structure is so basic, and it is so important to be in agreement about it, that one must now ask: Was Beethoven right or are Webern and Satie right?

I answer immediately and unequivocally, Beethoven was in error, and his influence, which has been as extensive as it is lamentable, has been deadening to the art of music.

Now on what basis can I pronounce such a heresy?

It is very simple. If you consider that sound is characterized by its pitch, its loudness, its timbre, and its duration, and that silence, which is the opposite and, therefore, the necessary partner of sound, is characterized only by its duration, you will be drawn to the conclusion that of the four characteristics of the material of music, duration, that is, time length, is the most fundamental. Silence cannot be heard in terms of pitch or harmony: It is heard in terms of time length. It took a Satie and a Webern to rediscover this musical truth, which, by means of musicology, we learn was evident to some musicians in our Middle Ages, and to all musicians at all times (except those whom we are currently in the process of spoiling) in the Orient.

Beethoven represents the most intense lurching of the boat away from its natural even keel. The derivation of musical thought from his procedures has served not only to put us at the mercy of the waves, but to practically shipwreck the art on an island of decadence. Last night, in a discussion, I was willing to grant that there may be different physical evidences of structural principles. Today I will not be so pacific. There can be no right making of music that does not structure itself from the very roots of sound and silence—lengths of time. In India, rhythmic structure is called Tala. With us, unfortunately, it is called a new idea.   [2]

"Instantaneous and Unpredictable"

Text for a program booklet, 1952

written in response to a request for a manifesto on music, 1952 } instantaneous   and unpredictable

nothing is accomplished by writing a piece of music }   our ears are
"   "   "   " hearing "   "   "   "   now
"   "   "   " playing "   "   "   "   in excellent condition
                                                                        [3]

ERROR

From 45' for a Speaker, a lecture/piece, 1954

Error is drawing a straight line between anticipation of what should happen and what actually happens. What actually happens is however in a total not linear situation and is responsible generally. Therefore error is a fiction, has no reality in fact. Errorless music is written by not giving a thought to cause and effect. Any other kind of music always has mistakes in it.   [4]

COMPOSITIONAL TECHNIQUES

From "Lecture on Nothing," published in Incontri Musicali, *August 1959*

All I know about method is that when I am not working I sometimes think I know something, but when I am working, it is quite clear that I know nothing.   [5]

I am still really thoroughly puzzled by this way of composing by observing imperfections in paper. It is this being thoroughly puzzled that makes it possible for me to work. I am puzzled by hearing music well played too.
   If I'm not puzzled it wasn't well played.   [6]

From "History of Experimental Music in the United States,"
Darmstädter Beiträge, *1959*

Morton Feldman divided pitches into three areas, high, middle, and low, and established a time unit. Writing on graph paper, he simply inscribed numbers of tones to be played at any time within specified periods of time.
   There are people who say, "If music's that easy to write, I could do it." Of course they could, but they don't.   [7]

From a conversation with Richard Kostelanetz, 1967/8

You can have art without even doing it. All you have to do is change your mind. You don't even have to have any skill.   [8]

EXPERIMENTAL MUSIC

From an address to the Music Teachers National Association, Chicago, 1957

Formerly, whenever anyone said the music I presented was experimental, I objected. It seemed to me that composers knew what they were doing, and that the experiments that had been made had taken place prior to the finished works, just as sketches are made before paintings and rehearsals precede performances. But, giving the matter further thought, I realized that there is ordinarily an essential difference between making a piece of music and hearing one. A composer knows his work as a woodsman knows a path he has traced and retraced, while a listener is confronted by the same work as one is in the woods by a plant he has never seen before.

Now, on the other hand, times have changed; music has changed; and I no longer object to the word "experimental." I use it in fact to describe all the music that especially interests me and to which I am devoted, whether someone else wrote it or I myself did. What has happened is that I have become a listener and the music has become something to hear. Many people, of course, have given up saying "experimental" about this new music. Instead, they either move to a halfway point and say "controversial" or depart to a greater distance and question whether this "music" is music at all.

For in this new music nothing takes place but sounds: those that are notated and those that are not. Those that are not notated appear in the written music as silences, opening the doors of the music to the sounds that happen to be in the environment. This openness exists in the fields of modern sculpture and architecture. The glass houses of Mies van der Rohe reflect their environment, presenting to the eye images of clouds, trees, or grass, according to the situation. And while looking at the constructions in wire of the sculptor Richard Lippold, it is inevitable that one will see other things, and people too, if they happen to be there at the same time, through the network of wires. There is no such thing as an empty space or an empty time. There is always something to see, something to hear. In fact, try as we may to make a silence, we cannot. For certain engineering purposes, it is desirable to have as silent a situation as possible. Such a room is called an anechoic chamber, its six walls made of special material, a room without echoes. I entered one at Harvard University several years ago and heard two sounds, one high and one low. When I described them to the engineer in charge, he informed me that the high one was my nervous system in operation, the low one my blood in circulation. Until I die there will be sounds. And they will continue following my death. One need not fear about the future of music.   [9]

COMMUNICATION

From a lecture composed of quotations
from writings by Cage and others, late 1950s

NICHI NICHI KORE KO NICHI: EVERY DAY IS A BEAUTIFUL DAY.

What if I ask thirty-two questions?
What if I stop asking now and then?
Will that make things clear?
Is communication something made clear?
What is communication?
Music, what does it communicate?
Is what's clear to me clear to you?
Is music just sounds?
Then what does it communicate?
Is a truck passing by music?
If I can see it, do I have to hear it too?
If I don't hear it, does it still communicate?

If while I see it I can't hear it, but hear something else, say an egg-beater,
    because I'm inside looking out, does the truck communicate or the egg-
    beater, which communicates?
Which is more musical, a truck passing by a factory or a truck passing by a
    music school?
Are the people inside the school musical and the ones outside unmusical?
What if the ones inside can't hear very well, would that change my question?
Do you know what I mean when I say inside the school?
Are sounds just sounds or are they Beethoven?
Is there such a thing as silence?
Even if I get away from people, do I still have to listen to something?
Say I'm off in the woods, do I have to listen to a stream babbling?
Is there always something to hear, never any peace and quiet?
If my head is full of harmony, melody, and rhythm, what happens to me when
    the telephone rings, to my piece and quiet, I mean?
And if it was European harmony, melody, and rhythm in my head, what has
    happened to the history of, say, Javanese music, with respect, that is to say, to
    my head?
Are we getting anywhere asking questions?
Where are we going?
Is this the twenty-eighth question?
Are there any important questions?
"How do you need to cautiously proceed in dualistic terms?"
Do I have two more questions?
And, now, do I have none?   [10]

TRADITION

From "History of Experimental Music in the United States"

Once in Amsterdam, a Dutch musician said to me, "It must be very difficult for
you in America to write music, for you are so far away from the centers of tradition." I had to say, "It must be very difficult for you in Europe to write music,
for you are so close to the centers of tradition."   [11]

SERIALISM

From "Lecture on Nothing"

I have nothing against the twelve-tone row; but it is a method, not a structure.
We really do need a structure, so we can see we are nowhere. Much of the music I love
uses the twelve-tone row, but that is not why I love it. I love it for no reason.   [12]

From a conversation with Michael Zwerin,
published in the Village Voice, January 6, 1966

What is free about a tone row? You have to run up and down that row as though
you were a mouse in a trap.   [13]

DISCIPLINE

From a conversation with Richard Kostelanetz, 1967/8

The way I was educated I was not given the meaning of discipline. I was told that if I were going to be a composer I should know harmony, counterpoint, and all those things. You are told that you have to study those things, although they are of no use to you ultimately, and that you learn those things in order later to give them up when finally you get around to self-expression. But this isn't the nature of discipline. True discipline is not learned in order to give it up, but rather in order to give oneself up. Now, most people never even learn what discipline is. It is precisely what the Lord meant when he said, give up your father and mother and follow me. It means give up the things closest to you. It means give yourself up, everything, and do what it is you are going to do. At that point, what have you given up? Your likes, your dislikes, etc. When it becomes clear, as it now becomes to so many people, that the old disciplines need no longer be taken seriously, what is going to provide the path to the giving up of oneself?   [14]

From a response to a letter criticizing Satie, Musical America, *April 1, 1951*

When life is lived, there is nothing in it but the present, the "now-moment" (I quote Meister Eckhart); it is thus impossible to speak of being ahead of one's time or of historical development. When life is lived, each one is "the most honored of all creatures" (I quote the Buddha), living in "the best of all possible worlds" (I quote Voltaire), and when this is done there is "no silliness" (I quote my former wife, Xenia Cage). Art when it is art as Satie lived it and made it is not separate from life (nor is dishwashing when it is done in this spirit).   [15]

SATIE

From an imaginary conversation with Satie, Art News Annual, *1958*

To be interested in Satie one must be disinterested to begin with, accept that a sound is a sound and a man is a man, give up illusions about ideas of order, expressions of sentiment, and all the rest of our inherited aesthetic claptrap.

It's not a question of Satie's relevance. He's indispensable.   [16]

SCHOENBERG AS TEACHER

From "Indeterminacy," a lecture composed of stories, first given in 1958

When Schoenberg asked me whether I would devote my life to music, I said, "Of course." After I had been studying with him for two years, Schoenberg said, "In order to write music, you must have a feeling for harmony." I explained to him that I had no feeling for harmony. He then said that I would always encounter an obstacle, that it would be as though I came to a wall through which I could not pass. I said, "In that case I will devote my life to beating my head against the wall."

[17]

APHORISMS

The best thing to do about counterpoint is what Schoenberg did: teach it. ("45' for a Speaker") [18]

If one feels protective about the word "music," protect it and find another word for all the rest that enters through the ears. ("45' for a Speaker") [19]

I have nothing to say and I am saying it and that is poetry as I need it. ("Lecture on Nothing") [20]

Silence is all of the sound we don't intend. There is no such thing as absolute silence. (Zwerin conversation) [21]

I'm not interested in whether any of my works are good or bad. (Kostelanetz conversation) [22]

We are going to have to get over the need for likes and dislikes. (Kostelanetz conversation) [23]

Milton Babbitt
b. 1916

As early as the 1930s Babbitt was beginning to develop logical extensions of twelve-tone principles that would lead to the development of integral serialism in the years following World War II. In the 1950s he did pioneering work in electronic music, helping to create the room-sized synthesizer at Columbia University with which he assembled his first electronic works. Long interested in popular music, Babbitt wrote pop songs and played jazz during his youth in Mississippi, and he later composed several film scores and a musical. He has often used his talents as a compelling writer and speaker to defend "difficult" twentieth-century music, as in the 1958 article (reproduced here in its complete form) made infamous by its title—not Babbitt's, but an editor's.

"WHO CARES IF YOU LISTEN?"

Essay in High Fidelity, *1958*

This article might have been entitled "The Composer as Specialist" or, alternatively, and perhaps less contentiously, "The Composer as Anachronism." For I am concerned with stating an attitude towards the indisputable facts of the status and condition of the composer of what we will, for the moment, designate as "serious," "advanced," contemporary music. This composer expends an enormous amount of time and energy—and, usually, considerable money—on the creation of a commodity which has little, no, or negative commodity value. He is, in essence, a "vanity" composer. The general public is largely unaware of and uninterested in his music. The majority of performers shun it and resent it. Consequently, the music is little performed, and then primarily at poorly attended concerts before an audience consisting in the main of fellow professionals. At best, the music would appear to be for, of, and by specialists.

Towards this condition of musical and societal "isolation" a variety of attitudes has been expressed, usually with the purpose of assigning blame, often to the music itself, occasionally to critics or performers, and very occasionally to the public. But to assign blame is to imply that this isolation is unnecessary and undesirable. It is my contention that, on the contrary, this condition is not only inevitable, but potentially advantageous for the composer and his music. From my point of view, the composer would do well to consider means of realizing, consolidating, and extending the advantage.

The unprecedented divergence between contemporary serious music and its listeners, on the one hand, and traditional music and its following on the other, is not accidental and—most probably—not transitory. Rather, it is a result of a half-century of revolution in musical thought, a revolution whose nature and consequences can be compared only with, and in many respects are closely analogous to, those of the mid-nineteenth-century revolution in mathematics and the twentieth-century revolution in theoretical physics. The immediate and profound effect has been the necessity for the informed musician to re-examine and probe the very foundations of his art. He has been obliged to recognize the possibility, and actuality, of alternatives to what were once regarded as musical absolutes. He lives no longer in a unitary musical universe of "common practice," but in a variety of universes of diverse practice.

This fall from musical innocence is, understandably, as disquieting to some as it is challenging to others, but in any event the process is irreversible; and the music that reflects the full impact of this revolution is, in many significant respects, a truly "new" music. Apart from the often highly sophisticated and complex constructive methods of any one composition, or group of compositions, the very minimal properties characterizing this body of music are the sources of its "difficulty," "unintelligibility" and—isolation. In indicating the most general of these properties, I shall make reference to no specific works, since I wish to avoid the independent issue of evaluation. The reader is at liberty to supply his own instances; if he cannot (and, granted the condition under discussion, this is a very real possibility), let him be assured that such music does exist.

First. This music employs a tonal vocabulary which is more "efficient" than that of the music of the past, or its derivatives. This is not necessarily a virtue in itself, but it does make possible a greatly increased number of pitch simultaneities, successions, and relationships. This increase in efficiency necessarily reduces the "redundancy" of the language, and as a result the intelligible communication of the work demands increased accuracy from the transmitter (the performer) and activity from the receiver (the listener). Incidentally, it is this circumstance, among others, that has created the need for purely electronic media of "performance." More importantly for us, it makes ever heavier demands upon the training of the listener's perceptual capacities.

Second. Along with this increase of meaningful pitch materials, the number of functions associated with each component of the musical event also has been multiplied. In the simplest possible terms, each such "atomic" event is located in a five-dimensional musical space determined by pitch-class, register, dynamics, duration, and timbre. These five components not only together define the single event, but, in the course of a work, the successive values of each component create an individually coherent structure, frequently in parallel with the corresponding structures created by each of the other components. Inability to perceive and remember precisely the values of any of these components results in a dislocation of the event in the work's musical space, an alteration of its relation to all other events in the work, and—thus—a falsification of the composition's total structure. For example, an incorrectly performed or perceived dynamic value results in destruction of the work's dynamic pattern, but also in false identification of other components of the event (of which this dynamic value is a part) with corresponding components of other events, so creating incorrect pitch, registral, timbral, and durational associations. It is this high degree of "determinacy" that most strikingly differentiates such music from, for example, a popular song. A popular song is only very partially determined, since it would appear to retain its germane characteristics under considerable alteration of register, rhythmic texture, dynamics, harmonic structure, timbre, and other qualities.

The preliminary differentiation of musical categories by means of this reasonable and usable criterion of "degree of determinacy" offends those who take it to be a definition of qualitative categories, which—of course—it need not always be. Curiously, their demurrers usually take the familiar form of some such "democratic" counterdefinition as: "There is no such thing as 'serious' and 'popular' music. There is only 'good' and 'bad' music." As a public service, let me offer those who still patiently await the revelation of the criteria of Absolute Good an alternative criterion which possesses, at least, the virtue of immediate and infallible applicability: "There is no such thing as 'serious' and 'popular' music. There is only music whose title begins with the letter 'X' and music whose title does not."

Third. Musical compositions of the kind under discussion possess a high degree of contextuality and autonomy. That is, the structural characteristics of a given work are less representative of a general class of characteristics than they are unique to the individual work itself. Particularly, principles of relatedness, upon which depends immediate coherence of continuity, are more likely to evolve in the course of the work than to be derived from generalized assumptions. Here again greater and new demands are made upon the perceptual and conceptual abilities of the listener.

Fourth, and finally. Although in many fundamental respects this music is "new," it often also represents a vast extension of the methods of the other musics, derived from a considered and extensive knowledge of their dynamic principles. For, concomitant with the "revolution in music," perhaps even an integral aspect thereof, has been the development of analytical theory, concerned with the systematic formulation of such principles to the end of greater efficiency, economy, and understanding. Compositions so rooted necessarily ask comparable knowledge and experience from the listener. Like all communication, this music presupposes a suitably equipped receptor. I am aware that "tradition" has it that the lay listener, by virtue of some undefined, transcendental faculty, always is able to arrive at a musical judgment absolute in its wisdom if not always permanent in its validity. I regret my inability to accord this declaration of faith the respect due its advanced age.

Deviation from this tradition is bound to dismiss the contemporary music of which I have been talking into "isolation." Nor do I see how or why the situation should be otherwise. Why should the layman be other than bored and puzzled by what he is unable to understand, music or anything else? It is only the translation of this boredom and puzzlement into resentment and denunciation that seems to me indefensible. After all, the public does have its own music, its ubiquitous music: music to eat by, to read by, to dance by, and to be impressed by. Why refuse to recognize the possibility that contemporary music has reached a stage long since attained by other forms of activity? The time has passed when the normally well-educated man without special preparation can understand the most advanced work in, for example, mathematics, philosophy, and physics. Advanced music, to the extent that it reflects the knowledge and originality of the informed composer, scarcely can be expected to appear more intelligible than these arts and sciences to the person whose musical education usually has been even less extensive than his background in other fields. But to this, a double standard is invoked, with the words "music is music," implying also that "music is just music." Why not, then, equate the activities of the radio repairman with those of the theoretical physicist, on the basis of the dictum that "physics is physics"? It is not difficult to find statements like the following from the New York *Times* of September 8, 1957: "The scientific level of the conference is so high . . . that there are in the world only 120 mathematicians specializing in the field who could contribute." Specialized music on the other hand, far from signifying "height" of musical level, has been charged with "decadence," even as evidence of an insidious "conspiracy."

It often has been remarked that only in politics and the "arts" does the layman regard himself as an expert, with the right to have his opinion heard. In the realm of politics, he knows that this right, in the form of a vote, is guaranteed by fiat. Comparably, in the realm of public music, the concertgoer is secure in the knowledge that the amenities of concertgoing protect his firmly stated: "I didn't like it" from further scrutiny. Imagine, if you can, a layman chancing upon a lecture on "Pointwise Periodic Homeomorphisms." At the conclusion, he announces: "I didn't like it." Social conventions being what they are in such circles, someone might dare inquire: "Why not?" Under duress, our layman discloses precise reasons for his failure to enjoy himself; he found the hall chilly, the lecturer's voice unpleasant, and he was suffering the digestive aftermath of a poor dinner. His interlocutor understandably disqualifies these reasons as irrelevant to the content and value of the lecture, and the development of mathematics is left undisturbed. If the concertgoer is at all versed in the ways of musical lifemanship, he also will offer reasons for his "I didn't like it"—in the form of assertions that the work in question is "inexpressive," "undramatic," "lacking in poetry," etc., etc., tapping that store of vacuous equivalents hallowed by time for: "I don't like it, and I cannot or will not state why." The concertgoer's critical authority is established beyond the possibility of further inquiry. Certainly he is not responsible for the circumstance that musical discourse is a never-never land of semantic confusion, the last resting place of all those verbal and formal fallacies, those hoary dualisms that have been banished from rational discourse. Perhaps he has read, in a widely consulted and respected book on the history of music, the following: "to call him (Tchaikovsky) the 'modern Russian Beethoven' is rootless, Beethoven being patently neither modern nor Russian. . . ." Or, the following, by an eminent "non-analytic" philosopher: "The music of Lourié is an ontological music. . . . It is born in the singular roots of being, the nearest possible juncture of the soul and the spirit. . . ." How unexceptional the verbal peccadilloes of the average concertgoer appear beside these masterful models. Or, perhaps, in search of "real" authority, he has acquired his critical vocabulary from the pronouncements of officially "eminent" composers, whose eminence, in turn, is founded largely upon just such assertions as the concertgoer has learned to regurgitate. This cycle is of slight moment in a world where circularity is one of the norms of criticism. Composers (and performers), wittingly or unwittingly assuming the character of "talented children" and "inspired idiots," generally ascribed to them, are singularly adept at the conversion of personal tastes into general principles. Music they do not like is "not music," composers whose music they do like are "not composers."

In search of what to think and how to say it, the layman may turn to newspapers and magazines. Here he finds conclusive evidence for the proposition that "music is music." The science editor of such publications contents himself with straightforward reporting, usually news of the "factual" sciences; books and articles not intended for popular consumption are not reviewed. Whatever the reason, such matters are left to professional journals. The music critic admits no comparable differentiation. He may feel, with some justice, that music that presents itself in the market place of the concert hall automatically offers itself to public approval or disapproval. He may feel, again, with some justice, that to omit the expected criticism of the "advanced" work would be to do the composer an injustice in his assumed quest for, if nothing else, public notice and "professional recognition." The critic, at least to this extent, is himself a victim of the leveling of categories.

Here, then, are some of the factors determining the climate of the public world of music. Perhaps we should not have over looked those pockets of "power" where prizes, awards, and commissions are dispensed, where music is adjudged guilty, not only without the right to be confronted by its accuser, but without the right to be confronted by the accusations. Or those well meaning souls who exhort the public "just to listen to more contemporary music," apparently on the theory that familiarity breeds passive acceptance. Of those, often the same well-meaning souls, who remind the composer of his "obligation to the public," while the public's obligation to the composer is fulfilled, manifestly, by mere physical presence in the concert hall or before a loudspeaker or—more authoritatively—by committing to memory the numbers of phonograph records and amplifier models. Or the intricate social world within this musical world, where the salon becomes a bazaar, and music itself becomes an ingredient of verbal canapés for cocktail conversation.

I say all this not to present a picture of a virtuous music in a sinful world, but to point up the problems of a special music in an alien and inapposite world. And so, I dare suggest that the composer would do himself and his music an immediate and eventual service by total, resolute, and voluntary withdrawal from this public world to one of private performance and electronic media, with its very real possibility of complete elimination of the public and social aspects of musical composition. By so doing, the separation between the domains would be defined beyond any possibility of confusion of categories, and the composer would be free to pursue a private life of professional achievement, as opposed to a public life of unprofessional compromise and exhibitionism.

But how, it may be asked, will this serve to secure the means of survival for the composer and his music? One answer is that after all, such a private life is what the university provides the scholar and the scientist. It is only proper that the university, which—significantly enough—has provided so many contemporary composers with their professional training and general education, should provide a home for the "complex," "difficult, and "problematical" in music. Indeed, the process has begun; and if it appears to proceed too slowly, I take consolation in the knowledge that in this respect, too, music seems to be in historically retarded parallel with now sacrosanct fields of endeavor. In E. T. Bell's *Men of Mathematics,* we read: "In the eighteenth century the universities were not the principal centers of research in Europe. They might have become such sooner than they did but for the classical tradition and its understandable hostility to science. Mathematics was close enough to antiquity to be respectable, but physics, being more recent, was suspect. Further, a mathematician in a university of the time would have been expected to put much of his effort on elementary teaching; his research, if any, would have been an unprofitable luxury. . . ." A simple substitution of "musical composition" for "research," of "academic" for "classical," of "music" for "physics," and of "composer" for "mathematician," provides a strikingly accurate picture of the current situation. And as long as the confusion I have described continues to exist, how can the university and its community assume other than that the composer welcomes and courts public competition with the historically certified products of the past, and the commercially petrified products of the present?

Perhaps for the same reason, the various institutes of advanced research and the large majority of foundations have disregarded this music's need for means of survival. I do not wish to appear to obscure the obvious differences between musical composition and scholarly research, although it can be contended that these differences are no more fundamental than the differences among the various fields of study. I do question whether these differences, by their nature, justify the denial to music's development of assistance granted these other fields. Immediate "practical" applicability (which may be said to have its musical analogue in "immediate extensibility of a compositional technique") is certainly not a necessary condition for the support of scientific research. And if it be contended that such research is so supported because in the past it has yielded eventual applications, one can counter with, for example, the music of Anton Webern, which during the composer's lifetime was regarded (to the very limited extent that it was regarded at all) as the ultimate in hermetic, specialized, and idiosyncratic composition; today, some dozen years after the composer's death, his complete works have been recorded by a major record company, primarily—I suspect—as a result of the enormous influence this music has had on the postwar, nonpopular, musical world. I doubt that scientific research is any more secure against predictions of ultimate significance than is musical composition. Finally, if it be contended that research, even in its least "practical" phases, contributes to the sum of knowledge in the particular realm, what possibly can contribute more to our knowledge of music than a genuinely original composition?

Granting to music the position accorded other arts and sciences promises the sole substantial means of survival for the music I have been describing. Admittedly, if this music is not supported, the whistling repertory of the man in the street will be little affected, the concert-going activity of the conspicuous consumer of musical culture will be little disturbed. But music will cease to evolve, and in that important sense, will cease to live. [1]

From an interview in Soundpieces, *1975*

COMMENTS ON "WHO CARES IF YOU LISTEN?"

I gave a lecture at Tanglewood in 1957 about the state of the contemporary composer. The then-editor of *High Fidelity* heard it and asked me to write it down. I had been improvising it and didn't want to write it down, but they had a copy of the tape, and asked me if I would take it and put it into some kind of publishable shape. The title of the article as submitted to *High Fidelity* was "The Composer as Specialist." There was no imputation whatsoever of "who cares if you listen," which as far as I am concerned conveys very little of the letter of the article, and nothing of the spirit. Obviously the point was that I cared a great deal who listened, but above all *how* they listened. I was concerned about the fact that people were not listening. But theirs, of course, was a much more provocative title, and journalists are concerned to provoke, and do.

I'm very distressed by this, because inevitably the article is what I'm known by, and I don't really care to be known at all if I have to be known by that. The piece was reprinted twice in anthologies, and I asked in both cases that my original title be restored, along with some of the sentences. Some of the sentences had been changed in *High Fidelity*, not because of my alleged obscurity, but because at the last moment some new advertisements came in, so they just cut a few phrases and sentences to make room. That is the story of "Who Cares If You Listen?," my most celebrated achievement.

Now, of course, I don't mean to disavow the article—not all of it—by any means. Some of it is unintelligible because of the cuts, but I am not apologizing for or disclaiming the article—I am deeply concerned about the title and what it signifies, because most people don't go beyond the title.

Q: Could you tell us precisely what it was that you had in mind then, and how you feel about those ideas today?

A: It wasn't "who cares if you listen." It was this: If you're not going to take our activities in as serious and dignified a manner as we take them, then of course we don't want you to listen. I don't offer my music for the approval or disapproval of those who have no serious concern to find out what we do in our music, or why we're doing it. It is certainly not music for the unlettered, nor is anything most of my colleagues do for the unlettered. If you want to find out what we're doing and how we're doing it, we'd be only too happy to tell you about it. That article was a very simple, brief introductory attempt to do so.

There was a time when we thought that perhaps we could gain some kind of appropriate position among intellectuals in other fields by appealing not to their capacity to hear the soundness of our music—they have little musical background—

but by the sense of our words. Of course, it turned out that our words went as unheeded as our music went unheard. If anything seems to offend people more than taking music seriously, it's taking talking about music seriously. The result was that people whom we thought would at least recognize that we were trying to be responsible and informative were irritated by our insistence that any music was to be taken seriously. Most of my colleagues in other fields regard music as something that is obliged to provide them with some sort of surcease from the demands of their really important pursuits.   [2]

COMPOSER EXPLICATIONS

There are enormous hazards in a composer attempting to invoke words in explication of his music. Obviously, the words themselves, if they're going to have any genuine correlation with the unfamiliar musical event, are going to be very unfamiliar. I'm going to have to depend on concepts that derive from musical and analytical processes that will be at least as unfamiliar as my music.

The things that I could say about my music are likely to be overladen with misunderstandings. For example, I could say that all of my music is twelve-tone. What does that possibly mean? It possibly means that someone will connect it with all of the misunderstandings and all of the bad books on the subject. "Twelve pitches where you *can't* repeat one until all have been stated" or "whatever goes up may go sideways," and a heap of other such imperatives and permissives, which if they were the conditions for music to be characterized as twelve-tone music, then a twelve-tone work would not be discoverable anywhere in the world of serious music.

On the other hand, I don't wish it to be presumed that the question of "twelve-tone" is an irrelevant one. Very often, the attitude seems to be that to inform the audience that the piece is "twelve-tone" is downright anti-social and undemocratic. To be sure, the listener doesn't have to be aware that it is twelve-tone, but those fundamental relationships which are available within any twelve-tone piece are going to provide the basic musical relations. If he construes this piece in a different way, fine, let me hear how he does it, but don't let me hear him say that the music doesn't make any or much sense, and then have him explain with respect to a completely inappropriate language frame.

It's the difference between hearing a triad and hearing that it *is* a triad. I imagine that many people who listen to the *Eroica* Symphony do not realize that what they hear in the beginning is what we normally come to call a "major triad. " But what they are hearing is still a "major triad. " The man on the street is not aware of the problems of grammaticality, and how difficult it is to speak of grammaticality, but he speaks and understands grammatical English. So the question of internalized twelve-tone properties is very important. But how could he hear these relationships in any satisfactory way if he's heard perhaps one twelve-tone piece, and no late Beethoven String Quartet?   [3]

ELECTRONIC MUSIC

The synthesizer permits me to hear what I'm doing as I do it, and that's terribly important, because we have so little notion of what we can and do hear, as human beings and as trained human beings. Here is a good place to stop for that question, "But what about the human element?" If the questioner is ignorant, this question is most interesting. If the questioner is hostile, it's most offensive. The answer is that never before has a music been so completely dependent upon human capacities, because those uninformed machines can do that and only that which a composer specifies in every precise detail. Never before did one's ideas have to be notated so precisely, clearly, completely, and accurately; it was neither necessary nor possible in the past. Moreover, since these machines can produce "anything," the only boundaries are the humanly meaningful. What we must know now is, beyond the capacities of the machines, how do we hear? what do we hear? and that asks us questions about all kinds of music, both electronic and non-electronic.   [4]

From a lecture at the University of Wisconsin, 1983

THE DEVELOPMENT OF SEPARATE TRADITIONS

Fifty years ago, when I was a young student of music, we were told, "Look, you're dramatizing yourself. This new music, this music of Schoenberg, Webern, even Stravinsky, is not really that new. It seems new because you're too close to it and because you're part of it, but you're dramatizing yourself and you're making the whole thing a melodramatic situation. You just wait. Either this music will fall into the normal repertoire and will be played as often as the *Surprise* Symphony, or it will simply disappear like an illusion without a future, one of the transitory, evanescent things."

Well, of course, you know, neither has happened. Instead, we've developed different repertoires. The music that is still almost never played by orchestras (I don't want to mention specifics; I don't have to since they're all pretty much the same), and which is not at all in the repertoire of the so-called music lover, not only has become the cornerstone of most young composers' work but also is regarded as a matter of fact, a part of the past. It's already become part of the tradition. The situation of Schoenberg is typical—he was never in fashion and now he's become old-fashioned.   [5]

SCHOENBERG, BERG, AND WEBERN; CONTEXTUALITY

Those middle-period works of Schoenberg, the middle-period works of Berg, the middle-period works of Webern . . . are to as large an extent as possible self-referential, self-contained, and what I'm given to call "contextual." Contextuality merely has to do with the extent to which a piece defines its material within itself.

Now there are obvious hazards here. The problem of contextuality again is a problem of the listener, it's a problem of the composer, it's a problem of the performer. Just consider what is involved. It means that when you come to hear such a piece, you are listening to a piece that is going to use perhaps physical materials that are familiar, but very little else that is familiar. You're going to have to proceed with this piece by a complete concentration on the piece as piece. You're going to have very little that you can carry with you from your memory of former pieces, very little that you carry by way of your experiences of past music. In other words, it is not very communal. . . .

But it had all these new rewards; it had all these new possibilities. The idea of writing a piece that is self-referential, self-contained, is of course an intriguing one, an exciting one, but contextuality is after all a relative thing. Any piece of music is contextual to the extent that when you say, in talking about a piece, that this is related to that, that this is derived from that, that this is a return to that, you're talking contextually. It's a matter of degree, and matters of degree can be crucial where musical intelligibility is concerned. Later, Schoenberg said that the difficulty with this middle period music was indeed the fact that with this contextual approach they could not create structures of great enough length, of great enough complexity. Now immediately that's a very bewildering statement. *Erwartung* isn't long enough? *Erwartung* doesn't have enough notes per square inch? There are very few pieces that have more. He didn't mean that kind of superficial complexity; he didn't mean that kind of superficial temporal length. He meant structural length; he meant structural complexity; he meant degree of structural determination, structural richness. The solution to this problem . . . for Schoenberg was, of course, the musical formulation of the twelve-tone idea.

――――― ♪ ―――――

It used to be said frequently . . . that the trouble with the whole twelve-tone idea is that it's too mechanical, too mechanistic, and it forces too many things upon you. You don't have the great freedom of will that artists of the past enjoyed. The truth is that if anyone is concerned to dismiss a whole body of music—and it's a rather futile and undesirable pastime—I would suggest you could say quite the opposite. You could say the trouble with any twelve-tone work, by virtue of the whole notion of the twelve-tone concept, is that it's too contextual. It's too self-contained. The communal aspect shared by a twelve-tone work, and therefore what you can bring from one twelve-tone work to another or even from one piece of the same composer to another, is really not enough. [6]

From an interview with Laura Karpman, Perspectives of New Music, *1985*

MUSIC AND MATHEMATICS

Any music can be regarded as mathematical; the question is, is that the way one wants to hear a piece of music? It's not a very interesting way because it doesn't produce a very interesting construal of the music or very interesting mathemetics, because most of the mathematics that are invoked by those who wish to invoke it as a justification for a way of writing music is the most rudimentary mathematics. It doesn't give rise to the most rudimentary music and that is my point—the two questions are utterly irrelevant. [7]

SERIALISM

I have never thought of the twelve-tone system as imposing certain constraints. It has opened the way to certain modes of thinking about musical progression, structure, richness, and reach of the relationships, of relatedness, depth, and scope of reference, in a way that I could extend personally, that interested me more, and that was simply not available with regard to so-called tonal material. [8]

European and American Composers

From "On Having Been and Still Being an American Composer,"
Perspectives of New Music, *1989*

The presence of ever-increasing numbers of European musicians among us deprovincialized us by their presence and denationalized us by our awareness of the causes of this presence, even though even some of them transported such already familiar depreciations of American music as: "Of course, Gershwin is the best American composer; of course, he's not *really* a composer, but that's American music for you." And this proposition has persisted down through the intervening decades, with only the composer's name changed to protect the insult's contemporaneity.

——— ♪ ———

Almost all American composers act in accord with or react against a "thinking about" music, a "knowing that" whose diversity yet defines a common domain, while the Continental composers share common aspirations, shaped not by educational orientation and institutions, but by "real world" political and public institutions. The Continental composer may be obliged to court program directors of radio stations, but also he can expect to encounter even conductors—for example—who not only share his nationality and cultural background but have the authority and professional ambition to perform works other than the riff-raffish displays of evanescently flashy timbral patinas which make life easy for the America conductor, his performers, his audience, and his employers, and yet are permitted to count as a generous gesture to contemporary music. . . .

The Continental composer may guide his professional behavior with a view to enjoying the material rewards of genuine celebrity; the American composer of highly "cultivated" music, with no illusions as to who are the cultural heroes in a people's cultural democracy, may attain bush-league celebrity, with many of the disadvantages of materially genuine celebrity and but few of the advantages. Our most egalitarian of countries has produced, almost necessarily by way of self-preservation, the most remarkable of elites in all realms of creative intellection, and in music—so micro and yet so completely messy a sub-realm—the defensive strategies of survival of its elite have to be applied on many fronts: against that coercive coalition, that union of journalists, media meddlers, performers, and even (some) music historians who perpetuate the axiological illogic of the European ("the best American composer is ... ") with "the best contemporary music is ... ," and when the shocked demurrer takes the form of "but that music is simply silly," the satisfied response is: "of course it's silly, but that's contemporary music for you." The best—as identified by me (us), without any derivation from the analytical through the normative—is silly. Underlying this illicit "is—ought" conversion is the unmistakable implication that they, particularly the music historians, possess so superior an overview and—even—"aesthetic sense" that they know that "non-silly" music of any consequence cannot be written in our time, for if it could they would be the ones to write it. So we who attempt to do just that are kidding ourselves; we should be grateful that we, in our lack of superior historic perspective, are more to be pitied than censured. But still we can only wonder how those, no matter how highly developed their aesthetic and historical sensibilities, who presumably no longer depend upon McGuffey's Eclectic Readers for their literary satisfaction, hail its musical clone as music suitable for adult consumption, and, if their words of appreciation of these works are the most interesting things they can find to say about them, how they possibly can find the works themselves interesting. [9]

APHORISMS

There's nothing a know-nothing resents more than someone who knows something; he knows plenty of nothing and nothing's plenty for him. (*Perspectives of New Music* essay) [10]

Of course, we don't revel in our difficulties. Believe me, the performance of our music is no revel. (University of Wisconsin lecture) [11]

If the best thing a composer can be is dead, the next best thing he can be is German. One of the worst things he can possibly be, still, is American. (University of Wisconsin lecture) [12]

"THE HYPOTHETICAL OTHER"

From the Perspectives of New Music essay

When asked to identify the audience for whom he composed, the American composer Igor Stravinsky replied: "The Hypothetical Other." I—who have been obliged too often to confess that I try to write the music which I would most like to hear, and then am accused of self-indulgence, eliciting the ready admission that there are few whom I would rather indulge—I am prepared to confess that I, too, have composed for a Hypothetical Other, but—to paraphrase another American thinker—I have met my Hypothetical Other, and he is I. [13]

Leonard Bernstein
1918–1990

Bernstein's profusion of talents made it difficult for him to be satisfied within a single branch of musical activity. By the time he became the first American-born conductor of the New York Philharmonic in 1958, he had composed ballets, a film score, two symphonies, the operas Trouble in Tahiti *and* Candide, *and the musicals* On the Town *and* West Side Story. *His charisma and boundless energy gave him a spectacular presence as a performer. Com-*

bined with his appetite for erudition, these same qualities made him an engaging teacher and an effective popularizer of classical music—roles he assumed in the majority of his published writings.

HEARING VERSUS LISTENING

From "An Imaginary Conversation," 1962

It's not easy to listen to a piece and really know and feel what's going on in it all the time. It may be easy to *take*, or pleasant to hear for many people; it may evoke fanciful images in the mind, or bathe them in a sensuous glow, or stimulate, or soothe, or whatever. But none of that is *listening*. And until we have a great listening public, and not just a passively *hearing* one, we will never be a musically cultured nation.   [1]

COMPOSERS, AUDIENCES, AND TONALITY

From the introduction to The Infinite Variety of Music, 1966

My dear and gentle Reader:

Everyone says that this is a critical moment in the history of music. I agree, but double in spades: it is a *scary* moment. The famous gulf between composer and audience is not only wider than ever: it has become an ocean. What is more, it has frozen over; and it shows no immediate signs of either narrowing or thawing.

It has been claimed that the abovementioned gulf first appeared as a tiny fissure the moment a composer first set down his personal message, conceived in his own unconscious rather than in the collective unconscious of the sacred/secular community. This may well be; and, if true, makes our gulf hundreds of years old. But throughout this period—even in the wildest years of Romanticism—there has always been some relation between composer and public, a symbiotic interaction that has fed both. The composer has been the manipulator of musical dynamics, responsible for change and growth, creating the public taste and then satisfying it with the appropriate nutriment; while the public, *quid pro quo,* has nourished him by simply being interested. Any new opera, by Monteverdi, Rossini, Wagner or Puccini has in its time invariably been an occasion for curiosity, speculation and excitement. Likewise a new symphony of Haydn or Brahms, a new sonata of Scarlatti or Chopin.

This is no longer true, nor has it been true in our century. The First World War seemed to mark a full stop: Debussy, Mahler, Strauss, and the early Stravinsky barely made the finish line; they were the last names in that long era of mutually dependent composer and public. From then on it became a hassle: composer *versus* public. For fifty years now audiences have been primarily interested in music of the past; even now they (you) are just catching up with Vivaldi, Bellini, Buxtehude, Ives. The controversy backs and fills about Wagner, as though he were Stockhausen. We (you) are still discovering Haydn symphonies, Handel operas. And it still requires a monumental effort of concentration for the average concertgoer to absorb the *Eroica* as a full, continuous formal experience. To say nothing of *Elektra, Pelléas*, or Mahler's Seventh. Gentle reader, be frank and admit it.

What this means is that for fifty years the public has not anticipated with delight the premiere of a single symphonic or operatic work. If this seems too strong a statement, then fight back; remind me of the glaring exceptions: *Porgy and Bess* (can show tunes make an opera?); Shostakovich's Seventh Symphony (a wartime enthusiasm inflated to hysteria by the competition of broadcast networks); *Mahagonny* (a local quasi-political phenomenon). The list could go on; but these works were all exceptions, and their delights anticipated chiefly for nonmusical reasons. . . .

We could conceivably look at this drastic change with equanimity, form a quasi-scientific opinion about its causes, and even project an objective theory as to its probable future course—if it were not for the fact that we are simultaneously living with such an incredible boom in musical activity. Statistics are soaring: more people are listening to more music than ever before. And it is the intersection of these two phenomena—the public's enormous new interest in music, plus their total lack of interest in *new* music, the musical bang plus the musical whimper—that has created this scary moment. . . .

Pop music seems to be the only area where there is to be found unabashed vitality, the fun of invention, the feeling of fresh air. Everything else suddenly seems old-fashioned: electronic music, serialism, chance music—they have already acquired the musty odor of academicism. Even jazz seems to have ground to a painful halt. And tonal music lies in abeyance, dormant.

Having said that I believe this musical crisis to be transitory in nature, I must now say where the transition may be leading, and why. I think that the key is to be found in the nature of music itself. It is an art so distinct, so utterly different from all other arts, that we must be careful not to assign to it values and dynamics it does not have. This is the mistake so many people make who follow the arts as a whole and try to deduce generalizations about them. What works in other arts does not necessarily work in music. Let us, for the sake of argument, try for a generalization. What is the nature of this crisis in all the arts today? We are constantly hearing negative phrases: anti-art, anti-play, anti-novel, anti-hero, non-picture, non-poem. We hear that art has become, perforce, art-commentary; we fear that techniques have swallowed up what used to be known as content. All this is reputed to be lamentable, a poor show, a sad state. And yet look at how many works of art, conceived in something like these terms, prosper, attract a large following, and even succeed in moving us deeply. There must be something good in all this negativism.

And there is. For what these works are doing is simply moving constantly toward more poetic fields of relevance. Let us now be specific: *Waiting for Godot* is a mightily moving and compassionate non-play. *La Dolce Vita,* which deals with emptiness and tawdriness, is a curiously invigorating film, even an inspiring one. Nabokov's non-novel *Pale Fire is* a thrilling masterpiece, and its hero, Charles Kinbote, is a pure non-hero. Balanchine's most abstract and esoteric ballets are his prize smash hits. De Kooning's pictures can be wonderfully decorative, suggestive, stimulating and very expensive. This could become a very long list indeed; but there is one thing that it could not include—a piece of serious anti-music. Music cannot prosper as a non-art, because it is basically and radically an abstract art, whereas all the other arts deal basically with real images—words, shapes, stories, the human body. And when a great artist takes a real image and abstracts it, or joins it to another real image that seems irrelevant, or combines them in an illogical way, he is poeticizing. In this sense Joyce is more poetical than Zola, Balanchine more than Petipa, Nabokov more than Tolstoy, Fellini more than Griffith. But John Cage is *not* more poetical than Mahler, nor Boulez more so than Debussy.

Why must music be excluded from this very prosperous tendency in the arts? Because it is abstract to start with; it deals *directly* with the emotions, through a transparent medium of tones which are unrelated to any representational aspects of living. The only "reality" these tones can have is *form*—that is, the precise way in which these tones interconnect. And by form I mean the shape of a two-note motive as well as of a phrase, or of the whole second act of *Tristan*. One cannot "abstract" musical tones; on the contrary they have to be *given* their reality through form: up-and-down, long-and-short, loud-and-soft.

And so to the inescapable conclusion. All forms that we have ever known— plain chant, motet, fugue, or sonata—have always been conceived in *tonality,* that is, in the sense of a tonal magnetic center, with subsidiary tonal relationships. This sense, I believe, is built into the human organism; we cannot hear two isolated tones, even devoid of any context, without immediately imputing a tonal meaning to them. We may differ from one another in the tonal meaning we infer, but we infer it nonetheless. We are stuck with this, and always will be. And the moment a composer tries to "abstract" musical tones by denying them their tonal implications, he has left the world of communication. In fact, it is all but impossible to do (although Heaven knows how hard composers have been trying for fifty years)—as witness the increasingly desperate means being resorted to— chance-music, electronic sounds, noteless "instructions," the manipulation of noise, whatnot.

It has occasionally occurred to me that music could conceivably exist, some distant day, ultimately detached from tonality. I can't hear such music in my head, but I am willing to grant the possibility. Only that distant day would have to have seen a fundamental change in our physical laws, possibly through man's detaching himself from this planet. Perhaps he has already begun, in his space chase, the long road to that New Consciousness, that Omega point. Perhaps we are some day to be freed from the tyranny of time, the dictatorship of the harmonic series. Perhaps. But meanwhile we are still earth-based, earth-bound, far from any Omega point, caught up in such old-fashioned things as human relationships, ideological, international, and interracial strife. . . .

It can be no mere coincidence that after half a century of radical experiment the best and best-loved works in atonal or 12-tone or serial idioms are those works which seem to have preserved, against all odds, some backdrop of tonality—those works which are richest in tonal implications. I think offhand of Schoenberg's Third Quartet, his Violin Concerto, his two Chamber Symphonies; almost all of Berg's music; Stravinsky in *Agon* or *Threni;* even Webern in his Symphony or in his second Cantata—in all of these works there are continuous and assertive spectors of tonality that haunt you as you listen. And the more you listen, the more you are haunted. And in the haunting you feel the agony of longing for tonality, the violent wrench away from it, and the blind need to recapture it.

We will recapture it. That is the meaning of our transition, our crisis. But we will come back to it in a new relationship, renewed by the catharsis of our agony . . . And music will survive. [2]

OBSERVATIONS

From an address at the University of Chicago, 1957

I should think that most composing by almost any composer happens lying down. Many a time my wife has walked into my studio and found me lying down and has said, "Oh, I thought you were working, excuse me!" And I *was* working, but you'd never have known it. [3]

Even those composers who call themselves "experimental" composers (and who are dedicated to the idea of writing music that is different from all other music that preceded it, making their music valuable only because it is different from other music) are admitting their recognition of the presence of an art that preceded their own, because their art is still being written in terms of the art that preceded it— only . . . in antithesis instead of imitation. [4]

I know that I always think of an audience when I write music—not as I plan to write music, not as I am actually writing it—but somewhere in the act of writing there is the sense haunting this act of the people who are going to hear it. [5]

You can always tell whether it [music] has come from an inner place or an outer place. And the people who can tell best, strangely enough, are not the critics and not other composers, but the public. . . . Even if they are listening to a quartet by Webern and they don't like Webern, they know that it's real, that Webern was a real composer. And the reason for this is that they can sense the communication. They can tell that the music comes from an inner place and wasn't just made up out of somebody's head. [6]

JAZZ AS AN INFLUENCE ON COMPOSERS

From a television script, 1959

Many American composers since Gershwin have turned jazz to far subtler and more complex uses than he did. For many of them jazz entered their blood stream, became part of the air they breathed, so that it came out in their music in new, transformed ways, not sounding like jazz at all, but unmistakably American. Such composers as Copland, Harris, Schuman, and even Sessions and Piston, have written music that is American without even trying, the result of an unconscious metamorphosis of jazz elements or jazz feelings. This has been one of the strongest conditioning forces of the American musical language. [7]

MOZART

From a television script, 1959

Mozart is *all* music; there is nothing you can ask from music that he cannot supply. [8]

From "An Imaginary Conversation"

I could talk myself hoarse about Mozart on a thousand television shows and never convey to you a fraction of the insight and knowledge you could gain from an hour of playing Mozart sonatas all by yourself. [9]

MAHLER AND OTHERS

From an article in High Fidelity, September 1967

The first spontaneous image that springs to my mind at the mention of the name *Mahler* is of a colossus straddling the magic dateline *1900*. There he stands, his left foot (closer to the heart!) firmly planted in the rich, beloved nineteenth century, and his right, rather less firmly, seeking solid ground in the twentieth. Some say he never found this foothold; others (and I agree with them) insist that twentieth-century music could not exist as we know it if that right foot had not landed there with a commanding thud. Whichever assessment is right, the image remains: he straddled. Along with Strauss, Sibelius and, yes, Schoenberg, Mahler sang the last rueful songs of nineteenth-century romanticism. But Strauss's extraordinary gifts went the route of a not very subjective virtuosity; Sibelius and Schoenberg found their own extremely different but personal routes into the new century. Mahler was left straddling; his destiny was to sum up, package, and lay to ultimate rest the fantastic treasure that was German-Austrian music from Bach to Wagner. [10]

COPLAND

From an article in the Schwann catalogue, 1975

Like his Biblical namesake, he has functioned as the High Priest of American music, the gentle but forceful leader and taste-maker, adored by his disparate tribes for his flexibility, facility, and immensely appealing articulateness. And yet this is a superficial portrait—this benign bestower of the Golden Calf. For within this pleasant and reassuring persona called Aaron lives the mysterious anima of the brother Moses, the stern and stammering lawgiver. It is as though the amiable, cultivated Aaron provided the public voice for the harsh and resolute prophet that rages within. And it is this inner voice that ultimately informs the whole Copland musical corpus, uniting all its flexibility and "eclecticism" into a significant and lasting whole. Those critics who speculate, not quite sympathetically, on how the same composer could have written the pop-toned *Music for the Theatre* and the thornily severe *Connotations* should listen more carefully. They will find in both works, and in all others in between, that unmistakably consistent Mosaic voice, attenuated, adorned, or mollified to varying degrees according to the changing visibility of the Aaronic vestments, of the gleaming, opulent priestly breastplate.   [11]

Conducting versus Composing

From a written statement, October 15, 1946

It is impossible to me to make an exclusive choice among the various activities of conducting, symphonic composition, writing for the theater, and playing the piano. What seems right to me at any given moment is what I must do, at the expense of pigeonholing or otherwise limiting my services to music. I will not compose a note while my heart is engaged in a conducting season; nor will I give up writing so much as a popular song, while it is there to be expressed, in order to conduct Beethoven's Ninth. There is a particular order involved in this, which is admittedly difficult to plan; but the order must be adhered to most strictly. For the ends are music itself, not the conventions of the music business; and the means are my private problem.   [12]

CHAPTER THIRTEEN

Györgi Ligeti

Ned Rorem

Pierre Boulez

Luciano Berio

Gunther Schuller

Hans Werner Henze

Karlheinz Stockhausen

Györgi Ligeti

b. 1923

Ligeti received his training in Budapest, later teaching at the Academy of Music there. Among his first models as a composer were Bartók and Stravinsky. He left Hungary in 1956 after the failure of the revolution, settling in Germany and continuing to teach. At this time he also became interested in electronics, and the voice of his mature compositions began to emerge. Since then he has opened himself up to a wide variety of influences, from sub-Saharan drumming to the ideas of the philosopher Karl Popper, often adapting them in a practical fashion toward the development of compositional techniques.

From an interview with Péter Várnai, 1978

STYLISTIC NORMS

Since today there is no accepted norm in musical language everybody must find his own. We are forced to look for something new, which puts me right at the opposite pole from nostalgia or neotonality. I feel that to revert to the great tradition of the past is tantamount to taking refuge in "safe" music. There is another way of continuing the work of the great masters of the past, composing at the same level as represented, say, by the late Beethoven sonatas, but in a new language, a new style. There is a task for you! Going back to the same musical idiom will not do. . . .

I should welcome a generally accepted musical language, such as tonality used to be. In the context of tonality it was of extraordinary interest when Liszt invented a new modulation no one had ever heard before. Since we now have no universal language, such events are no longer imaginable. Serialism, which Boulez had thought would gain universal currency, turned out to be a mere episode in musical history. [1]

MUSICAL FASHIONS

You can observe a certain alternation of fashions in the history of music, in which a more experimentally minded period is followed by one leaning more toward tradition. I do not speak of fashion in a derogatory sense, I simply mean trends. Machaut and Landini started something genuinely new, which was very experimental. The Flemish school then developed it into some form of classical style. Also, Monteverdi's *seconda prattica* represented an immensely bold step when it first appeared, but had turned into old-fashioned, stuffy conformism by the time of Bach's sons. In my opinion the time for new, decisive innovations always comes when a particular musical tradition has run out of steam. Just think of Debussy coming after Saint-Saëns and Fauré. There are periods when the renewal of musical language is of little consequence. There is not much new in Mozart's musical language compared to the novelty of the Mannheim school and of J. C. Bach. Mozart created something outstandingly new but not in the technical aspects of musical language. I think that a change in style is brought on partly by the potentiality inherent in the music of a period and partly by a transformation of the general cultural context. In Central Europe after the collapse of Nazism there was a cultural vacuum, which was filled by Stravinsky, Hindemith, Schoenberg, and Webern. Then a number of composers, bursting with new ideas, happened to come together in Darmstadt. It had to be in Germany, where the cultural vacuum was most pronounced; Germany, after all, was in the eye of the storm. All that has changed by now. There has now been a period of ten years marked by some form of consolidation, of the wrong kind, I should say. In many areas I have become aware of a marked trend back to romanticism. Some people call it nostalgia—the French say "retro"; it has become chic, it is all the rage. We can never tell what will ultimately come from a fashion—the Mannheim style was also a fashion in its time. As far as I am concerned, I did not follow Stockhausen or Cage when they were the guiding stars but went on in my own way. Now we find nostalgia in the same dominant position, and again I do not follow this trend either but remain independent.   [2]

CONFORMITY

There are official composers who dress up in a dinner suit and Bohemian ones who wear jeans. I do not wear either. In every country and every system there are official composers and the complete outsiders. It seems very disturbing that I do not belong to either group. In spite of that I usually get very good reviews, but most critics are discomfited by my not fitting into either mold. What can I do? My position in this respect is the same as what I have said about my music, I think. There must be some kind of order, but not too much of it, and it should not be dogmatic. But there must not be disorder either.   [3]

Music should not be normal, well-bred, with its tie all neat.   [4]

MUSIC AND MONEY; FILM MUSIC

Being a well-known composer, as I have been since *Apparitions* [1957], does not necessarily mean that you are well paid. The few performances of my works did not bring in much; I was reduced to a Bohemian, almost "clochard" existence. Yet I refused to write film music, even in those days, although it would have been very lucrative. I was afraid that it would compromise my talent. I wanted to be radical and not to compromise my ideas. This may sound pompous, but that was the aim I set myself in life. When, in the early '60s, I could have had the opportunity to write film music without any stylistic preconditions, I still refused. I did not wish to get into the world of cinema; I had the feeling it was a world that would corrupt you. The first commission for film music is soon followed by the next. You quickly get used to the idea of what mood is required for a particular sequence, you are influenced by the knowledge of what atmosphere is wanted as background for particular scenes, you compose with a stopwatch, minding the seconds: all that has a corrupting effect. I do not think that Mozart would have been able to write his quartets dedicated to Haydn if he had composed film music earlier.   [5]

THE TEACHING OF COMPOSITION

I am constitutionally an anti-educationalist, and in any case you cannot teach composition. You can teach the technical aspects of it, harmony, musical form, counterpoint, orchestration. My requirement is that everybody who intends to compose what you call modern music—any kind of modern music—should be perfectly familiar with tertian harmony, Palestrina and Bach counterpoint, should be able to write fugues and should be conversant with musical forms. This is an indispensable knowledge even if as a composer he will not use it. That was my conclusion after studying with Ferenc Farkas, and also with Sandor Veress, Kadosa, and Jardanyi. I was lucky to have had the opportunity to learn all the rules of traditional musical technique. They served me more than I can say, in everything I did, be it micropolyphony, multilayered textures, or anything else. Without the Palestrina exercises I learned through Jeppesen I would never have been able to work out intricate micropolyphonic textures. I would swear by the importance of traditional techniques. But there is also a negative side to studying composition. Whereas I find it extremely important to learn how to handle sonata form or rondo form, I am totally against the use of traditional forms for present-day melodic, harmonic, or rhythmic material. Knowing how to analyze traditional forms is indispensable, but God save us from atonal sonatas. [6]

SCHUMANN

Schumann's internal weaving of lines, both very dense and unsystematic, is not really contrapuntal; it consists in figures and ornaments run wild. It is very original, and in some ways profoundly affects the development of his formal structures. It gives the impression of a musical form that has overflowed the banks. [7]

MAHLER

The ambition in Mahler is such a wonderful failure. His ambitious overall forms somehow always fail; it is really touching. You find in his music a gap between the symphonic aspirations and the result, which came in for very harsh criticism at the time. The opinion was that his music tends to disintegration. The apparent lack of logic in his forms was not understood, whereas I am particularly attracted by that rent quality, his *Zerrissenheit* [raggedness]. Mahler is a composer you can admire and feel compassion for at the same time. [8]

PHILOSOPHIES; VARIOUS COMPOSITIONS

My music is a continuous flow, unbroken by bars, like a Gregorian melody. You could not analyze it according to Riemann's rules. [9]

I have always been fascinated by machines that do not work properly; in general, by the external world of technology and automation, which engenders, and puts people at the mercy of, bureaucracies. Transposed into music, the ticking of malfunctioning machinery occurs in many of my works, including the Second Quartet. [10]

In the early '60s I was also interested in other areas of form and expression, in a frantic, tormented quality of sound that may seem like a disorderly, wild gesticulation, haphazard and completely uncontrolled. . . . At the same time I was really trying to find ways of transforming this "superexpressiveness" into something cool, as if to put such a wild musical gesticulating in a glass case, to see it as we see objects exhibited in a museum. [11]

Technically speaking, I have always approached music texture through part-writing. Both *Atmosphères* and *Lontano* have a dense canonic structure. But you cannot actually hear the polyphony, the canon. You hear a kind of impenetrable texture, something like a very densely woven cobweb. I have retained melodic lines in the process of composition, they are governed by rules as strict as Palestrina's or those of the Flemish school, but the rules of this polyphony are worked out by me. The polyphonic structure does not actually come through, you cannot hear it; it remains hidden in a microscopic, underwater world, to us inaudible. I call it micropolyphony (such a beautiful word!). All in all, you cannot hear my music as it appears on paper. Of course, while actually composing each piece I worked on what we hear, as we hear it. The technical process of composition is like letting a crystal form in a supersaturated solution. The crystal is potentially there in the solution but becomes visible only at the moment of crystallization. In much the same way, you could say that there is a state of supersaturated polyphony, with all the "crystal culture" in it but you cannot discern it. My aim was to arrest the process, to fix the supersaturated solution just at the moment before crystallization. [12]

Ned Rorem
b. 1923

Rorem began his formal musical studies with Leo Sowerby at the age of fifteen and continued at Northwestern University, Curtis Institute, and the Juilliard School. Like Virgil Thomson, with whom he studied orchestration in 1944, Rorem spent several years in France and holds an avowed preference for French musical ideals over German ones. As a composer, he is best known for his songs, of which he has written well over a hundred. Equally wide is his fame as an author and diarist, with more than a dozen books to his credit.

From Music from Inside Out, 1959–67

"THE INTERNATIONAL LANGUAGE"

Music is probably the least international of languages. During two years in Morocco I never encountered a native who could fathom our formal music any more than our Christian values. Only in the past century and to us of the West do Strauss's sheep or Ravel's sad birds, Respighi's trees or Honegger's engine, signify themselves in sound through habit and suggestion. And yet, when he knows what it represents, who, hearing Britten's "Sick Rose," for instance, can restrain a spinal chill when that wormlike horn bores into the flower's heart? An Arab would not *see* this as we do—through the ears. We also, were we not told beforehand of the intended association, would miss our guess nine times out of ten even with such broad themes as love and war, festivity and madness. [1]

COMPOSERS AND COMPOSITION

Composers today are suspiciously articulate: many pass more time explaining than composing. . . . If a recent London critic can be believed, the current state of music presents a variety of solutions in search of a problem, the problem being to find somebody left to listen.

The future's measure of our creative pulse may well prove to be the sciences. They have seduced many an artist (yet cannot afford to be seduced by art). One doesn't criticize a method, just the method's results. Poems and pictures are already retreating from methods of obscurantism. Music, not yet. But then music always lags behind the other arts, and all art lags when the world is in trouble.

In any case, there is little truly new in composition, the language having been complete for about a half-century. Of music being composed the finest isn't worried about novelty-at-any-price. It is worried about expressive innovation. With the standardization of both audiences and composing techniques, individual expressivity seems about the one lasting goal.

The true advance guard is freedom—that of being honest about one's own creative logic on one's own terms. Little such freedom exists when art grants priority to style over content.* The liberation will doubtless come, as in the past, through a great man. I, for one, do not yet perceive him among musicians; fresh talent today is busy elsewhere. But let us hope he will arrive before the dwindling need of formal beauty finally vanishes. [2]

Composers often avoid concerts because they are saturated with their own music, because they are weary of standardized programs exalting virtuoso rather than creator, and because (when their works are represented) they are intimidated. The intimidation is either from dismay at a possible bad performance for which they are blameless, or from schizophrenia at hearing notes which no longer directly concern them and over which they've relinquished control.

They are usually a little impatient while their music is played: it sounds better or worse but never the same as what they heard in the inner ear. When impatience becomes gratifying, it's a transference of how they hope their audience is reacting. Their own reaction is doubtless most objective when alone with recordings.

Although acclaim is agreeable, it is foreign to the composer's basic elation. For that elation is exercised only in the hermetic act of writing music, and is of such unique magnitude and mystery that it is not only irrelevant but impossible to depict in words. [3]

Inspiration, as such, is no special concern of the composer. There is nothing much he can do about it anyway. He takes it for granted and goes on from there. However, he can do something about the tailoring of his technical resources. If his craft

---

* Today the "style" is to consider style and content as one. [Rorem]

is not ready to construct a suitable lodging for the eventual visit of Inspiration, Inspiration will turn around and leave.

Brahms one day was confronted by a lady who unctuously inquired: "How do you make your slow movements so beautiful?" He replied with his legendary gruffness: "Because the publishers order them that way!" He was unconcerned with the hoped-for response which would have been: "Inspiration falls from heaven in my dreams."

Alas! Music of dreams becomes trash in the morning. Anyone can discover beautiful noise in revery. The composer's job is to communicate an organization of this sound. Inspiration through dreams is less dependable for the artist than for the prophet. How many times will a composer awaken full of wisdom, to find that as the day progresses his ecstasy evaporates when given utterance, and at nightfall only banalities have been scribbled? The work of art seldom springs from a gratuitous source. [4]

From An Absolute Gift, 1978

MASTERPIECES

People suggest that I sneer at musical masterpieces. It's not a sneer, it's awe taken for granted. I won't deny the fact of masterpieces (though some are my cup of tea while others are straight medicine). We are preconditioned to this one, another we "discover," but both kinds, once swallowed, can't stay with us daily, or we'd have time for nothing else—for searching out new masterpieces, maybe composing one ourselves. Since rarely now I sit down and listen to, say, Beethoven's Fifth, the very rareness permits fresh surprise: Why, it *is* marvelous! despite the fact that we *know* it's marvelous. [5]

SCANDALS

Scandal in music seems to be gone. Earlier in the century the biggest *causes célèbres* were scandals, and all except *Sacre* were vocal works: *Pierrot, Noces, Wozzeck, Four Saints*. But those sixties firecrackers of, say, Berio and Salzman and Austin spluttered insofar as they offered themselves as outrageous. Perhaps the scandal of Vietnam dwarfed such adventures. In any case true scandal can't be planned, and might come today only via the quintessentially pristine. Meanwhile the current example of an *enfant terrible* is not even an Alice Cooper or a loud Lukas Foss, but a muffled Morton Feldman or a gentle George Crumb. [6]

SACRED AND PROFANE

The sacred and profane styles, so-called, of so many, are indistinguishable. Wagner's *Parsifal* and *Venusberg*, Poulenc's *Mamelles* [*de Tiresias*] and *Stabat* [*Mater*], Britten's *War Requiem* and *Death in Venice* are brewed from the same irrepressible perfumes. Composers speak one language only, though they can speak it well or poorly depending on the weather. Or depending on God, who sometimes arranges that their holy music is not "as good as" their sin tunes. [7]

CHURCH MUSIC

Ask not what music can do for the Church, but what the Church can do for music. Performances are generally lousy, there's little money in it for composers, and the congregation doesn't come for the melodies. To include the parishioners by writing tunes facile enough for them is to treat music not as an art—as an end in itself for the Lord's glory—but as a means to keep folks awake. To overemphasize audience participation is to condescend, to suppose that listening is not participatory.   [8]

CRITICS

A critic's chief crime, as the composers see it, rests in a casual viewpoint toward new music. Admittedly most new music, like most everything, is mediocre and the critic must say so; but let him say so with sorrow, not sarcasm. His problem is partly occupational, for good criticism abounds in related fields. Movie, art, dance and drama critics review mostly the new. Only music critics must still think up phrases for Beethoven because only they review performance equally with what's performed.   [9]

APHORISMS

The more we know someone's music the more we know how it should *not* go. (*An Absolute Gift*)   {10}

Art is a misquotation of something heard. Thus, it becomes a quotation of something never heard. (*Knowing When to Stop*)   {11}

From Knowing When to Stop, *1994*

MUSIC AS REPRESENTATION (1959/94)

The sea reminds me of Debussy's *La mer*; *La mer* never reminds me of the sea. But if a picture recalls the sea, the sea conjures up no picture of anything beyond itself. In this sense, water is as abstract as music, but a picture of water *represents* an abstraction. Whatever title Debussy may have chosen, his work is finally enjoyed as sheer music. If a novice were told that the three movements of this piece illustrated three times of day, not on the sea but in a city, he wouldn't know the difference.   {12}

LISTENING TO BEETHOVEN

I immersed myself {c. 1940} in the late quartets, dissecting the scores, pondering the discs (mainly the Busch ensemble), and fearing that the lack was in me and not in Ludwig when his airs didn't click, when "it" didn't happen, when the involuntary mental erection impelled by True Art failed to materialize. I never got—still don't get—the point of Beethoven. Far from weeping, I nod;

my guilty love of Debussy and (shame!) Poulenc was as disconcerting as my preferring sugar to pasta, or preferring men to women. Would Beethoven acquire new meaning when I "matured"? [13]

RAVEL

From An Absolute Gift

His rhythmic sense, characteristically French, is vague, except where consciously italicized.

He made no pretense at being a contrapuntalist, and his few stabs at canon (with the exception of the ecstatic false fugue at the close of *L'Enfant*) are banal.

He was a harmonist born. His harmonies, both in their vertical selves and in sequence, contain the inevitability of greatness, are almost embarrassingly tactile, and are always recognizable as his despite their providing the unique base for all chordal progressions in pop music internationally for fifty years.

His tunes, spun out for mile upon silver mile, locate him in a camp far from Beethoven or even Debussy, both of whom glued together (always ingeniously) their truncated fragments.

His instrumental hues (again characteristically French) are unadulterated. But if the French have always been noted for economical means, which in turn are the roots of taste, no one has ever focused on taste in, say, Franck or Fauré.

What is called Ravel's wit is his removal, when choosing texts to set, from sober adult romance. . . .

The effects of his music, assumed to be restrained and upper-class (so as to distinguish them easily from Debussy's), are really nonintellectual and replete with voluptuous yearning. [14]

POULENC

An appreciation, 1963, from Music from Inside Out

Like his name he was both dapper and ungainly. His clothes came from Lanvin but were unpressed. His hands were scrubbed, but the fingernails were bitten to bone. His physiognomy showed a cross between weasel and trumpet, and featured a large nose through which he wittily spoke. His sun-swept apartment on the Luxembourg Gardens was grandly toned in orange plush, but the floors squeaked annoyingly. His social predilections were for duchesses and policemen, though he was born and lived as a wealthy bourgeois. His villa at Noizay was austere and immaculate, but surrounded by densely careless arbors. There he wrote the greatest vocal music of our century, all of it technically impeccable, and truly vulgar. He was deeply devout and uncontrollably sensual.

In short, his aspect and personality, taste and music, each contained contrasts which were not alternating but simultaneous. In a single spoken paragraph he would express terror about a work in progress, hence his need for a pilgrimage to the Black Virgin's Shrine at Rocamadour; his next breath extolled the joys of cruising the Deauville boardwalk. This was no *non sequitur* but the statement of a whole man always interlocking soul and flesh, sacred and profane; the double awareness of artists, and of their emulators, the saints.   [15]

CAGE

From Knowing When to Stop

John Cage was very much around [New York City, 1940s], and we met often, mainly at Lou Harrison's dark loft on Bleecker Street. . . . Already tireless in the promotion of his selflessness, he seemed a dime-store Descartes pushing "Je pense, donc je suis" as though he'd coined the phrase. If everything's art, as Cage would claim, then anything's art; and if nothing is truly ugly (a heap of corpses at Belsen?), as he also would claim, then is anything truly beautiful? His undefined terms make for easy chuckles and a soft-centered coterie, while his non-egoist stance makes for lasting publicity of that stance. All contradiction is brooked with a permanent smile, like that of so-patient Mormons who, because they're going to heaven and you're not, can afford magnanimity. . . .

I was bowled over one evening when John brought forth *Either/Or* by my piquant landsman Kierkegaard, of whom I'd never heard, and began to read aloud. . . . Less overwhelming was the premiere a few years later of Cage's most notorious piece, *4'33"*, scored for a performer who remains silent by his instrument for four minutes and thirty-three seconds. Hadn't Harold Acton, in one of his novels from the twenties, proposed the identical philosophy? (The music dwells in the audience's fidgety thoughts and in the random outside din during the prescribed minutes.) John has been dining out for two generations on Acton's uncredited notion.

What a fake! Yes, but a fake what?   [16]

From An Absolute Gift

Cage, like most household utensils, gets rusty and needs resharpening from time to time. His arguments grow lax: he justifies poetry with poetry, thereby stopping conversation.   [17]

From An Absolute Gift

BOULEZ

Boulez has been for thirty years not the *enfant terrible* but the intellectual conscience of music. His early works were eerily reasonable in their avoidance of easy sensuality, and his creative influence was nothing if not a triumph of style over content. He did not flirt with the ear, and it was with the eye that we examined, on paper, the labyrinth of his processes, processes worked out for piano solo or for instruments of one family where color mixtures could not take precedence over profile.   [18]

COMPOSING

Laziness is due not to too few but to too many notions, all fully realized. They aren't waiting to be born, but to be notated, and oh the drudgery, because they exist, almost complete—at least theatrically—there on the staves of the brain. The hours spent writing them down could be better spent thinking them up. Or so I reason, and get sick. [19]

My three mottos for songwriting: Use only good poems—that is, convincing marvels in English of all periods. Write gracefully for the voice—that is, make the voice line as seen on paper have the arched flow which singers like to interpret. Use no trick beyond the biggest trick—that is, since singing is already such artifice, never repeat words arbitrarily, much less ask the voice to groan, shriek, or rasp. I have nothing against special effects; they are just not in my language. I betray the poet by framing his words, not by distorting them. [20]

Pierre Boulez
b. 1925

A pupil of Olivier Messiaen and René Leibowitz, Boulez absorbed the principles of serialism and went on to construct his own musical language, uncompromising in its complexity and vigorous in its expression. In 1971 he began a controversial six-year tenure as music director of the New York Philharmonic, upsetting many subscribers by dramatically increasing the programming of twentieth-century music. In 1976 he received extensive funds from the French government to create a new organization dedicated to electronic music, the Institut de Recherche et Coordination Acoustique/Musique, or IRCAM. Boulez's plentiful intellectual resources and his outspoken, provocative manner, evident in his many writings, have helped to make him one of the most visible composers of his generation.

THE EVOLUTIONARY CYCLE OF ARTISTIC LANGUAGES
From "The Composer As Critic," 1954

As a first approximation in tracing the evolution of any art, we can establish various fluctuations, some gradual and others violent. On the one hand there are periods during which a language is being established, its potentialities explored; and these are on the whole periods of stability marked by a certain primordial peace guaranteed by the quasi-automatic nature of what is happening. On the other hand there are periods of destruction and discovery, with all the accompanying risks that have to be taken in responding to new and unfamiliar demands. In the first period there is not much critical writing apart from a few turgid polemical pieces of no more than passing interest; but in the second there are passionate discussions of fundamental problems raised by the weakening of automatic responses, the impoverishment of means of expression and a diminishing power of communication. [1]

THE STIMULUS TO COMPOSE
From an essay based on lectures given at Darmstadt in 1960

What in fact is the stimulus to compose? Well, it may be an entirely abstract formal idea, quite divorced from any "content," in which case the intermediary processes needed for its realization will gradually present themselves to the composer's mind, so that the original overall plan will reshape itself by means of a number of subsidiary "local" discoveries. Alternatively the stimulus may come from some purely instrumental feeling, a sound-picture demanding certain types of writing, which will generate the musical idea best suited to produce the desired effect; and in that case the outer envelope will have to find its own suitable content. Again, it may be some linguistic enquiry, which will lead to the discovery of forms of which the composer had in the first place no idea, or the use of certain instrumental combinations that had not at first occurred to him. The outline and sense of a work will sometimes be quite clear to the composer from start to finish, while in other cases actual starting points may be defined and become clear only after a long and difficult working-over. Or again the initial plan may be so modified during the course of composing that the composer has to go back and "recalibrate" the whole piece.

It is only very seldom that the composer finds himself in the presence of a world that he has glimpsed, like Schoenberg, in a single flash of heightened awareness, a world he then has to bring into actual existence. This "theological" aspect of the composer's task is more an aspiration than a fact (" . . . and you shall be like gods"), since it implies a most improbable degree of knowledge.   [2]

EAST AND WEST

From an interview in The World of Music, *1967*

I'm against this talk of parallels, this system of comparison. I find that people form a too sentimental and emotional idea of Oriental music. They now dive into it like tourists setting off to visit a landscape that is about to vanish. For they know very well that these musical civilizations are on the verge of extinction and so set out to sight-see while they still can. Such people imagine that they are deriving from these forms of music a measure of wisdom and contemplation, supposedly in relation to our Western world of movement. But movement is life. There is a great foolishness in the Westerner who goes to India, and I detest this idea of a "lost paradise." It is one of the most odious forms of affectation.

The music of Asia and India is to be admired because it has reached a stage of perfection, and it is this perfection that interests me. But otherwise the music is dead. In the course of time other languages arrive at the same maturity, but what is important is that which endures.   [3]

From a lecture at Sainte-Etienne, May 1968

EXPERIMENTATION AND NOSTALGIA

When one has had one's fill of experimenting, there comes a nostalgia for the past, a nostalgia for childhood, and attempts are made to camouflage this nostalgia by returning to certain things and integrating them as best one can in the world of today by means of a clumsy dialectic. . . . I can only say that such nostalgias have no interest for me; they are purely individual phenomena, of purely individual interest and quite unable to contribute to a future in the framework of history. I think that, quite the opposite, what we must face at the present time is a return to the future, seeking a way out of our strict disciplines and imagining the future with a certain freedom, which, combined with voluntary discipline, will give our contemporary language a chance of becoming more truly universal.   [4]

Resistance to Change

The musical world is indeed one of the most conservative of all and almost the most enclosed. You cannot expect such a world to be quickly transformed, because it is governed by economic imperatives extremely difficult to control.

Try, for instance, simply as a matter of organization, to modify the constitution of an orchestra. You will see that you will almost certainly encounter deep hostility, from both public and players, who will tell you that it has worked very well as it is: why should it not continue to do so, with a few adjustments? The fact that must now be faced is that it will not continue unless a profound remedy is discovered—and how is that to be done? By organizing either concert halls or actual concerts in a much more flexible way. There is a great deal of talk about free music, music in a state of "becoming," from the point of view of composition, but as soon as this music "in the state of becoming" reaches the stage of practical performance, we all come up against the fatal rigidity of structures.   [5]

Cultural Conditioning

In every listener there is a creator, who asks to express himself by means of another personality only because he himself lacks the creative gift. The composer is exactly like you, constantly on the horns of the same dilemma, caught in the same dialectic—the great models and an unknown future. He cannot take off into the unknown. When people tell me, "I am taking off into the unknown and ignoring the past" it is complete nonsense. Only if one were an Eskimo and found oneself in the middle of civilization, would it be possible to ignore the past. A certain modicum of civilization is needed, of course, in order to be able to share in our means of expression. Anyone born here, anyone whose first experiences of expression and of culture have been in Western Europe, is completely conditioned and cannot help himself. It will be possible for him to escape and to discover ways of eluding his formation, but he will never be able to escape his basic conditioning.   [6]

Research

From an address, April 20, 1979

Research is not the dry desert of logic, not the cramping and imprisoning of live forces, not the squared-out plan of a town that no one could be interested in building, not the security of a universe hedged in by definitions. Research is like a hunger: it grips you until you satisfy it; and then it returns. This hunger cannot be satisfied once and for all and then be got rid of and forgotten.   [7]

Rhythm

From "Stravinsky Remains," Musique russe, 1951/3

One can think that, since the end of the Renaissance, rhythm has not been considered a peer of the other musical components and that the best part of it has been left to intuition and good taste.

To find the most rational attitude toward rhythm in our occidental music, one must return to Philippe de Vitry, Guillaume de Machaut, and Guillaume Dufay. Their isorhythmic motets are decisive testimony to the constructive value of rhythmic structures in relation to the different sequences implied by the cadences.

[8]

From "Eventually ... ," Revue musicale, 1952

Serialism

Most of our contemporaries would seem to be unaware of what happened in Vienna with Schoenberg, Berg, and Webern. That is why, even though it may become irksome, one still must describe, shorn of all prophetic legend and all admiring, exclamatory style, the real achievement of the three Viennese. The dodecaphonists find themselves involved in the present misunderstanding of this subject for a reason. Organizing *congresses*—those of specialists playing at initiate ceremonies for fearful beginners—falsely doctrinaire, absurdly conservative, they lord it in stupid repletion for the greater glory of the avant-garde. They have adopted the serial system, whether in the comfortable belief that nothing but vulgar ruse exists outside that orthodoxy or with the intention of erecting a salutary guardrail. This is an attitude that does not even have the advantage of being uncertain.

In another camp, the serial system is considered under some aspects that are not without flavor!

The deaf find in it nothing but artifice, decomposition, and decadence (see above ...). A possible reaction might be a smile that certainly will have passed beyond commiseration.

The sentimental do not witness the implantation of chaos without terror, but in the legitimate anxiety not to allow the present situation to bypass them, they try to make use of chaos in order to oppose to it—and it is, let it be clearly understood, a symbol of our epoch—the classic vocabulary. Puffing from that sketchy exploit, they hold themselves freed of fear.

They are close to the libertarians or libertines who are not at all terrified, in principle, by all the technical research. They make those interesting acquisitions theirs, but, in the name of *liberty,* defend themselves from being *prisoners* of the system. They want *music* above everything, or at least what they proclaim to be music: they do not want to lose sight of *lyricism* (who will ever penetrate the mystery of the concepts covered by that vague word?). Their biggest preoccupation is of a rather encyclopedic order. They want to lock up all of history after monophony. They allow themselves the illusion of being vast and innumerable.

As for the generous, their reasonings take divergent paths. They try to persuade you that the serial discoveries are old, that all that was known in 1920. Now one should create the *new,* and in support of that brilliant thesis, they cite to you fake-Gounods, pseudo-Chabriers, champions of clarity, elegance, and refinement, eminently *French* qualities. (They adore mixing Descartes and *haute couture.*) They are convinced adepts of the time machine. The fashion in which they explore is, furthermore, unspeakable.

Finally, there will be the indulgent, who consider dodecaphony a venereal disease, who consider that having had a turbulent youth is logical, almost well-mannered, and—why not?—glorious. But it becomes inexcusable if one relapses after the delay granted to madness has expired.

The dodecaphonists themselves at times acquiesce to some of these points of view. Otherwise they are plunged into their restricted manifestation of minorities in exile, exactly like some semi-secret, gently illuminated, or moderately speculative association. Or, the second eventuality is that they can give themselves over, as a group or individually, to frenetic arithmetic masturbation. For in their necessitous speculation they have forgotten to go beyond the elementary stage of arithmetic. Do not ask them for anything more: they know how to count up to twelve and in multiples of twelve. Excellent spirits as apostles and disciples.

So dodecaphonists and independents labor under the ensign of *liberty.* Humor has it that the avant-garde glorifies the liberty of agreed-to discipline, whereas the conservatives favor anarchic freedom. The latter, in particular, consumed by disquiet over what they call the *multiplicity of techniques*—a pompous phrase in support of a notorious ineptitude. All that mediocrity still legislates for the majority; it is a survival that is breaking up. Nothing of it but anecdotes can endure.

What can we conclude? The unexpected: I, in turn, assert that any musician who has not experienced—I do not say understood, but, in all exactness, experienced—the necessity for the dodecaphonic language is USELESS. For his whole work is irrelevant to the needs of his epoch.

I hasten to give precise answers to the laggards who still assert that the series is a purely arbitrary, artificial creation by a master outside the moral code. It seems sufficiently evident that the epidemic of chromaticism after Wagner was notorious; Debussy will not contradict that. Thus the serial technique is nothing but the bringing to light of musical problems in ferment since 1910. It is not a decree; it is an authentication. A close analysis of Schoenberg's Opus 23 allows us to take very precise account of the transition effected in what may be called ultrathematization—where thematic intervals become absolute intervals freed of the rhythmic figures, capable of assuming by themselves the writing and structure of the work, able to move from horizontal unfolding to vertical coagulation.   [9]

INTELLECTUALISM

Since the nineteenth century, the word "intellectual" has been the most outrageous epithet when aimed at a creator working in the so-called arts of expression. Thus one faces some confusions. The dodecaphonists in particular have been the objects of that accusation. But, contrary to what generally has been said about them—which has been nothing but hearsay—they mostly have had no intelligent comprehension of the musical phenomena of our time. They have been satisfied to rest on bases acquired with destructive purposes by their predecessors; these they apply, in the manner of the later Schoenberg, to an antihistorical course. We are asked to take such a larval academicism as intellectualism, whereas it is merely the secretion of limited spirits short of expedients.

Sometimes, nonetheless, the confusions are other than anecdotal. The "intellectual artist" almost answers to this definition: he establishes *his* theory in a closed circuit, he strongly wants to convince others of the efficacy and availability of that theory; for that reason, making newness a sort of proof, he sets out to produce works that finally have no criterion other than that of proof by newness. If the creation is bad, there is a rush to treat him with contempt as a theoretician, clockmaker, etc. If the creation is good, there is an equal rush to assert that it is not the theoretician who should enlist agreement, that his theories are not very important, given that he has produced a beautiful work. To reach that glorification, they forget all relation of cause and effect, which, in the contempt case, they themselves placed in evidence.

But why should we be ashamed of our technique? I retort to the contrary and assert that the reproach of intellectualism is ill-founded because it starts from an erroneous understanding—when it is not stained with bad taste—of the interpenetrating role of sensibility and intelligence in all creation. Let us not forget that in music, expression is intrinsically linked to the language, to the very technique of the language. Music is perhaps of all phenomena the one least dissociable from all its means of expression in the sense that its own morphology is what in the first place gives an account of the perceptible evolution of the creator. Thus one sees that those reproaches of intellectualism are wrongheaded because the formal means supply the only possible communication. I am not being paradoxical when I say that the more complex the formal means are, the less they are perceived intellectually by the listener. Analysis, then, is impossible during the course of a performance; and even when one has analyzed a complex structure, experience shows that the best-constructed forms—and therefore the least visible forms—are recomposed as heard and again challenge the analytic intelligence by submerging it. One could mention many works thought of as simple in which one perceives—this time in a very intellectual way—the schematic character precisely because it is foreseeable.

These schemas, which content those who reject the sin of intellectualism, are culpable as much for their gratuitousness, their arbitrariness, as for their *a priori*. They cannot lead to any consequence but sterility solidified outside the circuit. Even if they are pompously baptized *liberty*, even if they are justified in the name of lyric expression, nothing but their proneness to sclerotic tendencies is thus justified or baptized.

As a last recourse, however, there is protest in the name of the creative imagination. One must bow very low to minds with such fertile imagination. They are odd, for the rest, these protestants, in holding that faculty to be so fragile that it will not bear direction. In fact, I have already noted that it is not only fragile, but also very weak—whereas they proclaim it all-powerful; they fall, all unaware, upon all the caltrops of the worst commonplaces. On the contrary, I have the tendency to find that the imagination requires some of these springboards supplied by the formal means put at its disposal by a technique that dares to be called by its own name.

Thus we reach that unbearable question of formalism. The final residue of romanticism, it always conceives of theoretical research as a closed cycle not coinciding with creations, properly speaking, as I have already mentioned. Let us free ourselves of that obsolete legend: it cannot be thus, under pain of mortal asphyxia. A consciously organizing logic is not independent of the work to whose creation it contributes; it is linked to it in a reversible circuit, for what leads to the evolution of technique is the need to make precise what one wants to express; that technique reinforces the imagination, which then projects itself toward the unperceived; and thus, in a perpetual play of mirrors, creation is pursued; organization, living and lived, leaving possible all the acquisitions, enriching itself with each new experience, completing itself, even changing accentuation. I shall say more: it is by the glorification of rhetoric itself that music is justified. Otherwise it remains only laughable anecdote, noisy grandiloquence, or morose libertinage.   [10]

ANALYSIS AND CONTEXT

From "' ... Auprès et au loin,'" 1954

It is completely ineffective to take account of a work by means of *a posteriori* investigation; it is equally ineffective to examine a work by imposing upon it a system of references to which it was anterior. The attempt to analyze a Bach piece in relation to a study of pitches and registers is just as vain as trying to compare a Webern structure literally to a Beethoven structure. The work, then, imposes the choice of the means with which to approach it: which by no means guarantees that in such a procedure one will inescapably overtake the composer's intuition. We need not busy ourselves about the mechanism that leads to the work, but rather with the work itself, which, once composed—by the mere fact that it has been achieved—casts into night all the preliminary procedures. The achievement implies abolition of what might have been: chance abolished, but without forgetting the element of chance which can intervene in that abolition. What absolute masterpiece could aim to remain outside that situation? That should not permit us to forget that events did not coincide for the composer from the outset to give a "sound phenomenon." Creation is in some part analytical. By accident, notebooks containing sketches by great musicians have been preserved for us, and in certain cases reading those manuscripts—in inks of various colors—can be very instructive. The sound "phenomenon"—which there may be too much tendency to believe indissociable—was often attained by successive approaches to a satisfactory state. Some examples of that are especially striking in Beethoven: the first sketch of the scherzo of his Ninth Symphony is marked *"Ende Langsam,"* and one can still read below the notation of the theme: *"Fuge."* To speak once more of creation for which the material is selected in view of its possibilities, all foreseen, is to give proof of a determinist Utopia of curiously hybrid nature. The same is true of any harping on "English horn" melodies, sonatas with "specifically" pianistic or "specifically" violinistic themes; misunderstandings of that sort are very tenacious and reflect a very deeply rooted religious mentality; the composer is God and his clairvoyance embraces the entire work from the moment he decides to create it.   [11]

From an address to the Arnold Schoenberg Institute, March 16, 1987

What is analysis? Is it just the description of the reality of the musical object, a kind of objective, impersonal description? An analysis of this sort is certainly important for the definition of a work of art, but it can be totally unimaginative and have nothing to do with creativity. For a composer it is essential to find himself in works by other composers. Perhaps his approach, his analysis, will be wrong and not correspond at all, or only in part, to the creative process of another composer. What is important is the result the analysis has on himself. I can give three examples of that:

The first one I remember very well is Messiaen analyzing the *Rite of Spring*. He was searching for his own truth, and he spoke of living characters in his rhythmical analysis of Stravinsky. Of course, it was not at all the essence of Stravinsky's rhythms as such, but it was Messiaen's rhythm seen through the magnifying glass of Stravinsky.

The second example was Stockhausen's well-known analysis of Webern. His analysis was based on density, which, of course, Webern was not interested in at all. Webern was interested only in canonic writing, and density was a consequence. But Stockhausen wanted to see density, so he saw density; that was the consequence which was important for him. The analysis was "wrong," but it was fruitful for him, and that was what was very important.

When I analyzed the Études by Debussy I did not look at all for a kind of tonal process, but I looked much more for an interval process, my own "process" of composing. I am sure it was not Debussy's intention to compose only with intervals; he was much more taken with a kind of tonal language. But what was most important to me, at least at the time, was the interval substance of the language. I was perhaps wrong in my analysis of Debussy's creative process but I was right for myself because it became part of my creative process. So you do not speak about the work, but the work speaks about you.   [12]

From the Schoenberg Institute address

EMPIRICAL AND THEORETICAL APPROACHES TO COMPOSING

You define your language according to two types of behavior. The first is empirical. You write music, and through this tangible experience of the act of writing you discover how you can achieve some of the goals you have set for yourself. You experiment with reality, with the experience of the process of writing. The solutions, of course, are your own individual solutions that vary according to each case you meet, so that every time you come up against this problem you have to find a "momentary" solution, one might say. But sometimes, after having found a certain number of solutions, you pull them all together and see the general aspects which give them a certain unity.

But there is also a theoretical approach. Perhaps I speak especially for myself because I am more drawn toward a mixture of both approaches. But, you can analyze in a more abstract manner the problems you have come up against when composing, and this can also be very helpful. This theoretical approach should not be discarded as being too intellectual or dehumanized. Technique is an essential part of language, and we are sometimes too easily satisfied with solutions we think good; whereas in reality, it was our memory that was at the bottom of the source of the solutions. Then a certain amount of laziness is involved, and not our imagination. I am always very suspicious when I have these instinctive solutions in front of me, because instinct is generally a kind of reservoir of solutions. The more you progress in your evolution, the more material you have in this reservoir because you have found a number of solutions for different works you have written which you think are satisfactory, and these solutions, more or less consciously and sometimes not consciously at all, are present in your current work. The solution which always comes to mind first is the one you have already experienced and therefore you already know how to use it. Even if you think it is new, it is not new, obviously, because it is instinctive. . . .

The empirical and theoretical approaches complement each other, and are both necessary. I believe in that very strongly. They are like two mirrors that reflect your personality. The mirror of technique reflects the imagination, and the mirror of imagination reflects the technique. [13]

LEARNING AND TECHNOLOGY

Learning should be a very quick process. Basically, by learning what we call the *métier*—harmony, counterpoint—one comes to understand the evolution of language, the historical process of evolution. Once you have mastered these categories, you can think for yourself, and you are on your own. You become an autodidact. At one point or another, you have to be self-taught. This is the only way you can find your own language. You are an autodidact by will, and not by chance. When you compare language and its elements with what you want to express, you can begin to extrapolate and begin to build your own house on safe ground. This experience of writing is as necessary as ever, now that technology does exist. You cannot just play around with these new toys, you have to invent according to a technological potential, and your musical language needs to be solidly anchored in order to be able to work out the necessary vocabulary while using it. I must say, as the head of an institute like IRCAM, such institutes are plagued by people who think they are doing some marvelous thing just by playing around with technology. You can see immediately that their musical thinking is extremely weak, because they have never really thought through how the musical ideas can be developed. It is very easy to find very good sounds to synthesize and to marvel at them and say, "I have discovered something." But, it is much more difficult to invent a dialectic exchange with these sounds and to control the relationship between the structure of a composition and the sound material as such. [14]

MODERN OPERA

From an interview in Der Spiegel, *1967*

I do not allow myself to be taken in by the tremendous activity of certain opera houses. I still maintain that since Alban Berg's *Wozzeck* and *Lulu,* no one has written an opera worth talking about.

I don't think it's possible to bring about a new movement simply through commissions. It would be like saying that all you need is a doctor in order to bring a child into the world. Other, more important things must happen first. . . .

[In my conception of opera] the text must really be conceived directly for the musical theater. It must not be an adaptation of literary material, as is always the case today. . . . It would be an experiment, in which text and music were conceived simultaneously.

Q: M. Boulez, do you think you could realize your conception of a modern musical theater in our very conventional opera houses?

A: Certainly not. That brings us to another reason why there is no modern opera today. The new German opera houses look modern on the outside, but inside they're thoroughly old-fashioned. It's basically impossible to present modern operas in a house that mostly does the standard repertoire. It's unthinkable. The most expensive solution would be to blow up the opera houses. But don't you think it would also be the most elegant?

Q: But since no administrator is about to take this suggestion—

A: Then you could use the existing opera houses for the standard repertoire: Mozart, Verdi, Wagner, up to Berg or so. For new operas, it's essential to add experimental theaters.   [15]

PLURALISM

From a panel discussion, Paris, c. 1985

Ah! Pluralism! There's nothing like it for curing incomprehension. Love, each one of you in your corner, and each will love the others. Be liberal, be generous toward the tastes of others, and they will be generous to yours. Everything is good, nothing is bad; there aren't any values, but everyone is happy. This discourse, as liberating as it may wish to be, reinforces, on the contrary, the ghettos, comforts one's dear conscience for being in a ghetto, especially if from time to time one tours the ghettos of others. The economy is there to remind us, in case we get lost in this bland utopia: there are musics that bring in money and exist for commercial profit; there are musics that cost something, whose very concept has nothing to do with profit. No liberalism will erase this distinction.
[16]

POST-MODERNISTS AND POST-MODERNISM

From an interview in Andrew Ford's Composer to Composer, *1988*

I find that these people are tired; they are afraid of complications, of complexity, and they say that we cannot communicate with an audience because our music is too complex. Okay, so what are they doing? They are going back to something. For me, that's impossible because history never goes backwards. And when I see people who are writing pseudo-Mahler... well, there's enough Mahler for me, I don't need pseudo-Mahler. . . .

I don't see a future for modernism; I don't see a future for post-modernism. You are not modern—you are merely expressing yourself according to the coordinates of your time, and that's not being modern, that's being what you are. All kinds of references, for me, are absolutely useless. I want to be myself. Period. I really can't see any interest in going back to a lost paradise. For me there is no paradise and there is no loss—of any kind.   [17]

APHORISMS AND OBSERVATIONS

I believe that music should be collective hysteria and spells, violently of the present time—following the lead of Antonin Artaud and not in the direction of simple ethnographic reconstruction in the likenesses of civilizations more or less remote from ours. ("Proposals," 1948)   [18]

More and more I imagine that an effective creator must take delirium into account and—yes—organize it. ("Sound and Word," 1958)   [19]

Innovation is possible only after the completest possible digestion of the past. ("Schoenberg the Unloved?" 1974)   [20]

The very active composer is always a thief—he makes use of every single thing he can put his hands on. (Schoenberg Institute address)   [21]

I like people who are not trying to catch the spirit of the time, but who create the spirit of the time. (*Composer to Composer*)   [22]

BERLIOZ

From an article in High Fidelity/Musical America, *1969*

What Berlioz brought to music is so singular that it has not yet been truly absorbed, has not become an integral part of tradition. Whereas Wagner, for example, has given rise to fanatical admirers as well as detractors, Berlioz still seems to be isolated. He stands at a point where customary judgment cannot be easily applied. I think we must see the principal reason for this in the fact that a large part of his oeuvre has remained in the realm of the imaginary. No one dreams of denying that his works exist or of maintaining that they cannot be incorporated into our musical heritage, for he resembles Wagner in having fully as much practical sense as imagination. One of the permanent aspects of his character is just such a mixture of realism and fantasy—and his realism could be every bit as meticulous as his fantasy could be extravagant. [23]

SATIE

From an article in the Revue musicale, 1952

Satie's humor, the best of it—"la maître d'Arceuil." Wonderful as a title—as long as there is no music attached. [24]

"SCHOENBERG IS DEAD"

From a revised version of an article of the same title that originally appeared in Score, May 1952

Schoenberg's discoveries were essentially morphological. That evolutive progression started from the post-Wagnerian vocabulary and reached "suspension" of the tonal language. One can detect very well-defined tendencies even in *Verklärte Nacht*; the First Quartet, Opus 7; and the *Kammersymphonie*; but it is only in certain passages in the scherzo and the finale of the Second Quartet, Opus 10, that one can watch a true attempt at revolution. All the works just mentioned therefore are, in a way, preparations; I believe that today we may be allowed to regard them chiefly from a documentary point of view.

Suspension of the tonal system is achieved effectively in the Three Pieces for Piano, Opus 11. Thereafter, the experiments become more and more penetratingly acute and lead to the renowned *Pierrot lunaire*. I note three remarkable phenomena in the writing of these scores: the principle of constantly efficacious variation, or nonrepetition; the preponderance of "anarchic" intervals—presenting the greatest tension relative to the tonal world—and progressive elimination of the octave, the tonal world par excellence; and a manifest attempt to construct contrapuntally.

These three characteristics already diverge, if they do not contradict. In fact, the principle of variation can be accommodated only badly with rigorous (read: scholastic) contrapuntal writing. One observes a sharp internal contradiction in the exact canons in particular, where the consequent textually reproduces the antecedent—both the sound-figures and the rhythmic figures. When, on the other hand, these canons are produced at the octave, extreme antagonism ensues between a succession of horizontal elements ruled by a principle of abstaining from tonality and vertical control placing the strongest tonal constituent in sharp relief.

———— ⚉ ————

It even seems that in the sequences of Schoenberg's creations that began with the Serenade, Opus 24, he found himself outridden by his own discovery; the no man's land of rigor can be located in the Five Pieces for Piano, Opus 23.

The last point of equilibrium, Opus 23 clearly is the inauguration of serial writing, into which the fifth piece—a waltz—introduces us: each of us may be permitted to meditate on that very "expressionistic" meeting of the first dodecaphonic composition with a type-product of German romanticism ("Prepare oneself for it by serious immobilities," Satie might have said).

And there we are, in the presence of a new organization of the sound-world. A still-rudimentary organization that will be codified with the Suite for Piano, Opus 25, and the Wind Quintet, Opus 26, and will attain conscious schematization in the Variations for Orchestra, Opus 31.

That exploration of the dodecaphonic realm may be bitterly held against Schoenberg, for it went off in the wrong direction so persistently that it would be hard to find an equally mistaken perspective in the entire history of music.

I do not make this assertion gratuitously. Why?

I do not forget that establishment of the series came, with Schoenberg, from ultrathematization in which, as I said above, thematic intervals could be considered absolute intervals released from all rhythmic or expressive obligation. (The third piece of Opus 23, developing on a succession of five notes, is particularly significant in this respect.)

It behooves me to acknowledge that this ultrathematization remains the underlying idea of the *series,* which is only its purified outcome. In Schoenberg's serial works, furthermore, the confusion between theme and series is explicit enough to show his impotence to foresee the sound-world that the series demands. Dodecaphonism, then, consists of only a rigorous law for controlling chromatic writing; playing only the role of regulating instrument, the serial phenomenon itself was not, so to speak, perceived by Schoenberg. . . .

The preclassic or classic forms ruling most of the architectures have no historic link to the dodecaphonic discovery; thus an inadmissible hiatus is produced between infrastructures related to the tonal phenomenon and a language in which one again perceives the laws of organization summarily. Not only does the proposed project run aground—such a language was not consolidated by such architectures—but also the opposite happens, which is to say that those architectures annihilate the possibilities of organization inherent in the new language. The two worlds are incompatible, and Schoenberg had attempted to justify one by the other.

One cannot call that procedure valid, and it produced results that could have been anticipated: the worst sort of misunderstanding. A warped "romantico-classicism" in which the good intentions are not the least unattractive element. One certainly gave no great credit to the serial organization by not allowing it its own modes of development, but substituting other, apparently surer ones. A reactionary attitude that left the door ajar for all the more or less disgraceful holdovers.

The persistence of accompanied melody, for example; of counterpoint based upon a principal part and secondary parts (*Hauptstimme* and *Nebenstimme*). We are in the presence of a very unhappy heritage owed to scarcely defensible scleroses of a certain bastard language adopted by romanticism. Nor is it only in the limited conceptions, but equally in the writing itself, that I see reminiscences of a dead world. Under Schoenberg's pen, in fact, there abounded—not without producing irritation—the clichés of redoubtably stereotyped writing representing, there too, the most ostentatious and obsolete romanticism. I refer to those constant anticipations, with expressive leaning on the key note; I mean those false appoggiaturas; or, again, those formulas of arpeggios, of devices, of repetitions, which sound terribly hollow and deserve to be called what they are: "secondary parts." Finally, I indicate the morose, disagreeable use of a derisively poor—call it ugly—rhythmic, in which tricks varying the classic rhythmic are disconcerting in their credulity and ineffectuality.

How could we, without weakness, relate ourselves to an *oeuvre* manifesting such contradictions? If only it manifested them within a rigorous technique, the only safeguard! But what are we to think of Schoenberg's American period, during which the greatest disarray and most deplorable demagnetization appeared? How could we, unless with a supplementary—and superfluous—measure, judge such lack of comprehension and cohesion, that re-evaluation of polarizing functions, even of tonal functions? Rigorous writing was abandoned in those works. In them we see appearing again the octave intervals, the false cadences, the exact canons at the octave. Such an attitude attests to maximum incoherence—a paroxysm in the absurdity of Schoenberg's incompatibilities. Ought one not to have pressed forward to a new methodology of the musical language instead of trying to reconstitute the old one? So monstrous an uncomprehending deviation leaves us perplexed: in the Schoenberg "case" a ruinous "catastrophe" occurred which doubtless will remain cautionary. . . .

We must keep ourselves from considering Schoenberg as a sort of Moses who died in view of the Promised Land after having brought down the Tables of the Law from a Sinai that some people obstinately want to confuse with Walhalla. (During that time, the dance before the Golden Calf was in full swing.) We certainly owe him *Pierrot lunaire* . . . , and some other very enviable works. This will not give offense to the environing mediocrity that wants, very speciously, to limit the ravages to "Central Europe."

Nonetheless, it has become indispensable to demolish a misunderstanding that is full of ambiguity and contradictions: it is time to neutralize the setback. That rectification will be accomplished not by any gratuitous bragging, much less by any sanctimonious fatuity, but by rigor free of weakness and compromise. Therefore I do not hesitate to write, not out of any desire to provoke a stupid scandal, but equally without bashful hypocrisy and pointless melancholy:

SCHOENBERG IS DEAD.   [25]

STRAVINSKY'S *FIREBIRD*

From a note to a recording, c. 1968

I see in *Firebird* a kind of greed to take possession of already existing music and transmute it into an aggressively personal object. This virulent determination to take possession of music and transform its whole aspect and appearance, and the youthful zest of the whole conception, are very remarkable; and all the more so because the historical antecedents of the musical material are so plainly visible. This places us in a perfect position to appreciate the passion with which the ferment of a creative idea impels a composer to embark on his first work.   [26]

WEBERN AND BERG

Webern's work, . . . once one has grasped its essence and its vocabulary (and of course I am referring particularly to the last works), does not require a series of different readings. It is like a picture by Mondrian. You can see its perfection and it is very striking, being stripped down to the absolute minimum—a truly austere kind of perfection; but when you see it again at a later date, it offers you nothing further. . . .

On the other hand (and I am deliberately taking an example from a period that no longer concerns me) if I look at certain paintings by Cézanne, their complexity, their references, their infinity of architectural and textural detail all offer so many levels of interpretation that I can look at them five times, ten times, and still feel that I have not accounted for every small detail of their texture. Well, there are often times in Berg when I have this impression of an extremely difficult work, whose texture is very hard to grasp completely. Despite the fact that they communicate so readily to the listener, Berg's are works to go back to five or six times, especially the large-scale ones.   [27]

SHOSTAKOVICH

Remark to a Belgian journalist, September 1993

The vogue for Shostakovich astonishes me. I would give his entire output for some little Stravinsky pieces like the Three Clarinet Pieces or the [Four] Russian Songs.
                                                                                                       [28]

HENZE'S OPERAS

From the interview in Der Spiegel

Henze's works are certainly not modern operas. They make me think of a slick hairdresser who embraces a completely superficial modernism. . . . Henze is like de Gaulle—he puts out crap every time and still believes he's king. . . . A Beatles record is definitely cleverer than a Henze opera, and shorter as well.   [29]

PERSONAL AMBITIONS

From the essay "Freeing Music," 1971

What I want to do is to change people's attitude. They have inherited their tastes from the past and look only to the past—to museums, as it were—for their music, while all the time there is live, living music in the world around them. My aim is to promote in every field the ideas of today. We cannot spend our whole lives in the shadow of the huge tree of the past. People nowadays have developed a kind of defense mechanism and are more interested in preserving than creating, like the Romans in the third and fourth centuries. No generation that fails to question the achievements of the past has a hope of achieving its own potential or exploiting its vital energies to the full.

In the past some of my quips have caused surprise—when, for instance, I suggested that it was not enough to add a moustache to the Mona Lisa: it should simply be destroyed. All I meant was just to urge the public to grow up and once for all to cut the umbilical cord attaching it to the past. The artists I admire—

Beethoven, Wagner, Debussy, Berlioz—have not followed tradition but have been able to force tradition to follow them. We need to restore the spirit of ir-reverence in music. [30]

Luciano Berio
b. 1925

Trained first by his father and grandfather, both organists, and then by G. F. Ghedini at the Milan Conservatory, Berio took an interest in electronic music and in 1955 opened Italy's first electronic music studio. In 1963 he moved to the United States, where he held a series of teaching positions. The awareness of history that emerges in his writings is equally evident in his music: some of his works incorporate "found" objects, which range from folk songs to pages out of Mahler, while his Sequenzas *for different solo instruments effectively distill the instrumental traditions of several centuries into a unified virtuoso technique. Berio's music also frequently incorporates elements of drama, and sometimes even of public spectacle or carnival, to witty and striking effect.*

From a series of interviews
with Rossana Dalmonte and Bálint András Varga, 1980–81

MUSICAL MEANINGS

I think that all ways of making, listening to and even talking about music are right in their way. When music has sufficient complexity and semantic depth, it can be approached and understood in different ways. Most commercial songs, and for that matter the sonic wallpaper and the musical tombolas [bingo games] of the self-styled avant-garde, can only be listened to on one level: but there's also music that can be heard on many levels, and is continually generating musical meaning. The more simple and one-dimensional a musical discourse is, the more diffuse and im-mediate its relationship to everyday reality. The more concentrated and complex it is, the more complex and selective are its social relations, and the more ramified its meanings. So that a song can express a moment of human work and emotion, and it is an immediately "useful" instrument to people at different times of the day or year: but you can replace one with another. Whereas complex musical works are irreplaceable moments in a historical process. Think of Beethoven and Schoen-berg: their musical thought often seems to have a positively excessive semantic depth. There's enough for everyone, and always a bit left over which remains in the shadows, waiting for a different approach. I don't believe people when they say "I don't understand this music, will you explain it to me?" It means they don't understand themselves and the place they occupy in the world, and that it doesn't occur to them that music is also a product of collective life. Sometimes I have a strange feeling that musical processes can be more intelligent than the people who produce and listen to them—that the cells of those processes, like the chromo-somes of a genetic code, can be more intelligent than the perceptive organs that should be making sense of them. It's as if music were miming one of the most incredible of natural processes: the passage from inanimate to animate life, from molecular to organic forms, from an abstract and immobile dimension to a vital and expressive one. Music must be capable of educating people to discover and create relations between different elements (as Dante said in the *Convivio*, "music is all relative"), and in doing that it speaks of the history of man and of his musical resources in all their acoustic, and expressive, aspects. [1]

INSTRUMENTS

I think it's very important to understand—which is why I'm insistent about it—that a musical instrument is in itself a piece of musical language. To try to invent a new one would be as futile and pathetic as trying to invent a new grammatical rule for our language. The composer can only contribute to the transformation of musical instruments by using them, and trying to understand *post factum* the complex nature of the transformations. . . .

No one has ever been able to change the violin. After 350 years it is still the same—if you exclude the bow and its technique and what the strings are made of, all of them things that have helped to increase its carrying power. [2]

VIRTUOSITY

I hold a great respect for virtuosity even if this word may provoke derisive smiles and even conjure up the picture of an elegant and rather diaphanous man with agile fingers and an empty head. Virtuosity often arises out of a conflict, a tension between the musical idea and the instrument, between concept and musical substance. . . . As is well-known, virtuosity can come to the fore when a concern for technique and stereotyped instrumental gestures gets the better of the idea, as in Paganini's work—which I'm very fond of, but which didn't really shake up the history of music, although it did contribute to the development of violin technique. Another instance where tension arises is when the novelty and the complexity of musical thought—with its equally complex and diverse expressive dimensions—imposes changes in the relationship with the instrument, often necessitating a novel technical solution (as in Bach's Violin Partitas, Beethoven's last piano works, Debussy, Stravinsky, Boulez, Stockhausen, etc.), where the interpreter is required to perform at an extremely high level of technical and intellectual virtuosity. Finally, as I've often emphasized, anyone worth calling a virtuoso these days has to be a musician capable of moving within a broad historical perspective and of resolving the tension between the creativity of yesterday and today. My own *Sequenzas* are always written with this sort of interpreter in mind, whose virtuosity is, above all, a virtuosity of knowledge. (I've got no interest in, or patience for, those who "specialize" in contemporary music.) [3]

TRANSCRIPTIONS

The history of transcription has yet to be written, and if I were still teaching, that is something that I'd like to go into with my students. I'd start with Monteverdi's *Orfeo* ("This ritornello was played by two ordinary violins . . . ") and then pause over

Bach transcribing Bach. I'd take a quick look at Liszt: his transcriptions and paraphrases, which combine cosmopolitan high fashion with a concern for popularization, made an enormous contribution to the evolution of piano technique and to the exchanging of musical influences, but they have little to do with his great personality as a composer. I'd take an equally quick look at Busoni: his great personality as a transcriber has little to do with his rather frustrating work as a composer. Thus I'm interested in transcription when it's part of a design, a coherent and homogeneous musical vision, even though at times it's primarily motivated by considerations of practicality and custom. Then I'd look at Schoenberg transcribing himself and Brahms, Ravel transcribing himself, and Stravinsky transcribing "everything." I'd also look at isolated but very significant episodes such as Maderna transcribing Gabrieli, Ghedini transcribing Frescobaldi and Kagel who also transcribes literally everything. But the real object of this course would be to arrive at unconscious transcription, in other words, forms of transcription that are completely assimilated into the creative process. Here we are no longer dealing with transcription as a genre (don't forget that for centuries the practice of transcription had a function analogous to that of records), but as part of the ups and downs of creativity: when, that is, you have a single musical vision (a single project, they say these days) going through different and self-sufficient formulations before arriving at the definitive realization, decanted from (or destroying) all the others. There are three works that particularly interest me in this respect: *Noces* (there are three versions of this Stravinskian masterpiece), Stockhausen's *Kontrapunkte* (the first, unperformable version was for a huge orchestra: I have the impression that Stockhausen was "born" precisely by reducing, that is, transcribing this work for ten instruments), and Boulez's *Notations* (a large work for orchestra that transcribes and amplifies some short pieces for piano written in 1947). Naturally, I would contribute to the project with my *Chemins,* and also my Concerto for Two Pianos and Orchestra where, from time to time, the two solo instruments coexist with their image reflected and transcribed in the orchestra.   [4]

ELECTRONIC INSTRUMENTS

Commercial synthesizers aspire to be musical jacks-of-all-trades, and because of their specific characteristics they end up taking over from the composers who use them. A composer can't think musically with those machines, and ends up impoverished by them in one way or another. At best, they produce fascinating sound effects that help to accentuate one of the greatest problems of our time: the distance and the indifference between music's acoustic and conceptual dimensions. . . .

One of the most alarming things about synthesizers is that they are not precise. One of the most interesting is that they are constructed on modular criteria, and are thus open, for better and for worse. But they're not musical instruments.   [5]

Twenty or thirty years ago the musician shaped technical means of non-musical origin (oscillators, filters, tape recorders, etc.) to his own ideas and visions, whereas during the last ten or fifteen years one gets the impression that technical development has got the upper hand, and that the composer is struck dumb in the face of the new resources created expressly for him.   [6]

The Teaching of Composition

I think that once a certain basis has been established, a young composer has to carry on by himself and hunt out the things that he needs. As far as I'm concerned, that basis is first counterpoint, and then analysis. Not that I'm nostalgic for the great days of counterpoint, but I don't yet know of any other means of getting a student to train himself systematically in linking up his brain and his ears. There's no need to be too finicky about this: any type of counterpoint will do, provided it's being taught by a responsible teacher and is placed coherently within its historical and technical context: the Burgundians, Palestrina, Bach, Fux, Cherubini and, why not, Dubois. The pupil must of course be young, must be steered away from making an ideology out of counterpoint, and must learn it as he would the rules of a game. In other words, you've got to make sure that, later on, this experience of counterpoint doesn't transform itself into a regressive refuge, a reactionary technical instrument. . . .

I don't believe in authoritarian teaching, but I do believe in discipline. And I don't believe in being self-taught, either. I'm always suspicious of those who label themselves in this way: it usually means that their technical capabilities are fragile.

[7]

Critics and Criticism

I don't see the musical, cultural or even social usefulness of someone who has to write articles every week for the dailies or weeklies, and does *nothing else.* In their place I'd go mad after a fortnight. When I go to a concert and hear a Schubert sonata for the nth time, marvelously interpreted by Pollini or Brendel, I sometimes wonder in dismay what on earth I would write if I were a critic and wanted to avoid the usual panegyrics, the usual fountain of useless words. Who knows, I'd probably end up doing the same thing as everyone else to avoid going hungry. But I wonder whether in the long run a profession of that sort, always concentrated on other people's work, always busy giving judgment on what other people are doing (other people of today, not yesterday) doesn't end up damaging your intellectual and moral fiber. . . .

The critic's job is an uncertain and fragile one, and I suppose that it's because of that that even esteemed and refined scholars—overcome by the boredom of their semi-profession—sometimes permit themselves the most unforgivable forms of spitefulness, so as to amuse themselves a little and make their young friends laugh. I think that criticism can be useful when it knows how to criticize itself. But it's so difficult! Real criticism, which doesn't confine itself to little weekly articles, thus has its own autonomy, its own history, its own "poetics" and therefore its own needs. . . .

But there's nothing seriously wrong in all this, nor can anything dramatic really occur because in the end, as we all know, in the exercise of musical criticism—as in nature—nothing is created and nothing is *really* destroyed. [8]

Music and the Marketplace

Music doesn't escape the law of the market place. America, which is undoubtedly the most musical country in the world (in the sense that the majority of people have a direct and real contact with music making), has a very high standard of performance, a staggering number of orchestras—and an American orchestral musician earns in a week what his Italian equivalent earns in a month, with a more or less equal cost of living. Musical creativity doesn't escape the law of the market either. The most lively, authentic and interesting forms of American creativity are to be found in commercial music and, perhaps, in the really advanced research on music created with computers or synthesizers (linked to the electronics and computer industries). In the middle, between these two extremes—rock, pop, disco and jazz on the one hand, and "technological" and digital music on the other (extremes which in America often overlap and influence each other on the level of pure *sound*)—there's the music of serious composers, which naturally has no market. It lives inside academic citadels or else in the limbo of "foundations" that absorb and anaesthetize everything, even John Cage. In the United States the "serious" composer is materially well off, but his music is less fortunate, despite appearances. It is fairly often performed but has nobody to really address itself to, no cultural or spiritual destination, even subconsciously. In other words, it lacks a real "market" of musical ideas that strive to represent a possible stage of being. It is fundamentally a music of solitude because, ironically, it lacks the vehicle of a market in a society where market value seems to be the necessary prerequisite for the recognition of anything at all, even the very things that the market inevitably destroys: human and cultural ideals. [9]

IMPROVISATION

Rare, fleeting moments of interest apart (when the musicians involved were of considerable quality), improvisation has been a haven for dilettantes, who may be fluent in inventing socio-musical alibis but are in most cases quite incapable of evaluating and analyzing themselves in relation to any historico-musical perspective. Improvisation during the baroque era was somewhat like jazz improvisation in that it based itself upon a harmonic (and therefore a rhythmic and metric) structure that was clear and, as it were, unanimous. Nowadays improvisation presents a problem: above all because there's no true unanimity of discourse among the participants, only, once in a while, a unanimity of behavior. . . .

I don't believe that musical thought needs improvisation to develop itself, to manifest itself in finished form, and to make itself useful to other people in one way or another. What it needs is a more stable and selective medium. Jazz improvisation is another matter, because it is based on the rapid extraction of musical modules and instrumental gestures from the great reservoir of memory, and it is also based on speed of reaction to one's partners and to oneself—it's somewhat similar to the rapid reflexes involved in the act of speech. [10]

FOLK MUSIC AND ART MUSIC

I have a Utopian dream, though I know it cannot be realized: I would like to create a unity between folk music and our music—a real, perceptible, understandable continuity between ancient, popular music-making, which is so close to everyday work, and our music. [11]

Observations

It seems to me that history is rather ungenerous with today's younger composers, and sometimes I have the impression that it has no need of them. To put it in a rather intolerant and authoritarian way, you might say that they themselves have been intolerant and ungenerous with history, so history is getting its own back.   {12}

Poetry has always looked at music nostalgically—as though at an unattainable possibility.   {13}

In the end, I do not believe in chance as far as music is concerned. It is simply a deception. The musical process is so complex that even if the composer doesn't want to suggest or impose any intentionality, the performer will do it in his place.   {14}

Puccini and Opera

Puccini introduced the rhythm and the psychological mobility of everyday life into the musical theatre. He didn't articulate this through large-scale musical structures, but through a continually fragmented time-flow that nonetheless preserves its inner logic and unity. The time of the action and musical time are completely homogenous: the two levels are part of the same process. This is one of the reasons for the direct impact of Puccini—so that *La Bohème* offers one more solution to a perennial problem. Indeed, one of the most difficult and interesting (and least discussed) aspects of the musical theatre of all ages has been precisely this question of inventing temporal conventions that extend the relationship between words and dramatic action on one hand, and music on the other, making it flexible and dialectical. This search has always gone on under different names and pretexts. From tragedy to comedies with music, from "poetry, handmaid of music" to "music, handmaid of poetry," from intermezzos to the conventions of Italian melodrama, from the Wagnerian suspension of time to verismo, from cinematic cutting in *Wozzeck* to Stockhausen's spatio-temporal voyages into cosmic light. Puccini's experiment with time is very close to Debussy's, albeit using more rudimentary methods. Debussy effectively invented a new musical time, articulated through the repetition and continually transformed return of short elements that constantly change their function. . . .

After Puccini there was only *"puccinismo."* Puccini's only heir, and that a negative one, was Respighi, whose operatic aspirations got more and more dessicated as he fattened out the Puccinian orchestra.   {15}

Stravinsky's *Agon*

Agon is a triumph not only of invention and, in its own way, of awareness and of courage, but also of the transformation of materials. Onto a subcutaneous tissue (as Schoenberg would have called it), that is, a harmonic structure that glides from G major to a Webernian series (and back again) through various stages of chromatic corruption, there unfolds in remorseless, exemplary and naïve fashion, the hyper-intelligent parable of a "short history of music" that performs a lucid but tragic autopsy on itself under the pretext of a game.   [16]

WEBERN AND THE RELATIONSHIP OF TEXT TO MUSIC

Anton Webern carries with him the last echo of the romantic Lied; in his work the relation between text and music is inextricable, and I wouldn't like to say which has primacy from the formal point of view. Indeed, I'd rather say the contrary: that his musical processes and procedures are so intense and concentrated, and so strongly spiritually charged, that they impose their own dimension on [the texts by] Hildegard Jone—and that these in turn lend themselves admirably to all the sinuosities and truncations of Webern's music. It was above all with Mozart and Schubert that the pre-established forms of poetic narration coincided with the music in a miraculous fashion, and on all levels including the psychological. Then music and poetry spoke the same language, and all it needed was a minimal disjunction between the two (for example, a melodic variation when repeating the same poetic strophe) to open up abysses of sense: think of Schubert's *Winterreise* or Schumann's *Dichterliebe* and what happens in them to the relation between poetic strophe and musical "strophe." In other words, poetry and music move symmetrically and analogically not only on the rhetorical level, but also on that of *langue* and *parole*. But you'd look in vain for that in Webern. Indeed, Webern's vocal music always emits something indefinable, a sort of expressive stupor that derives from a certain impassivity (I would hardly dare to call it indifference) of the music in the face of the text. Even when the discourse becomes strophic, this impassivity remains, as for example in the final part of the second Cantata (where the text is "ground up" by a quadruple crab canon repeated three times) which becomes an icy machine of divine contemplation, an implacable prayer. However, the relationship between text and music in Webern is sufficiently complex and ambiguous to permit all sorts of considerations, some of them very contrasting. I don't believe it's necessarily the text that confers a formal sense on the music, or in any way functions as a formal support for it. It's rather the type of relation or "conflict" with the text and, above all, the type of vocal writing that one chooses—or by which one lets oneself be chosen—that has formal consequences.   [17]

SINFONIA

I'd had it in mind for a long time to explore from the inside a piece of music from the past: a creative exploration that was at the same time an analysis, a commentary and an extension of the original. This follows from my principle that, for a composer, the best way to analyze and comment on a piece is to do something, using materials from that piece. The most profitable commentary on a symphony or an opera has always been another symphony or another opera. My *Chemins* are the best analyses of my *Sequenzas,* just as the third part of my *Sinfonia* is the most developed commentary that I could have possibly produced on a piece by Mahler.
[18]

Gunther Schuller

b. 1925

A musical polymath, Schuller has made his mark as a horn player, conductor, composer, educator, publisher, recording producer, essayist, and scholar of jazz and ragtime. While still in his teens he joined the orchestra of the New York City Ballet, also becoming active in jazz. In 1957 he coined the term "third stream" to describe a particular music resulting from the confluence of jazz and classical. He has worked in this style as well as in his own purely contemporary classical idiom. In the 1970s Schuller's recordings with the New England Conservatory Ragtime Ensemble sparked a revival of interest in Scott Joplin and ragtime. His books on the origins and early history of jazz have become standard references. Schuller's teaching career has included a decade as head of the New England Conservatory of Music and two decades as a teacher and administrator of contemporary music at the Tanglewood Music Center.

THIRD STREAM

From an article in Saturday Review, *May 13, 1961*

I first used the term "Third Stream" in a lecture three or four years ago, in an attempt to describe a music that was beginning to evolve with growing consistency. For lack of a precise name, one was forced at the time to describe it either in a lengthy definition or in descriptive phrases comprising several sentences. I used the term as an adjective, not as a noun. I did not envision its use as a name, a slogan, or a catchword . . . nor did this imply a "canonization," as one critic facetiously put it; nor, least of all, did I intend the term as a commercial gimmick. Such a thought evidently comes most readily to some people's minds in a society in which commercial gimmickry is an accepted way of life. Ultimately, I don't care whether the term "Third Stream" survives. In the interim it is no more than a handy descriptive term. It should be obvious that a piece of Third Stream music is first of all music, and its quality cannot be determined solely by categorization. . . .

I am fully aware that, individually, jazz and classical music have long, separate traditions that many people want to keep separate and sacred. I also recognize the right of musicians in either field to focus their attention entirely on preserving the idiomatic purity of these traditions. It is precisely for these reasons that I thought it best to separate from these two traditions the new genre that attempts to fuse "the improvisational spontaneity and rhythmic vitality of jazz with the compositional procedures and techniques acquired in Western music during 700 years of musical development." I felt that by designating this music as a *separate, third* stream, the two other main streams could go their way unaffected by attempts at fusion. I had hoped that in this way the old prejudices, old worries about the purity of the two main streams that have greeted attempts to bring jazz and "classical" music together could, for once, be avoided. This, however, has not been the case. Musicians and critics in both fields have considered this Third Stream a frontal attack on their own traditions. . . .

In *my* understanding of the term, Third Stream music must be born out of respect for and full dedication to *both* the musics it attempts to fuse. (This is more than one can say for the pop song or rock-'n'-roll commercializers of jazz, about whom, ironically, I have heard no serious complaints.) The lifting of external elements from one area into the other is happily a matter of the past. At its best Third Stream can be an extremely subtle music, defying the kind of easy categorization most people seem to need before they can make up the minds whether they should like something or not. As [the Modern Jazz Quartet's] John Lewis once put it to me in a conversation: "It isn't so much what we see (and hear) in the music of each idiom; it is more what we do *not* see in the one that already exists in the other." Certainly both musics can benefit from this kind of cross-fertilization, in the hands of gifted people. For example, the state of performance in classical music at the professional level today is, despite all we hear about our skilled instrumentalists, rather low. Most performances touch only the surface of a work, not its essence; and this is most true of the performance of contemporary music. If virtuosic perfection at least were achieved, one could—in a forgetful moment—be satisfied with that. But one cannot even claim this, since the leisurely attitude of the majority of classical players toward rhythmic accuracy is simply appalling, and would seem so to more people were it not so widespread as to be generally accepted. There is no question in my mind that the classical world can learn much about timing, rhythmic accuracy, and subtlety from jazz musicians, as jazz musicians can in dynamics, structure, and contrast from the classical musicians.   [1]

"TOWARD A NEW CLASSICISM?"

From a lecture of the same title, Goucher College, October 15, 1978

We composers should remember that after all the artistic, aesthetic battles have been fought and all injustices to misunderstood composers rectified, the audience—the large over-all audience, in short, the culture—is the final arbiter of that which survives. These societal verdicts can come early, or late, and at first may be confused and even misled. But sooner or later, as if with the aid of some marvelous artistic gyroscope, the ultimate assessment is made, and usually remains for a very long time.

I am a composer, and so I have thought about these things all of my life. But I have also been a fighter and activist for new music for many decades, as a performer, as a teacher, as a lecturer. Perhaps naïvely, I used to take great comfort in the notion that almost all new art, particularly if it is radically new, is at first rejected or greeted with apathy, and that it takes a generation or two for the audience to catch up with the front runners. By that time, of course, they are no longer front runners, but are either dead or well-ensconced in the pack, and have now been replaced by a new group of front runners. I resigned myself to the notion that the complexities of Schoenberg, Webern, and Ives would have to wait their thirty- to forty-year turn to be resolved and understood. The problem is that it is no longer thirty years; it's getting to be sixty years. And my earlier optimism has long ago been replaced by a growing discomfort that that old axiom really never had much substance. It was an illusion, a hope. Despite the best efforts of thousands of well-meaning people on both the producer and the consumer side, things have not changed significantly, and at best we seem to be in a sort of stalemate, with no one having quite the right pawns and queens and kings and bishops to move to a clear checkmate.

I feel that the problem goes much deeper than the changed specifics of the language: atonality, free rhythms and meters, disjunct melodies and themes, stream-of-consciousness forms, etc. It is a question of having been seduced into the pursuit of complexity and intellectualism for their own sakes.

Now complexity and intellectual qualities in and of themselves are not necessarily bad or destructive. Several hundred Bach fugues, a lot of Beethoven's last works, and some of the best music of our century are a clear proof of that. But it is finally a question of balance: how much of the one as against how much of the other. And if we can, with our sophisticated minds and sophisticated techniques and sophisticated new (electronic) instruments, push our music to the limits of comprehensibility, ought we not at the same time to balance that with a commensurate infusion of emotion, simplicity, comprehensibility, and humanism?

If there is one characteristic common to the great masterpieces of our Western musical tradition, it is that they use and coordinate all the elements of music fully. And innovators in the past, be they Monteverdi, Beethoven, or Wagner—moved forward *on all fronts*: harmony, melody, rhythm, form, and so on. That fullness, that richness of experience we associate with the great music of the past, an experience in which all of our listening and feeling faculties are involved—that is something we are given only in the rarest of circumstances today. When have we had music that gave you goosepimples, that made you choke with emotion, that brought tears to your eyes?

When I propose a "new classicism" I do not mean neo-classicism as we once knew it, or a return to the past in terms of style and certain fashions of the past, but rather a turning back to those profound verities—and, dare I say, human truths—that are common to all great music, whether of the baroque or the romantic or the modern era. In other words, it is not so much a "return to" as an "analogy to." I dream of finding contemporary analogies to that glorious past from which we still have much to learn and which we should not merely discard. Nor is my new classicism merely a new form of conservatism. It is in fact the opposite: a daring confrontation with certain rather disturbing realities and a radical move to gain back much of what we lost. It is not so much about conserving the past, but rather about accessibility and communication with our lost audience. It is to bring the past *through renewal* to the present, to translate that which is eternal in the past into our contemporary terms—to find the contemporary analogy to those past cumulative traditions, not only by discarding and omitting, but by rediscovering and truly adding. . . .

A new classicism could take many forms and speak in many musical tongues. My own personal view of such a renaissance—particularly as it is expressed in my own music—is bound to be but one among many. But in whatever form or shape,

I see it not as a mere return to the past nor on the other hand a total abandonment of the skills and techniques we have acquired in the twentieth century, but rather a richer, more homogeneous balance of the old with the new, of the traditional with the experimental, of the expressive with the intellectual, of the need to communicate with the need to try the unheard, the unseen, the unproven.   [2]

DEMOCRACY IN MUSIC

From a lecture at New York University, 1980

"Democracy" in music doesn't work. The concept of majority rule is basically anti-creative, by definition anti-individualistic. Bach, Beethoven, Brahms, or Stravinsky did not create by common consent or committee vote. Neither did Caruso or Casals or Furtwängler or Mitropoulos or Michelangelo. In the absence of absolutes and in the knowledge that unequivocal, perfected standards of decision and evaluation cannot be achieved, I would rather take my chances with some form of benign dictatorship. You can always argue against it, oppose it, and try to dislodge it. But at least it is something to depose. And it is often enlightened.   [3]

"ELITISM VERSUS POPULISM"

From an article in Keynote, 1982

The old and much bandied-about [argument] of "elitism versus populism" . . . is—at least as it is usually exploited—specious and based on totally false assumptions. For it is usually used to pit the "disadvantaged" against the "advantaged," and attempts to make people who cherish quality music look like autocrats, snobs, and eggheads, in insinuating that there is something anti-democratic and un-American about considering Duke Ellington superior to the Plasmatics or Mozart greater than John Lennon. Indeed the elitism-versus-populism argument is completely mythical, a polemical sleight-of-words invented by clever ignoramuses to becloud the real issue: namely, that quality, creativity, and high craftsmanship can and do exist in all forms and categories of music. So can and do their opposites: mediocrity and absence of quality. No form of musical expression is either inherently blessed with quality or intrinsically devoid of it.

The anti-elitists obscure the real issues further by invoking audience statistics and sales figures, as if mass consumption and mass appeal automatically equate with quality. Not content with the fact that certain commercial/popular musics already attract tens of millions of buyers (consumers), these apostles of populism feel put upon if some of us occasionally dare to suggest that most of this music is trivial *as music* and not of lasting relevance. . . . Moreover, populists constantly confuse commercial musics, which may be quite inane, with vernacular musics that may represent ethnic or folk traditions of great beauty and artistic integrity. We live in a time and a country of cultural pluralism. There isn't only one good music; there are many. One may like only one, but there are many. And all of these musics, which coexist (and even cohabit on occasion), are capable of high-quality inspired art—and low-quality inferior art. . . .

Now in a culturally pluralistic society, such a diverse array of likes and dislikes would not in itself be bad, *if* those likes and dislikes were based on a free choice and if the commercial musics didn't have such a total stranglehold on our people.

The sad truth is that the majority of Americans never has a chance to make a choice, to make a contact with the myriad variety that comprises the full available musical spectrum. . . . Why is it that 215 million Americans' musical diet consists of rock and pop, while only 10 million are able to enjoy other kinds of music as well? Is it because rock and pop are better musics than Beethoven or Ellington and those 215 million are driven to top-40 music by its superior quality? The answer is obvious. The answer has nothing to do with quality. In our consumerist society, what sells is deemed good—and that to me is the ultimate cultural debasement.   [4]

JAZZ AND CLASSICAL

From a preconcert lecture, New York City, December 3, 1983

In the 1920s when classical composers like Aaron Copland in America, Darius Milhaud and Ernst Krenek in Europe, discovered jazz, they were first and foremost captivated by the sounds and effects of jazz, the new brass mutes, the new instrumental techniques, the new instruments like the saxophones or the percussion, then either not in use at all in classical music or not used in the way that jazz musicians were utilizing these instruments. Indeed, these composers were impressed by the emphasis on wind and percussion instruments, and the solo virtuosity of the individual players in what was, after all, essentially a chamber ensemble approach, quite removed from the massive sounds of symphony orchestras with their large string sections. It is also true, alas, that that is about all those composers heard in jazz—the sonoric surface of the music. They did not, for example, realize that they were in most cases—Milhaud was a notable exception—listening to dance bands, not true improvised jazz. As a result they were blissfully unaware of the fact that jazz was a primarily improvisatory, spontaneous form of musical expression.

In classical music a "beautiful" sound is that which is deemed fashionable at a particular time and place—and these fashions do, of course, change from time to time, every three or four generations perhaps. In jazz, on the other hand, there is no such thing as a beautiful sound. It is up to the individual to create *his* sound—if it is within his creative capacities to do so—one that will best serve his musical concepts and style. In any case, in jazz the sound, timbre, and sonority are much more at the service of individual self-expression, interlocked intimately with articulation, phrasing, tonguing, slurring, and other such stylistic modifiers and definers.

The true jazz artist is generally unimpressed by technique for its own sake. He is generally trying to tell a story, trying to make a personal statement, trying to say something on his instrument that has perhaps not been said before in just such a way. The true jazz artist is creative not just in the on-the-spot invention of musical statements, that is, *his* choice of notes, shapes, phrases, rhythmic figures, but also creative in the way he approaches his instrument. He does this often in ignorance or defiance of the orthodox training methods by which classical players learn their instruments. Many jazz players, especially in the older days, were self-taught. I'm sure it never occurred to Louis Armstrong to stop at high C because that's where some exercise book left off. Similarly, it never occurred to him to use one kind of tonguing or articulation, as most classical trumpet players do. He used whatever tonguing and articulation his ear commanded him to use and in the process invented articulations, phrasings, and rhythmic configurations never heard before.   [5]

"ANTI-GUGGENHEIM, PRO-ESTERHÁZY"

From an interview with James Hoffmann and Joseph Maneri,
Boston, November 1985

Q: Audiences and performers still enjoy Esterházy music, but not Guggenheim music. Why?

A: There are three major parts to that problem. I would put first the plain historical fact that in the early part of this century, and again thirty years later, there were two basic major musical revolutions which changed the language of music so fundamentally that audiences, and even to some extent musicians and conductors, have not yet really caught up with those profound changes. It took Koussevitzky ten to fifteen years to educate an audience for new music in Boston.* At first he met tremendous resistance from audiences, from his Board of Trustees, from everybody; but he stuck it out and by the time he got through, say by 1945, I think he had one of the most intelligent, literate, sophisticated audiences in the world. And by extension, it carried over into the recordings that he made, and so educated not just the community of Boston, but the larger community of the country and eventually the world.

The next point to be made in relation to this problem is that of education, [which is necessary] in order to achieve at least a minimal comprehension of our twentieth-century musical language. And here I do not just mean education in the formal sense, as in schools, but also in the broader sense in which we become educated by the environment and cultural climate that surrounds us. The main culprit here is television, most especially network television, nowadays the prime educator of the average American. There is no art or culture or fine music on TV. The schools are also not doing the job of educating in the arts, and for the foreseeable future I don't see that they can do very much because all of those problems are resolvable only in the political and economic arena. You have to turn to Public Television to see a program on Van Gogh or hear a program of classical music or great jazz. The statistics on this subject are very clear: on the best night that

---

* The Russian-born Serge Koussevitzky (1874–1951) was conductor of the Boston Symphony Orchestra from 1924 to 1949. During this time he commissioned works from a long list of composers, including Bartók, Copland, Harris, Hindemith, and Stravinsky, programming many of the new pieces repeatedly so that audiences would become familiar with them.

Public Television can produce, it will get only four percent of the American view-ing audience.

The third part of the problem is, frankly, the reality that a lot of music today is bound to be less than great. We forget that we look at history in a telescoped retrospective in which all the bad music of the past has been sifted out. Leaf through a major music encyclopedia and you will find many composers who now are accorded at least a small paragraph in which it says the composer was born in 1712, died in 1795, and wrote thirty-seven operas, fifty-seven cantatas, nineteen symphonies and innumerable chamber works. The implication is—and rightly so—that the music was competent, correct, but probably unoriginal, not particu-larly creative. The poor folks who had to hear that music and others like it in that composer's lifetime were undoubtedly complaining about the amount of bad music. Likewise, we live in a situation today where we hear all the bad and indif-ferent music, along with the good.

We composers and professionals have, of course, to some extent or other the ability to discriminate between bad and good. But the average lay person does not, really cannot. And why should he? Imagine some fellow, who has been dragged to a concert by his wife, who hears first an overture in a familiar language, and then suddenly comes an onslaught of atonal, for him mixed-up, unintelligible sounds. It may be a frightful piece of junk or it may be a masterpiece. He will not be able to tell which; and indeed, even we fellow composers might have trouble telling. Put all these three parts together and you have a fundamental anti-Guggenheim, pro-Esterházy attitude.   [6]

ELLINGTON

From an article in High Fidelity, *November 1974*

If I dare to include Ellington in the pantheon of musical greats—the Beethovens, the Monteverdis, the Schoenbergs, the prime movers, the inspired innovators—it is precisely because Ellington had in common with them not only musical genius and talent, but an unquenchable thirst, an unrequitable passion for translating the raw materials of musical sounds into his own splendid visions. But that is still too general, something that can be said even of minor composers.

What distinguishes Ellington's best creations from those of other composers, jazz and otherwise, are their moments of total uniqueness and originality. There are many such flashes in his *oeuvre,* and it is a pity that they are virtually unknown to most non-jazz composer colleagues. Perhaps this is due to the fact that you can-not go into the nearest music store or library and obtain the orchestral scores of Duke Ellington. There is no Ellington *Gesamtausgabe,* alas, although this is some-thing that should become someone's life work. However, even if such scores ex-isted, they still would not readily disclose the uniqueness of which I speak. For Ellington's imagination was most fertile in the realm of harmony and timbre, usu-ally in combination. And as played by some of the finest musicians jazz has ever known, the specific effect produced in performance and on records is such that no notation has yet been devised to capture it on paper.

It was part of Ellington's genius—what I called earlier his fierce determination and unquenchable thirst—to assemble and maintain for over forty years his own private orchestra, comprising musicians more remarkable in their *individuality* than those of any symphony orchestra I know. Not since Esterházy had there been such a private orchestra—and Esterházy was not a composer. But like Haydn, who practiced daily on that band of Austrian/Hungarian musicians to develop the symphonic forms we now cherish, so Ellington practiced on his "instrument." This is a luxury we other composers simply do not know, and the whole experience of writing consistently for a certain group of musicians is a phenomenon we have never savored.

In Ellington's case, collaboration of such intimacy and durability was bound to produce unique musical results. These can be heard on literally hundreds of Ellington orchestra recordings in varying degrees of "uniqueness." When that alchemy worked at its best, the result was such as cannot be heard anywhere else in the realm of music. [7]

Hans Werner Henze
b. 1926

A prolific composer in many genres, Henze studied in his native Germany and attended Leibowitz's seminars on serialism. In 1946 he moved to Italy, primarily for political reasons. His music is often eclectic and is always intricately constructed and highly dramatic. His commitment to the ideals of the left emerges in some of his numerous stage works, as well as in his writings about music, many of which are contained in Music and Politics, Collected Writings, 1953–81, *the source for these excerpts.*

ART, ARTISTS, AND POLITICS
From "The Artist As Outsider," Essays, 1964

The bourgeois artist, or one who feels himself to be socially secure, tends to disintegrate the material at his disposal while he is creating, whereas the alienated one, the outlaw, puts all his energy into achieving the opposite with the same material, namely to try to integrate himself at all costs. This is something that has occurred at all periods and in all the arts, though it should be added that the longing for integration is peculiar to the alienated artist, who strives for a social form that corresponds to his isolation—one or other form of minority with which he sympathizes, and which moves his sensual and spiritual substance. He will not aim to reconcile himself with the fundamental tendencies of the ruling ideas of his time. He looks for understanding not among *nouveau-riche*, middle-class consumers, but among individuals or minorities with whom he believes he can communicate. Thus both his behavior and the form of his works are implicitly provocative, and more or less consciously he makes this provocation his goal. [1]

From "Music Is Inevitably Political," Zuricher student, *June 1969*

If a committed artist wishes to articulate his commitment—for instance if he is a composer who writes orchestral music—he has to rely on the modern symphony orchestra if he wants to use the resources of a large ensemble. He has to rely on record companies or radio stations, and to depend for everything on what the system has to offer. He undoubtedly finds himself in a dilemma.

One shouldn't try to fool oneself; the artist is dependent, no matter what, even if only on the dole.

——— ⁂ ———

One idea prevalent in the West is altogether wrong. There are those people who say that all previous music has been bourgeois music, and must therefore be done away with. It is not just that it seems odd that, under capitalism, some people want to do away with something that is humanistically essential—while others are trying to do away with capitalism by means of a humanistically essential revolution—but that wanting to do away with art is completely inhuman, unmarxist, and monstrous. [2]

From "The Task of Revolutionary Music," Neue Musikzeitung, *February/March 1971*

The theory that for music to become new it would be sufficient to develop new forms is a formalist notion. I am concerned with the struggle of the working class, and with the struggle of the many who want to leave their class. I try to recognize their problems, and come to the conclusion that they are mine. I try to bring about a dialectical contact. That was not the case in my music before. My content has thus become different. New content requires new forms. In the process of deepening this new content, and through contact with my new listener, new structures will also become visible. [3]

From a letter published in the Deutsche Volkszeitung, *May 9, 1974*

The notion that opera is "bourgeois" and an obsolete art form is itself one of the most outdated, tedious, and musty notions. There are, to be sure, outmoded styles, outdated and tedious productions, and slipshod routine that make it difficult for many theater-lovers and young comrades to grasp the content of the works being performed. . . . But this art form contains riches that are among the most beautiful inventions of the human spirit. They belong to all people; they were not written for the ruling class, but in a spirit of human brotherhood. Anyone who has seen, for example, how young workers and peasants in Havana have made symphonic music and opera their own, and how they fill the opera house, *their* opera house, to listen to *their* composers, Mozart, Verdi, Caturla, Beethoven, and Brouwer, will no longer be able to retain any doubts about which direction progressive cultural work must take—certainly not that of doing away with one of the fundamental factors of our culture.

It is not opera that is reactionary. What is bourgeois is a (undialectical) belief in linear progress, titillated by fashionable notions, frustrated and elitist, which calls for different forms of music and music making as if to escape reality, to bypass it: forms that could not exist at all, because they would have no basis (in the political and philosophical sense). Progress in art (and in artistic life) is conceivable only in connection with social progress. One must start at the foundations.   {4}

From "The Message of Music," essay
based on a lecture at the Brunswick Chamber Music Festival, 1959

LANGUAGE AND MUSIC

Language and music are two parallel spheres that are often connected; more than half of all existing music consists of settings of words. This relationship has diverse forms; sometimes music seizes violently upon language, and crushes it in its embrace, or sometimes language wants to seize upon music; they both can degrade but also can elevate one another. This is a phenomenon as old as music itself. In recent years more has been said about the division than about the possible connections; doubts have been raised whether any *rapprochement* is still possible unless music, whose purity is damaged by language, obliterates words and robs them of their meaning and origins, so that it can absorb them in this purified form, as sound. There are musicians who in language see only the words, and in musical phrases only the individual notes. In the words and single notes only the sound delights them (just as a few decades ago the noise of motors and hooters was considered by some to have musical potential). They wish to see the components separated from the movement or delivery of a musical or linguistic phrase. But it seems to me that such separation makes language into an intellectually unsatisfying thing: a hybrid that oscillates between disjointed meaninglessness, and a noise inferior to music, the organized art of sound; in every respect inferior to language, the highly formed art of thought.   {5}

THE COMPOSER AND THE PAST

The difficulty in which unknown music—conceived with new and unknown methods—repeatedly finds itself is to make itself intelligible. Intelligible: not so as to flatter philistines, not to delight stupid reactionaries, but in the sense that this music, set against centuries of experience, must undergo a trial of strength that only naïveté or ignorance could allow it to underestimate or reject.   {6}

The notes of the equal-tempered system, irrespective of the order in which they are conceived and the perspective in which they are viewed, offer themselves anew to the present as an unknown, uncharted field. For if Stravinsky or dodecaphony had a different conception of the treatment of notes from their predecessors and successors, how has this exhausted the notes themselves? Why should they have become superannuated because they were fixed for a time in specific systems? They are a resilient raw material that does not change. Only we change, in our attitude towards this raw material. Insofar as we realize the extent to which we are burdened by history, the burden disappears. We must be able to separate notes in their determinateness and their intrinsic properties from their history, to recognize their power. Once an awareness of the prehistory of notes, and of their experiences and tragedies during the last five hundred years, enters our subconscious and becomes a part of us, a patrimony that supports us and to which we owe nothing and everything—the human and logical desire for exactness and independence—once we no longer see ourselves oppressed by history but sustained by it, we can make a fresh start with freedom. [7]

From "Tradition and Cultural Heritage," interview in Die Welt, July 13, 1966

I believe that the road from Wagner's *Tristan* to Mahler and Schoenberg is far from finished, and with *The Bassarids* I have tried to go further along it. I am not prepared to relinquish what the centuries have passed on to us. On the contrary; "One must also know how to inherit; inheriting, that, ultimately, is culture." That was Thomas Mann's view, and I willingly subscribe to it.

One of the most important things for which I should like my music to be known is the vulnerability of its sounds—a fact too frequently forgotten. Also, an awareness of the symbolic quality of music that has passed into history. Anybody who consciously wants to free himself from it falls into an absurd nothingness where there are no precedents. He is committing an intellectual *lapsus,* and music takes its revenge by summoning up undesired associations. Music makes fun, as it were, of the musician. It passes him by. [8]

From "Music As a Means of Resistance," essay based on a lecture at the Technical University, Berlin, January 28, 1963

THE MATHEMATICAL AND THE CHAOTIC

In its urgency to become sound, in its haste to come into the world, to make itself manifest, music by its nature tends to make manifestos superfluous. The path it takes is never expected, required, prescribed. Music ignores theoretical correctives, and dissolves dogma whenever it wishes. Its realms are neither reification nor chaos; it spreads itself between these two poles, knowing about both of them, but existing only in the tension between them, by which it is energized. An awareness of urgent harmonized forms, formal ciphers, and idioms is needed to master chaos, a chaos that would be as boring and just as ugly as a completely reified work. Infinitude, boundlessness, explosions, and chaotic images are needed to resist oppression by the mathematical, which is just as much a part of the static raw material of music as the disordered and chaotic. All the misfortunes, doubts, and age-old torments of music-making are embodied in the knowledge of this polarity. [9]

OBSERVATIONS

The significance of chamber music is that in dealing with the intimate it can attain the ineffable. Chamber music conceives itself as a world of sound that has external boundaries but no internal ones. [10]

Old forms seem to me, as it were, like classical ideals of beauty, no longer attainable but still visible in the far distance, stirring memory like dreams; but the path toward them is filled with the age's greatest darkness and is the most difficult and the most impossible. To me it seems the only folly worth living for.   [11]

From "The Artist As Bourgeois Hero," program note on Elegy for Young Lovers, 1975

ART AND THE SUBCONSCIOUS

The argument, as you can read in every newspaper, is that the artist ideally creates from his subconscious. Now it may well be that, when the artist of our time switches off his intellect, or restricts it to purely mechanical functions, he may indeed babble one or two truths in the process—and this might even cast a beam of light on to his intellect. But it is not exactly a good sign for a society that only the inarticulate and the inebriated speak the truth, or are prepared to speak it. The trouble is that the artist usually manages to draw only errors and lies from his subconscious. He in fact draws from it only what has been put into it, and if the drawing out is unconscious, the putting in was usually very much conscious.
[12]

THE ARTIST-GENIUS

Aesthetically speaking, the personal existence of the artist is accidental; the essential thing is his production. The artist-genius, as the nineteenth century conceived him, made this aesthetic presupposition an ethical absolute; that is to say, he claimed to represent the highest, most authentic mode of human existence.
Accept this claim, and it follows that the artist-genius is morally bound by a sacred duty to exploit others whenever such exploitation will benefit his work, and to sacrifice them whenever their existence is a hindrance to his production.   [13]

MAHLER

From a program note on Mahler's Second Symphony, November 1975

With the increasing distance of time, Mahler's music has lost what a quarter of a century ago still prevented many from approaching it, namely its semantic affinities with Jugendstil. With hindsight its greatness can be recognized, and two things become visible: first, that we have here a continuation of the great German symphonic tradition; and second, that music is here radically called into question. For the first time in musical history, music is interrogating itself about the reasons for its existence and about its nature. The demands it makes on itself are on a level with the age from which it originates; it is a knowing music, with the same tragic consciousness as Freud, Kafka, Musil. Its provocation lies in its love of truth and in its consequent lack of extenuation. Like all great music, it too comes from the singing and dancing of the people; but that in no sense makes it simple; no, it makes everything real, and really difficult.   [14]

WEBERN

From "The Composer As Interpreter," interview
in the Frankfurter Opernhefte, *May 10, 1975*

Webern's conception of music and his taste are elements of a homespun musical thinking, in contrast with that of such men as Mahler and Berg, which opened different doors and linked music more inwardly with life, not least because they looked on their age with their senses open and therefore reflected its intellectual and political tendencies with sensitivity and awareness. This is specifically expressed in the fact that with Mahler and Berg music becomes critical, self-critical; it calls music into question, and questions itself, whereas with Webern it is uncritically affirmative. Music in a state of decomposition is brought back as a state of purity there as if nothing had happened; as if there were no class struggle, no imperialism, no wars, as if society were in order; as though everything were as untouched as blades of grass high in the Alps. [15]

METHODS AND BELIEFS

From a response to a review, the Rheinische Post, *May 11, 1957*

I have never yet allowed myself to belong to any group or school. I love music very much, but I detest politicking, the struggle for or against something in music; music reaches people of its own accord, when it wants to. It cannot be imposed, can hardly be explained, cannot be propagated; leading articles make it no better and no worse. We Germans with our renowned, incomparable, and vigorous musical life often tend to consign music to categories, to theoretical values, instead of applying liberal individual criteria. Many people read about music instead of listening to it; this may be pleasurable, but it is not the same thing, and does not necessarily always further their understanding of music. . . .

When I start a work I never have a plan, a preconceived opinion or a theory to direct me. I do not think so little of music that I fancy I know more than it does. Thus with each new composition everything is difficult and problematical until I have found a way—call it, if you will, a technique—in which I can express myself clearly. But the value of this technique dies out when the composition is finished; some lessons and experiences are perhaps carried forward, but the next work is bound to present problems different from those I expect. [16]

From an interview in Für wen komponieren Sie eigentlich? *1971*

I have taken the decision that in my work I will embody all the difficulties and all the problems of contemporary bourgeois music, and that I will, however, try to transform these into something usable, into something the masses can understand. Now that does not mean that I want to operate on the level of commercial music and "hits." But neither do I think, on the other hand, that there is any place for worry about losing elite notions of value. [17]

Karlheinz Stockhausen
b. 1928

After a traditional musical education, Stockhausen began composing electronic music in 1953, and was associated for decades with the avant-garde institutions of Cologne and Darmstadt. His mysticism and his interest in drawing on fields outside music helped win attention for his works in art and general cultural circles, while his dramatic iconoclasm and his incorporation of spatial aspects made him one of the few composers to enjoy a large following among younger audiences. Stockhausen's extensive writings offer a detailed view of his aesthetic and philosophical positions.

From Jonathan Cott's
Stockhausen: Conversations with the Composer, *1973*

"WE ARE ALL TRANSISTORS"

We are all transistors in the literal sense. Waves arrive, antennae receive them, and the so-called high fidelity system plays them back as directly as possible without distorting them too much. And a human being is always bombarded with cosmic rays which have a very specific rhythm and structure, and they transform his atomic structure and by that his whole system. And if we're too much involved with our personal ego, desires, interests, people, whatever it is, then these rays become focused on us as individuals with our tiny private problems. But when we more and more forget ourselves—I mean try to make ourselves pure in the state of reception and transmission—then this current passes through. And if you have a special talent—that you have no merits for, it's just given to you—to work in sound, light, or in gestures as a dancer, then you can use what you have in order to concretize what comes through you, and then that communication is possible. You become a focus. The current goes through you, and then it goes to the others through you.

I've had several letters during the last weeks from very young people in Germany who are literally turned on. They make music in small groups at night in the forest, trying to make the music in harmony with the sound in the forest. And they are really trying to catch waves from distant stars. I want to show you these letters of eighteen-, nineteen-year-olds. I think there's a new generation, a new consciousness. Those guys, what they describe! For example, in the last letter that I got from a young man, he tells how he listened to shortwave sounds over earphones for several hours over a period of several nights. And then one evening he heard the Third and Fourth Regions of *Hymnen*. He listened to them again for four hours, meditating in between the sections and then focusing on the waves. And he said that in the nine megahertz Region all of a sudden he hit a point where he flipped out. He completely went off and had a cosmic trip.

I know this young man. He wasn't on drugs, and he's very brilliant and thinks and speaks very logically. He asked me if I knew about these waves. And I didn't.

All I know is that I've come on very strange situations when I've performed with shortwave radios together with other instruments. And I always need at a certain moment to tune in certain shortwaves. Because they're not only the result of interferences from the terrestrial vibrations of all those private and public radio stations, ships, and Morse code stations, but in addition to this new quality which results from these interferences, there are also all the quasar waves. And I'm definitely sure that there are a lot of rhythmetized waves coming from outside of our solar system. These are very important things to deal with. And if young people have such experiences, then I take it as real.   [1]

THE SPIRIT

I think the ultimate goal of a creative person is to transform his whole existence as a person into a medium that's more timeless, more spiritual. All my energy goes into the music; and it's not really my music. I don't ultimately know what my music has to do in this world and what it means. Because it must be filled with new meanings, with other people, other spirits. I'm commissioned, so to speak, by a supernatural power to do what I do. I think the spirit, as a personal spirit, will be the music itself, so I don't have to take care of it anymore; it begins to have its own life, and sometimes when I meet it again, I hardly recognize it.   [2]

I have not been able up to now to materialize myself completely within a machine, in an object, though I have been able in a few moments of my life at a very high state of consciousness to identify completely with an animal or with a plant. Maybe others have that power. I don't see any reason why spirit cannot materialize in any form.   [3]

THE POWER OF WAVES

People in advertising and politics know very well what sounds do to the masses. Oh yes. The Khmer people in Cambodia moved thirty- and forty-ton stones, with elephants pushing and people pulling on ropes. Trumpet blowers who periodically blew very sharp signals had an important function, helping to synchronize thousands of people pulling at the rope in order to move such stones even one inch. Sounds can do anything. They can kill. The whole Indian mantric tradition knows that with sounds you can concentrate on any part of the body and calm it down, excite it, even hurt it in the extreme. There are also special mantras, naturally, that can lift the spirit of a person up into supernatural regions so that he leaves his body.

This information must be taught in schools; it's more important than writing and arithmetic. We must know what the waves do to us—all the waves, most of the waves have no names, cosmic rays constantly bombarding and penetrating our bodies. The astrologists have an elaborate knowledge of what certain constellations of other planets do to the human body. Our bodies are preconditioned, having been born under certain influences of the stars, which are enormous magnets, that's just what they are. So the magnetic field of a person is predetermined by certain magnetic constellations. When you record something on a tape recorder what else do you do but magnetize very small elements of metal which are on the tape, and these molecules are ordered in certain patterns that, when they're reproduced, make sound. [4]

THE GREAT ARTIST

We always think that the great artist should be a person who embraces the whole world as much as possible and integrates rather than chops things up. But there are people who have written practically only songs or only a certain kind of piece in one style and have done beautiful work. We think of Goethe as a greater artist than … Mörike, for example. But Mörike had his own qualities. So going very deep and specializing on one point is also necessary in the total situation. [5]

THE TRADITIONAL VERSUS THE NEW

At the beginning of my career, I pointed out that in traditional music—Webern also included—musicians always showed the same figure in different light. This is the kaleidoscopic idea of variation, transformation, and development; and all these dramatic forms were based on this principle. It's like the idea of theater which derives from the Greek drama where you have the figures—characters who go through the whole play, through all stages of dramatic situations, until they die, at which point the play is over. (In classical sonatas, the recapitulations presented the material unchanged from the beginning—and then the movement was over. But of course the development sections became more and more important.) All the early twelve-tone composers treated the series as a *theme* to be developed. They transposed it, added sounds, showed it in mirror form, but they always had a thematic concept. And composers like Boulez, Pousseur, and myself criticized this when we were young, pointing out that though the serial concept might have given birth to a completely new musical technique—by getting rid of thematic composition—composers like Schoenberg and Berg still couldn't get away from it. What I said then was that in traditional music you always see the same object— the theme or the motive—in a different light, whereas in the new music there are always new objects in the *same* light. By the "same light" I meant a set of proportions—no matter what appeared in these proportions: the relationships became more important than what was being related. In this way you could constantly create new configurations by working with a series of proportions and, as we've said the other day, the proportions could be applied once to time, once to space. This created completely different musical figures, allowing us to move away from the thematic concept. [6]

MUSICAL MEANING

From the foreword to Robin Maconie's
The Works of Karlheinz Stockhausen, *1990*

Let no one suppose that the composer may be better able to interpret the musical vibrations transmitted through him, than a commentator who immerses himself, body and soul, in this music. All the commentaries that have ever been, and those yet to be written, all the thoughts and dreams and impressions and visions and actions that my music arouses in its hearers, all these, no less, add up to the meaning of this music—something that must always remain largely a mystery, never totally to be comprehended by a single individual. The resonance is different in every person, for each stands on a different rung of the ladder of spiritual self enhancement. [7]

COMPOSITION TODAY

From an interview in Andrew Ford's Composer to Composer, 1992

The fascination of sound visions; the fascination of being a very good engineer: these two things are the permanent problem of modern composition. There are younger composers—my students—who only react to associative composition. They sit down and what comes comes, and they hear a lot of other music. Several of my students, who have become very well known now, they listen to my music while they are composing, or they watch television while they compose in order to get enough stimuli. Some kind of mixture comes out of this. There are certain chameleons among present-day composers—they call themselves post-modernists—and they mix everything they can steal, and paint the stolen elements with different colors so that you cannot identify them immediately. They are enormous garbage containers of pre-existing sound figures and clichés and out of this source comes something else. There is no unifying spirit. It's the opposite: the will *not* to have a unifying spirit, to have everything and to combine everything in an unusual fashion. I think that is a big mistake. [8]

COMPARISON WITH BOULEZ

From Stockhausen: Conversations with the Composer

I think that perhaps the basic difference between Boulez and myself is that my interests have always somehow been more prospective, God knows why. Prospective in the sense that I've posed problems that couldn't be solved at the moment, that were futuristic, and that necessitated a complete change in the manner of teaching musicians, in constructing and using these instruments. Whereas Boulez is a more practical man, not moving too far away from what is available and where we are. [9]

CHAPTER FOURTEEN

Toru Takemitsu

Sofia Gubaidulina

Steve Reich

Philip Glass

John Harbison

Oliver Knussen

Toru Takemitsu

1930–1996

In his music Takemitsu sought a fusion of East and West, in the spiritual and expressive dimensions as well as in technical aspects such as scoring, form, and motivic play. He once stated that his goal was "to achieve a sound as intense as silence." Born in Tokyo, he studied music there and in 1951 helped to found an experimental workshop for the blending of ancient Japanese and modern Western musical methods. From the 1970s until his death he taught and lectured extensively in the United States and Europe.

From "A Composer's Diary," 1962

SOUND AND SILENCE

The fear of silence is nothing new. Silence surrounds the dark world of death. Sometimes the silence of the vast universe hovers over us, enveloping us. There is the intense silence of birth, the quiet silence of one's return to the earth. Hasn't art been the human creature's rebellion against silence? Poetry and music were born when man first uttered a sound, resisting the silence. By scraping one object against another or by scouring a surface, pictorial art was born.

By the time of the Renaissance, art increasingly carried the taint of man. In the historical diversification of the arts, together with modern intellectualism, the very nature of art itself was threatened. In our time many of the arts have become exclusive and self-contained, each within its own narrow domain; no amount of verbal defense or theory will enrich such art.

Confronting silence by uttering a sound is nothing but verifying one's own existence. It is only that singling out of one's self from the cavern of silence that can really be called "singing." That is the only "truth" that should concern artists, otherwise we will never really face the question of art's reality. (Viewed this way, descriptive music is a cowardly art.) It is in silence that the artist singles out the truth to sing or sketch. And it is then that he realizes his truth exists prior to everything. This is the love of art, and at the same time is something that could be called "the world." These days too many arts have left the meaning of silence behind.   [1]

THE NATURE OF COMPOSITION

I wish to free sounds from the trite rules of music, rules that are in turn stifled by formulas and calculations. I want to give sounds the freedom to breathe. Rather than on the ideology of self-expression, music should be based on a profound relationship to nature—sometimes gentle, sometimes harsh. When sounds are possessed by ideas instead of having their own identity, music suffers. This would be my basic rule, but it is only an idea and naturally I must develop a practical method. One way might be through an ethnological approach. There may be folk music with strength and beauty, but I cannot be completely honest in this kind of music. I want a more active relationship to the present. (Folk music in a "contemporary style" is nothing but a deception.)

Because the writer of popular tunes looks at his world with too much detachment, it falls to the composer to deal with the real thoughts and emotions of his time. In this welter of contemporary life it is only through his own sense of worth and by proving himself that a composer is able to relate to tradition in the most faithful sense.

———— ⚡ ————

I love collaborating. While I don't take individual efforts lightly, I'm afraid that such efforts may tend to become self-centered without relationships beyond themselves. Establishment of the ego is a prerequisite for modern times. But to be fastidious in blocking out others would soon result in one's own death. There would be no circulation of air. Too often these days creativity is nothing but the invention of methods. When aesthetics becomes so sharp and distinguished, art becomes weak. Really, expression is nothing but the maximum realization and proving of self. If that is true I don't see that it makes sense to hold onto conventional techniques. I am afraid of attitudes lapsing into convenient routines. . . .

I am a composer whose thoughts are only the early glimmering of awareness of someone who regards composing as his profession. As a composer—not an inventor—I don't need patents. Things I think of must have been thought of by others already. That is why it is fitting that I be a composer, since I am not concerned about thinking thoughts that no one else might ever think. I just want to make sure that while I am thinking those thoughts that anyone might think, I am doing it in my very own way. Therefore, I think I don't mind if things are not always all my own.

Theoretically, the coexistence of two individualities is a contradiction. I am not trying to eliminate that contradiction by working in collaboration. On the contrary, by experiencing stronger contradictions I hope to know reality. Is not the effort in reconciling differences the real exercise for life? Contradiction will result in movement, and that will make the air circulate.

Hereupon, being is not being. Therefore, being is being. —Daisetsu Suzuki

Composition should be something that truly has being, something that should have arisen from the composer's own turbulent interaction with reality. For the composer, reality is nothing more than sounds. And for sounds to come into being they must reverberate through the composer, becoming one with him. The technique of constructing sounds through mathematical formulas is trivial. If music consisted only of inventing and constructing sounds I could well do without being a composer. If there is a sound that is alive, some kind of order will naturally exist. That is why we think the singing of birds is beautiful, truly beautiful.

The work of inventing and constructing music really holds no interest for me. I want to carve away the excess sound finally to grasp the essential single sound.

[2]

Listening

From Sound, Word, Man *(written with Junzo Kawada), 1980*

When one listens to a bird song in a natural circumstance, he hears other natural noises as having the same importance. In a natural environment, the noises should not hinder the act of listening. Rather, innumerable sounds help one to really listen.

Establishing many auditive focal points is one (objective) side of composing, and trying to listen to one voice in many sounds is another side.

First, devote yourself to a simple act of listening. Only then will you understand the purpose of music.   [3]

East and West

From a lecture at the Japan Society, New York City, July 6, 1988

I believe that cultures do converge and gradually form themselves into a cluster. Furthermore, that very often what occurs in the fusion of cultures goes beyond what can be predicted from cultural influences flowing back and forth. What we see today is a Japan deeply influenced by the West, by Europe and the United States, and we see increasing numbers of Westerners who are deeply impressed by Eastern cultures. More and more, East and West are being evaluated on equal terms. But we're not there yet: fundamental differences still remain.

Take, for example, the case of John Cage, who is known for introducing the principles of chance, of randomness, into his music. To me, if this process is taken to its extreme, randomness becomes just the opposite—it seems terribly logical. To the Japanese listener the principle becomes rather tiresome (not in the case of Cage, but in extreme cases). However, I must express my deep and sincere gratitude to John Cage. The reason for this is that in my own life, in my own development, for a long period I struggled to avoid being "Japanese," to avoid "Japanese" qualities. It was largely through my contact with John Cage that I came to recognize the value of my own tradition. In his own way, John Cage was influenced by Zen through his encounters with the Zen master Daisetsu Suzuki. It doesn't really matter what came first or who was influenced by whom. What is important in the long run is that it is possible for us to understand each other. Recently I talked with John Cage about just this point and we were in complete agreement.
[4]

In the essence of our music I think there are things that are perhaps very different from Western music—a sense of time, a sense of space, and a sensitivity to color and tone. But I don't want to say that as Orientals, or as Japanese, we have any particular monopoly on these qualities in music. There are gaps, certainly, in the traditions of the West and of the East, but in studying each other's music and learning from each other's music we are, together, beginning to fashion a "universal egg" of communication between cultures.

In our present world severe demands are made on the artist and the creator. Some artists have succumbed to the contradictions, the problems, of national systems and nationalism. But, as we all strive for an ideal world, what we must do is find what is genuine in ourselves, the unique qualities in ourselves, and affirm these in a universal fashion. We must all share this common goal. The role of the artist is to serve as a bridge for all men to accomplish this and the artist must be fully and completely aware of this task. For Japanese to be learning from the West, and for Westerners—Europeans and Americans—to be deepening their appreciation of Oriental culture, is a difficult undertaking, a very serious one that we must all confront. I'm not sure that our mutual intercultural understanding is complete or has reached an ideal state yet. There are still problems that separate us: senses of differences of race and color. These are the things that we must strive to transcend. [5]

"FIXED" AND "PORTABLE" MUSIC

From an interview, July 1988

On this globe, roughly speaking, there are two different kinds of music: one which is portable, possible to carry; and one which is never carried, not portable. Of course, all Japanese traditional music was originally imported from outside—from China, Korea, Laos—and then it was "Japanized" over a long period. So, in studying Japanese music I have also studied the original music—Chinese music, South Vietnamese music, Indonesian music. I have visited many places: China, Indonesia, Australia. Indonesian music is so refined, especially gamelan music. Many of the instruments are made from metal, so the instruments are portable. However, the music belongs to the land. . . .

In the West, ancient European music still belonged to the land. But modernizations began, perhaps in the Renaissance. The interval was divided and divided and divided, and everything about the instruments became so functional—very good to carry abroad, like Christianity! Now the problem is how to integrate the differences. Modernism, I mean, industrialism and everything, is finding difficulty in coming up with solutions. [6]

CONTACT WITH AMERICAN MUSIC

From the Japan Society lecture

Throughout World War II nearly all Western music was prohibited in Japan. Except for the music of the Axis countries, we had no chance at all to hear other forms of Western music. Toward the end of the war, as the American forces were preparing to invade Japan, the Japanese military constructed bases deep in the mountains. I was fourteen years old at the time, and was conscripted to work at one of these mountain bases. It was far from Tokyo and all the young conscripts like myself lived in a kind of rough barracks. For me the experience was an extremely bitter one. We were not real soldiers, and the soldiers treated us very harshly. Not all of them, of course; there were a few exceptions.

One day, one of the military officers took a number of us to the very back of the barracks where he had a record player and a number of records. There was no needle to play the records, but this officer had carefully sharpened a piece of bamboo, and using it as a needle he was able to play the records for us. One of the first records that he put on was the French chanson, "Parlez-moi de l'amour." For me, hearing that music came as an enormous shock. I was stunned, and for the first time I suddenly realized the splendid quality of Western music. Later, after the war, when the Americans arrived in Japan, they soon established a radio station for the American troops. At that time I was sick and had to spend every day in bed. With my ears turned to the radio I spent all my time listening to music on the U.S. Armed Forces Network. . . . [Later] I also went very, very frequently to the library of the Civil Information and Education branch of the U.S. Occupation government. There I also sought out American music. Through hearing the music of Roy Harris, Aaron Copland, Walter Piston, Roger Sessions, and such great American composers, I was introduced to an unknown world, and I gradually began to develop a sense of my own musical taste. For me, after having tasted the bitter, miserable experiences of the war years, this music seemed full of hope.   [7]

"IMAGINARY SOUNDSCAPES"

From a lecture at Studio 200, Tokyo, April 30, 1984

In my music there is no constant development as in the sonata; instead, imaginary soundscapes appear. A single element is never emphasized with development through contrast. The listener need not understand the different operations discussed here. Actually, I have my own theories of structure and systematic procedure, but I wish to avoid overemphasizing these. My music is composed as if fragments were thrown together unstructured, as in dreams. You go to a far place and suddenly find yourself back home without having noticed the return.   [8]

MUSICAL IDENTITY

From Mirror of Tree, Mirror of Grass, 1975

To deny the Europe that is inside of me is to negate myself. By that action, the poignant value of traditional Japanese music is also lost.   [9]

From the Japan Society lecture

For a long while, I permitted myself to gaze only into the mirror of Western music and Western art. However, one day I chanced to see a performance of the Bunraku puppet theater and was very surprised by it. It was in the tone quality, the timbre, of the *futazao* shamisen, the wide-necked shamisen used in Bunraku, that I first recognized the splendor of traditional Japanese music. I was very moved by it and I wondered why my attention had never been captured before by this Japanese music. I wondered, perhaps, if it wasn't precisely the fact that I had studied Western music so deeply that enabled later to be so moved by the Bunraku music that I heard. Had I never been under the sway of Western music I know my appreciation of Japanese music would have been very different. I think this is an extremely important point. From that time on I devoted a great deal of energy—as much as possible—to studying Japanese musical traditions, with particular attention to the differences between Japanese music and Western music. With great diligence I tried to bring forth the sensibilities of Japanese music that had always been within me. [10]

Sofia Gubaidulina
b. 1931

Already facing hurdles by virtue of her gender and ethnicity (her father was Tatar, her mother part Jewish), Gubaidulina encountered further obstacles to official Soviet recognition when she began composing music with spiritual and religious overtones. She became known in the West through the advocacy of a few performers and subsequently made a series of visits to Europe and the United States; since then her fame has increased dramatically both at home and abroad.

From an interview, 1991
ORIGINS AS A COMPOSER

I was born in 1931, and when I was five years old I heard the conversations of my parents and their reactions [to the Stalinist Terror], especially in 1937 and 1938. I lived in an atmosphere in which everyone was aware of everything: for example, in the street in which we lived, a woman who was the best and most noble of us all was the first to be arrested. Everyone was ready at any moment, when they heard the knock at the door, to be taken away. Everyone knew it and lived in dread. . . .

A human being, even under the most difficult conditions, even in a murderous atmosphere, must have something to hold sacred. I remember extremely well my impressions at five years of age, when I began to have some understanding: all my life was gray and I felt good only when I entered the door of the music school. From that moment I felt myself in a sacred space. I heard the sounds coming from the halls, I felt the bond that united the students, and everything came together in that polytonal harmony of sounds, and I wanted to live in that world. [1]

SERIALISM

What does the twelve-tone system mean? This system, so attractive, has defined the ideas and awareness of composers for a great part of this century. Let's try to see what is at the base of its attraction. Theorists have explained that serialism is the result of the evolution of the musical language, but what are the existential reasons a system based on the equality of tones is preferable to a system founded on their hierarchical organization? Here we must answer that there is nothing intrinsically better about a system founded on equality; I think both systems are necessary.

Permit me to suggest a metaphor drawn from agriculture. There's a season for harvesting fruit, another in which seeds germinate, and yet another in which one prepares the ground for planting. Our century has confronted the problem of how to prepare the ground in order to plant and harvest new crops. In this preparatory phase, the earth must be leveled and reduced to an even density, thus bringing it into a different condition. The artists of our century have often been engaged in such a process of dematerialization. Naturally they have been artists of very different temperaments, such as Picasso, Schoenberg, or Webern; they may be lyrical, abstract, or tragic temperaments, but all of them have worked with the same intention, to prepare the ground for new harvests. Such an approach presupposes a substantial faith in the intrinsic quality of one's material; precisely for that reason I would define this approach as classical.

There is another position, however, that I would define as postclassical, and that is an approach that doesn't believe truth is immanent in the material, but arises only from the comparison between diverse types of material. This approach begins with a nucleus of thought that is capable of joining together all these different types of material. This type of consciousness, in my opinion, belongs to a musician such as Alfred Schnittke, for example.   [2]

THE SACRED

I think of "the sacred" as an ethical category, but the idea of religion as a universal idea of communication. If concepts of the sacred are defined historically, it means they are products of human history, but if instead we speak of a religious idea that exists outside of history we approach a cosmic concept that seems to me important not only for our human mentality, but also for the development of the world. Without these more general religious ideas one can't live, because they are the roots of existence. Often religion is defined literally according to its Latin root, *religare*, to reconnect or rebind—that is, as a reestablishment of communication, and for we musicians a concept of this sort is perfectly comprehensible; we have very concrete ideas about such a process. Binding together diverse elements, leading them back toward a center, is a characteristically musical idea, and also an existentially tragic idea that represents the essence of the spiritual world. Every human being feels the need to re-connect, and art is one way to express that need.   [3]

DEMATERIALIZATION

In many contemporary composers there exists a tendency to dematerialization, to the progressive dissolution of the harmonic fabric. One of the characteristics of our time is to have chosen the way of "interior-ness" with a resolve unknown in past eras. The exploration of the internal and the intimate through psychoanalysis is one obvious demonstration of this tendency. In order to penetrate our inner life it is necessary to unravel the material quilt that conceals our spirituality. This is why the music of our time has so often engaged processes of dematerialization, the dismantling of form, often adopting a stance of renunciation that sometimes oversteps the threshold of silence. . . .

I am firmly convinced that we find ourselves now in a new period of "archaism." We have dissolved sonic structures used for so long in order to descend into a new profundity, and find ourselves in a completely dark and unknown space. For this reason I feel so close to the tendency of Luigi Nono to use ideas of dispersed space, to make them live in the pauses of his *Quartetto*, to use them to build a temple made of silences. And in such a work of construction it seems to me that the most appropriate building material is the symbol, which is the most striking character-istic of all archaic art. Such symbols are made of ancient materials, used daily in the most banal way, but uprooted from their former contexts so that they can be used with a symbolic meaning. Thus it is with the rests in Nono's *Quartetto*, and with the pizzicati in my own Third Quartet, where all the energy is concentrated in the fingers that pluck the strings as long as is bearable; only then may the per-formers return to playing with the bow. Pizzicati, harmonics, glissandi do not appear as variations of color, but as symbols that allude to a different sonic con-dition.   {4}

ART AND TIME

Art poses the objective of creating a time that I would call the continual present. In the dimension of temporality as we usually experience it, the present is always elusive, suspended between a past that is no longer and a future that is not yet. From the perspective of art the present acquires a superior force of concentration on objects and concepts—it escapes from temporality. To be realized, however, this process of transfiguration requires the sacrifice of temporality—a sacrifice that, as T. S. Eliot has explained very well, becomes an act of expiation.   {5}

KABALEVSKY AND KHACHATURIAN

Kabalevsky behaved in a way that was completely contrary to my ideals. I recall his total lack of understanding of his students' works. He often said, "Why do our students write such sad music? In our country we have no reason to be sad." For me, such statements mean that the man understood nothing. Khachaturian didn't say things like that, but his position was not dissimilar. He lived too well in every sense, and I consider him an excessively materialistic artist.   [6]

STRAVINSKY'S NEOCLASSICAL PERIOD

In my opinion, [in works like *Apollon musagète* and *Perséphone*] some extraordinary apparations occur. When the soul of a composer confronts memories, it is as though it is embarking on a voyage into a labyrinth. It is a complicated voyage in which the soul never fully enters into a particular object. The musician con-tinues to contemplate the objects from a certain distance because, although they are found in memory, recollections can only be contemplated from afar. It hap-pens very rarely, in my opinion only a couple of times, that Stravinsky succeeds in eradicating the distancing perspective of memory and identifies completely with the objects he is contemplating.   [7]

SHOSTAKOVICH'S "SIMPLER" WORKS

The life of an artist is much more complicated than people think. The need to be radical manifests itself externally at some times, but not at others. This hope for progress cannot be reflected in all phases of the creative process, in every fragment of an artist's work. You go forward following your own road, and you can't always be gazing at the highest peaks. I remember that one of my piano teachers once told me, "You must listen to everyone and obey no one." I'm sure that Shostakovich, Ravel, and Bartók did exactly that when they were criticized for not being radical enough.   [8]

COMPOSITIONS OVER THE PAST THREE DECADES

From an interview, mid-1990s

I really can't say that any radical shift has taken place in my work, or any unexpected change in my way of thinking. . . . It seems to me that I have been traveling through my soul the whole time, in a definite direction, always further and further and further. . . . Today my work is concerned with rhythm and form, while at that time it concentrated on tonal color and pitch. What I mean is that with me there is indeed some sort of technical development, but the conceptual line, in my opinion, has always remained the same.   [9]

Steve Reich
b. 1936

Reich's teachers included William Bergsma, Vincent Persichetti, Darius Milhaud, and Luciano Berio, but his musical identity derives as much from non-Western influences such as African drumming, Balinese gamelan, and Hebrew cantillation. In 1966 he founded his ensemble, Steve Reich and Musicians, developing and performing with them his first signature works of shifting rhythmic patterns overlying a hypnotic pulse.

THE WESTERN TRADITION; INFLUENCES

From an interview in Soundpieces, 1980

All music that we know and love, for whatever reason—and certainly Bach, Stravinsky, and Bartók are at the top of this list—is clearly, "hearably" from a certain time and place. Since the roots of the Second Viennese School were obviously where and when they were, for an American in the 1950s, '60s, or '70s to take this over lock, stock, and barrel is a little artificial. The sounds that surrounded America from 1950 through 1980—jazz and rock and roll—cannot be ignored. They can be refined, filtered, rejected, or accepted in part, but they can't be ignored, or you're an ostrich; you're ill-informed. To ape another culture of another time has to have a certain sterility as a result. It's like taking a plant that grows in another very different environment; you have to build a hothouse, a miniature tropical environment, to keep it alive. That's what museums are for, and that's why it's important to have orchestras that play the music that they do; I'm all for that. But in terms of living composers, I don't think that you can pretend you are someone who is completely divorced from this time and place. And that's very much how I've dealt with non-Western music; I avoid sounding like it, because I think that would be absurd.   {1}

At the age of fourteen, I first heard Bach, Stravinsky, and bebop—Charlie Parker and Miles Davis. That nexus of tastes—Baroque music, Stravinsky, and jazz—stayed with me ever since. That spoke to something that was waiting to be spoken to inside of me, and since then I've followed that path.   {2}

I'm obviously a Western composer, and so naturally I like to be understood as one. It's quite erroneous to think that I'm involved in some pursuit that has nothing to do with or is a complete break from Western tradition. Specifically, the way to connect my music to the Western tradition is not to look at what comes immediately behind me chronologically, the series of post-Webern compositions. Though if you want to do that, then look at Webern himself. Look at the number of notes on a page, think of the reduction involved in what he was doing, and the organization that went on in serial music. Actually, there's a great similarity between that and my early pieces, like *Piano Phase*: the severity and clarity of the organization. A very different kind of sound, but a very pared-down, severely organized kind of music.   {3}

From an interview in Andrew Ford's Composer to Composer, *1991*

MINIMALISM

I don't mention that word at all.   {4}

HARMONIC STASIS

The person who first worked in [the] area of harmonic stasis was definitely La Monte Young—there's no question about that. And the second person who worked in this area, who was influenced by La Monte Young, was Terry Riley—there's no question about that either. And the third person who worked in this area was myself. And through me, who met and influenced Philip Glass in New York, that's really the chain of transmission. Everyone, except the last person on line there, seems to agree with the history.   {5}

POLITICAL ART

I don't believe that political art serves a function and that we must get it out there at the barricades: I think that's hogwash. *The Threepenny Opera* had absolutely no effect in stopping the Nazis; *Guernica* is a masterpiece but it didn't stop Franco or Hitler or Mussolini for two seconds.   {6}

Philip Glass
b. 1937

While in Paris studying with Nadia Boulanger in 1964, Glass met the sitarist Ravi Shankar, who offered him the job of transcribing some ragas. The experience led Glass to re-evaluate his identity as a composer. Returning to New York City in 1967, he established himself among the "downtown" artists and writers and began creating the works that led to the repetition-based style for which he first became known. His reputation was firmly established with the opera Einstein on the Beach, *premiered in 1976. He has since written numerous other operas as well as film scores, ballets, mixed-media pieces, and pop songs.*

From an interview in Soundpieces, 1980
TEACHERS VERSUS COMPOSERS

You learn different things from composers; mainly you learn tricks. From people like Boulanger you learn technique—it's not the same thing. There's a lot of things you can learn from composers if they're willing to teach you . . . : ways of writing out a score so you can see the whole piece without turning the page, for example. Those are the kinds of things that I learned most from other composers, to the extent that they were willing to impart those things; sometimes they aren't.   [1]

THE CLUB SCENE

The most important and vital new music scene today, for me, has been in the clubs. The New Wave scene is basically another form of non-commercial music. . . . I find [the New Wave bands'] approach to their music serious, lively, risky; these guys are doing all the things that artists are supposed to be doing. It's a hand-to-mouth trip. I don't know any of them that are doing it for the money. If they thought they were, they'd be crazy; even the successful ones aren't making that much money. It's not about money. You're more likely to find people in the straight music world who are interested in money. This is almost an art rock trip, but it's not that arty either; it's something more committed than that, and it's very serious.   [2]

From Music by Philip Glass, 1987
THE EXISTENCE OF ART

One might venture to say that art objects—be they paintings, string quartets, or plays—don't exist or function by themselves as abstract entities. They function and become meaningful only when there are people present to experience them. When put that way, one old riddle is answered very easily. When the tree falls in the forest, does it make a sound if no one is there to hear it? The answer, of course, is no. Yet many people still act as if Art somehow has an independent existence all its own.   [3]

Serialism

In the hands of a talented composer, serial composition could produce highly expressive and often ingenious music, and it became fashionable, almost mandatory, among composers growing up after World War II. Probably its intellectual rigor and sheer difficulty for creator, performer and listener made it seem almost automatically worthwhile, regardless of how it actually came out. After the premiere of a new piece, it was not uncommon to hear the remark, "It's actually much better than it sounds"(!). Such attitudes seem more and more incomprehensible today, but it was only a few years ago that they were taken quite seriously.

Though there were many gifted and energetic composers and performers dedicated to Serialism, the music to this day has not found a general public acceptance. In spite of this rather obvious drawback, its adherents over the years have at times been very influential, controlling performance opportunities and commissions, while developing a critical following to make up for its other shortcomings. In this way, the music business is much like any other, political skills and alliances counting for a great deal.

This, then, was the music that appeared to dominate the world of serious concert music in the mid-1960s. It was music I had studied as a student, and any further exercise of that kind interested me not at all. To me, it was music of the past, passing itself off as music of the present. After all, Arnold Schoenberg was about the same age as my grandfather!

Occasionally the "Domaine Musicale" would play a work by an American such as Earle Brown, John Cage or Morton Feldman, and they always came as a breath of fresh air after so much heavy European didacticism.   [4]

From an interview, 1990

The Composer's Voice

At the age of nineteen or twenty, very few composers have many original ideas or know who they are. Most of us write the music our teachers write—and I think, in fact, that's a good method. You learn a lot about music. You learn about finishing pieces, and how they work. My own voice really came to me, I would say, in 1965. It was a good ten years after I began seriously studying music that I really had any original ideas. And it wasn't until 1969 that I wrote any pieces that are still in my repertoire.   [5]

The first problem a composer has is to find his own voice, his own style, and the second problem he has is to get rid of it. I'm more concerned with finding diversity within a style than finding or recognizing one style. I'm always hoping one day to write a piece that no one will know who wrote it.   [6]

Minimalism

About the word *minimalism*: First, historically, it's a journalistic invention—at least, in its application to music. It was first used in 1971 by Tom Johnson, a writer for the *Village Voice*, who was also a composer. It probably derives from the visual arts movement of the time. The progenitors of Minimalism in art were Robert Morris and Donald Judd and Sol LeWitt. . . .

The term was used in music in a very broad way. I knew about thirty composers who were writing in an antiestablishment style. Antiestablishment for those days meant writing not dodecaphonic or serial music. They were a whole generation writing in a totally rhythmically oriented way. Several became known as Minimalists. I didn't like the name for a long time. I thought what was interesting about this generation of people were their differences and not their similarities, which has turned out to be the case. However, since then, I must say, we've been called much worse things. Now "Minimalism" doesn't sound so bad.   {7}

From Soundpieces

COMPOSITIONS

I remember in Paris in '65, a young conductor asked me to write a piece, and I wrote him one of these repetitive pieces, and he actually became quite nasty about it. That was when I first realized what kind of reaction I was going to get with this music. . . .

Originally I was unprepared for that. It seemed to me that the music was so simple, so transparent, what was there to be angry about? Of course, that was precisely what there was to be angry about. I had, perhaps without intending it—although it's really hard to know—challenged so many precepts of the modernist tradition at that point. In fact, you could almost have defined my music in terms of polarities: If Stockhausen jumped all over the place, my music stayed in a very limited range. . . . In fact, I wasn't thinking about that [polarities] at all. I was just trying to write some music, and it came out that way—for a variety of reasons, partially having to do with my discontent with contemporary music at that time.   [8]

On some level, the music depends on and aims at a very visceral reaction. I think there's sufficient intellectual content in the music; someone could go through a score like *Einstein* and find a lot there just on the level of analysis. But I don't think that's what the response of the audience is about. Then again, I think that may have been true [in the case of] someone like Wagner too.   {9}

For me, what sets [my] music apart is the fact that it's non-narrative; and because it is non-narrative, we don't hear it within the usual time frame of most musical experiences. As I look at most other music, I see that it takes ordinary time, day-to-day time—what I call colloquial time—as a model for its own musical time. So you have story symphonies and story concertos—even the modernist tradition continues that to a large extent. . . .

When music doesn't deal with subjects and treatments, as in my music, which is often a process where the musical material and its evolution become part and parcel of the structure of the music, then you don't have the psychological access to the music [as you do in narrative music]. . . . When people say to me that the music is druggy or trancey or this or that, I think they're confused; they're confusing a variety of experiences that share in common their difference from ordinary life, but which have vast differences between them. On the simplest level: This is music that, at least for me, requires a state of attentiveness, or provokes one; whereas, clearly there are drugged and hypnotic states that are various states of sleep. [10]

From Music by Philip Glass

EINSTEIN ON THE BEACH (1975)

Conceptual development, with the director Robert Wilson

We began with the subject. Since neither of us knew what that would be, this involved lengthy discussions, and we used up several lunches on that item alone. Bob has always been interested in famous historical figures, and I recall that he proposed Charlie Chaplin as the major character of our work, but I couldn't see how that could be done. It seemed to me too complex a problem to present, on the stage, a character who had been one of the great performers of modern times. Adolf Hitler was another of Bob's suggestions, but this subject was just too "loaded."

I countered Hitler with Mahatma Gandhi, but I suppose that Gandhi as a subject did not have for Bob the rich associations he did for me, and the discussion passed on. At one point, Bob suggested Albert Einstein, and that immediately clicked. As a child, Einstein had been one of my heroes. Growing up just after World War II, as I had, it was impossible not to know who he was. The emphatic, if catastrophic, beginning of the nuclear age had made atomic energy the most widely discussed issue of the day, and the gentle, almost saintlike originator of the theory of relativity had achieved the 1940s version of superstar status. [11]

It never occurred to us that *Einstein on the Beach* would have a story or contain anything like an ordinary plot. . . . I saw *Einstein on the Beach* more as a portrait opera. In this case the portrait of Einstein that we would be constructing replaced the idea of plot, narrative, development, all the paraphernalia of conventional theater. Furthermore, we understood that this portrait of Einstein was a poetic vision. Facts and chronology could be included (and indeed were) in the sequence of movements, images, speaking and singing. Conveying that kind of information, though, was certainly not the point of the work. [12]

Fundamental to our work was the assumption that the audience itself completed the work. The statement is no mere metaphor; we meant it quite literally. In the case of *Einstein on the Beach*, the "story" was supplied by the imaginations of the audience, and there was no way for us to predict, even if we had wanted to, what the "story" might be for any particular person. [13]

First performances at the Metropolitan Opera, New York City, 1976

For many who were there on those two evenings, it no doubt was their first time in an opera house anywhere. I remember standing backstage during the second Sunday's performance, watching the audience with one of the higher-up administrators of the Metropolitan Opera.

He asked me, "Who are these people? I've never seen them here before."

I remember replying very candidly, "Well, you'd better find out who they are, because if this place expects to be running in twenty-five years, that's your audience out there." {14}

WORK HABITS

In my student days, I knew a lot of composers, many of them more talented than myself. But I learned one thing most of them did not: good work habits. When I was still a teenager, I forced myself to write music during a set period every morning, and I also forced myself to stop at one in the afternoon. I refused to take down musical ideas at other hours, even when they came to me. You might say I trained the Muse to come calling at *my* hours, not hers. And it worked. For years now, I have gotten my ideas in the mornings, and never in the afternoon. {15}

John Harbison
b. 1938

Harbison's musical interests were evident by his high school years, during which he studied violin, viola, piano, voice, and tuba, as well as music theory. His composition teachers included Boris Blacher, Roger Sessions, and Earl Kim. For many years Harbison has taught at the Massachusetts Institute of Technology, also appearing as a choral and orchestral conductor in Boston. He has been composer-in-residence with the orchestras of Pittsburgh and Los Angeles. Harbison's music synthesizes a variety of influences into a richly textured personal style whose elements are often familiar but whose shapes and syntax are unexpected.

From a series of lectures at the Berkshire Music Center, Summer 1984

MUSIC HISTORY

I have come to believe that a composer begins early constructing his own history of music, one that has nothing to do with the official hierarchies. The writings of Wagner, Debussy, and Stravinsky attest to the efficacy of this practice and, increasingly in modern times, composers from Boulez to Rochberg have also written history to lead inexorably to them.

We must do this.

We must begin with the standard version. We can't intentionally omit Haydn or Beethoven or Wagner or Berg from our studies because they don't appeal to us. We must study and learn "the classics" on faith. Not to do so means that our eventual, personal history will be too parochial to be useful.

But very soon, as we go along, our appetites take more and more initiative. At each stage of life the hierarchy seems inviolate; then, lo and behold, a few years later it has shifted. At each moment we must mobilize our versions of the past behind us like support troops.

Here is how it went for me: in adolescence Mozart string quintets and Bach cantatas, Stravinsky *Symphony of Psalms*, Bartók *Concerto for Orchestra*. With jazz groups: Kern and Gershwin songs. Oscar Peterson, later Horace Silver. And I freely admit the Four Freshmen, Nat King Cole. This is the most impressionable time. Everything from these years is indelible. If we really cared about teaching music we'd do it then, and before, and then leave people alone.

During college: more Stravinsky, some Hindemith and Dallapiccola. Bach and Mozart even more preponderant. Discovery of Monk and Parker. Against my teachers' will—suspicion that Wagner might be both corrupting *and* great.

After college: Schütz a revelation of five hundred more things music can do. Schoenberg likewise but the price higher. Verdi, from complete misunderstanding to adoration, triggered by Sessions' remark "one scene of *Falstaff* is worth the whole *Ring* to me" (this from a lifelong Wagnerian). Bach still central, due to my performances of over forty of his cantatas, Mozart in a state of estrangement due to a discovery that I couldn't perform him convincingly.

Out of school, on my own: forbidden fruits like Varèse, Cage, Bellini, D. Scarlatti; none challenge Bach or Schumann or Stravinsky as a daily diet, but they suggest I may not be who I think I am.

Early maturity: finally ready for Schubert, who wrote the best piece in every genre he really tackled. English music, especially Tippett, suddenly speaks. Finally grown up to Sessions. Demanding more and more linguistic density, but paradoxically hearing something in some of the minimal music of the 70s.

Along with bearing witness to these changing appetites comes the need for a potential theoretical framework. My first important redrawn historical boundary places the Second Viennese School at the end of an era, not at the beginning. (This harmonizes with an astrological conclusion of Yeats in *A Vision*, as well as with Toynbee.) This done, Monteverdi also shifts into a similar role. The compositional task becomes one of rebuilding and reconnecting, rather than following a dialectic line.

The full availability of four centuries of history, plus music from other cultures and from popular culture, is a recent resource for composers, but it slows and confuses our development. We must early and ruthlessly begin understanding what is for *us*, and what is distracting. The older we get the more we must telescope and distort it for our own purposes. It should be used as we use texts for setting: freely, lovingly, brutally.   [1]

CRITICS

The dignified and correct position on music criticism for the composer seems to be this one: "I don't read the critics, I don't care what they say, that can't possibly affect me." I regard it with suspicion, just as I do the pronouncements of my intellectual friends: "I never watch television, I can't imagine why anyone would watch television."

Both carry an air of moral superiority, in fact they *are* morally superior, but we degenerates who read criticism (maybe not within the first week), or watch TV, suspect that such lofty indifference to the health hazards of our culture may not always be on the level.

I read music reviews, my own and others, and consider them important factors in the survival struggles of our profession. Some years ago I attempted not to read them, but found that the ones from "important" papers, especially the cruel and disparaging ones, were always clipped and mailed to me by close friends and relatives. I also found my curiosity killing me.

I am also not going to claim indifference to what I read. Though I seem either unwilling or unable to alter my approach to answer or fulfill the evaluations, and thus have found myself impervious to them in actual artistic action, I am anything but impervious in emotional terms. I admit to having lost days and weeks of work to insults and misunderstandings, even from writers I can't respect. And if the writer is one I believe in, I wind up considering other professions.

The reasons: sensitivity to public humiliation, inability to find effective avenues of response. Also on more vulnerable levels: all composers have some insecurities and doubts, and critics, good and bad, will, by luck or perspicacity, occasionally hit them on the nose.

I am also not going to claim indifference to praise. I am especially happy when a good listener cares for what I have done. I have also accepted with pleasure praise from someone whose view I would otherwise not regard seriously! Which of us has not dismissed a given critic as a charlatan, then when he says something positive, we abjectly clip it and include it on our dossier? Those words, those pieces of paper become legal tender or filthy lucre in our struggle for recognition and economic survival, they become a chronicle of our defeats and victories, and yet they have so little to do with what it is really about.

We know we can never satisfy the critics, because they want something that they already know about, that is easy to write about, or that confirms their own inner plans for music. And they can never satisfy us. We want to be loved, but worse and more, we want to be *understood*, even if not loved, and that, in art as in life, is simply asking too much.   [2]

TECHNIQUE

It is important that some of what we study early on provide an abstract frame in which to explore simply relationships between tones. But technical deficiencies in today's music, if it is possible to identify them, stem less from educational gaps than from a lack of ongoing curiosity—a willingness to accept one's type or label. Composers need continuing practice, as players do. Some of this may be done in public, but the endless adaptation of our techniques also can be done in our sketchbooks, as submusic, throughout our composing lives. It can also be done in the steady thinking we must do about our art, away from the page, between pieces.

We know that many composers "stayed in school" throughout their creative lives, strengthening their muscles to handle the pressure of new ideas. We have many canons from Mozart and Schoenberg, part of their daily habits, far more than doodles, because both of these composers were constantly and restlessly acquiring skills as they went along. Mozart's excitement upon discovering Bach was due to the rarity of an encounter with one who could do more in some ways than he could, and whose skills must thus be added in. Numerous unfinished Bachian pieces attest to his determination, in mid-career, to enlarge his resources by assimilating an initially intractable set of principles.

While Mozart and Schoenberg were also given to remarkable displays of technical problem-solving brilliance in their music, other composers took a different attitude. The maintenance of their technical prowess was more a reserve arsenal, shown in glimpses but mainly held as capital. We know that Verdi stayed at practice fugue-writing throughout his career. It is hardly in evidence during "La Donna è mobile"—a bit more audible in the opening of the first scene of *Aïda*, triumphantly revealed at the end of *Falstaff*. But he felt that even his simplest tunes required the ability, all in reserve, to do virtually anything (Handel seems to have shared this assumption).

For though we associate the presence of technique with its display, in moments no listener can miss, it is also an essential factor in the so-called artless moment. Nothing is more wearing, or less durable, than the composer writing constantly at the limit of his technique, however impressive it is.   [3]

CONTROL

Commentators and audience members speak of the accessibility or difficulty of a piece as if composers really have a choice in these matters. I suppose it is good public relations for composers to perpetrate the myth that we are always in total control. I believe that in our less high-pressure tasks we can be. In writing music for a specific public occasion, or for a television program, or for a dance by circus elephants, we have to be able to shoot for an exact mark. But in our highest-striving work, when we seek out the livest, high-yeast material, we can't be fully in the driver's seat: the ideas, if they are really alive, have their own life, and sometimes all our planning, expectation and habits must be prepared for adjustment, or abandonment. It is not a lack of technique that causes this lack of willful control. In fact, it takes a lot of ready technique to deal with the unforeseen situations that can arise when the material has strong legs.

Most of us composers, after we have had the experience of having a piece veer off to a different place than we expected or planned, begin to realize that our freedom of choice is an illusion. We cannot choose the kind of music we write—accessible, difficult, complex, simple—any more definitively than we choose our shoe size or our hair color.

We can and must do things to maximize our abilities—if we write too many notes and confuse our intentions we can try to be more economical; if we are too monochromatic and over-refined we must strive for the clearest contrasts. But we can't change our basic nature, only discover it, so that audiences and critics who take credit for our accessibility or bristle at our difficulty are assuming more control of our fates than we have. "He sold out," we often hear, as a comment about an accessible piece the hearer didn't like. But no one ever sold out! Instead, their character, their genes, their fatal pull emerges. The result may be great, it may be weak and venal, but it is beyond planning and design. Its realization can be hastened, but never *determined* by the pull of the market place. (Besides, the yield from a "sell-out," at least in concert music, is so paltry it is hardly worth the trouble.)   [4]

CONCERT MUSIC AND POPULAR MUSIC

From a lecture at the Massachusetts Institute of Technology,
Autumn 1988

When I teach a course in music repertoire I am especially aware of my students' listening habits, of the sounds that make up their world. About half would come to a Haydn-Mozart-Beethoven class wearing earphones. For the most part it was not those composers playing into those ears, in fact for up to ten hours of the day it was rock. Now for three hours a week in class and for a few hours more outside, they concentrated on the classical pieces we studied. But I remember thinking what a small window of time these composers were offered when at the close of the class I saw earphones go back on, and the faint steady splash of cymbals signaled their return to the normal milieu.

Those few hours of concentrated listening to Haydn are not enough for him to change the aural chemistry of the young listener, shaped by louder, more repetitive, more casually attended sounds many other hours on end. It is like trying to balance a body chemistry conditioned by bags of potato chips with an occasional handful of sunflower seeds. . . .

Earphones are yet another device that isolates us from each other. The grand coming-together occasions of the past are faded—the political rally, the camp meeting, the parade, the circus have been co-opted by television. Our collective events are the football game and the rock concert. These are loud, assaultive events, obviously entertaining and viscerally involving. But the last surviving arena in which we speculate and reflect together is the classical concert, and it depends on a desire to follow intricate and expressive sounds over long time spans, sometimes at very low levels of audibility, and to do so most crucially in a group, a group that shares the experience.   [5]

From a fundraising letter for a new music group, 1987

Compared to the economic fact of rock music, all concert music, even involving stars like Pavarotti and Perlman, is commercially ephemeral, and its struggles and triumphs a side street.

In those terms, new music ensembles like Collage work in an alley off a side street. Our breweries and distilleries are located upstairs in the rear, and we are overdue on the rent.

Is it possible that this is where we belong, that rather than being prophets and poets and visionaries, we are irrelevant neurotics singing into our armpits?

The Playmate of the Month lists "contemporary music" as one of her interests! But it is not Jacob Druckman and Andrew Imbrie she fancies, it is the Stray Cats and Duran Duran. "She's right," says my friend the literature professor, who reads Updike and Bellow, looks at Poons, and endorses that very contemporary music: "Michael Jackson, Madonna, and Prince are the Mozarts and Beethovens of today. Music lives, you guys just haven't caught on!"

What Tina Turner expresses and what Roger Sessions expresses are different things. Sessions's recent death robbed me of one of my most persistent fantasies, to have Tina introduce him to America at some gonzo pan-musical epiphany. But the fact remains that different musics aim very differently. The finer they are the more they overlap, but in general rock seeks to embody rebellion against parent and society, extrovert sexuality, aggression of a more or less tolerable kind, and the childlike need for loudness, reiteration, and pulsation. The rock performer is expected to swagger, flaunt, and harangue, to give the impression that he will live forever without impediment. Concert music, while touching these at times, seeks transcendence, the awareness of death, the control of time, the hope, not the certainty, of immortality. These quests take place *within* the music. If concert music fails to undertake this calling, this quest, it doesn't deserve our care. Our secret fear is that our present back alley address comes partly from our failure to *distinguish* ourselves from popular music, in terms of the magnitude of our aims, the poignance of our hopes, the grotesqueness of our failures. [6]

Oliver Knussen
b. 1952

Knussen earned international attention when, at fifteen, he led the London Symphony Orchestra in the premiere of his First Symphony. As an artistic director and conductor Knussen has been an advocate for contemporary music in his native United Kingdom and in the United States. Not highly prolific, he writes brilliantly orchestrated works whose sophistication is often balanced with spontaneity and subtle humor. Knussen's interest in composing for children is manifest in his first opera, Where the Wild Things Are *(1981), written with author and illustrator Maurice Sendak.*

COMPOSING FOR CHILDREN

From an article on Peter Maxwell Davies in Tempo, *March 1978*

This music [Maxwell Davies's *O Magnum Mysterium*] must have appeared outrageously difficult in all respects to most music educators at that time [1960], yet it proceeded from the premise that children will respond best to music that presumes their serious attention and that, while remaining technically within their capacities, extends their concepts of what is musically possible for them—and, indeed, of what music itself is.

This attitude to youth and music is of course implicit in Britten's music for children, which became progressively less compromising as time went on. . . . Working on serious large-scale projects of this kind will draw out the gifts of children who are intrinsically musical, and the more casual (or indeed hostile) participants will not feel condescended to. Meanwhile the chronically musical child—who often feels like an outcast—will at last be able to find some kind of common concern with his classmates. [1]

COMPOSER RECORDINGS

From "Self-Observation," an article in a festschrift for George Perle, 1996

Would-be interpreters ignore composer-conducted or -played recordings at their peril. Composers may not be the best people to judge what the music behind the notes is ultimately about, but they certainly know how it goes, simply, in terms of tempo and articulation.   [2]

MOZART'S THEMATIC CATALOGUE

From an interview with Andrew Ford, 24 Hours, September 1994

In 1991, Mozart's own thematic catalogue came out in facsimile. The idea of some-one sitting down every week or two and, as a matter of course, jotting down the first four bars of what he'd done struck me very forcefully. *Don Giovanni* doesn't look any more important than the lowliest of contradances in this context. It looks as if Mozart had no preconceptions about the value of what he was doing, other than that he had to write a piece for this or that occasion; he did it as well as he could and that was that. The whole business of "Where do I fit in the world?" or "What am I try-ing to say?" shouldn't be present—maybe it should be present when you're think-ing about the piece, but not while you're actually writing.   [3]

STRAVINSKY'S LATE WORKS

From an interview for Deutsche Grammophon, 1995

Stravinsky's late works have fascinated me ever since they first came out. So much is said with so few notes—there is abundant wit even in the most austerely com-posed textures—and the notes themselves are like rocks, they get stronger and stronger and righter and righter the more you know them. *The Flood* is like an in-credible comic-strip race through Genesis, very entertaining and theatrical, but expressed through some of the most advanced-sounding serial music Stravinsky ever composed.   [4]

BRITTEN

From the 24 Hours interview

What I find the most rewarding feature of Britten's music—especially pieces like the *Nocturne* or *Curlew River* or the Third Quartet—is that there's a very appre-hensible surface which works because he was a terrific craftsman, but underneath it there's something else very strong. Although the harmony is triadic-tonal, or modal-tonal if you like, Britten's methods are nevertheless an attractive counter-pole, in some ways, to Schoenberg's. The network of relationships is probably just as rich, it's just that the terms in which they're expressed are not the same at all. If you examine *Death in Venice* from a motivic point of view, it is manically integrated, rather like late Webern, although the time scale and the manner are anything but Webernesque.

For me, Britten is one of those composers who, rather than trying to do something new and different for its own sake, says something important with means that can communicate very directly. He deals with imponderables in a very commonsensical way. [5]

CARTER

From notes to a compact disc, 1992

While it is certainly true that Carter's orchestral music is formidably complex in effect, it is never gratuitously so and is always rewardingly conceived for the individual instruments involved. The rhythmic elaboration is the result of layering simple pulses (variously related), the lines are made of clearly identifiable intervallic patterns, the harmonic characters are sharply defined and their progress carefully controlled. In other words, the basic compositional principle is common sense. It is because the resultant framework is at the service of prodigious inventiveness that the listener will need several hearings to find a path through the highly ordered jungle of aural images into which these basic ingredients are moulded; and these in turn are employed to articulate an unbroken musical argument that is in a state of rapid evolution from beginning to end, even if the proportions of individual movements (which define the progress of that constant growth) seem almost classical. . . . Carter is, to my mind, the greatest present-day musical dramatist in the instrumental sphere. [6]

TAKEMITSU

From a memorial speech, New York, May 13, 1996

Takemitsu's music defines a world of paradoxes.

One usually has a sense of immense spaciousness—but the works are often short, and the music units from which the pieces are built are self-contained, and almost always very brief

One remembers long silences—but in actuality these are less long than highly charged and colored by their contexts.

The atmosphere seems to be consistently peaceful—but Takemitsu's orchestral climaxes are often immensely forceful (Peter Lieberson likens them to changes in the weather).

It all sounds spontaneous to the point of seeming to be almost improvised—but every event is plotted with the most painstaking precision. Just when one seems to be on familiar terrain, a close look at his myriad notations for dynamics, nuances, and fluctuations of pace makes one realize that this world is very much Takemitsu's own. [7]

OBSERVATIONS

Listening to a Debussy piano étude is a bit like watching a film of Houdini getting out of an impossible knot. (*24 Hours* interview) [8]

I don't think about the audience when I'm composing, partly because I'm very rarely the reason they decide to buy a ticket or not. (Colloquium at Harvard University, November 1995)   [9]

I much prefer to be bewitched for five minutes than hypnotized for an hour. (Program note, March 1994)   [10]

APPROACH TO COMPOSING

From an interview in Paul Griffiths's
New Sounds, New Personalities, 1985

I don't regard a high degree of self-scrutiny as anything less than necessary. I was fortunate in that my first teacher, John Lambert, insisted on the avoidance of easy formulae or padding—unjustified literal repetition of any kind in particular—which is an attitude I suspect he partly inherited from his teacher Nadia Boulanger. I think this is probably the root of my obsession with following through the implications of what you could call musical cross-hatching. For example, in the first interlude of *Where the Wild Things Are* there's a long horn melody over mixed piano and harp arpeggios on each beat. The arpeggiated chords start at two notes and build to twelve, while the actual harmony shifts gradually. Now the way those chords are distributed and arpeggiated each time was more than a week's work. It may seem nonsensical to fuss that way, particularly as this is only one of three or four layers operating in that section, but the point to me is that you can focus your ear, if you so choose, on that accompaniment figure and find that those arpeggiations are doing something constructive. . . .

Realistically, I suppose, one's approach must be to ensure that the idea and broad design of a work is crystal clear to anyone who wants to be receptive to it—which implies also a willingness on the part of the listener to try to get onto its wave-length in return. The working out of other, less immediately perceptible levels must be carried out with the same degree of care, obviously to facilitate the clearest possible articulation of form, also to try to achieve a model balance between order and spontaneity or fantasy, and finally because I think any other attitude amounts to a contempt for the art itself. There is absolutely no justification for applying mass production criteria to the composition of serious music today: alarmingly few people want it, and the sheer quantity of music being written far exceeds any real demand for it, particularly in the orchestral field.   [11]

I think the expressive character of music is very dangerous stuff to be dealing with consciously if you're a composer. Obviously you make certain observations as you go. . . . But otherwise one decides what it is one wants to write, and then simply does it as best one can, often learning how to compose it as you go. You don't plumb your depths to write a terribly self-expressive piece. You do it with technique, and hope that it talks back to you when you finally hear it. I suspect Brahms worked the same way, or Tchaikovsky or Berg, who certainly all approached the actual composition rationally, however affecting the end product.   [12]

From "Self-Observation"

Aspects of my music that I am most often asked to explain (timbre, rhythm) are the aspects that I habitually leave entirely to intuition or, rather, that appear to dictate their own details according to context; while those aspects to which I have devoted a great deal of effort and research (proportion, harmony and movement in general) are scarcely commented upon by the outside world. Of course, this may be a form of compliment in that perhaps they appear to be achieved effortlessly, but I suspect that the truth of the matter is that all these things are merely means to an end, and the effectiveness of that end to the listener is all that counts.

Questions that arise are probably about things that don't work. I know which pieces of mine I like, which achieve what I set out to do, but the relationships between these self-judgments and external "success" are unpredictable to say the least. And for the composer to attempt to define his or her own thumbprints is fatal, I think—as a wise composer once said to me, one would then run the risk of trying to write what one thought one's own music ought to sound like.   [13]

From the Deutsche Grammophon interview

I don't set much store by what counts today as "accessible," much of which seems to me to be muzak. I certainly don't begin any piece of music with what you might call a stylistic agenda. I try to let the piece tell me what it wants to sound like, though of course one has technical means of assessing this, and influencing it to a degree. My operas with Maurice Sendak are a special case because I chose to make them, as it were, out of the sort of music I loved as a child, and I suspect that this had certain stylistic after-effects, which I tried to purge (because of the danger of unthinking sentimentality) by applying much stricter compositional means to the music I've written in the decade or so since the operas. However I am not implying that I try to avoid being accessible—comprehensibility of the musical idea seems to me to be a commonsense-ical given, however complex what you are trying to say may be. I find pieces like [Stockhausen's] *Gruppen* or Carter's Concerto for Orchestra or [Boulez's] *Pli selon pli* quite accessible enough, thank you, given the musical issues with which they deal. But at the same time it isn't right to simply dismiss music that expresses itself with far fewer notes just because of what it is.   [14]

MUSIC AND "MORALITY"

Written statement, July 8, 1996, based on remarks at the Harvard colloquium

You hear quite a few youngish composers today speak of the tyranny of serialism during the time they were students, and perhaps it's true that composers of my generation were encouraged to be myopically focused on only one area of possibilities for structural thinking. But I was a student myself during the later stages of the "serial orthodoxy," and can report that if you kept your independence of outlook (without which one probably shouldn't be a composer anyway) it was a marvelous time to absorb and argue ideas pro and contra. However, in recent years the terms "serial" and "tonal" have erroneously become accepted designations of style rather than systematic basis, equated with "complex" versus "accessible" and, by implication, "elitist" versus "popular," together with the quasi-moralistic baggage that comes with these notions. Now, I'm in the lucky position that my music seems to me to be all of these things at once, so I find this all rather more amusing than anything else. There is nothing intrinsically superior about a tonal piece, or an anti-tonal or serial piece, any more than there is between a work on a religious theme and a piece that deals entirely with abstract ideas. But one might question the "moral" stance of those who abruptly jettison their entire creative past in a vain attempt to court popularity through the adoption of a manner in which "easy listening" masquerades as spiritual depth. The only serious reason to compose today, when the very existence of what we do is under threat from many sides, is to defend the survival of whatever values made one want to put pen to paper in the first place.   [15]

SOURCES

The list below contains bibliographic data for all sources. After each source are the reference numbers (in brackets) for the passages taken from that source. Each reference number is followed by the page number where the excerpt begins in the source. Translations prepared especially for this book are listed with the name of the translator or editor responsible. Most translations, including those from published sources, have been edited for continuity of style. Some have been revised; where this is the case, the name of the editor principally responsible for the revisions is noted.

Sources cited three or more times have been given abbreviated listings in the chapter notes. The full listings are as follows:

American Composers on American Music: A Symposium Edited by Henry Cowell (Stanford, Calif.: Stanford University Press, 1933).

Andrew Ford, *Composer to Composer: Conversations about Contemporary Music* (St. Leonards, New South Wales: Allen & Unwin, 1993).

Cole Gagne and Tracy Caras, *Soundpieces: Interviews with American Composers* (Metuchen, N.J.: Scarecrow Press, 1982).

Hans Gal, *The Musician's World* (New York: Arco, 1966).

La Mara [pseud. of Marie Lipsius], *Briefe hervorragender Zeitgenossen an Franz Liszt* (Leipzig: Breitkopf & Härtel, 1895); trans. Morgenstern.

Jay Leyda and Sergei Bertensson, *The Musorgsky Reader* (New York: Norton, 1947); translation rev. Morgenstern.

Ludwig Nohl, *Letters of Distinguished Musicians*, trans. Lady Wallace (London: Longmans, Green, 1867); translation rev. Morgenstern.

Marc Pincherle, *Musiciens, peints par eux-mêmes* (Paris: Cornuau, 1939); trans. Morgenstern.

Nicolas Slonimsky, *Lexicon of Musical Invective*, 2nd edition (Seattle: University of Washington Press, 1969).

CHAPTER ONE

Hildegard

Carol Neuls-Bates, *Women in Music* (New York: Harper & Row, 1982). [1] 18

Marchetto

F. Alberto Gallo, *Music of the Middle Ages*, vol. 2, trans. Karen Eales (Cambridge: Cambridge University Press, 1985). [1] 114

Guillaume de Machaut

Letters of Composers through Six Centuries, ed. Piero Weiss (Philadelphia: Chilton [1967]). [1] 1; [2] 2

Guillaume de Machaut, *La fonteinne amoureuse*, bilingual edition, ed. R. Barton Palmer (New York: Garland, 1993); trans. Fisk. [2] 12

————, *Le Jugement du roy de Behaigne & Remède de fortune*, ed. James I. Wimsatt and William W. Kibler (Athens: University of Georgia Press, 1988); trans. Fisk. [3] 189.

Tinctoris

Ronald Woodley, "The *Proportionale musices* of Iohannes Tinctoris: A Critical Edition, Translation, and Study" (D.Phil. diss., University of Oxford, 1982). [1] 311

Oliver Strunk, *Source Readings in Music History* (New York: Norton, 1950). [2] 198

Palestrina

Henry Coates, *Palestrina* (New York: Pellegrini & Cudahy, 1949). [1] 22; [2] 4; [3] 18

Byrd

Edmund H. Fellowes, *William Byrd*, 2d ed. (London: Oxford University Press, 1948). [1] 149

The Collected Vocal Works of William Byrd, ed. Edmund H. Fellowes, vol. 14 (London: Stainer & Bell, 1949). [2] ix

Caccini

Prima fiorituri del melodramma italiano, ed. Francisco Mantica, vol. 2 (Rome: Raccolte Claudio Monteverdi, 1930); trans. Morgenstern. [1] 1

Morley

Thomas Morley, *A Plaine and Easie Introduction to Practicalle Musicke* (1597; reprint, London: Oxford University Press, 1937). [1] 180; [2] 162; [3] 1; [4] 121; [5] 177; [6] 179; [7] 181

Monteverdi

Tutte le opere di Claudio Monteverdi, ed. G. Francesco Malipiero (Asolo: n.p., 1926–42); trans. Morgenstern. [1] 5: preface; [4] 8: preface

Louis Schneider, *Claudio Monteverdi* (Paris: Perrin, 1921); trans. Morgenstern. [2] 138

Henry Prunières, *Monteverdi: His Life and Work* (New York: Dutton, 1926). [3] 284

Schütz

Heinrich Schütz: Gesammelte Briefe und Schriften, ed. Erich H. Müller (Regensburg: Bosse, 1931); trans. Morgenstern. [1] 64; [2] 128; [3] 192

Gal, *The Musician's World*. [4] 28

CHAPTER TWO

Purcell

J. A. Westrup, *Purcell* (New York: Pellegrini & Cudahy, 1949). [1] 69

John Playford, *Introduction to the Skill of Music*, rev. edition (1700). [2] 134

Couperin

François Couperin, *Oeuvres complètes*, vol. 1 (Paris: L'Oiseau Lyre, 1933); trans. Morgenstern. [1] 25; [2] 26; [3] 28; [4] 41

————, *Les Nations* (1726); trans. Fisk. [5] preface

Telemann

Willi Kahl, *Selbstbiographien deutscher Musiker des xviii. Jahrhunderts* (Cologne: Staufen, 1948); trans. Morgenstern. [1] 205; [2] 206

Rameau

Jean Philippe Rameau, *Nouveau système de musique théorique* (1726); trans. Morgenstern. [1] 106; [2] 42; [3] 43; [4] 105
——, *Observations sur notre instinct pour la musique et son principe* (1726); trans. Morgenstern. [5] 3; [6] 2; [7] 61
——, *Code de musique pratique* (1760); trans. Morgenstern. [8] 23

J. S. Bach

Hans T. David and Arthur Mendel, *The Bach Reader* (New York: Norton, 1945). [1] 120; [2] 122; [3] 246; [4] 257; [5] 259; [6] 276; [7] 329; [8] 334

Marcello

Benedetto Marcello, "Il teatro alla moda," trans. Reinhard G. Pauly, *Musical Quarterly* 35 (1948). [1] 372; [2] 380

CHAPTER THREE

C. P. E. Bach

C. P. E. Bach, *Essay on the True Art of Playing Keyboard Instruments*, trans. and ed. William J. Mitchell (New York: Norton, 1949). [1] 79; [2] 147; [3] 367
Nohl, *Letters*. [4] 54; [5] 55

Gluck

Nohl, *Letters*. [1] 3; [2] 8
Gal, *The Musician's World*. [3] 52

Haydn

Nohl, *Letters*. [1] 107
Letters of Mozart, ed. Hans Mersmann, trans. M. M. Bozman (reprint, New York: Dorset, 1986). [2] 226
Willi Reich, *Joseph Haydn: Leben, Briefe, Schaffen* (Lucerne: Stocker, 1946); trans. Morgenstern. [3] 160; [4] 161; [5] 162
Georg August Greisinger, *Biographische Notizen über Joseph Haydn*, ed. Franz Grasberger (1809; reprint, Vienna: Kaltschmid, [1954]); trans. Morgenstern. [6] 61; [7] 61; [8] 17

Mozart

Mozart Briefe und Aufzeichungen: Gesamtausgabe, ed. Wilhelm A. Bauer and Otto Erich Deutsch (Kassel: Bärenreiter, 1962–63); trans. Fisk. [1] 2:68; [2] 2:69; [3] 2:83; [4] 2:228; [5] 2:304; [6] 2:378; [10] 3:301; [12] 2:397; [16] 3:272; [17] 3:161; [18] 3:167; [19] 3:245
The Letters of Mozart and His Family, trans. and ed. Emily Anderson (London: Macmillan, 1938). [7] 937; [8] 801; [9] 813; [11] 875; [13] 800; [14] 316
G. N. Nissen, *Biographie W. A. Mozarts* (1828); trans. Fisk. [15] 662
Gal, *The Musician's World*. [20] 108

CHAPTER FOUR

Beethoven

Beethoven: Letters, Journals, and Conversations, ed. and trans. Michael Hamburger (New York: Pantheon, 1952). [1] 36; [2] 46; [3] 35; [4] 72; [8] 198; [9] 194; [10] 153; [11] 161; [12] 237; [13] 34; [14] 76; [16] 55; [17] 68; [18] 212

Beethoven's Letters, ed. A. C. Kalischer (London: Dent, 1909). [5] 140

Musikerbriefe, ed. Ernst Bücken (Wiesbaden: Dieterich, n.d.); trans. Morgenstern. [6] 84

Friedrich Kerst, *Beethoven: The Man and the Artist as Revealed in His Own Words*, trans. Henry E. Krehbiel (New York: Huebsch, 1905). [7] 26

Thayer's Life of Beethoven, ed. Elliot Forbes (Princeton, N.J.: Princeton University Press, 1967). [15] 1:88

Hedwig M. von Asow, *Ludwig van Beethoven: Heiligenstädter Testament* (Vienna: Doblinger, 1957); trans Fisk. [19] 9

Spohr

Louis Spohr, *Autobiography*, trans. anon. (London: n.p., 1865); translation rev. Morgenstern. [1] 1:45; [2] 1:186; [3] 2:81

Weber

Carl Maria von Weber, *Sämmtliche Schriften*, ed. Georg Kaiser (Berlin: Schuster & Loeffler, 1908); trans. Morgenstern. [1] 252; [2] 224; [4] 397

Gal, *The Musician's World*. [3] 148

Nohl, *Letters*. [5] 209

Rossini

Lettere di G. Rossini, ed. G. Mazzatinti and F. G. Manis (Florence: Barbera, 1902); trans. Morgenstern. [1] 2; [2] 190; [3] 251; [6] 342

Herbert Weinstock, *Rossini: A Biography* (London: Oxford University Press, 1968). [4] 284

Interviews and Encounters with Verdi, ed. Marcello Conati, trans. Richard Stokes (London: Gollancz, 1984). [5] 20

La Mara, *Briefe*. [7] 305

Schubert

O. E. Deutsch, *Franz Schubert's Letters and Other Writings*, trans. Venetia Savile (New York: Knopf, 1928). [1] 25; [2] 28; [3] 52; [4] 96

————, *Franz Schubert's Briefe und Schriften* (Munich: Müller, 1922); trans. Morgenstern. [5] 62

The New Grove Dictionary of Music and Musicians. ed. Stanley Sadie (London: Macmillan, 1980). [6] 16:770

CHAPTER FIVE

Berlioz

Hector Berlioz, *Memoirs*, trans. Rachel Holmes and Eleanor Holmes, rev. Ernest Newman (New York: Knopf, 1932). [1] 13; [2] 408; [3] 410; [4] 98; [6] 154; [7] 65; [8] 318; [9] 65; [10] 289; [11] 376; [12] 487

Nat Shapiro, *An Encyclopedia of Quotations about Music* (Garden City, N.Y.: Doubleday, 1978). [5] 123

Glinka

Octave Fouque, *Glinka d'après ses mémoires et sa correspondance* (Paris: Heugel, 1880); trans. Morgenstern. [1] 10; [4] 83

Oskar von Riesemann, *Monographien zur Russischen Musik* (Munich: Drei-Masken, 1923); trans. Morgenstern. [2] 79; [3] 98

Mendelssohn

Felix Mendelssohn-Bartholdy, *Letters*, ed. Gisella Selden-Goth (New York: Pantheon, 1945). [1] 81; [5] 277; [6] 313; [7] 260; [10] 296

Gal, *The Musician's World*. [2] 158; [3] 164; [4] 171; [9] 214

Peter Sutermeister, *Felix Mendelssohn-Bartholdy: Lebensbild mit Vorgeschichte* (Zurich: Ex-Libris, 1949); trans. Morgenstern. [8] 210

Paul Mendelssohn-Bartholdy and Carl Mendelssohn, *Letters of Felix Mendelssohn*, trans. Lady Wallace (Philadelphia: Leypoldt, 1894). [11] 113

Chopin

Chopin's Letters, coll. Henryk Opienski, trans. E. L. Voynich (New York: Knopf, 1931). [1] 129; [2] 133; [3] 154; [5] 394

Gal, *The Musician's World*. [4] 196

The Journal of Eugène Delacroix, trans. Walter Pach (New York: Grove Press, 1961). [6] 148; [7] 195; [8] 586

Schumann

Karl Storck, *The Letters of Robert Schumann*, trans. Hannah Bryant (New York: Dutton, 1907). [1] 43; [2] 51; [3] 70; [4] 79; [6] 237; [7] 252; [8] 256; [9] 58; [25] 135; [28] 227; [34] 222; [36] 103; [37] 130; [43] 224; [45] 250; [46] 251; [47] 278; [49] 69; [50] 132

Robert Schumann, *Music and Musicians*, trans. and ed. Fanny Raymond Ritter (London: Reeves, 1877). [5] 110; [11] 59; [12] 66; [13] 74; [14] 84; [15] 84; [16] 73; [17] 77; [19] 203; [20] 14; [21] 205; [22] 411; [24] 413; [30] 122; [32] 304; [35] 54; [38] 268; [39] 4; [41] 145; [42] 152; [44] 352

Robert Schumann, *On Music and Musicians*, ed. Konrad Wolff, trans. Paul Rosenfeld (New York: Pantheon, 1946). [10] 38; [18] 72; [23] 30; [26] 87; [27] 102; [29] 106; [31] 172; [33] 114; [40] 142; [48] 252

Liszt

Franz Liszt, *Gesammelte Schriften* (Leipzig: n.p., 1880–82); trans. Morgenstern. [1] 5:231; [2] 3:32; [3] 6:267; [4] 6:51; [6] 3:32; [8] 3:44; [9] 1:10

———, *Briefe* (Leipzig, n.p., 1893); trans. Morgenstern. [5] 1:123

Gal, *The Musician's World*. [7] 218

Arthur Holde, "Unpublished Letters by Beethoven, Liszt, and Brahms," *Musical Quarterly* 32 (1946). [10] 283

Wagner

Richard Wagner's Prose Works, trans. William Ashton Ellis (New York: Broude Brothers, 1893–94). [1] 2:18; [4] 3:82

The Correspondence of Wagner and Liszt, 2d ed., rev. W. Ashton Ellis, trans. Francis Hueffer, vol. 2 (1897; reprint, New York: Vienna House, 1973). [2] 84; [3] 119

Verdi

Franz Werfel and Paul Stefan, *Verdi: The Man and His Letters* (New York: Fischer, 1942). [1]

145; [2] 173; [3] 175; [4] 185; [5] 251; [6] 303; [7] 336; [8] 343; [9] 364; [10] 124; [11] 301; [12] 299; [15] 402; [16] 431; [17] 363; [18] 365; [19] 346; [20] 372; [21] 261
Gal, *The Musician's World*. [13] 270; [14] 272

CHAPTER SIX

Lalo

Pincherle, *Musiciens*. [1] 179; [2] 172

Smetana

Ernst Rychnowsky, *Smetana* (Stuttgart: Deutsche Verlagsanstalt, 1924); trans. Morgenstern. [1] 263; [2] 263; [3] 264
La Mara, *Briefe*. [4] 2:121

Brahms

Letters of Clara Schumann and Johannes Brahms, ed. Berthold Litzmann, trans. anon. (New York: Longmans, Green, 1927). [1] 1:67; [4] 2:16; [10] 1:241
Johannes Brahms in Briefwechsel mit Joseph Joachim (Berlin: Deutsche Brahms-Gesellschaft, 1912); trans. Morgenstern. [2] 1:150
Eduard Hanslick, *Am Ende des Jahrhunderts* (Berlin: Allgemeiner Verein für deutsche Literatur, 1899); trans. Morgenstern. [3] 381; [5] 379
Richard Heuberger, *Erinnerungen an Johannes Brahms*, ed. Kurt Hofmann (Tutzing: Schneider, 1976); trans. Fisk. [6] 93; [7] 56; [9] 73
Max Kalbeck, *Johannes Brahms: The Herzogenberg Correspondence*, trans. Hannah Bryant (New York: Dutton, 1909). [8] 286

Borodin

V. V. Stassov, *Alexandre Borodin*, trans. [into French] Alfred Habets (Paris: Fischbacher, 1893); trans. [into English] Morgenstern. [1] 2:118; [3] 2:121
Leyda and Bertensson, *The Musorgsky Reader*. [2] 173

Cui

César Cui, *La musique en russie* (Paris: Fischbacher, 1880). [1] 4; [2] 73
Slonimsky, *Lexicon*. [3] 230; [4] 208; [5] 137

Saint-Saëns

Camille Saint-Saëns, *Musical Memories*, trans. Edwin Gile Rich (Boston: Small, Maynard, 1919). [1] 14
———, *Au courant de la vie* (Paris: Dorbon-Aîné, 1914); trans. Morgenstern. [2] 16
"Lettres de Saint-Saëns et Camille Bellaigue," *Revue des deux mondes* 8 (1936); trans. Morgenstern. [3] 538; [4] 535; [5] 539
Pincherle, *Musiciens*. [6] 155
Slonimsky, *Lexicon*. [7] 102

CHAPTER SEVEN

Bizet

Georges Bizet, *Lettres*, ed. Louis Ganderax (Paris: Calmann-Levy, 1908); trans. Morgenstern. [1] 118; [2] 123; [3] 144; [6] 135; [8] 311; [9] 322

Hughes Imbert, *Portraits et études* (Paris: Fischbacher, 1894); trans. Morgenstern. [4] 164; [5] 180

Bizet, *Lettres à un ami, 1865–72*, ed. Edmond Galabert (Paris: Calmann-Levy, 1909); trans. Morgenstern. [7] 184

Musorgsky

Gal, *The Musician's World*. [1] 357

Leyda and Bertensson, *The Musorgsky Reader*. [2] 138; [3] 192; [4] 199; [5] 360; [6] 111; [7] 419

Tchaikovsky

Modeste Tchaikovsky, *The Life and Letters of Peter Ilyich Tchaikovsky*, trans. Rosa Newmarch (New York: Lane, 1906). [1] 250; [5] 259; [6] 372; [10] 281; [11] 306; [12] 311

Piotr Ilyich Tchaikovsky, *Letters to His Family: An Autobiography*, trans. Galina von Meck (New York: Stein and Day, 1981). [2] 89; [3] 213; [4] 110; [7] 417; [8] 246; [9] 119; [13] 171; [14] 507; [15] 534

Dvořák

Otakar Šourek, *Antonín Dvořák: Letters and Reminiscences*, trans. Roberta Finlayson Samsour (New York: Da Capo Press, 1985). [1] 152; [3] 170; [4] 71; [5] 158; [6] 167

Antonín Dvořák, "Music in America," *Harper's New Monthly Magazine* 90 (1895). [2] 429

Grieg

Edvard Grieg, "Mozart," *Century Magazine* 55 (1897). [1] 140

————, "Robert Schumann," *Century Magazine* 47 (1894). [2] 440; [3] 447

Rimsky-Korsakov

Leyda and Bertensson, *The Musorgsky Reader*. [1] 406

Nicolas Rimsky-Korsakov, *Principles of Orchestration*, trans. Edward Agate (London: Russian Music Agency, 1922). [2] 2

Gerald Abraham, *Rimsky-Korsakov* (London: Duckworth, 1945). [3] 72

Slonimsky, *Lexicon*. [4] 248

Fauré

Gabriel Fauré, *Opinions musicales* (Paris: Rieder, 1930); trans. Morgenstern. [1] 94; [2] 24; [4] 101; [5] 139

————, "Souvenirs," *Revue musicale* 3 (1922); trans. Morgenstern. [3] 3

CHAPTER EIGHT

Janáček

Janáček's Uncollected Essays on Music, ed. and trans Mirka Zemanová (London and New York: Boyars, 1989). [1] 76; [3] 60; [5] 121; [6] 39; [7] 55; [8] 99; [9] 46; [12] 183; [13] 188; [15] 186; [16] 123

Bohumír Štědroň, *Leoš Janáček: Letters and Reminiscences*, trans. Geraldine Thomsen (Prague: Artia, 1955). [2] 70; [4] 90; [10] 168; [11] 34; [14] 60; [18] 183

Intimate Letters: Leoš Janáček to Kamila Stösslová, ed. and trans. John Tyrrell (Princeton, N.J.: Princeton University Press, 1994). [17] 27

Puccini

Giuseppe Adami, *Letters of Giacomo Puccini*, trans. Ena Makin (Philadelphia: Lippincott, 1931). [1] 164; [2] 177; [3] 243; [4] 90; [5] 91; [6] 130; [7] 146; [8] 169; [9] 176; [11] 265; [12] 270
Vincent Seligman, *Puccini among Friends* (London: Macmillan, 1938). [10] 138

Wolf

Hugo Wolf, *Musikalische Kritiken* (Leipzig: Breitkopf & Härtel, 1912); trans. Morgenstern. [1] 10; [2] 35; [3] 96; [4] 212; [8] 125
Frank Walker, *Hugo Wolf* (New York: Knopf, 1952). [5] 159; [6] 155
The Music Criticism of Hugo Wolf, ed. and trans. Henry Pleasants (New York: Holmes & Meier, 1978); translation rev. Fisk. [7] 186

Mahler

Alma Mahler, *Gustav Mahler: Briefe* (Vienna: Zsolnay, 1924); trans. Morgenstern. [1] 146; [2] 296; [3] 187; [4] 191; [5] 462; [15] 228; [18] 162
————, *Gustav Mahler: Erinnerungen und Briefe* (Vienna: Bermann-Fischer, 1949); trans. Morgenstern. [6] 69; [8] 367; [11] 308
————, *Gustav Mahler: Memories and Letters*, trans. Basil Creighton (London: John Murray, 1946). [7] 175; [9] 201; [10] 178; [12] 207; [14] 92; [16] 175; [19] 183
Arnold Schoenberg, *Style and Idea*, ed. Leonard Stein, trans. Leo Black (London: Faber & Faber, 1984). [13] 42
Bruno Walter, *Gustav Mahler*, trans. supervised by Lotte Walter Lindt (New York: Schocken, 1974). [17] 26

Delius

Lionel Carley, *Delius: A Life in Letters*, vol. 2 (Aldershot, England: Scolar Press, 1988). [1] 9; [2] 19; [3] 79; [4] 191; [5] 191
Frederick Delius, "At the Crossroads," *The Sackbut* 1 (1920). [6] 205
Clare Delius, *Frederick Delius: Memories of My Brother* (London: Nicholson & Watson, 1935). [7] 198

Debussy

Claude Debussy: Lettres, ed. François Lesure (Paris: Hermann, 1980); trans. Fisk. [1] 39; [2] 128; [3] 147; [7] 40; [22] 160; [25] 270
Jacques Durand, *Lettres de Claude Debussy à son éditeur* (Paris: Durand, 1927); trans Fisk ([4] and [14]) and Morgenstern (all others). [4] 158; [9] 164; [14] 150; [24] 85; [28] 55; [32] 176
François Lesure and Roger Nichols, *Debussy Letters*, trans. Roger Nichols (Cambridge, Mass.: Harvard University Press, 1987). [5] 76; [10] 77; [23] 178; [29] 41; [31] 72
Claude Debussy through His Letters, ed. and trans. Jacqueline M. Charette (New York: Vantage Press, 1990). [6] 205; [8] 70; [26] 18; [30] 17
————, *Monsieur Croche the Dilettante Hater*, trans. B. N. Langdon Davies (New York: Viking, 1928). [11] 33; [12] 92; [13] 177; [15] 108; [16] 143; [17] 130; [19] 187; [20] 41; [21] 70
Edward Lockspeiser, *Debussy: His Life and Mind* (Cambridge: Cambridge University Press, 1978). [18] 2:68
————, *Debussy* (New York: Pellegrini & Cudahy, 1949). [27] 56

Strauss

Richard Strauss, *Betrachtungen und Erinnerungen* (Zurich: Atlantis, 1949); trans. Morgenstern. [1] 44; [2] 45; [3] 47; [4] 101; [5] 134; [6] 91
Richard Strauss and Hugo von Hofmannsthal, *Briefwechsel* (Zurich: Atlantis, 1952); trans. Morgenstern. [7] 343; [8] 348; [9] 362; [10] 485
Gal, *The Musician's World.* [11] 395

Nielsen

Carl Nielsen, *Living Music*, trans. Reginald Spink (Copenhagen: Wilhelm Hansen, 1968). [1] 32; [2] 51; [3] 66; [4] 47; [5] 15
Robert Simpson, *Carl Nielsen, Symphonist* (London: Dent, 1952). [6] 192

Busoni

Ferruccio Busoni, *Sketch of a New Esthetic of Music*, trans. T. Baker (New York: G. Schirmer, 1911). [1] 3; [2] 7; [3] 22; [4] 24; [5] 15; [6] 23; [7] 43
———, *Letters to His Wife*, trans. Rosamund Ley (London: Arnold, 1938). [8] 229; [10] 78; [11] 287
Edward J. Dent, *Ferruccio Busoni* (London: Oxford University Press, 1933). [9] 230

Satie

Erik Satie, "Mémoires d'un amnésique," *Revue S.I.M.* 10 (1914); trans. Morgenstern. [1] 69
The Writings of Erik Satie, ed. and trans. Nigel Wilkins (London: Eulenberg, 1980). [2] 82; [14] 84; [15] 96; [16] 104; [18] 79; [19] 79; [20] 84
Ornella Volta, *Satie Seen through His Letters*, trans. Michael Bullock (London and New York: Boyars, 1989). [3] 189; [10] 149; [12] 147; [13] 89
———, *Erik Satie: Ecrits* (Paris: Editions Champs Libres, 1981); trans. Fisk. [4];166
Pierre-Daniel Templier, *Erik Satie*, trans. Elena L. French and David S. French (Cambridge, Mass.: MIT Press, 1969). [5] 7; [6] 7; [7] 64; [8] 66; [9] 1; [17]32
Rollo H. Myers, *Erik Satie* (London: Dobson, 1948). [11] 32; [21] 65

CHAPTER NINE

Vaughan Williams

Ralph Vaughan Williams, *National Music* (London: Oxford University Press, 1934). [1] 3; [2] 13; [3] 92; [5] 102
Hubert Foss, *Ralph Vaughan Williams* (London: Harrap, 1952). [4] 23

Reger

Max Reger: Briefwechsel mit Herzog Georg II von Sachsen-Meiningen, ed. Hedwig von Asow and E. Müller von Asow (Weimar: Böhlau, 1947); trans. Morgenstern. [1] 91
Max Reger, *Briefe eines deutschen Meisters*, ed. Else von Hase-Koehler (Leipzig: Koehler & Amelang, 1928); trans. Morgenstern. [2] 77; [4] 39
Nicolas Slominsky, *Music since 1900*, 4th ed. (New York: Scribner's, 1971). [3] 80

Rachmaninoff

Oskar von Riesemann, *Rachmaninoff's Recollections,* trans. Dolly Rutherford (New York: Macmillan, 1934). [1] 144; [2] 158; [3] 155; [4] 98; [5] 205
David Ewen, "Music Should Speak from the Heart," interview with Rachmaninoff, *The Etude* 59 (1941). [6] 804

Schoenberg

Arnold Schoenberg: Letters, ed. Erwin Stein, trans. Eithne Wilkins and Ernst Kaiser (Berkeley and Los Angeles: University of California Press, 1987). [1] 27; [4] 55; [7] 72; [8] 186; [9] 210; [10] 224; [11] 218; [15] 259; [16] 50; [19] 23; [21] 43; [22] 248; [23] 243; [24] 250

Jelena Hahl-Koch, *Arnold Schoenberg, Wassily Kandinsky: Letters, Pictures and Documents*, trans. John C. Crawford (London: Faber, 1984). [2] 23; [3] 60; [6] 74

Juliane Brand, Christopher Hailey, and Donald Harris, *The Berg-Schoenberg Correspondence* (New York: Norton, 1987). [5] 303

Arnold Schoenberg, *Style and Idea*, trans. Dika Newlin (New York: Philosophical Library, 1950). [12] 103

Alma Mahler, *Gustav Mahler: Memories and Letters*, trans. Basil Creighton (London: John Murray, 1946). [13] 190

Willi Reich, *Alban Berg*, trans. Cornelius Cardew (New York: Vienna House, 1974). [14] 71

Henry Cowell and Sidney Cowell, *Charles Ives and His Music* (New York: Oxford University Press, 1955). [17] 114n

Anton Webern, *Six Bagatelles* (Vienna: Universal, 1924). [18] foreword

Merle Armitage, *George Gershwin* (New York: Longmans, Green, 1938). [20] 97

Ives

Charles Ives, *Essays before a Sonata, The Majority, and Other Writings*, ed. Howard Boatwright (New York: Norton, 1970). [1] 97; [2] 80; [3] 94; [4] 71; [5] 84; [6] 117; [12] 86; [13] 21

————, *114 Songs* (Redding, Conn.: [Charles Ives], 1922). [7] "Postface"

————, *Memos*, ed. John Kirkpatrick (New York: Norton, 1972). [8] 52; [9] 32; [10] 130; [11] 196; [14] 114; [15] 44; [16] 115; [17] 47

Ravel

Maurice Ravel, "Lettre au Comité de la Ligue Nationale pour la défense de la musique française," *Revue musicale* 19 (1938); trans. Morgenstern. [1] 70

Hélène Jourdan-Mourhange, *Ravel et nous* (Geneva: Editions du milieu de monde, 1945); trans. Morgenstern. [2] 81

Ravel, "L'oeuvre de Chopin," *Courier musical* 8 (1910); trans. Morgenstern. [3] 31

————, "Concerts Lamoureux." *Revue S.I.M.* 8 (1912); trans. Morgenstern. [4] 63; [8] 62

H. H. Stuckenschmidt, *Maurice Ravel: Variations on His Life and Work*, trans. Samuel R. Rosenbaum (Philadelphia: Chilton, 1968). [5] 138; [6] 229; [9] 202; [10] 82; [11] 149; [13] 230; [14] 215

Rice Institute Pamphlet (Houston: Rice Institute, 1928). [7] 131

M. D. Calvocoressi, "Ravel's Letters to Calvocoressi," *Musical Quarterly* 27 (1941). [12] 17

Falla

Manuel de Falla, *Escritos* (Madrid: Comisaria General de la Música, 1947); trans. Morgenstern. [1] 122

CHAPTER TEN

Bloch

Ernest Bloch, "Man and Music," trans. Waldo Frank, *Seven Arts Magazine* 1 (1917). [1] 495

Mary Tibaldi-Chiesa, *Ernest Bloch* (Turin: Paravia, 1933); trans. Morgenstern. [2] 29

Bartók

Béla Bartók, "Race Purity in Music," *Modern Music* 19 (1942). [1] 153
———, "The Significance of Folk Music to Modern Music," trans. Eva Hajnal-Kouyi, *Tempo* 14 (Winter 1949–50). [2] 19; [6] 21
———, "The Liszt Problem," trans. Colin Mason, *Monthly Musical Record* 78 (1948). [3] 200
Serge Moreux, *Béla Bartók*, trans. G. S. Fraser and Erik de Mauny (London: Harvill, 1953). [4] 92
Béla Bartók Essays, ed. Benjamin Suchoff (London: Faber, 1976). [5] 469

Stravinsky

Igor Stravinsky, *Chronicle of My Life* (London: Gollancz, 1936). [1] 247; [7] 91; [26] 189; [37] 14
———, *Poetics of Music in the Form of Six Lessons*, trans. Arthur Knodel and Ingolf Dahl (Cambridge, Mass.: Harvard University Press, 1947). [2] 34; [3] 37; [4] 12; [5] 56; [6] 81
Igor Stravinsky and Robert Craft, *Expositions and Developments* (1960; reprint, London: Faber Music, 1981). [8] 101; [9] 102; [18] 71; [20] 83; [21] 63; [27] 64; [34] 98; [38] 46; [39] 148; [40] 142; [42] 145
———, *Conversations with Igor Stravinsky* (1957; reprint, London: Faber Music, 1979). [10] 34; [11] 35; [12] 132; [13] 115; [14] 107; [15] 107; [16] 28; [17] 26; [22] 116; [23] 107; [28] 20; [29] 44; [30] 75; [33] 41; [41] 46
———, *Memories and Commentaries* (1959; reprint, London: Faber Music, 1979). [19] 113; [31] 64; [35] 104
Nat Shapiro, *An Encyclopedia of Quotations about Music* (Garden City, N.Y.: Doubleday, 1978). [24] 126; [25] 252
Vera Stravinsky and Robert Craft, *Stravinsky in Pictures and Documents* (London: Hutchinson, 1979). [32] 605
Igor Stravinsky [and Robert Craft], "Stravinsky: The Last Interview," *New York Review of Books,* July 1, 1971. [36] 4

Kodály

Zoltán Kodály, "New Music for Old," *Modern Music* 3, no. 1 (1925). [1] 27
———, "Bartók, le folkloriste," *Revue musicale* 212 (April 1925); trans. Morgenstern. [2] 37

Webern

Humphrey Searle, "Conversations with Webern," *Musical Times* 81 (1940). [1] 405
Alban Berg et al., *Arnold Schönberg*, symposium booklet (Munich: Piper, 1912); trans. Morgenstern. [2] 85
Musiker über Musik, ed. Josef Rufer (Darmstadt: Stichnote, 1956); trans. Morgenstern. [3] 216

Berg

Nicolas Slonimsky, *Music since 1900* (New York: Norton, 1937); translation rev. Fisk. [1] 543
Willi Reich, *Alban Berg* (Vienna: Reichner, 1937). [2] 152; [3] 175

Varèse

Contemporary Composers on Contemporary Music, ed. Elliot Schwartz and Barney Childs (New York: Holt, Rinehart & Winston, 1967). [1] 196; [2] 196; [3] 196; [4] 199; [5] 201; [6] 207

CHAPTER ELEVEN

Prokofiev

H. H. Stuckenschmidt, *Neue Musik* (Berlin: Suhrkamp, 1951); trans. Morgenstern. [1] 338; [2] 342; [3] 347

Honegger

Arthur Honegger, *Je suis compositeur* (Paris: Conquistador, 1951); trans. Morgenstern. [1] 102; [2] 86; [3] 164; [4] 175

Milhaud

Darius Milhaud, *Notes without Music*, trans. Donald Evans (New York: Knopf, 1953). [1] 82; [2] 62; [3] 55; [4] 105; [5] 102; [6] 164

Still

American Composers on American Music. [1] 182
William Grant Still and the Fusion of Cultures in American Music, ed. Robert Bartlett Haas (Los Angeles: Black Sparrow Press, 1972). [2] 122; [3] 134; [4] 114

Hindemith

Paul Hindemith, *A Composer's World* (Cambridge, Mass.: Harvard University Press, 1952). [1] 38; [2] 104; [3] 177; [4] 121

Thomson

Virgil Thomson, *The State of Music* (New York: Morrow, 1939). [1] 8; [2] 10; [3] 109; [4] 207; [8] 188; [21] 131; [27] 216
———, *The Art of Judging Music* (New York: Knopf, 1948). [5] 293; [6] 148; [11] 146; [17] 186
———, *The Musical Scene* (New York: Knopf, 1945). [7] 58; [9] 85; [10] 4; [13] 4; [14] 118; [16] 108; [19] 227; [24] 218
———, *Music Right and Left* (New York: Holt, 1951). [12] 126; [26] 189
———, "The Ives Case," *New York Review of Books*, May 21, 1970. [15] 10
———, "George Gershwin," *Modern Music* 13, no. 1 (1935). [18] 14
———, "Aaron Copland," no. 6 of "Contemporary American Composers," *Modern Music* 9 (1932). [20] 70
———, *A Virgil Thomson Reader* (Boston: Houghton Mifflin, 1981). [22] 375
John Rockwell, "A Conversation with Virgil Thomson," *Parnassus: Poetry in Review* 5 (1977). [23] 420; [25] 422

Sessions

Roger Sessions, "On the American Future," *Modern Music* 17 (1940). [1] 72
———, *The Musical Experience of Composer, Performer, Listener* (Princeton, N.J.: Princeton University Press, 1950). [2] 4; [3] 72; [4] 77; [5] 70; [6] 123; [7] 99
———, *Questions about Music* (Cambridge, Mass.: Harvard University Press, 1970). [8] 11; [9] 150
Andrea Olmstead, "Roger Sessions: A Personal Portrait," *Tempo* 127 (December 1978). [10] 15; [11] 15
Gagne and Caras, *Soundpieces*. [12] 358

Cowell

American Composers on American Music. [1] 12; [2] 132; [3] 44

Gershwin

Merle Armitage, *George Gershwin* (New York: Longmans, Green, 1938). [1] 225
American Composers on American Music. [2] 186
Hyman Sandow, "Gershwin Presents a New Work," *Musical America*, August 18, 1928.
[3] 12

Chávez

American Composers on American Music. [1] 167

Poulenc

Francis Poulenc, "Feuilles Americains," *Table ronde* 30 (1950); trans. Morgenstern. [1] 68;
[2] 74; [3] 75
Roland Gelatt, "A Vote for Francis Poulenc," *Saturday Review of Literature*, January 28,
1950. [4] 57

Copland

Aaron Copland, "A Modernist Defends Modern Music," *New York Times Magazine*, De-
cember 25, 1949. [1] 11
———, "Fresh and Different," *New York Times Magazine*, March 13, 1955. [2] 27
Gagne and Caras, *Soundpieces.* [3] 107; [11] 108; [26] 111
Copland, *Music and Imagination* (Cambridge, Mass.: Harvard University Press, 1952). [4]
69; [5] 8; [6] 10; [7] 13; [14] 29; [18] 37; [23] 62; [24] 2
———, *Copland on Music* (New York: Norton, 1963). [8] 131; [9] 134; [10] 264; [12]
37; [13] 39; [15] 35; [16] 126; [17] 34; [25] 45
———, "Contemporaries at Oxford," *Modern Music* 9 (1931). [19] 22
American Composers on American Music. [20] 102
The New Music Lover's Handbook, ed. Elie Siegmeister (New York: Harvey House, 1973).
[21] 542
Copland, Review of Benjamin Britten's *The Rape of Lucretia*, *Notes* 4 (March 1947). [22]
190

Seeger

Carol Neuls-Bates,*Women in Music* (New York: Harper & Row, 1982). [1] 309

Chapter Twelve

Shostakovich

Dmitri Shostakovich, *Lettres à un ami: Correspondance avec Isaac Glikman*, preface and commentaries by Isaac Glikman, trans. [into French] Luba Jurgenson (Paris: Albin Michel,
1994); trans. [into English] Fisk. [1] 155; [5] 218; [10] 276; [15] 191; [20] 26; [22]
88; [23] 160; [27] 71; [28] 81; [29] 294; [33] 119
Testimony: The Memoirs of Dmitri Shostakovich, as related to and ed. by Solomon Volkov,
trans. Antonina W. Bouis (New York: Harper & Row, 1979). [2] 196; [3] 234; [4] 162;
[6] 129; [7] 42; [8] 60; [9] 40; [11] 32; [12] 198; [13] 35; [14] 36; [18] 134; [19] 183;
[21] 154; [25] 218; [26] 229

Elizabeth Wilson, *Shostakovich: A Life Remembered* (Princeton, N.J.: Princeton University Press, 1994). [16] 54; [17] 90; [25] 470; [32] 409; [33] 30; [34] 89
"Amity Is Voiced by Shostakovich," *New York Times*, October 25, 1959. [34] 13

Messiaen

Olivier Messiaen, *Technique of My Musical Language*, trans. John Satterfield (Paris: A. Leduc, 1956). [1] 1
Claude Samuel, *Conversations with Olivier Messiaen*, trans. Felix Aprahamian (London: Stainer & Bell, 1976). [2] 34; [3] 51; [6] 111
Almut Rössler, *Contributions to the Spiritual World of Olivier Messiaen*, trans. Barbara Dagg and Nancy Poland (Duisberg, Germany: Gilles & Francke, 1986). [4] 57; [5] 30; [7] 45; [8] 32
Olivier Messiaen, *Music and Color: Conversations with Claude Samuel*, trans. E. Thomas Glasow (Portland, Ore.: Amadeus Press, 1994). [9] 249
Harriet Watts, "Canyons, Colours and Birds: An Interview with Olivier Messiaen," *Tempo* 128 (1979). [10] 4

Carter

Elliott Carter, *The Writings of Elliott Carter* (Bloomington: Indiana University Press, 1977). [1] 217; [2] 284; [11] 48; [13] 262; [17] 302; [18] 192
Ford, *Composer to Composer.* [3] 8
Allen Edwards, *Flawed Words and Stubborn Sounds: A Conversation with Elliott Carter* (New York: Norton, 1971). [4] 80; [5] 57; [6] 89; [7] 67; [10] 62; [12] 63; [14] 63; [15] 64; [16] 65; [19] 50; [20] 91
Gagne and Caras, *Soundpieces.* [8] 95; [9] 8

Cage

John Cage, *Silence* (Middletown, Conn.: Wesleyan University Press, 1961). [1] 3; [3] xii; [4] 167; [5] 109; [6] 165; [7] 72; [9] 7; [10] 41; [11] 73; [12] 125; [17] 261; [18] 165; [19] 190; [20] 109
Richard Kostelanetz, *John Cage: An Anthology* (New York: Da Capo Press, 1991). [2] 81; [8] 12; [14] 13; [22] 20; [23] 31
Michael Zwerin, "A Lethal Measurement," interview with Cage, *Village Voice*, January 6, 1966. [13] 8; [21] 12
John Cage, Letter to the editor, *Musical America*, April 1, 1951. [15] 26

Babbitt

Milton Babbitt, "Who Cares If You Listen?," *High Fidelity*, February 1958. [1] 38
Gagne and Caras, *Soundpieces.* [2] 36; [3] 40; [4] 43
Babbitt, *Words about Music,* ed. Stephen Dembski and Joseph Straus (Madison: University of Wisconsin Press, 1987). [5] 165; [6] 167; [11] 166; [12] 180
Laura Karpman, "An Interview with Milton Babbitt," *Perspectives of New Music* 23, no. 2 (spring–summer 1985). [7] 81; [8] 81
Babbitt, "On Having Been and Still Being an American Composer," *Perspectives of New Music* 27, no. 1 (fall–winter 1989). [9] 107; [10] 112; [13] 112

Bernstein

Leonard Bernstein, *The Infinite Variety of Music* (New York: Simon & Schuster, 1966). [1] 20; [2] 9; [3] 273; [4] 278; [7] 64; [8] 80; [9] 24
——, "Mahler: His Time Has Come," *High Fidelity,* September 1967. [10] 53
——, *Findings* (New York: Simon & Schuster, 1982). [11] 314; [12] 103

Chapter Thirteen

Ligeti

György Ligeti, *Ligeti in Conversation* (London: Eulenberg, 1983). [1] 32; [2] 29; [3] 51; [4] 14; [5] 24; [6] 71; [7] 78; [8] 77; [9] 14; [10] 16; [11] 15; [12] 14

Rorem

Ned Rorem, *Music from Inside Out* (New York: Braziller, 1967). [1] 12; [2] 31; [3] 98; [4] 113; [15] 121
———, *An Absolute Gift* (New York: Simon & Schuster, 1978). [5] 46; [6] 57; [7] 50; [8] 49; [9] 56; [10] 221; [14] 220; [17] 150; [18] 151; [19] 43; [20] 24
———, *Knowing When to Stop* (New York: Simon & Schuster, 1994). [11] 103; [12] 269; [13] 173; [16] 232

Boulez

Pierre Boulez, *Orientations*, ed. Jean-Jacques Nattiez, trans. Martin Cooper (Cambridge, Mass.: Harvard University Press, 1986). [1] 106; [2] 76; [3] 421; [4] 447; [5] 449; [6] 454; [7] 526; [20] 326; [24] 324; [26] 361; [30] 481
———, *Notes of an Apprenticeship*, trans. Herbert Weinstock (New York: Knopf, 1968). [8] 143; [9] 146; [10] 179; [11] 188; [18] 71; [19] 58; [25] 268
———, "The Composer and Creativity," *Journal of the Arnold Schoenberg Institute* 11 (1988). [12] 110; [13] 112; [14] 114; [21] 115
"Spiegel-Gespräch," unsigned interview, *Der Spiegel,* September 1967; trans. Fisk. [15] 172; [29] 166, 174
Pierre Boulez and Michel Foucault, "Contemporary Music and the Public," trans. John Rahn, *Perspectives of New Music* 24, no. 1 (fall–winter 1985). [16] 8
Ford, *Composer to Composer.* [17] 23; [22] 28
Pierre Boulez, "Berlioz and the Realm of the Imaginary," *High Fidelity/Musical America,* March 1969. [23] 43
———, *Conversations with Celestin Deliege*, trans. Robert Wangermee (London: Eulenberg, 1976). [27] 24
Frans C. Lemaire, *La Musique du xxe siècle en Russie* ([Paris]: Fayard, 1994); trans. Fisk. [28] 207n

Berio

Luciano Berio, *Two Interviews*, interviews by Rossana Dalmonte and Bálint András Varga (London and New York: Boyars, 1985). [1] 22; [2] 91; [3] 90; [4] 112; [5] 40; [6] 121; [7] 75; [8] 133; [9] 55; [10] 81; [11] 148; [12] 78; [13] 143; [14] 146; [15] 48; [16] 65; [17] 115; [18] 107

Schuller

Gunther Schuller, *Musings: The Musical Worlds of Gunther Schuller* (New York: Oxford University Press, 1986). [1] 115; [2] 174; [3] 257; [4] 259; [5] 29; [7] 47
James Avery Hoffmann and Joseph Gabriel Maneri, "A Conversation with Gunther Schuller," *Perspectives of New Music* 24, no. 2 (spring–summer 1986). [6] 243

Henze

Hans Werner Henze, *Music and Politics*, trans. Peter Labanyi (Ithaca, N.Y.: Cornell University Press, 1982). [1] 65; [2] 168; [3] 197; [4] 217; [5] 84; [6] 87; [7] 90; [8] 145; [9] 125; [10] 130; [11] 133; [12] 109; [13] 110; [14] 157; [15] 154; [16] 82; [17] 180; [18] 153

Stockhausen

Jonathan Cott, *Stockhausen: Conversations with the Composer* (New York: Simon & Schuster, 1973). [1] 24; [2] 53; [3] 29; [4] 81; [5] 103; [6] 224; [9] 93
Robin Maconie, *The Works of Karlheinz Stockhausen* (Oxford: Oxford University Press, 1990). [7] v
Ford, *Composer to Composer*. [8] 145

CHAPTER FOURTEEN

Takemitsu

Toru Takemitsu, *Confronting Silence*, trans. and ed. Yoshiko Kakudo and Glenn Glasow (Berkeley: Fallen Leaf Press, 1995). [1] 17; [2] 4; [8] 106
Noriko Ohtake, *Creative Sources for the Music of Toru Takemitsu* (Aldershot, England: Scolar Press, 1993). [3] 20; [9] 62
Toru Takemitsu, "Contemporary Music in Japan," *Perspectives of New Music* 27, no. 2 (spring–summer 1989). [4] 198; [5] 203; [7] 199; [10] 201
Toru Takemitsu with Tania Cronin and Hilary Tan, "Afterword," *Perspectives of New Music* 27, no. 2 (spring–summer 1989). [6] 211

Gubaidulina

Gubaidulina, vol. 2 of *Autori Vari*, ed. Enzo Restagno (Turin: Edizioni di Torino, 1991); trans. Nichols. [1] 10; [2] 27; [3] 55; [4] 82; [5] 88; [6] 12; [7] 18; [8] 21
Interview with Gubaidulina, quoted in booklet to Sony compact disc SK 53960 (Gubaidulina's piano works, Andreas Haefliger, piano), 1995. [9] n.p.

Reich

Gagne and Caras, *Soundpieces*. [1] 309; [2] 309; [3] 311
Ford, *Composer to Composer*. [4] 64; [5] 63; [6] 67

Glass

Gagne and Caras, *Soundpieces*. [1] 212; [2] 224; [8] 213; [9] 226; [10] 214
Philip Glass, *Music by Philip Glass*, ed. Robert T. Jones (New York: Harper & Row, 1987). [3] 36; [4] 13; [11] 29; [12] 32; [13] 35; [14] 53; [15] xv
Philip Glass, interview by Josiah Fisk, transcribed and ed. from tape recording, Boston, October 4, 1990. [5] n.p.; [6] n.p.; [7] n.p.

Harbison

John Harbison, "Six Tanglewood Talks (1, 2, 3)," *Perspectives of New Music* 23, no. 2 (spring–summer 1985). [1] 13; [2] 19
———, "Six Tanglewood Talks (4, 5, 6)," *Perspectives of New Music* 24, no. 1 (fall–winter 1985). [3] 49; [4] 51
———, lecture at MIT, fall 1988 (transcript supplied by the composer). [5] n.p.
———, fundraising letter for Collage New Music Ensemble, 1987. [6] n.p.

Knussen

Oliver Knussen, "Peter Maxwell Davies's 'Five Klee Pictures,'" *Tempo* 124 (March 1978). [1] 17
———, "Self-observation," article for George Perle festschrift (forthcoming; manuscript supplied by the composer). [2] n.p.; [13] n.p.

Andrew Ford, "Songs without Voices," 24 Hours (program magazine of ABC Radio, Australia), September 1994. [3] 39; [5] 40; [8] 42

Oliver Knussen: Debut on Deutsche Grammophon, publicity brochure from Deutsche Grammophon, July 1995.[4] n.p.; [14] n.p.

Oliver Knussen, notes for Virgin Classics compact disc VC7 91503-2 (music of Elliott Carter conducted by Knussen, 1992). [6] n.p.

———, memorial speech for Toru Takemitsu, Japan Society, New York (transcript supplied by the composer). [7] n.p.

———, remarks at a colloquium at Harvard University, November 27, 1995 (transcribed Fisk). [9] n.p.

———, program note for a concert in the Hague, March 1994. [10] n.p.

Paul Griffiths, New Sounds, New Personalities: British Composers of the 1980s in Conversation with Paul Griffiths (London: Faber Music, 1985). [11] 57; [12] 63

Oliver Knussen, statement written for Composers on Music (Snape, England, July 8, 1996). [15] n.p.

ACKNOWLEDGMENTS

The editor is grateful for the permission to reproduce selected excerpts from the following copyrighted sources:

Milton Babbitt, *Words about Music*. Copyright © 1987 by Stephen Dembski and Joseph Straus. Reprinted by permission.

Luciano Berio, *Two Interviews*. Copyright © 1981 by Laterza; copyright © 1981 by Balínt András Varga. English version copyright © 1985 by Marion Boyars Publishers. Reprinted by permission of Marion Boyars Publishers Ltd.

Leonard Bernstein, *The Infinite Variety of Music*. Copyright © 1962, 1963, 1966 by Leonard Bernstein; copyright © 1966 by the Leonard Bernstein Foundation, Inc. Reprinted by permission of Bantam Doubleday Dell Publishing Group, Inc., and Amberson, Inc.

Pierre Boulez, *Notes of an Apprenticeship*, trans. Herbert Weinstock. Copyright © 1966 by Éditions du Seuil. Reprinted by permission of Georges Borchardt, Inc.

Pierre Boulez, *Orientations*, ed. Jean-Jacques Nattiez, trans. Martin Cooper. Copyright © 1981, 1985 by Christian Bourgeois. English translation copyright © 1986 by Faber and Faber Ltd. and the President and Fellows of Harvard College. Reprinted by permission of Harvard University Press and Faber and Faber Limited.

John Cage, *Silence*. Copyright © 1961 by John Cage and Wesleyan University Press. Reprinted by permission of University Press of New England.

Elliott Carter, *The Writings of Elliott Carter*. Reprinted by permission of Indiana University Press.

Aaron Copland, *Music and Imagination*. Copyright © 1952 by the President and Fellows of Harvard College. Reprinted by permission of Harvard University Press.

Jonathan Cott, *Stockhausen: Conversations with the Composer*. Copyright © 1973 by Jonathan Cott. Reprinted by permission.

Allen Edwards, *Flawed Words and Stubborn Sounds: A Conversation with Elliott Carter*. Copyright © 1971 by W. W. Norton & Co., Inc. Reprinted by permission of W. W. Norton & Co., Inc.

Andrew Ford, *Composer to Composer*. Copyright © 1993 by Andrew Ford. Reprinted by permission of Allen & Unwin Pty. Limited.

Andrew Ford, "Songs Without Voices." Copyright © 1994 by Andrew Ford. Reprinted by permission.

Cole Gagne and Tracy Caras, *Soundpieces: Interviews with American Composers*. Copyright © 1982 by Cole Gagne and Tracy Caras. Reprinted by permission of Scarecrow Press.

Philip Glass, *Music by Philip Glass*. Copyright © 1987 by Dunvagen Music Publishers, Inc. Reprinted by permission of HarperCollins Publishers, Inc.

INDEX